T0205302

Lecture Notes in Computer Science 13335

More information about this series at https://link.springer.com/bookseries/558

Heidi Krömker (Ed.)

HCI in Mobility, Transport, and Automotive Systems

4th International Conference, MobiTAS 2022
Held as Part of the 24th HCI International Conference, HCII 2022
Virtual Event, June 26 – July 1, 2022
Proceedings

Editor
Heidi Krömker
Technische Universität Ilmenau
Ilmenau, Germany

ISSN 0302-9743 ISSN 1611-3349 (electronic)
Lecture Notes in Computer Science
ISBN 978-3-031-04986-6 ISBN 978-3-031-04987-3 (eBook)
https://doi.org/10.1007/978-3-031-04987-3

This Springer imprint is published by the registered company Springer Nature Switzerland AG
The registered company address is: Gewerbestrasse 11, 6330 Cham, Switzerland

Foreword

Human-computer interaction (HCI) is acquiring an ever-increasing scientific and industrial importance, as well as having more impact on people's everyday life, as an ever-growing number of human activities are progressively moving from the physical to the digital world. This process, which has been ongoing for some time now, has been dramatically accelerated by the COVID-19 pandemic. The HCI International (HCII) conference series, held yearly, aims to respond to the compelling need to advance the exchange of knowledge and research and development efforts on the human aspects of design and use of computing systems.

The 24th International Conference on Human-Computer Interaction, HCI International 2022 (HCII 2022), was planned to be held at the Gothia Towers Hotel and Swedish Exhibition & Congress Centre, Göteborg, Sweden, during June 26 to July 1, 2022. Due to the COVID-19 pandemic and with everyone's health and safety in mind, HCII 2022 was organized and run as a virtual conference. It incorporated the 21 thematic areas and affiliated conferences listed on the following page.

A total of 5583 individuals from academia, research institutes, industry, and governmental agencies from 88 countries submitted contributions, and 1276 papers and 275 posters were included in the proceedings to appear just before the start of the conference. The contributions thoroughly cover the entire field of human-computer interaction, addressing major advances in knowledge and effective use of computers in a variety of application areas. These papers provide academics, researchers, engineers, scientists, practitioners, and students with state-of-the-art information on the most recent advances in HCI. The volumes constituting the set of proceedings to appear before the start of the conference are listed in the following pages.

The HCI International (HCII) conference also offers the option of 'Late Breaking Work' which applies both for papers and posters, and the corresponding volume(s) of the proceedings will appear after the conference. Full papers will be included in the 'HCII 2022 - Late Breaking Papers' volumes of the proceedings to be published in the Springer LNCS series, while 'Poster Extended Abstracts' will be included as short research papers in the 'HCII 2022 - Late Breaking Posters' volumes to be published in the Springer CCIS series.

I would like to thank the Program Board Chairs and the members of the Program Boards of all thematic areas and affiliated conferences for their contribution and support towards the highest scientific quality and overall success of the HCI International 2022 conference; they have helped in so many ways, including session organization, paper reviewing (single-blind review process, with a minimum of two reviews per submission) and, more generally, acting as goodwill ambassadors for the HCII conference.

This conference would not have been possible without the continuous and unwavering support and advice of Gavriel Salvendy, founder, General Chair Emeritus, and Scientific Advisor. For his outstanding efforts, I would like to express my appreciation to Abbas Moallem, Communications Chair and Editor of HCI International News.

June 2022 Constantine Stephanidis

HCI International 2022 Thematic Areas and Affiliated Conferences

Thematic Areas

- HCI: Human-Computer Interaction
- HIMI: Human Interface and the Management of Information

Affiliated Conferences

- EPCE: 19th International Conference on Engineering Psychology and Cognitive Ergonomics
- AC: 16th International Conference on Augmented Cognition
- UAHCI: 16th International Conference on Universal Access in Human-Computer Interaction
- CCD: 14th International Conference on Cross-Cultural Design
- SCSM: 14th International Conference on Social Computing and Social Media
- VAMR: 14th International Conference on Virtual, Augmented and Mixed Reality
- DHM: 13th International Conference on Digital Human Modeling and Applications in Health, Safety, Ergonomics and Risk Management
- DUXU: 11th International Conference on Design, User Experience and Usability
- C&C: 10th International Conference on Culture and Computing
- DAPI: 10th International Conference on Distributed, Ambient and Pervasive Interactions
- HCIBGO: 9th International Conference on HCI in Business, Government and Organizations
- LCT: 9th International Conference on Learning and Collaboration Technologies
- ITAP: 8th International Conference on Human Aspects of IT for the Aged Population
- AIS: 4th International Conference on Adaptive Instructional Systems
- HCI-CPT: 4th International Conference on HCI for Cybersecurity, Privacy and Trust
- HCI-Games: 4th International Conference on HCI in Games
- MobiTAS: 4th International Conference on HCI in Mobility, Transport and Automotive Systems
- AI-HCI: 3rd International Conference on Artificial Intelligence in HCI
- MOBILE: 3rd International Conference on Design, Operation and Evaluation of Mobile Communications

List of Conference Proceedings Volumes Appearing Before the Conference

1. LNCS 13302, Human-Computer Interaction: Theoretical Approaches and Design Methods (Part I), edited by Masaaki Kurosu
2. LNCS 13303, Human-Computer Interaction: Technological Innovation (Part II), edited by Masaaki Kurosu
3. LNCS 13304, Human-Computer Interaction: User Experience and Behavior (Part III), edited by Masaaki Kurosu
4. LNCS 13305, Human Interface and the Management of Information: Visual and Information Design (Part I), edited by Sakae Yamamoto and Hirohiko Mori
5. LNCS 13306, Human Interface and the Management of Information: Applications in Complex Technological Environments (Part II), edited by Sakae Yamamoto and Hirohiko Mori
6. LNAI 13307, Engineering Psychology and Cognitive Ergonomics, edited by Don Harris and Wen-Chin Li
7. LNCS 13308, Universal Access in Human-Computer Interaction: Novel Design Approaches and Technologies (Part I), edited by Margherita Antona and Constantine Stephanidis
8. LNCS 13309, Universal Access in Human-Computer Interaction: User and Context Diversity (Part II), edited by Margherita Antona and Constantine Stephanidis
9. LNAI 13310, Augmented Cognition, edited by Dylan D. Schmorrow and Cali M. Fidopiastis
10. LNCS 13311, Cross-Cultural Design: Interaction Design Across Cultures (Part I), edited by Pei-Luen Patrick Rau
11. LNCS 13312, Cross-Cultural Design: Applications in Learning, Arts, Cultural Heritage, Creative Industries, and Virtual Reality (Part II), edited by Pei-Luen Patrick Rau
12. LNCS 13313, Cross-Cultural Design: Applications in Business, Communication, Health, Well-being, and Inclusiveness (Part III), edited by Pei-Luen Patrick Rau
13. LNCS 13314, Cross-Cultural Design: Product and Service Design, Mobility and Automotive Design, Cities, Urban Areas, and Intelligent Environments Design (Part IV), edited by Pei-Luen Patrick Rau
14. LNCS 13315, Social Computing and Social Media: Design, User Experience and Impact (Part I), edited by Gabriele Meiselwitz
15. LNCS 13316, Social Computing and Social Media: Applications in Education and Commerce (Part II), edited by Gabriele Meiselwitz
16. LNCS 13317, Virtual, Augmented and Mixed Reality: Design and Development (Part I), edited by Jessie Y. C. Chen and Gino Fragomeni
17. LNCS 13318, Virtual, Augmented and Mixed Reality: Applications in Education, Aviation and Industry (Part II), edited by Jessie Y. C. Chen and Gino Fragomeni

18. LNCS 13319, Digital Human Modeling and Applications in Health, Safety, Ergonomics and Risk Management: Anthropometry, Human Behavior, and Communication (Part I), edited by Vincent G. Duffy
19. LNCS 13320, Digital Human Modeling and Applications in Health, Safety, Ergonomics and Risk Management: Health, Operations Management, and Design (Part II), edited by Vincent G. Duffy
20. LNCS 13321, Design, User Experience, and Usability: UX Research, Design, and Assessment (Part I), edited by Marcelo M. Soares, Elizabeth Rosenzweig and Aaron Marcus
21. LNCS 13322, Design, User Experience, and Usability: Design for Emotion, Well-being and Health, Learning, and Culture (Part II), edited by Marcelo M. Soares, Elizabeth Rosenzweig and Aaron Marcus
22. LNCS 13323, Design, User Experience, and Usability: Design Thinking and Practice in Contemporary and Emerging Technologies (Part III), edited by Marcelo M. Soares, Elizabeth Rosenzweig and Aaron Marcus
23. LNCS 13324, Culture and Computing, edited by Matthias Rauterberg
24. LNCS 13325, Distributed, Ambient and Pervasive Interactions: Smart Environments, Ecosystems, and Cities (Part I), edited by Norbert A. Streitz and Shin'ichi Konomi
25. LNCS 13326, Distributed, Ambient and Pervasive Interactions: Smart Living, Learning, Well-being and Health, Art and Creativity (Part II), edited by Norbert A. Streitz and Shin'ichi Konomi
26. LNCS 13327, HCI in Business, Government and Organizations, edited by Fiona Fui-Hoon Nah and Keng Siau
27. LNCS 13328, Learning and Collaboration Technologies: Designing the Learner and Teacher Experience (Part I), edited by Panayiotis Zaphiris and Andri Ioannou
28. LNCS 13329, Learning and Collaboration Technologies: Novel Technological Environments (Part II), edited by Panayiotis Zaphiris and Andri Ioannou
29. LNCS 13330, Human Aspects of IT for the Aged Population: Design, Interaction and Technology Acceptance (Part I), edited by Qin Gao and Jia Zhou
30. LNCS 13331, Human Aspects of IT for the Aged Population: Technology in Everyday Living (Part II), edited by Qin Gao and Jia Zhou
31. LNCS 13332, Adaptive Instructional Systems, edited by Robert A. Sottilare and Jessica Schwarz
32. LNCS 13333, HCI for Cybersecurity, Privacy and Trust, edited by Abbas Moallem
33. LNCS 13334, HCI in Games, edited by Xiaowen Fang
34. LNCS 13335, HCI in Mobility, Transport and Automotive Systems, edited by Heidi Krömker
35. LNAI 13336, Artificial Intelligence in HCI, edited by Helmut Degen and Stavroula Ntoa
36. LNCS 13337, Design, Operation and Evaluation of Mobile Communications, edited by Gavriel Salvendy and June Wei
37. CCIS 1580, HCI International 2022 Posters - Part I, edited by Constantine Stephanidis, Margherita Antona and Stavroula Ntoa
38. CCIS 1581, HCI International 2022 Posters - Part II, edited by Constantine Stephanidis, Margherita Antona and Stavroula Ntoa

39. CCIS 1582, HCI International 2022 Posters - Part III, edited by Constantine Stephanidis, Margherita Antona and Stavroula Ntoa
40. CCIS 1583, HCI International 2022 Posters - Part IV, edited by Constantine Stephanidis, Margherita Antona and Stavroula Ntoa

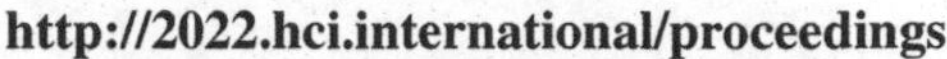

http://2022.hci.international/proceedings

Preface

Human-computer interaction in the highly complex field of mobility and intermodal transport leads to completely new challenges. A variety of different travelers move in different travel chains. The interplay of such different systems, such as car and bike sharing, local and long-distance public transport, and individual transport, must be adapted to the needs of the travelers. Intelligent traveler information systems must be created to make it easier for travelers to plan, book, and execute an intermodal travel chain and to interact with the different systems. Innovative means of transport are developed, such as electric vehicles and autonomous vehicles. To achieve the acceptance of these systems, human-machine interaction must be completely redesigned.

The 4th International Conference on HCI in Mobility, Transport, and Automotive Systems (MobiTAS 2022), an affiliated conference of the HCI International (HCII) conference, encouraged papers from academics, researchers, industry, and professionals, on a broad range of theoretical and applied issues related to mobility, transport, and automotive systems and their applications.

For MobiTAS 2022, researchers were primarily concerned with focal points revolving around the technical capabilities which make it possible to develop new interactions for driving tasks. The enrichment of reality with virtual 3D content and the scenario-based representation of complex tasks in autonomous driving have a major role to play here. But taking advantage of these new technical possibilities requires a fundamental understanding of users' mobility requirements. Young users have new mobility requirements, and the future benefits of new forms of mobility must be methodically explored. Driver information and assistance systems must be developed cost-effectively on the one hand and with a high emotional benefit on the other. The studies on automated driving show how the test environments for user-centered developments can be designed. Micro-mobility and urban mobility occupy a special place, as the different mobility offers must be combined here.

One volume of the HCII 2022 proceedings is dedicated to this year's edition of the MobiTAS conference and focuses on topics related to designing interactions in the mobility, transport, and automotive context; human-centered design of automotive systems; driver information and assistance systems; and studies on automated driving, as well as micro-mobility and urban mobility.

Papers of this volume are included for publication after a minimum of two single-blind reviews from the members of the MobiTAS Program Board or, in some cases, from members of the Program Boards of other affiliated conferences. I would like to thank all of them for their invaluable contribution, support, and efforts.

June 2022 Heidi Krömker

4th International Conference on HCI in Mobility, Transport, and Automotive Systems (MobiTAS 2022)

The full list with the Program Board Chairs and the members of the Program Boards of all thematic areas and affiliated conferences is available online at

http://www.hci.international/board-members-2022.php

4th International Conference on HCI in Mobility, Transport, and Automotive Systems (MobiTAS 2022)

Program Board Chair: **Heidi Krömker**, Technische Universität Ilmenau, Germany

- Angelika C. Bullinger, Chemnitz University of Technology, Germany
- Bertrand David, Ecole Centrale de Lyon, France
- Marco Diana, Politecnico di Torino, Italy
- Cyriel Diels, Royal College of Art London, UK
- Chinh Ho, University of Sydney, Australia
- Christophe Kolski, Université Polytechnique Hauts-de-France, France
- Josef F. Krems, Chemnitz University of Technology, Germany
- Lena Levin, VTI, Swedish National Road and Transport Research Institute, Sweden
- Matthias Rötting, Technische Universität Berlin, Germany
- Philipp Rode, Volkswagen Group, Germany
- Thomas Schlegel, Karlsruhe University of Applied Sciences, Germany
- Felix Wilhelm Siebert, Technical University of Denmark, Denmark
- Ulrike Stopka, Technische Universität Dresden, Germany
- Tobias Wienken, CodeCamp:N GmbH, Germany
- Xiaowei Yuan, Beijing ISAR User Interface Design Limited, China

The full list with the Program Board Chairs and the members of the Program Boards of all thematic areas and affiliated conferences is available online at

http://www.hci.international/board-members-2022.php

HCI International 2023

The 25th International Conference on Human-Computer Interaction, HCI International 2023, will be held jointly with the affiliated conferences at the AC Bella Sky Hotel and Bella Center, Copenhagen, Denmark, 23–28 July 2023. It will cover a broad spectrum of themes related to human-computer interaction, including theoretical issues, methods, tools, processes, and case studies in HCI design, as well as novel interaction techniques, interfaces, and applications. The proceedings will be published by Springer. More information will be available on the conference website: http://2023.hci.international/.

General Chair
Constantine Stephanidis
University of Crete and ICS-FORTH
Heraklion, Crete, Greece
Email: general_chair@hcii2023.org

http://2023.hci.international/

Contents

Micro-mobility and Urban Mobility

Designing Interactions in the Mobility, Transport, and Automotive Context

How to Support Rapid Prototyping of Virtual Content for Automotive AR Head-Up Displays?

Bilal Azzam[1,2](✉), Johannes Tümler[2], and Korinna Bade[2]

[1] Volkswagen AG, Wolfsburg, Germany
bilal.azzam@volkswagen.de
[2] Anhalt University of Applied Sciences, Köthen, Germany
{johannes.tuemler,korinna.bade}@hs-anhalt.de

Abstract. Emerging AR applications for vehicles, and especially for AR HUDs, are current topics for modern assistance systems to support drivers in their driving tasks. Prototyping of AR experiences is presented in current research in immersive authoring tools to overcome complexities and entry barriers for designers and psychologists. However, these are not applicable to navigation displays for AR HUD. This paper presents a qualitative study with concept developers in their domain to determine the characteristics of AR applications that the HUD should possess. The different dimensions of the problems and properties of the required information are presented. The different facets of associated issues and information requirements are also discussed. These facets and its corresponding information are categorized in different levels of complexity of the navigation context, which are not typically part of the development of standard AR applications. Technological entry barriers introduce additional complexity levels for the concept developers. More specifically, the representation of dynamic virtual objects on displays in dynamic environments complicates the development as there is no suitable evaluation platform meeting the requirements of the concept developers.

Keywords: Augmented Reality · AR HUD · Development process · HMI prototyping

1 Introduction

Augmented Reality (AR) refers to virtual information used to supplement the user's view of the real world [2]. In the automotive domain, AR is used to present assisting virtual information within the driver's field of view, such as navigational information, street signs and speed limits. The aim is to reduce the driver's mental workload associated with the need to combine information from multiple sources in the vehicle (e.g. speed indicator) and on the road. Abdi and Meddeb demonstrated that reducing mental workload could lead to less driving errors and therefore in less traffic accidents [1]. Bauerfeind et al. and Sandbrink showed that due to the ever-growing number of vehicles and the resulting traffic load, using

H. Krömker (Ed.): HCII 2022, LNCS 13335, pp. 3–20, 2022.
https://doi.org/10.1007/978-3-031-04987-3_1

AR as assisting technology in the vehicle will become increasingly important [3, 16]. Therefore, novel prototyping methods and tools are required in order to create supportive and compelling AR visualizations for use in vehicles.

1.1 Development of AR Applications

AR applications exist in different forms:

- Handheld AR: A device such as a tablet PC or smartphone is held by at least one hand. A live camera video is displayed on the device's screen and virtual content is merged into the video feed.
- Head-worn AR: Users wear see-through devices (e.g. a Microsoft HoloLens) on their head. They see the real-world environment combined with spatially registered 3D content that is superimposed on the environment within their line of sight.
- Projection-based AR: The position of user's head is tracked. A static or movable projector projects additional content on the surrounding environment, resulting in an AR view [11].

In this work, we refer to the examples above as *standard AR applications.* They apply different kinds of displays (monitor, projector) to present spatially registered 3D content. Users see the content and can interact with it, in which case the content reacts to the users' commands in real-time (Fig. 1).

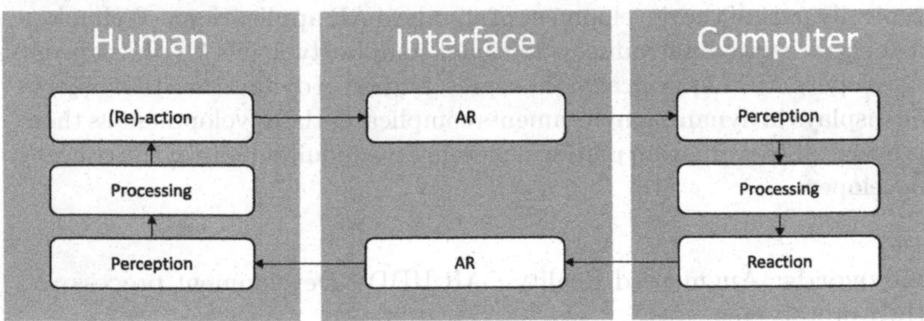

Fig. 1. Augmented Reality serves as the interface between human and computer.

The development steps for standard AR applications are known and already supported by numerous frameworks. Software developers, UX designers, and application specialists usually work in teams. The planned target platform defines the necessary SDKs for the development. 3D objects and their behaviors are created and imported. One important step is the spatial mapping of the 3D data to a world coordinate system. This process may need spatial markers, model-based or feature-based tracking approaches and specific mapping procedures. Specialized AR-relevant workflows and authoring tools such as Unity

MARS[1] can be used if the physical space of the users is unknown to the developers. The application will then be deployed to the target platform and gradually tested, refined and published upon completion.

The development of assisting AR applications in the automotive domain can require the consultation from psychologists and human factors experts in addition to the standard developer team. Since the use of AR in the car has the potential to distract the driver, the cognitive perception of the displayed content can be investigated and explored in a joint effort by designers and psychologists. Such procedure could lead to significantly more development iterations compared to standard AR applications. In addition, some technical requirements of SDKs created for release on certain AR platforms may not be as available and applicable in the vehicle. In standard AR applications it is usually sufficient to use in-built sensors to recognize simple surfaces, building or room structures to map augmented content. In the vehicle, the mapping process can be a lot more complex: AR content must be adapted not only to the user's position and dynamics but also to vehicle dynamics and dynamic changes in the environment.

It is not unusual that new AR concepts are developed while the target vehicle platform is not yet available, making the implementation of such AR concepts extremely challenging. To our knowledge, no public SDKs exist to facilitate the AR software development of in-vehicle Head-Up-Displays (HUDs). Therefore, any development is done on prototype setups or in simulated virtual vehicles. This can lead to additional iterations in the product development cycle, introducing undesirable delays and conflicts between hardware architecture requirements and user experience.

1.2 Prototyping and Evaluation of AR HUD Concepts

Crucial AR HUD development phases must be iterated several times (see Sect. 1.1).

1. Ideation: Creative concept development by discussing and brainstorming ideas.
2. Prototyping: Idea and concept visualization.
3. Development: Software implementation including definition of behaviors, trigger events, markers etc. of the final experience.
4. Evaluation/Testing: Testing the implemented concept in a simulator and/or in the real driving experience.
5. Presentation: Final concept presentation depending on the project dependencies and environments.

According to Mueller and Thoring, the prototyping phase is characterized by a visualization of ideas prior to their implementation in a finished product [13]. Such tangible visualization allows assessment, testing and refinement at a low cost. Nebeling and Madier as well as Rudd et al. distinguish between low fidelity

[1] https://unity.com/products/unity-mars.

to high fidelity prototyping [14,15]. Low fidelity prototyping is a simple and low cost method to quickly represent ideas. The skills related entry barrier is low allowing individuals from different professional backgrounds to participate in the prototyping process. However, low fidelity prototypes comprise limited functions and interaction techniques. A low fidelity technique like paper prototyping in AR lacks immersion, does not provide a spatial view or a 3D-prototype. High fidelity prototypes on the other hand can include the full range of functions and be fully interactive, which is associated with higher costs and a longer implementation time. As an AR-prototyping technique, high fidelity prototyping offers specific advantages [5,7,12]:

- It provides a high level of immersion allowing the user to experience the virtual content as seamlessly embedded into the real world.
- It ensures higher ecological validity, increasing the extent to which findings from test setups can be applied to real-world situations.

To achieve a high fidelity of AR prototypes for automotive AR HUDs, expert level skills in 3D modelling, behavior programming and rendering as well as knowledge of specialized software (e.g. Blender and Unity 3D) are required. Often, this part of development is completed by experts instead of AR concept creators.

1.3 Motivation and Goals

Concept developers of automotive AR HUD visualizations cannot rely solely on low- or medium-fidelity prototyping. They would greatly profit from being able to work with a high fidelity prototyping environment considering its higher ecological validity. Therefore, the following study was designed to gain a deeper understanding of the automotive AR HUD concept development process by focusing on the following research questions:

- Needs and requirements: Why do concept developers want a high fidelity prototyping environment? What needs should be met by a high fidelity prototyping environment?
- Pain points, hurdles and entry barriers: What keeps concept developers from working with a high fidelity prototyping environment? How can these challenges be overcome?

2 Related Work

In 2020, Freitas et al. reviewed literature dealing with tools and techniques for AR prototyping and ranked them according to the following categories [7]:

1. Resulting prototype fidelity: the level of similarity between the resulting prototype and the final product ranging from high to low. For example, the paper prototyping technique generates a low fidelity prototype whereas prototyping in Unity produces a high fidelity prototype.

2. Required skill level: skill level required to use the tool in accordance with the resulting prototype fidelity. For example, paper prototyping is ranked low in both categories, since sketching on paper in 2D requires does not require specialized expert skills, while prototyping in Unity is ranked highest in both categories.

Depending on the context and the desired results, developers may have to consider a trade-off between prototype fidelity, fidelity in AR and the necessary skill level when choosing an appropriate AR prototyping tool/technique.

At best, an AR prototyping tool or technique should allow a high prototype fidelity, be easy to use for individuals of variable skill levels while also producing a high fidelity in AR. Typically, this combination is rare and difficult to achieve, since producing high fidelity in AR is challenging without expert skills. Freitas et al. cite the following tools/techniques that fulfill the aforementioned criteria [7]. GestureWiz developed by Speicher and Nebeling is a tool for gesture-based interaction with virtual objects [17]. The tool was realized via the so-called Wizard of Oz approach, in which a person (the wizard) recognizes the user's gestures and mirrors them allowing users to realistically prototype gestures for interaction with virtual objects. With PintAR by Gasques et al. users can digitally sketch their ideas on handhelds in 2D, allowing an easy creation without expert skills [8]. Using Head-mounted displays (HMDs) users can view and interact with their prototypes in 3D with high levels of immersion. Using Holobuilder by Speicher et al. users can easily create AR-based instruction manuals for industrial applications [18]. According to Freitas et al., the Holobuilder tool is similar to PowerPoint [7].

In their user study, De Sá and Churchill implemented a mobile AR application as a high, low and mixed fidelity prototype [6]. Their results showed that the mixed fidelity approach was sufficient in this use case. Interestingly, users expected a higher fidelity of the high fidelity prototype than it could deliver, which could be a source of irritation and introduce additional challenges during the implementation process.

According to Freitas et al., PapAR by Lauber et al. is a technique that produces a low prototype fidelity and a low level of fidelity in AR [7,10]. Since no expert skills are required, ideas can be easily expressed and visualized. With PapAR, users prototype on two layers separate layers. This approach is particularly suitable for AR, since one layer can represent the real world and the transparent layer can be used to add AR objects to the scene. While the PapAR technique retains the low skill level requirements, it increases the ecological validity of traditional paper prototyping. FrameBox and MirrorBox by Broy et al., increase the fidelity level by expanding paper prototyping with a third spatial dimension and don't require expert skills to use them [4]. Both Lauber et al. and Broy et al. have applied their tools and techniques to prototype infotainment systems in automotive HUDs [4,10].

3 Use Case and Implementation

To find out how AR concept developers work, the study implemented a use case where participants developed an AR concept for an AR HUD. Therefore each participant was given a Lego City package containing a street layout, traffic lights, and street signs. With the help of two toy cars, the scenario was a traffic situation of a left turn with an oncoming car. This specific situation is complex since it required the participants to orchestrate two cars about traffic regulations, traffic lights, and street signs. Additionally, the participants were provided Play-Doh in different colors for prototyping 3D objects. It allows shaping the objects in any way. A laptop stand helped the study director observes the whole setup from the best angle. The setup (see Fig. 2) was neither validated nor used before. The study took a qualitative approach in which participants' rule

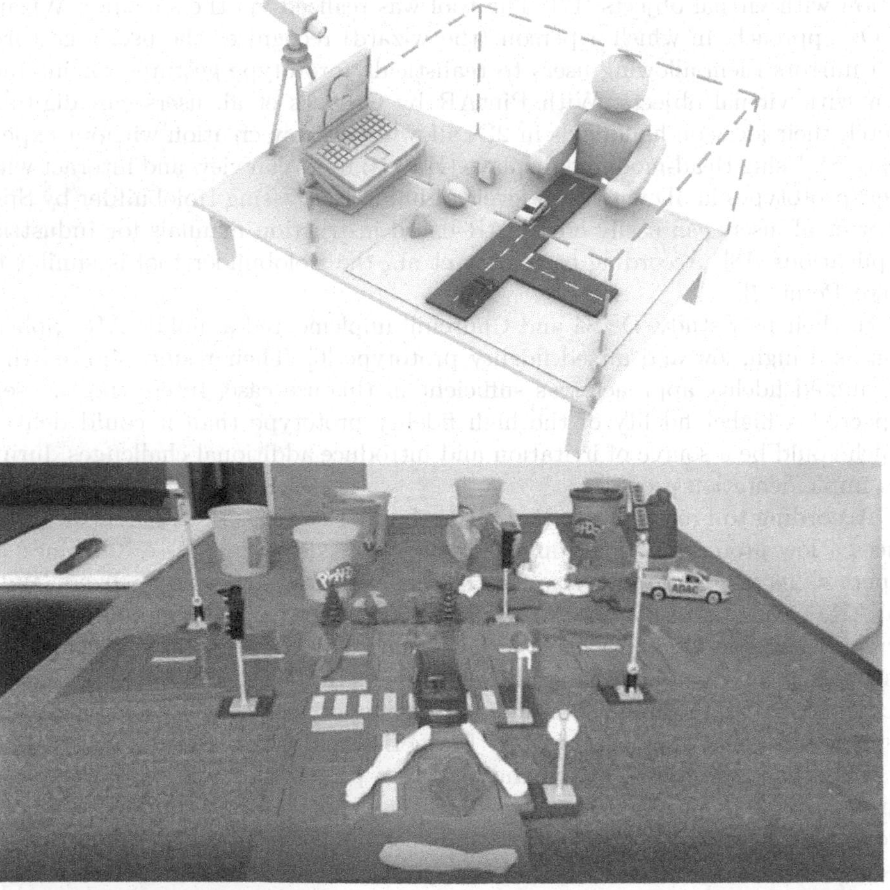

Fig. 2. Study setup - planned setup draft (top) actual setup from a participant (bottom)

sets for development and thought processes were evaluated using a systematic content analysis of video recordings and interviews.

With the help of the traffic scenario and Play-Doh, the concept developer could visualize his thoughts during the interview, supporting the process's creativity. The study aimed at observing the participants while completing a given task and gaining insights into their very own development processes concerning:

- What and where are pain points and hurdles for concept developers in their daily work?
- Which methodical and technical aid do concept developers wish for if they would get a HMI that would help them with their problems?

This refers to the guiding research questions presented in Sect. 1.3 and were the structuring part of the conducted interview.

4 Procedure and Evaluation

The user study took place in the first half of 2021. Due to the Covid-19 pandemic it had to be done remotely. N = 8 participants from automotive industry took part without compensation. All of the deliberately chosen participants were AR concept experts working with AR for a minimum of three years and daily. Here, we call them *concept developers*.

Three of them were psychologists, and five were either visual or interaction designers. Three participants held a Ph.D. degree, and the others had a master's degree. It is important to note here that these concept developers usually have technical knowledge, regardless of their specific education. The participants are experts in their field to create concepts, but they do not have all the necessary technical skills implement AR concepts in the vehicle themselves. In total, the study took around three to four hours per participant. Additionally, the participants received their working materials in home office.

With the help of the study director, who was connected remotely via video camera, they set up the traffic scenario with the two toy cars (see Fig. 2). Based on the setup, the study director explained the study in detail. The procedure depicted an exemplary development process divided into the phases described in Sect. 1.2.

The evaluation or testing phase was not part of the study because the participants were to be asked at what point in the development process they would conduct an assessment. Thus, the evaluation questions have moved on to the other phases. The development and presentation phases were classified as interview phases because the participants answered them hypothetically. Finally, ideation and prototyping were classified as working phases since they required the participants to work with the setup, for example, kneading 3D objects from play-doh. Here, the participants first had some time to fulfill the task and think aloud while the study director was observing. Afterward, the study director conducted the interview, depending on whether the questions were answered beforehand.

In addition to general questions, he asked contextually and phase-specific questions, such as questions regarding the experience and a theoretical HMI supporting the participants in the respective phase. Next, each phase is described in detail (Fig. 3):

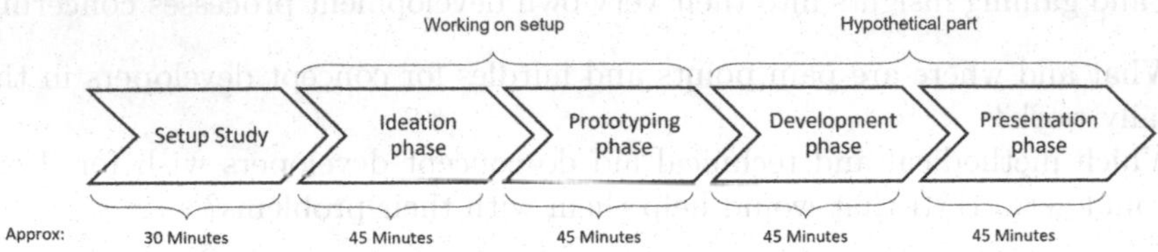

Fig. 3. Procedure of the study

1. Ideation: Participants had 15 min to develop possible traffic scenarios and how to support the driver in this situation in the given task. Afterwards, the interview was conducted. The questions mainly revolved around a theoretical HMI to support the participants during the ideation process.
2. Prototyping: The prototyping phase proceeded analogue to the previous phase. The participants used their time to specifically think about the implementation of the navigation concepts from the previous ideation phase. The questions mainly revolved around a theoretical HMI to support the participants during the prototyping process. Additionally, the interviewer asked questions regarding the implementation of virtual objects.
3. Development: The development phase was conducted as an interview only. The interviewer asked questions about the 3D modelling process, the implementation of virtual objects and behavior programming.
4. Presentation/Transfer: The presentation/transfer phase was conducted as an interview only. The interviewer mainly asked questions about the use case presentation. Lastly, participants were interviewed about other possible use cases, issues and hurdles experienced during the development of navigation concepts for AR HUDs.

The study was evaluated according to Kuckartz' structured content analysis [9]. The main thematic categories were derived from the research questions described in Sect. 1.3. The transcripts were coded using the thematic categories. Subsequently, all text lines with the same codes were compiled into a matrix. New subcategories were inductively formed based on the compiled matrix. In a next step, the resulting matrix was re-coded using the differentiated category system summarized in Table 1.

Table 1. Summary of the differentiated category system

User experience	AR authoring	Mobility functions
• Ease of use	• 2D-Tools	• Timing and procedures
• Object modelling	• Primitives	• Information loss
• Annotation notes	• Tangible prototyping	• Driver perspective
	• Scenarios and components	• Spatial contextualization
	• Version management	• Special features

5 Results

Every participant described a complete theoretical prototyping HMI for the end customer and could distinguish between basic terms and elements like virtual objects, objects related to the traffic scenario and behavior of the virtual and street elements. Table 2 shows a summarized overview of the main outcomes. In some study runs, it had become apparent that the ideation and prototyping phases could not be separated, as the participants had already began to integrate virtual content and prototype while still in the ideation phase. Therefore, it was essential for them to work with the virtual content at an early stage and specify their thoughts in the spatial context of the task.

Table 2. Overview of the main outcomes of the specific phases during the study

Working phase	Ideation phase	Prototyping phase	All phases
Completion	Naming of features	Casual and spatial description	Willingness to experience in real environment
Heat map		Driver-HUD-relation	
Mental model		Relation to daily work	
		Spatial reference	
		Description of behavior	

The evaluation of the working parts showed that almost every participant pointed out significant areas where information should be displayed. The participants named them maneuver or stopping points (shown in Fig. 4). In general, it is important to point out that every participant can be characterized as one of the following two types of concept developers: the ones who describe their concept in a more structure-controlled and those who express their idea in a more sequence-controlled way. This influenced their designed concepts and how they explained them. The difference became especially noticeable during the traffic events, like a traffic light that turns red. The structure-controlled developer recognized elements that could trigger an event and proactively described the event occurring. The sequence-controlled developer usually only paid attention to possible events during the maneuver or the route and inevitably brought the car into an event. Thus, it happened four times that concept developers who took a sequence-controlled approach did not name the elements that could have been triggered in the scene. In the following, the two types shall be called structure and sequence developers. Table 3 presents each types properties.

Table 3. Structure and sequence developers

Developer	Property	Description
Structure	Description of user story	Possible events around the car
	Type of reaction to events	Proactive
	Note	Needed more complex information
Sequence	Description of user story	Linear on maneuver
	Type of reaction to events	Reactive
	Note	Were faster but ignored information

Figure 4 shows a compilation of the maneuver points of the scene, where AR content could be presented. In particular, it has been demonstrated here that the augmentation must take place far in front of the vehicle. The concept developer wants to control the timing of the display concerning vehicle position and speed. External triggers, such as traffic lights or crosswalks, are independent and can be displayed in regard to their importance. This figure is a compilation of the experts. Not all of them required the use of maneuver points. In comparison, others have explicitly marked some spatially in the scene.

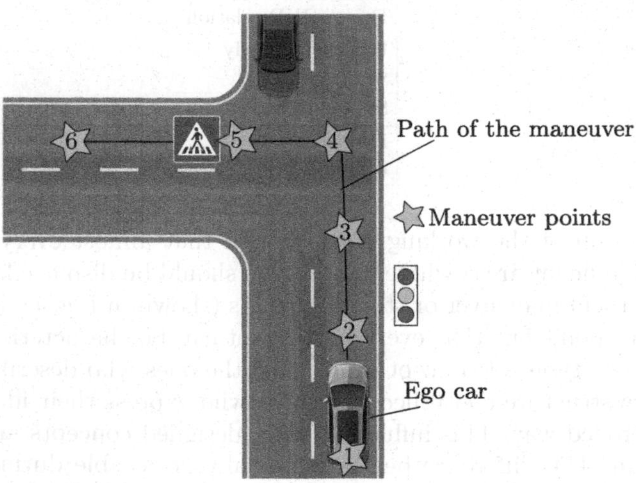

Fig. 4. Maneuver points (extracted from the videos of the study)

The ideation phase has shown that the concept developers, in particular, have indirect requirements for a development environment that do not necessarily have to be technical. One participant, in particular, emphasized that he needed the opportunity to collaborate with others and work on the concepts.

> "[...] I need to collaborate with other persons, so multiple people need to see things together simultaneously. [...] whenever you work with AR and so on, especially the HUD, [...], even when you make studies, either you or the participant can see it. [...]"

The summarized results of the prototyping phase are shown in Table 4. They were assigned to the respective subcategories that emerged during the evaluation.

Table 4. Results of the prototyping phase

Subcategory	Summarized result
Description of all created virtual objects with Play-Doh	They have a spatial or causal relationship. Spatial is for registration of objects in the world coordinate system of reality, and causal is concerning road users, functional entities (such as traffic lights), or the driver himself
	The type of object generated can be described as single objects that change their shape concerning the emerging information. Another concept has been described as a permanent transformation of things throughout the maneuver so that recurring patterns can be generated
Relation between HUD and driver	The augmentation must always be one step ahead for the driver to react to the information in time
	The concept must also not overwhelm the driver. It must leave him a decision not to be forced to follow it
Comparison of the work in the study and daily work	Working with virtual dough would be very good. The spatial and tangible creation of virtual objects pleases almost everyone in the study setup
	2D graphics are almost always created in daily work extended to three-dimensional space
Location of objects in scene	These depend on speed, distance to the driver, and the current amount of information in the display
Description of the behavior in general terms	The behavior was described based on emergent maneuver elements in the study setup
	They should be similar to the animation functionalities in Microsoft PowerPoint
	Common behaviors mentioned and used in the majority are changing the size of the virtual object, fading in and out based on distance, and pulsing

In the development phase, critical elements of development were asked. The summary shows aspects of the daily work of the concept developers. For example, Fig. 5 shows that half of the test persons are confident to prototype the concept created in the study, whereas 7 out of 8 would commission the development in their everyday work. This is due to time constraints, lack of competence in terms of knowledge about the car, or the ability to develop the concept with high visual quality for a presentation.

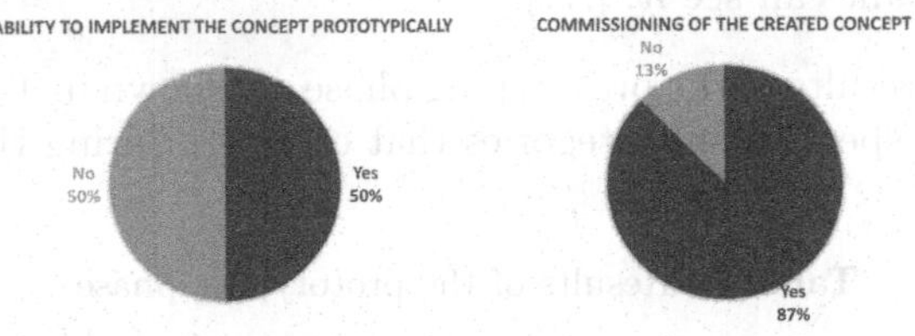

Fig. 5. Comparison of results in development

The effort was as high or very high by seven of the eight subjects (see Fig. 6). However, the evaluation was complex since they have a corresponding assignment in their daily work and can only estimate the actual effort. Whether prototypical or not, the development is a black box that the software developers implement.

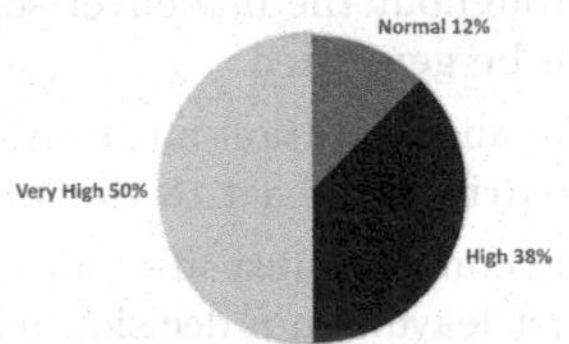

Fig. 6. Effort of programming

In the final phase of the study, only one participant communicated to show the customer's result in an AR HUD. The responses after the previous experience were characterized by alternative or no solutions. The following quote shows this: "[...] usually we can't present the product's final state. [...]". A large number was characterized by partial solutions, which can be attributed to two features of the presentation:

1. Only partial solutions are presented in partial functionalities based on triggers in simulated worlds and not under real circumstances.
2. The target group very much determines the presentation platform, and videos or presentations of moving images are shown, which, however, can represent the entire concept. The target audience includes potential customers, the general public, testers with specific characteristics or management.

In addition to the core results of the four phases, the participants were also asked about their willingness to evaluate the experience at this point, i.e., with the result generated in each stage. Table 2 shows partial statements of the respective phase.

Table 5. Willigness to evaluate

Phase	Quote
Ideation	"That avoids possible dead ends that you might only realize much later in the project if you skip this immersion phase in reality"
	"So it is necessary to test the whole thing at an early stage, so that you don't realize after two years of development that the concept works with one person, but not with the other"
Prototyping	"[...] In a real situation it feels different than just in a micro world, like here now. I will understand something different than you. In my head something completely different happens than in yours and above all [...] also something completely different happens than in that of the future users"
Development	"Yep and on almost daily basis really. that's critical at that point"
	"Only at the end, I wouldn't want to see every little change I make in the real conditions but when I say ok I am done with this phase then I would want to experience it. [...] In the earlier phases it was more important to experience earlier because you were testing a concept, here it is at the end to confirm that everything works"

At the end of the study, the participants were asked to name the most significant problem from their point of view. The following summarized list shows the result:

- spatial understanding of the user are the biggest learning costs of AR
- to get into presentation mode
- to setup study settings
- mandatory reference to the environment combined with the limitation of the field of view
- create ideas in the ideation phase
- transition between the phases: media change or further tools needed
- getting good quality and stable data
  - occlusion is still a big problem
  - precise localization of the car and the environment are hard to process.

In summary, the statements on the last question are a good example of the different focal points and dimensions that concept developers in the automotive industry deal with as so called non-technical experts. In essence, as with the usual AR development process, the focus is on technical problems. They become apparent by naming technical difficulties in development and transferring results between different media or platforms. Further on, procedural difficulties also become apparent, presented by a lack of cooperation in the development of virtual objects in the context of navigation for an AR HUD. At several points in the interviews, the desire for a collaboration environment was expressed.

6 Discussion

The results of the expert study essentially show how multidimensional the development of AR applications is in the automotive context. Half of all test persons had the confidence to prototype their personally created concept, which shows that the necessary technical basis exists to understand and name the general problems. In many places, however, clear so-called "black boxes" were called in which concept developers do not know what is happening or how the concepts are implemented. Therefore, in addition to strong design and programming skills, technical understanding of the vehicle and platform-specific development skills for the AR HUD are also needed.

This is particularly evident in the individual platform decisions made in day-to-day work. No holistic evaluation platform exists that meets the needs of concept developers. In most cases, partial solutions are created that are tested in simulation environments concerning experience or functionality. This clarifies that although all concept developers develop navigation concepts for AR HUDs, they have individual development processes about their decisions.

Indeed, there is a difference in whether a proof of concept is evaluated on slides, videos, simulated virtual worlds, or the actual target platform. This is shown by the statements in Table 5 regarding immersive evaluation. The study design allowed participants to manage their analyses and tasks spatially and tangibly. Even without an explicit question within the interview, almost all participants still positively mentioned it. Especially in the first two phases of the development process, the subjects' spatial representation of all components and interrelationships helped.

As expected, the lo-fi prototyping environment used in the study helped the participants to understand the development process better. Even though the methodology is not a validated approach, it can be used as a first creative development building block in many places. No technical skills are necessary, and it is multi-user capable. This means that hardware setup can be used for simple virtual objects, their placement, and composition for creation and communication. The biggest weakness, which also became apparent within the study, is the ability to represent behavior. Alliterations and steps in the user story have to be done manually.

Especially the first two phases show the difference for the creation of navigation concepts in an automotive context besides the advantages of spatial and tangible AR prototyping environments known so far in the literature. The structure and sequence developer show that the mental models and the language used to describe the user story significantly influence the requirements of a prototyping environment. For example, the structural descriptions showed that increased knowledge of the vehicle's environment and possible occurring events in the environment is needed. On the other hand, the sequential descriptions showed the importance of knowledge about the vehicle's behavior, the components of navigation, procedures, and routines of the concept and the driver.

The analysis of the participants' description and approach supports the explicit multidimensional complexity of the automotive context of the generated AR application. The narrowing of the task helps this. The participants created their concept for only one maneuver. The processes would be significantly more complex in the context of an entire navigation route with multiple maneuvers and possible events in the process.

The traffic elements provided in the study, such as the crosswalk or the traffic light, were in all cases used either as anchors for virtual objects or as sources of information by the participants. This shows that the requirement for an immersive authoring tool is not only in the functional support of the concept developer, such as creating virtual objects or the description of animations and behavior. In particular, knowledge about the existence and function of the natural world is essential. Specifically, this means that the concept developer wants to know the state of the traffic light and interpret this information in his concept and present it to the driver in an appropriate way in the AR HUD.

Subdivision of the study into several phases may have influenced the participants by providing a thought pattern. Still, it helped structure the questions regarding the research question and all relevant items. Generally, the study was held according to the fixed standardized scheme, where the participants first had time for themselves, bouncing around some ideas. Afterwards, they were interviewed by the study director. The interview questions were the same with every participant, but subquestions in dialogue differed according to what each participant said before.

Covid-19 and the consequent limitations lead to several hurdles and problems in conducting the study. It was planned to observe and interview the participants in their presence. In the end, the study had to be moved to each participant's home, sending the set up to the participants and the study director conducting the study remotely. Next to technical issues, distractions at the participants' homes may have led to disruptions and delays. This also reflects in the evaluation, when some parts of the recording were incomprehensible and impossible to transcribe. Moreover, several participants had to back out due to Covid-19.

7 Conclusion

Domain-specific analysis for an AR authoring tool can add several complexity levels to the general problem of developing AR for in-vehicle use:

- Complexity of technology of the vehicle and suitable simulation environments.
- Complexity of traffic and other entities like real world elements and their functions (e.g. traffic lights) in relation to the vehicle.
- Complexity of behavior that can be addressed to own vehicle, other road users and the virtual objects.

A schematic representation of the complexity levels are shown in the Fig. 7.

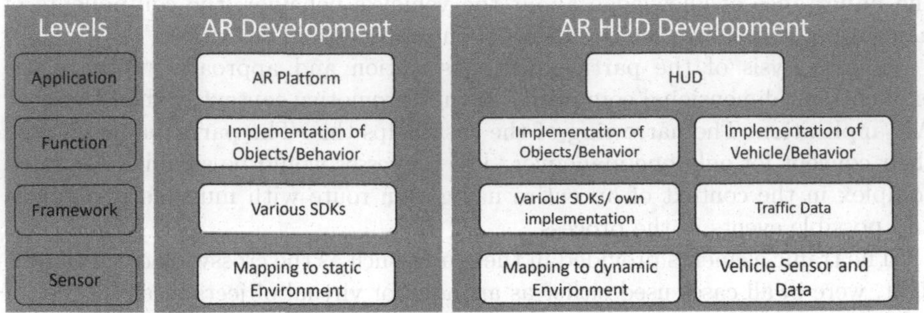

Fig. 7. Different complexities in developing AR- and AR HUD applications

Our guiding research questions have helped us understand the issues and dimensions involved in developing AR concepts for vehicle drivers. On the one hand, these are the consideration of the levels of complexity within the development and the inclusion of the individual aspects of the mobility domain that are not known in AR development for concepts. Thus, extensive knowledge about spatial and flow-oriented contexts is necessary, and the interaction with entities from traffic, environment and virtual objects is an essential requirement for creating AR concepts for vehicle drivers.

Because of the context explained so far, the complexities shown, and the wishes expressed by the concept developers, it is confirmed that a high fidelity and immersive authoring tool is beneficial for high ecological validity. Here all rules and information of the automotive mobility domain must be included. In addition to these rules, a multi-user evaluation in the target platform of the AR HUD is helpful.

A lo-fi prototyping environment leads to lower quality of developed AR concepts for vehicle drivers, higher production costs in terms of late changes in process, and a lack of understanding of the concept idea between developer, presenter, and customer.

One exemplary use case could be a rule-based development environment for a navigation concept that is related to a traffic light. Based on the traffic light's state, the concept would change its color to the represented status of the traffic light. This rule-based development should provide all necessary demands from ideation to presentation and speak the concept developer's language to achieve the best experience.

In the future, we plan to evaluate an immersive authoring tool for AR concepts for vehicle drivers to investigate the development process and the acceptance of such a development environment of a concept developer.

Conflict of Interest Statement. Bilal Azzam is employed by Volkswagen AG. The study was conducted and financed by Volkswagen AG. The authors declare no competing conflict of interest. The results, opinions and conclusions expressed in this publication are not necessarily those of Volkswagen AG.

References

1. Abdi, L., Meddeb, A.: In-vehicle augmented reality system to provide driving safety information. J. Vis. **21**(1), 163–184 (2017). https://doi.org/10.1007/s12650-017-0442-6
2. Azuma, R.T.: A survey of Augmented Reality, vol. 6, pp. 355–385. https://doi.org/10.1162/pres.1997.6.4.355
3. Bauerfeind, K., Drüke, J., Bendewald, L., Baumann, M.: When does the driver benefit from AR-information in a navigation task compared to a head-up display? Results of a driving simulator study. In: Proceedings of the Human Factors and Ergonomics Society Europe, pp. 219–230 (2019)
4. Broy, N., Schneegass, S., Alt, F., Schmidt, A.: FrameBox and MirrorBox: tools and guidelines to support designers in prototyping interfaces for 3D displays (2014)
5. Carter, S., Mankoff, J., Klemmer, S.R., Matthews, T.: Exiting the cleanroom: on ecological validity and ubiquitous computing. Hum.-Comput. Interact. **23**(1), 47–99 (2008). https://doi.org/10.1080/07370020701851086
6. De Sá, M., Churchill, E.: Mobile augmented reality: exploring design and prototyping techniques (2012)
7. Freitas, G., Pinho, M.S., Silveira, M.S., Maurer, F.: A systematic review of rapid prototyping tools for augmented reality. In: 2020 22nd Symposium on Virtual and Augmented Reality, pp. 199–209. IEEE Computer Society, Los Alamitos (2020). https://doi.org/10.1109/SVR51698.2020.00041
8. Gasques, D., Johnson, J.G., Sharkey, T., Weibel, N.: What you sketch is what you get: quick and easy augmented reality prototyping with PintAR. In: Brewster, S., Fitzpatrick, G., Cox, A., Kostakos, V. (eds.) CHI 2019: Proceedings of the 2019 CHI Conference on Human Factors in Computing Systems, pp. 1–6. Association for Computing Machinery, New York (2019). https://doi.org/10.1145/3290607.3312847
9. Kuckartz, U.: Qualitative Text Analysis: A Guide to Methods, Practice & Using Software. London (2014). https://doi.org/10.4135/9781446288719
10. Lauber, F., Böttcher, C., Butz, A.: PapAR: paper prototyping for augmented reality. In: Boyle, L.N., Kun, A.L., Pearce, B., Szostak, D., Osswald, S. (eds.) AutomotiveUI 2014, pp. 1–6. Association for Computing Machinery, New York (2014). https://doi.org/10.1145/2667239.2667271
11. Menk, C., Koch, R.: Truthful color reproduction in spatial augmented reality applications. IEEE Trans. Visual. Comput. Graph. **19**(2), 236–248 (2012)
12. Milgram, P., Kishino, F.: A taxonomy of mixed reality visual displays. IEICE Trans. Inf. Syst. **E77–D**(12), 1321–1329 (1994)
13. Mueller, R.M., Thoring, K.: Understanding artifact knowledge in design science: prototypes and products as knowledge repositories. In: AMCIS 2011 Proceedings - All Submissions, p. 216 (2011). http://aisel.aisnet.org/amcis2011_submissions/216
14. Nebeling, M., Madier, K.: 360proto: making interactive virtual reality & augmented reality prototypes from paper. In: Brewster, S., Fitzpatrick, G., Cox, A., Kostakos, V. (eds.) CHI 2019: Proceedings of the 2019 CHI Conference on Human Factors in Computing Systems, pp. 1–13. Association for Computing Machinery, New York (2019). https://doi.org/10.1145/3290605.3300826

15. Rudd, J., Stern, K., Isensee, S.: Low vs. high fidelity prototyping debate (06022022). https://www.yumpu.com/en/document/read/32856502/low-vs-high-fidelity-prototyping-debate
16. Sandbrink, J.: Gestaltungspotenziale Für Infotainment-Darstellungen Im Fahrzeug. Springer, Wiesbaden (2019). https://doi.org/10.1007/978-3-658-23942-8
17. Speicher, M., Nebeling, M.: GestureWiz: a human-powered gesture design environment for user interface prototypes. In: Mandryk, R., Hancock, M., Perry, M., Cox, A. (eds.) CHI 2018: Proceedings of the 2018 CHI Conference on Human Factors in Computing Systems, pp. 1–11. Association for Computing Machinery, New York (2018). https://doi.org/10.1145/3173574.3173681
18. Speicher, M., Tenhaft, K., Heinen, S., Handorf, H.: Enabling industry 4.0 with holobuilder. In: Cunningham, D.W., Hofstedt, P., Schmitt, I. (eds.) INFORMATIK 2015, vol. 246, pp. 1561–1575 (2015)

Creating Geopositioned 3D Areas of Interest from Fleet Gaze Data

Jan Bickerdt[1(✉)], Christian Gollnick[1], Jan Sonnenberg[1], and Enkelejda Kasneci[2]

[1] Volkswagen AG, 38440 Wolfsburg, Germany
{Jan.Bickerdt,Christian.Gollnick,Jan.Sonnenberg}@volkswagen.de
[2] Eberhard Karls Universität Tübingen,Tübingen, Germany
Enkelejda.Kasneci@uni-tuebingen.de

Abstract. In order to observe driver's attention levels, different approaches are followed. They include simple methods counting driver input changes [6], machine learning based approaches based on driver input [17], and methods considering additional inputs such as environmental data and eye tracking data [3–5,7,12,16]. Recent studies have proposed geopositioned 3D AOIs as a tool for driver intention observation. Geopositioned 3D AOIs are three dimensional Areas (boxes), with fix geopositiones (e.g. GPS) which have to be observed for a safe completion of driving maneuvers. Examples are pedestrian waiting areas, crosswalks, and traffic light. Creating these AOIs by hand is a tedious task with ample room for potential errors, as the created AOIs might differ from the real AOIs drivers look at. We therefore propose a pipeline to generate real 3D AOIs from gaze clouds. To generate relevant gaze clouds we use the points of closest encounter in fleet gaze data collected in a driving simulator setup. The results show that the generation of 3D AOIs from fleet data is possible and the created AOIs are mostly consistent with the expected AOIs.

Keywords: Eye tracking · Automotive · Areas of interest · Fleet data

1 Introduction

Recently, the idea of using geopositioned 3D AOIs for gaze analysis has been proposed [2]. Geopositioned 3D AOIs are different from traditional AOIs, as they are defined as 3D cuboids in fix geostationary positions (e.g. GPS) and not as pixel coordinates on an image. They could be compared to bounding boxes, with the main difference being their independence from physical objects. Meaning, they can be used to define environmental areas like pedestrian waiting areas.

This approach of defining AOIs at fixed geopositions demonstrates an short term alternative and a long term addition to object based AOIs/bounding boxes (BB). Unlike BB, AOIs are not reliant one the existence or rather the systems awareness of an object. As the vehicle does not need to detect surrounding objects only a reduced sensor set, consisting of eye tracking and GPS, is

H. Krömker (Ed.): HCII 2022, LNCS 13335, pp. 21–34, 2022.
https://doi.org/10.1007/978-3-031-04987-3_2

required to use 3D AOIs. As driver monitoring is now part of the Euro NCAP requirements [14,15] and EU regulation [21], these sensors could be available in all production cars in the near future. They could be used to study drivers gaze behavior, find irregular observation behavior, and therefore improve traffic safety. In the more distant future 3D AOIs could be used to enhance the performance of next generations Advanced Driver Assistance Systems (ADAS). By combining object detection with 3D AOIs new methods for driver attention and driver intention estimation could be developed.

Up to this point, using 3D AOIs in a real world setting required extensive knowledge of the environment and traffic conditions in order to manually define them. One way to make 3D AOIs easier to use, would be the generation based on fleet gaze data. This could lead to the discovery of important traffic areas previously missed by researchers and could allow for the detection of distractions.

We propose the use of fleet gaze data, as it allows for the creation of AOIs at positions deemed important/interesting by the majority of drivers, and enables comparison of individual gaze behavior with the overall gaze behavior.

The main contribution of this article is as follows: (1) A method to determine similar gaze goals between different viewers is established. (2) The OPTICS algorithm is used to determine clusters in the generated point cloud. (3) Based on these clusters a method to generate and optimize 3D AOIs is shown.

The remaining article is structured as follows: Sect. 2 summarizes the preceding work exploring driver intention prediction and gaze analysis in urban scenarios. Additionally, the experimental setup and the data preparation is explained. Section 3 deals with the data preprocessing and the methods used for driver intention prediction. Performance metrics are introduced and explained. In Sect. 4, the results are presented and analyzed. Existing limits and further steps are highlighted in Sect. 5. The last section summarizes the findings and concludes this work.

2 Related Work

To generate geopositioned 3D AOIs from gaze data, it is important to find the gaze target. There are multiple ways to estimate the targets position [22]. Firstly, the intersection of the two gaze vectors of the participants eyes can be calculated. This requires very accurate gaze data. To achieve the required level of accuracy, head stabilization is required. Driving requires free head movement, this approach is therefore not suitable for our use case. Secondly, the two gaze vectors can be combined into one average vector. If an environmental point cloud is available, the point closest to the gaze vector can be calculated and used as the gaze target. As one of the advantages of 3D AOIs is the reduction of sensors like LIDAR, the use of LIDAR generated point clouds is not possible.

The next step is the generation of clusters from the found point cloud. Because point clouds are a common representation of LIDAR data and are often used in ADAS, numerous algorithms for point cloud clustering exist. Song et al. use clustering to reduce the complexity of point clouds [20]. Their approach produces a predefined number of clusters. As the number of 3D AOIs is unknown, this approach is not applicable for our use case. Hannaneh et al. use clustering to optimize point cloud analysis [13]. While this approach sounds promising, the way this algorithm clusters is meant to optimize parallel computing and can lead to unwanted cluster shapes. Miheal et al. introduced the OPTICS (Ordering Points To Identify the Clustering Structure) algorithm [1].

To analyze the quality of the results, a baseline is needed. A lot of previous work has been done on eye tracking in intersections. Lemonnier et al. show that gaze interaction with traditional vehicle AOIs like speedometer, and mirrors, depends on the environment and task, as well as the familiarity of the stimuli [10,11]. It also has been shown, that simpler environments can lead to a decrease in visual observations [23]. Most methods use either vehicle AOIs or traffic/environmental objects for eye tracking analysis. We could not find any articles defining the relevant, object independent gaze targets.

3 Research Questions and Methods

3.1 Research Questions

Can gaze data from a group of driver's be combined to generate 3D AOIs?
Do the generated 3D AOIs match the predicted 3D AOIs?
Can generated 3D AOIs be used to obtain new information about the drivers gaze behavior?

3.2 Dataset

The used dataset has been provided by Bickerdt et al. [2]. It contains data from 74 participants, with a male to female ratio of 11/63. The documented average age is 39.4 with a standard deviation (SD) of 10.5 years. 42 participants have more than 20 years of driving experience, with an average of 12 years and a SD of 4.7 for the remaining participants. The yearly driven kilometers are 18k km with a SD of 7.5k km. A pretest was performed to determine participant's visual acuity, contrast perception and color perception. All participants achieved at least 100% acuity, were able to identify the color test plates, and could perceive the minimum displayable contrast. The data was recorded in a driving simulator with five 3.05 m × 1.89 m screens equipped with color calibrated projectors. This equates to a coverage of 245° × 39° of the users field of view. Additionally three displays positioned behind the user provided a usable mirror setup. This setup allows for almost 360° of coverage fo the participants field of view. The recorded data contains vehicle data (e.g. speed, position, steering angle, etc.), environmental data (e.g. surrounding objects, traffic light status), and eye tracking data (eye position, head position, gaze direction, etc.). The environment consisted of a complex urban intersection with high and low amounts of traffic, depending on the performed scenario. The dataset consists of three different scenarios. "Turn left", "Crossing", and "Turn right". "Turn left" has been performed with different variations. The implemented variations are daytime (night/day) and traffic amount (high/low). To determine the driver's gaze, the simulators cockpit was equipped with a SmartEye Pro remote eye tracking system. Consisting of three IR GigE cameras with 1.3 MP resolution, the eye tracking system achieves an accuracy of up to 0.5 °C in estimating the gaze direction [18,19], under optimal conditions.

3.3 Predefined 3D AOIs/Ground Truth

According to the minimum required attention (MiRA)-theory defined by Kirchner et al. the driver can be "considered attentive [...]" by "sampling sufficient information [...] to be able to to form and maintain a good enough mental representation of the situation" [9]. We defined our ground truth based on this requirement. For a better identification of the observations required we adapted the three phases for intersection crossing "Entering", "Crossing", and "Leaving" as described by Geruschat et al. [8] (see Fig. 1). Applying the MiRA-theory and the three phases to the used scenarios leads to the 3D AOIs visualized in Fig. 2 and the predicted gaze-3D AOI interactions shown in Table 1.

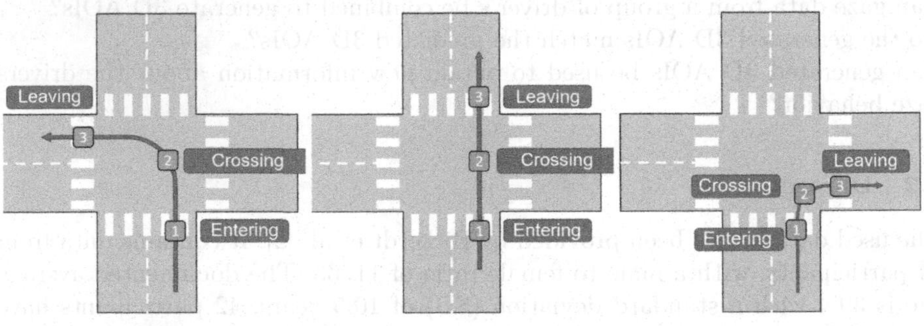

(a) Segments of the "turn left" driving maneuver. (b) Segments of the "crossing intersection" driving maneuver. (c) Segments of the "turn right" driving maneuver.

Fig. 1. Based on vehicle deceleration and environmental interaction, the maneuvers can be divided into different segments, "Entering", "Crossing", and "Leaving". This subdivision allows for a better understanding of the created AOIs.

3.4 Point Cloud Generation

To create create 3D AOIs, we propose to use a combination of the aforementioned approaches. A point cloud can be created by using a combined two eye gaze vector and finding the point of closest encounter with the other participant's gaze vectors. The created point cloud can then be used to generate 3D AOIs by performing a density based clustering algorithm.

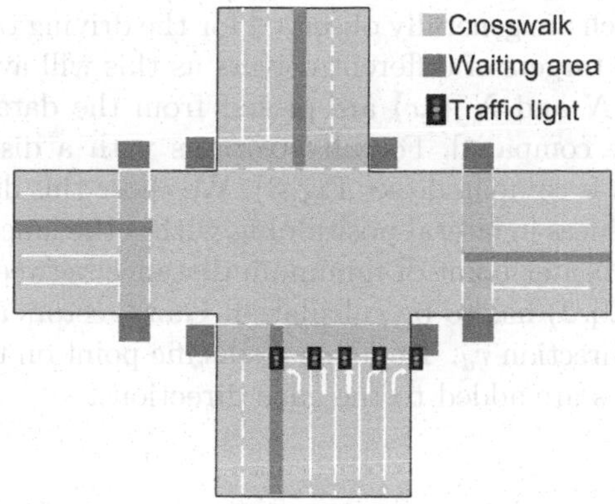

Fig. 2. Predefined AOIs. Pedestrian waiting areas are orange. Crosswalks are yellow. (Color figure online)

Table 1. Expected AOI interactions divided by maneuver and maneuver phase. Necessary AOI observation is marked with x. Additional, useful AOI observation is marked with +. AOI positions are abbreviated for better readability. The first two letters identify the road junction, and the next two letters specify the position on that road junction (**Lo**wer, **Le**ft, **Up**per, **Ri**ght). For example, "LoRi Crosswalk" is the crosswalk on the right side of the lower road, behind the traffic lights. The traffic lights are numbered from left to right.

AOIs\Maneuver	Turn left			Crossing			Turn right		
Phase	Entering	Crossing	Leaving	Entering	Crossing	Leaving	Entering	Crossing	Leaving
LoLe Crosswalk	+	+		+	+		+	+	
LoRi Crosswalk	x	x		x	x		x	x	
LeLo Crosswalk			+						
LeUp Crosswalk			x						
UpLe Crosswalk						+			
UpRi Crosswalk						x			
RiUp Crosswalk									+
RiLo Crosswalk									x
LoLe Waiting Area									
LoRi Waiting Area	+	+		+	+		+	+	
LeLo Waiting Area									
LeUp Waiting Area			+						
UpLe Waiting Area									
UpRi Waiting Area						+			
RiUp Waiting Area									
RiLo Waiting Area									+
Trafficlight 1	x	+							
Trafficlight 2				x	+				
Trafficlight 3				x	+				
Trafficlight 4							x	+	
Trafficlight 5							x	+	

To find areas which are generally observed for the driving task, it is important to compare the gaze targets of different drivers as this will average out outliers. Firstly, two driver (N and $N+x$) are picked from the dataset. Secondly, the vehicle positions are compared. For all positions with a distance of less than 0.25m, the gaze data is compared (see Fig. 3). We chose this distance, as roughly equates to the differences in lateral positioning within the lane. In order to create the point could, the center point of minimum distance between the gaze vectors $\boldsymbol{r}_1$ (Eq. 1) and $\boldsymbol{r}_2$ (Eq. 2) has to be calculated. Gaze vectors are defined as gaze origin $\overrightarrow{r_o}$ plus gaze direction $\overrightarrow{r_d}$. To define a specific point on the gaze vector the multiplicators t and s are added to the gaze directions.

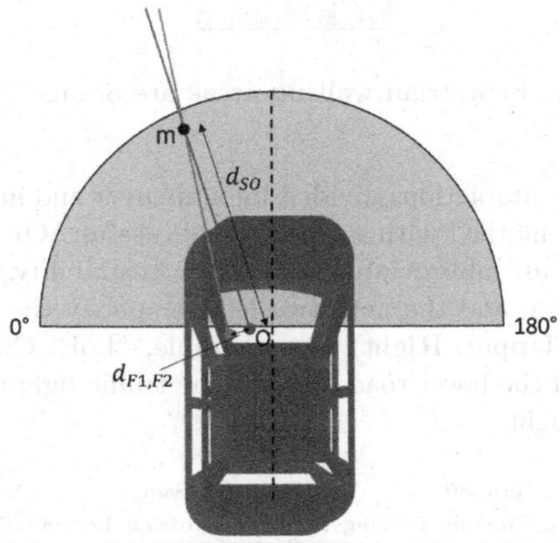

Fig. 3. Schematic representation of the algorithm used to find the center point of minimum distance between two drivers' gaze. Gaze vectors, from different participants ($F1, F2$), originating (O) in a distance smaller than 0.25 m ($d_{F1,F2}$) are compared to find the points of minimum distance (d_{SO}) and calculate the center point of minimum distance (m). (Eqs. 1–6)

$$\overrightarrow{r_1} = \overrightarrow{r_{1o}} + \overrightarrow{r_{2d}t} \tag{1}$$

$$\overrightarrow{r_2} = \overrightarrow{r_{2o}} + \overrightarrow{r_{2d}s} \tag{2}$$

To find the center point of minimum distance, the points of minimum distance have to be found for each gaze vector. This is possible by finding the minimum solution for Eq. 3. p represents a point on the gaze vector of driver 2.

$$d = ((\overrightarrow{r_{1o}} + \overrightarrow{r_{1d}t}) - p)^2 \tag{3}$$

Rearranging the formula results in Eqs. 4 and 5.

$$t = \frac{((\overrightarrow{r_{2o}} - \overrightarrow{r_{1o}}) \cdot \overrightarrow{r_{1d}})(\overrightarrow{r_{2d}} \cdot \overrightarrow{r_{2d}}) + ((\overrightarrow{r_{1o}} - \overrightarrow{r_{2o}}) \cdot \overrightarrow{r_{2d}})(\overrightarrow{r_{1d}} \cdot \overrightarrow{r_{2d}})}{(\overrightarrow{r_{1d}} \cdot \overrightarrow{r_{1d}})(\overrightarrow{r_{2d}} \cdot \overrightarrow{r_{2d}}) - (\overrightarrow{r_{1d}} \cdot \overrightarrow{r_{2d}})^2} \tag{4}$$

$$s = \frac{((\overrightarrow{r_{1o}} - \overrightarrow{r_{2o}}) \cdot \overrightarrow{r_{2d}})(\overrightarrow{r_{1d}} \cdot \overrightarrow{r_{1d}}) + ((\overrightarrow{r_{2o}} - \overrightarrow{r_{1o}}) \cdot \overrightarrow{r_{1d}})(\overrightarrow{r_{1d}} \cdot \overrightarrow{r_{2d}})}{(\overrightarrow{r_{1d}} \cdot \overrightarrow{r_{1d}})(\overrightarrow{r_{2d}} \cdot \overrightarrow{r_{2d}}) - (\overrightarrow{r_{1d}} \cdot \overrightarrow{r_{2d}})^2} \quad (5)$$

With Eq. 6 the center point of minimum distance can be calculated from the found t and s. It is important to use the center point of minimum distance instead of the gaze intersection, as intersections in 3D space are highly unlikely while small distances occur often.

$$m = \frac{(\overrightarrow{r_{1o}} + \overrightarrow{r_{1d}}t) + (\overrightarrow{r_{2o}} + \overrightarrow{r_{2d}}s)}{2} \quad (6)$$

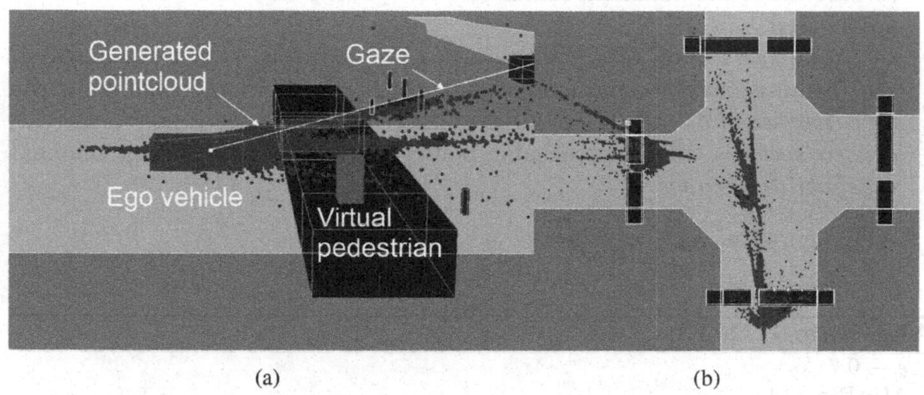

Fig. 4. Visualization of the point cloud generated for the "turn left" maneuver in a side view (a) and a bird view (b). Gaze points are represented by blue dots, the ego vehicles is visualized as gray bounding box, and the predefined AOIs are shown as black boxes with yellow edges. (Color figure online)

The process is repeated to all positions between all drivers. This generates a 3D point cloud (see Fig. 4)

To reduce noise, points inside the vehicle i.e. within a 1.5 m radius of the driver as well as points behind the driver are deleted. Additionally, points above or below −1 m/+10 m have been deleted, as they can no longer be attributed to a relevant area.

3.5 OPTICS Algorithm

Next, 3D AOIs are generated from the remaining point cloud. To do so, the point clouds need to be clustered. As the presented task requires the finding and splitting of a previously unknown number of clusters, in unknown dimensions, and density, we use the unsupervised clustering algorithm "Ordering Points To Identify the Clustering Structure" (OPTICS) [1]. This algorithm clusters datapoints based on three adjustable parameters.

- ϵ, the maximum distance two points can have for them to be considered neighboring.
- *MinPts*, the minimum number of neighboring points required for a center-point.
- *minclustersize*, the minimum number of points per group required to be a cluster.

To explain the algorithm, some additional values need to be defined:

- ϵ-environment, the set of points within a distance of ϵ to a point o.
- *corepoint*, a point o with at least *MinPts* points within its' ϵ-environment.
- *coredistance*, the minimum radius of a *corepoint* o in which *MinPts* points are located.
- *reachabilitydistance*, of a point p, in a ϵ-environment is, at its' maximum, the distance between *corepoint* o and point p, and at its' minimum, the *coredistance* of o.
- *orderedseeds* is a list of reachable points sorted by their current minimal *reachabilitydistance*

The algorithm works as follows:

Algorithm 1. OPTICs

```
ε ← 0.7
MinPts ← 4
minclustersize ← 40
while NOT unprocessedPoints.empty() do
    Point_o = unprocessedPoints.pop()
    Point_o.processed = TRUE
    Point_o.getcoredistance(Point_o.epsilon-environment, MinPts)
    OrderedFile.add(Point_o)
    OrderedSeeds ← Point_o.epsilon-environment.sortByReachability()
    while NOT OrderedSeeds.empty() do
        Point_p = OrderedSeeds.pop()
        Point_p.processed = TRUE
        unprocessedPoints.remove(Point_p)
        Point_p.getcoredistance(Point_p.epsilon-environment, MinPts)
        OrderedFile.add(Point_p)
        OrderedSeeds.sortIn(Point_p.epsilon-environment)
    end while
end while
RETURN OrderedFile
```

The used parameters provided the best results for our use case.

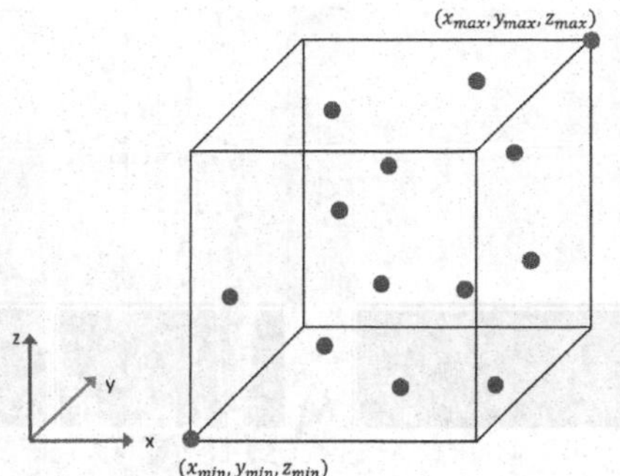

Fig. 5. Visualization of the AOI generation process. The highest and lowest x-, y-, and z-values in a cluster are taken as the limits of the AOI.

Based on the clusters generated by the OPTICS algorithm, 3D AOIs can be generated. To define the size and position of the AOIs, the minimum and maximum coordinates are taken form the points in each cluster (see Fig. 5).

3.6 AOI Optimization

Visual inspection of the generated AOIs reveals that even though the general direction seems correct, they are in close proximity to the vehicle. To correct this, we apply an inverse Gaussian shift along the vector generated from the average gaze origin and the AOI center. This results in a bigger shift for AOIs further distanced to the gaze origin (see Fig. 6). The last step of AOI optimization is the merging of AOIs. If the distance between AOIs is smaller than 1 m, they are merged into bigger clusters. This reduces the number of overlapping and close 3D AOIs and can therefore reduce memory required to store the 3D AOIs, as well as the computation time for algorithms. The clusters are merged after they are shifted, to combine clusters at their final position. Adjusting the OPTICS algorithm to generate bigger clusters by tuning the parameter would result into less defined AOIs, therefore reducing the resolution of the generated result.

4 Results

We defined the AOIs we expected to be relevant for driving on a complex, urban intersection as ground truth. As mentioned in Related Work (Sect. 2), the three driving maneuvers are divided into three parts “entering intersection”, “crossing intersection”, and “leaving intersection”. Based on these phases, and the areas crucial for safely performing the maneuver, we came up with the AOIs shown in Fig. 2. These areas contain traffic lights, crosswalks and pedestrian waiting areas. Drivers need to/should observe these AOIs to detect potential accident risks (see Table 1).

Comparing the predefined 3D AOIs with the generated 3D AOIs reveals that, while there is an overlap, the AOIs are not identical. For the “Turn left” maneuver, the generated AOIs mostly overlap with the predicted AOIs (see Fig. 7a).

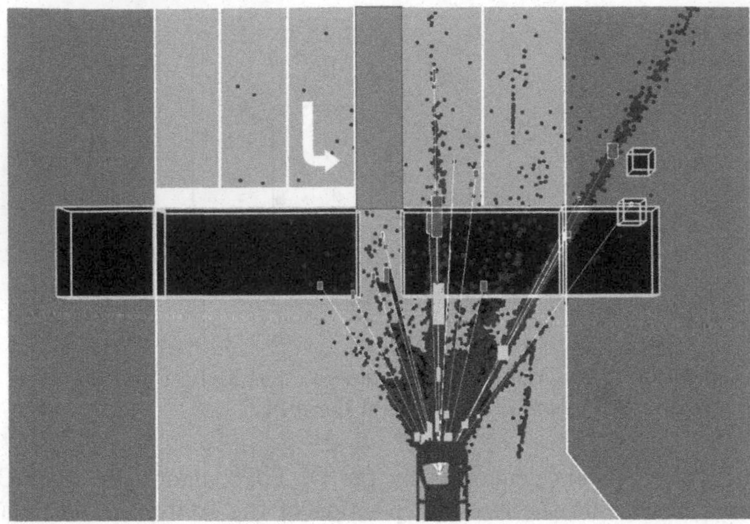

Fig. 6. Visualization of the inverse Gaussian push applied to the AOIs, along the vector defined by the gaze origin and the AOI center. Generated AOIs in yellow, pushed AOIs in red, and predicted AOIs in black. (Color figure online)

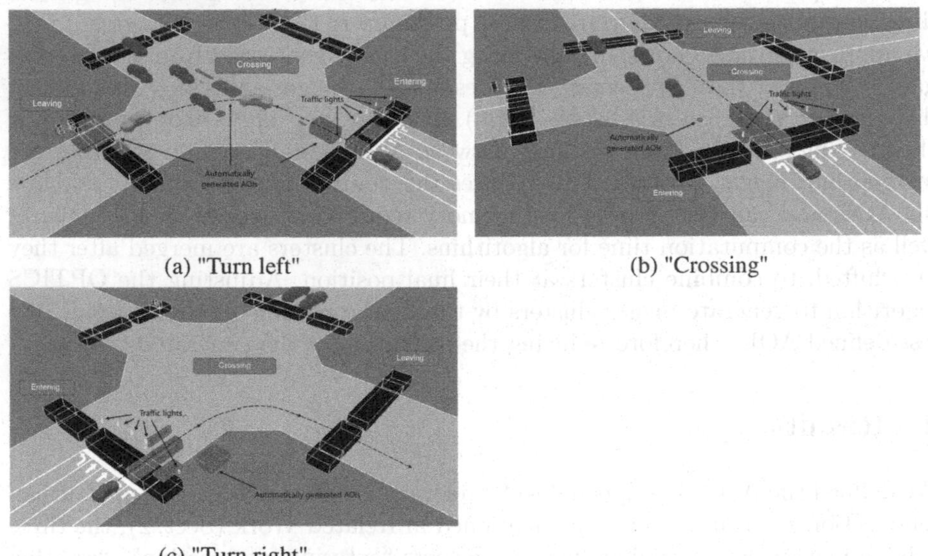

(a) "Turn left"

(b) "Crossing"

(c) "Turn right"

Fig. 7. Comparison of the generated AOIs and predefined AOIs for the driving maneuvers. Predefined AOIs are black with yellow edges. Generated AOIs are red. (Color figure online)

It is notable that a unforeseen group of AOIs is positioned at the center of the intersection. The AOIs generated for crossing (Fig. 7b) are mostly located at the "Entering" phase. It is interesting to see, that the biggest AOI is mostly in front of the lane, which has been used for the maneuver. No AOIs have been generated for the phases "Crossing" and "Leaving". In Fig. 7c the generated AOIs for the "Turn right" maneuver are visualized. The AOIs are spread over both turning lanes with an unforeseen AOI on the right sidewalk. No AOIs have been generated for the phases "Crossing" and "Leaving".

5 Discussion

As shown in the last section, the generated 3D AOIs only partially match the predefined 3D AOIs. The found differences can lead to a deeper understanding of traffic situation, as there are multiple possible reasons why AOIs exist at unforeseen locations, why some predicted AOIs have no generated counterpart, and why the generated AOIs have different shapes.

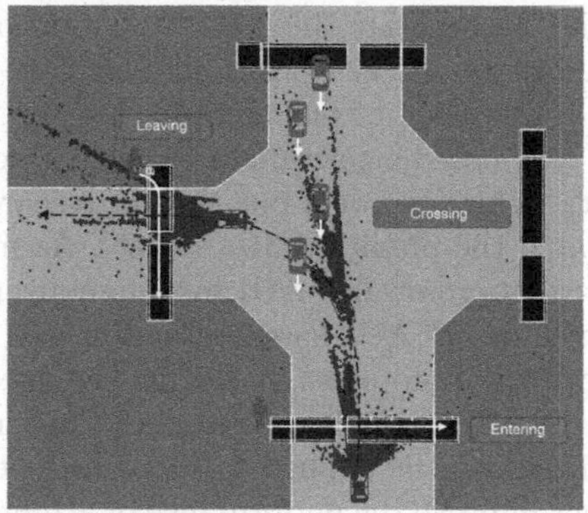

Fig. 8. Schematic visualization of the turn left maneuver with point clouds and scene objects.

Firstly, the unforeseen locations can be explained by analyzing the maneuver phases. The "Crossing" phase of the "Turn left" maneuver has a set of unpredicted AOIs (see Fig. 7a). We expected the participant to focus on the "upper left crosswalk" AOI, as oncoming traffic starts from there. This is not the case. As the vehicles start at the same time, they meet in the middle, and the participants focused their attention onto the closest vehicles. The further distanced, oncoming vehicles might have been observed via peripheral vision, but as it is not possible to predict that with the used sensor set, AOIs are created at the area participants' gaze focuses on.

Secondly, analyzing the generated AOIs reveals, that for the maneuvers "crossing" and "turn right", only the phase "Entering" generated AOIs, while there are generated AOIs for all the phases of the "turn left" maneuver. There are multiple possible explanations for this phenomenon. For the "turn right" maneuver, the "crossing" phase is very short, which could cause the drivers' to immediately focus their attention onto the "leaving" phase. While this could explain the absence of generated AOIs for this phase, it would not explain the lack of AOIs for the other phases. We believe, the other reason for this is, the lack of traffic participants/accident hazards for these maneuver phases, found in the used dataset. This means, the drivers do not need to closely observe the predicted AOIs to safely perform the maneuvers. In contrast, the "turn left" maneuver required the crossing of the oncoming traffic, which resulted in the generation of additional AOIs (see Fig. 8).

Thirdly, the differences in shape can partially be explained by the fact that the generated AOIs are maneuver specific, while the predicted AOIs are maneuver overarching. Combining the generated AOIs in the lower, right part of the intersection would result in an AOI similar to the predicted AOI. We chose not to combine the generated AOIs, as we believe, the benefits of having different AOIs for the respective maneuvers outweigh the downsides caused by the additional memory needed to store more AOIs.

The results show, that it is possible to generate geopositioned 3D AOIs from gaze data. This answers our first research question "Can gaze data from a group of driver's be combined to generate 3D AOIs?". Additionally, the generated AOIs can be positioned at unforeseen positions and have unpredicted shapes. This could be seen as a downside of our method, but we belief it can be used to further improve 3D AOI based algorithms and extract additional information from the available data, which answers our second research question "Do the generated 3D AOIs match the predicted 3D AOIs?". As mentioned before, the division of the "lower, right crosswalk" AOI into maneuver specific AOIs could improve the performance of 3D AOI based intention and attention prediction algorithms. Furthermore the unforeseen AOIs for the "crossing" phase of the "turn left" maneuver, and at the sidewalk of the "turn right" maneuver can provide additional insight into the applied safeguarding behavior. Additionally these AOIs could further improve the performance of attention/intention prediction algorithms. The unforeseen AOIs could also allow for the identification of distractions, which answers our last research question "Can generated 3D AOIs be used to obtain new information about the drivers gaze behavior?".

Even though the absence of generated AOIs for the "crossing" and "leaving" phases of the maneuvers "crossing" and "turn right" could be explained by the lack of traffic participants at this part of the environment, there could be other causes for it. Further studies, with additional traffic participants are needed to better understand this phenomenon.

It is also important to address the fact that the used data was collected in simulator setting. In the real world additional distractions could lead to a more complex environment and therefore decrease the accuracy of the found 3D AOIs.

6 Conclusion

In summary, a method to generate geopositioned, 3D AOIs from fleet gaze data has been proposed. By calculating the point of closest encounter for the gaze vectors of different drivers, a point cloud is created. The OPTICs algorithm is used to determine density based cluster from the point cloud. By preprocessing and merging the found clusters geopositioned 3D AOIs are created. It has been shown, that the generated AOIs can differ from the predicted AOIs, based on the traffic volume and traffic events. The expected limitations of this approach have been presented. The shown results enable a number of interesting research topics. One possible subject is distraction detection. By finding 3D AOIs which are not part of the driving context distracting features could be found. This would require a semantic classification of the found AOIs, which might be possible by analyzing the drivers' gaze behavior. Another possibility for semantic classification could be the comparison of the AOI with map data, to find AOIs which are positioned outside of the traffic environment. Another interesting field of research is the test of this methods real time capabilities and adaptiveness. It could be possible to adapt the 3D AOIs to changes in the environment in real time, by continuously comparing established AOIs to the AOIs generated by the drivers gaze behavior. This approach could also be used to identify reoccurring effects e.g. distractions or obstacles caused by rush-hour traffic. Combining the found AOIs with vehicle data e.g. emergency braking could lead to the identification of potential road hazards for the driver and other traffic participants. Additionally by comparing the found 3D AOIs with data found by other environmental sensors a relevance rating for different sensor data could be created. An new sensors could be evaluated for their usefulness.

References

1. Ankerst, M., et al.: OPTICS: ordering points to identify the clustering structure. ACM SIGMOD Rec. **28**(2), 49–60 (1999). https://doi.org/10.1145/304181.304187
2. Bickerdt, J., Sonnenberg, J., Gollnick, C., Kasneci, E.: Geopositioned 3D areas of interest for gaze analysis, pp. 1–11, September 2021. https://doi.org/10.1145/3409118.3475138
3. Bozkir, E., Geisler, D., Kasneci, E.: Assessment of driver attention during a safety critical situation in VR to generate VR-based training. In: Neyret, S., Kokkinara, E., Franco, M.G., Hoyet, L., Cunningham, D.W., Świdrak, J. (eds.) SAP 2019: ACM Symposium on Applied Perception 2019, pp. 1–5 (2019). https://doi.org/10.1145/3343036.3343138
4. Braunagel, C., Kasneci, E., Stolzmann, W., Rosenstiel, W.: Driver-activity recognition in the context of conditionally autonomous driving. In: 2015 IEEE 18th International Conference on Intelligent Transportation Systems - (ITSC 2015), pp. 1652–1657 (2015). https://doi.org/10.1109/ITSC.2015.268
5. Doshi, A., Trivedi, M.M.: Investigating the relationships between gaze patterns, dynamic vehicle surround analysis, and driver intentions. In: IEEE Intelligent Vehicle Symposium. IEEE (2009). https://doi.org/10.1109/IVS.2009.5164397, https://ieeexplore.ieee.org/abstract/document/5164397
6. Fletcher, L., Loy, G., Barnes, N., Zelinsky, A.: Correlating driver gaze with the road scene for driver assistance systems. Robot. Auton. Syst. **52**(1), 71–84 (2005). https://doi.org/10.1016/j.robot.2005.03.010
7. Fletcher, L., Zelinsky, A.: Driver inattention detection based on eye gaze–road event correlation. Int. J. Robot. Res. **28**(6), 774–801 (2009). https://doi.org/10.1177/0278364908099459

8. Geruschat, D.R., Hassan, S.E., Turano, K.A.: Gaze behavior while crossing complex intersections. Optom. Vis. Sci. **80**, 515–528 (2003). https://doi.org/10.1097/00006324-200307000-00013, https://pubmed.ncbi.nlm.nih.gov/12858087/
9. Kircher, K., Ahlstrom, C.: Minimum required attention: a human-centered approach to driver inattention. Hum. Factors **59**(3), 471–484 (2017). https://doi.org/10.1177/0018720816672756
10. Lemonnier, S., Brémond, R., Baccino, T.: Gaze behavior when approaching an intersection: dwell time distribution and comparison with a quantitative prediction. Transp. Res. F: Traffic Psychol. Behav. **35**(4), 60–74 (2015). https://doi.org/10.1016/j.trf.2015.10.015
11. Lemonnier, S., Désiré, L., Brémond, R., Baccino, T.: Drivers' visual attention: a field study at intersections. Transp. Res. Part F: Traffic Psychol. Behav. **69**, 206–221 (2020). https://doi.org/10.1016/j.trf.2020.01.012, https://www.sciencedirect.com/science/article/pii/S1369847819301597
12. Mavely, A.G., Judith, J.E., Sahal, P.A., Kuruvilla, S.A.: Eye gaze tracking based driver monitoring system. In: 2017 IEEE International Conference on Circuits and Systems (ICCS), pp. 364–367 (2017). https://doi.org/10.1109/ICCS1.2017.8326022
13. Najdataei, H., Nikolakopoulo, Y., Gulisano, V., Papatriantafilou, M.: Continuous and parallel lidar point-cloud clustering. In: IEEE International Conference on Distributed Computing Systems (ICDCS), vol. 38. IEEE (2018). https://ieeexplore.ieee.org/document/8416334
14. Euro NCAP: Euroncap-roadmap-2025-v4 (2017). https://cdn.euroncap.com/media/30700/euroncap-roadmap-2025-v4.pdf
15. Euro NCAP: Assessment protocol - safety assist (2019). https://cdn.euroncap.com/media/53156/euro-ncap-assessment-protocol-sa-v902.pdf
16. Rong, Y., Akata, Z., Kasneci, E.: Driver intention anticipation based on in-cabin and driving scene monitoring. In: 2020 IEEE 23rd International Conference on Intelligent Transportation Systems (ITSC), pp. 1–8 (2020). https://doi.org/10.1109/ITSC45102.2020.9294181
17. Sayed, R., Eskandarian, A.: Unobtrusive drowsiness detection by neural network learning of driver steering. Proc. Inst. Mech. Eng. Part D: J. Automob. Eng. **215**(9), 969–975 (2005). https://doi.org/10.1243/0954407011528536
18. Smart Eye: Smart eye pro (2014). http://smarteye.se/wp-content/uploads/2014/12/Smart-Eye-Pro.pdf
19. SmartEye: Smarteyepro (2019). https://smarteye.se/research-instruments/se-pro/
20. Song, H., Feng, H.Y.: A global clustering approach to point cloud simplification with a specified data reduction ratio. Comput.-Aided Design **40**, 281–292 (2008). https://doi.org/10.1016/j.cad.2007.10.013, https://www.sciencedirect.com/science/article/pii/S0010448507002448
21. European Union: Regulation (EU) 2019/2144 of the European parliament and of the council. Official Journal of the European Union (2019)
22. Wang, H., Antonelli, M., Shi, B.E.: Using point cloud data to improve three dimensional gaze estimation. In: Annual International Conference of the IEEE Engineering in Medicine and Biology Society, vol. 39. IEEE (2017). https://doi.org/10.1109/EMBC.2017.8036944, https://ieeexplore.ieee.org/abstract/document/8036944
23. Werneke, J., Vollrath, M.: Where did the car come from? Attention allocation at intersections. In: Modelling of drivers' behaviour for ITS design. Loughborough University (2012). https://www.humanist-vce.eu/fileadmin/contributeurs/humanist/Berlin2010/2b_Werneke.pdf

Exploring New Depths: How Could Passengers Interact with Future In-Car Holographic 3D Displays?

Maryia Kazhura[1,2](✉)

[1] Technische Universität Berlin, 10623 Berlin, Germany
[2] Volkswagen AG, Berliner Ring 2, 38436 Wolfsburg, Germany
maryia.kazhura@volkswagen.de

Abstract. Holographic 3D (H3D) displays have the potential to enhance future car interiors and provide users with a new dimension of visual and interactive experience, offering a larger depth range than other state of the art 3D display technologies. In this work, a user-elicited gesture set for 3D interaction with non-driving related tasks was built and evaluated. As the H3D technology itself is still in development, mixed reality headsets (Hololens 1 and 2) were used to emulate a virtual H3D display. In a gesture-elicitation study, N = 20 participants proposed mid-air gestures for a set of 33 tasks (referents) displayed either within or outside of participants' reach. The resulting set of most mentioned proposals was refined with a reverse-matching task, in which N = 21 participants matched referents to videos of elicited gestures. In a third evaluation step, usability and memorability characteristics of the user-elicited gesture set were compared to those of an expert-elicited alternative using a between-subjects design with N = 16 participants in each group. Results showed that while both sets can be learned and recalled comparably well, the user-elicited gesture set was associated with a higher gesture suitability and ease, a higher perceived intuitiveness and a lower perceived mental effort. Implications for future H3D in-car interfaces are discussed.

Keywords: Natural user interaction · Gestural input · Gesture elicitation · Holographic 3D · Mixed reality · Hololens

1 Introduction

As our society becomes increasingly digitized and experience driven, user experience plays an increasingly important role in the automotive industry [2,38] and purchasing experiences can make people happier than purchasing material goods [73]. Auto-stereoscopic 3D (S3D) displays have the potential to improve user experience [8], declutter information dense environments through depth layering [6,7,9,13,45,61,62,81] and increase perceived attractiveness of displayed content [7–9]. However, the recommended depth range for S3D displays is limited due to mismatched accommodation (focal depth) and vergence (inward eye-rotation to

H. Krömker (Ed.): HCII 2022, LNCS 13335, pp. 35–61, 2022.
https://doi.org/10.1007/978-3-031-04987-3_3

avoid double image) depth cues, also referred to as the accommodation-vergence conflict (AVC) [39,58]. The AVC has been associated with eye strain, visual discomfort, fatigue, headaches [16,25] and even visually-induced motion sickness [28,29,65,70]. Light-field displays - a more advanced type of 3D display technology, are not affected by the AVC but lose image resolution at larger distances in front of the screen [34]. Holographic 3D (H3D) displays on the other hand do not suffer from any of these constraints. By reconstructing the amplitude and phase of light in a 3D scene, H3D provides the full range of natural depth cues and the largest depth without loss of image resolution [58]. As a result, H3D can expand the design space for in-car interaction by extending the depth range in which users can interact with digital content without visual discomfort.

With increasing availability of virtual, augmented and mixed reality devices, 3D gestural interfaces have gained popularity with multiple studies discussing successful implementations of a wide variety of freehand 3D interaction techniques, as summarized in [78]. Microsoft for example, implemented a complex set of gestures for mid-air interaction with holograms in mixed reality using their Hololens 2 [44]. In the automotive domain, gestural interfaces have mostly been investigated in the context of driving safety with the aim to reduce driver's display glance times during secondary tasks like infotainment or car functions controls [17,19,43,56]. However, level 4 automation [52] could allow passengers to engage in more complex non-driving related tasks [52,80] which could involve more complex gestures with greater range of movement.

From a usability perspective, hand gestures should be intuitive and logical, easy and quick to perform, easy to remember and ergonomic [1,50,67]. User input is intuitive when the user can effectively interact with a system by subconsciously utilizing pre-existing knowledge acquired from past interface experiences [3,46]. However, design of gestural interaction techniques is often influenced by the limitations of the hand-tracking technology used [63,78]. As a result, gestures are often selected based on their tracking accuracy rather than their logical interpretation and ergonomic qualities [32]. Contrary to this technology-driven approach, the user-centered approach focuses on intuitiveness and users' expectations rather than technical performance of hand-tracking devices [32,50]. In the so-called gesture elicitation method, suitable gestures are determined by showing participants the effects of a specific action (also called referent) and asking them to propose suitable gestures that would cause that effect [50,82,83]. Gesture elicitation studies have been conducted to develop mid-air gesture sets (often referred to as 'vocabularies') for a multitude of applications ranging from smart TV [37,75,84] and smart home controls [22] to augmented reality [55,57], in-car S3D displays [79] or others summarized in [77] and [76].

Gestural interfaces are usually developed for a specific application. Thus, a set of gestures will match the application it was designed for [5,50]. It is therefore useful to compare new elicited gestures with existing gesture vocabularies to evaluate whether some interaction techniques can be re-purposed for new emerging applications [5]. In addition to the application context, other factors like the hologram scale can also influence elicited gestures [55,57]. In the context of H3D displays, hologram distance presents an additional possible influence.

In their work, [50] propose to evaluate elicited gesture vocabularies with two follow-up tests: reverse-matching the elicited gestures with their corresponding referents [37] and a memorability evaluation [48]. Especially with regard to the latter, user-elicited gestures can be easier to learn and memorize than gestures designed by experts [48].

The purpose of this work was to investigate how non-expert users would use gestures to interact with non-driving related tasks in the context of future in-car H3D passenger displays. This paper presents the results of three consecutive studies: 1. Gesture elicitation to build a set of suitable gestures 2. Reverse-matching task to refine the user-elicited gesture set and 3. Memorability evaluation of the refined user-elicited vocabulary in comparison to an alternative expert-elicited set of gestures. Preliminary results from studies 1 and 2 have been presented during the poster session at the 20th International Conference on Mobile and Ubiquitous Multimedia (MUM 2021) [35].

2 Study 1: Gesture Elicitation

Study 1 was performed with the goal to elicit a set of intuitive 3D gestures to interact with possible use cases for future in-car holographic 3D displays. To explore the effect of hologram distance on elicited gestures, the holograms were presented in two conditions: within and outside of participants' reach.

2.1 Method

Apparatus. The study was performed at the passenger's site of a seating buck. A black 24 × 20 cm large plastic plate was placed 80 cm in front of the seated participant to serve as a placeholder for a future passenger display. Because the holographic 3D display is still in development, the holograms were displayed on a Microsoft Hololens 1 in a 20 × 16 cm virtual display screen window within the placeholder area. To visualize the effects of each referent, 3D scenes were created using the Unity3D game engine to show the 3D objects within each scene in their "before" and "after" states, demonstrating the effect of a referent. No animations were used to visualize the transitions from one state to the other to eliminate any influence on participants' mental models and expectations [55]. In the within reach condition, 3D objects appeared 40 cm in front of the virtual display screen or as far as the virtual display screen. In the outside of reach condition, 3D objects appeared 120 cm behind the virtual display screen or as close as the virtual display screen. A camera was placed behind the seating buck to film participants' hands. Images of the setup are depicted in Fig. 1.

Selection of Referents. Referents were derived from possible use cases identified through a series of expert workshops, by following the domain-specific design approach [10] in which tasks are designed with specific domain knowledge

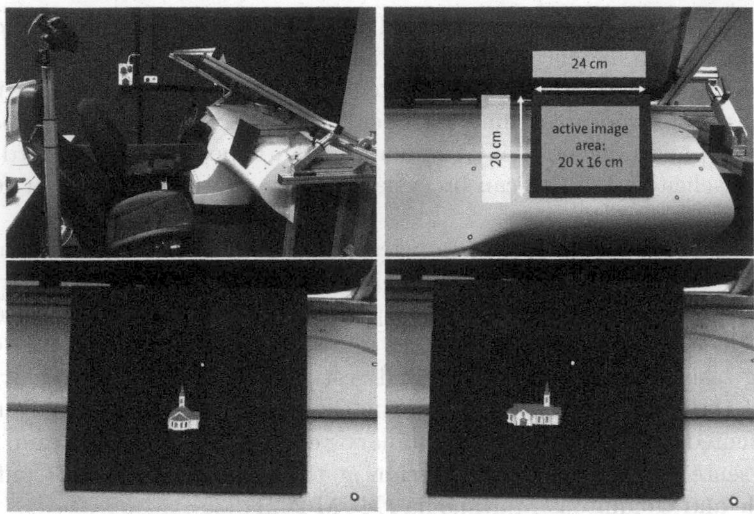

Fig. 1. Top row: Seating buck and the placeholder with the active visible window area within which the holograms appeared. Bottom row: Example hologram of a 3D object in its 'before' (left image) and 'after' (right image) state representing the effect of the referent 'rotate counterclockwise around vertical axis'.

in mind. The resulting 33 referents can be summarized to the following categories: manipulate interface (activate/deactivate objects, browse menus/lists, open/close interface elements), manipulate object (move in x/y/z, rotate around x/y/z, scale, remove) and manipulate map (move in x/y, scale, rotate around z). To avoid undesirable clipping effects, large-scale objects like maps are best placed at screen level distance or behind. Therefore, all map related tasks were only shown in the outside of reach condition, resulting in 25 referents in the within reach condition and 33 in the outside of reach condition. The referents within each condition were presented in a fixed sequence to form use scenarios told from a user's perspective [14,55].

Procedure. The study followed a within design in which each participant completed both conditions. Participants with intact stereoscopic vision, as measured by the entrance test of the Butterfly Stereo Acuity Test, completed a preliminary questionnaire to collect information about their age, gender, handedness, vision correction and usage of touchscreens, gestural controls, augmented/mixed reality, virtual reality and video games. After a short introduction to how holographic 3D displays work, the conditions were presented in a randomized order. For each referent in the scenario, participants first viewed a 3D scene in its original state and received a verbal description of the referent in question, followed by the 'after' view of the scene demonstrating the effect of that referent. To counteract the effect of legacy bias, which refers to the influence of previous experience on the first suggestion that comes to mind [47,83], participants were instructed to suggest at least two suitable gestures, then choose their preferred option [79]. The preferred gesture proposal was then rated in terms of its suitability (*'The gesture I chose is a good match for the intended purpose'*) and ease (*'The gesture I picked is easy to perform'*), each on a 7-point Likert scale (-3 = strongly disagree, 0 = undecided, 3 = strongly agree) [37,57,83]. The procedure was repeated for each referent within each condition. Participants were instructed to think aloud and their hands were videotaped for later categorization of the elicited gestures.

Sample. 20 participants (13 males, 7 females) with a mean age of 39.65 years (SD = 11.93) and no background in interaction or user interface design were recruited for this study. 17 participants were right-handed, 2 left-handed and 1 participant was ambidextrous. 95% of participants used touchscreens on a daily basis. 80% of participants never used augmented or mixed reality devices and 50% of participants had no previous experience with gestural controls.

2.2 Results

Agreement. In total, 1160 preferred gestures were elicited - 500 in the within and 660 in the outside of reach condition. Video recordings of elicited gestures were grouped following the loosened constraint introduced by [57], allowing gestures to be similar but not necessarily identical within each group. Identical gestures were grouped to variants. Variants with identical movement path but minor hand pose variations were summarized to groups [57]. As a result, 272 gesture variants summarized to 160 groups were identified in the within and 364 variants summarized to 223 groups in the outside of reach condition. Agreement rates (AR) were then calculated based on the gesture groups according to the equation provided by [74], which is an updated version of the original equation by [82]. The overall average agreement rate across all referents in the within reach condition was $AR = 0.31$ ($SD = 0.17$) and $AR = 0.29$ ($SD = 0.17$) in the outside of reach condition. The chance-corrected agreement according to [69] was $K_F = 0.30$ in the within reach condition and $K_F = 0.26$ in the outside of reach condition. All calculated agreement rates represent a medium agreement according to [74]. Statistical testing against a null-hypothesis to compare the agreement rates between conditions was not applied, following the advice by [69]. Agreement rates per referent in each condition are illustrated in Fig. 2. The most frequently proposed gesture groups were included in the gesture set, resulting in 29 distinct gestures. Some referents produced a tie and only 9 referents produced different gestures for within and outside of reach interaction. The resulting list of referents, most mentioned gestures and the corresponding agreement rates are provided in Table 1.

Gesture Ratings. Average suitability ratings ranged between 5.95 and 6.85 across all referents in the within and between 5.90 and 6.65 in the outside of reach condition. The standard variations of the suitability ratings ranged between 0.37

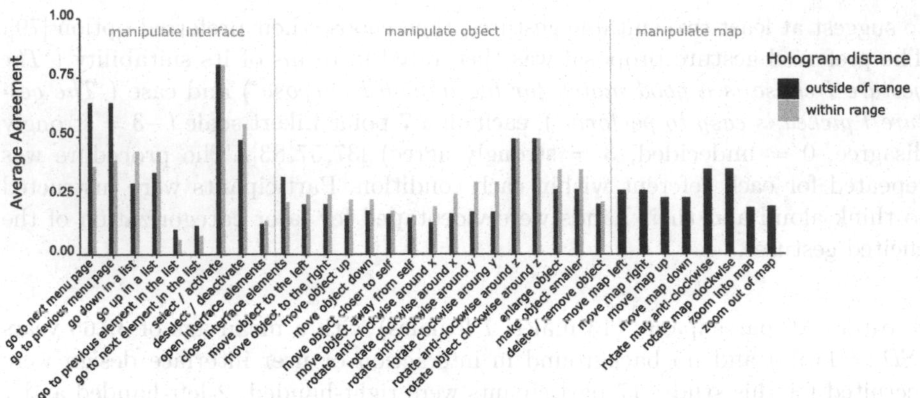

Fig. 2. Agreement rates per referent and condition. The axes are defined according to the left-handed coordinate system: the positive x, y and z axis point right, up and forward, respectively.

and 1.08 in the within and between 0.60 and 1.02 in the outside of reach condition. Average ease of use ratings ranged between 6.25 and 6.80 across all referents in the within and between 6.05 and 6.80 in the outside of reach condition. Standard deviations of ease ratings ranged between 0.41 and 0.81 in the within and between 0.44 and 1.15 in the outside of reach condition. The results indicate that participants were consistently confident in the suitability and ease of their proposed gestures.

Participants' Feedback and Mental Models. Multiple participants pointed to the importance of user feedback to indicate whether their input was successful and found it more convenient to physically manipulate 3D objects if they appeared within reach. One participant noted that elderly users might have issues with gestures that involve spreading fingers or wrist rotation. Some participants suggested using eye gaze instead of touch to select or activate elements. The transcribed think aloud protocols were used to extract the thought processes and mental models behind gesture proposals. The summarized results for the most mentioned gestures are described in the following section.

Menus and Lists. Slide or swipe like on a smartphone when paging through, scroll up or down like on a smartphone when going through a vertical list. When elements are arranged behind each other, swipe the first element away to go forward in the list or swipe in the opposite direction to swipe the previous element back into view. Alternatively, swipe towards self to shift the list forward or swipe away from self to push the list back. Finger can be used instead of hand when precision is needed, objects appear close or are small.

Select or Activate. Push the button or tap like on a smartphone. Tap the element again to reverse the selection. Selection is expected to open an application or to activate an element. If an element has been activated, it is expected to be automatically deactivated once a different element is activated. Explicit gesture to deselect or deactivate an object or element is perceived as unnecessary.

Open and Close Interface Elements. Tap into screen or move hand into view and the system is expected to automatically display the interface, like with other known systems (touchscreens, in-car infotainment system, video player). Tap somewhere else in screen (in-between the control elements) to 'click' the interface away. When interface floats within reach, swipe it away and out of view like it's a floating object.

Rotate 3D Object Around x, y and z. 3D object is perceived as something that can be grabbed and turned in hand like a solid object in the real world. Rotating around the forward z-axis is like turning a knob.

Rotate 3D Map Around z (bird view). Rotate like it's a paper map on the table or like turning a volume knob. Similar to how a map is rotated on a touchscreen.

Move 3D Object in x and y. Mark or activate the object, then drag it in any direction. Object is expected to follow the fingertip. Alternatively, when object is outside of reach, push it to the left or right of the screen with palm.

Move 3D Map in x and y. Mark a location on the map with finger by pointing at it (like on a touchscreen), then move finger in any direction. Map is expected to follow the fingertip.

Move 3D Object Closer or Away from Self. When object is within reach, it is perceived as something that can be grabbed and pulled towards self like a solid object. When object is outside of reach, palm can be used as proxy and its movement translates to the object. Push the object away from body with palm like with a real object.

Scale Object or Map. Pinch-to-zoom gestures like on a touchscreen.

Remove Object. With the hand, push or wipe the object out of the display.

2.3 Discussion

The obtained average and corrected agreement rates are in line with other gesture elicitation studies in the field [78]. Agreement rates were generally lower for referents that required spatial, depth-related actions (e.g. 'move an object closer towards self'). This could be due to a lack of participants' experience with 3D interaction in space, as interaction in depth is not available in traditional touchscreen interfaces. A majority of the elicited gestures was adapted from touchscreen interfaces and demonstrates the influence of previous interface experience, which has been observed in other gesture elicitation studies [37,53,57,60,75].

Table 1. Referents, most mentioned gestures, agreement rates (AR) and the number of mentions of the respective gesture group (n). Gestures proposed exclusively in the outside of reach condition are marked with a *. The axes are defined according to the left-handed coordinate system: the positive x, y and z axis point right, up and forward, respectively. CW = clockwise, CCW = counterclockwise.

ID	Referent	Most mentioned gesture	AR within (n)	AR outside (n)
1	Go to next page	Swipe left with hand	0.37 (11)	0.64 (16)
2	Go to previous page	Swipe right with hand	0.40 (11)	0.64 (16)
3*	Move map left	Point at the map with one/two fingers and slide left		0.27 (10)
4*	Move map right	Point at the map with one/two fingers and slide right		0.27 (10)
5*	Move map up	Point at the map with one/two fingers and slide up		0.24 (9)
6*	Move map down	Point at the map with one/two fingers and slide down		0.24 (9)
7*	Rotate map CCW	Grab from the front with spread fingers and turn wrist CCW		0.36 (12)
8*	Rotate map CW	Grab from the front with spread fingers and turn wrist CW		0.36 (12)
9*	Zoom into map	Spread thumb and index finger		0.20 (7)
10*	Zoom out of map	Pinch thumb and index finger		0.20 (7)
11	Select/activate	Tap/point at the object with one/two fingers	0.81 (18)	0.81 (18)
12	Deselect/deactivate	Tap/point at the object with one/two fingers	0.55 (15)	0.48 (14)
13.1	Move object closer towards self	Grab and pinch with multiple fingers and pull towards self	0.18 (7)	
13.2*	Move object closer towards self	Stretch arm out and move palm towards self		0.17 (6)
14	Rotate object CW around y	Grab from below with spread fingers and turn wrist CW	0.31 (11)	0.18 (8)
15	Rotate object CCW around y	Grab from below with spread fingers and turn wrist CCW	0.31 (11)	0.18 (8)
16	Rotate object CCW around x	Grab from the side with spread fingers and turn wrist CCW	0.20 (9)	0.13 (7)
17	Rotate object CW around x	Grab from the side with spread fingers and turn wrist CW	0.25 (10)	0.17 (8)
18	Rotate object CCW around z	Grab from the front with spread fingers and turn wrist CCW	0.49 (14)	0.49 (14)
19	Rotate object CW around z	Grab from the front with spread fingers and turn wrist CW	0.49 (14)	0.49 (14)

(*continued*)

Table 1. (*continued*)

ID	Referent	Most mentioned gesture	AR within (n)	AR outside (n)
20	Move object away from self	Push away from body with palm	0.16 (7)	0.17 (6)
21.1	Move object left	Touch/point at object with one/two fingers and slide left	0.25 (8)	0.25 (8)
21.2*	Move object left	Push to the left with palm		0.25 (8)
22.1	Move object right	Touch/point at object with one/two fingers and slide right	0.25 (8)	0.23 (8)
22.2*	Move object right	Push to the right with palm	0.23 (8)	
23	Move object up	Touch/point at object with one/two fingers and slide up	0.23 (8)	0.16 (6)
24	Move object down	Touch/point at object with one/two fingers and slide down	0.23 (8)	0.18 (6)
25	Make object larger	Spread thumb and index finger	0.36 (11)	0.27 (9)
26	Make object smaller	Pinch thumb and index finger	0.36 (11)	0.27 (9)
27	Remove/delete object	Swipe away with hand in a large diagonal motion	0.22 (8)	0.21 (8)
28.1	Go forward to next element	Swipe to the side with one/two fingers	0.06 (3)	
28.2	Go forward to next element	Swipe towards self with one/two fingers	0.06 (3)	
28.3*	Go forward to next element	Swipe to the side with hand		0.11 (6)
29.1	Go back to previous element	Swipe away from self with hand	0.08 (4)	
29.2*	Go back to previous element	Swipe to the opposite side with hand		0.12 (6)
30.1	Go down in a list	Swipe up with one/two fingers	0.44 (11)	
30.2*	Go down in a list	Swipe up with hand		0.30 (10)
31.1	Go up in a list	Swipe down with one/two fingers	0.44 (11)	
31.2*	Go up in a list	Swipe down with hand		0.35 (11)
32.1	Open interface elements	Tap/point at the screen with one/two fingers	0.14 (6)	0.13 (5)
32.2*	Open interface elements	Hold hand up in front of the screen (stop sign)		0.13 (5)
33.1	Close interface elements	Swipe interface away with hand	0.22 (6)	
33.2*	Close interface elements	Tap/point at the screen again with one/two fingers		0.33 (6)

This legacy bias was present, despite using the increased production technique as a countermeasure. This could be due to the low effectiveness of increased production. [24] showed that increased production of up to three suggestions did not decrease the amount of proposed gestures influenced by legacy bias.

87.90% of all observed gestures were performed using only the dominant hand. The elicited gestures were similar in both conditions, indicating that participants preferred to remain consistent rather than introducing new techniques for interactions with close or distant holograms. A similar observation was noted by [79], who found that move and rotate operations with objects behind the screen were often performed in mid-air using proxy objects. However, agreement rates associated with physical manipulations of 3D objects were generally lower in the outside of reach condition, with particularly large differences found for rotation around the x and y axis. The think aloud protocols revealed that the rotation technique was largely derived from interactions with physical objects in the real world, because participants perceived the 3D object as something they could grab and manipulate as if it was actually there. Combined with mentions of preference towards holograms within reach, these findings suggest that physical manipulations of 3D objects and rotation in particular, may be less intuitive when the 3D object appears outside of physical reach. This is further supported by [64], who found that direct input interaction with true 3D displays was improved when the 3D object was positioned less than 36 cm away from the input device (e.g. hand).

3 Study 2: Reverse-Matching

Study 2 was designed with the goal to remove less suitable gestures by reverse-matching elicited gestures to their referents [37,50,67,84]. The referent 'deselect/deactivate' was removed based on participants' feedback from study 1. The remaining 32 referents were grouped to 24 tasks by summarizing the dichotomous referents for rotation around x, y, z and movement in x and y. Rotation was depicted clockwise around the axis of rotation, thus reducing the number of gesture videos to 26.

3.1 Method

Procedure. The reverse-matching task was performed using an online questionnaire. At the beginning of the questionnaire, participants were asked to provide information about their age, gender, handedness and usage of touchscreens, gestural controls, augmented/mixed reality, virtual reality and video games. This was followed by a short introduction to H3D displays, the gesture elicitation process from Study 1 and the referents. During the subsequent reverse-matching task, participants viewed representative videos of the elicited gestures in a randomized order and chose the referent for which each depicted gesture seemed most suitable. Multiple choice input was allowed and participants were encouraged to add comments about their responses.

Suitability Measure. Based on the assumption that a suitable gesture should ideally evoke the referent in mind for which it has been designed for [37], the suitability of a gesture was measured by calculating the number of correct pairings between the gesture and the correct referent.

Sample. 21 participants (17 males, 4 females) with a mean age of 38.76 years ($SD = 10.46$) and no background in interaction or user interface design completed the reverse-matching questionnaire. None of the participants took part in study 1. All participants reported using touchscreens on a daily basis. 62% never used augmented or mixed reality devices and 52% had no previous experience with gestural controls.

3.2 Results

A detailed list of all gesture-referent mappings with the respective suitability scores is provided in Table 2. Based on the resulting suitability scores, gesture-referent mappings with scores below 10 were removed from the gesture set. Gesture to remove/delete object can be replaced by a 'delete' button. The gestures to open and close interface elements were changed to the second most popular proposal from the gesture elicitation study - swipe up with hand to open interface elements and swipe down with hand to close them. Gesture 17 was removed from the vocabulary in favor of its more suitable counterpart (Gesture 16). Swipe gestures with hand or finger were matched to the same referents with similar suitability scores and were hence grouped together. The resulting refined set of 23 gesture-referent pairings is summarized in Fig. 3.

3.3 Discussion

Gestures resembling touchscreen techniques and physical manipulations of real-world objects produced the highest suitability scores. It can be assumed that these gestures trigger knowledge built from previous experiences with touchscreen interfaces and real-world physical interactions [31]. Overall, the majority of the techniques in the refined gesture set (select, rotate, scale, swipe through pages) is very similar to gestures elicited in studies exploring 3D interaction with mixed reality [55,57] and in-car stereoscopic 3D displays [79].

4 Study 3: Memorability Evaluation

Study 3 was a memorability study inspired by [37,48,50] to compare the memorability and user experience characteristics of the refined user-elicited gesture set with an alternative gesture set elicited from experts. A between-subjects design was applied with 'gesture set' (user-elicitied vs. expert-elicited) as the between-subjects factor.

Table 2. Gesture-referent mappings and the corresponding suitability scores n. The axes are defined according to the left-handed coordinate system.

ID	Referent	Gesture	n
3	Make object smaller	Pinch thumb and index finger	21
9	Select/activate	Tap/point at the object with one/two fingers	20
11	Make object smaller	Spread thumb and index finger	20
3	Zoom out of map	Pinch thumb and index finger	19
11	Zoom into map	Spread thumb and index finger	19
16	Move object closer towards self	Grab and pinch with multiple fingers and pull towards self	18
15	Rotate object around z	Grab from the front with spread fingers and turn wrist	18
10	Move object away from self	Push away from body with palm	18
13	Go down in a list	Swipe up with finger	18
8	Move map vertically	Point at the map with finger and slide down	18
1	Go to the next page	Swipe left with hand	17
4	Rotate object around y	Grab from below with spread fingers and turn wrist	17
12	Rotate object around x	Grab from the side with spread fingers and turn wrist	17
8	Move object vertically	Tap/point at object with finger and slide down	17
7	Move map horizontally	Point at the map with finger and slide left	17
20	Go up in a list	Swipe down with finger	17
6	Move map horizontally	Point at the map with finger and slide right	17
7	Move object horizontally	Tap/point at object with finger and slide left	16
6	Move object horizontally	Tap/point at object with finger and slide right	16
23	Go down in a list	Swipe up with hand	16
24	Go up in a list	Swipe down with hand	16
2	Move map vertically	Point at the map with finger and slide up	16
5	Go to previous page	Swipe right with hand	15
2	Move object vertically	Tap/point at object with finger and slide up	15
17	Move object closer towards self	Stretch arm out and move palm toward self	14
19	Go forward to next element	Swipe towards self with finger	13
15	Rotate map	Grab from the front with spread fingers and turn wrist	12
21	Go back to previous element	Swipe away from self with hand	11
25	Move object horizontally	Push to the left with palm	9
14	Remove/delete object	Swipe away with hand in a large diagonal motion	9
22	Open interface elements	Hold hand up in front of the screen (stop sign)	9
14	Close interface elements	Swipe interface away with hand	9
9	Open interface elements	Tap/point at the screen with finger	8
26	Move object horizontally	Push to the right with palm	6
1	Go forward to next element	Swipe left with hand	3
18	Go forward to next element	Swipe left with finger	2
9	Close interface elements	Tap/point at screen with finger	2
5	Go back to previous element	Swipe right with hand	0

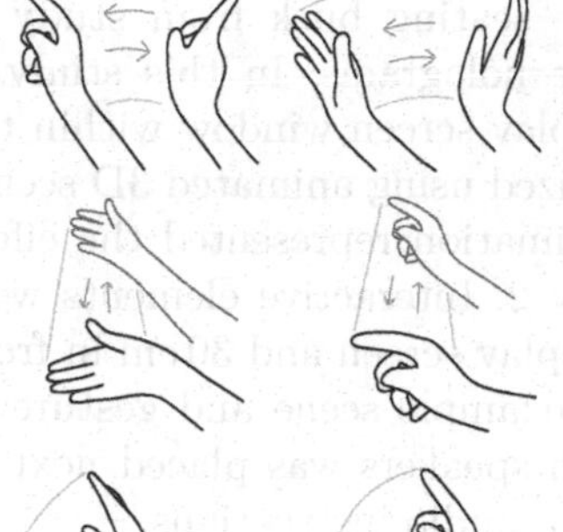

Swipe gestures
Page through menus or a list of elements arranged horizontally
Swipe back and forth through a list of elements arranged behind each other
Scroll up and down in a list of objects arranged vertically
Swipe up to open interface elements and down to close them

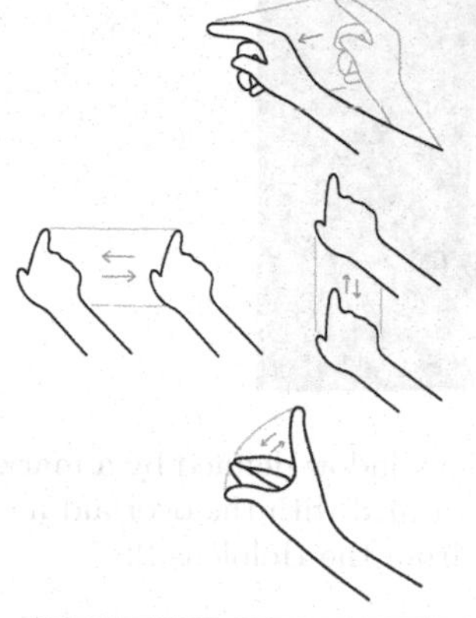

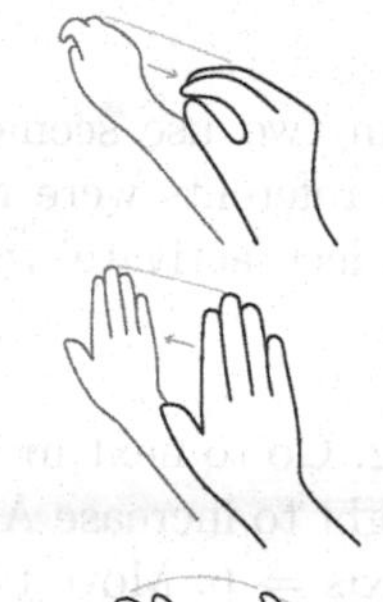

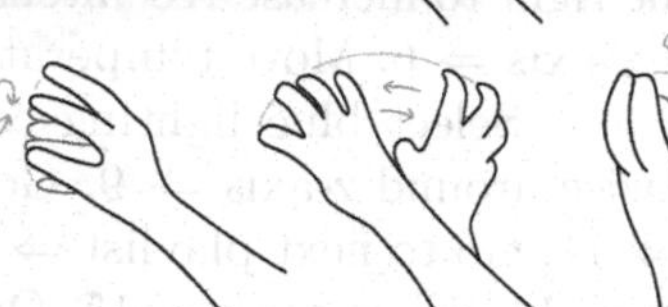

Fig. 3. Refined user-elicited gesture set. The axes are defined according to the left-handed coordinate system.

4.1 Method

Apparatus. The study was carried out in the seating buck from study 1. A Microsoft Hololens 2 was used to display the holograms. In this study, a 24×13.5 cm large marker defined the virtual display screen window within the black placeholder plate. The referents were visualized using animated 3D scenes created with the Unity3D game engine. Each animation represented the effect of a specific gesture-referent mapping from study 2. Interactive elements were placed within reach only - between the virtual display screen and 30 cm in front of the virtual display screen. Figure 4 shows an example scene and gesture as seen in the Hololens 2. An external monitor with speakers was placed next to the seating buck to play videos of the gestures and audio instructions.

Fig. 4. 3D map displayed within the virtual display screen window defined by a marker on the black placeholder. A pinch-to-zoom gesture is performed with the overlaid hand mesh to provide additional occlusion cues. Image taken from the Hololens 2.

Scenarios. The animated scenes were presented in two use scenarios. 12 of the 16 reversible gestures designed for dichotomous referents were represented with only one direction of movement. The referent 'select/activate' was included multiple times.

Scenario 1 consisted of 17 tasks: 1. Select menu ⇒ 2. Go to next menu page ⇒ 3. Select settings ⇒ 4. Move intensity slider to the right to increase AC intensity ⇒ 5. Rotate slider bar counterclockwise around x-axis ⇒ 6. Move temperature slider to the left to decrease AC temperature ⇒ 7. Select blue lighting color ⇒ 8. Rotate lighting control knob counterclockwise around z-axis ⇒ 9. Go to previous menu page ⇒ 10. Select music player ⇒ 11. Go to next playlist ⇒ 12. Select playlist ⇒ 13. Go down in the list of songs ⇒ 14. Select song ⇒ 15. Open music player interface ⇒ 16. Move volume slider up to increase volume ⇒ 17. Close music player interface.

Scenario 2 consisted of 13 tasks: 1. Select navigation ⇒ 2. Pull introduced 3D model closer towards self ⇒ 3. Enlarge the 3D model ⇒ 4. Rotate 3D model clockwise around y-axis ⇒ 5. Push 3D model away from self ⇒ 6. Select 'Buy' ⇒ 7.Go to next element in the list behind the first ⇒ 8. Select element ⇒ 9. Rotate map clockwise in bird-view perspective ⇒ 10. Move map up ⇒ 11. Move map left ⇒ 12. Zoom out of the map ⇒ 13. Select destination on the map.

Expert-Elicited Gesture Set. 5 experts whose daily work involves research and creation of innovative augmented, virtual and mixed reality applications for in-car passengers participated in a workshop to elicit expert-defined gestures. The expert-elicited gesture set is displayed in Fig. 5.

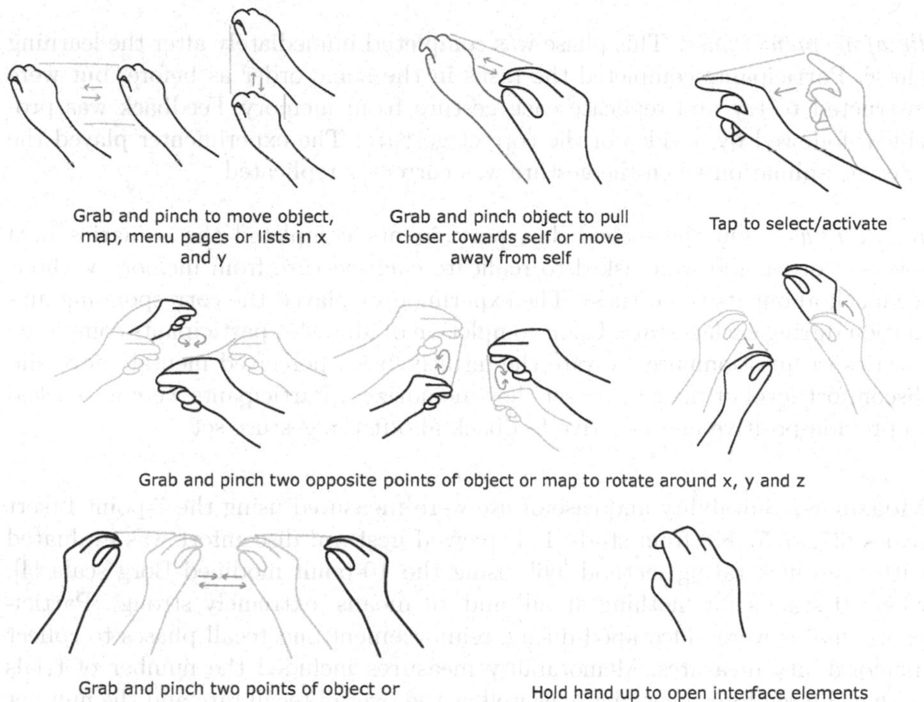
Grab and pinch to move object, map, menu pages or lists in x and y
Grab and pinch object to pull closer towards self or move away from self
Tap to select/activate
Grab and pinch two opposite points of object or map to rotate around x, y and z
Grab and pinch two points of object or map to scale up and down
Hold hand up to open interface elements
Put hand down and wait to close interface elements

Fig. 5. Expert-elicited gestures. The axes are defined according to the left-handed coordinate system.

Procedure. The study took place on two consecutive days with the learning and reinforcement phases completed on day one and the recall phase completed on day two. On the first day, participants with intact stereoscopic vision, as measured by the entrance test of the Butterfly Stereo Acuity Test, completed the preliminary questionnaire from study 1 and received a short introduction to H3D displays. Participants were asked to focus exclusively on the gestures, not the visual appeal of the interface. All interactions were carried out using the Wizard-of-Oz method [84]. Using an external controller, the experimenter played the referent animation while the participant was executing the corresponding gesture.

Learning Phase. On day 1, Scenarios 1 and 2 were presented in a randomized order for the first time. Each referent was introduced with an audio instruction and a video of the corresponding gesture. Participants were instructed to repeat the gesture 4 times to gain an assessment of the gesture's discomfort level [66]. After four training executions, participants were asked to perform the gesture for a fifth time, which is when the experimenter played the referent animation. Participants then rated the gesture's suitability, ease and discomfort level. Each gesture was rated only once, following its first occurrence in the scenario.

Reinforcement Phase. This phase was completed immediately after the learning phase. Participants completed the tasks in the same order as before, but were instructed to try and replicate each gesture from memory. Feedback was provided, followed by a video of the correct gesture. The experimenter played the referent animation when the gesture was correctly replicated.

Recall Phase. On the second day, participants completed the scenarios in a reversed order and were asked to replicate each gesture from memory without feedback about its correctness. The experimenter played the corresponding animation during each gesture. Upon completion of all tasks, participants completed a series of questionnaires to rate the intuitiveness, perceived mental effort and discomfort level of the gesture set they memorized. Participants were also asked to provide positive and negative feedback about the gesture set.

Measures. Suitability and ease of use were measured using the 7-point Likert scales [37,37,57,83] from study 1. Perceived gestural discomfort was evaluated with the quick rating method [66], using the 10-point modified Borg scale [4], where 0 stands for 'nothing at all' and 10 means 'extremely strong'. Participants' hands were videotaped during reinforcement and recall phases to collect memorability measures. Memorability measures included the number of trials during the reinforcement phase, as well as the overall recall rate and the number of errors during the recall phase. A higher number of trials required to replicate the gesture correctly reflects a higher learning difficulty [37]. Correct recalls are defined by [48] as gestures with the same number of hands, fingers, contacts and the same general movement shape. Non-correct recalls were either association errors, when participants failed to associate the correct gesture with the referent in question, or partial gesture errors, if the gesture was similar but with some noticeable differences [48]. A reversible gesture performed in the wrong direction of movement was not classified as an error, because it would elicit a correct response from the system just not in the expected direction. Perceived intuitiveness of each gesture set was measured using the INTUI questionnaire for intuitive interaction [71]. The INTUI assesses four components of intuitive interaction: effortlessness, verbalizability, magical experience and gut feeling, plus an additional question measuring global intuitiveness. The resulting 17 items are rated on a 7-point scale between two bipolar statements. Perceived mental effort was rated using the German SEA scale (scale for assessing subjectively experienced effort) [15], which provides a single rating scale ranging from 0 to 220 where higher numbers are associated with a higher perceived mental effort.

Sample. Data was collected from 32 participants who did not take part in any of the previous studies. One group of 16 participants (11 male, 5 female, 15 right- and 1 left-handed) with the mean age of 39.88 (SD = 10.48) learned the user-elicited gesture set. The other group of 16 participants (13 male, 3 female, 15 right- and 1 left-handed) with the mean age of 40.88 (SD = 10.84) learned the expert-elicited gesture set. All except one participant in the expert-elicited group used touchscreen devices on a daily basis. 37.5% of participants in the user-elicited and 43.8% in the expert-elicited group had no previous experience with gestural controls. 95% of participants in the user-elicited and 68.8% in the expert-elicited group never used augmented or mixed reality devices.

4.2 Results

Visual inspection of distributions of memorability and gesture rating measures revealed that these were not normal. Hence, Wilcoxon rank-sum tests were performed to analyze differences between groups. The significance threshold was set to $\alpha = .10$ to increase statistical power, given the small sample size. Statistical testing was not applied to INTUI, discomfort and SEA ratings from the post-recall questionnaires, due to uncertainty caused by recall bias. Table 3 provides a summary of the results.

4.3 Discussion

The expert-elicited gesture set was criticized for the use of two-hand gestures for scaling and rotation (7 mentions) and the lack of convenient swipe, slide and pinch-to-zoom gestures known from touchscreen interfaces (8 mentions). 4 participants described the expert-elicited gesture set as intuitive and easy to use. Participants in the user-elicited group criticized the discomfort of the rotation gesture (4 mentions) and the lack of feedback during input (3 mentions). 8 participants described the user-elicited gesture set as intuitive and easy to use. Statistical analysis of memorability measures revealed no significant differences between groups, both gesture sets were memorized similarly well with recall rates above 90%. However, analysis of the gesture ratings revealed that participants who learned the user-elicited gestures rated the gestures as significantly more suitable and easy to use than participants who learned the expert-elicited gestures. The difference in gesture discomfort ratings was marginally non-significant, but in favor of the user-elicited gesture set. Descriptive analysis further showed that

Table 3. Descriptive statistics with means, standard deviations and medians, Wilcoxon rank-sum test results and respective effect sizes. (r).

Measure	User-elicited		Expert-elicited		W	p	r
	M (SD)	Md	M (SD)	Md			
Num. of trials	1.20 (0.70)	1.00	1.15 (0.43)	1.00	129.00	.99	−.00
Recall rate	0.90 (0.11)	0.95	0.93 (0.09)	0.95	144.00	.55	−.11
Num. of association errors	1.69 (1.99)	1.00	1.19 (1.33)	1.00	114.00	.56	−.09
Num. of partial gesture errors	0.44 (0.63)	0.00	0.31 (0.60)	0.00	113.00	.50	−.12
Avg. gesture suitability	5.83 (0.59)	6.00	5.55 (0.53)	6.00	120.00	.08	−.31
Avg. gesture ease	6.11 (0.59)	7.00	5.89 (0.57)	7.00	121.50	.09	−.30
Avg. gesture discomfort	0.88 (0.45)	0.00	1.13 (0.55)	1.00	236.00	.11	−.28
INTUI effortlessness	5.93 (1.05)	6.00	5.45 (1.23)	6.00			
INTUI verbalizability	6.29 (0.80)	6.50	6.19 (0.82)	6.00			
INTUI magical experience	5.16 (1.37)	5.00	4.63 (1.28)	5.00			
INTUI gut feeling	3.69 (1.67)	3.00	3.31 (1.62)	3.00			
INTUI global intuitiveness	5.44 (0.89)	6.00	5.00 (1.32)	5.00			
Perceived mental effort	34.81 (23.41)	21.00	42.38 (25.34)	35.00			
Post-recall discomfort	1.19 (0.83)	1.00	1.44 (1.09)	1.00			

the user-elicited gesture set was rated higher on all INTUI scales. This could be the result of a lower domain transfer distance [12] in the user-elicited gesture set. The large number of touchscreen techniques decreases the distance between the new application domain introduced in this study and touchscreens as the main origin of prior knowledge. The ability to utilize knowledge from past experiences is a core characteristic of intuitive systems [3,12,46]. It is, however, important to note that results from the post-recall questionnaires should be interpreted with caution, as 9 participants in the expert-elicited group and 10 participants in the user-elicited group failed to reproduce the gesture set without association errors and were therefore affected by recall bias. The remaining unaffected participants rated the user-elicited gesture set higher on all INTUI scales except magical experience, lower on the perceived mental effort scale and slightly higher on the perceived discomfort level scale.

5 General Discussion

Implications for Future In-Car Holographic 3D Interfaces. The large number of observed hand pose variants during the gesture elicitation study demonstrates that future hand-tracking systems should be trained to recognize a variety of hand poses. Context-aware user interfaces could be applied to allow a greater flexibility of user input by predicting the intention behind the gesture [54].

Every interactive system can be greatly improved with feedback [49] and lack of thereof was a recurrent theme in Studies 1 and 3. Feedback can be introduced through multiple channels. For instance, visual feedback that signals a successful contact with a virtual button has been shown to increase the accuracy of 3D mid-air touch [68]. Mid-air haptic feedback produced by focused ultrasonic air pressure [26,27,30,72] is another intriguing channel that can be applied in vehicles [18] to improve the interaction experience with mid-air gestural interfaces [21,41].

Visual 3D user interface (UI) design was not specifically addressed in the present work, but has been found to be an influential factor on users' ability to understand which gesture should be used for a specific task [11]. 3D interfaces in particular, can deviate visually from traditional user interfaces and have the potential to introduce new interaction techniques to utilize the spatial properties of 3D UIs. To make 3D UIs as unambiguous as possible, UI elements could be designed to convey affordances [51] that match the intended 3D interaction technique.

Interface elements and 3D objects that allow direct physical manipulation should be displayed within reach, whenever possible. During study 1, it was observed that when holograms appeared outside of reach participants instinctively extended their arm, which can cause a higher fatigue and muscle stress compared to a bent arm posture [23,36,40]. Rotation techniques that require flexion of the wrist can also cause additional discomfort and should therefore not be assigned to frequently performed tasks [59]. Two-hand gestures seem to be less favored for in-car interaction and are therefore not recommended.

Lastly, the observed similarities between the proposed user-elicited gesture set and mid-air gestures suggested for other 3D applications [55,57,79] demonstrate that future 3D UIs may rely on universal interaction techniques, applicable to a variety of display technologies and application contexts. A consolidation of all suggested techniques into a standardized 3D interaction vocabulary could help bridge the gap between different 3D devices that support mid-air gestures and allow users to enjoy 3D UIs without the requirement to memorize new interaction techniques with each emerging application and device.

Limitations. The studies reported in this work were subject to some limitations. Study 1 was designed as an exploratory investigation in which the experimenter interacted with participants to make inquiries about their thought process. As a result, some participants may have been engaged to a greater degree than others, which could have had an effect on the quantity and quality of their proposals. Another limitation is that cultural background was not accounted for. Past research suggests that cultural and demographic background can influence gesture proposals and preferences [33,42]. Furthermore, the proposed user-elicited gesture set was not evaluated in a moving vehicle or tested for tracking accuracy and robustness, which are important quality criteria for gestural interfaces [1]. In a moving car, acceleration and vehicle body movement could make precise targeting and manipulation more difficult [79]. A lack of objective measures in study 3 is another limitation to consider. The Wizard-of-Oz approach rendered time measures unreliable and all usability, effort and discomfort measures were based on post-recall subjective questionnaires, which in some cases were affected by recall bias caused by falsely memorized gestures.

Objective measures of fatigue such as oxygen consumption [20], consumed muscle endurance [23] or muscle activity [36] could be an alternative and provide additional insights. Reliable time measures with implemented interactions in real-time would also help assess the robustness and efficiency of the proposed gestures.

6 Conclusions and Future Work

Automated driving could elevate cars to experience platforms for non-driving related content. H3D displays can deliver the largest depth range with the most natural 3D experience, expanding the design space for 3D UIs and spacial interactions in cars. As of today, the majority of users have only limited experience with 3D interaction, which highlights the need for intuitive and easy to learn interaction techniques. This paper presents an intuitive and memorable user-elicited gesture set for interaction with menus, system interfaces, 3D objects and maps.

The lack of tactile feedback was a major critique point. Future work could therefore focus on investigating effective feedback concepts to enhance mid-air gestural interaction and improve the overall experience. If possible, gesture sets proposed for in-car use should be evaluated in a moving vehicle. Additional evaluations with objective performance, effort and discomfort measures would be valuable. Visual interface design as well as cultural background are additional factors that could be considered in future investigations.

Conflicts of Interest. The author is employed by Volkswagen AG. The study was conducted and financed by Volkswagen AG. The author declares no competing conflict of interest. The results, opinions and conclusions expressed in this publication are not necessarily those of Volkswagen AG.

References

1. Barclay, K., Wei, D., Lutteroth, C., Sheehan, R.: A quantitative quality model for gesture based user interfaces. In: Proceedings of the 23rd Australian Computer-Human Interaction Conference, OzCHI 2011, pp. 31–39. Association for Computing Machinery, New York (2011). https://doi.org/10.1145/2071536.2071540
2. Bengler, K.: Driver and driving experience in cars. In: Meixner, G., Müller, C. (eds.) Automotive User Interfaces. HIS, pp. 79–94. Springer, Cham (2017). https://doi.org/10.1007/978-3-319-49448-7_3
3. Blackler, A., Hurtienne, J.: Towards a unified view of intuitive interaction: definitions, models and tools across the world. MMI-Interaktiv **13**, 36–54 (2007). https://eprints.qut.edu.au/19116/
4. Borg, G.: Borg's Perceived Exertion and Pain Scales. Human Kinetics, Champaign (1998)
5. Bowman, D.A., et al.: New directions in 3D user interfaces. Int. J. Virtual Real. **5**(2), 3–14 (2006). https://doi.org/10.20870/IJVR.2006.5.2.2683

6. Broy, N., Alt, F., Schneegass, S., Henze, N., Schmidt, A.: Perceiving layered information on 3D displays using binocular disparity. In: Proceedings of the 2nd ACM International Symposium on Pervasive Displays, PerDis 2013, pp. 61–66. Association for Computing Machinery, New York (2013). https://doi.org/10.1145/2491568.2491582
7. Broy, N., Alt, F., Schneegass, S., Pfleging, B.: 3D displays in cars: exploring the user performance for a stereoscopic instrument cluster. In: Proceedings of the 6th International Conference on Automotive User Interfaces and Interactive Vehicular Applications, AutomotiveUI 2014, pp. 1–9. Association for Computing Machinery, New York (2014). https://doi.org/10.1145/2667317.2667319
8. Broy, N., André, E., Schmidt, A.: Is stereoscopic 3D a better choice for information representation in the car? In: Proceedings of the 4th International Conference on Automotive User Interfaces and Interactive Vehicular Applications, AutomotiveUI 2012, pp. 93–100. Association for Computing Machinery, New York (2012). https://doi.org/10.1145/2390256.2390270
9. Broy, N., Guo, M., Schneegass, S., Pfleging, B., Alt, F.: Introducing novel technologies in the car: conducting a real-world study to test 3D dashboards. In: Proceedings of the 7th International Conference on Automotive User Interfaces and Interactive Vehicular Applications, AutomotiveUI 2015, pp. 179–186. Association for Computing Machinery, New York (2015). https://doi.org/10.1145/2799250.2799280
10. Chen, J., Bowman, D.A.: Domain-specific design of 3D interaction techniques: an approach for designing useful virtual environment applications. Presence: Teleoper. Virtual Environ. **18**(5), 370–386 (2009). https://doi.org/10.1162/pres.18.5.370
11. Chen, L., Wu, W.: Evaluation of the influence of interface symbols on user hand-gestures in augmented reality. In: Rebelo, F. (ed.) AHFE 2021. LNNS, vol. 261, pp. 814–821. Springer, Cham (2021). https://doi.org/10.1007/978-3-030-79760-7_98
12. Diefenbach, S., Ullrich, D.: An experience perspective on intuitive interaction: central components and the special effect of domain transfer distance. Interact. Comput. **27**(3), 210–234 (2015). https://doi.org/10.1093/iwc/iwv001
13. Dünser, A., Billinghurst, M., Mancero, G.: Evaluating visual search performance with a multi layer display. In: Proceedings of the 20th Australasian Conference on Computer-Human Interaction: Designing for Habitus and Habitat, OZCHI 2008, pp. 307–310. Association for Computing Machinery, New York (2008). https://doi.org/10.1145/1517744.1517796
14. Dzida, W., Freitag, R.: Making use of scenarios for validating analysis and design. IEEE Trans. Softw. Eng. **24**(12), 1182–1196 (1998). https://doi.org/10.1109/32.738346
15. Eilers, K., Nachreiner, F., Hänecke, K.: Entwicklung und überprüfung einer skala zur erfassung subjektiv erlebter anstrengung (1986)
16. Emoto, M., Niida, T., Okano, F.: Repeated vergence adaptation causes the decline of visual functions in watching stereoscopic television. J. Display Technol. **1**(2), 328 (2005)
17. Fariman, H.J., Alyamani, H.J., Kavakli, M., Hamey, L.: Designing a user-defined gesture vocabulary for an in-vehicle climate control system. In: Proceedings of the 28th Australian Conference on Computer-Human Interaction, OzCHI 2016, pp. 391–395. Association for Computing Machinery, New York (2016). https://doi.org/10.1145/3010915.3010955

18. Georgiou, O., et al.: Haptic in-vehicle gesture controls. In: Proceedings of the 9th International Conference on Automotive User Interfaces and Interactive Vehicular Applications Adjunct, AutomotiveUI 2017, pp. 233–238. Association for Computing Machinery, New York (2017). https://doi.org/10.1145/3131726.3132045
19. Graichen, L., Graichen, M., Krems, J.F.: Evaluation of gesture-based in-vehicle interaction: user experience and the potential to reduce driver distraction. Hum. Factors **61**(5), 774–792 (2019). https://doi.org/10.1177/0018720818824253
20. Hansberger, J.T., et al.: Dispelling the gorilla arm syndrome: the viability of prolonged gesture interactions. In: Lackey, S., Chen, J. (eds.) VAMR 2017. LNCS, vol. 10280, pp. 505–520. Springer, Cham (2017). https://doi.org/10.1007/978-3-319-57987-0_41
21. Harrington, K., Large, D.R., Burnett, G., Georgiou, O.: Exploring the use of mid-air ultrasonic feedback to enhance automotive user interfaces. In: Proceedings of the 10th International Conference on Automotive User Interfaces and Interactive Vehicular Applications, AutomotiveUI 2018, pp. 11–20. Association for Computing Machinery, New York (2018). https://doi.org/10.1145/3239060.3239089
22. He, Z., Zhang, R., Liu, Z., Tan, Z.: A user-defined gesture set for natural interaction in a smart kitchen environment. In: 2020 13th International Symposium on Computational Intelligence and Design (ISCID), pp. 122–125 (2020). https://doi.org/10.1109/ISCID51228.2020.00034
23. Hincapié-Ramos, J.D., Guo, X., Moghadasian, P., Irani, P.: Consumed endurance: a metric to quantify arm fatigue of mid-air interactions. In: CHI 2014, one of a CHInd, pp. 1063–1072. Association for Computing Machinery, New York (2014). https://doi.org/10.1145/2556288.2557130
24. Hoff, L., Hornecker, E., Bertel, S.: Modifying gesture elicitation: do kinaesthetic priming and increased production reduce legacy bias? In: Proceedings of the TEI '16: Tenth International Conference on Tangible, Embedded, and Embodied Interaction, TEI 2016, pp. 86–91. Association for Computing Machinery, New York (2016). https://doi.org/10.1145/2839462.2839472
25. Hoffman, D.M., Girshick, A.R., Akeley, K., Banks, M.S.: Vergence-accommodation conflicts hinder visual performance and cause visual fatigue. J. Vis. **8**(3), 1–30 (2008). https://doi.org/10.1167/8.3.33
26. Hoshi, T.: Compact ultrasound device for noncontact interaction. In: Nijholt, A., Romão, T., Reidsma, D. (eds.) ACE 2012. LNCS, vol. 7624, pp. 502–505. Springer, Heidelberg (2012). https://doi.org/10.1007/978-3-642-34292-9_45
27. Hoshi, T., Takahashi, M., Nakatsuma, K., Shinoda, H.: Touchable holography. In: Wigdor, D. (ed.) ACM SIGGRAPH 2009 Emerging Technologies, p. 1. ACM, New York (2009). https://doi.org/10.1145/1597956.1597979
28. Howarth, P.A.: Potential hazards of viewing 3-D stereoscopic television, cinema and computer games: a review. Ophthalmic Physiol. Opt. J. Br. Coll. Ophthalmic Opticians (Optometrists) **31**(2), 111–122 (2011). https://doi.org/10.1111/j.1475-1313.2011.00822.x
29. Hwang, A.D., Peli, E.: Instability of the perceived world while watching 3D stereoscopic imagery: a likely source of motion sickness symptoms. i-Perception **5**(6), 515–535 (2014). https://doi.org/10.1068/i0647
30. Inoue, S., Makino, Y., Shinoda, H.: Active touch perception produced by airborne ultrasonic haptic hologram. In: Colgate, J.E. (ed.) IEEE World Haptics Conference 2015, pp. 362–367. IEEE, Piscataway (2015). https://doi.org/10.1109/WHC.2015.7177739

31. Jacob, R.J., et al.: Reality-based interaction: a framework for post-wimp interfaces. In: Proceedings of the SIGCHI Conference on Human Factors in Computing Systems, CHI 2008, pp. 201–210. Association for Computing Machinery, New York (2008). https://doi.org/10.1145/1357054.1357089
32. Jahani, H., Kavakli, M.: Exploring a user-defined gesture vocabulary for descriptive mid-air interactions. Cogn. Technol. Work **20**(1), 11–22 (2017). https://doi.org/10.1007/s10111-017-0444-0
33. Jiang, H., et al.: Demographic effects on mid-air gesture preference for control of devices: implications for design. In: Black, N.L., Neumann, W.P., Noy, I. (eds.) IEA 2021. LNNS, vol. 223, pp. 379–386. Springer, Cham (2022). https://doi.org/10.1007/978-3-030-74614-8_47
34. Kara, P.A., Cserkaszky, A., Tamboli, R., Barsi, A., Martini, M., Balogh, T.: Light-field capture and display systems: limitations, challenges, and potentials. In: Hahlweg, C.F., Mulley, J.R. (eds.) Proceedings of the SPIE 10746, Novel Optical Systems Design and Optimization XXI, 1074604, p. 1074604 (2018). https://doi.org/10.1117/12.2320564
35. Kazhura, M.: User-elicited gestural interaction with future in-car holographic 3D displays. In: Poster Session at the 20th International Conference on Mobile and Ubiquitous Multimedia (MUM 2021), Leuven, Belgium, 5–8 December (2021). https://doi.org/10.1145/3490632.3497832
36. Kim, J.H., Ari, H., Madasu, C., Hwang, J.: Evaluation of hologram distances in reducing shoulder stress during augmented reality interactions. Proc. Hum. Factors Ergon. Soc. Ann. Meeting **64**(1), 868–871 (2020). https://doi.org/10.1177/1071181320641201
37. Kühnel, C., Westermann, T., Hemmert, F., Kratz, S., Müller, A., Möller, S.: I'm home: defining and evaluating a gesture set for smart-home control. Int. J. Hum. Comput. Stud. **69**(11), 693–704 (2011). https://doi.org/10.1016/j.ijhcs.2011.04.005
38. Kun, A.L., Boll, S., Schmidt, A.: Shifting gears: user interfaces in the age of autonomous driving. IEEE Pervasive Comput. **15**(1), 32–38 (2016). https://doi.org/10.1109/MPRV.2016.14
39. Lambooij, M., IJsselsteijn, W., Fortuin, M., Heynderickx, I.: Visual discomfort and visual fatigue of stereoscopic displays: a review. J. Imaging Sci. Technol. **53**(3), 030201 (2009). https://doi.org/10.2352/J.ImagingSci.Technol.2009.53.3.030201
40. Lou, X., Li, X., Hansen, P., Feng, Z.: An empirical evaluation on arm fatigue in free hand interaction and guidelines for designing natural user interfaces in VR. In: Chen, J.Y.C., Fragomeni, G. (eds.) HCII 2020. LNCS, vol. 12190, pp. 313–324. Springer, Cham (2020). https://doi.org/10.1007/978-3-030-49695-1_21
41. Matsubayashi, A., Makino, Y., Shinoda, H.: Direct finger manipulation of 3D object image with ultrasound haptic feedback. In: Proceedings of the 2019 CHI Conference on Human Factors in Computing Systems, pp. 1–11. Association for Computing Machinery, New York (2019). https://doi.org/10.1145/3290605.3300317
42. Mauney, D., Howarth, J., Wirtanen, A., Capra, M.: Cultural similarities and differences in user-defined gestures for touchscreen user interfaces. In: Extended Abstracts on Human Factors in Computing Systems, CHI 2010, pp. 4015–4020. Association for Computing Machinery, New York (2010). https://doi.org/10.1145/1753846.1754095

43. May, K.R., Gable, T.M., Walker, B.N.: Designing an in-vehicle air gesture set using elicitation methods. In: Proceedings of the 9th International Conference on Automotive User Interfaces and Interactive Vehicular Applications, AutomotiveUI 2017, pp. 74–83. Association for Computing Machinery, New York (2017). https://doi.org/10.1145/3122986.3123015
44. Microsoft: Mixed reality documentation: Direct manipulation with hands. https://docs.microsoft.com/en-us/windows/mixed-reality/design/direct-manipulation
45. Mizobuchi, S., Terasaki, S., Häkkinen, J., Heinonen, E., Bergquist, J., Chignell, M.: The effect of stereoscopic viewing in a word-search task with a layered background. J. Soc. Inform. Display **16**(11), 1105 (2008). https://doi.org/10.1889/JSID16.11.1105
46. Mohs, C., et al.: Iuui - intuitive use of user interfaces. In: Hassenzahl, M., Bosenick, T., Müller-Prove, M., Peissner, M. (eds.) Tagungsband UP06, pp. 130–133. Fraunhofer Verlag, Stuttgart (2006). https://dl.gi.de/handle/20.500.12116/5992
47. Morris, M.R., et al.: Reducing legacy bias in gesture elicitation studies. Interactions **21**(3), 40–45 (2014). https://doi.org/10.1145/2591689
48. Nacenta, M.A., Kamber, Y., Qiang, Y., Kristensson, P.O.: Memorability of pre-designed and user-defined gesture sets. In: Proceedings of the SIGCHI Conference on Human Factors in Computing Systems, CHI 2013, pp. 1099–1108. Association for Computing Machinery, New York (2013). https://doi.org/10.1145/2470654.2466142
49. Nielsen, J.: Usability Engineering. Kaufmann, Amsterdam (1994)
50. Nielsen, M., Störring, M., Moeslund, T.B., Granum, E.: A procedure for developing intuitive and ergonomic gesture interfaces for HCI. In: Camurri, A., Volpe, G. (eds.) GW 2003. LNCS (LNAI), vol. 2915, pp. 409–420. Springer, Heidelberg (2004). https://doi.org/10.1007/978-3-540-24598-8_38
51. Norman, D.A.: The Design of Everyday Things. Basic Books, New York (2013). Revised and expanded edition
52. On-Road Automated Driving (ORAD) committee: Taxonomy and Definitions for Terms Related to Driving Automation Systems for On-Road Motor Vehicles, June 2018. https://doi.org/10.4271/J3016_201806
53. Ortega, F.R., et al.: Gesture elicitation for 3D travel via multi-touch and mid-air systems for procedurally generated pseudo-universe. In: 2017 IEEE Symposium on 3D User Interfaces (3DUI), pp. 144–153. IEEE, Piscataway (2017). https://doi.org/10.1109/3DUI.2017.7893331
54. Perera, M.: Personalised human device interaction through context aware augmented reality. In: Proceedings of the 2020 International Conference on Multimodal Interaction, ICMI 2020, pp. 723–727. Association for Computing Machinery, New York (2020). https://doi.org/10.1145/3382507.3421157
55. Pham, T., Vermeulen, J., Tang, A., MacDonald Vermeulen, L.: Scale impacts elicited gestures for manipulating holograms: implications for AR gesture design. In: Proceedings of the 2018 Designing Interactive Systems Conference, DIS 2018, pp. 227–240. Association for Computing Machinery, New York (2018). https://doi.org/10.1145/3196709.3196719
56. Pickering, C.A., Burnham, K.J., Richardson, M.J.: A research study of hand gesture recognition technologies and applications for human vehicle interaction. In: 2007 3rd Institution of Engineering and Technology Conference on Automotive Electronics, pp. 1–15. IEEE Xplore, Piscataway (2007). https://ieeexplore.ieee.org/document/4383638

57. Piumsomboon, T., Clark, A., Billinghurst, M., Cockburn, A.: User-defined gestures for augmented reality. In: Kotzé, P., Marsden, G., Lindgaard, G., Wesson, J., Winckler, M. (eds.) INTERACT 2013. LNCS, vol. 8118, pp. 282–299. Springer, Heidelberg (2013). https://doi.org/10.1007/978-3-642-40480-1_18
58. Reichelt, S., Häussler, R., Fütterer, G., Leister, N.: Depth cues in human visual perception and their realization in 3D displays. In: Javidi, B., Jung-Young, S., Thomas, J.T., Desjardins, D.D. (eds.) Proceedings Volume 7690: Three-Dimensional Imaging, Visualization, and Display 2010 and Display Technologies and Applications for Defense, Security, and Avionics IV, vol. 7690 (2010). https://doi.org/10.1117/12.850094
59. Rempel, D., Camilleri, M.J., Lee, D.L.: The design of hand gestures for human-computer interaction: lessons from sign language interpreters. Int. J. Hum. Comput. Stud. **72**(10–11), 728–735 (2015). https://doi.org/10.1016/j.ijhcs.2014.05.003
60. Ren, Z., Jiang, B., Deng, L.: Research of interactive gesture usability of navigation application based on intuitive interaction. In: Kurosu, M. (ed.) HCII 2020. LNCS, vol. 12182, pp. 96–105. Springer, Cham (2020). https://doi.org/10.1007/978-3-030-49062-1_6
61. Russell, V., Steven, P.W., Dean, E.N.: Effective declutter of complex flight displaysusing stereoptic 3-D cueing. Technical report. ADA279764, NASA Hampton VA Langley Research Center, Hampton, VA, April 1994. https://apps.dtic.mil/sti/pdfs/ADA279764.pdf
62. Sandbrink, J., Vollrath, M., Krems, J.F.: Gestaltungspotenziale für Infotainment-Darstellungen im Fahrzeug: Dissertation, AutoUni - Schriftenreihe, vol. 132. Springer Fachmedien Wiesbaden, Wiesbaden (2019). https://doi.org/10.1007/978-3-658-23942-8
63. Schmidt, A.: Following or leading? The HCI community and new interaction technologies. Interactions **22**(1), 74–77 (2015). https://doi.org/10.1145/2692980
64. Serrano, M., Hildebrandt, D., Subramanian, S., Irani, P.: Identifying suitable projection parameters and display configurations for mobile true-3D displays. In: International Conference on Human-Computer Interaction with Mobile Devices and Services (MobileHCI 2014), Toronto, ON, Canada, pp. 135–143, September 2014. https://hal.archives-ouvertes.fr/hal-01414974
65. Solimini, A.G.: Are there side effects to watching 3D movies? A prospective crossover observational study on visually induced motion sickness. PLoS ONE **8**(2), e56160 (2013). https://doi.org/10.1371/journal.pone.0056160
66. Son, M., Jung, J., Park, W.: Evaluating the utility of two gestural discomfort evaluation methods. PLoS ONE **12**(4), e0176123 (2017). https://doi.org/10.1371/journal.pone.0176123
67. Stern, H.I., Wachs, J.P., Edan, Y.: Designing hand gesture vocabularies for natural interaction by combining psycho-physiological and recognition factors. Int. J. Semant. Comput. **02**(01), 137–160 (2011). https://doi.org/10.1142/S1793351X08000385
68. Ting, C.H., Jen, T.H., Chen, C.H., Shieh, H.P.D., Huang, Y.P.: 3D air-touch user interface with high touch accuracy on stereoscopic displays. J. Display Technol. **12**(5), 429–434 (2016). https://doi.org/10.1109/JDT.2015.2495176
69. Tsandilas, T.: Fallacies of agreement: a critical review of consensus assessment methods for gesture elicitation. ACM Trans. Comput.-Hum. Interact. **25**(3), 1–49 (2018). https://doi.org/10.1145/3182168

70. Ujike, H., Watanabe, H.: Effects of stereoscopic presentation on visually induced motion sickness. In: Woods, A.J., Holliman, N.S., Dodgson, N.A. (eds.) Stereoscopic Displays and Applications XXII, vol. 7863, pp. 357–362. SPIE (2011). https://doi.org/10.1117/12.873500
71. Ullrich, D., Diefenbach, S.: Intui. exploring the facets of intuitive interaction. In: Ziegler, J., Schmidt, A. (eds.) Mensch & Computer 2010: Interaktive Kulturen, pp. 251–260. Oldenbourg Verlag, München (2010). https://dl.gi.de/handle/20.500.12116/7107
72. Ultraleap: Ultrahaptics knowledge base. https://developer.ultrahaptics.com/knowledge-base/
73. van Boven, L., Gilovich, T.: To do or to have? That is the question. J. Pers. Soc. Psychol. **85**(6), 1193–1202 (2003). https://doi.org/10.1037/0022-3514.85.6.1193
74. Vatavu, R.D., Wobbrock, J.O.: Formalizing agreement analysis for elicitation studies: new measures, significance test, and toolkit. In: Proceedings of the 33rd Annual ACM Conference on Human Factors in Computing Systems, CHI 2015, pp. 1325–1334. Association for Computing Machinery, New York (2015). https://doi.org/10.1145/2702123.2702223
75. Vatavu, R.D., Zaiti, I.A.: Leap gestures for TV: insights from an elicitation study. In: Proceedings of the ACM International Conference on Interactive Experiences for TV and Online Video, TVX 2014, pp. 131–138. Association for Computing Machinery, New York (2014). https://doi.org/10.1145/2602299.2602316
76. Villarreal-Narvaez, S., Vanderdonckt, J., Vatavu, R.D., Wobbrock, J.O.: A systematic review of gesture elicitation studies: what can we learn from 216 studies? In: Proceedings of the 2020 ACM Designing Interactive Systems Conference, DIS 2020, pp. 855–872. Association for Computing Machinery, New York (2020). https://doi.org/10.1145/3357236.3395511
77. Vogiatzidakis, P., Koutsabasis, P.: Gesture elicitation studies for mid-air interaction: a review. Multimodal Technol. Interact. **2**(4), 65 (2018). https://doi.org/10.3390/mti2040065
78. Vuletic, T., Duffy, A., Hay, L., McTeague, C., Campbell, G., Grealy, M.: Systematic literature review of hand gestures used in human computer interaction interfaces. Int. J. Hum. Comput. Stud. **129**, 74–94 (2019). https://doi.org/10.1016/j.ijhcs.2019.03.011
79. Weidner, F., Broll, W.: Interact with your car: a user-elicited gesture set to inform future in-car user interfaces. In: Proceedings of the 18th International Conference on Mobile and Ubiquitous Multimedia, MUM 2019. Association for Computing Machinery, New York (2019). https://doi.org/10.1145/3365610.3365625
80. Wiegand, G., Mai, C., Holländer, K., Hussmann, H.: InCarAR: a design space towards 3D augmented reality applications in vehicles. In: Proceedings of the 11th International Conference on Automotive User Interfaces and Interactive Vehicular Applications, AutomotiveUI 2019, pp. 1–13. Association for Computing Machinery, New York (2019). https://doi.org/10.1145/3342197.3344539
81. William Wong, B.L., Joyekurun, R., Mansour, H., Amaldi, P., Nees, A., Villanueva, R.: Depth, layering and transparency: developing design techniques. In: Proceedings of the 17th Australia Conference on Computer-Human Interaction: Citizens Online: Considerations for Today and the Future, OZCHI 2005, pp. 1–10. Computer-Human Interaction Special Interest Group (CHISIG) of Australia, Narrabundah (2005). https://doi.org/10.5555/1108368.1108406

82. Wobbrock, J.O., Aung, H.H., Rothrock, B., Myers, B.A.: Maximizing the guessability of symbolic input. In: CHI 2005 Extended Abstracts on Human Factors in Computing Systems, CHI EA 2005, pp. 1869–1872. Association for Computing Machinery, New York (2005). https://doi.org/10.1145/1056808.1057043
83. Wobbrock, J.O., Morris, M.R., Wilson, A.D.: User-defined gestures for surface computing. In: Proceedings of the SIGCHI Conference on Human Factors in Computing Systems, CHI 2009, pp. 1083–1092. Association for Computing Machinery, New York (2009). https://doi.org/10.1145/1518701.1518866
84. Wu, H., Wang, J., Zhang, X.L.: User-centered gesture development in TV viewing environment. Multimed. Tools Appl. **75**(2), 733–760 (2014). https://doi.org/10.1007/s11042-014-2323-5

Establishment and Validation of Flight Crew Training Cost Model

Xianxue Li(✉) and Tingying Song

Shanghai Aircraft Design and Research Institute, No. 5188 JinKe Road, PuDong New District, Shanghai 201210, China

lixianxue@comac.cc

Abstract. As one of the important part of civil aircraft's life cycle cost, training cost is the key factor for manufacturer's consideration of market competitiveness and for airline's aircraft procurement. A mathematical model of flight crew training cost is established to study the impact of cockpit layout, human machine interface and operational procedure to different type of aircraft's flight crew training cost. This model is validated by using typical aircraft's training cost and can be used to explain and predict flight crew's training time.

Keywords: Aircraft · Training cost · Model

1 Introduction

As one of the important part of civil aircraft's life cycle cost, training cost is the key factor for manufacturer's consideration of market competitiveness and for airline's aircraft procurement.

In this study, a mathematical model of flight crew training cost is established to study the impact of cockpit layout, human machine interface and operational procedure to different type of aircraft's flight crew training cost. This model is validated by using typical aircraft's training cost and can be used to explain and predict flight crew's training time.

2 Methods

2.1 Composition of the Training Cost

The aircraft's life cycle training cost is composed of several parts, the most important parts are initial training, transition training and retraining. Since the cost of retraining is constant for different types of aircraft, this paper pays more attention on the initial training and transition training.

Initial training and transition training are divided into theoretical training, emergency training and simulator training which the cost of simulator training accounts for the maximum proportion. So the flight crew's training cost mainly depends on the simulator training time, as shown in Fig. 1.

H. Krömker (Ed.): HCII 2022, LNCS 13335, pp. 62–71, 2022.
https://doi.org/10.1007/978-3-031-04987-3_4

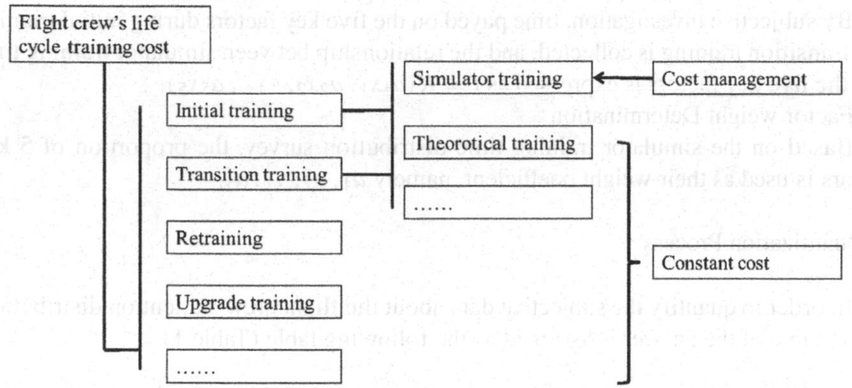

Fig. 1. Composition of flight crew's life cycle's training cost

Specially, flight crew's life cycle cost is the sum of different year's present training cost as follows:

$$LCC = \sum\nolimits_{i=0}^{T} C_i \cdot (P/F, r, i)$$

which:
LCC——life cycle cost;
i——the i year;
T——life cycle time;
C_i——the training cost in the i year;
(P/F, r, i) ——composed interest present value coefficient.

Further C_i can be divided into several training cost such as initial training, transition training, upgrade training, retraining, type A transfer training and type B transfer training in the i year.

$$C_i = \sum \xi_{ij} Y_j$$

Which: Y_j is the training cost of the type j training, $\xi_{i,j}$ is boolean variable.

2.2 Model Establishment

The goal of mathematical model is to explain the relationship between the key factor and flight crew's life cycle cost. According to formula 1 and formula 2, $Y_j = C_{Theory} + A_k t_j$,which C_{theory} is the theory training cost, A_k is the simulator cost per hour, t_i is the simulator training time. The simulator training time for upgrade training, retraining, type A transfer training and type B transfer training is same for different aircraft types. Finally, the most important work is to define the relation between training time of initial training and transition training and five key factors which are cockpit layout familiarity, theory knowledge, operative skill, procedure performance, and crew resource management.

By subjective investigation, time payed on the five key factors during initial training and transition training is collected, and the relationship between simulator training time and the five key factors is expressed as $t = K(a_1x_1, a_2x_2, \cdots, a_5x_5)$.

Factor weight Determination

Based on the simulator training time distribution survey, the proportion of 5 key factors is used as their weight coefficient, namely $a_1, a_2, \ldots a_5$.

- Quantization Process

In order to quantify the subjective data about the flight crew's attention distribution, a map table of the answer is assumed as the following table (Table 1).

Table 1. Survey answer map table

Answer	Unnecessary	Very small	Normal	Much	Very much
Quantization date	0	0.2	0.5	0.8	1

According to the survey, the level of concern and the mapping ratio about cockpit layout familiarity, theory knowledge, operative skill, procedure performance, and crew resource management during initial training and transition training are established as shown in Table 2 and Table 3.

Table 2. Mapping ratio of initial training

	Cockpit layout familiarity	Theory knowledge	Operative skill	Procedure performance	Crew resource management	Weighted average	Training cost	Mapping ratio K
Weighted average	0.43	0.57	0.73	0.70	0.63	62.75	80.00	1.27
Weight coefficient	20.00	14.50	27.50	25.50	12.50			

2.3 Modeling Validation

In order to validate the correction of the model, we collect the date for A320 initial training, B737 initial training, transition training from A320 to A330, transition training from A330 to A320, transition training from B737 to B777 and transition training from B777 to B737 which 3 senior instructor participated in the survey. The validation results are as shown in Table 4.

From the comparison between actual training cost and calculated training cost from model, we can see the difference is relative small which the training cost model is validated.

Table 3. Mapping ratio of transition training

	Cockpit layout familiarity	Theory knowledge	Operative skill	Procedure performance	Crew resource management	Weighted average	Training cost	Mapping ratio K
Weighted average	0.20	0.47	0.53	0.56	0.54	44.12	16	0.36
Weight coefficient	20.00	14.50	27.50	25.50	12.50			

Table 4. Validation results

	X1	X2	X3	X4	X5	Actual training cost	K	Calculated cost	Diffenence
A320 initial training	0.53	0.74	0.62	0.71	0.5	80	1.27	79.67	0%
	0.335	0.84	0.59	0.8	0.8	80	1.27	83.19	4%
	0.47	0.74	0.59	0.71	0.8	80	1.27	81.86	2%
B737 initial training	0.395	0.44	0.71	0.79	0.8	80	1.27	81.22	2%
	0.53	0.8	0.8	0.7	0.2	80	1.27	81.98	2%
	0.29	0.74	0.71	0.71	0.8	80	1.27	81.48	2%
A320-A330 transition	0.08	0.74	0.5	0.5	0.5	16	0.36	16.23	1%
	0.305	0.56	0.41	0.5	0.2	16	0.36	14.67	−8%
	0.21	0.56	0.41	0.7	0.5	16	0.36	17.17	7%
A330-A320 transition	0.04	0.56	0.71	0.53	0.8	56	1.05	54.49	−3%
	0.245	0.5	0.71	0.53	0.5	56	1.05	53.95	−4%
	0.41	0.68	0.76	0.5	0.2	56	1.05	56.85	2%
B737-B777 transition	0.365	0.44	0.5	0.62	0.2	56	1.05	47.97	−14%
	0.305	0.5	0.5	0.5	0.5	56	1.05	48.35	−14%
	0.5	0.56	0.71	0.8	0.8	64	1.05	71.36	12%
B777-B737 transition	0.275	0.26	0.71	0.59	0.8	64	1.05	56.47	−12%
	0.04	0.56	0.71	0.53	0.8	56	1.05	54.49	−3%
	0.18	0.5	0.71	0.71	0.8	56	1.05	61.33	10%
	0.245	0.5	0.71	0.53	0.5	56	1.05	53.95	−4%
	0.41	0.68	0.76	0.5	0.2	56	1.05	56.85	2%

X1: Cockpit layout familiarity
X2: Theory knowledge
X3: Operative skill
X4: Procedure performance
X5: Crew resource management

3 Model Application and Analysis

To analyze the training cost difference between different key training scenario, the following scenarios are compared: A320 to A330 transition, A330 to A320 transition, B737 to B777 transition, B777 to B737 training, Boeing to A320 transition and Airbus to B737 transition.

3.1 Cockpit Layout Familiarity

The cockpit layout is divided into 7 parts: FCU/MCP, CDU/MCDU, flight controls, communication panel, instrument displays, new added panels and other panels. The time used to be familiar with these cockpit panels during the transition training scenarios is calculated and compared as shown in Fig. 2 and Fig. 3.

From the results of Fig. 2 and Fig. 3, we can see that transition training from other aircraft types to B737 such as B777 to B737, Airbus to B737 requires more time to be familiar with the flight controls. New added panels also need more time and flight controls need less time to be familiar from B737 to B777 and from A320 to A330.

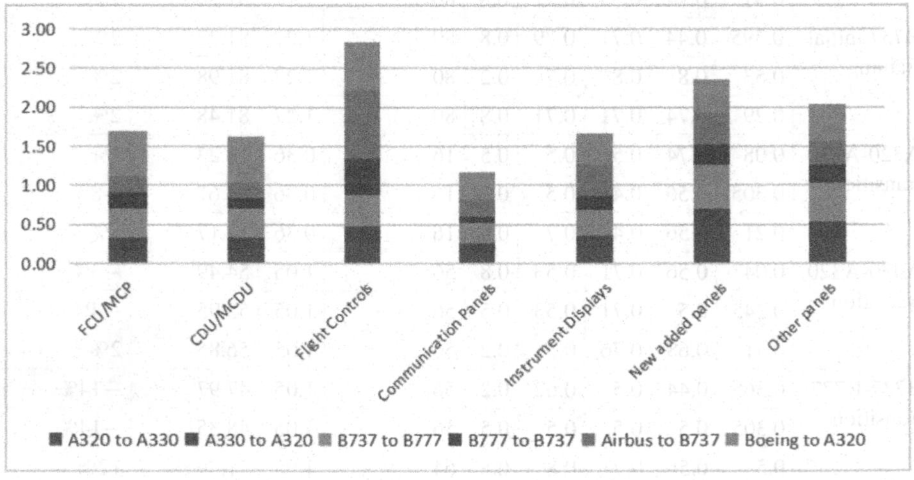

Fig. 2. Time used to be familiar with the cockpit layout (subjective survey)

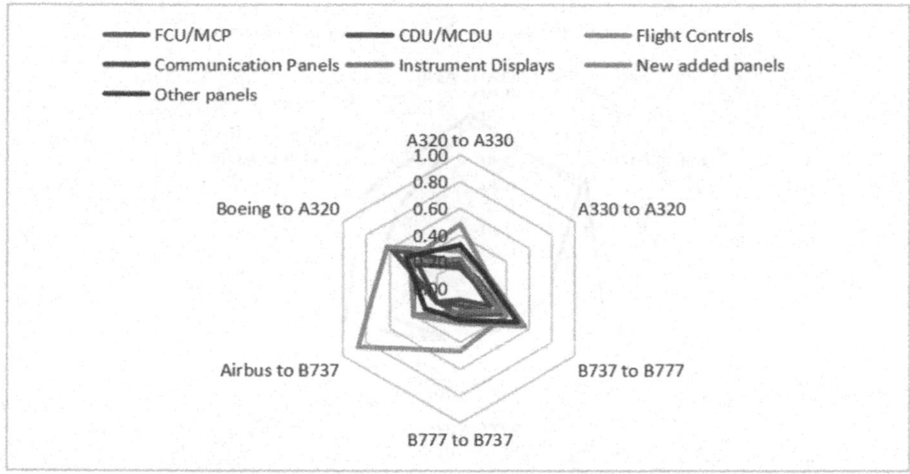

Fig. 3. Time used to be familiar with the cockpit layout

3.2 Theory Knowledge

The theory knowledge composed of aircraft related knowledge and aircraft irrelevant knowledge and the training time of these knowledge is calculated and compared as shown in Fig. 4 and Fig. 5.

From the results of Fig. 4 and Fig. 5, we can see that the time spared on aircraft related knowledge and aircraft irrelevant knowledge is almost the same. It needs more time to study the aircraft related knowledge during transition training from Airbus to B737 and from Boeing to A320. However, it needs less time during transition training from B737 t0 B777 and from A320 to A330, the time saved can be used on the aircraft irrelevant knowledge.

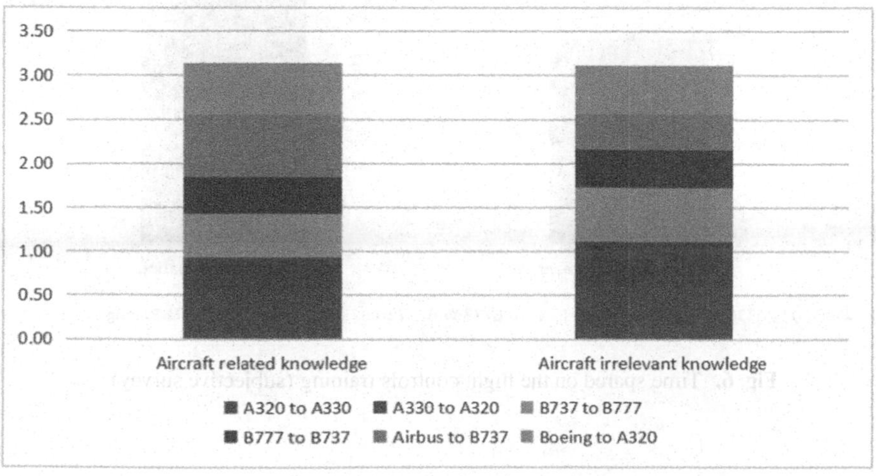

Fig. 4. Time spared on the theory knowledge (subjective survey)

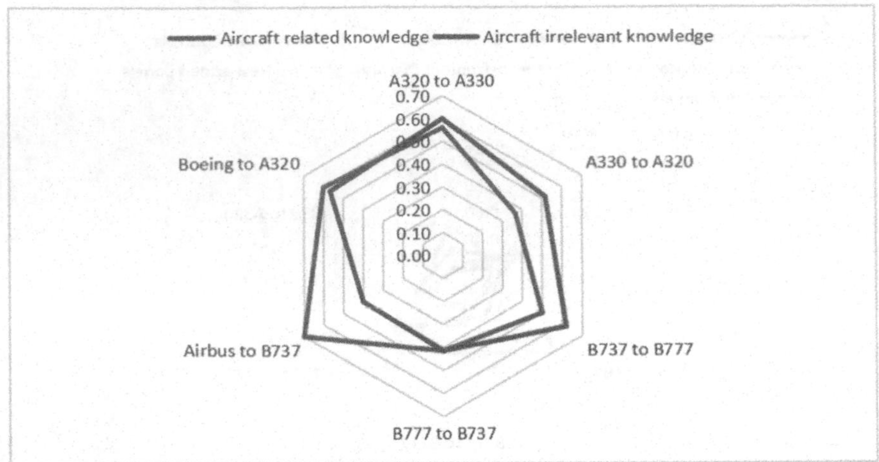

Fig. 5. Time spared on the theory knowledge

3.3 Flight Controls

The flight controls composed of automation equipment and manual manipulation and the training time is calculated and compared as shown in Fig. 6 and Fig. 7.

From the results of Fig. 6 and Fig. 7, we can see that the time spared on the training of manual manipulation is more than the time spared on the automation equipment training, especially for the transition training from B777 to B737 and from Airbus to B737.

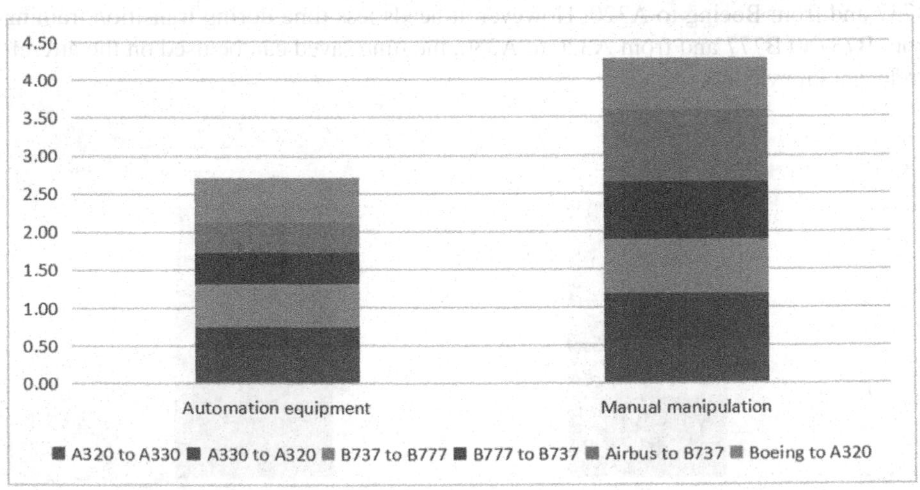

Fig. 6. Time spared on the flight controls training (subjective survey)

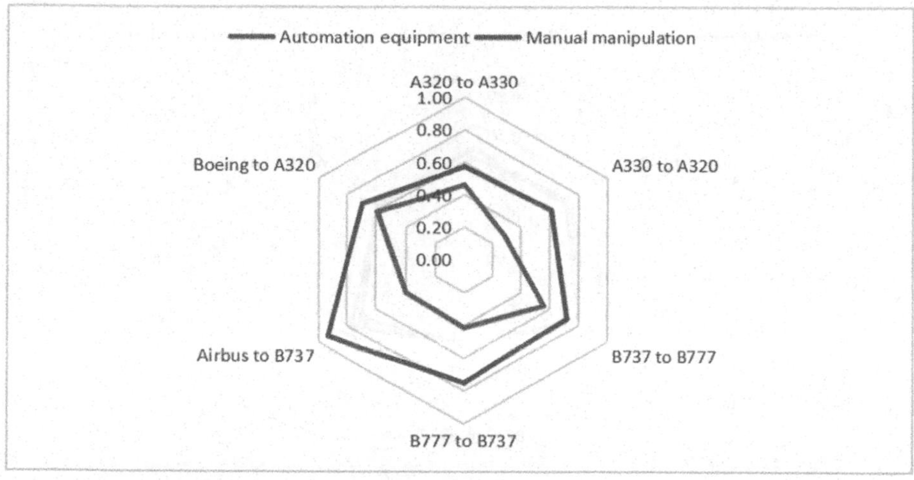

Fig. 7. Time spared on the flight controls training

3.4 Procedure Performance

Procedure is divided into SOP, supplementary procedure, abnormal and emergency procedure. The training time spared on the procedure is calculated and compared as shown in Fig. 8 and Fig. 9.

From the results of Fig. 8 and Fig. 9, we can see that the training time spared on the SOP, supplementary procedure, abnormal procedure and emergency procedure is almost the same, abnormal and emergency procedure training needs relative more time.

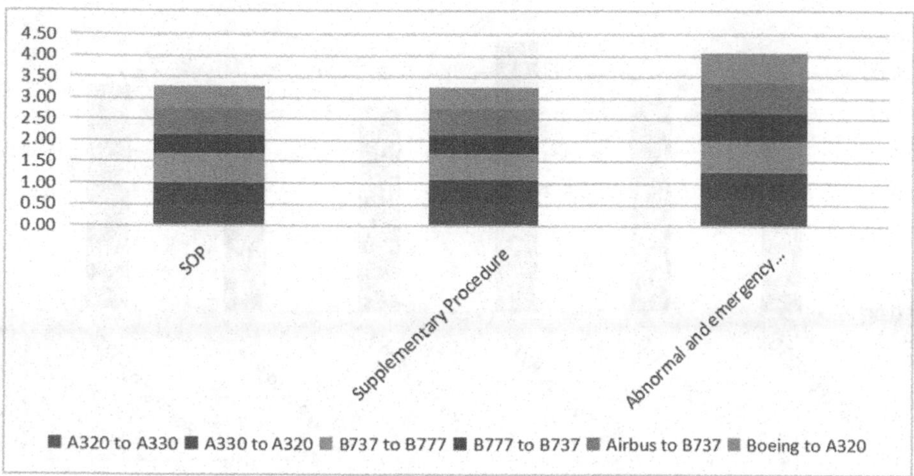

Fig. 8. Time spared on the procedure training (subjective survey)

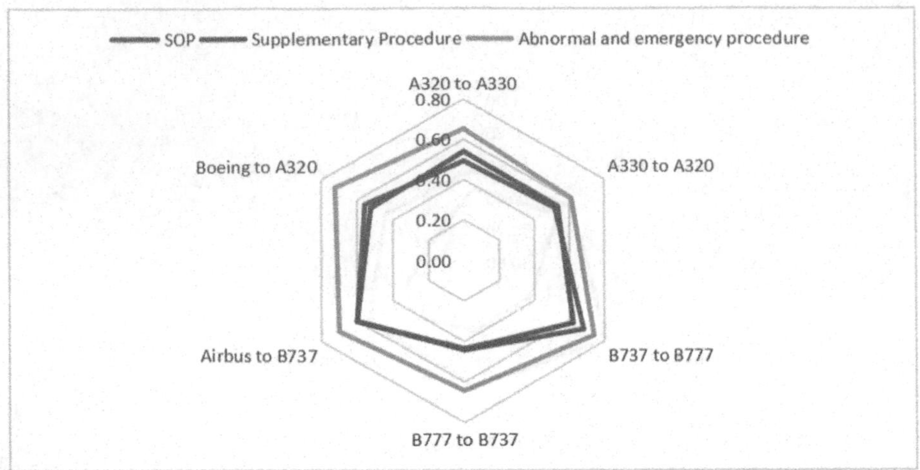

Fig. 9. Time spared on the procedure training

3.5 Crew Resource Management

The training time spared on the crew resource management is calculated and compared as shown in Fig. 10.

From the results of Fig. 10, we can see that the training time spared on the crew resource management is almost the same.

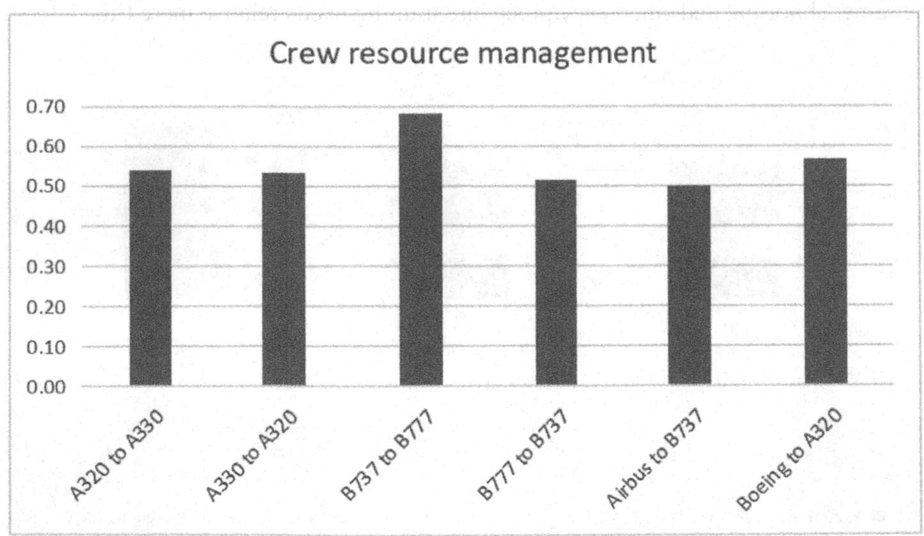

Fig. 10. Time spared on crew resource management training

4 Conclusions

In summary, a mathematical model of flight crew training cost is established and validated. And this model can be used to predict the training cost based on the cockpit design proposal and reversely modify the cockpit design proposal.

Omniverse-OpenDS: Enabling Agile Developments for Complex Driving Scenarios via Reconfigurable Abstractions

Zilin Song, Yicun Duan, Wangkai Jin, Shuchang Huang, Shuolei Wang, and Xiangjun Peng(✉)

User-Centric Computing Group, University of Nottingham, Ningbo, China
shiangjunpeng@gmail.com
https://unnc-ucc.github.io

Abstract. We present ***Omniverse***, a set of configurable abstractions for efficient developments of complex driving events during simulated driving scenarios. The goal of ***Omniverse*** is to identify the inefficiency of existing scenario implementations and provide an alternative design for ease-of-implementations for simulated driving events. We first investigate the standard code base of driving scenarios and abstract their overlapped building blocks through mathematical models. Then, we design and implement a set of flexible and configurable abstractions as an external library, to allow further developments and adaptions for more generalized cases. Finally, we validate the correctness and examine the effectiveness of ***Omniverse*** through standard driving scenarios' implementations, and the results show that ***Omniverse*** can (1) save 42.7% development time, averaged across all participants; and (2) greatly improve the overall user experience via significantly improved readability and extendability of codes. The whole library of ***Omniverse*** is online at https://github.com/unnc-ucc/Omniverse-OpenDS.

Keywords: Cognitive driving simulators · Configurable abstractions · Mathematical modeling · Driving scenarios

1 Introduction

Driving scenarios, which refer to a series of driving events conducted by external agents, are important for in-lab simulations to provide pre-determined events (e.g., takeover, back a vehicle and etc.) during the driving simulation. These scenarios are responsible to restore the demanded events so that participants can be capable to experience, which allows researchers to collect relevant statistics for validations and examinations of their proposals/hypotheses (e.g., [3]). However, with the increasing demands for the integration of multiple driving events (i.e. to form more complicated scenarios), the efficiency of implementations becomes

Z. Song and Y. Duan—Equal contributions.

H. Krömker (Ed.): HCII 2022, LNCS 13335, pp. 72–87, 2022.
https://doi.org/10.1007/978-3-031-04987-3_5

the major bottleneck for future in-lab simulation, which can be summarized into the following two outstanding issues.

First, the complex combinations of supporting libraries, for the creations of driving scenarios, amplifies the difficulty of their concrete implementations. Driving simulators initializes environmental factors through Graphic Engines (e.g., [4]), but handle driving events through a separate library. This separation incurs the hardship for code reuses and adaptions since different software components can result in great obstacles for simulator-to-library interactions (e.g., variations in Programming Languages, Data Structures and etc.). Moreover, the growing complexity of demanded driving scenarios amplifies such a development gap, namely to frequently adapt and re-implement past implementations according to specific requirements (e.g., region-based characteristics, specific transportation regulations and even cultural differences [12,22,25]).

Second, the high volume of required details on driving scenarios' implementations significantly limit the capability of generalizations from existing codes. Simple driving events are actually implemented through the naive and straight-forward method, by setting every position point and determining the time duration with sufficient details. Such detailed implementations require developers to perform an extensive amount of extra efforts to calculate and examine its feasibility, for instance, while involving braking events through setting the accelerator velocity. And these implementations are very hard to be reused since they are event-specific, which substantially increase the difficulty of the actual implementations.

Hence, it becomes critical to implement complicated driving scenarios, due to the limitations from the complex integration of multiple libraries and the lack of potential code reuses and adaption, which subsequently affects the overall efficiency and prolongs the overall research (using driving simulations). **Our goal** in this paper is to design and implement a series of effective abstractions of elementary driving events, and examine the practical impacts of these abstractions via real-world studies. Through the code base study about the template scenarios from existing driving simulators, we make the following three **key observations** about the missing pieces for efficient driving scenarios' implementations, including: (1) **High-level Modeling** to describe specific building blocks for driving events during simulated studies; (2) **Flexible Abstractions** to create, adjust and adapt different objects and factors for effective and accurate driving events, instead of getting hands on the detailed-but-redundant codes; and (3) **Developer Toolkits** to allow extensible and adaptive re-implementations agilely.

We design and build ***Omniverse***, which consists of multiple driving event models based on the OpenDS driving simulator [19] and aims to quickly generate driving events to achieve agile developments of driving scenarios. The aim and the key idea of ***Omniverse*** is abstracting driving events into mathematical models and figuring out the relationships between each variable. When developers want to use ***Omniverse*** to build driving events, they only need to call specific functions with a few variables and then, ***Omniverse*** can automatically generate all the needed codes. The whole development of ***Omniverse*** can be divided into three parts: The first part is to identify representative driving events, which need to be common enough so that this set of abstractions can cover (almost) all driving scenarios; Second, based on these representative events, we simplify and abstract a group of models to facilitate with these representative events; and third, we design and implement code templates based on the abstracted models, and fuse them as an external library ***Omniverse***.

We examine the effectiveness of ***Omniverse*** through an empirical user study, by recruiting 12 volunteers with programming experiences of driving scenarios. The experiment is divided into three stages. First, all participants need to spend 5 h on training to make sure they are familiar with OpenDS and ***Omniverse***. Then, each participant needs to finish two given diving scenarios with a fixed number of driving events: one is implemented in default way and another needs to use ***Omniverse***. And the time they use will be recorded to support further analysis. Finally, every participant is required to finish two questionnaires at the end of the experiment. Based on their feedback, we conclude that ***Omniverse*** can greatly improve the overall efficiency and user experiences than the conventional approach. We believe ***Omniverse*** has great potential in practice and we expect such an idea to be extended in other driving simulators.

Specifically, we make the following three major contributions in this paper:

- We address outstanding issues on building driving scenarios in terms of the efficiency and user experiences, which prevents the potential for complex driving simulations.
- We design and implement ***Omniverse***, an external library for efficient creations of complex driving events. ***Omniverse*** consists of a series of configurable abstractions which can be used to efficiently build driving events.
- We quantitatively evaluate the effectiveness of ***Omniverse*** by carrying out experiments with 12 volunteers, and results suggest that ***Omniverse*** can significantly improve the efficiency when building driving scenarios in OpenDS simulators.

The rest of this paper is organized as follow. Section 2 provide background and motivation of ***Omniverse***. Section 3 presents the design and implementations of ***Omniverse***. Section 4 elaborates the experimental methodology and results for ***Omniverse***.

2 Background and Motivation

The background and motivation of ***Omniverse*** is provided in the following two subsections. For the background, we outline the reasons why driving simulators are important for in-lab driving simulations and how do these simulators function with the customization of driving scenarios. Then, we introduce the driving simulator we focus on in this paper - OpenDS, a widely-used cognitive driving simulator. Finally, we summarize three key challenges to build driving scenarios as the motivation to develop ***Omniverse***.

2.1 Driving Simulations and Driving Scenarios in OpenDS

With the rapid increase in the demand of personalized Human-Vehicle Interaction (HVI), there are a growing amount of studies being carried out for characterizing in-vehicle drivers and exploring potential designs (e.g. [6,8,11,18,26, 28,30,32]. Due to the consideration of the safety and resource constraints, most studies need to be carried out in the laboratory and use some tools to provide a realistic driving experience [2,10,13,17,21,23]. Therefore, as one of the key components for in-lab HVI study, driving simulators play a significant role in such studies due to the following reasons: First, driving simulators can be regarded as a framework and developers need to build driving scenarios for proper uses. To meet the requirements of different studies, most open-source driving simulators can allow customization of driving scenarios [1,7,19]. As a result, it's essential to spend a considerable amount of time to familiarize with driving simulators, and the development costs can be considerably high. Therefore, an easy-to-use and powerful driving simulator can greatly contribute to the promotion of HVI research [20,31]. Second, a driving simulator plays a significant role in the quality of simulation-based experiments [9,14,24,31]. Beyond the visualization supports, there are also built-in functions in driving simulators to be used for the collection of drivers' statistics [16,29].

OpenDS is an open-sourced driving simulator to support in-lab driving simulations [19]. To use OpenDS, developers need to implement driving scenes and scenarios in advance, since driving scenes provide environmental simulations and driving scenarios consist of all events within the whole simulation. A driving scene mainly includes necessary static model files like road or building; and a driving scenario contains all driving events within a particular scene model. As different driving simulators have different implementations for extending driving scenarios, and we use OpenDS hereby as a motivating example to illustrate how driving scenarios are implemented: a complete driving scenario in OpenDS consists of model files and XML files. As Fig. 1 shown, after concluding the design phase of all driving events (i.e. needed in a particular scenario), developers first need to use professional modeling software (e.g., JMonkeyEngine3 [15]) to build the required scene models, and ensure those models can be visualized by OpenDS. Then, developers need to import those models by modifying the XML [5] files and adjust various parameters (e.g., size, rotation degrees and etc.) to satisfy the design requirements. Next, all dynamic changes in a driving scenario need to be written by developers, via built-in functions and programming regulations of OpenDS, including the interactions between vehicles, the change of traffic lights and etc. Moreover, developers can achieve finer-grained adjustments via detailed parameters in OpenDS, such as maximum rotation angle, braking distance, acceleration and etc. Though this set of built-in functions can be considered powerful and broad, it's still quite challenging for scenario developments since a very simple scenario requires hundreds of parameters to be configured manually. Also, since OpenDS cannot synchronize display changes with adjusted parameters, developers need to execute the whole scenario for a time with each modification, to validate whether these changes are effective. Therefore, more efforts are spent to fine-tune these parameters than to construct the basic scenario, which substantially results in huge burdens on the development of driving scenarios.

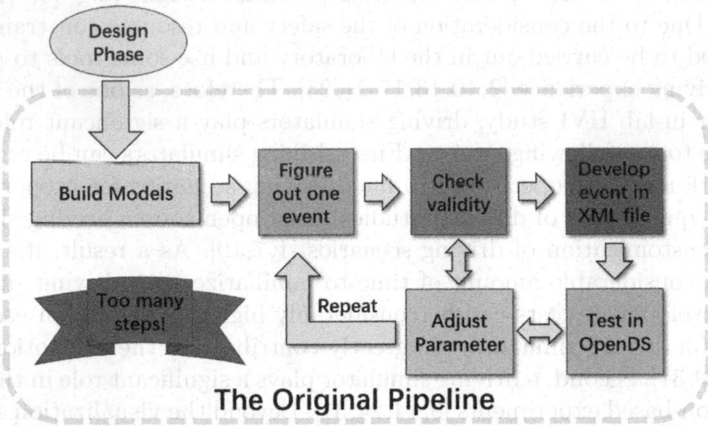

Fig. 1. The process of building scenario, using OpenDS as a motivating example.

2.2 Redundant Implementations of Driving Scenarios in OpenDS

As covered above, the process of building driving scenarios is very complex and demands a considerable amount of effort. For example, a simple driving scenario with 6 driving behaviours (e.g., turn on and overtake) needs more than 6,000 lines of codes in the OpenDS simulator, and most of these codes demand fine-grained configurations in terms of detailed parameters. By exploring the code base of OpenDS, we find that there are a large number of highly-repetitive codes in the implementations of driving scenarios in OpenDS, and we use an example to showcase such an issue. Figure 2 gives out an example of how existing implementations of driving scenarios contain highly-redundant lines of codes. Therefore, exploring opportunities to reduce this redundancy, by providing reconfigurable abstractions, can greatly relax the constraints of implementing driving scenarios for simulations.

2.3 Motivation

This work aims to address and takes the first attempt to solve a critical but usually ignored issue: **how to efficiently construct a complicated scenario for in-lab driver simulations?** Towards this problem, we summarize that there are three key challenges, which motivate this work: (1) **Developer Wall:** the construction of driving events has a large amount of prerequisite of detailed OpenDS designs and implementations. As a result, programmers need to take a

```
<wayPoint id="WayPoint_0_1"><translation><vector jtype="java_lang_Float" size="3"><entry>-6.4</entry><entry>0</entry><entry>-430</entry>
</vector></translation><speed>50</speed></wayPoint>
<wayPoint id="WayPoint_0_2"><translation><vector jtype="java_lang_Float" size="3"><entry>-6.4</entry><entry>0</entry><entry>-350</entry>
</vector></translation><speed>50</speed></wayPoint>
<wayPoint id="WayPoint_0_3"><translation><vector jtype="java_lang_Float" size="3"><entry>-6.4</entry><entry>0</entry><entry>170</entry>
</vector></translation><speed>50</speed><trafficLight>TrafficLight.00_04</trafficLight></wayPoint>

<wayPoint id="WayPoint_1_1"><translation><vector jtype="java_lang_Float" size="3"><entry>-6.4</entry><entry>0</entry><entry>215</entry>
</vector></translation><speed>40</speed></wayPoint>
<wayPoint id="WayPoint_1_2"><translation><vector jtype="java_lang_Float" size="3"><entry>-6.4</entry><entry>0</entry><entry>407</entry>
</vector></translation><speed>50</speed></wayPoint>
<wayPoint id="WayPoint_1_3"><translation><vector jtype="java_lang_Float" size="3"><entry>-6.4</entry><entry>0</entry><entry>958.5</entry
></vector></translation><speed>50</speed></wayPoint>
<wayPoint id="WayPoint_1_4"><translation><vector jtype="java_lang_Float" size="3"><entry>-4</entry><entry>0</entry><entry>966</entry></
vector></translation><speed>50</speed></wayPoint>
<wayPoint id="WayPoint_1_5"><translation><vector jtype="java_lang_Float" size="3"><entry>1</entry><entry>0</entry><entry>973.5</entry></
vector></translation><speed>50</speed></wayPoint>
<wayPoint id="WayPoint_1_6"><translation><vector jtype="java_lang_Float" size="3"><entry>9</entry><entry>0</entry><entry>978</entry></
vector></translation><speed>50</speed></wayPoint>
<wayPoint id="WayPoint_1_7"><translation><vector jtype="java_lang_Float" size="3"><entry>17</entry><entry>0</entry><entry>981.5</entry>
</vector></translation><speed>50</speed></wayPoint>
```

Fig. 2. An example of highly-redundant codes in a scenario file.

lot of energy to become familiar with how to build a driving event that can be run on the simulator; (2) **Effort Gap:** the workloads of building these driving events are often large and significant, with the growing complexity of corresponding scenarios. Due to the code of building the scene being highly similar, it can be very complex work when modifying complex driving scenarios especially when the editor is not a producer. Besides, with the large amounts of parameters, setting and adjusting can also be troublesome; and (3) **Hard to Get Right:** the lack of relevant abstractions lead to poor organization and constructions of implementations. In OpenDS, since the route of the automatic driving is artificially set in advance, it may cause multiple different variables for the same type of driving event in the same scenario in comparative experiments, which further lead to a large number of issues when testing and verifying whether those driving events are implemented as designed.

3 Omniverse Design

We make the key observation that there are mathematical relationships between many parameters within a driving scenario, which can be abstracted and reused for different driving events by exploiting some common parameters. By doing so, if we exploit these relationships via abstracted models, we can accurately implement driving events in a correct manner by automatically generating these parameters. To this end, the design principle of ***Omniverse*** is to maximize the reuse of abstracted models as much as possible, so the implementations of hands-tuned parameters can be as few as possible, which substantially reduce the overall development burdens. The design of ***Omniverse*** consists of two major components: Abstraction Design and Automatic Filling. For the model, in fact, due to so many variables in OpenDS, adding all the related variables will make the model too complex to calculate. As a result, we can select a part of the representative parameters from a large number of parameters to consist of the model. After getting models, we need to integrate all the models into ***Omniverse*** and this is related to the Automatic Filling part.

3.1 Abstraction Design

To better understand the design choice of Abstraction Design in ***Omniverse***, the autopilot function in OpenDS needs to be properly described in advance. In driving scenarios, there are multiple waypoints to be defined for each different vehicle. As shown in Fig. 3, a waypoint is represented in the scenario using a red block. These waypoints can be regarded as a sequence of three-dimensional coordinate points, and the autopilot function allows vehicles to operate based on their own route, formed by automatically connecting these waypoints. When the vehicle performs automatic driving, it can only comply with some rules during transportation (e.g. red light parking and anti-collision and etc.). Moreover, these waypoints can be used as a switch to trigger some particular events (e.g. enforcing changes of traffic lights), which are usually used to effectively control the variables of the demanded experiments.

Fig. 3. An example of waypoints in OpenDS. (Color figure online)

In ***Omniverse***, each model is abstracted from a set of real driving events. The result of a model is the 3D coordinates of several points which can be used to define corresponding waypoints later. Based on the inputted parameters, ***Omniverse*** can automatically generate the corresponding codes. We use Turning as the example since it's one of the most representative driving events, to showcase how we achieve Abstraction Design in ***Omniverse***. The Turning event includes a right-angle turn driving event and a U-Turn driving event, which both can be seen as a part of an arc, the difference is the size of its central angle. To simplify the design, we can assume that this behavior occurs on the same plane, which means that the z-axis coordinate is constant. Therefore, we only need to consider the changes of x-axis and y-axis.

This brings out another issue: as the waypoint in OpenDS follows a sequential order, it's essential to allow ***Omniverse*** to generate waypoints in an accurate order. We follow the example above to explain our key insights. This issue can be concretely described explained as follow. As the driving route can be viewed as a part of an arc, the abstraction requires X-value to derive the corresponding Y-value. However, this calculation formula involves square arithmetic and generally, every X-value input corresponds to two Y-values. More interestingly, according to the angle between the diameter of the semicircle and the X-axis, one X-value can generate one Y-value or two Y-values. Therefore, it's essential to provide correctness guarantees to safeguard the generations of driving events.

To solve the above issue, we first assume the turn angles for all events are less than 180 °C. Then we can convert all possible cases to the simplest case, which means each X-value only corresponds to one Y-value. After satisfying the simplest condition, we need to facilitate such conversions with the default configurations of the coordinate system. For the Turning model, since generated parameters are not sufficient to resolve this issue, we need to divide Turning events into two parts, turn left and turn right and the only difference between them is the turning direction. With the Start Position, End Positions and the turning direction, we can derive the angle of the rotation. After settling all details within an event, we need to derive the centre of the semicircle and then facilitate with the coordinate system.

3.2 Automatic Filling

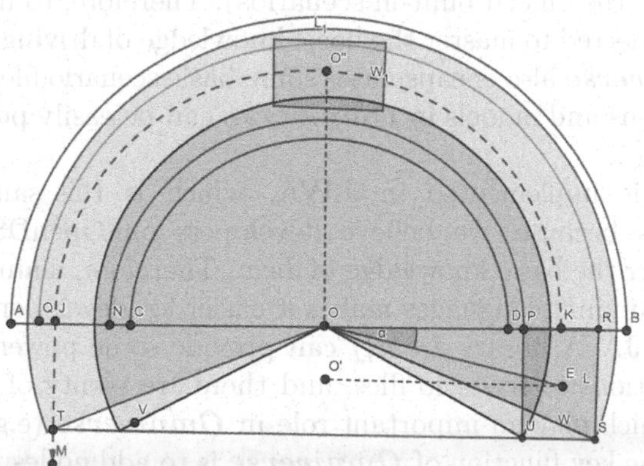

Fig. 4. A visualization of our U-Turn Model.

We synthesize the above considerations to construct a set of abstractions, to provide Automatic Filling for auto-generated waypoints. We describe U-Turn Model as a representative example. As shown in Fig. 4, ***Omniverse*** abstracts the U-Turn driving event as a semicircle. Before exploiting relationships between each variable, we first identify all variables, which need to be regarded as inputted parameters. In this case, the following parameters are included: 3D coordinates of the beginning of the behavior (X_1, Y_1, Z_1), 3D coordinates of the end of the event (X_2, Y_2, Z_2), the width of the road D, the length and width of the vehicle L and W. All these variables can be derived from OpenDS. Before Automatic Filling, a series of checking functions are performed to ensure the inputted parameters are legal. For instance, one of the basic requirements is that the road width should be large enough to prevent a vehicle from colliding with the inside/outside of the road, during the entire driving event. After that, Automatic Filling derive all intermediate waypoints by using the formulation (e.g. a circle ($X^2 + Y^2 = R^2$)). Note that developers can manually configure how many waypoints need to be generated since the number of generated waypoints represents the tradeoffs between the extent of realistic scenarios and the computational costs. Finally, all generated waypoints can be saved as a driving event, which can be directly used by the driving simulator.

3.3 Implementation Details

Omniverse is designed as an external library, and each abstracted model is individually encapsulated as a method. Currently, ***Omniverse*** focuses on the creations of driving events. Since there are an extensive amount of parameters to be considered when building a driving scene and scenario from scratch, the purpose of ***Omniverse*** aims to provide complementary supports with automatic scene generations [27]. Different from building driving scenes, developing a driving scenario demands a certain extent of programming experiences (e.g. quickly modifying the official built-in scenarios). Therefore, to use ***Omniverse***, developers are expected to master the basic knowledge of driving simulators (e.g. OpenDS). ***Omniverse*** also encapsulates some basic scenario files from OpenDS, so that all functions and models in ***Omniverse*** can be easily ported/integrated with the simulator.

Omniverse is implemented in JAVA, which is the same language as OpenDS. This is because, we believe developers on OpenDS simulator are assumed to master the basic knowledge of Java. Therefore, maintaining the consistency of programming languages makes it easier for developers to use ***Omniverse***. Also, the JAVA library *Dom4j* can provide some powerful functions to support modifications to scenario files, and there are plenty of universal auxiliary functions which play an important role in ***Omniverse*** (e.g., input/output files and etc.). The key function of ***Omniverse*** is to add nodes (i.e. waypoints). As shown in Fig. 5, the mechanism of this function can be roughly described as follows. This function (1) first read the scenario files and trace the position to add nodes; (2) then read all the same existing nodes and locate to the end of the last node; and (3) finally fill the node with its attributes, and assign attribute values based on the code regulations in OpenDS.

```
@SuppressWarnings("unchecked")
public void addwaypoint(String id, float[] pos,int sp) {

    Element wayPoints = getauto(doc).element("wayPoints");
    List<Element> list = wayPoints.elements();

    //int num = list.size() -1;

    Element wayPoint =  wayPoints.addElement("wayPoint");

    //Element wayPoint = null;
    //list.add(num, wayPoint);
    wayPoint.addAttribute("id", id);//

    Element translation = wayPoint.addElement("translation");
    Element speed =  wayPoint.addElement("speed");
    speed.setText(String.valueOf(sp));
    Element vector = translation.addElement("vector");
    vector.addAttribute("jtype", "java_lang_Float");
    vector.addAttribute("size", "3");
    Element entry = vector.addElement("entry");
    Element entry2 = vector.addElement("entry");
    Element entry3 = vector.addElement("entry");
    list = vector.elements();
    list.get(0).setText(String.valueOf(pos[0]));
    list.get(1).setText(String.valueOf(pos[1]));
    list.get(2).setText(String.valueOf(pos[2]));
}
```

Fig. 5. An example to add nodes/waypoints using Dom4j.

Figure 6 shows a part of the U-Turn model implementation. The *setnum* function is used to change the number of the generated nodes. As covered above, the more points generated, the smoother the vehicle's driving trajectory. Note that an excessively-dense route can cause errors in simulation, due to potential crashes within OpenDS. There are five input parameters needed in this function. The first three parameters are the Vehicle Width, Vehicle Length and Road Width. These parameters are used to check whether the vehicle can finish this event as expected since the oversized vehicle cannot turn around on a narrow road. The function *check* is used to check if the input is legal whenever the *model* function is called. After the input parameters are guaranteed to be valid, it automatically generates the path and writes them into a file, based on the abstracted model and the inputted parameters; and the last two parameters are the Start Point and Finish Point, which represents the start and end positions of these driving events in the driving scenarios. The mechanism of this function is as follows. First, this function generates all needed parameters by using the five inputted parameters, and checking whether this driving event is legal. After passing the check, it continually generates other parameters, which are used to form the final results. After getting these results, it calls other functions, such as *addwaypoints* function, to generate codes based on the result.

```
public void turn_left(float car_width, float car_length, float road_width, float[] start, float[] end) {

    int condition = poisition_check_left(start, end);
    float[] fina_pos = {25,0,-100};
    float r, R, min, max;
    float[] ori_pos = {(start[0]+end[0])/2, (start[2]+end[2])/2};
    if(condition == 0) {
        min = Math.min(start[0], end[0]);
        max = Math.max(start[0], end[0]);
        r = (Math.abs(max-min)-road_width)/2;
        R = r+road_width;

    }else {
        float l = (float) Math.sqrt((Math.pow((start[0] - start[0]), 2) + Math.pow((start[2] - start[2]), 2)));
        start[0] = l/2;
        start[2] = -car_length/2;
        end[0] = -l/2;
        end[2] = -car_length/2;
        r = (l-road_width)/2;
        R = r+road_width;
        min = Math.min(start[0], end[0]);
        max = Math.max(start[0], end[0]);
    }

    float k = (end[2] - start[2])/(end[0]-start[0]);

    if(!check(r,R,car_width,car_length,road_width)) {
        System.out.println("Invaild condition!");
        System.exit(0);
    }
```

Fig. 6. An example implementation of U-Turn model (in part).

4 Experimental Study

We design and perform an empirical study to examine the effectiveness of ***Omniverse***. The details of this study are described as follows. We first elaborate our consideration in terms of ethical issues. Then we cover the methodology and the procedure of our study. Finally, we present study results and perform an in-depth analysis based on the feedback from the questionnaire.

4.1 Ethical Issue Statement

For all human-participated research, we inform all participants that their data may be used for research purposes, and all participants give their full consent. All experiments are done anonymously and only anonymous feedback is collected in experiments. Since no identity information is needed (e.g. personal names, ages) in our study, we ensure that no personal information of all participants was collected or leaked in any form, which guarantees that all participants' privacy is not compromised.

4.2 Study Methodology and Procedure

Since ***Omniverse*** is developed for developers with Java programming experience and OpenDS simulator, we recruited twelve relevant volunteers in this study and all participants are at least computer science undergraduates or above, and some of them are also have experience in developing driving scenarios using OpenDS. There are three stages in our study. First, all participants are trained for five hours to make sure they are capable to build driving events in OpenDS. After training, they are divided into two groups with six people in each group; second, each group is required to build two pre-specified scenarios based on the provided template. The first scenario contains four driving events and the second one contains sixteen driving events. All these events are supported to use ***Omniverse***. During the study, one group is required to use ***Omniverse*** and the other is not. We record the duration of their developments to examine the overall efficiency. We create two rounds to ensure all groups can use ***Omniverse***; and third, each participant needs to finish a questionnaire for examining user experiences. The content of this questionnaire involves the following aspects: Whether users are satisfied with ***Omniverse*** in terms of ease-to-use? Are models in ***Omniverse*** are designed reasonably? Shortcomings of ***Omniverse*** and possible improvements. The questionnaire combines ratings and comments to allow participants to supply their comments as comprehensively as possible.

4.3 Study Results

Figure 7 reports the results in terms of the improved efficiency when using ***Omniverse***. We make the two observations. First, ***Omniverse*** improves the efficiency when developers build driving events in OpenDS. For the first scenario, participants can benefit from ***Omniverse*** with 30.1% less time on average, compared with the conventional approach. For the second scenario, participants can benefit from ***Omniverse*** with 55.2% less time on average. Second, the benefits

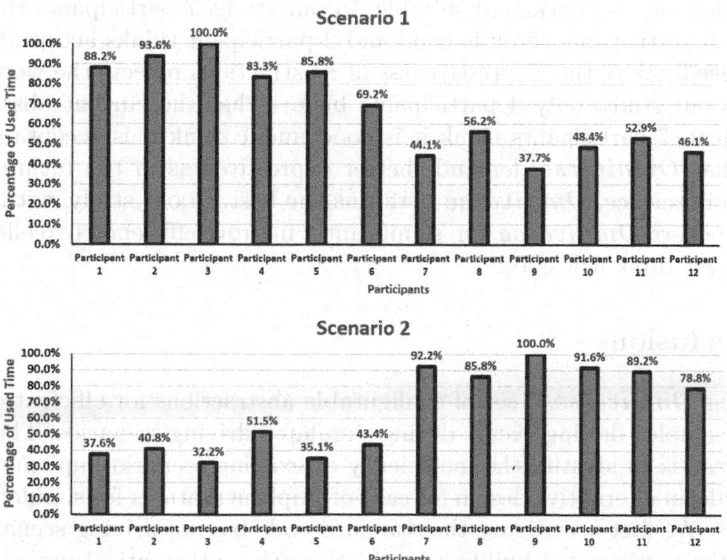

Fig. 7. Percentage of Time to build driving scenarios using ***Omniverse***, compared with the conventional approach.

of ***Omniverse*** varies across different goals of driving scenarios. ***Omniverse*** provides more benefits in the second scenario (55.2%), because the number of driving events increases. This confirms that ***Omniverse*** can benefit the construction of complex driving scenarios.

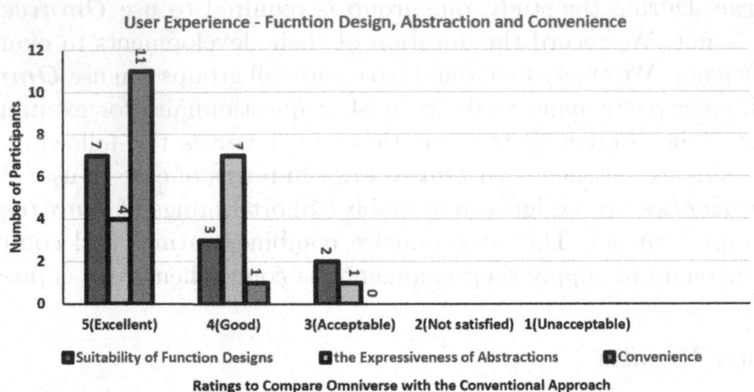

Fig. 8. Results on User Experience when using ***Omniverse***, compared with the conventional approach.

Figure 8 reports the results on user experience when using ***Omniverse***, in terms of the Suitability of Function Designs, the Expressiveness of Abstractions and the Convenience. We make three observations. First, the designs of ***Omniverse*** functions are considered suitable. In our study, 7 participants think it is excellent, 3 participants think is good and 2 participant thinks acceptable. Second, the feedback of the Expressiveness of Abstractions reflects the worst experience. In our study, only 4 participants believe that the current abstractions are excellent, 7 participants think it is good and 1 think it is acceptable. This reflects that ***Omniverse*** demands better expressiveness in the future. Third, for the Convenience, ***Omniverse*** performs the best. In our study, with 11 participants believe ***Omniverse*** can significantly improve efficiency (excellent) and 1 participant think it is good.

5 Conclusions

We present ***Omniverse***, a set of configurable abstractions for efficient developments of complex driving events during simulated driving scenarios. The goal of ***Omniverse*** is to identify the inefficiency of existing scenario implementations and provide an alternative design for ease-of-implementations for simulated driving events. We first investigate the standard code base of driving scenarios and abstract their overlapped building blocks through mathematical models. Then, we design and implement a set of flexible and configurable abstractions as an external library, to allow further developments and adaptions for more generalized cases. Finally, we validate the correctness and examine the effectiveness of ***Omniverse*** through standard driving scenarios' implementations, and the results suggest ***Omniverse*** can greatly improve the efficiency and user experiences when building complex driving scenarios. The whole library of ***Omniverse*** is online at https://github.com/unnc-ucc/Omniverse-OpenDS.

Acknowledgements. We thank anonymous reviewers in HCI'22 for their valuable feedback. We thank for all members of User-Centric Computing Group at the University of Nottingham Ningbo China for the stimulating environment. This work was started as Zilin Song's internship and undergraduate thesis at the University of Nottingham Ningbo China.

References

1. Alvarez, I., Rumbel, L., Adams, R.: Skyline: a rapid prototyping driving simulator for user experience. In: Proceedings of the 7th International Conference on Automotive User Interfaces and Interactive Vehicular Applications, pp. 101–108 (2015)
2. Bella, F.: Driving simulator for speed research on two-lane rural roads. Accid. Anal. Prev. **40**(3), 1078–1087 (2008)
3. Boyle, L.N., Lee, J.D.: Using driving simulators to assess driving safety (2010)
4. Brand, J.G.: Graphics for a 3D driving simulator. Bachelor thesis, Center for Intelligent Information Processing Systems, University of Western Australia (2008)
5. Bray, T., Paoli, J., Sperberg-McQueen, C.M., Maler, E., Yergeau, F., Cowan, J.: Extensible markup language (XML) 1.0 (2000)
6. Dawson, J.D.: Practical and statistical challenges in driving research. Stat. Med. **38**(2), 152–159 (2019)
7. Dosovitskiy, A., Ros, G., Codevilla, F., Lopez, A., Koltun, V.: Carla: an open urban driving simulator. In: Conference on Robot Learning, pp. 1–16. PMLR (2017)
8. Duan, Y., Liu, J., Jin, W., Peng, X.: Characterizing Differentially-Private Techniques in the Era of Internet-of-Vehicles. Technical Report-Feb-03 at User-Centric Computing Group, University of Nottingham Ningbo China (2022)
9. Fouladinejad, N., Fouladinejad, N., Abd Jalil, M., Taib, J.M.: Modeling virtual driving environment for a driving simulator. In: 2011 IEEE International Conference on Control System, Computing and Engineering, pp. 27–32. IEEE (2011)
10. Hassan, B., Berssenbrügge, J., Al Qaisi, I., Stöcklein, J.: Reconfigurable driving simulator for testing and training of advanced driver assistance systems. In: 2013 IEEE International Symposium on Assembly and Manufacturing (ISAM), pp. 337–339. IEEE (2013)
11. Huang, Z., et al.: Face2Multi-modal: in-vehicle multi-modal predictors via facial expressions. In: Adjunct Proceedings of the 12th International Conference on Automotive User Interfaces and Interactive Vehicular Applications, AutomotiveUI 2020, Virtual Event, Washington, DC, USA, 21–22 September 2020, pp. 30–33. ACM (2020). https://doi.org/10.1145/3409251.3411716
12. Jin, W., Duan, Y., Liu, J., Huang, S., Xiong, Z., Peng, X.: BROOK Dataset: A Playground for Exploiting Data-Driven Techniques in Human-Vehicle Interactive Designs. Technical Report-Feb-01 at User-Centric Computing Group, University of Nottingham Ningbo China (2022)

13. Jin, W., Ming, X., Song, Z., Xiong, Z., Peng, X.: Towards emulating internet-of-vehicles on a single machine. In: 13th International Conference on Automotive User Interfaces and Interactive Vehicular Applications, AutomotiveUI 2021, Leeds, United Kingdom, 9–14 September 2021 - Adjunct Proceedings, pp. 112–114. ACM (2021). https://doi.org/10.1145/3473682.3480275
14. Kaptein, N.A., Theeuwes, J., Van Der Horst, R.: Driving simulator validity: some considerations. Transp. Res. Rec. **1550**(1), 30–36 (1996)
15. Kusterer, R.: jMonkeyEngine 3.0 Beginner's Guide. Packt Publishing Ltd. (2013)
16. Lee, W.S., Kim, J.H., Cho, J.H.: A driving simulator as a virtual reality tool. In: Proceedings of the 1998 IEEE International Conference on Robotics and Automation (Cat. No. 98CH36146), vol. 1, pp. 71–76. IEEE (1998)
17. Li, X., Rakotonirainy, A., Yan, X.: How do drivers avoid collisions? A driving simulator-based study. J. Safety Res. **70**, 89–96 (2019)
18. Liu, J., et al.: HUT: Enabling High-UTility, Batched Queries under Differential Privacy Protection for Internet-of-Vehicles. Technical Report-Feb-02 at User-Centric Computing Group, University of Nottingham Ningbo China (2022)
19. Math, R., Mahr, A., Moniri, M.M., Müller, C.: OpenDS: a new open-source driving simulator for research. GMM-Fachbericht-AmE 2013, vol. 2 (2013)
20. Niezgoda, M., Kamiński, T., Ucińska, M., Kruszewski, M.: Effective methods for drivers research with use of a driving simulator. J. KONES **18**, 309–316 (2011)
21. Papantoniou, P., Yannis, G., Christofa, E.: Which factors lead to driving errors? A structural equation model analysis through a driving simulator experiment. IATSS Res. **43**(1), 44–50 (2019)
22. Peng, X., Huang, Z., Sun, X.: Building BROOK: A Multi-modal and Facial Video Database for Human-Vehicle Interaction Research, pp. 1–9 (2020). https://arxiv.org/abs/2005.08637
23. Saxby, D.J., Matthews, G., Hitchcock, E.M., Warm, J.S., Funke, G.J., Gantzer, T.: Effect of active and passive fatigue on performance using a driving simulator. In: Proceedings of the Human Factors and Ergonomics Society Annual Meeting, vol. 52, pp. 1751–1755. Sage Publications, Los Angeles (2008)
24. Song, Z., Wang, S., Kong, W., Peng, X., Sun, X.: First attempt to build realistic driving scenes using video-to-video synthesis in OpenDS framework. In: Adjunct Proceedings of the 11th International Conference on Automotive User Interfaces and Interactive Vehicular Applications, AutomotiveUI 2019, Utrecht, The Netherlands, 21–25 September 2019, pp. 387–391. ACM (2019). https://doi.org/10.1145/3349263.3351497
25. Sun, X., et al.: Exploring personalised autonomous vehicles to influence user trust. Cogn. Comput. **12**(6), 1170–1186 (2020). https://doi.org/10.1007/s12559-020-09757-x
26. Wang, J., Xiong, Z., Duan, Y., Liu, J., Song, Z., Peng, X.: The importance distribution of drivers' facial expressions varies over time! In: 13th International Conference on Automotive User Interfaces and Interactive Vehicular Applications, AutomotiveUI 2021, Leeds, United Kingdom, 9–14 September 2021 - Adjunct Proceedings, pp. 148–151. ACM (2021). https://doi.org/10.1145/3473682.3480283
27. Wang, S., et al.: Oneiros-OpenDS: an interactive and extensible toolkit for agile and automated developments of complicated driving scenes. In: International Conference on Human-Computer Interaction (2022)
28. Wang, W., Cheng, Q., Li, C., André, D., Jiang, X.: A cross-cultural analysis of driving behavior under critical situations: a driving simulator study. Transport. Res. F: Traffic Psychol. Behav. **62**, 483–493 (2019)

29. Weir, D.H.: Application of a driving simulator to the development of in-vehicle human-machine-interfaces. IATSS Res. **34**(1), 16–21 (2010)
30. Xiong, Z., et al.: Face2Statistics: user-friendly, low-cost and effective alternative to in-vehicle sensors/monitors for drivers. In: International Conference on Human-Computer Interaction (2022)
31. Yang, Y., Hu, J., Chen, D.: Research on driving knowledge expert system of distributed vehicle driving simulator. In: 2007 11th International Conference on Computer Supported Cooperative Work in Design, pp. 693–697. IEEE (2007)
32. Zhang, Yu., Jin, W., Xiong, Z., Li, Z., Liu, Y., Peng, X.: Demystifying interactions between driving behaviors and styles through self-clustering algorithms. In: Krömker, H. (ed.) HCII 2021. LNCS, vol. 12791, pp. 335–350. Springer, Cham (2021). https://doi.org/10.1007/978-3-030-78358-7_23

Oneiros-OpenDS: An Interactive and Extensible Toolkit for Agile and Automated Developments of Complicated Driving Scenes

Shuolei Wang(✉), Junyu Liu, Haoxuan Sun, Xiaoxing Ming, Wangkai Jin, Zilin Song, and Xiangjun Peng

User-Centric Computing Group, University of Nottingham Ningbo China, Ningbo, China
`shiangjunpeng@gmail.com`
`https://unnc-ucc.github.io/`

Abstract. We present ***Oneiros***, an interactive toolkit for agile and automated designs and developments of driving scenes for OpenDS driving simulator. ***Oneiros*** is the first response to address and tackle the key challenge of in-lab driving simulations: how to enable efficient designer-programmer cooperation, to design and develop complicated driving scenes. Our response is to design and build ***Oneiros***, which enables a single designer to design, rectify and implement complicated driving scenes without programmers' helps. This is credited to the integration of both GUIs and Automated Code Generation in ***Oneiros***. Our empirical study, among 11 designers with experiences in designing driving scenes, indicates that ***Oneiros*** can significantly improve the productivity by increasing user-friendliness. The executable and source codes of ***Oneiros*** are online at https://github.com/unnc-ucc/Oneiros-OpenDS.

Keywords: Automated code generation · Cognitive driving simulators · Driving scenes · GUI

1 Introduction

Driving scenes of in-lab simulations (e.g. roads, buildings, lights, etc.) are essential to create near-to-reality environmental factors during driving procedures, which guarantee effective validations and evaluations of advanced Human-Vehicle Interaction designs. The creation of driving scenes requires interdisciplinary expertise, and usually involves researchers with diverse expertise, to ensure the correctness of designs and effective implementations of them. However, such characteristic has significantly limited flexibility and efficiency of creating complicated driving scenes for in-lab simulations. In summary, it can be described as **the gap between scene designers and programmers**. We divide such gap into the following two aspects.

S. Wang and J. Liu—Stands for equal contributions.

H. Krömker (Ed.): HCII 2022, LNCS 13335, pp. 88–107, 2022.
https://doi.org/10.1007/978-3-031-04987-3_6

First, the Natural Difficulty of Generating Driving Scenes has been a Great Obstacle for a While. The requirements of simulated driving scenes are far beyond simple environmental decorations but also involve multiple other factors in the reality (e.g. Gravity). Therefore, some parts of driving scenes are usually implemented by extra toolkits (e.g. Physical Engines for Gravity). However, the low efficiency of developments in extra toolkits (e.g. Physical Engines) has been considered as one of the greatest issues in practice (e.g. complicated dependency, low-level coding, etc.). These difficulties also amplify the issue about reusing existing driving-scene templates, and substantially incur extremely time-consuming designs and developments. For instance, though recent efforts attempt to provide a set of general abstractions for agile developments in terms of Physical Engines [14], it's still challenging to integrate them for driving-scene developments.

Second, the *Human-In-The-Loop* Characteristic has Amplified the Non-Balance of Workloads and Prolonged the Whole Pipeline. Since the designs and developments of driving scenes require multiple expertise, both designers and programmers have to involve and the collaboration might significantly endanger the overall productivity. For instance, designers are capable to investigate and draft designs quickly, and they are highly possible to adjust and rectify them later after previewing the designs. However, these adjustments and rectifications add huge burdens on the programmers, due to the inefficiency in driving-scene developments. Particularly, as mentioned above, the problem can become more serious while programmers are not experienced with domain-specific toolkits (e.g. Physical Engines), which demands extra efforts for pre-training.

Therefore, there is an essential and urgent need for an alternative to incorporate designers and programmers, for efficient creation of complicated driving scenes (Sect. 2). To this end, we make the following two key observations about the important obstacles during designer-programmer cooperation when developing driving scenes: (1) Preview Functions are very important to allow designers for introspection and rectifications of their designs. This is naturally difficult in existing driving simulators, because all driving scenes have to be loaded and displayed; (2) Graphical User Interfaces are also very important to ease designers for creation, adjustments and adaptions of different objects and factors. This is not realistic in existing driving simulators, because all driving scenes have to be implemented by hands-on coding.

Our goal in this paper is to provide a toolkit for more efficient and agile developments of complicated driving scenes. In this work, we centralize our efforts on a widely-used and open-sourced driving simulator OpenDS [27]. After exploring the code base of OpenDS, we retrieve the key insight for potential automation: most codes of generating objects and factors (in the process of building driving scenes) are formatted regularly, and can be easily abstracted as internal functions, according to a large number of source codes regarding existing driving scene templates. Moreover, these abstracted functions can be linked and triggered by relevant users through an easy-to-use Graphical User Interface (GUI), via appropriate organizations and implementations.

We present ***Oneiros***, an interactive toolkit for agile and automated designs and developments of complicated driving scenes, for OpenDS cognitive driving simulator. The **key idea** of ***Oneiros*** is to integrate a *Graphical User Interface* for interaction, along with several *Automated Code Generators* for specific categories of objects and factors. There are three major novelties of ***Oneiros***: (1) GUI-based Scene Operators allow designers to use a GUI for additions, deletions and adjustments of any objects/factors in draft driving scenes; (2) Automated Code Generators enable automated transformations from high-level designs into low-level implementations, without hands-on implementations; and (3) Flexible Preview Functions allow designers for quickly previewing their designs, so that they can decide whether more adjustments/rectifications are needed (Sect. 3).

In addition to the above key functionalities, our implementation of ***Oneiros*** is considered as a comprehensive prototype. We provide an example to walk through the pipeline of ***Oneiros***, which covers as many functionalities as we can. The current version of ***Oneiros*** contains many functionalities for user-friendly interactions. For example, ***Oneiros*** supports users to change their viewpoints, and Zoom in/out for better visualizations, for both drafting and previewing stages. All driving scenes, created through ***Oneiros***, can be directly utilized by OpenDS driving simulator without any modifications. Our implementations of ***Oneiros*** have 5K lines of codes in Java, and the developments are still actively continuing (Sect. 4).

We examine the effectiveness of ***Oneiros*** through an empirical user study, by recruiting 11 participants with design experiences of driving scenes (Sect. 5). The procedure of this study consists of three major steps. We first allow all participants to investigate and come up with their own design choices of driving scenes. Then, we provide training sessions for two approaches: (A) designer-programmer Cooperation, and (B) Oneiros. Next, all participants are asked to develop their driving scenes in both approaches and provide feedback. Based on their feedback, we conclude that ***Oneiros*** is a more productive and user-friendly approach than the conventional one. We believe ***Oneiros*** has great potentials in practice and discuss major takeaways from our user study (Sect. 6).

More specifically, we make three key contributions in this paper:

- We address the challenges about the designs and developments of complicated driving scenes, and identify key opportunities to tackle these issues. We observe the needs of key functionalities, to resolve such inefficiencies.
- We propose ***Oneiros***, an interactive toolkit for agile and automated designs and developments of complicated driving scenes. ***Oneiros*** focuses on OpenDS driving simulator, which contains 5K lines of codes.
- We perform an empirical study of ***Oneiros***, by enabling 11 participants to compare it with the conventional pipeline. The results indicate that ***Oneiros*** can significantly improve the levels of productivity with much more user-friendliness, which further supports the promising future of ***Oneiros*** and its variants.

The rest of this paper is organized as follows. Section 2 introduces the background and motivation of ***Oneiros***. Section 3 gives an overview of ***Oneiros*** and elaborates its key components one-by-one. Section 4 elaborates detailed implementations of ***Oneiros***, and give an example to demonstrate many functionalities as possible. Section 5 presents the experimental methodology and the results for ***Oneiros***. Section 6 discusses challenges and potentials of ***Oneiros***.

2 Background and Motivations

In this section, we provide background and motivation of ***Oneiros*** by presenting related work. We first identify the importance of driving simulators for Human-Vehicle Interaction, and the key component for realistic driving scenes (Sect. 2.1). Then, we briefly elaborate the widely-used cognitive driving simulator OpenDS, with its structural organization of OpenDS (Sect. 2.2). Next, we comprehensively address the gap between designers and programmers, in terms of complicated driving-scene creations (Sect. 2.3). Finally, we outline the motivation and our goal in this work (Sect. 2.4).

2.1 The Importance of Driving Simulators

Driving simulators are key enablers for many studies of Human-Vehicle Interaction in many aspects of research and practices. This is because (1) a large number of in-field studies are restricted by local laws or available resources; (2) some characterizations are very difficult to perform in common conditions (e.g. [2,8,37]). Therefore, driving simulators are considered necessary alternatives for efficient characterizations of Human-Vehicle Interaction designs. We use on-road studies as motivating examples hereby, which are (1) detecting drivers' drowsiness [19] and affective state [5]; (2) monitoring drivers' distraction state and situational awareness [1,20,21]; (3) building users' trust for autonomous vehicles in a virtual reality simulator [28];(4) analyzing aggressive driving style (e.g. road rage) [13]; (5) studying safety issues, such as vehicle accidents [11].

A driving simulation consists of various driving events (i.e. we denote them as scenarios) and environmental compositions (i.e. we denote them as scenes). In this work, we focus on driving scenes. While few of the existing driving simulators are based on the real-word maps [6,23,25], most of the simulators require pre-defined scenes (or maps) [3,4,7,8,10,29,30,32,33] for driving simulations. There are multiple design purposes for these simulators. For example, [3,10,30] are designed for inter-vehicle interactions and motion planning, [8,29,32,33] focus on physics modeling and real-world scenario rendering for end-to-end learning, and [4,7] simulate crowded traffic control in the urban area. For simulators which relies on pre-implemented driving scenes, it is essential to develop an efficient method for set up. However, driving scenes usually rely on Physical Engines to construct and deploy static models of different components (e.g. roads, buildings, traffic lights, sign models, etc.), which are usually achieved by external libraries. These libraries require low-level coding for concrete implementations, since they need to provide sufficient details and specifications of a scene. This is considered as a great obstacle to the development of driving scenes.

2.2 OpenDS: An Open-Sourced Driving Simulator

To motivate the needs of efficient creations for complicated driving scenes, we centralize our focus on a widely-used simulator to dive into more details. As one of the most widely-used simulators, OpenDS is an open-sourced driving simulator for cognitive driving studies [27]. It has four major components, and we elaborate them one-by-one. (1) JMonkeyEngine collects runtime information during the simulation, and provides on-the-fly generations of driving scenes (e.g. emulation of gravity, coordinates and etc.) [22]; (2) JBULLET inherits JMOnkeyEngine to support generations of static object models (e.g. road, traffic light, etc.) in pre-declared specifications of driving scenes [16]; (3) NIFTY-GUI provides interaction supports for dynamic changes of events (e.g. the change of traffic light, the motion of vehicles , etc.) [12]; and (4) LIGHTWEIGHT JAVA GAME LIBRARY supports the execution of user-defined scenarios during driving simulations [26]. Since the scope of this work lies on the driving scenes, we focus on the first two components[1].

2.3 The Conventional Approach to Create Driving Scenes

The creation of a driving scene requires multiple expertise, and we divide them into two types: designers and programmers. We observe that the conventional approach, to develop complicated driving scenes, is limited by the gap between designers and programmers. To better understand this gap, we use OpenDS simulator to demonstrate the workload distribution. Figure 1 shows the conventional approach to develop complicated driving scenes. Designers are responsible to propose designs of driving scenes and scenarios, and programmers are responsible to implement these. More specifically, programmers implement driving scenes in JMonkeyEngine and driving scenarios in OpenDS. The separation of design and implementations, to match individuals with corresponding expertise, seems very reasonable.

However, this approach brings significant challenges in practice. Designers create driving scenes and scenarios based on only a brief description, which requires multiple adjustments and rectifications. However, since the implementations are fully conducted by programmers, all adjustments and rectifications need to be vetted with designers, and then executed. These prolong the whole pipeline. Moreover, for complicated driving scenes, the number of object models can be hundreds. Such frequent interactions between designers and programmers can lead to significant overheads, due to possibly ineffective communications and feedback from designers. Note that driving scenarios usually need to be implemented after concluding the implementations of driving scenes. Therefore, this work focuses on how to improve the efficiency to develop driving scenes.

2.4 Motivation and Our Goal

Motivated by the inefficiency for the developments of complicated driving scenes, our goal is to provide a toolkit for more efficient and agile developments of

[1] Note that we use JMonkeyEngine throughout the paper, since JBULLET can be considered as a part of JMonkeyEngine for loading static models.

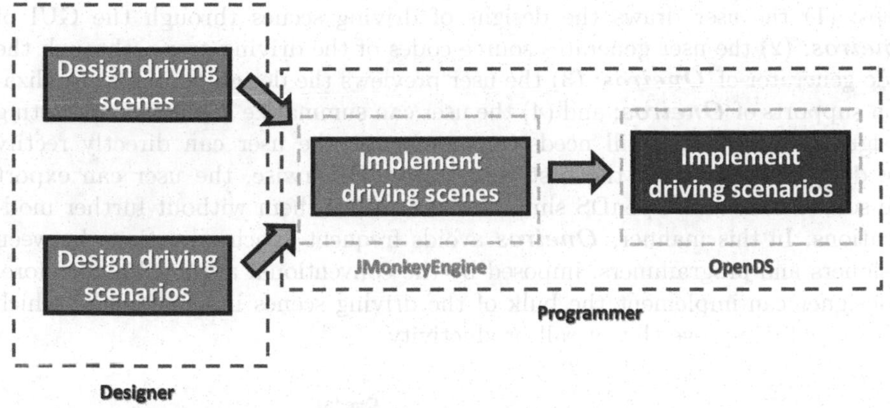

Fig. 1. A high-level distribution of workloads to designers and programmers.

complicated driving scenes. We conjecture that, if designers can independently undertake most implementations of driving scenes via a toolkit, the overall procedure can be significantly accelerated. Tailored to the need of such a toolkit, we derive two key requirements of such a toolkit: (1) Preview Functions are very important to allow designers for introspection and rectifications of their designs. This is naturally difficult in existing driving simulators, because all driving scenes have to be loaded and displayed; (2) Graphical User Interfaces are also very important to ease designers for creation, adjustments and adaptions of different objects and factors. This is not realistic in existing driving simulators, because all driving scenes have to be implemented by hands-on coding.

3 *Oneiros*: A High-Level Overview

To enable efficient designs and developments of complicated driving scenes, we present ***Oneiros***, an interactive and extensible toolkit for this purpose. ***Oneiros*** consists of three key ideas: (1) GUI-based Scene Operators allow designers to use a GUI for additions, deletions and adjustments of any objects/factors in draft driving scenes; (2) Automated Code Generators enable automated transformations from high-level designs into low-level implementations, without hands-on implementations; and (3) Flexible Preview Functions allow designers for quickly previewing their designs, so that they can decide whether more adjustments/rectifications are needed. In this section, we first introduce the workflow of ***Oneiros*** (Sect. 3.1). Then we introduce each key component respectively.

3.1 *Oneiros* Workflow

Oneiros enables a single designer to design, implement and adjust his/her own designs of driving scenes. Figure 2 shows that the workflow of a single designer to create his/her own driving scenes, with ***Oneiros***. There are essentially four steps: (1) the user draws the designs of driving scenes through the GUI of ***Oneiros***; (2) the user generates source codes of the driving scene, through the code generator of ***Oneiros***; (3) the user previews the design through visualization supports of ***Oneiros***; and (4) the user can summarize key issues of existing designs. If the design still needs improvements, the user can directly rectify the design by repeating the first three steps. Otherwise, the user can export the source code and OpenDS simulator can utilize them without further modifications. In this manner, ***Oneiros*** avoids frequent synchronizations between designers and programmers, imposed by the conventional approach. Therefore, a designer can implement the bulk of the driving scenes independently, which substantially improve the overall productivity.

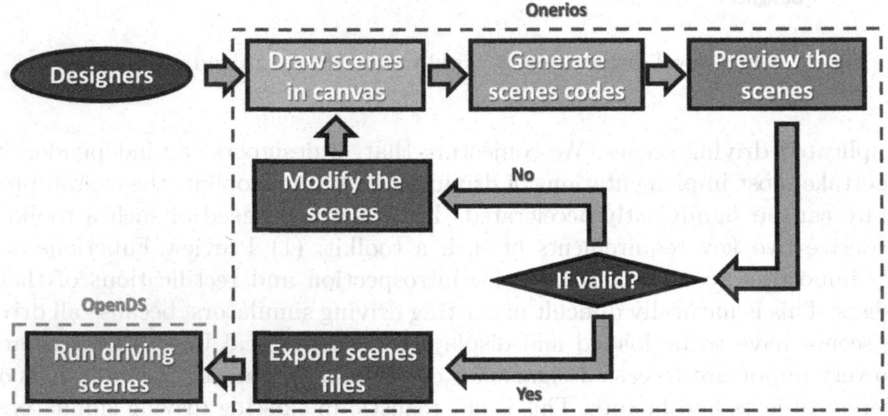

Fig. 2. A conceptual workflow of ***Oneiros***.

3.2 Component 1: GUI-Based Operators

The conventional approach requires the user to deal with low-level coding, and this has been a great obstacle in terms of productivity. Therefore, providing a user-friendly approach, to intuitively design and implement driving scenes, is essential for better efficiency. Hereby, we focus on how to reduce/avoid low-level coding, which is the key to simplifying the procedure of driving-scene creations.

Oneiros allows users to intuitively design and implement driving scenes via a sophisticated Graphical User Interface (GUI). When architecting the GUI of ***Oneiros***, the flexibility is the first-class consideration. Therefore, we form three major components of this GUI, including (1) Model Setup; (2) Canvas; and (3) Basic Operators. We provide details regarding each component one-by-one. For Model Setup, we consider the user can import the model and modify key attributes of the imported model accordingly. For Canvas, we consider the user can freely explore a user-defined space, and manipulate different models as free as they can. For Basic Operators, we consider the user can easily draw the driving scenes via painting and erasing, to provide a user-friendly interaction between the user and the software.

3.3 Component 2: Automated Code Generators

The capability to automatically generate the codes, according to drawn inputs, is the core of ***Oneiros***. This is motivated by the fact that: a large number of driving-scene implementations are frequently repeated and share common structures of codes. For instance, we consider architecting four intersections of roads in a driving scene and each intersection has four traffic lights with different orientations. In the conventional approach, the designer comes up with a single design using one intersection as an example, but the programmer needs to implement at least 16 traffic light models with different locations and orientations. However, ***Oneiros*** can simplify this procedure via Automated Code Generations, to create these traffic light models based on only drawn inputs.

Automated Code Generators, within ***Oneiros***, aim to significantly simplify the implementation workload of driving scenes. Our generator consists of three steps. (1) ***Oneiros*** transforms user-drawn scenes into a collection of key information; (2) ***Oneiros*** leverages existing code templates, derived from existing driving scenes, to automatically implement driving scenes based on the collected information (i.e. specification); and (3) ***Oneiros*** encapsulates/reorganizes all generated codes as a portable format, to ensure the visualizations and exportation can be achieved correctly.

3.4 Component 3: Preview Functions

The capability to preview the driving scenes, generated from Automated Code Generators, is also a key part of ***Oneiros***. This is motivated by the fact that: any decisions of adjustments/rectifications should be made based on the visualized driving scenes accordingly. Therefore, it's important for the user to preview their designs through visualization supports. Note that this capability is not supported in current driving simulators, so that they have to port their designs into the simulator for visualization.

Preview Functions, within ***Oneiros***, aim to enable the user to preview their designs of driving scenes. Our previewing supports have three major features, compared with full-simulator visualization: (1) ***Oneiros*** allows the user to take any viewpoint when previewing the whole scene; (2) ***Oneiros*** allows the user to traverse the whole scene in a user-defined manner, so that there are no blind spots for the user; and (3) ***Oneiros*** only partially takes advantage of the Physical Engines, which guarantees better performance in previewing.

4 *Oneiros*: Detailed Design

In this section, we introduce detailed designs within ***Oneiros***. We first cover the GUI of ***Oneiros*** (Sect. 4.1). Then we attempt to cover as many functionalities of ***Oneiros*** as possible, via concrete examples respectively (Sect. 4.2).

4.1 The GUI of *Oneiros*

The GUI of ***Oneiros*** is mainly composed of four parts. (1) Menu Bar; (2) Canvas; (3) Map Layer; and (4) Model Setup. Figure 3 shows a top-down visualized example, which contains Menu Bar (i.e. upper left), Canvas (i.e. the center), Map Layer (i.e. right), and Model Setup (i.e. left).

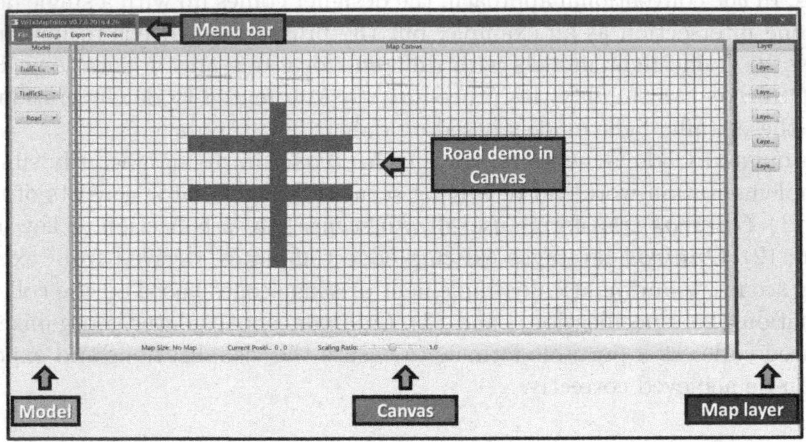

Fig. 3. An example of the GUI of ***Oneiros***.

Menu Bar. Menu Bar locates the left of the GUI, and there are four options including "File", "Setting", "Export" and "Preview". The "File" option contains all the functions related to the files, including new, open, save and save as map files; The "Setting" item contains the choices of user-defined characteristics, such as the brush and grid setting; The "Export" item contains the function that export the current scene to a simulator-compatible file; and the "Preview" item redirects to the function for previewing the scenes in real-time.

Canvas. Canvas occupies the largest portion of the GUI, which is in the center of the GUI. When the user triggers a new map operation, a grid will be automatically generated in the Canvas. Each cell in the grid represents the unit area in the driving scene. Users can implement their driving scenes, by filling in the corresponding positions on the Canvas (i.e. based on the position of the model in the driving scene). In order to provide tracking statistics, the bottom of the GUI has a bar to show the current stage of the Canvas, the coordinates of the current cell and the current scaling rate of grid pane. For instance, there is a demo of roads in the center of Fig. 3.

Map Layer. Map Layer locates in the right of the GUI, and the purpose of Map Layer is to allow users to manage multiple layers of a single driving scene.

Therefore, ***Oneiros*** allows users to put many models to different layers, and avoid the overlap between models occupying the same 2D position (i.e. the same 2D coordinates) with different heights (i.e. differences in 3D coordinates) on the canvas. It's notable to mention that Map Layer is an optional functionality, and users can simply ignore it if they don't plan to use it.

Model Setup. Model Setup locates in the left of the GUI, and it's an extensible part of ***Oneiros***. In our example, we demonstrate three types of models including "Road", "Traffic Light" and "Traffic Sign". Each type of model is represented as a button and they can be reconfigured by changing their attributes. For instance, for road models, there are two-lane, three-lane and four-lane road types. The user can select and reconfigure the model based on their needs, and then initialize them within the Canvas.

4.2 Demonstrations of *Oneiros*'s Functionalities

Oneiros has a comprehensive coverage of functionalities. Therefore, a single section is unable to cover all of them. Hereby, we demonstrate as many functionalities of ***Oneiros*** as possible, by walking through a single example. In this example, the assignment of a designer is described as follows.

> A designer is required to independently build a scene model for OpenDS driving simulator. The scene model should contain multiple roads with multiple intersections, in which roads may vary in terms of width and length. Traffic Signs should be implemented properly at each intersection. The designer is required to build such a model independently, without any assistance from the programmers. The results of this assignment are expected to be an executable scene file for OpenDS, without any further modifications.

With ***Oneiros***, this assignment is possible to be finished by a single designer. In the following, we describe representative functionalities of ***Oneiros*** by walking through the procedure to finish the above assignment, and provide concrete examples (i.e. visualized) to better understand how ***Oneiros*** works.

Step ①: Creating a New Map. The user would first create a map canvas through the "New" function in the Menu Bar. As shown in Fig. 4-(❶), when the user clicks the "New" button in the menu bar, the software will pop up a new interface to let the user enter the size of the canvas they want. After the user enters the size and clicks "New" to confirm, the map canvas is automatically generated.

Step ②: Drawing to Add Models. After creating a new map, the designer then adds a model at a specific position. He/She can import the models as he/she wants, select them via Model Setup, and then draw and add them onto the corresponding position on the map. As shown in Fig. 4-(❷), the red fills represent the roads, which are drawn by the designer.

Step ③: Zooming In/Out within Canvas. After drawing some basic Road models, the designer may adjust them due to the requirement "roads may vary in terms of width and length". Therefore, Zooming In/Out is very useful since the designer can take advantage of this functionality, to add some models in a smaller granularity (e.g. narrower or shorter roads). As shown in Fig. 4-(❸), the designer can use Zooming In/Out to observe either the parts of the scene or the whole driving scene conveniently.

Step ④: Adjusting the Direction of Models. After concluding the Road models, the designer can move to add models of Traffic Lights and Signs. However, in driving scenes, there are more considerations for these two models, compared with Road models. This is because both Traffic Lights and Signs can have different directions. More specifically, at an intersection of roads, there should be FOUR Traffic Light models, aligned as FOUR different directions for different driving directions. Therefore, it is necessary to allow users to adjust the models for different attributes (e.g. directions). ***Oneiros*** can support this functionality very well, and Fig. 4-(❹) shows such an example, where different models have different directions.

Step ⑤: Deleting Models within Canvas. When designing the driving scene via ***Oneiros***, it's understandable for the user to delete some models within Canvas, out of either adjustments/rectifications of designs or simple mistakes from careless manipulations. Therefore, ***Oneiros*** also supports deletion within Canvas. In this case, users can use the eraser to clear any stuff as they wish. This is as convenient as creating models within Canvas. Figure 4-(❺) showcases an example of selecting eraser for further deletion in ***Oneiros***.

Step ⑥: Adjusting Attributes of the Models. To adjust and rectify the draft, the designer needs to modify some attributes of different models. To ensure that the attributes are rich enough, ***Oneiros*** provides a separate operation to adjust detailed attributes of different models. For instance, to adjust attributes (e.g. the positions, directions and etc.), users only need to simply click the corresponding models. In addition, ***Oneiros*** can also allow such changes to be broadcast across many instances of the same models, if the user selects them together. As shown in Fig. 4-(❻), users can adjust/rectify the attributes of models by right-clicking the selected model/region. After users select the "Attributes" button, ***Oneiros*** will pop up a new window for listing detailed attributes for the users, and users can adjust them accordingly.

Step ⑦: Adjusting Environmental Factors. After concluding the designs and implementations of key parts within a driving scene, creating a more realistic scene also requires proper settings of environmental factors (e.g. Gravity,

Illumination and etc.). In this particular case, we use illumination as a motivating example. More specifically, illumination reflects that an object is brighter, when this object is facing the light direction, but darker, when it's on the other side. Driving scenes require the lighting functions to illuminate various models, for more realistic simulations. In ***Oneiros***, we consider the parameters of the lighting functions including light intensity and light direction. These parameters are pre-defined in the driving scenes by users of ***Oneiros***, and there are six directions of lighting to choose from. Users can set these parameters of lighting, based on the requirements of their driving-scene designs. An example, to change lighting in driving scenes, is shown in Fig. 4-(❼).

Step ⑧: Automated Code Generator. When all designs and implementations of driving scenes are finished, users need to export their designs as concrete implementations, and then port these implementations to the simulator without further modifications (i.e. OpenDS driving simulator in our case). As mentioned previously, ***Oneiros*** provides a full transformation from high-level abstractions in GUI into detailed implementations, which are directly compatible with OpenDS. Figure 4-(❽) shows an example, to transform a GUI-based design (shown in the left) into OpenDS-compatible implementations (which are successfully simulated by OpenDS, as shown in the right).

Putting All Functionalities Together. The above steps only cover basic functionalities of ***Oneiros***, because of the limited number of pages. However, the co-existence of all the above functionalities allows ***Oneiros*** to be very powerful in practice. We believe ***Oneiros*** can breed many more opportunities for complicated driving-scene creations.

5 User Study of *Oneiros*

In this section, we provide details about our user study of ***Oneiros***. We first introduce our study methodology. Then we provide concrete details of the procedure. Next, we present the results of our study. Finally, we identify the pros & cons of ***Oneiros*** based on the collected feedback. Our study aims to answer the following three questions:

- Can designers intuitively obtain better experiences by using ***Oneiros***, instead of following the conventional approach (i.e. collaborating with programmers)?
- Can ***Oneiros*** improve the efficiency of driving-scene designs and implementations for experienced designers?
- Are there any possible limitations and potential improvements for ***Oneiros***?

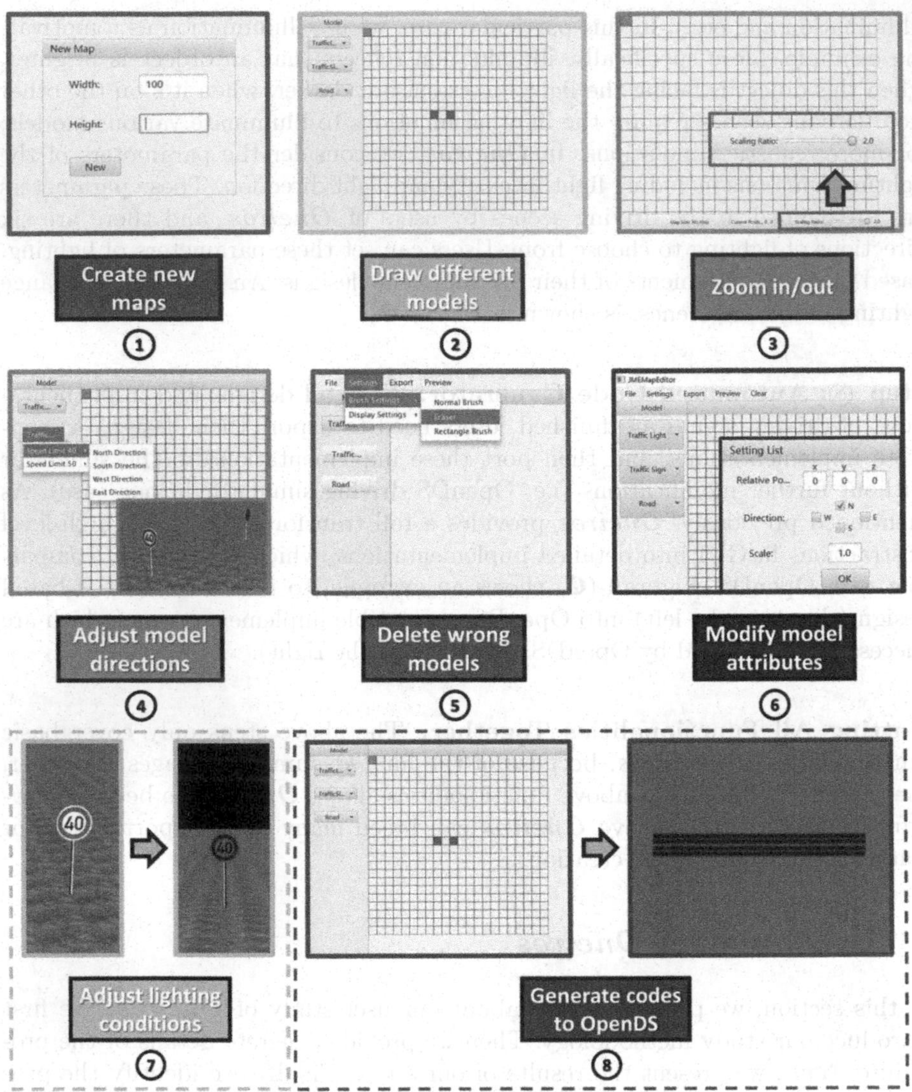

Fig. 4. Implementation details.

5.1 Ethical Issue Statement

For all human-participated research, we inform all participants that their data may be used for research purposes, and all participants give their full consents. All experiments are done anonymously and only anonymous feedback is collected in experiments. Since no identity information is needed (e.g. personal names, ages) in our study, we ensure that no personal information of all participants was collected or leaked in any form, which guarantees that all participants' privacy are not compromised.

5.2 Study Methodology

All participants are required to freely come up with two designs of driving scenes, with a similar level of complexity. After concluding designs, each participant has two stages during the study. First, all participants are required to use the conventional approach for building one of their own designs; and second, all participants are required to use ***Oneiros*** to build the other of their own designs. To support the first stage, we assign programmers with sufficient experience in creating driving scenes in OpenDS to cooperate with the designers. During each stage, all participants are required to record a diary of their developments, and fill in respective questionnaires when needed. We provide more details about the diary and questionnaires as follows.

- The diary requires participants to record their working hours, including their efforts in communicating with programmers, adjusting/rectifying designs and validating the implementations.
- The first questionnaire, for memorization purposes only, records users' experiences on the functionality, interactivity and convenience of the conventional approach via text comments.
- The second questionnaire collects users' experiences on the functionality, interactivity and convenience of using ***Oneiros*** by rating, and text comments are also optional. Note that all participants are allowed to view the first questionnaire, so that they can compare two approaches accordingly.

When rating Functionality, Interactivity and Convenience in the second questionnaire, every participant is provided 5 options including Much Worser, Worser, Neutral, Better and Much Better. We rephrase the words accordingly to ensure the participants can easily understand the concepts.

5.3 Study Procedure

In total, we recruit 11 participants by advertising our study via internal emails, among all students (i.e. 36) involving driving-scene designs previously in our lab. Therefore, we have to asynchronously perform the study for the conventional approach. All participants complete the study.

5.4 Study Results

In this section, we report our study results by first introducing improvements in terms of the efficiency, and then elaborating user experiences.

Efficiency Improvements - In Terms of Time. Results of the efficiency improvement are based on the diary. Figure 5 reports the results of saving time by using ***Oneiros***, compared with the conventional approach. We make three observations. First, there are 9 participants who save at least 32% time by using ***Oneiros***, compared with the conventional approach. Second, 1 participant saves up to 69% time by using ***Oneiros***. Third, 2 participants only save 5% and 11% time by ***Oneiros***. This is because these two participants are cold-start in using ***Oneiros***, without sufficient practices.

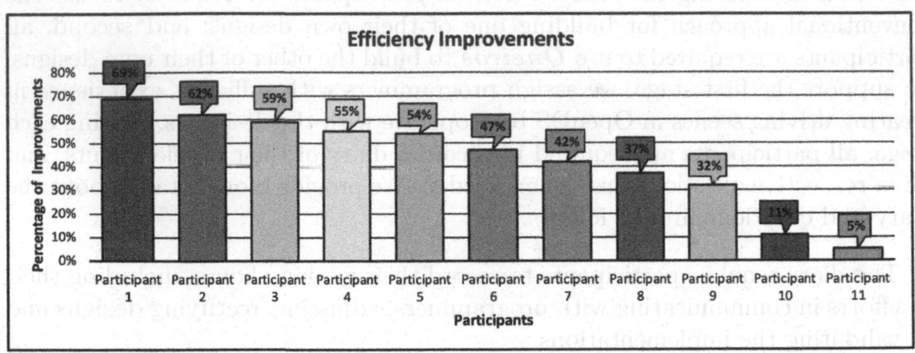

Fig. 5. Results of efficiency improvement (measured by diary-recorded time) by using ***Oneiros***, compared with the conventional approach.

User Experiences - In Terms of Functionality, Interactivity and Convenience. Results of user experience are based on the second questionnaire. Figure 6 reports the results of user experiences, in terms of Functionality (①), Interactivity (②) and Convenience (③) respectively. For Functionality, 1 participant thinks the functionality of ***Oneiros*** tool is good enough, 7 participants think is good, and 3 participants think the functionality is neutral; for Interactivity, all participants consider ***Oneiros*** is much more interactive than the conventional approach: 9 of them particularly enjoy the interactivity of ***Oneiros***; for Convenience, 4 participants think using ***Oneiros*** is much more convenient than the conventional approach, and 7 participants think ***Oneiros*** is more convenient. In summary, all participants are positive about Interactivity and Convenience of ***Oneiros***, and not negative about Functionality of ***Oneiros***, compared with the conventional approach.

6 Discussions and Limitations

In this section, we discuss the challenges and opportunities of ***Oneiros***, derived from our user study and retrospection. We first provide our insights from ***Oneiros***, in terms of efficiency improvements (Sect. 6.1). Then we cover our takeaways from ***Oneiros***, in terms of user experiences (including Functionality, Interactivity and Convenience) (Sect. 6.2). In addition, we also analyze and elaborate the limitations of ***Oneiros*** (Sect. 6.3).

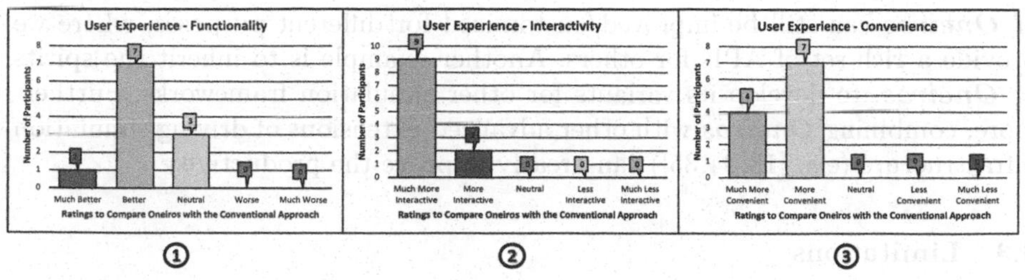

Fig. 6. Ratings for comparative user experiences, by first applying the conventional approach and then using ***Oneiros***. ① for Functionality, ② for Interactivity and ③ for Convenience.

6.1 Takeaways of Efficiency from *Oneiros*

Our user study on ***Oneiros*** demonstrates that all participants can save time by using ***Oneiros***. However, the variations of improvements imply several optimizations in potential, and we summarize them in the following three aspects. (1) the training of ***Oneiros*** is critical to enable a broad range of users, and the needs for a full documentation/manual might be essential; (2) the GUI of ***Oneiros*** can be improved for better interactions, and more engineering efforts are needed for this purpose; and (3) the organization of ***Oneiros*** can be adjusted/customized by the user, and we intend to provide more flexible supports for doing so without getting hands on source codes. Therefore, we believe there are a large amount of follow-up work for ***Oneiros*** and its variants. For instance, the characterization of different GUI designs for ***Oneiros*** can be very useful in practice, where we release the source codes for the implementations of ***Oneiros***. Improving the efficiency for driving simulations via ***Oneiros*** can greatly help with the characterization (e.g. personalization of driving behaviors [36,40], privacy protection [9,24]) and developments of Human-Vehicle Interaction techniques (e.g. datasets [17,31], collection of drivers' statistics [15,38,39]).

6.2 Takeaways of User Experiences from *Oneiros*

Our user study on ***Oneiros*** demonstrates that all participants are positive on Interactivity and Convenience, and they are not negative about Functionality of ***Oneiros***. Therefore, we conclude that ***Oneiros*** provides an effective alternative to collaborations with programmers, when developing driving scenes. We believe there are three key contributors to excellent user experiences of ***Oneiros***. (1) GUI-enabled designs for driving scenes avoid users to get hands on low-level coding, and the flexibility allows users to freely explore the design space; (2) Automated Code Generators safeguard the correct transformations from GUI-based designs to detailed implementations; (3) Preview Functions improves the efficiency for users to plan adjustments/rectifications of driving scenes, and this ensures the whole procedure can be carried out by a single designer. Therefore, we believe there are extensive opportunities for ***Oneiros***. For instance, the GUI of ***Oneiros*** can still be improved/customized for different purposes, where we provide a rich set of APIs for others. Another example is to inherit the spirits of ***Oneiros***, to develop its variants for other simulation frameworks. Furthermore, combining ***Oneiros*** with other advanced extensions of driving simulation infrastructure (e.g. [18,34,35]) can greatly improve the productivity.

6.3 Limitations

We hereby identify several limitations about ***Oneiros***. The first one is that users still need to manually configure the software running environment. Concretely, ***Oneiros*** can only be launched in specific system environment, which means that it requires installation and configurations of JMonkeyEngine, OpenDS, JVM, etc. Installations of these pre-required system environments can cause additional workloads for users and even unexpected problems. Besides, ***Oneiros*** can only build static driving scene models but cannot build completed driving scenarios, which should contain interactive models such as cars and pedestrian models. Currently, users need to use OpenDS to build scenarios after they implement the driving scenes in ***Oneiros***, which can be integrated into one system to save time and decrease additional workloads. The third aspect is that ***Oneiros*** cannot update driving scenes in real-time during the driving simulation. Specifically speaking, although ***Oneiros*** can generate driving scenes in OpenDS, it cannot lively update them in driving simulations. Therefore, the compatibility, functionality and interactivity of ***Oneiros*** should be further improved.

7 Conclusions

We present ***Oneiros***, an interactive and extensible toolkit for agile and efficient designs and developments of complicated driving scenes. ***Oneiros*** provides a sophisticated GUI, backed up by a powerful code generator. Therefore, a single designer can conclude the bulk of driving-scene designs and implementations, without any helps from programmers. We perform an empirical study of ***Oneiros***, and the results suggest great practicality of ***Oneiros***. We release both the executable and source codes of ***Oneiros*** at https://github.com/unnc-ucc/Oneiros-OpenDS.

Acknowledgements. We thank anonymous reviewers in HCI'22 and AutomotiveUI'21 for their valuable feedback. We thank for all members of User-Centric Computing Group at University of Nottingham Ningbo China for the stimulating environment. This work was started as Shuolei Wang's internship and undergraduate thesis at University of Nottingham Ningbo China.

References

1. Arkonac, S.E., Brumby, D.P., Smith, T., Babu, H.V.R.: In-car distractions and automated driving: a preliminary simulator study. In: Proceedings of the 11th International Conference on Automotive User Interfaces and Interactive Vehicular Applications: Adjunct Proceedings, AutomotiveUI '19, pp. 346–351. Association for Computing Machinery, New York (2019). https://doi.org/10.1145/3349263.3351505
2. Bella, F.: Driving simulator for speed research on two-lane rural roads. Accid. Anal. Prev. **40**(3), 1078–1087 (2008)
3. Bernhard, W., Espie, E.: Torcs - the open racing car simulator (2020). https://sourceforge.net/projects/torcs/
4. Best, A., Narang, S., Pasqualin, L., Barber, D., Manocha, D.: Autonovi-Sim: autonomous vehicle simulation platform with weather, sensing, and traffic control. In: 2018 IEEE/CVF Conference on Computer Vision and Pattern Recognition Workshops (CVPRW), pp. 1161–11618 (2018). https://doi.org/10.1109/CVPRW.2018.00152
5. Cai, H., Lin, Y., Mourant, R.: Study on driver emotion in driver-vehicle-environment systems using multiple networked driving simulators. DSC North America - Iowa City - September North America - Iowa City, September 2007
6. Cai, P., Lee, Y., Luo, Y., Hsu, D.: SUMMIT: a simulator for urban driving in massive mixed traffic. In: 2020 IEEE International Conference on Robotics and Automation (ICRA), pp. 4023–4029 (2020). https://doi.org/10.1109/ICRA40945.2020.9197228
7. Chao, Q., Jin, X., Huang, H.W., Foong, S., Yu, L.F., Yeung, S.K.: Force-based heterogeneous traffic simulation for autonomous vehicle testing. In: 2019 International Conference on Robotics and Automation (ICRA), pp. 8298–8304 (2019). https://doi.org/10.1109/ICRA.2019.8794430
8. Dosovitskiy, A., Ros, G., Codevilla, F., López, A.M., Koltun, V.: CARLA: an open urban driving simulator. CoRR abs/1711.03938 (2017). http://arxiv.org/abs/1711.03938
9. Duan, Y., Liu, J., Jin, W., Peng, X.: Characterizing differentially-private techniques in the era of internet-of-vehicles. Technical Report-Feb-03 at User-Centric Computing Group, University of Nottingham Ningbo China (2022)
10. Zhao, H., Cui, A., Cullen, S.A., Paden, B., Laskey, M., Goldberg, K.: Fluids: a first-order local urban intersection driving simulator. In: CASE (2018)
11. Hoffman, L., McDowd, J.M.: Simulator driving performance predicts accident reports five years later. Psychol. Aging **25**(3), 741 (2010)
12. Hohmuth, J.: Nifty Gui the manual 1.3.2 (2012). https://usermanual.wiki/Document/niftyguithemanual132.1944570287/help
13. Hu, H., Zhu, Z., Gao, Z., Zheng, R.: Analysis on biosignal characteristics to evaluate road rage of younger drivers: a driving simulator study*. In: 2018 IEEE Intelligent Vehicles Symposium (IV), pp. 156–161 (2018). https://doi.org/10.1109/IVS.2018.8500444
14. Hu, Y., Li, T., Anderson, L., Ragan-Kelley, J., Durand, F.: Taichi: a language for high-performance computation on spatially sparse data structures. ACM Trans. Graph. **38**(6), 201:1–201:16 (2019). https://doi.org/10.1145/3355089.3356506

15. Huang, Z., et al.: Face2Multi-modal: in-vehicle multi-modal predictors via facial expressions. In: Adjunct Proceedings of the 12th International Conference on Automotive User Interfaces and Interactive Vehicular Applications, AutomotiveUI 2020, Virtual Event, Washington, DC, USA, 21–22 September 2020, pp. 30–33. ACM (2020). https://doi.org/10.1145/3409251.3411716
16. JBullet: Jbullet-java port of bullet physics library (2010). http://jbullet.advel.cz/
17. Jin, W., Duan, Y., Liu, J., Huang, S., Xiong, Z., Peng, X.: BROOK dataset: a playground for exploiting data-driven techniques in human-vehicle interactive designs. Technical Report-Feb-01 at User-Centric Computing Group, University of Nottingham Ningbo China (2022)
18. Jin, W., Ming, X., Song, Z., Xiong, Z., Peng, X.: Towards emulating internet-of-vehicles on a single machine. In: AutomotiveUI '21: 13th International Conference on Automotive User Interfaces and Interactive Vehicular Applications, Leeds, United Kingdom, 9–14 September 2021 - Adjunct Proceedings, pp. 112–114. ACM (2021). https://doi.org/10.1145/3473682.3480275
19. Kiashari, S.E.H., Nahvi, A., Bakhoda, H., Homayounfard, A., Tashakori, M.: Evaluation of driver drowsiness using respiration analysis by thermal imaging on a driving simulator. Multimed. Tools Appl. **79**, 17793–17815 (2020). https://doi.org/10.1007/s11042-020-08696-x
20. Koohestani, A., Kebria, P., Khosravi, A., Nahavandi, S.: Drivers performance evaluation using physiological measurement in a driving simulator. In: 2018 Digital Image Computing: Techniques and Applications (DICTA), pp. 1–6 (2018). https://doi.org/10.1109/DICTA.2018.8615763
21. Koohestani, A., Kebria, P.M., Khosravi, A., Nahavandi, S.: Drivers awareness evaluation using physiological measurement in a driving simulator. In: 2019 IEEE International Conference on Industrial Technology (ICIT), pp. 859–864 (2019). https://doi.org/10.1109/ICIT.2019.8755188
22. Kusterer, R.: jMonkeyEngine 3.0 Beginner's Guide. Packt Publishing Ltd., Birmingham (2013)
23. Lima Azevedo, C., et al.: Simmobility short-term: an integrated microscopic mobility simulator. Transp. Res. Record: J. Transp. Res. Board **2622**, 13–23 (2017). https://doi.org/10.3141/2622-02
24. Liu, J., et al.: HUT: enabling high-utility, batched queries under differential privacy protection for internet-of-vehicles. Technical Report-Feb-02 at User-Centric Computing Group, University of Nottingham Ningbo China (2022)
25. López, P.Á., et al.: Microscopic traffic simulation using SUMO. In: Zhang, W., Bayen, A.M., Medina, J.J.S., Barth, M.J. (eds.) 21st International Conference on Intelligent Transportation Systems, ITSC 2018, Maui, HI, USA, 4–7 November 2018, pp. 2575–2582. IEEE (2018). https://doi.org/10.1109/ITSC.2018.8569938
26. LWJGL: LWJGL: Lightweight java game library (2010). https://www.lwjgl.org/
27. Math, R., Mahr, A., Moniri, M.M., Müller, C.: OpenDS: a new open-source driving simulator for research. In: Proceedings of the International Conference on Automotive User Interfaces and Interactive Vehicular Applications, Adjunct Proceedings, pp. 7–8 (2012)
28. Morra, L., Lamberti, F., Pratticó, F.G., Rosa, S.L., Montuschi, P.: Building trust in autonomous vehicles: role of virtual reality driving simulators in HMI design. IEEE Trans. Veh. Technol. **68**(10), 9438–9450 (2019). https://doi.org/10.1109/TVT.2019.2933601
29. Müller, M., Casser, V., Lahoud, J., Smith, N., Ghanem, B.: Sim4CV: a photo-realistic simulator for computer vision applications. Int. J. Comput. Vis. **126**(9), 902–919 (2018)

30. Naumann, M., Poggenhans, F., Lauer, M., Stiller, C.: CoInCar-Sim: an open-source simulation framework for cooperatively interacting automobiles. In: IEEE Intelligent Vehicles Symposium, pp. 1–6 (2018). https://doi.org/10.1109/IVS.2018.8500405
31. Peng, X., Huang, Z., Sun, X.: Building BROOK: a multi-modal and facial video database for human-vehicle interaction research, pp. 1–9 (2020). https://arxiv.org/abs/2005.08637
32. Richter, S.R., Hayder, Z., Koltun, V.: Playing for benchmarks. CoRR abs/1709.07322 (2017). http://arxiv.org/abs/1709.07322
33. Santara, A., et al.: Madras: Multi agent driving simulator. J. Artif. Intell. Res. **70**, 1517–1555 (2021)
34. Song, Z., Wang, S., Kong, W., Peng, X., Sun, X.: First attempt to build realistic driving scenes using video-to-video synthesis in OpenDS framework. In: Adjunct Proceedings of the 11th International Conference on Automotive User Interfaces and Interactive Vehicular Applications, AutomotiveUI 2019, Utrecht, The Netherlands, 21–25 September 2019, pp. 387–391. ACM (2019). https://doi.org/10.1145/3349263.3351497
35. Song, Z., Duan, Y., Jin, W., Huang, S., Wang, S., Peng, X.: Omniverse-OpenDS: enabling agile developments for complex driving scenarios via reconfigurable abstractions. In: International Conference on Human-Computer Interaction (2022)
36. Sun, X., et al.: Exploring personalised autonomous vehicles to influence user trust. Cogn. Comput. **12**(6), 1170–1186 (2020)
37. Tucă, A., Croitorescu, V., Oprean, M., Brandemeir, T.: Driving simulators for human vehicle interaction design. In: Balkan Region Conference on Engineering and Business Education, vol. 1. Sciendo (2015)
38. Wang, J., Xiong, Z., Duan, Y., Liu, J., Song, Z., Peng, X.: The importance distribution of drivers' facial expressions varies over time! In: AutomotiveUI '21: 13th International Conference on Automotive User Interfaces and Interactive Vehicular Applications, Leeds, United Kingdom, 9–14 September 2021 - Adjunct Proceedings, pp. 148–151. ACM (2021). https://doi.org/10.1145/3473682.3480283
39. Xiong, Z., et al.: Face2Statistics: user-friendly, low-cost and effective alternative to in-vehicle sensors/monitors for drivers. In: International Conference on Human-Computer Interaction (2022)
40. Zhang, Yu., Jin, W., Xiong, Z., Li, Z., Liu, Y., Peng, X.: Demystifying interactions between driving behaviors and styles through self-clustering algorithms. In: Krömker, H. (ed.) HCII 2021. LNCS, vol. 12791, pp. 335–350. Springer, Cham (2021). https://doi.org/10.1007/978-3-030-78358-7_23

Towards Scenario-Based and Question-Driven Explanations in Autonomous Vehicles

Yiwen Zhang, Weiwei Guo, Cheng Chi, Lu Hou, and Xiaohua Sun(✉)

College of Design and Innovation, Tongji University, Shanghai, China
{zhangyw,weiweiguo,1933633,xsun}@tongji.edu.cn

Abstract. Benefit from the progress in the field of explainable artificial intelligence (XAI), explanations have been increasingly prospective in the autonomous vehicle (AV) context. Providing explanations has been proved to be vital for human-AV interaction, but what and how to explain are still to be addressed. This study seeks to bridge the areas of XAI and human-AV interaction by combining perspectives of both users and researchers. In this paper, a conceptual framework of explanation models was proposed to indicate what aspects to explain in human-AV interaction. Based on the framework, we introduced a scenario-based and question-driven method, i.e., the SQX-canvas, to guide the workflow of generating explanations from users' demands in a certain AV scenario. To make an initial validation of the method, a co-design workshop involving researchers and users was conducted with four AV scenarios provided in forms of video clips. Participants produced explanation concepts and expressed their attitudes towards the AV scenarios following the "scenario, question and explanation" process. It was apparent that users' demands of explanations varied across scenarios, and findings as well as limitations were discussed. This method could provide implications for research and practice on facilitating transparent human-AV interaction.

Keywords: Autonomous vehicles · Explanations · Explainable AI · Scenario · User experience

1 Introduction

In the context of autonomous driving, the role of human driver gradually switches from a "active operator" to a "passive monitor". Human drivers may get sceptical or confused when they have to cooperate with the autonomous vehicles (AVs) controlled by artificial intelligence (AI) algorithms [24]. Thus, effective and transparent human-AV communication becomes increasingly vital. Explainable AI (XAI), which aims to open the "black-box" of AI algorithms, has gotten a lot of interest from academics in recent years, with the majority of them focusing on XAI technological solutions [1,3,21]. Explanations provided by AV have been proved to bring many benefits to the human-AV interaction (e.g., safety, trust,

H. Krömker (Ed.): HCII 2022, LNCS 13335, pp. 108–120, 2022.
https://doi.org/10.1007/978-3-031-04987-3_7

user experience) [9,15,24,26], but how these explanations should be generated and presented across scenarios is still open to be discussed.

To address this issue, this study aims to explore structured methodology to understand user's demand and envision what and how to explain in human-AV interaction scenarios. Starting from the analysis of human-AV shared control process, Sect. 3 depicted a conceptual framework containing three models of what to explain in human-AV interaction. Section 4 proposed a method, named SQX-canvas, to guide the researchers or designers how to discover users' demands for explanations in a certain scenario. The user's and researcher's perspectives are combined in this scenario-based and question-driven method. Further, a co-design workshop was organized to produce explanation concepts for four given AV scenarios, acting as an initial validation of this method. Findings and limitations are discussed in Sect. 5 to shed light on future work on explainable human-AV interaction.

2 Related Work

2.1 Human-Autonomous Vehicle Interaction

Although autonomous vehicles (AVs) above SAE Level 3 are still rare on the market, a large body of studies have focused on interaction between human and high-level AVs [13]. Human drivers can no longer perform driving tasks on the operational level, but they are still required to monitor and take over the control in shared control stages [14]. Avoiding "out of the loop" issues becomes critical in the field of human-AV interaction and attracted lots of attention from researchers [18]. It is commonly believed that making AV more transparent and understandable is beneficial to help the drivers cooperate with the AV effectively, and several HMI principles or guidelines for autonomous vehicles were proposed [5,7,20,25]. Pokam et al. investigated principles enhancing the transparency of human-AV interaction, and conducted an experiment with AR-HUD for validation [22]. While these guidelines and principles provide valuable insights into human-AV interaction, practical method is still lacking for researchers and practitioners to address specific design issues across scenarios.

2.2 Human-Centered Explainable AI

To deal with the opaqueness nature of AI or machine learning algorithms, explainable AI (XAI) techniques refer to methods that can explain why a certain prediction is achieved by the AI algorithm [1]. A large body of literature have focused on the techniques to improve the interpretability and explainability of machine learning algorithms [2,8], while it is not adequate for satisfying users' demand for explanations in a certain scenario [19]. Human-centric perspective has been indispensable in the XAI research, and a conceptual framework was proposed on how understanding people can inform XAI [28]. To address such issues in different scenarios, scenario-based design was introduced in the early stages of XAI system development, and the concept of "explainability scenario" worked as resources to understand the end-users' needs about the AI outputs [30]. Eiband et al. also proposed a five-stage participatory process for the transparent user interface design in intelligent systems, involving users, designers and providers [10]. To understand the real-world user demands for AI explanations, question probes were used to inform the design practices for user-centered XAI [16]. These methods have been initially adopted in the practices of high-stake fields, such as financial and medical decision-making assist, and there is a space to extend and integrate these methods to the design of human-autonomous vehicle interaction.

2.3 Explanations in Autonomous Vehicles

Apart from technical aspects, how to convey explanations in autonomous vehicles has been an increasingly promising topic [3,24]. Some studies focused on the content of explanations, indicating that the amount of information need to be optimized for an effective explanation [23]. Different categorized of information, such as "how" (effect) and "why" (cause) messages, can lead to different outcomes, and overload can be caused by containing too much information [15]. In terms of explanation forms, visual-auditory interfaces are most commonly used either in existing studies or commercial products [11,29,31]. While visual interfaces have advantages in constantly displaying complicated information, auditory interfaces can draw the drivers' attention and communicate semantic messages. Other modalities, such as vibrotactile signals, can also act as supplement for explanations [11]. The timing and priority of explanations also matter, while the necessity of providing explanations varies across scenarios [9,26]. Most existing studies looked into the single aspect of explanations and investigated its effects in AV context, while how to generate explanations matching users' expectations in specific scenarios is still little addressed.

3 What to Explain: A Conceptual Framework

In this study, we first aimed at discovering what to explain in the interaction process between the human and AV. According to the taxonomy of automated driving systems defined by SAE International [13], the role of automated driving systems (ADS) range from driving assistance (SAE Level 0) to fully autonomous driving (SAE Level 5). The AV's explanations becomes increasingly indispensable in ADS above SAE Level 3 (conditionally automated driving, CAD), especially in stages of human-vehicle shared control. Thus, it is reasonable to look into the shared control process where human drivers still need to interact with AV. Addressing aspects to be explained is an important step to achieve effective human-AV cooperation.

Typically, an automated driving system follows the perception, planning and control paradigm [21]. Receiving and fusing data from sensors (e.g. cameras, LiDAR, radars), the perception module can generate an understanding of the environment with mass information including object detection, semantic segments and multiple objects tracking, etc. [32]. These inputs were then sent to the planning module which makes decisions by calculating risks, planning behaviors and providing a motion trajectory [21]. Then the vehicle control was achieved by the instructions from the planning system outputs within the operational design domain (ODD). Before fully autonomous driving was launched, human drivers still have some responsibility for being part in the control loop. Meanwhile, human capabilities of perception, cognition and decision-making can also facilitate the shared control process.

Similar to a robot, AV is also an autonomous system that can act independently in a dynamic environment, making its own decisions in uncertain circumstances. To depict the key elements of transparency in human-robot interaction (HRI), Lyons [17] proposed a model consisting of both robot-to-human and human-to-robot transparency. Several sub-models were presented to cover different factors, i.e., intentional model, task model, analytical model, environment model, teamwork model and human state model. Therefore, we derived a conceptual framework of three models to illustrated how the models of explainability factors fitting in the shared control diagram based on the Lyons' HRI transparency model (see Fig. 1).

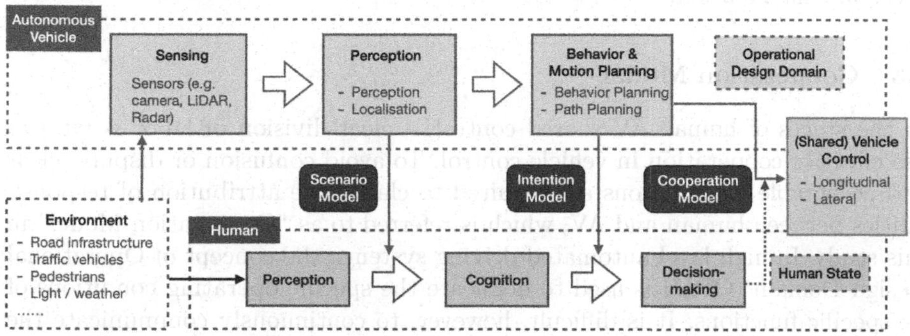

Fig. 1. A conceptual framework of human-autonomous vehicle interaction explainability models.

3.1 Scenario Model

Enhanced by multiple external and internal sensors, the AV has much more powerful capabilities of sensing and understanding the situation than human drivers. The outputs of perception system should not only be sent to the planning system, but also to the human's cognitive process in proper ways. Representations of dynamic environment elements are crucial aspects, including road infrastructures, traffic participants, as well as light and weather conditions, etc. And on top of this, actions and events occurred in the environment should also be communicated to human drivers to maintain the first two levels of situation awareness (perception and comprehension) [6]. Beyond the environment model, this model is referred to as a "Scenario Model" since it includes dynamic environment aspects as well as their temporal evolution that need to be explained [27]. Moreover, the goals of tasks performed by the ego AV are also within the scope of scenario model.

3.2 Intention Model

Autonomous vehicles will perform behavior and motion planning on the basis of the task goals and the awareness of situation. Clearly conveying the outputs of decision-making allows the human drivers to be aware of the AV's intention, which benefits the third level of situation awareness (projection). However, the underlying mechanisms of decision-making can be obscure due to the complexity and uncertainty existing in the situation. Lacking in explanations of decision-making can lead to miscalibrated trust in human drivers, causing undesirable or even fatal consequences [4]. Thus, the "Intention Model" consists of both "what" and "why" aspects regarding AV's decision-making, and explaining why the decision was made to human would be a rather challenging but essential issue. This model aims at assisting human drivers to keep an appropriate trust towards the AV, and supporting drivers to stay in the control loop and conduct necessary intervention.

3.3 Cooperation Model

In the stages of human-AV shared control, a clear division of labor is vital to the effective cooperation in vehicle control. To avoid confusion or dispute, clear and acceptable explanations are required to clarify the attribution of responsibilities between human and AV, which is referred to as "Cooperation Model" in this study. In high level automated driving systems, the concept of Operational Design Domain (ODD) is used to delineate the specific operating conditions of its specific functions. It is difficult, however, to continuously communicate the capability boundaries, applicable conditions and error possibilities of system to human in dynamic and complex situations. Moreover, the human states (e.g., emotional, cognitive and physical states) are also influencing factors to consider when involving human into the control loop [17]. This model is to facilitate the human-AV shared control on the execution level.

4 How to Explain: The SQX-canvas

4.1 Methodology

Based on the prior framework, we further envisioned how to excavate users' demand for explanations in certain scenarios, as well as how to communicate these explanations through HMI design concepts. A toolkit, named SQX-canvas, was developed to identify requirements of explanations in the AV context (see

Fig. 2). Inspired by the three models in human-AV interaction, the SQX-canvas is divided into three sections, i.e., Scenario, Question, and eXplanation. This toolkit actually works as a guide map for researchers and designers to follow the process and get output step by step with users involving in the loop. Next, how to operate each part is described separately.

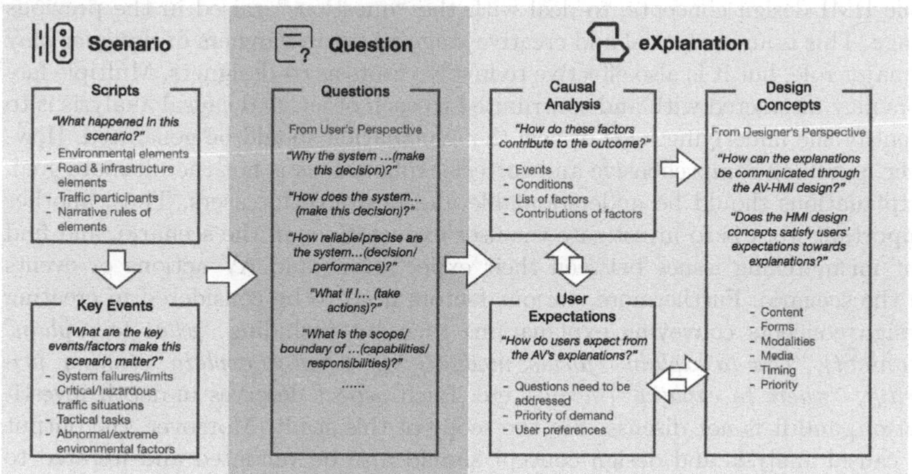

Fig. 2. Scenario-Question-eXplanation (SQX) canvas.

Scenario. This method begins with gaining an awareness of the scenario in which the AV is located, much similar to the "Scenario Model" of the previous framework. Environment elements and dynamic participants are like scenes and actors in a theater, but more importantly, actions and events link these scenes into a scenario [12]. Therefore, a script of the scenario should be built to illustrate *"what happened in this scenario"*. Then key events, actions or tasks need to be extracted from the script, such as system limits or failures and critical traffic situations. These core elements make this scenario worth investigating, and work as input materials for the next stage.

Question. The second stage is a core step to discover factors affecting users' experience by encouraging them to ask questions. The script provided in the first stage produce a sense of presence to users. They can refer to some given question patterns, and ask specific questions on factors making them confused, curious or uncomfortable. A question bank with several categories was adapted from a previous study on human-centered XAI [16]. Sample question categories include *"Why..."*, *"How..."*, *"What if..."*, *"How reliable..."*, which are relevant to AV's sensing and perception, decision-making process and the human-AV shared control. These questions also connect the technical XAI approaches with the user demand for explanations in certain scenarios. Questions produced in this stage can be further categorized by researchers and be sent to the next stage for analysis.

Explanation. The third stage aims at generating explanations, or even explainable HMI design concepts, to deal with the "questions" raised in the previous stage. This is an analytical and creative stage where researchers or designer play a major role, but it is also effective to involve users as co-designers. Multiple factors may interacted with and contributed to each other, and causal analysis is to identify the underlying logic of how the explanation should be generated. However, pursuing comprehensive and correct explanations is not the ultimate goal. Explanations should be understandable and desirable for users. Thus, another important work is to investigate the user expectations in the scenario, and find out mismatching issues between their expectations and AV actions or events in the scenario. Furthermore, various factors need to be considered in creating design concepts conveying explanations to users, including *"what to explain" (content), "how to explain" (forms, modalities), "when to explain" (timing, priority), "where to explain" (media)*, etc. Each aspect deserves in-depth investigation, and it is not discussed in the scope of this study. Moreover, the output of causal analysis and design concept should also be validated and iterated to better meet the user expectations.

4.2 Practice

To make an initial validation of the SQX-canvas, we conducted a co-design workshop involving both users and designers (see Fig. 3). The goal of this workshop is to generating explanations towards given AV scenarios following the "Scenario, Question and eXplanation" structure.

Participants. Since this workshop focused on validating the effectiveness of the method, we invited participants with some experience of interaction design or user experience. Totally 13 participants were recruited from academia or industry, and they were divided into four groups. Five PhD or master students in our lab worked as facilitators, with one in each group and one as a chief coordinator.

Materials. Key materials include the *SQX-canvas* and *AV scenario video clips.* The SQX-canvas shown in Fig. 2 was printed on a large worksheet in Chinese version, guiding the participants of each group through the process. Paper, postits, marker pens as well as cardboard, pipes, knives were prepared for simple prototypes. Outputs and insights can also be recorded on the worksheets.

AV Scenario Video Clips. To assist participants framing a real and concrete scenario for explanations, four video clips of AV scenarios were presented. These

Fig. 3. Workshops with the SQX-canvas toolkit. Left: Video of AV critical situation was projected on the screen. Right: The SQX-canvas worked as a guidance for the co-design workshop.

video clips were collected from the Internet, and they were recorded when a real car drove in the highway or urban road with automated driving system activated. Figure 4 described the four scenarios with video snapshot and scenario illustration in details.

Procedure. This workshop generally followed the Scenario, Question and eXplanation structure. After all participants were assigning into groups, they were presented the four video clips and required to choose one scenario as their topic. First they reconstructed the script of the scenario and extracted core events that matter. Next, they were instructed to switch their roles to users and ask questions about the scenario. Questions can be safety-critical or experience-related, and they were categorized with the assistance of facilitators. Then they were guided to analyze the relationships between factors indicated in their questions, and built their mental models towards the scenario. Their expectations on explanations provided by AV in the scenario were also expressed as drivers. Switching back to roles of designer, they envisioned how to explain the scenario to answer the questions they raised as "users". At last, they were encouraged to propose some design concepts to convey a certain explanation. Outputs of each step were recorded via photos, notes and sound recordings.

5 Summary and Discussion

5.1 Findings from the Workshop

Qualitative findings are the major outputs of this study due to its initial validation nature. First, the insights from the co-design workshop were summarized as follows.

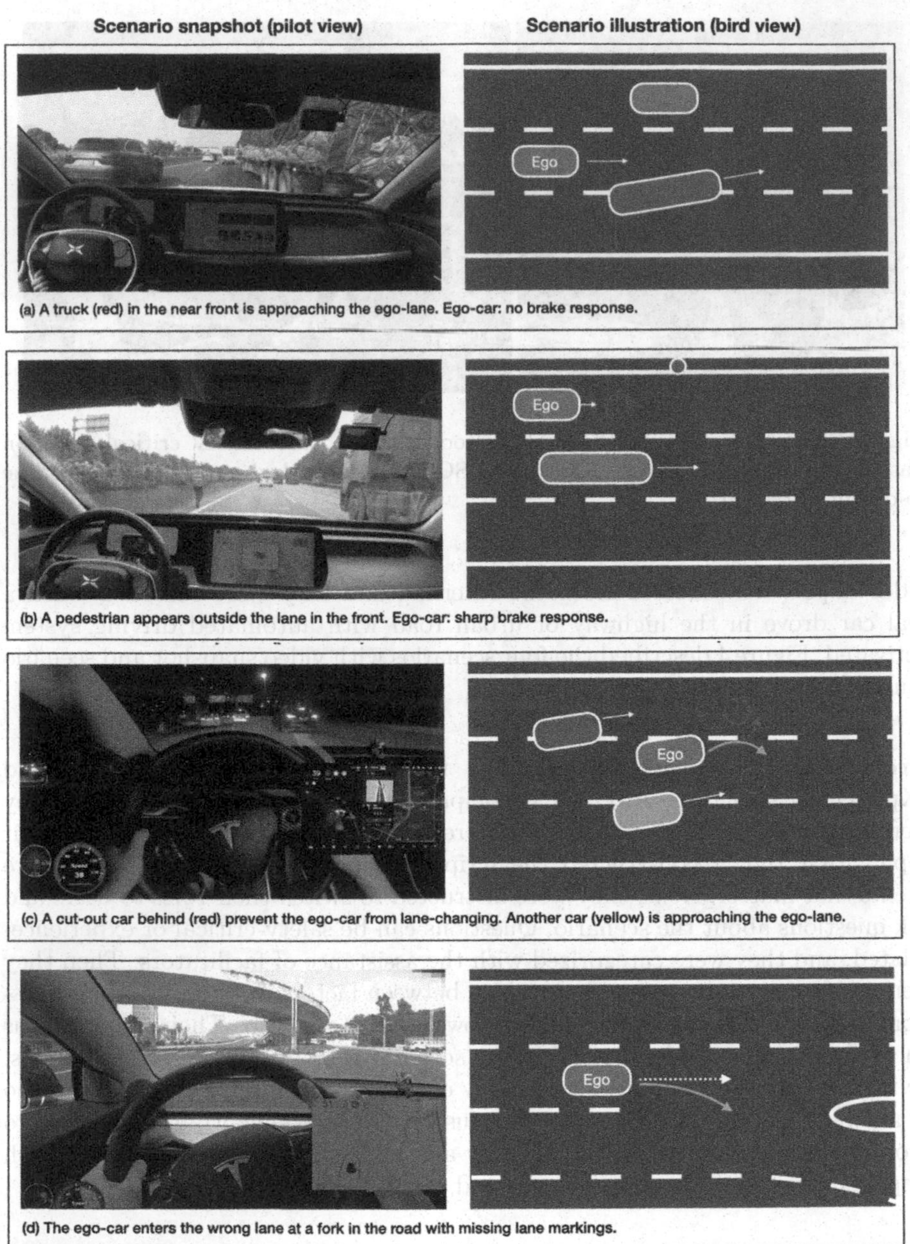

Fig. 4. Scenarios used in the workshop. Left: Video snapshots of scenarios. Right: Scenario illustration.

Scenario (a). The key focus of participants in this scenario is that why the AD system failed to detect the truck approaching the ego-lane, which greatly deviated from their expectations. Two possible explanation plans were proposed.

One is that the AD system should proactively explain its understanding of the scenario after driver's emergent brake, and ask the driver to input their considerations efficiently. Another is that given the sensing capabilities are still limited, potential risks in the surroundings need to be highlighted in forms more affordable for human monitors, such as AR-HUD.

Scenario (b). Different from the former scenario, participants in this group thought the AV's action was in line with expectations basically. However, there was also a space for explanations to mitigate the discomfort due to the emergent brake. This type of explanation is conciliatory and experience-related, which can be conveyed via soft voice from the VPA.

Scenario (c). This scenario was regarded as rather complex, and the core issue was considered to lie in the cooperation between AV and human. Excellent sensing capabilities of AD system were displayed in this scenario, but participants thought its lane-changing strategy was too conservative. A possible explanation plan is that the AV should present its lane-changing decision with an understanding of the scenario in advance, and wait for the driver's permission.

Scenario (d). Participants attributed the avoidable hazardous delegation to the misunderstanding caused by ambiguous lane-keeping decision. They argued that the path planning should be in line with the navigation goal, and the AV should explain its intention when conflicts may occur between task goals and dynamic motion planning.

5.2 The Value and Limitations of the Method

Through the practice in the workshop, this method showed its value on guiding works on how to make the AV more explainable to human, as well as limitations need to be further improved. In terms of value, this method, including both the framework and the SQX-canvas, is an effective tool for researchers or designers to organize their thoughts and work on envisioning explanations in human-autonomous vehicle interaction. It has a special advantage when users were involved in the process, collecting their feedbacks and excavating their demand for explanations, especially in early stages. Scenario-based and question-driven are two key features of this method. Scenario-based is beneficial for both researchers and respondents to build a in-depth understanding of a specific scenario, and they can express their thoughts more smoothly with a sense of presence. Question-driven makes the process more structural and actionable to produce concrete outputs step by step.

However, the workshop conducted in this study cannot provide the participants with a thorough and in-depth experience given the time and cost constraints. Although insightful opinions and findings were produced in this workshop, outputs were too rough in terms of design concepts of explanations. The switch of roles during the workshop was also challenging for participants. Actually, more work is required to sort and summarize the outputs by professionals after each stage, ensuring inputs to the next stage with good quality. Thus, the ideal execution of the method should be three or even more workshops separately with different kinds of participants involved.

Regarding the video materials used in this study, the automated driving system still showed great limitations in capabilities. This is also the fact with most AD system equipped in existing vehicles at present. Participants expressed great concern towards the system boundaries, leading to a negative attitude towards the cooperation with the AD system. Moreover, their demands for the explanations on decision-making mechanism appeared to be strong, but their requirements varied among scenarios with different complexity and criticality. Most participants agreed that the forms and content of communicating explanation matter in the cooperation between human and AV.

6 Conclusion

The goal of this study is to address the emerging issue that how to improve explainability in human-autonomous vehicle interaction. A conceptual framework of factors affecting the explanability was derived on the basis of human-AV shared control process, including the scenario, intention and cooperation model. In terms of how to explain in human-AV interaction, a scenario-based and question-driven method (i.e., the SQX-canvas) was proposed to involve both the roles of researchers and users. Then we organized a co-design workshop following the process: depicting the scenarios, asking specific questions and generating explanations through analysis. This workshop initially validated the effectiveness of this method on discovering users' demands of explanations in certain scenarios, while more in-depth analytical techniques were required to assist participants envisioning design concepts with high quality. This work contributes insights into the design for explainability in the AV context, and sheds light on the future HMI research empowered by XAI.

References

1. Adadi, A., Berrada, M.: Peeking inside the black-box: a survey on explainable artificial intelligence (XAI). IEEE Access **6**, 52138–52160 (2018)
2. Arya, V., et al.: One explanation does not fit all: a toolkit and taxonomy of AI explainability techniques. arXiv preprint arXiv:1909.03012 (2019)
3. Atakishiyev, S., Salameh, M., Yao, H., Goebel, R.: Explainable artificial intelligence for autonomous driving: a comprehensive overview and field guide for future research directions. arXiv preprint arXiv:2112.11561 (2021)
4. Banks, V.A., Plant, K.L., Stanton, N.A.: Driver error or designer error: using the Perceptual Cycle Model to explore the circumstances surrounding the fatal Tesla crash on 7th May 2016. Saf. Sci. **108**, 278–285 (2018). https://doi.org/10.1016/j.ssci.2017.12.023. https://www.sciencedirect.com/science/article/pii/S0925753517314212

5. Carsten, O., Martens, M.H.: How can humans understand their automated cars? HMI principles, problems and solutions. Cognit. Technol. Work **21**(1), 3–20 (2019). https://doi.org/10.1007/s10111-018-0484-0
6. De Winter, J.C., Happee, R., Martens, M.H., Stanton, N.A.: Effects of adaptive cruise control and highly automated driving on workload and situation awareness: a review of the empirical evidence. Transport. Res. F: Traffic Psychol. Behav. **27**, 196–217 (2014)
7. Debernard, S., Chauvin, C., Pokam, R., Langlois, S.: Designing human-machine interface for autonomous vehicles. IFAC-PapersOnLine **49**(19), 609–614 (2016)
8. Du, M., Liu, N., Hu, X.: Techniques for interpretable machine learning. Commun. ACM **63**(1), 68–77 (2019)
9. Du, N., et al.: Look who's talking now: implications of AV'S explanations on driver's trust, AV preference, anxiety and mental workload. Transp. Res. Part C: Emerg. Technol. **104**, 428–442 (2019)
10. Eiband, M., Schneider, H., Bilandzic, M., Fazekas-Con, J., Haug, M., Hussmann, H.: Bringing transparency design into practice. In: 23rd International Conference on Intelligent User Interfaces, pp. 211–223 (2018)
11. Eriksson, A., Petermeijer, S.M., Zimmermann, M., De Winter, J.C., Bengler, K.J., Stanton, N.A.: Rolling out the red (and green) carpet: supporting driver decision making in automation-to-manual transitions. IEEE Trans. Human-Mach. Syst. **49**(1), 20–31 (2018)
12. Geyer, S., et al.: Concept and development of a unified ontology for generating test and use-case catalogues for assisted and automated vehicle guidance. IET Intel. Transp. Syst. **8**(3), 183–189 (2014)
13. SAE International: J3016C: Taxonomy and Definitions for Terms Related to Driving Automation Systems for On-Road Motor Vehicles - SAE International (2021). https://www.sae.org/standards/content/j3016202104/
14. Kircher, K., Larsson, A., Hultgren, J.A.: Tactical driving behavior with different levels of automation. IEEE Trans. Intell. Transp. Syst. **15**(1), 158–167 (2014). https://doi.org/10.1109/TITS.2013.2277725. Conference Name: IEEE Transactions on Intelligent Transportation Systems
15. Koo, J., Kwac, J., Ju, W., Steinert, M., Leifer, L., Nass, C.: Why did my car just do that? Explaining semi-autonomous driving actions to improve driver understanding, trust, and performance. Int. J. Interact. Design Manuf. (IJIDeM) **9**(4), 269–275 (2015)
16. Liao, Q.V., Gruen, D., Miller, S.: Questioning the AI: informing design practices for explainable AI user experiences. In: Proceedings of the 2020 CHI Conference on Human Factors in Computing Systems, pp. 1–15 (2020)
17. Lyons, J.B.: Being transparent about transparency: a model for human-robot interaction. In: 2013 AAAI Spring Symposium Series (2013)
18. Merat, N., et al.: The "out-of-the-loop" concept in automated driving: proposed definition, measures and implications. Cogn. Technol. Work **21**(1), 87–98 (2019). https://doi.org/10.1007/s10111-018-0525-8
19. Miller, T.: Explanation in artificial intelligence: insights from the social sciences. Artif. Intell. **267**, 1–38 (2019)
20. Naujoks, F., Wiedemann, K., Schömig, N., Hergeth, S., Keinath, A.: Towards guidelines and verification methods for automated vehicle HMIS. Transport. Res. F: Traffic Psychol. Behav. **60**, 121–136 (2019)
21. Omeiza, D., Webb, H., Jirotka, M., Kunze, L.: Explanations in autonomous driving: a survey. IEEE Trans. Intell. Transp. Syst. (2021)

22. Pokam, R., Debernard, S., Chauvin, C., Langlois, S.: Principles of transparency for autonomous vehicles: first results of an experiment with an augmented reality human-machine interface. Cogn. Technol. Work **21**(4), 643–656 (2019). https://doi.org/10.1007/s10111-019-00552-9
23. Rezvani, T., Driggs-Campbell, K., Bajcsy, R.: Optimizing interaction between humans and autonomy via information constraints on interface design. In: 2017 IEEE 20th International Conference on Intelligent Transportation Systems (ITSC), pp. 1–6 (2017). https://doi.org/10.1109/ITSC.2017.8317686. iSSN: 2153-0017
24. Schneider, T., Hois, J., Rosenstein, A., Ghellal, S., Theofanou-Fülbier, D., Gerlicher, A.R.: Explain yourself! transparency for positive UX in autonomous driving. In: Proceedings of the 2021 CIII Conference on Human Factors in Computing Systems, pp. 1–12 (2021)
25. Schömig, N., et al.: Checklist for expert evaluation of HMIS of automated vehicles-discussions on its value and adaptions of the method within an expert workshop. Information **11**(4), 233 (2020)
26. Shen, Y., et al.: To explain or not to explain: a study on the necessity of explanations for autonomous vehicles. arXiv preprint arXiv:2006.11684 (2020)
27. Ulbrich, S., Menzel, T., Reschka, A., Schuldt, F., Maurer, M.: Defining and substantiating the terms scene, situation, and scenario for automated driving. In: 2015 IEEE 18th International Conference on Intelligent Transportation Systems, pp. 982–988. IEEE (2015)
28. Wang, D., Yang, Q., Abdul, A., Lim, B.Y.: Designing theory-driven user-centric explainable AI. In: Proceedings of the 2019 CHI Conference on Human Factors in Computing Systems, pp. 1–15 (2019)
29. Wiegand, G., Schmidmaier, M., Weber, T., Liu, Y., Hussmann, H.: I drive-you trust: explaining driving behavior of autonomous cars. In: Extended Abstracts of the 2019 CHI Conference on Human Factors in Computing Systems, pp. 1–6 (2019)
30. Wolf, C.T.: Explainability scenarios: towards scenario-based XAI design. In: Proceedings of the 24th International Conference on Intelligent User Interfaces, pp. 252–257 (2019)
31. Yan, F., Karaosmanoglu, S., Demir, A., Baumann, M.: Spatial visualization of sensor information for automated vehicles. In: Proceedings of the 11th International Conference on Automotive User Interfaces and Interactive Vehicular Applications: Adjunct Proceedings, pp. 265–270 (2019)
32. Yeong, D.J., Velasco-Hernandez, G., Barry, J., Walsh, J., et al.: Sensor and sensor fusion technology in autonomous vehicles: a review. Sensors **21**(6), 2140 (2021)

Human-Centered Design of Automotive Systems

Investigate the In-Vehicle Healthcare System Design Opportunities: Findings from a Co-design Study

Jiming Bai[1], Yaorun Zhang[1], Xu Sun[1,2](✉), Siyuan Zhou[1], Ruiheng Lan[1], and Xiaowu Jiang[3]

[1] Faculty of Science and Engineering, University of Nottingham Ningbo China, 199 Taikang East Road, Ningbo 315100, China
{jiming.bai,yaorun.zhang,xu.sun,siyuan.zhou, ruiheng.lan}@nottingham.edu.cn

[2] Nottingham Ningbo China Beacons of Excellence Research and Innovation Institute, 211 Xingguang Road, Ningbo 315100, China

[3] Ningbo Weizhi Digital Information Technology Co., Ltd., Building E, 655 Xueshi Road, Ningbo 315194, China
jxw@weizhiai.cn

Abstract. Many people spend a long time in vehicles in their daily commute, and they want their health condition to be taken care of during the journey. In line with this need, the advancement of smart technologies brings possibilities for ubiquitous healthcare. This work intends to explore users' expectations regarding an in-vehicle healthcare system (IVHS) and guide the development of relevant technologies. Four co-design workshops were organized with sixteen participants with diverse professional backgrounds. Over two hundred ideas were generated and categorized into seven groups, indicating seven promising perspectives in developing an IVHS. Furthermore, a conceptual framework was proposed based on the ideas collected from the workshops. The framework organized the expected functions of an IVHS into three groups, namely data collection, communication, and actuation. In combination with the literature review about relevant technologies, the framework pointed out some future research directions.

Keywords: Healthcare · Smart vehicle · Co-design

1 Introduction

1.1 Background

Healthcare is one of the keywords that have drawn worldwide attention in the era of the COVID-19 pandemic, which has also impacted the automotive industry. The idea of ubiquitous healthcare has grown in people's minds, and people want their health conditions to be taken care of all the time. People spend a long time in vehicles in daily commute, and the cockpit has been viewed as the third space of life besides home and

H. Krömker (Ed.): HCII 2022, LNCS 13335, pp. 123–133, 2022.
https://doi.org/10.1007/978-3-031-04987-3_8

workplace. Taking care of passengers' and drivers' wellbeing is a significant theme that deserves to be explored in depth. The advancement of technologies, such as the 5G communication platform [1], multifunctional sensors, artificial intelligence, and autonomous driving, have not only brought tremendous changes to the traditional car manufacturers but opened the possibility of in-vehicle healthcare systems (IVHSs).

In line with the increase of diversified demands on vehicle cockpit design, some leading automotive companies have already developed in-vehicle healthcare features. For example, Mercedes introduced a concept named ENERGIZING, which integrates a smartwatch to collect drivers' health data and then adapts the seat massage and ambient lights accordingly [2]. Besides, concepts such as Vehicle-to-Healthcare Everything (V2HX) communications [3], RFID-based smart automatic vehicle management systems [4] and elderly healthcare services in-vehicle [5] were continuously proposed by scholars from various perspectives to enhance the function of in-vehicle healthcare support strategy. However, it is not clear what the IVHS will be like in the future.

1.2 Relevant Studies

Vulnerable vehicle users who have health issues need special care during their journeys, especially when they drive. Researchers strived to mitigate the risks by monitoring the onset of attacks. Examples include the health monitoring systems developed for people with diabetes [6], who may suffer from hypoglycemia, obstructive sleep apnea and stroke. The detection and prevention of such symptoms require run-time monitoring of the person's physiological signals and environmental parameters, such as interstitial glucose, blood pressure, heart rate and rhythm, body temperature, respiration rate, and in-vehicle circulating oxygen levels [6, 7].

Apart from preventing health issues, the responses to medical emergencies in vehicles are also a significant healthcare-related concern. Delayed or improper first aid may deteriorate the victim's health condition or even result in death. Joseph and colleagues argued that it is a promising direction to install the first-aid robot in vehicles, though this idea faces challenges from both technological and legislative perspectives [8].

Tamizharasi et al. went a step further to involve hospitals and other healthcare infrastructures in their solution. Centered around the concept of "Telemedicine," the authors discussed challenges regarding the communication between the ego vehicle, other vehicles, and healthcare-related infrastructures [9]. *Telemedicine* refers to the healthcare services provided from a distance by utilizing information technologies and is often adopted in the diagnosis and management of chronic diseases such as asthma and diabetes [10]. Tamizharasi et al. proposed a multi-layer design architecture to take care of people with heart disease in vehicles, considering user interaction, data acquisition, data pre-processing, data transmission, data storage, and data security [9].

In addition to physical diseases, mental wellbeing also raised attention from various research. It was found that a guided slow breathing practice can reduce drivers' physiological stress [11]. Then, subtle interventions such as scents, assistants, music, ambient light, and the tone of voice can also be leveraged to relax drivers in a non-intrusive manner [12]. However, the effectiveness of these interventions may vary from person to person. Braun et al. developed a voice guide system personalized to drivers' personalities and tested in real driving. The result showed that friendly tone of voice assist is more effective for extroverted people pleasant in terms of bringing in pleasures [13].

A unique issue of in-vehicle healthcare is carsickness. Numerous studies attempted to predict carsickness through the integrated analysis of physiological signals, body instability and vehicle motion. It was found that people's susceptibility to motion sickness is related to their heart rate variability (HRV) [14], Vestibular-Ocular Reflex (VOR) [15], postural sway [16], and triaxial acceleration and triaxial angular velocity of the vehicle [17]. Some scholars have proposed a single multivariate equation to represent the complex processes leading to motion sickness, and others attempt to develop a multi-parameter automated computer simulation-based tool for predicting motion sickness in driving occupants [18, 19]. In terms of carsickness alleviation and prevention, some proven effective measures include increasing the design area of windows to reduce sensory conflict during the ride [20], reducing vibration and altering the riding position to reduce the sensation of motion sickness through active suspension system design [21].

The studies mentioned above discussed the technological opportunities for passengers with specific healthcare needs. However, healthcare is a broad term, including but not limited to the care of certain diseases. The concept of health management has enjoyed popular support. *Health management* was defined as actions for optimizing the person's health conditions, such as keeping track of their health status, avoiding risk factors, and keeping healthy habits [22]. Healthy people also have needs relevant to in-vehicle healthcare, and they are the majority among vehicle users. While researchers focus on specific issues, there is a lack of comprehensive understanding of links between users' expectations toward IVHSs and emerging technologies.

1.3 Objectives

This study aims to conduct design research to elicit user needs and explore the potential for healthcare solutions to be integrated into personal vehicles, bridging the gap between technology and its potential users of IVHSs.

2 Methodology

The principal method used in this qualitative study is co-design [23], in which stakeholders share the knowledge and experience with each other to produce innovative design ideas through creative collaboration. We organized four sessions of co-design activity with a total number of 16 participants (6 female, 10 male). Five of the participants were product experts from local automotive industries, mixed with normal car users. In order to understand different users' needs and create solutions from diverse perspectives, the other participants varied in age groups (aged from 20 to 45) and occupations (Engineers, designers, nurses, doctors, teachers, a marketing officer, and a sailor).

The sessions were organized by an experienced creative facilitator and went through four stages, namely purge, diverge, categorize, and evaluate. To start with, the facilitator briefly introduced the concept of intelligent cockpits and the goal of the workshop. The intelligent cockpit was described as equipped with advanced technologies, including various sensors, automated actuators, and wireless connections with other facilities. The participants were encouraged to generate ideas about how to take care of car users' health in an intelligent cockpit as more as possible. After the introduction, the participants were asked to write down their immediate ideas while speaking loudly to inspire others. After they ran out of their ideas, the facilitator let them think of vehicle cockpits that may harm their health and then develop ideas to reverse them. In this way, more novel ideas were generated.

In the next stage, participants were asked to categorize the generated ideas according to the concerns behind the ideas. For example, the idea of a bad air quality alarm and an in-vehicle air purifier are both concerning the in-vehicle air quality and thus go into the same category. In this stage, the participant had the opportunity to go through each other's ideas and achieve a mutual understanding. Moreover, while clarifying their concerns, many new ideas were generated. In the evaluation stage, each participant proposed a conceptual IVHS using no more than five ideas from the workshop and presented it to others. Lastly, a thematic analysis technique for qualitative data was employed to analyze the findings in this study.

3 Result

3.1 Data Arrangement

The participants came up with 207 ideas about a "healthy personal vehicle". Since ideas may repeat in these workshops, the total number of ideas could be reduced to 44 after merging similar ones. As for the categorization of ideas, since the categorizing names and standards were decided by participants (for letting them express their concerns), they varied in the four independent sessions. For ease of analysis, they were combined into 7 categories. The categories and ideas were organized in Table 1. The categories were ordered based on their frequency of being concerned in the evaluation stage (i.e., the number of the ideas in the category being selected by participants). The numbers in the bracket indicate the times an idea/category is selected.

Table 1. Results from co-design workshop

Categories	Expectations
Health emergency treatment (21)	• A first-aid robot that can perform basic treatments automatically (7) • A local haul network on which vehicles and passengers can publish emergencies and ask for help (6) • An automatic alarm that calls the hospital in emergent conditions (5) • Intuitive first-aid tools such as a cardiac pacemaker (2) • AR glasses that help doctors provide remote guidance • A seat that can be ejected out the car to rescue passengers (1)
Hygienic cabin (16)	• Automatic vacuum cleaner (6) • Automatic switch between inner and outer air circulation (4) • In-vehicle planting system (4) • Air quality detector and alarm (2) • A bacteria scanner that can evaluate the in-vehicle cleanliness (2) • In-vehicle air purifier (2) • Automatic disinfectant spray robot • Regular ultraviolet disinfection in the car • Oxygen generator that regulates air component automatically
Prevention of health risks (14)	• Runtime collection of users' physiological data to detect the onset of disease symptoms through various sensors (8) • Daily physical assessment and health advice (6) • Synthesize data from other healthcare devices and hospitals • Detect environmental risk factors such as allergens
Mental well-being (11)	• Make the vehicle a "vent chamber", (yell out/punchbag) (3) • Virtual psychologist (3) • Anthropomorphic companion avatar (2) • Switch to stress-relieving mode, a soothing environment (1) • Meditation guide (1) • In-vehicle games that relieve stress and depression • Social activities with other drivers nearby (1)
Comfortable sensory experience (7)	• Give massage through car seats to relax the muscle (3) • Automatically control environmental parameters balancing everyone's preference, humidity, temperature, and lighting brightness (3) • Positional adjustable in-vehicle screen (1) • Noise filtration • Alert for adjusting in-proper sitting postures • Vibration reduction seat • Alert for relaxation when detects excessive sitting • Screen with self-adapting brightness and contrast
In-vehicle rehabilitate activities (5)	• In-vehicle exercise equipment (2) • Monitoring sleep quality and sleep cycles (1) • Create a separate space for sleep through a wall of air (1) • Recommend restaurants and add to map navigation (1) • Adjust window filtration rate according to user activities • Medicine intake reminder • Medicine storage
Car sickness prevention and alleviation (3)	• Predict car sickness, and prevent • Use music/fragrance to alleviate carsickness • Car-sickness-free display (3)

3.2 Data Specification

The issue that received the most concern is the treatment of health emergencies, especially in life-threatening cases. Relevant ideas include various methods of providing first aid and a fast pass to hospitals. It is worth mentioning that the participants expressed their concern not only for car users but also for people nearby the vehicle. On the one hand, passengers and other vehicles will be informed about the emergency in the ego vehicle and make way for the vehicle or provide professional support. On the other hand, when health emergencies occur nearby, the ego vehicle would serve as a temporary ambulance.

The second-largest concern was the in-vehicle hygiene, including the hygienic issues in operation areas and the in-vehicle air quality. Participants expressed their expectation for frequent and automatic cleaning, freshening and disinfection, especially when it comes to the areas of frequent contact. Moreover, being informed about the hygiene condition in the vehicle was a significant demand as well.

Another major expectation from the participant was to prevent unknown health risks. There are vulnerable groups at risk and need special care to prevent the crisis from happening. Although our participants were not from those groups, they came up with ideas based on their experiences with their family members and friends. The ideas mainly focused on monitoring users' physiological indicators such as blood pressure and respiratory rate. In addition, the detection of environmental risk factors, such as allergens in the air, was also wanted. Apart from the vulnerable groups, healthy participants also wanted to get informed about their health condition. A daily physical check and health advice based on the check was highly expected.

Subsequently, in-vehicle care for mental health also received much attention. Stressfulness and loneliness were two of the most concerning issues. According to a participant, cars are where people may both accumulate stress and alleviate their stress. The original quote was: "I feel stressed when I drive to my workplace or to meet my clients. Even on my way back home, I feel stressed in thinking of my unfinished tasks and familial responsibilities. I may stay in my car and calm myself down before getting out." Furthermore, a participant commented that since vehicles are enclosed spaces, they can prevent disturbances and thus become proper places for psychological counseling and mindfulness activities. Besides, other ideas concerning coping with mental stress included detecting users' increased stress levels and applying various comforting interventions. As for the loneliness issue, vehicles were expected to play an accompanying role through an avatar. Besides, vehicles can also provide a platform for passengers in the ego vehicle to socialize with other vehicle users.

Next to that, participants related healthcare to comfortableness. Participants' concerns for comfortableness included the vibration, noises, odor, and lighting conditions. The personalized setting of these environmental parameters was favored. In addition, muscle fatigue caused by excessive sitting raised awareness among participants. Sitting posture adjustment and muscle relaxation were typical directions of solutions. Next, since screens are widely used in current cars, visual fatigue caused by excessive screen viewing was also concerned. Screen brightness, contrast and position were believed to affect the level of visual fatigue.

There are rehabilitate activities that benefit people's health. The ones mentioned in the workshops included exercise, proper rest, healthy diet and medicine intake. Participants expressed their expectations for making cars a better place for these activities. The participant who is doing a diet wished that the vehicle could help them make a diet plan and recommend restaurants on the way. Besides, a participant drove two hours every day and suffered from insufficient sleep. He wishes he could sleep during the journey when autonomous driving comes true. Similarly, several participants wanted to make use of the time on cars to exercise.

The last category is the issue of carsickness. Participants proposed several methods for preventing and alleviating carsickness based on their intuition, such as music and fragrance. Besides, carsickness induced by looking at screens attracted relatively more attention. Since many of them have the habit of using smartphones on cars, A carsickness-free display method was highly demanded.

3.3 Conceptual Framework of the In-Vehicle Health System in the Future

Based on the ideas generated in the co-design workshops, a conceptual framework of the IVHS was proposed (see Fig. 1). The framework described necessary components for realizing the generated ideas, including the needed information, actuators that perform the caring functions, and the communication between the ego vehicle, nearby traffic participants, devices, and other healthcare systems. The framework does not explain technical details. Instead, it pointed out what is needed for constructing the next generation of an IVHS.

Run time collection of data is essential for many of the proposed features. First, the system was expected to perform diagnosis and monitoring tasks. Then, some assistive features, such as body posture correction reminders, rely on run time detection of the users' dynamic status. Furthermore, the interventions need to be delivered at the right time and in the right way based on the recognition of the situation, known as Just-in-Time Adaptive Intervention (JITAI) [24].

The framework listed out required input information but did not indicate collection methods because there could be multiple ways of acquiring information. For example, the stress level could be assessed based on heart rate [25], or the combination of electrocardiogram (ECG) and electromyogram (EMG) [26]. Furthermore, not all the data is suitable to be collected in the in-vehicle context. Ju et al. concluded 15 types of health monitors suitable for use in vehicles [27]. They pointed out that unobtrusive in-vehicle sensors could support the monitoring of diseases relevant to heart, respiratory, epilepsy, psychological and cognitive disorders. However, the parameters related to blood, such as blood pressure and blood sugar, are not available. Compared to health status, the behavioral information and environmental information mentioned in the framework is relatively easy to acquire (E.g. see [28–30]).

Concerning the necessary communication mentioned in the framework, the concept of Vehicle to Everything (V2X) could be checked for reference. V2X includes the information exchange between the ego vehicle and other vehicles, pedestrians, infrastructures, and networks [31]. Communication technologies such as 5G network platform and cellular systems are evolving to support the versatile communication in V2X systems [32]. On this basis, Junaid et al. propose the concept of Vehicle to Healthcare Everything

(V2HX) to support vehicle-based healthcare services [3]. Security and privacy issues resulting from V2HX were seriously discussed because a person's health information is

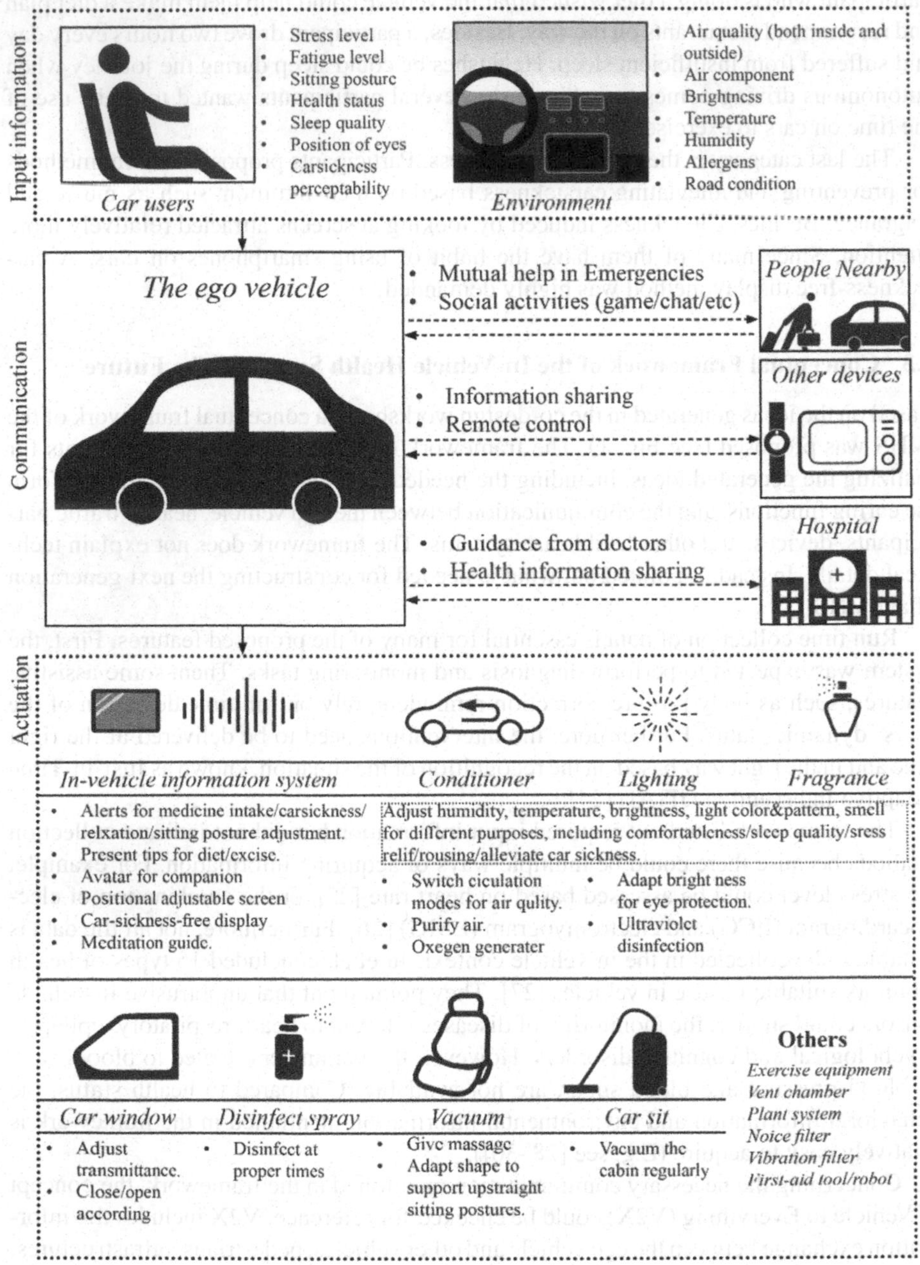

Fig. 1. A conceptual framework of an IVHS in the future.

sensitive, while healthcare information techniques are relatively vulnerable in cases of cyberattacks [3].

As for the actuation part of the framework, most actuators can apply their current functions and are automatically controlled according to the input information. However, some actuators do not exist in most personal vehicles, such as fragrances with adaptable odor, in-vehicle exercise equipment, intelligent first-aid tools, and automatic cleaning and disinfection devices. These indicate opportunities for product development.

4 Conclusion

The current qualitative research applied co-design methods to explore possible healthcare solutions in future personal vehicles. The ideas generated by end-users also reflected their concerns regarding in-vehicle healthcare. After organizing the data, we concluded seven categories of ideas, indicating seven major perspectives in developing IVHSs. However, the desirability of these perspectives is not the same. According to the evaluation in our study, the order of participants' demand from high to low was: (i) the treatment in health emergencies, (ii) in-vehicle hygiene, (iii) health risk prevention, (iv) care for mental wellness, (v) comfortable sensory experience, (vi) support for in-vehicle rehabilitate activities, (vii) prevention and alleviation of carsickness.

In order to collect diverse and comprehensive ideas, this study invited participants from different professional backgrounds, especially those with medical backgrounds and automotive industry backgrounds. Based on the ideas from the co-design workshop, we proposed a conceptual framework that contains all the features favored by the participants. This framework serves as a list of demands that pointed out promising research directions, such as a convenient monitor of blood parameters, the protection of privacy in healthcare information communications, and automatic first-aid device. The realization of these features requires engineers and designers to make further exploration.

5 Discussion

Most of the in-vehicle healthcare systems mentioned in the literature focused on preventing and treating health risks (e.g. [6–8]). However, it was found in this study that users also regarded hygiene, comfortableness and the support for healthy activities as significant factors that compose a healthy cockpit. Hygiene attracted the second most attention, only less than the treatment in health emergencies. This may be due to the particular concern about the spread of viruses and bacteria in the context of the current pandemic. Besides, many ideas for relieving stress and loneliness were put forward in the workshops, reflecting the need for caring for mental health in vehicles.

Some limitations of this study were well noted. First of all, although the involvement of experts and their knowledge ignited the participants' needs of their interaction with the intelligent cockpit, the presence of experts might have filtered the so-called "unrealistic fantasies" that could provide useful insights. Then, children and the elderly were not involved in this study for the ease of workshop organization. However, they may bring in novel ideas from their perspective. Moreover, since vehicles are complex systems, the trade-offs between technological constraints and costs need to be considered and balanced, which was not discussed in this study. Furthermore, it is anticipated that autonomous driving and shared vehicles will become common contexts of vehicle use. Although many of the healthcare solutions proposed in the current study are also applicable in these scenarios, a specialized exploration in these contexts is still needed in future studies.

References

1. Ullah, H., Nair, N.G., Moore, A., Nugent, C., Muschamp, P., Cuevas, M.: 5G communication: an overview of vehicle-to-everything, drones, and healthcare use-cases. IEEE Access **7**, 37251–37268 (2019)
2. ENERGIZING comfort control: Wellness while driving. https://media.daimler.com/marsMediaSite/ko/en/41880672. Accessed 05 Feb 2022
3. Chaudhry, J.A., Saleem, K., Alazab, M., Zeeshan, H.M.A., Al-Muhtadi, J., Rodrigues, J.J.: Data security through zero-knowledge proof and statistical fingerprinting in vehicle-to-healthcare everything (v2HX) communications. IEEE Trans. Intell. Transp. Syst. **22**(6), 3869–3879 (2021)
4. Pavithra, B., Suchitra, S., Subbulakshmi, P., Mercy Faustina, J.: RFID based smart automatic vehicle management system for healthcare applications. In: 2019 3rd International conference on Electronics, Communication and Aerospace Technology (ICECA), pp. 390–394. IEEE, Coimbatore, India (2019)
5. Park, S.J., Subramaniyam, M., Hong, S., Kim, D., Yu, J.: Conceptual design of the elderly healthcare services in-vehicle using IoT. SAE Technical Paper, 2017-01-1647, (2017)
6. Kerr, D., Olateju, T.: Driving with diabetes in the future: in-vehicle medical monitoring. J. Diabetes Sci. Technol. **4**(2), 464–469 (2010)
7. Dumitru, A.I., Mogan, G.L.: Aspects concerning drivers monitoring healthcare systems. Bulletin of the Transilvania university of Brasov. Eng. Sci. Ser. I **7**(1), 7 (2014)
8. Kurebwa, J.G., Mushiri, T.: Passenger car safety and emergency healthcare: a literature review. Procedia Manuf. **35**, 35–49 (2019)
9. Thirugnanam, T., Ghalib, M.R.: A new healthcare architecture using IoV technology for continuous health monitoring system. Heal. Technol. **10**(1), 289–302 (2019). https://doi.org/10.1007/s12553-019-00306-7
10. Mukhopadhyay, A.: QoS based telemedicine technologies for rural healthcare emergencies. In: 2017 IEEE Global Humanitarian Technology Conference (GHTC), pp. 1–7. IEEE, San Jose, CA, USA (2017)
11. Balters, S., Mauriello, M.L., Park, S.Y., Landay, J.A., Paredes, P.E.: Calm commute: guided slow breathing for daily stress management in drivers. Proc. ACM Interact. Mob. Wearable Ubiquitous Technol. **4**(1), 1–19 (2020)
12. Koch, K., et al.: When do drivers interact with in-vehicle well-being interventions? An exploratory analysis of a longitudinal study on public roads. Proc. ACM Interact. Mob. Wearable Ubiquitous Technol. **5**(1), 1–30 (2021)
13. Braun, M., Mainz, A., Chadowitz, R., Pfleging, B., Alt, F.: At your service: designing voice assistant personalities to improve automotive user interfaces. In: Proceedings of the 2019 CHI Conference on Human Factors in Computing Systems, pp. 1–11. Glasgow, Scotland, UK (2019)
14. Yokota, Y., Aoki, M., Mizuta, K., Ito, Y., Isu, N.: Motion sickness susceptibility associated with visually induced postural instability and cardiac autonomic responses in healthy subjects. Acta Otolaryngol. **125**(3), 280–285 (2005)

15. Bles, W., Bos, J.E., Kruit, H.: Motion sickness. Curr. Opin. Neurol. **13**(1), 19–25 (2000)
16. Smart, L.J., Jr., Stoffregen, T.A., Bardy, B.G.: Visually induced motion sickness predicted by postural instability. Hum. Factors **44**(3), 451–465 (2002)
17. Kamiji, N., Kurata, Y., Wada, T., Doi, S.I.: Modeling and validation of carsickness mechanism. In: SICE Annual Conference 2007, pp. 1138–1143. IEEE, Takamatsu, Japan (2007)
18. Bos, J.E., Bles, W.: Modelling motion sickness and subjective vertical mismatch detailed for vertical motions. Brain Res. Bull. **47**(5), 537–542 (1998)
19. Salter, S., Diels, C., Herriotts, P., Kanarachos, S., Thake, D.: Model to predict motion sickness within autonomous vehicles. Proc. Inst. Mech. Eng. Part D: J. Automob. Eng. **234**(5), 1330–1345 (2020)
20. Diels, C., Bos, J.E.: Self-driving carsickness. Appl. Ergon. **53**, 374–382 (2016)
21. DiZio, P., et al.: An active suspension system for mitigating motion sickness and enabling reading in a car. Aerosp. Med. Hum. Perform. **89**(9), 822–829 (2018)
22. Kobrinskii, B.A., Grigoriev, O.G., Molodchenkov, A.I., Smirnov, I.V., Blagosklonov, N.A.: Artificial intelligence technologies application for personal health management. IFAC-PapersOnLine **52**(25), 70–74 (2019)
23. Liu, J., Ma, D., Weimerskirch, A., Zhu, H.: A functional co-design towards safe and secure vehicle platooning. In: Proceedings of the 3rd ACM Workshop on Cyber-Physical System Security, pp. 81–90. Association for Computing Machinery, New York, United States (2017)
24. Nahum-Shani, I., et al.: Just-in-time adaptive interventions (JITAIs) in mobile health: key components and design principles for ongoing health behavior support. Ann. Behav. Med. **52**(6), 446–462 (2018)
25. Hakimi, N., Jodeiri, A., Mirbagheri, M., Setarehdan, S.K.: Proposing a convolutional neural network for stress assessment by means of derived heart rate from functional near infrared spectroscopy. Comput. Biol. Med. **121**, 103810 (2020)
26. Pourmohammadi, S., Maleki, A.: Continuous mental stress level assessment using electrocardiogram and electromyogram signals. Biomed. Signal Process. Control **68**, 102694 (2021)
27. Wang, J., Warnecke, J.M., Haghi, M., Deserno, T.M.: Unobtrusive health monitoring in private spaces: the smart vehicle. Sensors **20**(9), 2442 (2020)
28. Ran, X., Wang, C., Xiao, Y., Gao, X., Zhu, Z., Chen, B.: A portable sitting posture monitoring system based on a pressure sensor array and machine learning. Sens. Actuators A Phys **331**, 112900 (2021)
29. Chuang, M.C., Bala, R., Bernal, E.A., Paul, P., Burry, A.: Estimating gaze direction of vehicle drivers using a smartphone camera. In: Proceedings of the IEEE Conference on Computer Vision and Pattern Recognition Workshops, pp. 165–170. IEEE Computer Society (2014)
30. Lohani, D., Acharya, D.: Real time in-vehicle air quality monitoring using mobile sensing. In: 2016 IEEE Annual India Conference (INDICON), pp. 1–6. IEEE, Bangalore, India (2016)
31. Chen, S., et al.: Vehicle-to-everything (V2X) services supported by LTE-based systems and 5G. IEEE Commun. Stand. Mag. **1**(2), 70–76 (2017)
32. Ghosal, A., Conti, M.: Security issues and challenges in V2X: a survey. Comput. Netw. **169**, 107093 (2020)

User-Centered Development of a Route Planning App for Fragmented Automated Drives

Tobias Hecht(✉), Stefanie Weng, Alexander Drexl, and Klaus Bengler

Chair of Ergonomics, Department of Mechanical Engineering, Technical University of Munich, 85748 Garching, Germany
t.hecht@tum.de

Abstract. The introduction of SAE Level 3 and 4 will in the near future allow users to legally engage in a variety of non-driving related activities (NDRAs) during automated driving. However, automated driving functions will at first be available only on certain (predictable) segments of a drive, leading to fragmented journeys. To improve users' control over the route planning process and consequently best refine the acceptance and exploit the potential of NDRAs, the goal of this work was to develop a route planning software with focus on automation availability. Following a user-centered design process, different prototypes were iteratively designed and evaluated in small scale user studies. The final concept was implemented as an Android app; it featured individual travel profiles and the possibility of entering automated driving segments for certain time slots or durations. In a final study with 23 participants, usability, acceptance, and the fulfilment of user needs were evaluated. Participants executed six different tasks assumed to be representative for future use cases. Results show that the tasks were very well handled. User requirements were fulfilled to a high degree and usability ratings show a high mean SUS score of 81. Furthermore, a high intention to use became apparent.

Keywords: Automated driving · Route planning · User-Centered Development

1 Introduction

The introduction of SAE Level 3 (L3) and 4 (L4) automated driving functions will fundamentally change the usage of drive time in future automated vehicles (AVs): While in Level 2 (L2) and lower, the driver is still actively taking part in the driving task, users in L3 and L4 can legally engage in (visual-manual) non-driving related activities (NDRAs). The possibility of engaging in activities such as reading, playing games, watching videos, and working is perceived as a main benefit of automated driving [1]. Furthermore, it has the potential to positively influence the perceived value of travel time [2, 3] and the perceived usefulness of AVs [4]. The latter can – according to the Technology Acceptance Model [5] – be linked to intention to use and thus usage behavior

H. Krömker (Ed.): HCII 2022, LNCS 13335, pp. 134–150, 2022.
https://doi.org/10.1007/978-3-031-04987-3_9

(i.e., acceptance). Therefore, resulting user needs should be carefully addressed when designing driver-vehicle interaction for future AVs.

At first, automated driving functions will be available only on certain segments of a given journey, e.g., on highways or less complex city infrastructure [6]. This will cause planned transitions to and from manual driving at predictable points. Besides unplanned emergency take-overs, which are likely to occur less frequently [7], these transitions lead to fragmented drives in terms of automated driving. Since interruptions of NDRAs through transitions can lead to negative effects such as increased workload [8], several studies have investigated so-called predictive human-machine interface (HMI) designs to inform users about the length of current (and upcoming) segments of automated driving. Such HMI elements can positively influence users' acceptance [9], usability ratings [7, 9], and subjective workload levels [9], as well as take-over performance [10]. Furthermore, they can help build a correct mental model through increased system understanding [11].

Although huge effort has been undertaken to develop suitable internal and external HMI concepts for AVs (see [12] for an overview), the authors are not aware of any approach aiming at increasing users' control over the route planning process in terms of automated driving availability. Previous research on recommender systems, a technology that proactively suggests items of interest to users based on their objective behavior or stated preferences [13], has shown a positive effect of user control on user satisfaction [13], perceived quality of recommendations [14], cognitive load [15], and user acceptance [15]. In the domain of automated driving, the potential to include users in the route planning process has been demonstrated by [16] and [17]: While the first found a positive attitude towards accepting longer durations in exchange for fewer transitions, in [17] subjects reported a high willingness to accept longer travel times for a higher share of automated driving (resulting in 30% higher perceived value of travel time for automated driving). The idea of a route planner has been investigated by [18], the authors of which conducted a participatory design workshop to reveal user needs. Results show that users require having the ability to configure general travel profiles that can be used for fast and convenient route selection. Such profiles should contain preferences for on-time arrival and maximization of uninterrupted automated driving time. Calculated route alternatives should not only be displayed on a map (as in existing navigation systems) but should also be visualized in an abstract manner to enable a quick overview of manual and automated driving segments. These user needs have already been transferred into a first low-fidelity prototype for in-car touch navigation systems using the wireframing tool Balsamiq and following HMI best practice recommendations such as Nielsen's heuristics [19] and the Gestalt principles [20] (see Fig. 1). This work builds upon the prototype by [18].

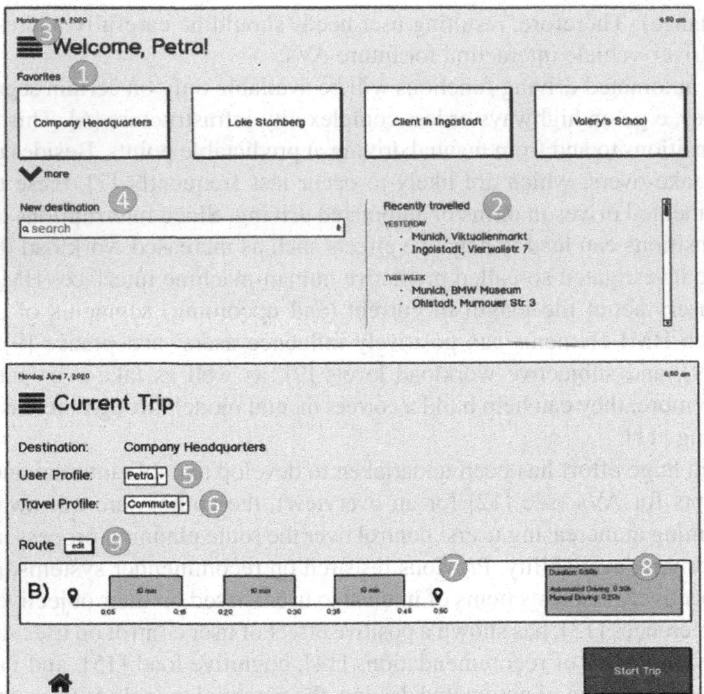

Fig. 1. Top: Home screen with favorite (1) and recently (2) travelled destinations, hamburger icon (3) to access an overflow menu, and a search bar for new destinations (4). Bottom: Overview of the currently planned drive with user (5) and travel profile (6), abstract drive visualization (7), and key information (8). Alternative route options can be accessed by pressing the edit button (9) [18].

2 Research Goals

While NDRAs play an important role for users of future AVs and a large effort has been undertaken to design internal HMIs of such systems according to user needs, research has not yet focused on integrating users in the route planning process when automation availability is limited. Giving users control over the route planning process to customize it according to their current needs can avoid interruptions and enable suitable NDRA engagement. Consequently, it is assumed to yield benefits comparable to those in recommender systems.

The overall goal of this work is, then, to develop a tool that supports users of future AVs with limited availability of the automated driving function into planning a drive according to their current needs. The concept should be highly usable, which means that it needs to be easy to learn, operated with high productivity, easy to remember, be pleasant to use, and have a low error rate [19]. Therefore, a user-centered design approach was pursued to build upon the existing prototype by [18]. A quantitative goal was to yield a "good" system usability scale (SUS) score of above 71.4 in a usability study [21].

3 User-Centered Design Process

A user-centered design process based on ISO 9241-210 [22] was followed (see Fig. 2). While the steps *understand context of use* (through a literature review) and *specify user requirements* (through a participatory design process) were conducted by [18], this work focused on the iterative development and evaluation of the concept. Different prototypes were designed and evaluated in three small-scale user studies (described in Sect. 3.1). The outcome of the concept design phase was implemented as an Android app, evaluated with an expert evaluation, and again improved (Sect. 3.2). Finally, the functional prototype was evaluated in an assessment study including both qualitative and quantitative evaluation (Sect. 3.3).

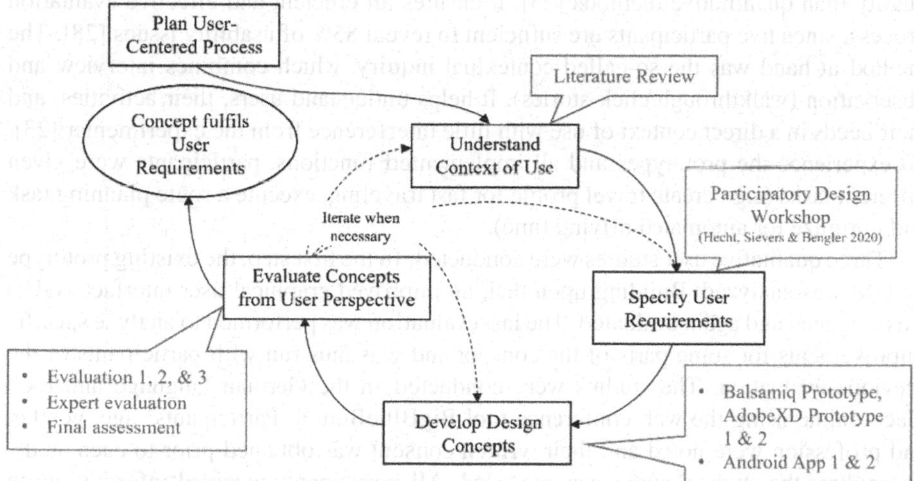

Fig. 2. User-Centered Design Process: The Balsamiq Prototype by [18] was evaluated in Evaluation 1. Subsequently, Adobe XD Prototype 1 and 2 were developed and evaluated (Evaluation 2 and 3). Then, Android App 1 was designed and evaluated by experts. Eventually, the app was updated (Android App 2) and evaluated (Final Assessment).

This work's wireframing prototypes were designed using Adobe XD. Compared to Balsamiq, which was utilized by [18], Adobe XD is more sophisticated and offers more options to share and discuss results (e.g., on smartphones). Based on Google's material design guideline, a color scheme was defined. According to [23], the font size for such an application should not be smaller than 10sp (scalable pixels). [24] further recommends 20sp for headings, 16sp for input text and list headers, and 14sp for regular texts, buttons, tabs, etc. Based on the considerations outlined above, the smallest font size used was 14sp.

Since more than 72% of all phones in Germany run Android [25], the concept was implemented as an Android app. This was done using the cross-platform framework Flutter for mobile user interface (UI) development. Compared to other cross-platform mobile frameworks such as Xamarin, NativeScript, and React Native, Flutter is the latest but already most popular one [26]. It uses the language dart for both GUI and function implementation and comes with its own widgets [27]. Visual Basic Code was used together with the Android emulator AVD Manager to run the code on an emulated Google Pixel 3a with a screen resolution of 2220 × 1080px (440dpi) for debugging. To use material design and its widgets, the Flutter Material Package was imported alongside with the Hex color Package.

3.1 Concept Design

Method. In the concept design phase, small-scale user studies were used to iteratively improve the concepts. This procedure is said to be cheaper, faster and with a higher quality than quantitative methods [23]. It ensures an efficient and effective evaluation process, since five participants are sufficient to reveal 85% of usability issues [28]. The method at hand was the so-called contextual inquiry, which combines interview and observation (walkthrough/click stories). It helps understand users, their activities, and their needs in a direct context of use with little interference from the experimenter [23]. To experience the prototypes and all implemented functions, participants were given different tasks (e.g., create travel profile for fast traveling, execute a route planning task and optimize for automated driving time).

Three qualitative user studies were conducted: In the first step, the existing prototype by [18] was analyzed. Building upon that, an improved graphical user interface (GUI) was designed and again evaluated. The last evaluation was performed to analyze specific improvements for some parts of the concept and was thus run with participants of the previous evaluation. The studies were conducted in the German language and took place online using the web conference tool BigBlueButton. Participants' age, gender, and profession were noted and their written consent was obtained prior to each study. To analyze the studies, audio was recorded. All participants received information on automated driving and the setting for which the tool was designed. To conduct the first study, the Balsamiq prototype (translated into German) was converted into a clickable PDF file and sent to participants who then shared their screen. For further prototypes, the share functionality of Adobe XD was used for the evaluation studies. In total, $N =$ 10 different participants with a diverse age, gender, and technology affinity background took part in the studies. Gender distribution amongst subjects was equal and the mean age was $M = 39.6$ years ($SD = 13.70$), ranging from 25 to 58 years. Participants owned a driver's license for $M = 21.40$ years ($SD = 13.70$). Seven subjects were working in different fields, three were students. On a 5-point Likert scale from 1 = *very low* to 5 = *very high*, participants rated their knowledge on automated driving as average (Mdn = 3). Their trust in automated driving from –2 = *I do not trust at all* to +2 = *I totally trust* was positive ($Mdn = 1$).

Results. The most significant difference compared to the Balsamiq prototype is obviously marked by the change from an in-car navigation tool to a mobile phone app as the outcome of the first study. All participants wanted to plan the routes on their phones.

This caused several changes, e.g., the vertical screen orientation and the need to additionally state starting point and date. In contrast to the prototype by [18], the final Adobe XD concept featured a travel profile triangle to adjust personal preferences regarding interruptions, automated driving share, and total duration (see Fig. 3). This was found to be easier to understand by the subjects. Furthermore, a maximum detour option was added in the travel profile settings as an outcome of the first study. To better fulfill the need for uninterrupted NDRA engagement, participants of the first study proposed to include the option to add desired automated driving segments on the home page. This was considered useful and was thus integrated in the following prototypes. It is possible to demand both time budgets (e.g., 20 min) and periods (e.g., from 2:30 to 3:00 o'clock) in the final prototype.

To improve navigation within the app, some pages were assigned headers with the respective page name. Moreover, a tab design was introduced for favorite and recently travelled destinations. A new color (dark green) was introduced as a call-to-action color. In line with Nielsen's heuristic no. 3 [19], a warning message was implemented when users exit without saving travel profile settings.

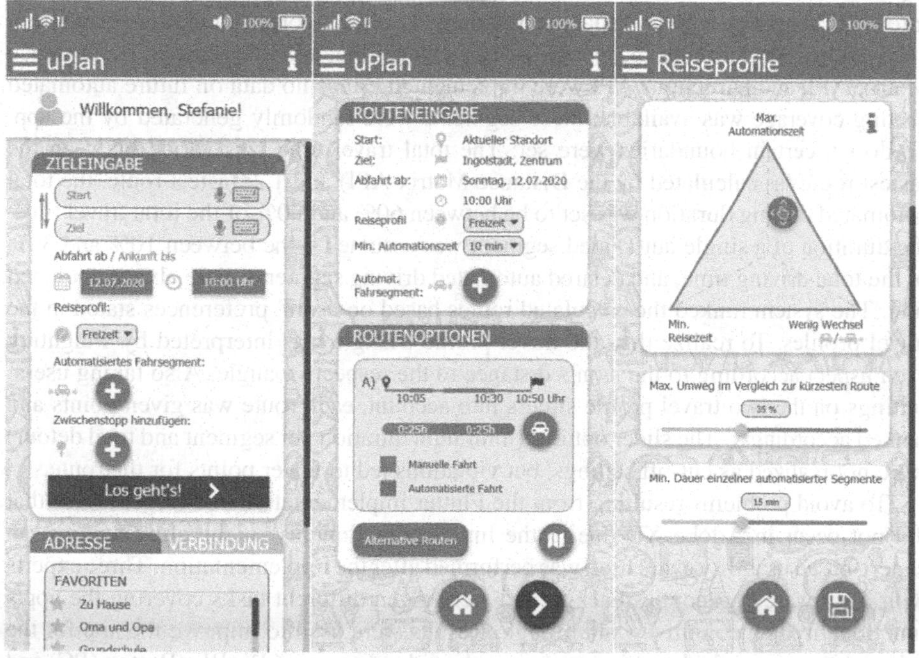

Fig. 3. Home screen, route overview, and travel profile setting screen (from left to right) of the Adobe XD prototype 2 (page 1 and 3 can be scrolled and are thus not fully displayed). The prototype was developed in German only.

Throughout all three studies, we noticed mainly elderly people having difficulties understanding some of the app's features. Also, the necessity for a tutorial, help texts or a basic version was expressed by some participants. Therefore, an info button was integrated in the header in Adobe XD prototype 1. However, participants of the evaluation 2 found the positioning to be suitable for global information only. Therefore, specific help will be integrated in the implementation phase. Furthermore, evaluation 2 investigated people's expectations regarding the reliability of predicted automated driving segments. Participants would understand deviations from the originally planned route. They expect the system to propose route changes during the drive in case the route planning is affected by traffic jams, constructions sites, etc.

3.2 Implementation

Method. In contrast to what was drafted in Adobe XD, the stopover function was omitted to ease the route calculation. This should nonetheless be implemented in future versions. To sensitize users to unforeseen changes, a disclaimer prior to the start of the navigation was integrated. A database was created to store data such as user and travel profiles, as well as favorite and recent destinations persistently using the Flutter SQFlite package for SQL databases. Multiple tables were created to ensure clarity and memory efficiency. SQL Joins were used to merge several tables into one and therefore connect correlating information from previously separated relations. To allow a route calculation to and from every address in Germany, the Google maps packages Places SDK, Maps SDK, Distance Matrix API, and Directions API were implemented. Since no data on future automated driving coverage was available, these segments were randomly generated by the app. To do so, certain boundaries were set: The total travel time was varied between the fastest route (as calculated by the Distance Matrix API) and 1.2*fastest route, the total automated driving duration was set to be between 60% and 90% of the total travel time, the duration of a single automated segment was assumed to be between 10% and 30% of the total driving time, and desired automated driving segments were always included first. The system ranked the calculated routes based on users' preferences stated in the travel profiles. To realize this, the travel profile triangle was interpreted by weighting each aspect according to the icon's distance to the respective angle. Also taking users' settings on the two travel profile sliders into account, each route was given points and ranked accordingly. The slider options (minimum duration per segment and total detour) were not realized as cut-off settings, but violations led to fewer points for the route.

To avoid problems resulting from the Flutter implementation and target issues that did not occur in Adobe XD due to the limited functionality of the click dummy, an expert-based usability evaluation was performed after the implementation. Three experts with a software ergonomics background were given different tasks covering the app's functionality in a cognitive walkthrough. Results were used to improve the app for the subsequent user study. Interviews were conducted online using BigBlueButton (PC) and Skype (to record experts' phone screens). The interviews lasted about 30 to 60 min.

Results. Experts suggested simplifying the design by omitting orange as an icon color as well as the background picture, which was rated as too playful. Moreover, the screen usage rate was seen as unsatisfactory. A zoom option featuring times was requested for the route overview, as was a separate color for the desired automated driving segment.

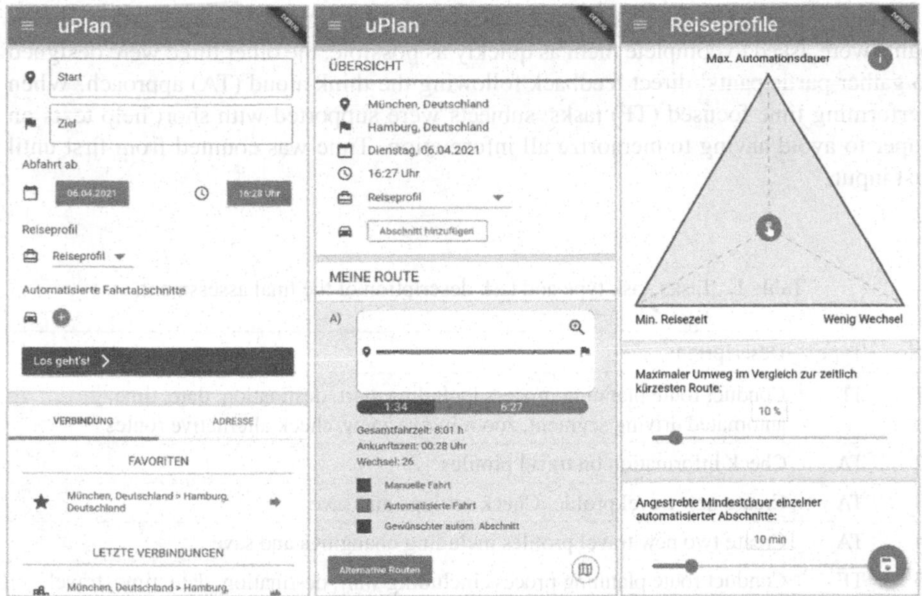

Fig. 4. Home screen, route overview, and travel profile setting screen of the final app prototype (from left to right; pages 1 and 3 can be scrolled and are thus not fully displayed). The app was developed in German only.

Further ideas for changes concern the home button (should be part of the overflow menu) and help texts for travel profiles in general and the triangle in specific. Other than that, experts rated the concept as a promising approach for future route planning and appreciated the quick and easy planning process with detailed voluntary customization options. Experts' ideas have been integrated, resulting in a modified design (see Fig. 4).

3.3 Final Assessment

Method. The goals of this final study were to evaluate the developed Android app and to assess to what degree the concept fulfills the previously derived user needs. Therefore, a usability study assessing both qualitative and quantitative metrics was performed.

Procedure and Metrics. Participants were welcomed and their written consent was obtained. A demographic questionnaire featuring questions on age, gender, automation experience, use of similar apps, and technology affinity (using the ATI-S [29] questionnaire) was followed by a short verbal introduction of the setting. Automated driving was introduced as a system that does not need supervision and is not capable of driving a full journey automated, leading to fragmented drives. The availability of the automation was described as highly predictable. The app was installed on a LG stylus 2 with a 5.7″ screen, running on Android 6. Thus, participants were asked to write an SMS and to use the native Android buttons (back, home, tab view) to familiarize themselves with the phone.

Then, six different tasks (see Table 1) were orally assigned. For three tasks, participants were asked to complete them as quickly as possible, the other three were designed to gather participants' direct feedback following the think aloud (TA) approach. When performing time focused (TF) tasks, subjects were supported with short help texts on paper to avoid having to memorize all information. Time was counted from first until last input.

Table 1. Tasks, task type and task description of the final assessment.

No	Type	Description
1	TF	Conduct route planning process including start, destination, date, time, automated driving segment, zoom in overview, check alternative routes
2	TA	Check information on travel profiles
3	TA	Create new travel profile. Check settings and save
4	TA	Create two new travel profiles including changings and save
5	TF	Conduct route planning process including start, destination, date, time, travel profile, check alternative routes
6	TF	Conduct route planning process including start, destination, date, time, travel profile, automated driving segment, zoom in overview, check alternative routes

Using the possibility of recording the phone screen and voices, task time (only TF) and quality (good/average/bad; only TF) was assessed. Good task quality requires no or only minor flaws in the task execution, average was defined as one to three mistakes, requiring the user to return or restart the operation. Accordingly, bad quality was rated for all tasks executions worse or with need to ask the experimenter.

After the completion of all tasks, participants were asked to fill another set of questionnaires including the system usability scale questionnaire (SUS [30]) and parts of the Technology Usage Inventory (perceived usefulness (PU) from [31], and intention to use (ITU) from [32], see Table 2). The SUS features ten items rated on a 5-point Likert scale resulting in total scores from 0 to 100. ITU and PU scores were calculated by summing up the respective items. Furthermore, subjects were asked to rate their overall satisfaction with the app on a 5-point Likert scale from 1 = *completely unsatisfied* to 5 = *very satisfied*.

In a structured follow-up interview, participants were confronted with seven statements resembling the user needs (see Table 2) and asked to rate them from 1 = *false* to 5 = *true*. Finally, additional comments and suggestions for improvement were solicited.

The Ethics Board of the Technical University of Munich provided ethical approval for this study. The corresponding approval code is 268/21 S-EB.

Table 2. Statements and questions of the post-study questionnaire.

Item	Question
PU1	Using this app would make travel planning more comfortable
PU2	This app would help me making the task of travel planning more convenient
PU3	I find this app useful for travel planning tasks
PU4	This app would support me in planning my future travels
ITU1	Would you use this app?
ITU2	Would you purchase this app?
ITU3	Would you want to have access to this app?
UN1	The app has been very good in helping me define my priorities for a current drive
UN2	The app has made it very easy to define a minimum automation duration
UN3	The app has made it very easy to set uninterrupted completion of a non-driving activity as a priority for the current drive
UN4	I really liked the ability to define and select from travel profiles
UN5	The app has been very good in helping me to choose a route that suits my current needs in a short time
UN6	All relevant data for the different routes were clearly provided by the app
UN7	Information on automated segments during the planned drive was presented very well

Sample. Due to the covid-19 pandemic, most of the subjects were recruited among employees of the chair of ergonomics at the Technical University of Munich. In total, 23 participants with a mean age of $M = 28.43$ years ($SD = 2.33$) took part in the study (13 male, 10 female). All of them were employed, fourteen in the field of automated driving. Six subjects indicated that they drive less than 5,000 km/year, four between 5,000 and 10,000 km/year, seven between 10,001 and 15,000 km/year, four between 15,001 and 20,000 km/year, and two more than 20,000 km/year. On a five-point Likert scale from 1 = *very low* to 5 = *very high*, subjects rated their knowledge on automated driving with a median of 4. Sixteen (69.57%) have experiences with L2 automated driving systems and a vast majority – 17 (73.91%) – is rather positive or positive towards the development of automated driving. The statement *"I trust an automated system that does not need to be monitored during automated driving, reliably recognizes its system limits, and prompts me in time to take over the driving task if necessary."* was rated with a median of 4 on a five-point Likert scale from 1 = *completely disagree* to 5 = *completely agree.* Using the ATI-S scale, the mean score of $M = 3.99$ indicates a rather tech-savvy sample [29]. Furthermore, the majority used Android as their phone operating system (60.87%; remaining: iOS).

Digital tools for route planning and navigation such as Google maps were frequently used by the subjects. Apps for travel planning with public transportation were well-known and used. Less popular were external navigation systems for in-vehicle use, integrated systems were more relevant (see Fig. 5).

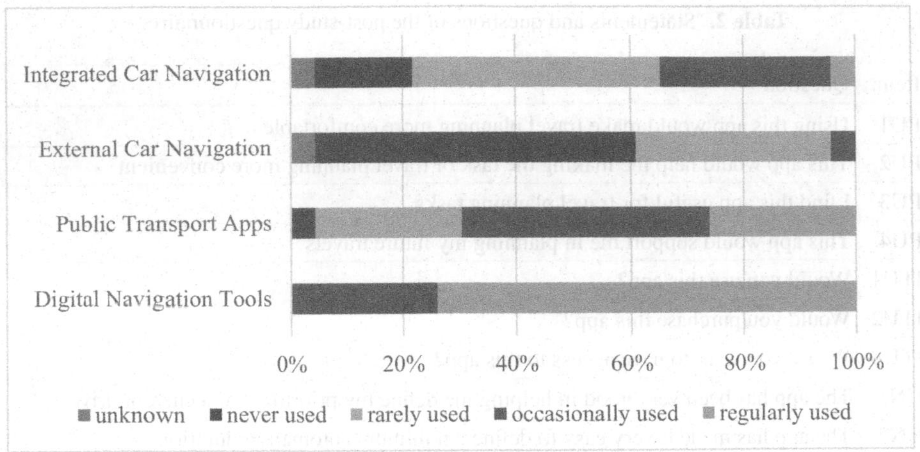

Fig. 5. Participants' reported app usage. $N = 23$.

Statistical Analysis. Statistical analysis was performed using JASP 0.14.1.0. To test the usability goal, Wilcoxon's signed-rank test was calculated against a specific value since the SUS scores were not normally distributed (Shapiro-Wilk: $p = .041$) and thus a one sample t-test could not be conducted. The alpha level was $\alpha = 0.05$.

Results. Overall, the three **time-focused tasks** were well handled. For the first route calculation, 19 trials were rated as "good," four as "average." The average rating was mainly due to problems entering the required automated driving segment, issues with the time picker, and forgetting to zoom in the route visualization. The second route planning task (without an additional segment) was well-handled by all subjects. In the third time-focused task, 18 trials were rated as "good," five as "average" (due to the same reasons as in task 1). The quantitative analysis of the time-focused tasks (see Fig. 6) reveals that the route planning process took $M = 2{:}25$ min ($SD = 0{:}30$ min) in the first contact situation (including adding desired automated driving segments and checking different alternatives). The second planning task (without automated segment) was much faster than the initial contact ($M = 1{:}37$ min, $SD = 0{:}19$ min). The third route planning process, which was very similar to the first, took less than two minutes on average ($M = 1{:}49$ min, $SD = 0{:}19$ min).

The **think-aloud tasks** were well handled, too. User comments targeted the help texts in the travel profile settings (understandability should be improved by using simpler language), the missing option of accessing the travel profile settings from the home screen, and the travel profile triangle (boundaries for touch point movements and visualization should be revised).

With a mean **SUS score** of $M = 80.65$ ($Mdn = 85$), the app was rated as "good" according to [21]. The calculated Wilcoxon test ($W = 226$, $p = .008$) shows that it was significantly better rated than the lower limit of "Good" (71.4) as defined in [21].

Based on the **perceived usefulness** subscale of the TUI, the app was rated as very useful for journey planning ($M = 25.13$, $SD = 3.17$) on a scale from 0 to 28 (the higher

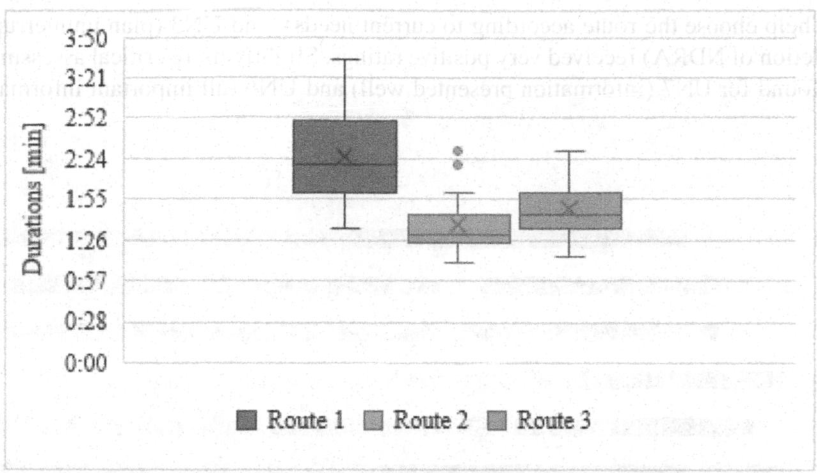

Fig. 6. Boxplots representing durations for a complete route planning process. A detailed description of the route planning tasks can be found in Table 1. $N = 23$.

values indicate higher usefulness). Furthermore, a high **intention to use** became apparent ($M = 25.83$, $SD = 21.81$) on a scale from 0 to 300 where lower values indicate higher intention to use (Fig. 7).

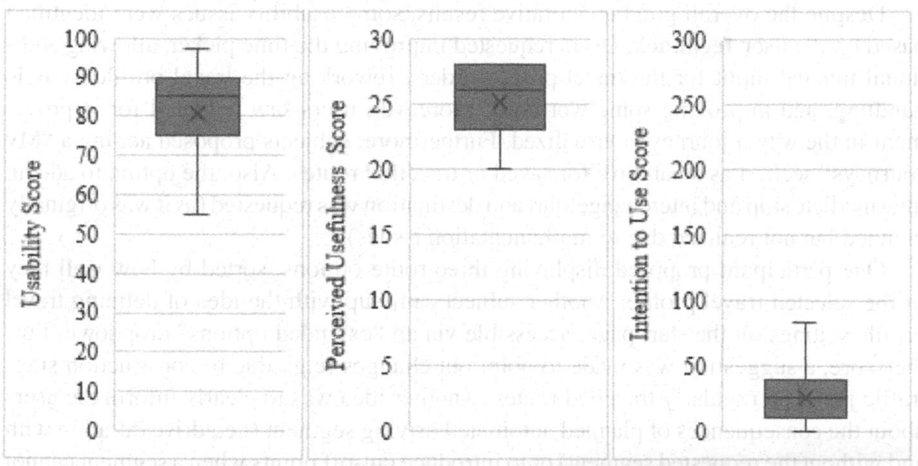

Fig. 7. Boxplots for usability, perceived usefulness, and intention to use (ITU). Lower ITU Score indicates higher ITU. $N = 23$.

The overall satisfaction with the app was rated with a median of 4; only one subject rated "2" and two rated "3" on a 5-point Likert scale (1 = *completely unsatisfied* to 5 = *very satisfied*).

Regarding the predefined **user needs**, subjects expressed overall satisfaction with the developed solutions (see Fig. 8). Especially UN4 (define and select travel profiles),

UN5 (help choose the route according to current needs), and UN3 (plan uninterrupted completion of NDRA) received very positive ratings. Slightly more critical assessments were found for UN7 (information presented well) and UN6 (all important information given).

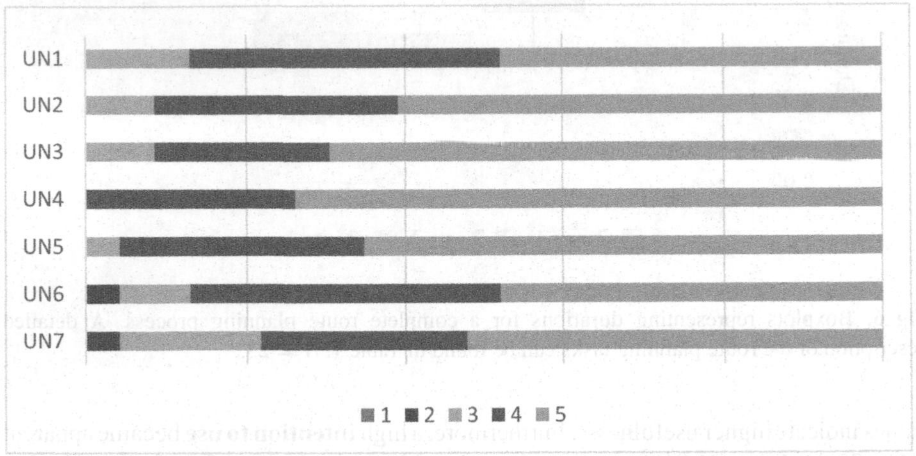

Fig. 8. User needs fulfilment (1 = *false* to 5 = *true*), see Table 2 for description. $N = 23$.

Despite the overall good quantitative results, some usability issues were identified based on the **user feedback**: Users requested improving the time picker, allowing additional manual input for the travel profile sliders, reworking the travel profile triangle handling, and improving some wordings. Moreover, users saw potential for improvement in the way a journey is visualized. Furthermore, subjects proposed adding a "My Journeys" section as an archive for saved or travelled routes. Also, the option to add an intermediate stop and interchange start and destination was requested (as it was originally planned but not realized due to implementation issues).

One participant proposed displaying three route options, sorted by how well they fit the selected travel profile. Another subject came up with the idea of defining travel profile settings on the start page, accessible via an "extended options" dropdown. Furthermore, a suggestion was made to point out changes (e.g., due to construction sites, traffic jams) on regularly travelled routes. Another idea was to clearly inform the users about the consequences of planned automated driving segment (i.e., drive duration with and without the requested segment) or to introduce cut-off points when a segment cannot be realized. Last, it was proposed to supplement the app with an extended planning tool for the PC, which would also allow for analysis and more sophisticated planning options taking advantage of the possibilities of a large screen and mouse and keyboard input.

4 Discussion and Outlook

The possibility of legally engaging in a variety of NDRAs while driving with SAE L3 and L4 automation changes the usage of drive time and poses new challenges for the domain of route planning software. With this work, we have developed a functional route planning app. Following the user-centered design process, different prototypes were iteratively evaluated in small-scale user studies and further improved. The final concept was implemented as an Android app, thus allowing realistic interaction and evaluation. In the end, a usability study with 23 participants was conducted to assess the concept's potential and further ideas for improvement. Despite some simplifications of the Android app prototype (e.g., no intermediate stops and limited map visualization), results show that the app is easy to use; only a few usability problems occurred. A complex route planning process takes less than two minutes on average and user requirements were fulfilled well. Furthermore, usability ratings show a good mean SUS score of 81. The app was rated as very useful for journey planning and most participants agreed that they would benefit from the app as it would make route planning more comfortable and more convenient. Furthermore, a high intention to use became apparent. Overall, participants were highly satisfied with the app.

Nonetheless, people lack experience with automated driving. Actual use might degrade these results, as might the known observation by the experimenter. Furthermore, despite the close integration of future users in the concept design phase (including elderly people), the final study suffers from a small, young, and technology-affine sample that possibly does not represent future users of (high-end) automated vehicles.

For the realized app concept, automated driving segment were randomly generated since AVs are not yet available on the market. The usefulness of the proposed concept most likely depends on automation availability and might diminish with vast automation coverage. Furthermore, the ratio between planned and unplanned transitions is unclear. A high rate of the latter can undermine the usefulness of the proposed route planner and must also be integrated into user communication. Thus, this concept has to be evaluated and possibly adapted when the technology has advanced further.

Future improvement of the app should, besides the reported simplifications, tackle different UI issues: Multimodal interaction concepts featuring speech input and output should be integrated, as well as a tutorial, and allowing for further UI-related settings (e.g., for font size, color theme). In [18], users requested that the system takes long-term experiences with the current user into account and include the driver state in the route planning process. Moreover, the ability to undertake changes in the route during the drive or the necessity of informing the user about inevitable route changes should be addressed (as in today's navigation systems). A concept for context-adaptive availability notification has been proposed by [33] and can serve as a starting point.

For future investigations, evaluating the app in connection with a driving simulator can lead to further insights. Thereby, route choices and their impact can be experienced in a more realistic setting and the influence on user acceptance can be evaluated better. Further, investigations on the influence of unplanned transitions and different prediction error rates can be assessed. However, one must keep in mind that such artificial settings can never fully picture real NDRA engagement, as activity choices depend on many factors [34] and NDRA engagement in turn has an influence on the evaluation of the journey [35]. Therefore, one might try to create a realistic and comparable scenario by instructing participants.

Finally, the ability to plan a fragmented automated drive before starting the actual ride might have an impact on people's behavior during the journey. The possibility of scheduling meetings, optimizing rides for automated driving time, and avoiding interruptions can potentially reduce users' intentional violations, e.g., engaging in NDRAs during SAE L2 automation (which is known to have a negative impact on monitoring behavior and traffic safety [36]). Also, continuing a visual-manual activity despite the need to take over manual control (i.e., task perseverance) after an automated driving segment can potentially be reduced. Thus, risk assessment research might add user control as a potential influencing factor to assess risks of future AVs.

This work proves the positive attitude of users towards being integrated into the route planning process when automation availability is limited to certain segment of a drive. Nonetheless, the app's usefulness will depend on future aspects of automated driving that are now yet fully clear, e.g., the prediction quality (i.e., uncertainty) of automation availability. Future evaluation might incorporate a setting closer to reality, e.g., in combination with a driving simulator and take a closer look at the influence of user control on intentional violations during a drive.

References

1. König, M., Neumayr, L.: Users' resistance towards radical innovations: the case of the self-driving car. Transp. Res. Part F Traffic Psychol. Behav. **44**, 42–52 (2017). https://doi.org/10.1016/j.trf.2016.10.013
2. DeSerpa, A.C.: A theory of the economics of time. Econ. J. **81**, 828 (1971). https://doi.org/10.2307/2230320
3. Wadud, Z., MacKenzie, D., Leiby, P.: Help or hindrance? The travel, energy and carbon impacts of highly automated vehicles. Transp. Res. Part A Policy Pract. **86**, 1–18 (2016). https://doi.org/10.1016/j.tra.2015.12.001
4. Naujoks, F., Wiedemann, K., Schoemig, N.: The importance of interruption management for usefulness and acceptance of automated driving. In: Proceedings of the 9th International Conference on Automotive User Interfaces and Interactive Vehicular Applications, Oldenburg, Germany, 24–27 September 2017
5. Davis, F.D.: Perceived usefulness, perceived ease of use, and user acceptance of information technology. MIS Q. **13**, 319 (1989). https://doi.org/10.2307/249008
6. ERTRAC: Connected Automated Driving Roadmap. ERTRAC Working Group Connectivity and Automated Driving No. 8, Brussels, Belgium (2019)
7. Holländer, K., Pfleging, B.: Preparing drivers for planned control transitions in automated cars. In: Abdennadher, S., Alt, F. (eds.) MUM 2018, 17th International Conference on Mobile and Ubiquitous Multimedia. Proceedings. 25 November–28 November 2018, Cairo, Egypt. The 17th International Conference, Cairo, Egypt, 25–28 November 2018, pp. 83–92. The Association for Computing Machinery, Inc., New York, New York (2018). ISBN 9781450365949
8. Speier, C., Valacich, J.S., Vessey, I.: The influence of task interruption on individual decision making: an information overload perspective. Decis. Sci. **30**, 337–360 (1999). https://doi.org/10.1111/j.1540-5915.1999.tb01613.x
9. Richardson, N.T., Flohr, L., Michel, B.: Takeover requests in highly automated truck driving: how do the amount and type of additional information influence the driver-automation interaction? MTI **2**, 68 (2018). https://doi.org/10.3390/mti2040068

10. Wiedemann, K.: Frühzeitige Informationen über Systemgrenzen beim hochautomatisierten Fahren; Universität Würzburg (2020)
11. Danner, S., Pfromm, M., Bengler, K.: Does information on automated driving functions and the way of presenting it before activation influence users' behavior and perception of the system? Information **11**, 54 (2020). https://doi.org/10.3390/info11010054
12. Bengler, K., Rettenmaier, M., Fritz, N., Feierle, A.: From HMI to HMIs: towards an HMI framework for automated driving. Information **11**, 61 (2020). https://doi.org/10.3390/info11020061
13. Pu, P., Chen, L., Hu, R.: Evaluating recommender systems from the user's perspective: survey of the state of the art. User Model User-Adapt. Interact. **22**, 317–355 (2012). https://doi.org/10.1007/s11257-011-9115-7
14. Harper, F.M., Xu, F., Kaur, H., Condiff, K., Chang, S., Terveen, L.: Putting users in control of their recommendations. In: RecSys 2015, Proceedings of the 9th ACM Conference on Recommender Systems, 16–20 September 2015, Vienna, Austria, New York, NY, USA. ACM Association for Computing Machinery, New York, NY (2015). ISBN 9781450336925
15. Jin, Y., Tintarev, N., Verbert, K.: Effects of personal characteristics on music recommender systems with different levels of controllability. In: Pera, S. (ed.) Proceedings of the 12th ACM Conference on Recommender Systems. RecSys 2018: Twelfth ACM Conference on Recommender Systems, Vancouver British Columbia Canada, 02 October 2018, pp. 13–21. ACM, New York, NY (2018). ISBN 9781450359016
16. Hecht, T., Kratzert, S., Bengler, K.: The effects of a predictive HMI and different transition frequencies on acceptance, workload, usability, and gaze behavior during urban automated driving. Information **11**, 73 (2020). https://doi.org/10.3390/info11020073
17. Lehtonen, E., Wörle, J., Malin, F., Metz, B., Innamaa, S.: Travel experience matters: expected personal mobility impacts after simulated L3/L4 automated driving. Transportation (2021). https://doi.org/10.1007/s11116-021-10211-6
18. Hecht, T., Sievers, M., Bengler, K.: Investigating user needs for trip planning with limited availability of automated driving functions. In: Stephanidis, C., Antona, M. (eds.) HCI International 2020–Posters. HCII 2020. CCIS, vol. 1226, pp. 359–366. Springer, Cham (2020). ISBN 978-3-030-50732-9. https://doi.org/10.1007/978-3-030-50732-9_48
19. Nielsen, J., Molich, R.: Heuristic evaluation of user interfaces. In: Chew, J.C., Carrasco, J.C., Carrasco Chew, J. (eds.) Empowering People, CHI 1990 Conference Proceedings the SIGCHI Conference, Seattle, Washington, United States, 1 April 1990–5 April 1990, pp. 249–256, Addison-Wesley, Reading, MA (1992). ISBN 0201509326
20. Rosson, M.B., Carroll, J.M.: Usability Engineering: Scenario-Based Development of Human-Computer Interaction, 1st edn. Academic Press, San Fancisco (2010). ISBN 9781558607125
21. Bangor, A., Kortum, P., Miller, J.: Determining what individual SUS scores mean: adding an adjective rating scale. J. Usability Stud. **4**, 114–123 (2009)
22. DIN Deutsches Institut für Normung e.V.: Ergonomics of human-system interaction-Part 210: human-centred design for interactive systems (2010). (DIN EN ISO 9241–210)
23. Cooper, A., Reimann, R., Cronin, D., Noessel, C.: About Face: The Essentials of Interaction Design; [the completely updated classic on creating delightful user experiences, 4. edn. [updated]; Wiley, Indianapolis, Ind. (2014). ISBN 9781118766583
24. Kennedy, E.: The Android/Material Design Font Size Guidelines. https://learnui.design/blog/android-material-design-font-size-guidelines.html#md-mobile. Accessed 23 Dec 2021
25. Bolkart, J.: Marktanteile der führenden mobilen Betriebssysteme an der Internetnutzung mit Mobiltelefonen weltweit von September 2010 bis September 2021. https://de.statista.com/statistik/daten/studie/184335/umfrage/marktanteil-der-mobilen-betriebssysteme-weltweit-seit-2009/. Accessed 23 Dec 2021

26. Liu, S.: Cross-platform mobile frameworks used by software developers worldwide from 2019 to 2021. https://www.statista.com/statistics/869224/worldwide-software-developer-working-hours/. Accessed 23 Dec 2021
27. Build apps for any screen. https://flutter.dev/?gclid=EAIaIQobChMI4I2-xP759AIVied3Ch2RrwCXEAAYASAAEgIOifD_BwE&gclsrc=aw.ds. Accessed 23 Dec 2021
28. Nielsen, J.: Why You Only Need to Test with 5 Users. https://www.nngroup.com/articles/why-you-only-need-to-test-with-5-users/. Accessed 23 Dec 2021
29. Franke, T., Attig, C., Wessel, D.: A personal resource for technology interaction: development and validation of the affinity for technology interaction (ATI) scale. Int. J. Hum. Comput. Interact. **35**, 456–467 (2019). https://doi.org/10.1080/10447318.2018.1456150
30. Brooke, J.: SUS–a quick and dirty usability scale. In: Jordan, P.W., Thomas, B., McClelland, I.L., Weerdmeester, B., (eds.) Usability Evaluation in Industry, pp. 189–194. Taylor & Francis, London (1996). ISBN 0-7484-0314-0
31. Disztinger, P., Schlögl, S., Groth, A.: Technology acceptance of virtual reality for travel planning. In: Schegg, R., Stangl, B. (eds.) Information and Communication Technologies in Tourism 2017, pp. 255–268. Springer, Cham (2017). ISBN 978-3-319-51168-9. https://doi.org/10.1007/978-3-319-51168-9_19
32. Kothgassner, O., Felnhofer, A., Hauk, N., Kastenhofer, E., Gomm, J., Krysprin-Exner, I.: TUI–Technology Usage Inventory: Manual. https://www.ffg.at/sites/default/files/allgemeine_downloads/thematische%20programme/programmdokumente/tui_manual.pdf
33. Danner, S., Feierle, A., Manger, C., Bengler, K.: Context-adaptive availability notifications for an SAE level 3 automation. MTI **5**, 16 (2021). https://doi.org/10.3390/mti5040016
34. Hecht, T., Darlagiannis, E., Bengler, K.: Non-driving related activities in automated driving–an online survey investigating user needs. In: Ahram, T., Karwowski, W., Pickl, S., Taiar, R. (eds.) Human Systems Engineering and Design II. IHSED 2019. AISC, vol. 1026, pp. 182–188. Springer, Cham (2020). ISBN 978-3-030-27928-8. https://doi.org/10.1007/978-3-030-27928-8_28
35. Susilo, Y., Lyons, G., Jain, J., Atkins, S.: Rail passengers' time use and utility assessment. Transp. Res. Rec. **2323**, 99–109 (2013). https://doi.org/10.3141/2323-12
36. Boos, A., Feldhütter, A., Schwiebacher, J., Bengler, K.: Mode errors and intentional violations in visual monitoring of level 2. In: IEEE ITSC 2020 Virtual Conference Proceedings. 23rd IEEE International Conference on Intelligent Transportation Systems, Virtual Conference, 20–23 September 2020

Gender Preference Differences in Color Temperature Associated with LED Light Sources in the Autopilot Cabin

Zhangchenlong Huang[1], Shanshan Wang[1], Ao Jiang[2](✉), Caroline Hemingray[3], and Stephen Westland[3]

[1] Beijing Normal University, Zhuhai, Zhuhai, China
[2] Imperial College London, ILEWG EuroMoonMars at ESTEC ESA, University of Leeds, London, UK
aojohn928@gmail.com
[3] School of Design, University of Leeds, Leeds, UK

Abstract. In an automated cockpit, the role changes from driver to passenger, with a greater focus on the in-cabin experience. The reasonable use of light sources will effectively improve the user cabin experience. In particular, we can effectively derive the preference for color temperature by the convergence of group selection for different groups of men and women.

In this study, systematic descriptive analysis, t-test, and one-way ANOVA were performed on the data yielded using questionnaires. The preference choices of 23 (11 male, 12 female) participants who came to China were studied under five different color temperature (CCT) lightings in the autopilot interior. The results demonstrated that there were disparities in terms of gender in the correlation of LED light sources in the autopilot cabin. Women preferred 3500K white light, and men preferred cooler than 5000K light during daytime in summer, while women preferred 3000K warm white light and men preferred 4000K cool white light during nighttime.

Moreover, passengers' alertness, visual comfort, and preference also differed under different color temperature environment brightness. Meanwhile, passengers' alertness, visual comfort, and preference were shown to have a significant positive correlation.

Keywords: Self-driving cars · Color temperature · Gender preference · Fatigue · Alertness

1 Introduction

Light sources are an important influencing factor in enhancing user experience [1]. Differences in light source color temperature evoke different feelings in users, whereby high color temperature lights make users feel calm and cold. In contrast, low color temperature lights make users feel warm and cozy. Due to gender differences, there is variability in the choice of light color temperature between men and women [2]. This

H. Krömker (Ed.): HCII 2022, LNCS 13335, pp. 151–166, 2022.
https://doi.org/10.1007/978-3-031-04987-3_10

study explores the correlation between gender differences and light color temperature preferences in the autopilot [3].

In previous studies, user acceptance (UA) and user experience (UX) [4] fluctuated depending on gender [5]. The perceptions of user experience (UX) and user acceptance (UA) in the automated cockpit substantially varied by gender, considering light comfort, intelligence, perceived behavioral control, trust, and fun. Furthermore, the type of task also affects the visual requirements; therefore, the space needs to be more detailed and tailored to the needs of different genders.

Usually, the combination of different color temperatures and illumination levels induces different emotions under the combination of low illumination levels (100 lx) and low color temperatures (3000 K). The performance values for higher psychological demands associated with operational tasks are usually lower. Therefore, we may be more apt to relax in low-intensity warm light lighting settings. High intensity (300–1000 lx) and high color temperature (4000–6500 K) will produce cooler light, resulting in better performance for operational tasks with higher mental demands. People are more likely to be alert in lighting settings of high illumination and high color temperature. Moreover, ambient temperature also affects the human judgment of color temperature preference; And the ambient temperature also affects people's judgment of color temperature preference, below the comfortable temperature (23 °C) will usually be more warm light. On the contrary, above the comfortable temperature will be more inclined to cool light [6]. Therefore, the choice of color temperature and illumination level in a given environment by alert researchers correlates with participants' mood and comfort level.

Currently, automotive interior lighting sources are light-emitting diodes (LEDs) as new lighting sources. They generate minimal heat, have a straightforward manufacturing process, have a small form factor, and can be turned on immediately with no rise time delay in the switching process [7]. They possess no flicker and no tribute and are well suited for lighting systems for reliability and safety in driving tasks with high requirements. The vehicle lighting applications in the vehicle for driving tasks concerning the U.S. APTA vehicle equipment lighting recommended guidelines should also consider the luminous efficiency of LED light sources, color rendering index, color temperature, and anti-glare. Therefore, to address these issues, the analysis and study of the applications of LED light sources in the interior lighting of the vehicle's automatic cockpit are crucial [8].

The color temperature of LEDs needs to be determined based on ergonomic experiments. LED light sources with color temperatures between 1000 K and 6000 K can be used for cabin lighting [9] The LED light spectrum is affected by the operating temperature of the LED chip, the current level, and the lens material; therefore, these factors must be controlled in practice to ensure lighting quality [10].

In addition to the use of LED lighting systems in automotive lighting, the Korean Motor Vehicle Safety Standards (KMVSS) were conducted on mainstream LED lamps [11], HID (High-Intensity Discharge) lamps, and halogen lamps in the market. Photometric characteristics, glare assessment, chromaticity (Fig. 1). We synthesized the Korean standard (KMVSS) and the vehicle equipment lighting guidelines (APTA) to examine the performance of LED lamps, comprehensively demonstrating their feasibility, as shown in Fig. 1 (Table 1).

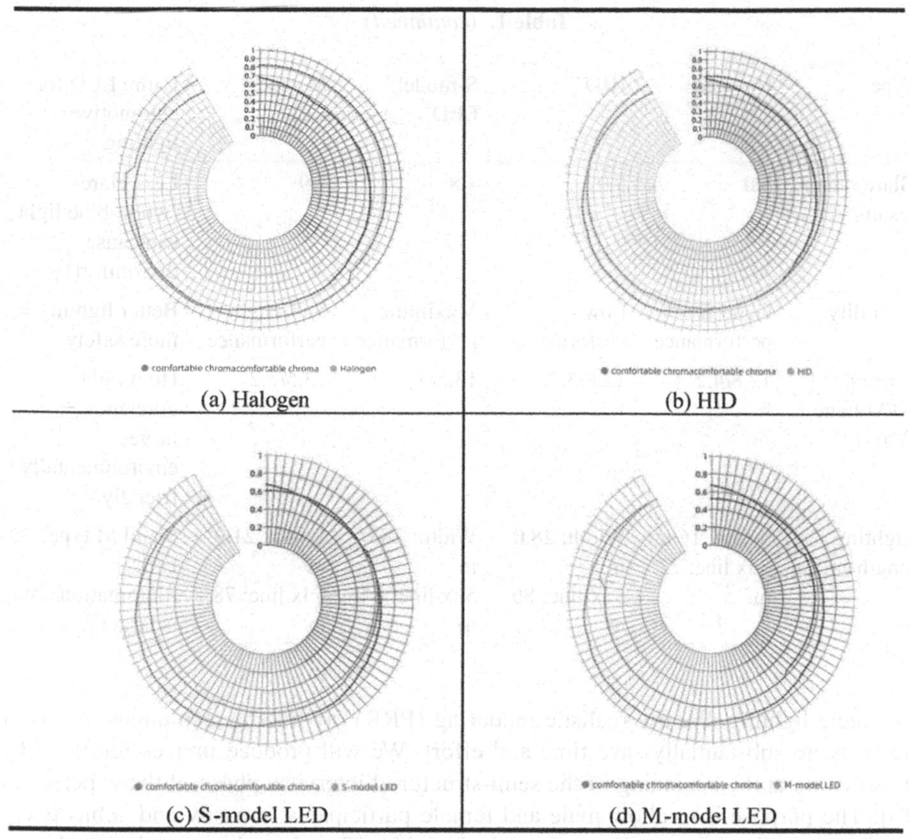

Fig. 1. (left) Halogen; HID; S-model LED; M-model LED chromaticity coordinates (mainly to assist in judging the glare level)

Table 1. Korean standard (KMVSS) on the vehicle with Halogen, HID, and LED lighting comparison

Type	Halogen	HID	S-model LED	M-model LED	Lamp LED for automotive lighting
Photometric properties MAX (unit: cd)	19, 977	21, 168	37, 737	26, 421	Stronger luminosity = greater vision

(continued)

Optical system color effects can be accurately and efficiently simulated on the current mainstream software LightTools [12]. In addition, one can use the color metrics in the evaluation function to optimize the system to achieve the best color performance in

Table 1. *(continued)*

Type	Halogen	HID	S-model LED	M-model LED	Lamp LED for automotive lighting
Glare rating results	5.0	5.0	4.8	4.9	Less glare (white-blue light can cause discomfort)
Visibility	General performance	Low performance	Maximum performance	Sub-High performance	Better lighting = more safety
Current (I)/Voltage (V)	12.8/4.2	12.8/3.2	13.5/3.3	13.5/3.2	High light efficiency = more environmentally friendly
Lighting length (m)	Width: 16 m 5 lx line: 72 m	Width: 28.0 m 5 lx line: 86 m	Width: 28.0 m 5 lx line: 84 m	Width: 21.9 m 5 lx line: 78 m	S and M type LED illumination area is larger

in-vehicle lighting. We use realistic rendering (PRR) ray-tracing techniques to render the scene to substantially save time and effort. We will produce images rendered by the software at the beginning of the semi-structured interview phase of the experiment [13]. The purpose is to allow male and female participants to easily and subjectively assess outstanding temperature preferences [14, 15]. (To reduce the cognitive burden on participants, we will discard some of the transitional color temperatures and retain only the "low, medium, and high" color temperature preferences), as illustrated in Fig. 2.

Fig. 2. Three spectra comparing the realistic rendering of the office scene: (a) 5000 K blackbody spectrum LED, (b) 2000 K fluorescence spectrum LED, and (c) 6000 K white phosphor LED

2 Experimental Setups

2.1 Participants

23 participants, 11 males, and 12 females, with normal visual function, were recruited. They did not have vision issues such as myopia and hypermetropia. The participants

were in good physical condition and had some cognitive and reading abilities. All participants were right-handed and were not practicing as professional athletes. Before the experiment, the procedures of the experiment were fully delineated to the participants, and informed consent forms were received. The experiment was conducted on December 26th at the Zhuhai campus of Beijing Normal University.

Generally, cooler light color temperature environments are more popular in warmer regions, while warm light color temperatures are more popular in colder regions. Henceforth, the geographical origin of the participants may affect the final experimental results or visual demand, which should be judged as a bias to this experiment. The experiment was conducted in China only with selected participants, who participated voluntarily and without payment support. This was determined to have no effect on the results of this experiment.

2.2 Experimental Scenarios and Their Parameter Settings

Passengers in the autopilot chamber simulate experimental scenarios by being in a full-size experimental silo with adjustable lighting of different color temperatures.

A box-type MVP with dimensions of 4420 mm in length, 1685 mm in width, and 1755 mm in height was used for the experiment. The seating positions were partitioned to achieve different functions (driver's seat, passenger's seat, and passenger's seat). Frosted stickers were applied to both the driver and passenger glass to prevent the outside environment from interfering with the participants. A solid-state light source was installed under the main and passenger seats. The parameters of this solid-state light source can be continuously adjusted, such as color temperature, luminous flux, and spectrum. The experimental seat size is 132 cm in length 49 cm in breadth with a tilt angle of 100°.

The sub-experimental scenario was devoid of external light sources other than the lights required for the experiment. In the temperature (18 ± 2) °C, relative humidity is 65%–77%. The vehicle surroundings were 28–32 dB, and the ambient light at night was 0.2 lx in the winter evening. Two illuminance meters were placed within the participants' comfortable viewing angle (30° to the left and right of the line of sight) to measure the actual light intensity and color temperature. As reported in this paper, all measured light intensity and color temperature values were measured on both sides of the testers.

Solid-state lighting equipment was simulated in the autopilot compartment, referring to the APTA vehicle lighting recommendations. 2 lighting devices and 2 controllers were used to set the color temperature in five levels.

2.3 Color Temperature Setting

This experiment was conducted on two groups of men and women as per gender disparities. A total of five different lighting modes were set, and specific illumination values and color temperatures are shown in Table 2. The night scene layout is illustrated in Figs. 3, 4, 5, 6 and 7. The daytime scene layout is shown in Figs. 8, 9, 10, 11, 12 and Table 3)

Table 2. Lighting settings in nighttime experimental scenes

Participants	Night illumination	Illumination	Color temperature
Male/Female	0.2 lx	750 lx	6500 k (warm white)
	0.2 lx	750 lx	5000 k (white)
	0.2 lx	750 lx	4000 k (cool white)
	0.2 lx	750 lx	3500 k (daylight color)
	0.2 lx	750 lx	3200 k (cool daylight color)

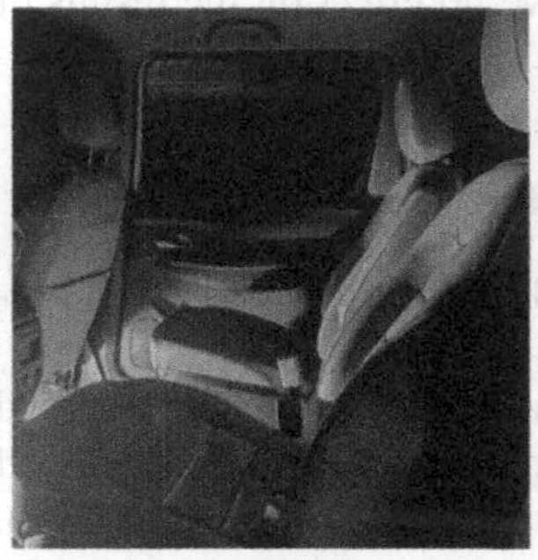

Fig. 3. 6500 K (warm white)

Fig. 4. 5000 K (white)

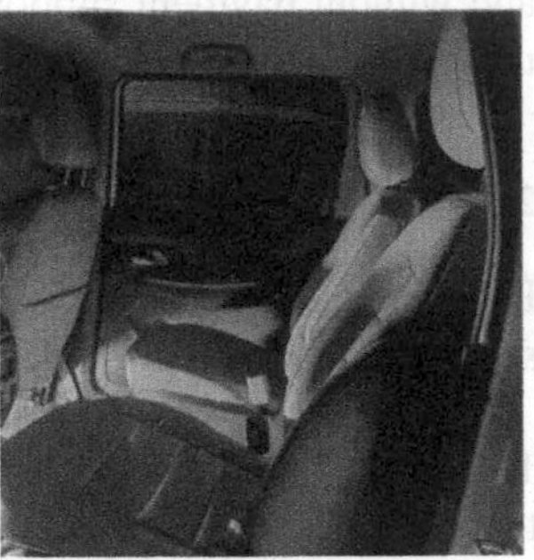

Fig. 5. 4000 K (cool white)

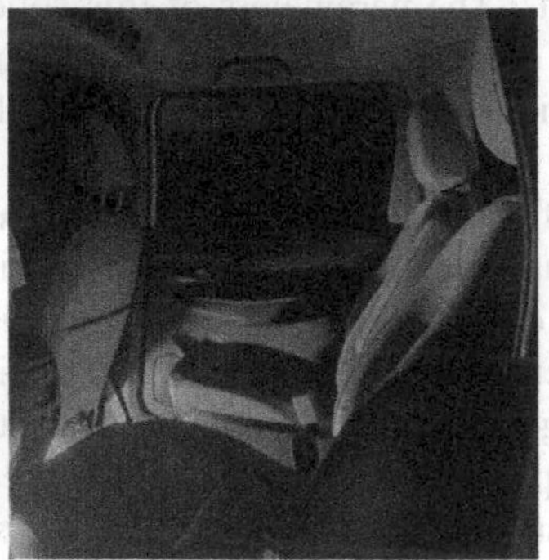

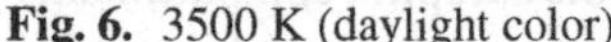

Fig. 6. 3500 K (daylight color)

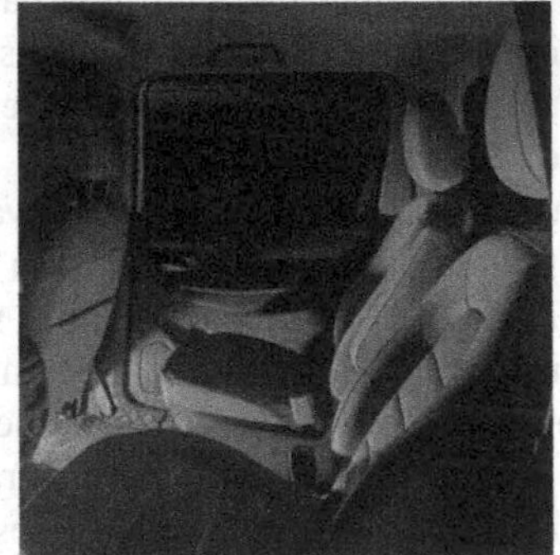

Fig. 7. 3200 K (cool daylight color)

Table 3. Lighting settings in daytime experimental scenes

Participants	Night illumination	Illumination	Color temperature
Male/Female	80000 lx	750 lx	6500 k (warm white)
	80000 lx	750 lx	5000 k (white)
	80000 lx	750 lx	4000 k (cool white)
	80000 lx	750 lx	3500 k (daylight color)
	80000 lx	750 lx	3200 k (cool daylight color)

Fig. 8. 6500 K (warm white)

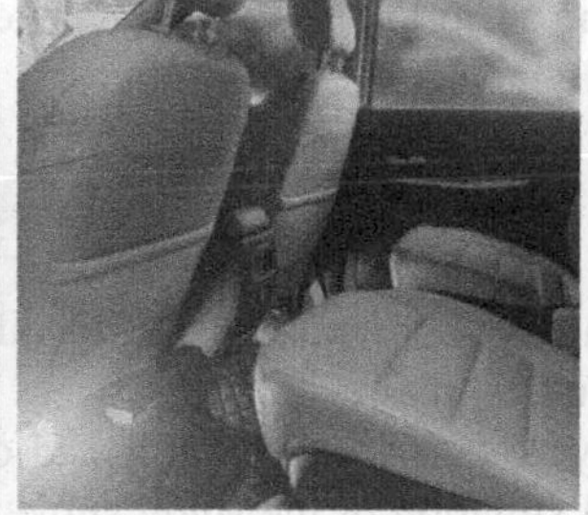
Fig. 9. 5000 K (white)

Fig. 10. 4000 K (cool white)

Fig. 11. 3500 K (daylight color)

Fig. 12. 3200 K (cool daylight color)

2.4 Procedures

We will first conduct a semi-structured interview with each male and female participant in the experiment. Participants are then asked to sit still for 10 min at night in 0.2 lx ambient light and then for 5 min at each color temperature to allow for acclimatization. Male and female participants were then asked to rate their subjective preference for each of the five different color temperature lights (CCT). The test was conducted daily from 6:00 to 9:00 p.m. and during the day from 12:00 to 15:00. 15 min would elapse between each color temperature to mitigate residual effects.

Semi-structured interviews elicited participants' expected judgments of different color temperature lighting. They expected judgments of brightness, color fidelity, expansiveness, pleasantness, clarity, relaxation, tension, depression, and fatigue for each color temperature environment.

The subjective preference score for comfort was designed to give participants a clear indication of which light or range of color temperatures made participants feel most comfortable. The scores measured the effects of passenger alertness, visual comfort, preference, and preference in three main dimensions. Alertness levels were measured by the Karolinska Drowsiness Scale [16], which was interpreted.

To ensure that the results of the subjective preference scores for comfort were as objective and accurate, the test design followed these four principles (1) to ensure that participants had the same degree of familiarity with the test questions (2) to ensure that participants had the same level of acceptance of the test questions (3) that the test-takers could accept the test method in a short period (4) that the test structure was as conducive to statistical and quantitative analysis.

2.5 Statistical Analysis

This paper mainly used data analysis software SPSS 26 and Excel to manage and analyze the data yielded from the questionnaire. In the process of data analysis, descriptive statistics, t-test, and one-way ANOVA were performed on the data obtained through the questionnaire. The actual situation of the study subjects was subsequently derived, and the reasons for the actual situation were discussed and analyzed. The descriptive statistics were used to answer the composition of the subjects and the analysis of the current situation; the t-test and the one-way ANOVA were used to answer distribution differences.

3 Study Results

3.1 Experimental Design

46 questionnaires were distributed in this experiment. A total of 23 participants in this study participated in the experiment (11 males and 12 females) Five different color temperatures (6500 K warm white; 5000 K white; 4000 K; cool white 3500 K; daylight color; 3200 K cool daylight color) with the same light intensity of 750 lx were screened, and the experiment was conducted in two different scenarios during the day and night.

3.2 Reliability and Validity Tests

Reliability refers to whether a certain evaluation method accurately reflects the real situation to be measured, i.e., the reliability of the evaluation index. It is an analysis of the stability and consistency of the measurement results. Reliability is influenced by random error, and the higher the reliability coefficient, the more reliable the measurement is. The reliability testing methods include retest reliability, replicate reliability, fold-and-half reliability, and internal consistency reliability (Intraclass Correlation Coefficient) analysis. In this study, Cronbach's Alpha Coefficient was used to test the reliability of the questionnaire, and the statistical data related to the reliability test of this evaluation index system were analyzed by spss26 statistical software, and the results are listed in Table 4.

The Cronbach coefficients for each subtest of the questionnaire ranged from 0.700 to 0.970. In general, a coefficient greater than 0.7 indicates high internal consistency and reliability, greater than 0.5 is considered reliable, and less than 0.35 indicates low internal consistency and reliability. The above results demonstrate that the coefficients of all the factors exceed 0.7, which fully meet the requirements and indicate that the internal consistency of the questionnaire is high.

In this paper, the questionnaire's exploratory factor analysis was conducted using SPSS 26.0 data analysis software, as measured by the KMO test values, Bartlett's spherical test, and cumulative variance contribution ratio. The test criteria are as follows: (1)

Table 4. Internal consistency test of the scores of each dimensional indicator of the pre-survey questionnaire (n = 70)

Indicators	Cronbach Alpha	Number of questions
Passenger alertness	0.876	5
Visual comfort	0.958	17
Color temperature preference	0.809	5
Total table	0.967	27

firstly, the size of thc KMO value is measured, and the KMO value needs to exceed the minimum academic standard of greater than 0.5; (2) secondly, the significance level of Bartlett's spherical test should be less than 0.01. In this paper, the KMO test and Bartlett's spherical test were first performed on the 24 measured question items of the sample, and the test results are shown in Table 5 below.

Table 5. KMO and Bartlett's test

KMO The number of sample suitability measures		0.833
Bartlett's sphericity test	Approximate cardinality	3283.796
	Degree of freedom	861
	Significance	0.000

As inferred from the table, the KMO value of the questionnaire is 0.833, which is greater than 0.5, and Bartlett's spherical test result is significant (Sig = 0.000), indicating that the overall validity of the questionnaire is acceptable and that each variable can be subjected to further exploratory factor analysis or validation factor analysis.

Table 6. KMO and Bartlett's test (n = 46)

Indicators	KMO	P
Passenger alertness	0.799	<0.001
Visual comfort	0.868	<0.001
Color temperature preference	0.731	<0.001
Total table	0.833	<0.001

The factor analysis revealed that the KMO values of the indicators ranged from 0.700–0.900, which was greater than the minimum academic standard of greater than 0.5, $p < 0.000$, indicating that the structural validity of the questionnaire was acceptable.

3.3 Descriptive Analysis

According to the results of the descriptive analysis, the average scores of passenger alertness, visual comfort, and color temperature preference are 4.4304, 4.3572, 4.3757, respectively, indicating that the overall level of passenger alertness is average, the overall level of visual comfort is high, and the color temperature preference is obvious.

Since t-tests, ANOVAs and correlations have the statistical prerequisite of normal data distribution. If the data is severely skewed, non-linear relationships between variables or pseudo-correlations, the conclusions are not deemed credible. Therefore, the normality test is performed before analyzing the regression model, as shown by the results. Under normal distribution, the skewness coefficient and kurtosis coefficient values should tend towards 0. When the skewness coefficient is greater than 3, and the kurtosis coefficient is greater than 8 the distribution is not normal. The skewed values close to 0 and peaks less than 8 for each dimension indicator in Table 6, the data are normally distributed (Table 7).

Table 7. Descriptive statistics

	N	Minimum value	Maximum value	Average value	Standard deviation	Skewness		Kurtosis	
	Statistics	Statistics	Statistics	Statistics	Statistics	Statistics	Standard error	Statistics	Standard error
Passenger alertness	46	3.00	6.40	4.4304	.75421	.407	.350	−.004	.688
Visual comfort	46	2.18	5.00	4.3572	.63330	−1.631	.350	3.650	.688
Color temperature preference	46	2.96	5.00	4.3757	.48896	−1.279	.350	1.590	.688

3.4 Variance Analysis

To explore the potential differences in light alertness and comfort between participants in which light or which range of color temperatures, t-tests, and ANOVAs were conducted in this study.

As inferred from the analysis results, there is a significant difference in the vigilance of gender under different color temperature lights ($F = 18.295$, $p = 0.000 < 0.0001$) (Figs. 13, 14 and Table 8).

Based on the results of the analysis, it is clear that there is a borderline significant difference in the comfort level of gender under different color temperature lighting ($F = 3.354$, $p = 0.076 > 0.05$) (Figs. 15 and 16) (Table 9).

3.5 Related Analysis

The Pearson correlation coefficient method is often used to describe the strength of the relationship between two variables. The results of the correlation analysis demonstrate

Table 8. Tests of between-subjects effects

Dependent variable: PA					
Source	Type III Sum of squares	df	Mean square	F	Sig.
Corrected model	23.463a	13	1.805	27.055	.000
Intercept	710.996	1	710.996	10658.274	.000
Gender	.576	1	.576	8.631	.006
Scenes	.054	1	.054	.812	.374
Gender * scenario	.003	1	.003	.051	.823
Gender * light type	9.763	8	1.220	18.295	.000
Gender * scene * lighting type	.004	2	.002	.027	.973
Error	2.135	32	.067		
Total	928.520	46			
Corrected total	25.597	45			

a. R Squared = .917 (Adjusted R Squared = .883).

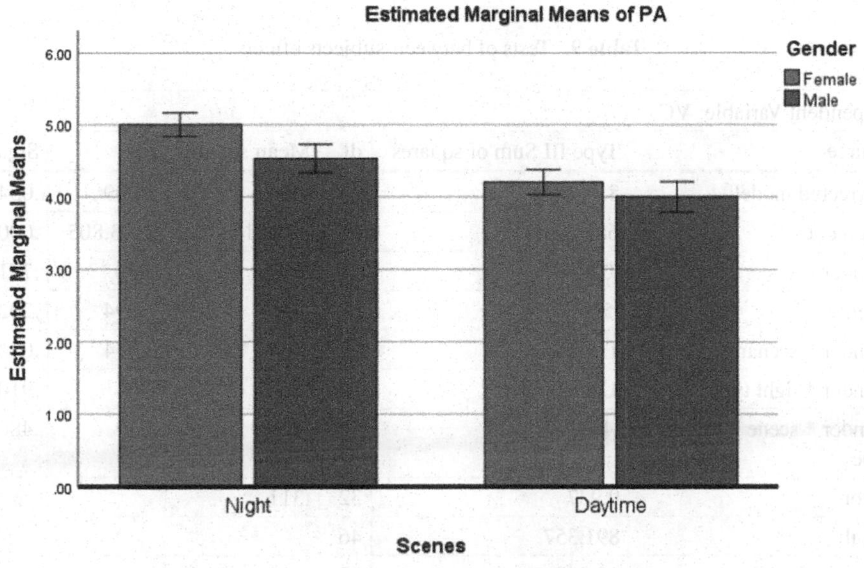

Fig. 13. Analysis of variance for different scenarios

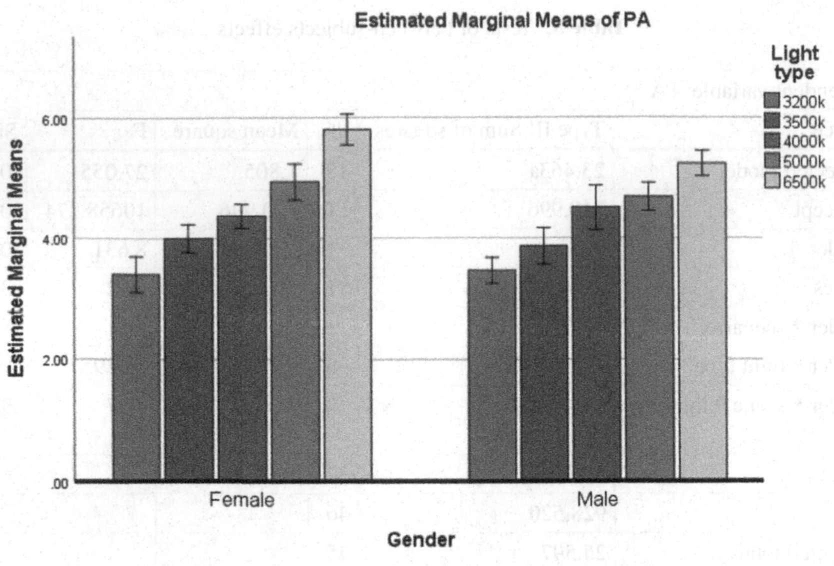

Fig. 14. Analysis of variance at different color temperatures

Table 9. Tests of between-subjects effects

Dependent Variable: VC					
Source	Type III Sum of squares	df	Mean square	F	Sig.
Corrected model	8.112a	13	.624	2.009	.054
Intercept	681.215	1	681.215	2193.805	.000
Gender	.027	1	.027	.086	.771
Scenes	.526	1	.526	1.694	.202
Gender * scenario	1.041	1	1.041	3.354	.076
Gender * light type	1.005	8	.126	.404	.910
Gender * scene * lighting type	.459	2	.229	.739	.486
Error	9.937	32	.311		
Total	891.357	46			
Corrected total	18.048	45			

a. R Squared = .449 (Adjusted R Squared = .226)

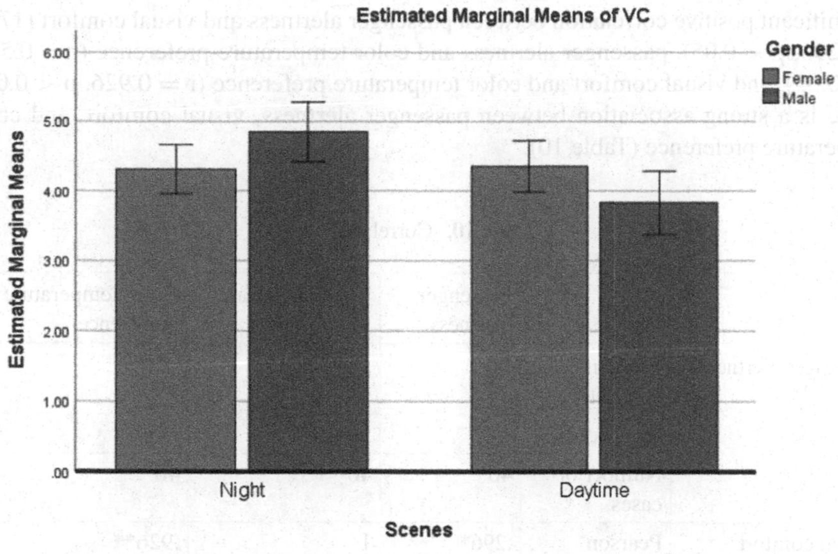

Fig. 15. Analysis of variance for different scenarios

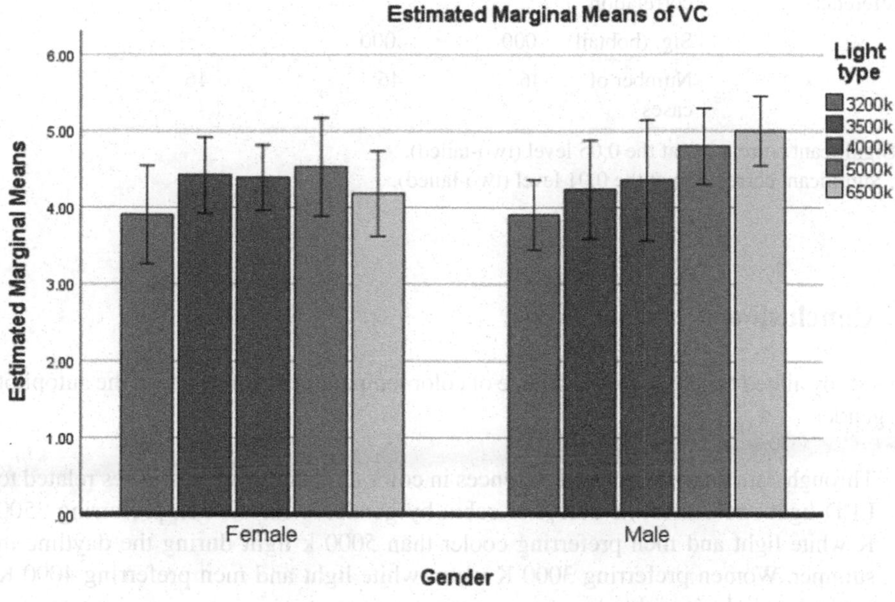

Fig. 16. Analysis of variance at different color temperatures

a significant positive correlation between passenger alertness and visual comfort [17] (r = 0.296, p < 0.05), passenger alertness and color temperature preference (r = 0.501, p < 0.05), and visual comfort and color temperature preference (r = 0.926, p < 0.05). There is a strong association between passenger alertness, visual comfort, and color temperature preference (Table 10).

Table 10. Correlation

		Passenger alertness	Visual comfort	Color temperature preference
Passenger alertness	Pearson correlation	1	.296*	.501**
	Sig. (bobtail)		.046	.000
	Number of cases	46	46	46
Visual comfort	Pearson correlation	.296*	1	.926**
	Sig. (bobtail)	.046		.000
	Number of cases	46	46	46
Color temperature preference	Pearson correlation	.501**	.926**	1
	Sig. (bobtail)	.000	.000	
	Number of cases	46	46	46

*. Significant correlation at the 0.05 level (two-tailed).

**. Significant correlation at the 0.01 level (two-tailed).

4 Conclusion

This study aimed to scrutinize the choice of color temperature preference in the autopilot by gender.

1) Through data analysis noted differences in color temperature preferences related to LED light sources in the autopilot cabin by gender, with women preferring 3500 K white light and men preferring cooler than 5000 k light during the daytime in summer. Women preferring 3000 K warm white light and men preferring 4000 K cool white light at night.
2) Moreover, with varying color temperature environments, brightness, passenger alertness, visual comfort, preference also possess differences. At the same time, passenger alertness, visual comfort, and preference have a significant positive correlation. It

can reduce visual fatigue, enhance user experience, and be calibrated to optimize energy consumption.

The passengers' preferences for the light color temperature through the automated cockpit are more interesting than the passenger's own choice. It is a direct automated activity, and the passenger is not involved in the decision-making process that may increase their cognitive burden.

This study proposes novel ideas for the design of the in-cabin experience and provides informative implications for differences in light and gender preferences in specific environments, as well as new ideas for differentiated customization in unmanned cabins.

References

1. Pakusch, C., et al.: Unintended effects of autonomous driving: a study on mobility preferences in the future. Sustain. **10**(7), 2404 (2018). https://doi.org/10.3390/su10072404
2. Marengo, L., Settepanella, S., Zhang, Y.X.: Towards a unified aggregation framework for preferences and judgments. Evol. Inst. Econ. Rev. **18**(1), 21–44 (2021). https://doi.org/10.1007/s40844-021-00200-w
3. Shreyas, V., Bharadwaj, S.N., Srinidhi, S., Ankith, K.U., Rajendra, A.B.: Self-driving cars: an overview of various autonomous driving systems. In: Kolhe, M.L., Tiwari, S., Trivedi, M.C., Mishra, K.K. (eds.) Advances in Data and Information Sciences. LNNS, vol. 94, pp. 361–371. Springer, Singapore (2020). https://doi.org/10.1007/978-981-15-0694-9_34
4. Sagnier, C., Loup-Escande, E., Valléry, G.: Effects of gender and prior experience in immersive user experience with virtual reality. In: Ahram, T., Falcão, C. (eds.) AHFE 2019. AISC, vol. 972, pp. 305–314. Springer, Cham (2020). https://doi.org/10.1007/978-3-030-19135-1_30
5. ACM Other conferences. Towards autonomous cars | Proceedings of the 6th International Conference on Automotive User Interfaces and Interactive Vehicular Applications (2022). https://dl.acm.org/10.1145/2667317.2667330. Accessed 10 Feb 2022
6. Zhu, Y., et al.: Effects of illuminance and correlated color temperature on daytime cognitive performance, subjective mood, and alertness in healthy adults. Environ. Behav. **51**(2), 199–230 (2017)
7. Lrc.rpi.edu. Interior Automotive Lighting | The Long and Lighted Road: Lighting and Driving | Lighting Futures | Programs | LRC (2022). https://www.lrc.rpi.edu/programs/futures/lf-auto/interior.asp
8. Shizhu, L., et al.: Effects and challenges of operational lighting illuminance in spacecraft on human visual acuity. In: Stanton, N. (ed.) AHFE 2021. LNNS, vol. 270, pp. 582–588. Springer, Cham (2021). https://doi.org/10.1007/978-3-030-80012-3_67
9. Blankenbach, K., Hertlein, F., Hoffmann, S.: Advances in automotive interior lighting concerning new LED approach and optical performance. J. Soc. Inform. Display **28**(8), 655–667 (2020)
10. Jiang, A., Yao, X., Schlacht, I.L., Musso, G., Tang, T., Westland, S.: Habitability study on space station colour design. In: Stanton, N. (ed.) AHFE 2020. AISC, vol. 1212, pp. 507–514. Springer, Cham (2020). https://doi.org/10.1007/978-3-030-50943-9_64
11. Kang, B., Yong, B., Park, K.: Performance evaluations of LED headlamps. Int. J. Automot. Technol. **11**(5), 737–742 (2010). https://doi.org/10.1007/s12239-010-0087-0
12. Synopsys.com. Lighting Design Software - LightTools | Synopsys Synopsys (2022). https://www.synopsys.com/en-us/optical-solutions/lighttools.html. Accessed 10 Feb 2022

13. Jiang, A., Foing, B.H., Schlacht, I.L., Yao, X., Cheung, V., Rhodes, P.A.: Colour schemes to reduce stress response in the hygiene area of a space station: a Delphi study. Appl. Ergon. **98**, 103573 (2022)
14. Yu, K., Jiang, A., Wang, J., Zeng, X., Yao, X., Chen, Y.: Construction of crew visual behaviour mechanism in ship centralized control cabin. In: Stanton, N. (ed.) AHFE 2021. LNNS, vol. 270, pp. 503–510. Springer, Cham (2021). https://doi.org/10.1007/978-3-030-80012-3_58
15. Jiang, A., Yao, X., Hemingray, C., Westland, S.: Young people's colour preference and the arousal level of small apartments. Color Res. Appl. **1**, 1–13 (2021). https://doi.org/10.1002/col.22756
16. Shamsul, M., Nur Sajidah, S., Ashok, S.: Alertness, visual comfort, subjective preference and task performance assessment under three advanced engineering. Forum **10**, 77–82 (2013)
17. Lu, S., et al.: The effect on subjective alertness and fatigue of three colour temperatures in the spacecraft crew cabin. In: Stanton, N. (ed.) AHFE 2021. LNNS, vol. 270, pp. 632–639. Springer, Cham (2021). https://doi.org/10.1007/978-3-030-80012-3_74

A Deep Dive into the China's Gen Z: How They Use and What They Expect for Their Cars

Qihao Huang[1(✉)], Guanyu Mao[1,2], Yelu Liu[1], Ya Wang[1], Xiaojun Luo[1], and Jifang Wang[1]

[1] Baidu Apollo Design Center, Shenzhen 518000, China
huangqihao@baidu.com, maoguanyu2020@email.szu.edu.cn
[2] College of Economics, Shenzhen University, Shenzhen 518000, China

Abstract. In the next half decade, there will be nearly 40 million potential Gen Z (or Gen Z for short) consumers in the Chinese market who will have a high propensity to buy cars. This study focuses specifically on Chinese Gen Z. It seeks to find out their car-buying preferences, lifestyles, how they understand and use their vehicles, and their daily driving needs, in the context of China. Our goal is to develop potential concepts and collect valuable insights from user research to guide our future product design. As a first step, we identified characteristics of Gen Z in China based on previous studies and industry research reports: Gen Z tends to focus on their feelings and needs, was born and lives on the Internet, and knows they have easy access to all the information they need, enjoys independence but also desires connectedness, uses the technology they are so good at, and loves Chinese culture. Next, we applied a qualitative method combining in-depth interviews and field observation. Twenty participants in China's first- tier cities, such as Beijing, Shanghai, and Shenzhen; second-tier cities, such as Changsha, Hunan, and Chengdu, Sichuan; and third-tier cities, such as Hengyang, Hunan, and Mianyang, Sichuan, had participated. The current study revealed that (a) Gen Z is good at gathering the information they need from KOLs on the Internet to select a suitable car for themselves; (b) a car is assigned multiple roles by Gen Z, such as a friend, a private space, and an assistant; (c) although there is no significant difference between Gen Z and their Millennial counterparts when it comes to car use scenarios, for instance, going to work, shopping, or organizing a road trip, they are more likely to have a connection with friends during a trip, so the connection between their car and the passenger or another car became more important. In addition to the detailed user needs to be highlighted in the scenarios, we also discussed the design possibilities to shape the future smart car based on Gen Z's needs for driver-automation shared control, digital cockpits, and their preferences for the car's interior and exterior decoration.

Keywords: Gen Z · Lifestyle · Car use scenarios · Driver-automation shared control · Digital cockpits

H. Krömker (Ed.): HCII 2022, LNCS 13335, pp. 167–183, 2022.
https://doi.org/10.1007/978-3-031-04987-3_11

1 Introduction

1.1 Research Background

By 2021, the total population of Gen Z (people born between 1995 and 2009) exceeds 280 million, accounting for 18.1% of China's total population [1]. Since 2016, Gen Z has gradually entered society to take over the division of labor. Their life status has shifted to the golden period of getting married and having children, becoming the new force in China's current Passenger Vehicle market. Meanwhile, with the transition from a product-driven economy to an experience-driven economy, sales in the car market are declining year by year, and many car manufacturers are looking for innovative ways to improve their business performance. They are trying to understand more and deeper about those potential car owners in China to make the future cars meet the preferences of the next generation of car owners and break through the sales bottleneck.

Definition of China's Gen Z. The name of Gen Z comes from Generation X and Generation Y. Generation X (people born between 1965 and 1980) was first shown in Canadian author Douglas Copeland's novel of the same name, Generation X: Tales for an Accelerated Culture [2]. It is then defined by fifteen years for a generation like Generation Y (people born between 1981 and 1995, also called Millennials). In its 2021 Consumer Report [1] for Chinese Society, Cyanhill Capital measures historical development and human growth against the 2003 SARS epidemic, which accelerated the spread of the Internet and public availability of information, and identifies the generation that reached age six in 2003 (born after 1997) as the beginning of Gen Z in China. According to CNNIC data [3], Internet penetration growth in China accelerated in 2001–2002 (when broadband connections became popular) and 2006–2007 (when smartphones and mobile Internet exploded). At the same time, we believe that this point in time (born after 1997) is too narrow as a node given the large regional and urban-rural differences in China, and the final definition of Gen Z in China mentioned in this paper is the generation born between 1995 and 2009, which also corresponds to Gen Z in the international community.

Characteristics of Gen Z in China. China's Gen Z grows up in an era of social stability and economic prosperity. Information is widely explosion on the Internet, and they know how to use the Internet skillfully and to easily get the information they need. In this context, their consumption is not limited to basic physical needs but focuses more on spiritual needs, not only for individual and unique styles and products but also more intense experiences. Gen Z emphasizes happiness and pleasure experiences in a rich living environment. PwC and SuperELLE [4], in their report "The Nation of Youth: Cultural Insights and Business Insights", describes the profile of Gen Z based on seven critical characteristics: (a) Independent Minds (they like to be unique and seek for their style), (b) Community Love (they eager to have a connection with the community), (c) Experience First (they focus on feelings of their own), (d) High Tech (they know how far technology can go), (e) Strong Spirits (they care about their health status, both physical and mental), (f) Diversity Matters (they live on multiple ways they enjoy to earn money and make a cool living), and (g) Cultural Confidence (they love Chinese culture). Chunling Li [5] believes that the change in values is important for the shift in consumer behavior.

Gen Z and the Vehicle Market in China. Research abroad on Gen Z covered various topics in consumer perspectives, perceptions of attitudes toward childcare [6], lifestyles [7], attitudes toward fashion [8], and other aspects. In recent years, there have also been some industry reports from the beauty [9], gaming [10], health [11] and other industries in China describing Gen Z consumers. As for the trend analysis of the car market, the Yiche Research Institute [12] predicts that the future buyers in the car market will show the trend of the new four: (a) they will be with higher education levels, (b) more of them will live in big cities, (c) there will be more single buyers, and (d) women will be a new big potential group of car buyers.

Over the past 20 years, sales in the Chinese passenger car market have steadily increased, but in 2018, passenger car sales began a steady decline. This is related to the significant decrease in the number of people born in 1990–1994 who want to spend money in the car market. Further, the population has experienced a steady decline after 1995, reducing the potential of some Gen Z car owners to buy cars and weakening their contribution to China's car market turnover. In addition, some of the private cars resold in the used car market are also bought by Gen Z, so China's private car consumption market is gradually moving into the share era. Both automotive companies and the automotive market are desperate to find new avenues for economic growth. The good news is that an online quantitative study conducted by Ipsos [13] shows that Gen Z has long considered driving a necessary skill in their fast-paced lives. 80% of Gen Z have already obtained their driver's license at college and usually plan to buy a car after they graduate or start working, unlike other generations who decide to buy a car after their jobs stabilize or after they get married and have children. With the rise of Chinese disposable income and the popularity of consumer credit, Gen Z's budget for car purchases is significantly higher than that of other generations. In addition, their unique insights about cars are also relevant to future car consumption.

1.2 Introduction to the Current Study

In this issue, this study was launched. We tried to discuss with Gen Z, including car owners and potential owners, about their lifestyles and values, car perceptions and preferences of vehicles, their driving scenarios, and expectations for future cars. This study is based on a qualitative approach, and three key steps are as follows (Fig. 1).

Fig. 1. Three key steps of the current study

As a first step, we identified characteristics of Gen Z in China based on previous studies and industry research reports to answer (a) "What kind of people should we design cars for?". Next, we applied a qualitative method combining in-depth interviews and field observation to sort out Gen Z's car scenarios and needs to clarify (b) "how to design cars for this generation of car owners in the future?". Finally, based on the research findings, we tried to cooperate with designers and explore (c) "how to design a suitable car for future car owners?".

2 Research Methodology

2.1 Participant

Twenty Gen Z users from five cities, recruited by an external consulting firm, participated in an in-home interview campaign. All users were paid after the interview ended.

Demographics. Gen Z differs across regions and between genders. As Gen Z is currently entering the workforce and school, their economic levels and life status vary. Therefore, the 20 Gen Z respondents, ten men and ten women, cover people with different life statuses, such as those studying in school, entering the workforce, getting married, and having children. Considering the requirements for driving experience and car ownership status, the respondents in this study were requested to be born between 1995 and 2001. They live in Tier 1–3 cities nationwide, including Tier 1 cities such as Shanghai, Beijing, and Shenzhen (Guangdong Province); Tier 2 cities such as Chengdu (Sichuan Province) and Changsha (Hunan Province); Tier 3 cities such as Mianyang (Sichuan Province) and Hengyang (Hunan Province).

Population Characteristics. All 20 users recruited were requested to match the seven elements of Gen Z from the PwC and SuperELLE report "The Nation of Youth: Cultural Insights and Business Insights" [4] mentioned above. We designed a value description matrix question for each attribute during the recruitment process. Those who met more than the criteria were considered to meet the feature, and qualified respondents were expected to meet at least three attributes. Overall, 20 respondents covered all seven characteristics.

Driving Experience and Car Ownership. All respondents had a driver's license and at least two-to-five-years driving experience based on the study objectives. They were also divided into owners and potential owners based on their car ownership. Ten of the owners owned the car that they decided to purchase. Ten car owners owned vehicles included new energy vehicles (Tesla, NIO), mainstream brands vehicles (BYD, Roewe, Mazda), and luxury brands vehicles (Audi, BMW); ten potential owners planned to purchase their car within three years, and their previous driving experience mainly came from their parents', friends' cars or rented cars.

2.2 Research Process

Desktop Research. Combining with industry research reports on Gen Z in china, we extracted the demographic characteristics of Gen Z to recruit users matching the characteristics of Gen Z on this basis.

On-site Interviews. We conducted in-person interviews with respondents in their homes to understand Gen Z's lifestyle and values and confirm industry research information. Besides, we aim to understand Gen Z's perceptions, preferences, and expectations for their cars and determine factors influencing their car purchase process. Further, we tried to understand Gen Z's car and travel scenarios and explore needs and pain points in travel scenarios. And at last, we discuss with them to study Gen Z's expectations for future cars in response to needs and pain points.

Environmental Observation. In the middle of the interviews, we observe and record the respondents' homes, their personal hobbies, and vehicles. This gives us a more concrete understanding of our users' lifestyles and perceptions.

2.3 Method of Analysis

We recorded user interview data using audio and video recordings and on-site transcription. The text analysis method was used for qualitative data to create journey maps of users' different car use scenarios. As an exploratory study, we started from the characteristics of Gen Z, and then mapped them to their car scenarios to better understand their car use scenario characteristics. Also, combining users' existing pain points, we derive users' core requirements about their car use through information clustering with the interview data.

3 Research Findings

3.1 Gen Z' Life States and Its Attitude Towards Cars

Life States of the Gen Z. Based on interviews and life observations, we classified the life status of Gen Z into four categories (Fig. 2): (a) Happy Lifestyle, (b) Traditional Comfort Lifestyle, (c) Career Chasing Lifestyle, and (d) Chaotic Fumbling Lifestyle. There are differences in the consumption concepts, decision-making basis, car perception, and Gen Z's current and future car purchases in the different styles.

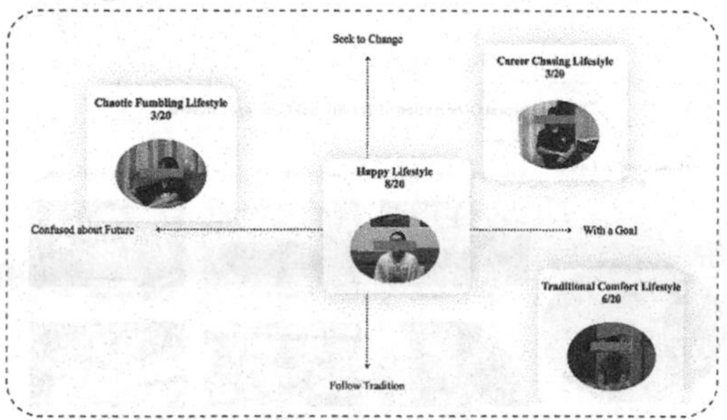

Fig. 2. Life states of the Gen Z

Happy Lifestyle. The lifestyle of these people is carefree, they live in the present and strive for self-satisfaction. This type of drivers is characterized by a better economic situation of the family, economic pressure is low, and women are more represented. They live their lives going with the flow, doing what they love and seeking personal happiness; they love to socialize and love to share their lives on social media. They love to enrich their lives with flower arrangements, potted plants, and decorative paintings. They are used to affordable luxury consumption, with consumer goods such as high-end skin care products, bags, and shoes, etc. They also like individual car decorations, place ornaments on the front of the car, the seats are often decorated with several personalized pillows and other decorations, and they also stick interesting exterior decorations on the body of the car (Fig. 3).

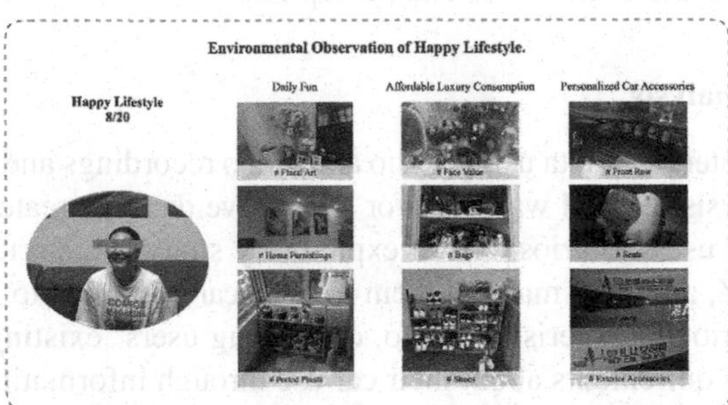

Fig. 3. Environmental observation of *Happy Lifestyle* Gen Z's home

Traditional Comfort Lifestyle. This kind of people strive for convenience, do not like pressure, but plan their life step by step. Respondents of this lifestyle has a more traditional family upbringing, lives in second and third tier cities, wants to have a stable and comfortable family life and career prospects, they use social media but spend less time with others and attach more importance to personal contacts. They love to create a warm home, decorate their desks and bedrooms, and the colors of the decoration are mostly based on coziness and warm tones. They all have their own hobbies, including Chinese Zither, a simple dubbing studio, designing a comfortable interior for their cars, such as soft and comfortable car seat cushions, and so on (Fig. 4).

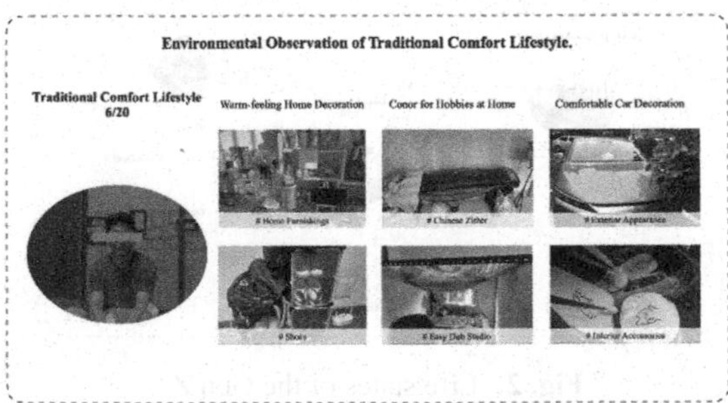

Fig. 4. Environmental observation of *Traditional Comfort Lifestyle* Gen Z's home

Career Chasing Lifestyle. Respondents of this lifestyle strive for professional success and have a strong desire for self-actualization. This type of car user generally has a higher income, lives in first-tier cities (represented by Shenzhen) and tends to be male. They strive for quality of life, have clear plans for the future, and work hard to achieve their career goals. They are also socially active and tend to use socializing as one of the ways to achieve their career goals. Most of them live near office buildings and have a high level of commercialization around them. They have enthusiastic hobbies like buying Garage Kits, motorcycle racing and so on. The requirement for their cars is cool interior and exterior decoration, including complete ambient lighting and body foils (Fig. 5).

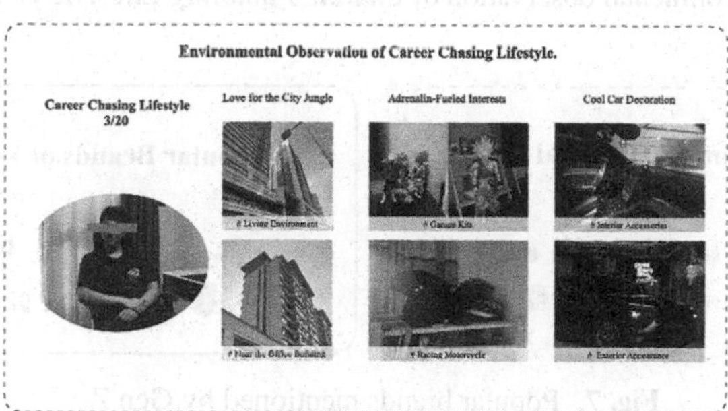

Fig. 5. Environmental observation of *Career Chasing Lifestyle* Gen Z's home

Chaotic Fumbling Lifestyle. This type of people is not clear about their future, they are eager for change but do not have the means to achieve it. This type of car user grows up in a rather conservative environment, does not have a high income, and usually lives in first-tier cities. They do not have a clear plan for the future and strive for complacency but are sometimes very confused; they use social media as a pastime, but their willingness to socialize is not very strong. Based on their purchasing power and living conditions, we can see that they like to buy simple and practical consumer goods such as dolls, ordinary bags and so on. They like a simple life, usually kill the time with their own hobbies, for instance, playing ukulele or violin to pass the time. They decorate their houses with wind chimes and prefer girly accessories. They also have foils on the outside of their bodywork, cushions, pendants, ornaments and DIY interiors on the inside of their cars and so on (Fig. 6).

The Consumption Concepts. When it comes to general consumer goods, Gen Z who strive for self-actualization are relatively indifferent to brand awareness, and their main need when buying products is practicality. However, the big brands offer Gen Z the security of quality assurance, while the many small brands and national brands fulfill Gen Z's attributes of patriotism and cultural trust, so some national brands have won Gen Z's favor. Gen Z is more brand-conscious than general consumption when it comes to car consumption, but their general consumption tendency is similar to general consumption, they pursue the brand that suits them and also readily accept domestic and new energy car brands. And as soon as China's Gen Z start to like a brand, they are relatively more loyal to brands (Fig. 7).

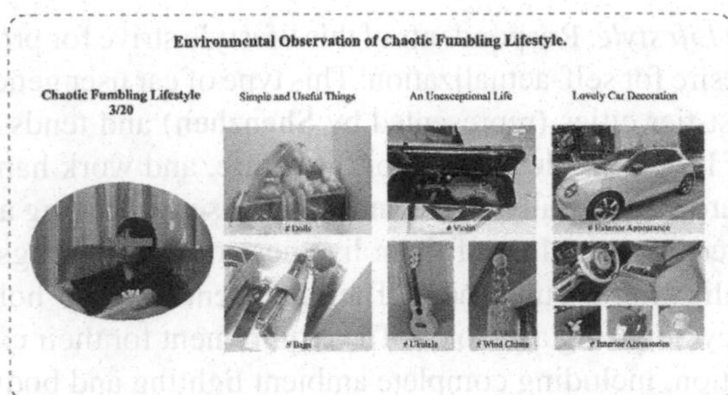

Fig. 6. Environmental observation of *Chaotic Fumbling Lifestyle* Gen Z's home

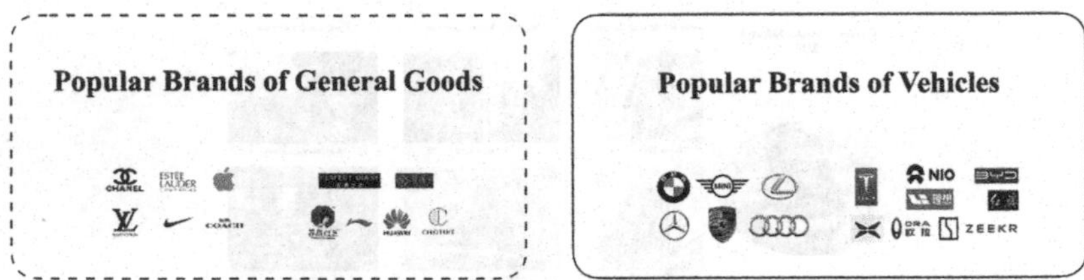

Fig. 7. Popular brands mentioned by Gen Z

The Information-Gathering Habit. At the same time, this Gen Z is good at using the Internet to gather information, and they like to "poke" through different channels when buying products. When they decide to buy a car, they like to pay attention to car vertical sales channels, e.g. autohome.com, dcdapp.com, bilibili.com, etc. Among them, KOL is also an important influencer, and some of this Ge Z find their favorite cars through rating and analysis by the KOLs. They are comprehensive and independent, want to live up to their own values and traditional consumer philosophy, so the practicality and design of the car play the most important role for them when buying a car. They focus on the interior, comfort, and intelligence of the car, but not on how important the intelligent driving characteristics of the car are (Fig. 8).

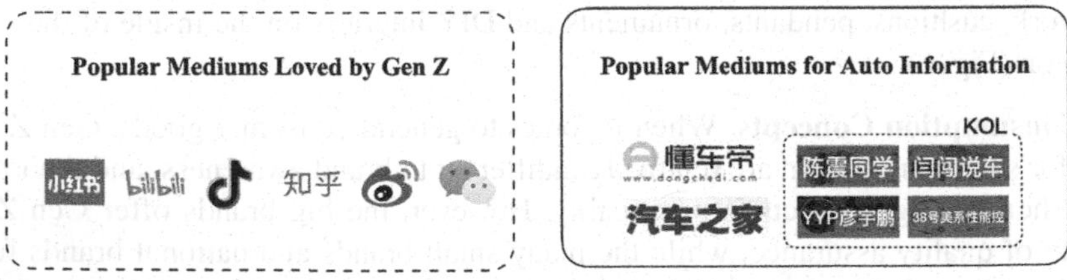

Fig. 8. Popular mediums in Gen Z's daily life

Perception of the Car. For Gen Z, the car is not only a means of transportation, but also a "big toy" that offers owners fun and an exciting driving experience. A car can be a mobile home or a private space that offers owners a place to relax alone. A car can also be a symbol of the owner's economic power, a representative of esthetic preferences and taste, and the owner's second business card. The car is something like a lover, a communicative friend, an assistant who helps the owner and a soul mate, because it can accompany the car owner all the time (Fig. 9). Gen Z owners believe that cars are chosen according to their needs and are business cards that can express their unique personalities, and they want the ideal future to be dedicated to their cars. They also hope that as their social status rises, the class of their next car will rise accordingly.

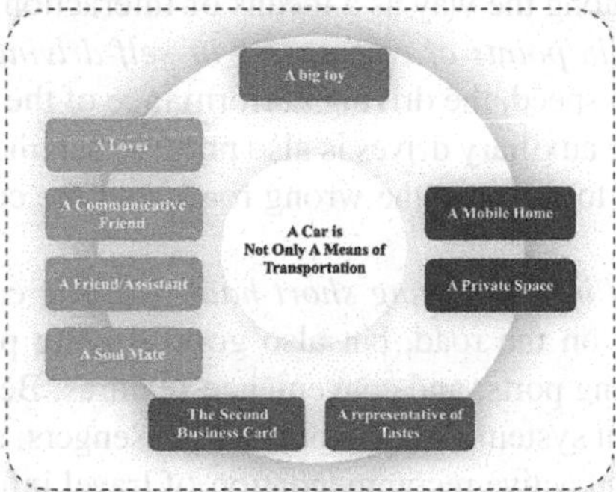

Fig. 9. A car is assigned multiple roles by Gen Z

3.2 The Car Use Scenarios of Gen Z

The lifestyle and consumer orientation of Gen Z are different. Still, the Gen Z's core car use scenarios are not different from those of previous Generations X and Y, such as commuting, city driving, short-distance driving, and long-distance driving. However, when combined with the characteristics of Gen Z, we can see some trends: (a) social connections between they and their companies are becoming more common, and (b) the scene of using the vehicle as a private space become more often. Based on the interview data, the current study sorts out six main types of car use scenarios of Gen Z (Fig. 10).

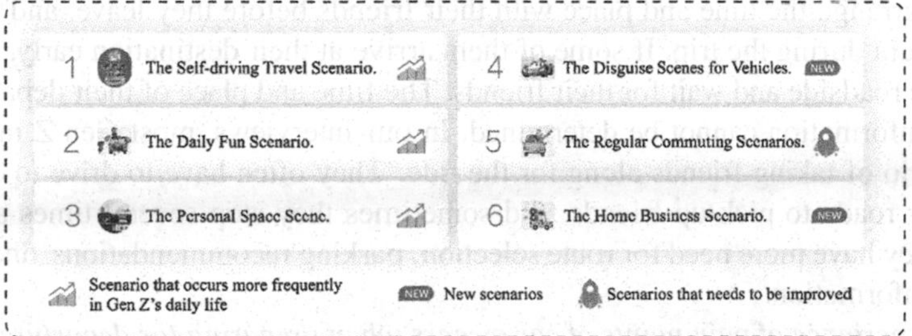

Fig. 10. Six main types of car use scenarios of Gen Z

The Self-driving Travel Scenario. Gen Z loves to travel with family and friends. They like to drive short distances to a place not far from home, especially on weekends and short holidays (for instance, the three-day International Labor Day holiday). And during the "Golden Week" (for instance, the seven-day National Day holiday) and long vacation periods, they, together with family or friends, will drive long distances mostly without a clear destination at the very first, creating the situation of multiple people taking turns at the wheel. Traveling together in multiple vehicles allows for more flexible itineraries, and they can book hotels nearby based on how far they are traveling. During our conversation, five people mentioned having travelled together in a group (usually with 3–5 cars). They would like to use the interaction between friends during the trip and the joy of traveling along the way as a means of interaction.

The experience of pain points of car owners in self-driving short haul. When the vehicle is running at high speed, the driving performance of the vehicle is poor, and the safety performance of the auxiliary drives is also poor. When the owner is driving on an unknown road, it is easy to drive on the wrong road, and the car also lacks navigation information.

Gen Z's expectations in self-driving short haul. (a) The car should have a larger trunk, weather alerts for on the road, but also good driving performance, reassuring driving aids, more charging ports, and convenience features. Besides, (b) it should also improve the entertainment system for the front and passengers, navigation transmission and navigation details, and active recommendation of travel information.

The experience of pain points of car owners during long distance driving. Car owners feel much fatigue during long-distance driving and are easily nervous when driving on special roads.

Gen Z's expectations during long distance driving. The car can intelligently check the condition of the car itself and relieve the owner's fatigue when driving.

The experience of pain points of car owners when traveling in groups. While traveling with multiple cars, car owners cannot communicate with each other in time and know the position of each other's car in time.

Gen Z's expectations when traveling in groups. Car owners and teammates can communicate with each other in real time, the car can show the position of teammates' cars, and the function of group travel can be optimized automatically.

The Daily Fun Scenario. Going out with friends is a much more common thing for most Gen Z. Whether they are traveling within the city or taking a longer or shorter trip, they will arrange the time and place with their friends before they leave, and they will contact them during the trip. If some of them arrive at their destination early, they will stop at the roadside and wait for their friends. The time and place of their departure and the road information cannot be determined. In our interviews, most Gen Z mentioned the scenario of taking friends along for the ride. They often have to drive to different, unfamiliar roads to pick up friends, and sometimes they stop several times along the way, so they have more need for route selection, parking recommendations, and sharing location information.

The experience of pain points of car owners when preparing for departure. It is not convenient to open the door or the trunk lid when holding something in the driver's hands, the make-up mirror in the car is small and the light tones are not natural.

Gen Z's expectations when preparing for departure. The car can open the door automatically when controlled by voice or remote control. More human comfort settings are also needed inside the car.

The experience of pain points of car owners while driving. Car owners are not safe when replying to chat messages while driving. Car owners do not know the agreed pickup location on an unknown road.

Gen Z's expectation while driving. The navigation map and AR navigation can tell the location of the person being picked up.

The experience of pain points of car owners before and after parking to pick up their friends. Car owners cannot fix the location of parking on unknown roads. When their friends are late, the inconvenience of parking on some roads leads to boredom while waiting in the nearest parking lot.

Gen Z's expectation when parking to pick up their friends. The car should accurately predict the arrival time according to the road conditions because the exact time and place are especially important to car owners. In addition, the nearest short-term parking lot should include the cost information of parking.

The experience of pain points of car owners when parking. It is difficult for car owners to park in large shopping malls because they cannot find parking spaces.

Gen Z's expectation when parking. The software in the car should improve parking information and parking guidance in commercial areas and should be able to connect with the owner's mobile app to find the parking space.

The Personal Space Scene. Gen Z, who are new to society or have not yet entered society, are very anxious and need an "independent space" to release their emotions. They use the car as a private space to temporarily relax from their worries and turn it into a multifunctional space to relax in the car after a trip or rest in the car during lunch break. Most of the respondents said they are currently dealing with many growing pains and sometimes have to be alone to think about their own staff. For Gen Z, the car is an excellent private space to develop the ability to start over. With the emergence of private cinemas and KTVs, cars also have a second meaning. Many car companies have given multiple identities to private spaces in cars, such as meditation rooms, cinemas, and KTVs.

The experience of pain points of the car owners when relax in the private space. The car's seats are not ergonomically designed and lack ventilation, heating and massage functions; the smart cockpit's media applications are not rich enough, and its accounts such as music and video are not linked.

Gen Z's expectations about smart cockpits. Cockpit seats should be designed to meet ergonomic requirements and increase comfort. Rich entertainment applications should be available in the cockpit, and the accounts of APP and cell phones in the vehicle can be connected.

The Disguise Scenes for Vehicles. Gen Z is also an avid car lover, they love driving and are willing to spend more money on car maintenance while taking cool photos of their cars. They then share the cool photos one their social medium like Weibo, but they care little about whether those photos are appreciated by others. However, if the car company's official account send "likes" to them, they will be happy. What's more, they go to the "Late Night Garage" (a brand for more fun car lifestyle) that specializes in cleaning and photographing vehicles to spruce up their cars (Fig. 11).

Fig. 11. Cool photos by the "Late Night Garage"

Depending on the shift in scenarios, they also expect different vehicles to be equipped with different services. For example, when Gen Z drives a car for pleasure, they have higher requirements for performance enhancement of their cars. If it is for family mobility and convenience, they have high expectations for comfort and cockpit space. They also expect the subsequent car maintenance team to be more professional and provide better services.

The Regular Commuting Scenarios. Gen Z, who have just entered the workforce, have a relatively fixed commute time, and those who are still in school also have a commuting scenario in which they drive to and from school. The driving scenario usually occurs on urban-rural roads, elevated roads, and urban highways, with fixed times and fixed routes. Gen Z will have incredible emotional highs and lows about being blocked in the driving process. The problem of long traffic jams and low number of parking spaces has always existed in the first-tire cities. As a result, users expect their new cars to have features that ease their anxiety, such as displaying parking information and automatically searching for parking spaces. Second- and third-tier cities, on the other hand, suffer from traffic chaos and tight parking spaces, and users expect improved automatic parking systems and synchronized information about road conditions on their cell phones or in their cars. A common feature in all cities is the lack of remote control of the vehicle and the lack of trust in assisted driving. Users also expect a borderless control system with optimized remote control, improved voice control, and education about the functions of assisted driving is also needed.

Due to the popularity of electric cars, Gen Z is more receptive to electric cars and loves technology-intensive products. Therefore, they will pay more attention to the location of charging stations along the route, the range of electric cars, and the efficiency of battery charging and replacement. Gen Z is used to and good at getting all kinds of information on the Internet. They want their in-vehicle systems to be updated and synchronized with the number of charging stations in their area before they charge and replace their batteries. They also expect charging stations to be somewhat closer to their homes, and finally, they want their electric cars to automatically shut off when they are fully charged so they do not have to incur the additional expense of locating a charging station.

The Home Business Scenario. Gen Z, early in their careers or starting their own businesses, typically use cars or SUVs as delivery vehicles when assisting businesses or their own small home-based businesses with deliveries. Gen Z has grown up with a diverse background. Some of the Gen Z who entered society early struggled for their family's business, so vehicles naturally became a tool for their business. During the time they are placing or picking up their cargo, their cars usually need more back seat space and a trunk with a wider opening angle, making it more convenient for them to place cargo.

3.3 Gen Z's Views on Intelligent Cars

By teasing out Gen Z's everyday car scenarios, we examine and sort out their pain points for the various modules and connections of the car itself, including human-machine collaboration, the digital cockpit, personalized interior, and exterior renovations obtain Gen Z's demand for future quality experiences (Fig. 12).

Fig. 12. Three aspects we discussed with Gen Z

Human-Machine Co-Driving. We talked about human-machine co-driving scenario with Gen Z, and here are what the Gen Z mentioned. In the human-machine co-driving scenario, the car owner must drive more carefully when the map system is navigating the vehicle. Therefore, aspects that can be optimized include the following: The destination and route displayed by the owner's mobile app can be synchronized with the car app. Based on the owner's driving habits and work schedule, the car can automatically set up navigation for the owner. When the navigation system is activated, it can offer the owner several routes to choose from. Navigation systems in cars should be sensitive and accurate, have many functions and have voice control. For example, the navigation system in the car uses voice control to change the route, but also needs to be intelligent to improve the efficiency of the trip and make the travel information more accurate. Aspects of the car navigation system that can be optimized include: It can help vehicle owners automatically avoid congested roads, it can send timely navigation information to vehicle owners based on road conditions and the location of other vehicles in the area, such as lane-level navigation announcements. It can also provide more detailed information about parking lots, such as the parking fees, etc.

Among the functions of autonomous driving, the intelligent function of automatic parking is the most preferred by Gen Z. The aspects that can be optimized by the car include improving the usage scenario of car parking, such as the function of parking at the ramp, improving the efficiency of car parking, and the need to improve the call mode of the owner to the car, such as the car automatically driving from the parking lot to the owner's location. Vehicle owners do not have high confidence in autonomous driving, but driver education remains important and can be strengthened to eliminate psychological resistance to autonomous driving. At the same time, the early warning function of such cars can automatically learn and adapt to the owner's driving habits. Among the aspects that can be optimized, the car can automatically adjust the sensitivity threshold of the assisted driving warning mode, so that the intervention time of assisted driving is more appropriate, which can avoid interfering with the normal driving of the car owner.

Digital Cockpit. Due to Gen Z group's preference for and use of smart products, cars with digital cockpits have gradually become one of Gen Z's first choices. For the in-car system, Gen Z expects a more intelligent interaction system for cell phone and car app. There should be a well-developed vehicle monitoring app in the car so that the owner can be warned in time if there is a problem. There should also be a senseless but stable Bluetooth connection in the cockpit so that the owner can connect wirelessly to CarPlay or CarLife in the car at any time. The owner's mobile entertainment app account can sync with the in-vehicle app and automatically switch to Bluetooth calls through the headset, depending on the conditions in the car. The cockpit should be equipped with a resourceful selection of entertainment in the car app, such as mainstream music playback, videos, games and karaoke for the car owner to enjoy, and so on. Owners use these content-rich apps in the car and operate entertainment apps with fine-grained voice controls, such as changing track lists, switching entertainment apps and more. The car should also be equipped with high-end immersive audio to enhance the entertainment experience for passengers, such as installing screens in the passenger and rear rows.

For the comfort configuration in the digital cabin, the hardware inside the cabin can also be optimized: the car's seats can be designed intelligently and scenario-based, and the ergonomic design of the seats should always be considered. In this way, the seat can become a high-end comfort. These features include a seat that can ventilate and dissipate heat, provide massage, and support the user's lower back. At the same time, the seat should also have a mode that allows the owner to rest and sleep in the car, and the rear seats of the car can have a one-touch folding function. The cockpit should be a more private space to meet the leisure and life needs of users. In addition, the car's features, such as ambient lighting, fragrance system, etc., should be more prominent. The car must also have a larger makeup mirror, the makeup lights must have a function to adjust the color temperature at the same time, and the refrigerator must also be installed in the car. The car should also have reasonable design to adapt to driving in strong light, such as reasonable tint and change the color of the glass in strong light and so on.

Aspects of the car's external hardware that can be optimized: The car's headlights should be intelligent and have a design suitable for night driving, such as adequate brightness, a function that allows the headlights to turn automatically when the car moves, and the ability to adjust the high and low beams automatically. The car's chassis should also be intelligent. It can raise automatically to make it easier for the owner to put things down. The trunk should also be intelligent, the trunk should have the function of automatic opening and induction opening, and the trunk should be larger so that the owner can divide the space more sensibly.

Gen Z expects cars to become fully automatic. Therefore, the following aspects can be optimized: Cars should have a senseless automatic unlocking function and be set to both memory and automatic setting. The intelligent car can automatically check if a part is defective and inform the owner in time. In addition, the car should have functions that adapt to the owner's driving style on rainy days, for example, the car can automatically defrost and dehumidify, automatically open the windshield wiper, the car mirror can be automatically heated, the car should be equipped with a reminder function for forgotten items, and the car can automatically close the lock when the owner leaves the car.

Since Gen Z has less driving experience than their Gen X and Y counterparts and many people like to drive to socialize, there are many features that can be optimized for safety alerts and convenience. For example, the car should have a monitoring system for driver attention and fatigue. The car can also provide timely voice warnings to remind the car owner to be careful when opening the door if a car is coming from behind. The cockpit should also be equipped with an integrated charging card and remind the owner in good time of the exact location of the next charging station if the car has no power. The steering wheel of the car should also be equipped with a voice-controlled start button.

In addition, we can optimize the social equipment in the cockpit: In the back of the car, there should be a charging port for cell phones and a power port for the trunk, and there should also be a rear reading light, and the brightness of the reading light can be automatically adjusted to the needs of the guests.

Personalized Interior and Exterior Design. Gen Z wants to show their personality through the exterior and interior of the car as well as the VPA image. Among them, female users show a strong interest in reflecting girly charm and unique exterior and interior design. As for the exterior of the car, the following aspects can be optimized: The car should have an individual shape, such as a young, sporty or cute design. The appearance of the car can be changed or filmed, the body should also be drawn and decorated. Then for the interior, the car can be suitable in terms of aspects including the car should be suitable for women's interior, such as the girl style or cute series, the car should also be a reflection of personal taste of the interior, such as rich ambient light colors, pendants, ornaments, cushions, seat cover lights and reflect the personality of the VPA image, and so on.

4 Summary

Gen Z values self-feeling and self-enjoyment; they grow up with the Internet and are heavy users of social media; they believe that smart products are part of life and everything can be connected; they are rooted in China and have a strong cultural sense of self with close ties to traditional concepts. Based on their life circumstances and their perceptions of car consumption, we divide Gen Z into four categories: the Happy Lifestyle, Traditional Comfort Lifestyle, Career Chasing Lifestyle, and Chaotic Fumbling Lifestyle. Combined with the survey, Gen Z has named the following six types of car scenarios: The Self-driving Travel Scenario, The Daily Fun Scenario, The Personal Space Scene, The Disguise Scenes for Vehicles, The Regular Commuting Scenarios, and The Home

Business Scenario. Combining the main issues in the above scenarios with the expectations for the car of the future, the three core opportunities were refined in the areas of human-machine co-driving, digital cockpit, personalized interior and exterior design.

This research provides the Baidu Map team and the Baidu Xiaodu Assistant team with the details of Gen Z driving behavior data in different scenarios. During a scenario reconstruction workshop, the research side gathers critical scenario-relevant information to collaborate with the design side to create design opportunities based on specific scenario characteristics, e.g., the commuting scenario of China's Gen Z. Finally, we work with the design side to implement relevant design opportunities and propose innovative solutions for different business directions.

5 Discussion

Gen Z, which grew up in an era of material prosperity with the rapid development of the Internet, places more emphasis on self-expression and individuality, and their values of enjoying the present, focusing on experiences, and over-consumption also lead to a marked difference between their automotive needs and consumption patterns and those of previous generations.

Vehicle manufacturers should accurately grasp the demand of Z customers and improve their competitiveness in all areas. At the design level, we should lead the trend, be both dynamic and fashionable, and reflect the sense of the future, innovation, and differentiation. At the product level, we should transform the car from a "functional tool" to a "mobile living space", pay attention to the quality of technology and materials, focus on the intelligence of the cabin, technology, and humanization. At the marketing level, we need to emphasize the combination of car and life, release Z customers into leisure and help them find their own style. At the channel level, we should focus on channel integration and diversification, create an ecosystem that covers a broader market, and build a complete service cycle to ensure service quality, technical capabilities, and local business policies. At the functional lever, we should provide consumers with a smarter experience, including optimizing assisted driving, automatic parking and other kinetic energy to help consumers make the entire driving process better and safer.

This study aims to capture the portrait of Gen Z and their main car use scenarios. The next research plan is to (a) segment the different types of Gen Z, explore the purchase models of Gen Z considering different consumer abilities and factors for car purchase, and provide opinions on future models for car manufacturers. (b) deepen Gen Z's attitudes and outlook toward autonomous driving and smart cockpits and explore the potential capabilities of autonomous driving and smart cockpits through user experiences; (c) combine quantitative research methods to collect data on a larger scale to further validate research findings and improve product experiences.

References

1. Cyanhill Capital: Definition and Characteristics of China's Gen Z: Consumer Report of the Year 2021. https://36kr.com/p/1310331587281670. Accessed 10 Feb 2022
2. Coupland, D.: Generation X: Tales for an Accelerated Culture. Abacus (1991)

3. China Internet Network Information Center: The 7th, 9th, 11th, 13th, 15th, 17th, 19th, 21st, and 23rd Statistical Survey Report on Internet Development in China. https://www.cnnic.net.cn/hlwfzyj/hlwxzbg/index.htm. Accessed 10 Feb 2022
4. PwC, SuperELLE: The Nation of Youth 2021: Cultural Insight and Business Impact Report. https://www.pwccn.com/en/services/deals-m-and-a/publications/young-power-china-white-paper-nov2021.html. Accessed 10 Feb 2022
5. Li, C.: Social changes and the Chinese youth issues. Youth Explor. 5–21 (2018)
6. Next100, Gen Forward: Millennials and Gen Z Want Affordable Child Care. https://thenext100.org/millennials-and-gen-z-want-affordable-child-care/. Accessed 10 Feb 2022
7. Orient Securities: The New Needs, New Culture, and New Economy: In-depth Economic Report on Gen Z. http://www.199it.com/archives/900600.html. Accessed 10 Feb 2022
8. Djafarova, E., Bowes, T.: 'Instagram made Me buy it': Generation Z impulse purchases in fashion industry. J. Retail. Consum. Serv. **59** (2021)
9. iResearch: Insight of Gen Z's Beauty and Skincare Consumption Report. https://report.iresearch.cn/report/202103/3748.shtml. Accessed 10 Feb 2022
10. Endata Inc: Understanding of the Gen Z's Entertainment Content Consumption Market. http://www.199it.com/archives/1324647.html. Accessed 10 Feb 2022
11. TANGUX, and BNU User Experience Center: China Health and Wellness White Paper (Youth Edition). https://zhuanlan.zhihu.com/p/446676590. Accessed 10 Feb 2022
12. Yiche Research Institute: How to handle Gen Z. https://news.yiche.com/hao/wenzhang/39937540/. Accessed 10 Feb 2022
13. Ipsos, and Bilibili: Gen Z Automotive Insights Report of the Year 2021. http://www.199it.com/archives/1316962.html. Accessed 10 Feb 2022

Effect of Age on Driving Behavior and a Neurophysiological Interpretation

Tianjian Li, Ruobing Zhao, Yi Liu, Xinyu Liu, and Yueqing Li(✉)

Department of Industrial and Systems Engineering, Lamar University, Beaumont, TX 77705, USA

yueqing.li@lamar.edu

Abstract. This study investigated the effect of age on driving behavior and provided a neurophysiological interpretation. Two age group of participants have driven on a 10-mile interstate highway on a driving simulator under different traffic density and driving mode. Driving performance, eye movement, brain activity, and subjective workload were measured. Results showed that age didn't affect the driving performance or brain activity. But the subjective workload and eye movement were significantly different among the two age groups. Moreover, drivers' subjective workload was not consistent with the eye movement. The study should provide insights to future studies about the effect of human factors in driving behavior.

Keywords: Automated vehicles · Age · Driving experience · fNIRS · Eye tracking

1 Introduction

World Health Organization found that the leading cause of death for young adults and children to be road traffic injuries (World Health Organization 2011). Young drivers do not have as much experience as older drivers, which results in their reckless driving behavior (Mueller and Trick 2012; Bao et al. 2020). According to National Highway Traffic Safety Administration (NHTSA), "in 2019, 31% of male drivers aged 15–20 years and 17% of female drivers aged 15–20 years who were involved in fatal crashes were speeding". Research showed that Teens are more likely than older drivers to speed and allow shorter headways (Simons-Morton et al. 2005). Young drivers' lack of experience not only affects their driving behavior, but it also affects their visual behavior (Konstantopoulos et al. 2010). Research observed that young drivers are less observant when driving in comparison to older drivers. Further research needs to be done to identify the effect of age on driving behavior of especially the young drivers.

H. Krömker (Ed.): HCII 2022, LNCS 13335, pp. 184–194, 2022.
https://doi.org/10.1007/978-3-031-04987-3_12

There are many research evaluating the effect of age on the driving behavior. Research with conventional vehicles showed that middle-aged drivers have a lower likelihood of being involved in severe crashes than younger and senior drivers (Derrig et al. 2002; Hijar et al. 2000; Norris et al. 2000; Zhang et al. 2000). As automated vehicles is more and more popular, impact of age on automated driving has also been investigated (Hartwich et al. 2018; Zhang et al. 2021; Sportillo et al. 2019; Wu et al. 2020; Li et al. 2019; Körber et al. 2016; Li et al. 2021). However, the results were not consistent. For example, one research found that older drivers take longer to respond and make decisions than younger drivers (Li et al. 2019). Another research found that older drivers were able to solve critical traffic events as well as younger drivers, though their operation methods were different (Körber et al. 2016).

This study aimed to evaluate the effect of age on driving behavior and provide a neurophysiological interpretation. Besides the driving performance, eye movement and brain activity were also used as neurophysiological indicators.

2 Methodology

2.1 Participants

Ten volunteers (2 females, 8 males) with valid driver licenses participated in the study. Among them, there were 5 young drivers (17–19 years old), and 5 old drivers (above 30 years old). The mean age of the young driver group is 18.2 (SD = 0.84). The mean age of the old driver group is 32.2 (SD = 05.50). All young drivers had less than 3 years driving experience (Mean = 2.6, SD = 0.89). All old drivers had more than 3 years driving experience (Mean = 8.8, SD = 4.49). All participants reported normal or corrected-to-normal visual acuity not taking stimulant and depressant drugs with 24 h before the experiment.

2.2 Equipment

Equipment included a driving simulator, an eye tracking device and a brain imaging device (Fig. 1). The driving simulator was the STISIM Drive ™ driving simulator equipped with a Logitech G27 steering wheel, floor-mounted pedals, an adjustable driver's seat, and three 23″ LED Dell monitors (1920 × 1080 resolution) with a 135° horizontal field of view in front of the driver's seat. Tobii pro glasses 2 was used to measure drivers' eye movement.

Fig. 1. Experiment setup

An 8 × 8 NIRSport2 system (NIRx Medical Technologies LLC, Germany) was used to measure the driver's prefrontal brain activity in hemodynamic responses. The system used optical signals with two wavelengths of 760 nm and 850 nm to output relative concentration changes of oxy-hemoglobin (HbO) and deoxy-hemoglobin (HbR). The configuration is shown in Fig. 2. fNIRS is an optical imaging hemodynamic technique to assess the functional activity in the human brain. Because of its advantage, fNIRS has been used in driving research to evaluate drivers' cognitive status (Yoshino et al. 2013; Unni et al. 2017; Zhao et al. 2021; Liu et al. 2021).

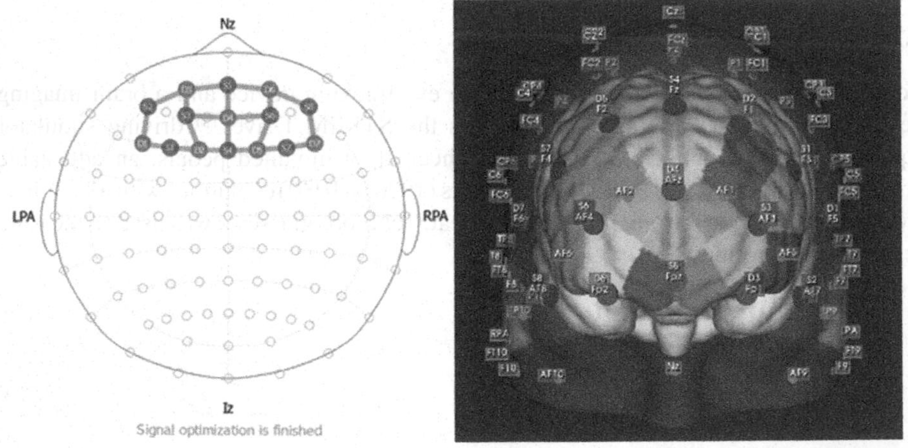

Fig. 2. FNIRS configuration

2.3 Independent Variables

There were two independent variables: traffic density and driving mode. Traffic density was designed following the rules of LOS (Level of Service). Level A, C and E were selected and simulated to represent low, medium and high traffic density, respectively. Two driving modes were provided: conventional driving, and partially automated driving, in which drivers only need to take over for lane changing by clicking the left/right button. In total, there were 6 different driving scenarios.

2.4 Dependent Variables

There were three types of dependent variables: driving performance, neurophysiological measurement, and subjective measurement. Driving performance included average speed and speed deviation. Neurophysiological measurement included eye movement (pupil dilation) and brain activity (oxygenated hemoglobin). Workload was measured by NASA TLX.

2.5 Task

In each scenario, participants were asked to drive 10 miles on a two-way rural interstate highway on the driving simulator. The speed limit was 60 miles/hour for low and medium traffic density, and 55 miles/hour for the high traffic density based on the rule of LOS. Participants were assigned to each scenario at a random order. During each drive, participants were required to perform the lane change and overtaking task when the vehicle ahead was much slower than the speed limit. In total, there were ten lane changing and overtaking tasks in each scenario. The experiment was conducted in a quiet, dimly lit room on campus.

2.6 Procedure

Participants were first given an instruction of the experiment and asked to complete a pre-questionnaire including demographic questions and personal driving experience questions. Then, a consent form was provided stating the task, procedure, benefits, and risks of the experiment. Next, participants were provided an at least 3 min practice drive to help them get familiar with the operation of the driving simulator. When they were ready, the experiment will begin. Participants were asked to obey the traffic rules and also keep their personal driving habits during the driving. After each scenario, participants were required to fill in a NASA-TLX questionnaire. At last, participants were provided with a post-questionnaire to evaluate their driving preferences as feedback. The whole experiment lasted around one and a half hours.

3 Results

3.1 Driving Performance

Results showed no significant difference of driving performance in both average speed and speed deviation in the two age groups.

3.2 Eye Tracking Measurement

Figure 3 and Fig. 4 are examples of old drivers and young drivers' heat map during driving. Figure 5 is an example of drivers' gaze visualization. The gaze path was dynamically visualized as a video scene throughout the timeline. The figures showed different patterns of eye movement among the two groups. For example, old drivers checked the rear mirror more frequently than the young drivers.

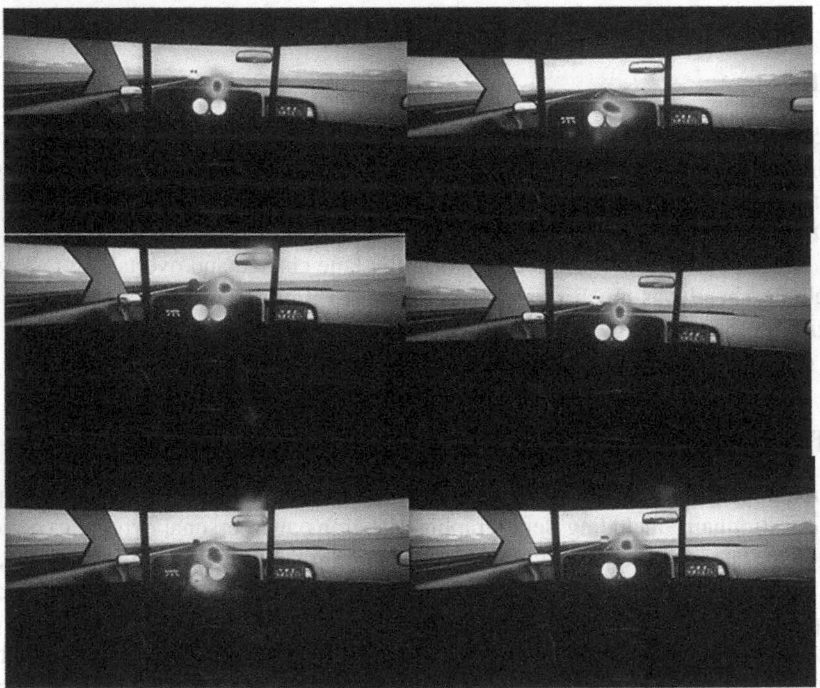

Fig. 3. An example of old drivers' heatmap (from left to right, up to down: automated and low traffic density, manual and low traffic density, automated and medium traffic density, manual and medium traffic density, automated and high traffic density, conventional and high traffic density)

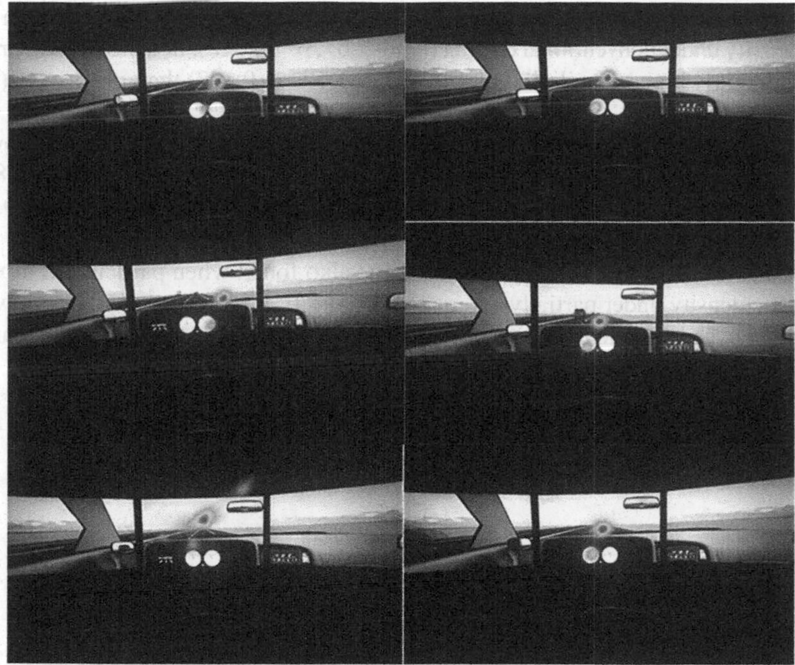

Fig. 4. An example of young drivers' heatmap (from left to right, up to down: automated and low traffic density, manual and low traffic density, automated and medium traffic density, manual and medium traffic density, automated and high traffic density, conventional and high traffic density)

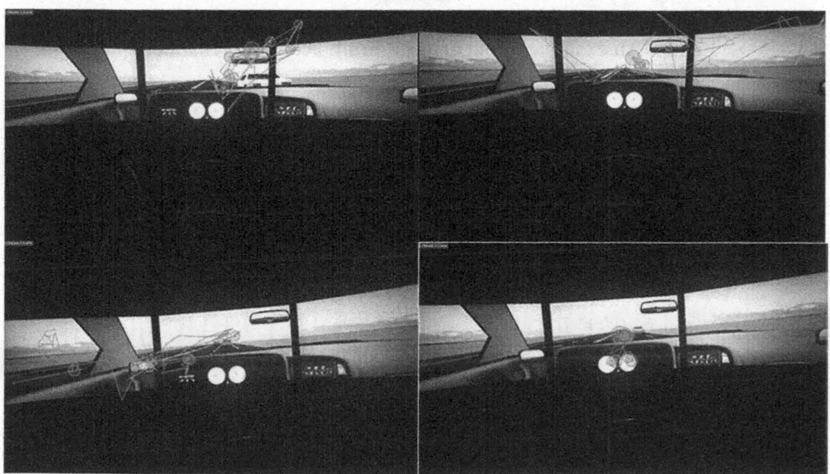

Fig. 5. An example of driver's gaze visualization (from left to right, up to down: old driver in automated driving, old driver in manual driving, young driver in automated driving, young driver in manual driving)

A significant difference in pupil dilation was found when participants drove in high traffic density under conventional driving ($t = -2.67, p = 0.028$), in which young drivers had significantly bigger pupil dilation ($M = 0.210, SD = 0.107$) than old drivers ($M = 0.056, SD = 0.072$).

A significant difference in pupil dilation was found when participants drove in medium traffic density under partially automated driving ($t = -2.68, p = 0.028$), in which young drivers had significantly bigger pupil dilation ($M = 0.116, SD = 0.104$) than old drivers ($M = -0.013, SD = 0.027$).

A significant difference in pupil dilation was also found when participants drove in high traffic density under partially automated driving ($t = -2.44, p = 0.041$), in which young drivers had significantly bigger pupil dilation ($M = 0.103, SD = 0.087$) than old drivers ($M = -0.008, SD = 0.053$).

3.3 Brain Activity

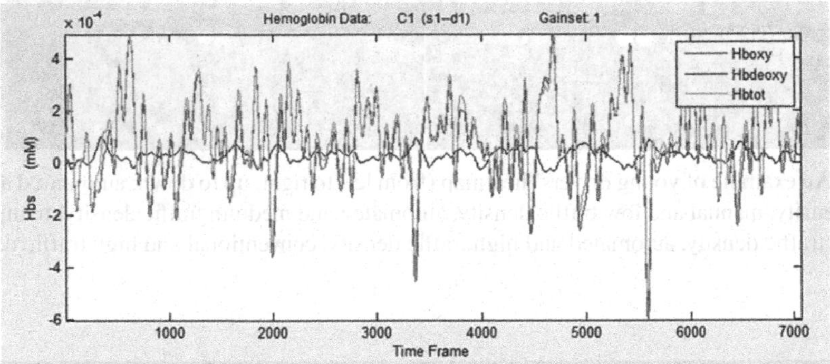

Fig. 6. An example of old drivers' brain activity in channel 1

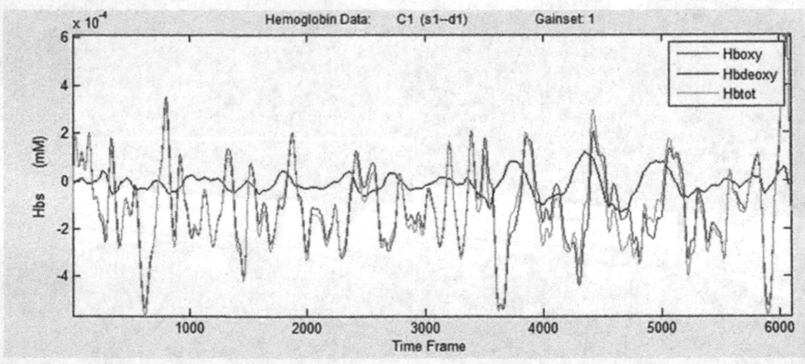

Fig. 7. An example of young drivers' brain activity in channel 1

Figure 6 and Fig. 7 show the raw fNIRS data of channel 1 in the time domain. The raw data then was processed to produce the Oxy-Hb concentration mapping for all hemodynamics states. Figure 8 is an example of young drivers' Oxy-Hb concentration mapping under different driving scenarios. A total of 20 channels were measured during the experiment. It shows different.

Results didn't show any significant difference in oxygenated hemoglobin during driving in the two groups.

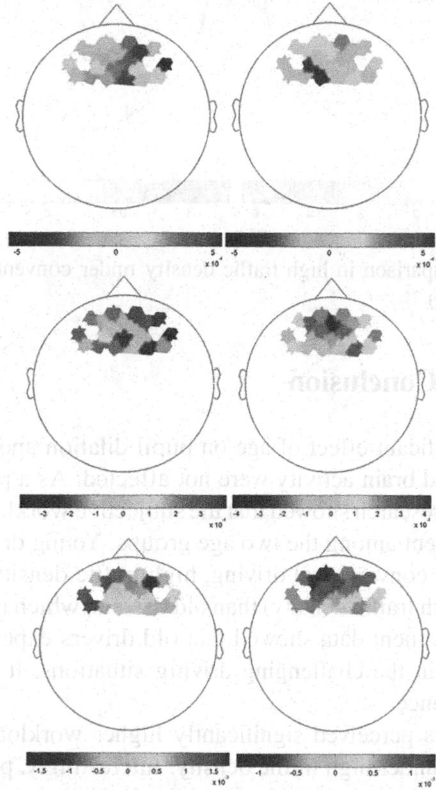

Fig. 8. An example of young drivers' Oxy-Hb concentration mapping for all hemodynamic states under different scenarios (from left to right, up to down: automated and low traffic density, manual and low traffic density, automated and medium traffic density, manual and medium traffic density, automated and high traffic density, conventional and high traffic density).

3.4 Workload

A significant difference in workload was found when participants drove in high traffic density under conventional driving ($t = 2.36$, $p = 0.046$). Old drivers had significantly higher workload ($M = 35.1$, $SD = 11.6$) than young drivers ($M = 20.3$, $SD = 7.8$). Figure 9 shows the Oxy-Hb comparison between the two age groups in high traffic density under conventional driving.

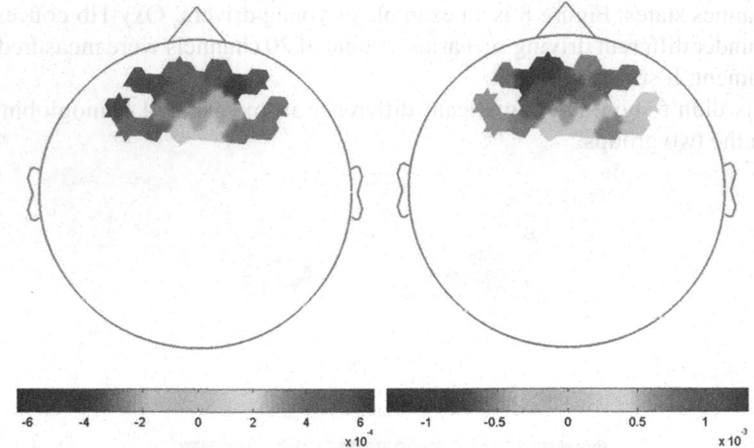

Fig. 9. Brain activity comparison in high traffic density under conventional driving (Left: old driver; Right: young driver)

4 Discussion and Conclusion

The study found a significant effect of age on pupil dilation and subjective workload. Driving performance and brain activity were not affected. As a preliminary study with limited sample size, the research showed that the subjective workload and eye movement were significantly different among the two age groups. Young drivers had significantly bigger pupil dilation (in conventional driving, high traffic density; partially automated driving, medium and high traffic density) than old drivers, which usually means a bigger workload. The eye movement data showed that old drivers experienced less workload than the young drivers in the challenging driving situations. It could be due to their enriched driving experience.

However, old drivers perceived significantly higher workload than young drivers in conventional driving under high traffic density. Interestingly, participants' subjective workload was not consistent with the neurophysiological indicators. Meanwhile, the heat map, gaze visualization and Oxy-Hb concentration mapping showed a different pattern in the two age groups.

Future research should recruit more participants, covering bigger age groups. More eye movement measurements (e.g., area of interest, revisit, fixation, etc.) should be used to investigate the driver's visual behaviors. Meanwhile, it needs to be identified if driving experience rather than age plays the role.

Acknowledgements. This research was partially supported by the Center for Advances in Port Management (CAPM) at Lamar University. Any opinions, findings, and conclusions or recommendations expressed in this material are those of the authors and do not necessarily reflect the views of the CAPM.

References

1. World Health Organization: Road traffic injuries, 21 June 2021. https://www.who.int/news-room/fact-sheets/detail/road-traffic-injuries
2. Mueller, A.S., Trick, L.M.: Driving in fog: the effects of driving experience and visibility on speed compensation and hazard avoidance. Accid. Anal. Prev. **48**, 472–479 (2012)
3. Bao, S., Wu, L., Yu, B., Sayer, J.R.: An examination of teen drivers' car-following behavior under naturalistic driving conditions: with and without an advanced driving assistance system. Accid. Anal. Prev. **147**, 1–7 (2020)
4. National Highway Traffic Safety Administration (NHTSA). Traffic Safety Facts 2019: Young Drivers (Report No. DOT HS 813 130). U.S. Department of Transportation, June 2021. https://crashstats.nhtsa.dot.gov/Api/Public/ViewPublication/813130externalicon
5. Simons-Morton, B., Lerner, N., Singer, J.: The observed effects of teenage passengers on the risky driving behavior of teenage drivers. Accid. Anal. Prev. **37**(6), 973–982 (2005)
6. Konstantopoulos, P., Chapman, P., Crundall, D.: Driver's visual attention as a function of driving experience and visibility. Using a driving simulator to explore drivers' eye movements in day, night and rain driving. Accid. Anal. Prev. **42**(3), 827–834 (2010)
7. Derrig, R.A., Sequi-Gomez, M., Abtahi, A., Liu, L.: The effect of population safety belt usage rates on motor vehicle-related fatalities. Accid. Anal. Prev. **34**(1), 101–110 (2002)
8. Hijar, M., Carrillo, C., Flores, M., Anaya, R., Lopez, V.: Risk factors in highway traffic accidents: a case control study. Accid. Anal. Prev. **32**(5), 703–709 (2000)
9. Norris, F.H., Matthews, B.A., Riad, J.K.: Characterological, situational, and behavioral risk factors for motor vehicle accidents: a prospective examination. Accid. Anal. Prev. **32**(4), 505–515 (2000)
10. Zhang, J., Lindsay, J., Clarke, K., Robbins, G., Mao, Y.: Factors affecting the severity of motor vehicle traffic crashes involving elderly drivers in Ontario. Accid. Anal. Prev. **32**(1), 117–125 (2000)
11. Hartwich, F., Beggiato, M., Krems, J.: Driving comfort, enjoyment and acceptance of automated driving – effects of drivers' age and driving style familiarity. Ergonomics **61**(8), 1017–1032 (2018)
12. Zhang, Q., Yang, X., Robert, L.: Drivers' age and automated vehicle explanations. Sustainability **13**(4), 1948 (2021)
13. Sportillo, D., Paljic, A., Ojeda, L.: On-road evaluation of autonomous driving training. In: 14th ACM/IEEE International Conference on Human-Robot Interaction (HRI), pp. 182–190. IEEE Press, Daegu (2019)
14. Wu, Y., et al.: Age-related differences in effects of non-driving related tasks on takeover performance in automated driving. J. Saf. Res. **72**, 231–238 (2020)
15. Li, S., Blythe, P., Guo, W., Namdeo, A.: Investigating the effects of age and disengagement in driving on driver's takeover control performance in highly automated vehicles. Transp. Plan. Technol. **42**(5), 470–497 (2019)
16. Körber, M., Gold, C., Lechner, D., Bengler, K.: The influence of age on the take-over of vehicle control in highly automated driving. Transp. Res. F: Traffic Psychol. Behav. **39**, 19–32 (2016)
17. Li, T., Zhao, R., Liu, Y., Li, Y., Li, G.: Evaluate the effect of age and driving experience on driving performance with automated vehicles. In: Stanton, N. (ed.) Advances in Human Aspects of Transportation, vol. 270, pp. 155–161. Springer, Cham (2021). https://doi.org/10.1007/978-3-030-80012-3_19
18. Yoshino, K., Oka, N., Yamamoto, K., Takahashi, H., Kato, T.: Functional brain imaging using near-infrared spectroscopy during actual driving on an expressway. Front. Hum. Neurosci. **7** (2013). https://doi.org/10.3389/fnhum.2013.00882

19. Unni, A., Ihme, K., Jipp, M., Rieger, J.W.: Assessing the driver's current level of working memory load with high density functional near-infrared spectroscopy: a realistic driving simulator study. Front. Hum. Neurosci. **11** (2017). https://doi.org/10.3389/fnhum.2017.00167
20. Zhao, R., Liu, Y., Li, Y., Tokgoz, B.: An investigation of resilience in human driving and automatic driving in freight transportation system. In: IIE Annual Conference, pp. 974–979. Norcross (2021)
21. Liu, Y., Zhao, R., Li, T., Li, Y.: An investigation of the impact of autonomous driving on driving behavior in traffic jam. In: IIE Annual Conference, pp. 986–991. Norcross (2021)

The Impact of Directional Road Signs Combinations and Language Unfamiliarity on Driving Behavior

Yi Liu, Ruobing Zhao, Tianjian Li, and Yueqing Li(✉)

Department of Industrial and Systems Engineering, Lamar University, 4400 S M L King Jr Pkwy, Beaumont, TX, USA

yli6@lamar.edu

Abstract. Twenty-one participants "drove" a simulated vehicle for one hour on an eight-lane rural highway. Data were aggregated from different scenarios (2 (Language: English, Spanish) × 2 (number of boards: 1, 3)). The results showed a significant main effect of language familiarity on driving performance. The higher standard deviations of speed and acceleration were found in Spanish condition. The research results showed that the impact of language familiarity on driving performance needs further research and attention.

Keywords: Signs combination · Language unfamiliarity · Driving simulator

1 Introduction

With the development of globalization, more and more people have the opportunity to travel and drive in unfamiliar countries (Yannis et al. 2007). However, it is a challenge for drivers to drive in an unfamiliar country with unfamiliar language road signs. Compared with domestic drivers, foreign drivers are more likely to drive dangerously due to their misunderstanding of unfamiliar road signs, which leads to more accidents. A global safety campaign study found that drivers' unfamiliarity with road signs is one of the contributing factors for foreigners' car accidents. (Foreign road can be deadly for the US, 2007). Researchers also found that foreign drivers lack understanding of traffic signs and markings compared to domestic drivers in US which results in higher accident rates (Dissanayak and John 2001).

Road signs are designed to provide critical cues for drivers, regardless of where drivers are from. The consequences of ignoring or misunderstanding these cues can cause drivers to make errors in judgment and increase their risk of accidents. Even with familiar language, changes in the combination of road signs can still cause distress to drivers. Surprisingly, there is no universally accepted standard for road signs. The relevant research on their impact on driving safety are still limited. Therefore, in order to fill this gap, this study aims to explore the impact of language familiarity and different combinations of multi-board road signs on drivers.

H. Krömker (Ed.): HCII 2022, LNCS 13335, pp. 195–204, 2022.
https://doi.org/10.1007/978-3-031-04987-3_13

2 Literature Review

2.1 Road Sign Combination

Directional road signs play an important role in daily highway traffic. One of the main functions of directional road signs is to guide the driver to the destination. With the development of urbanization, multi-board road signs are used to show enough information to drivers. However, a negative effect of multiple board signs is that they may be an external distractor for drivers. Study showed that distractions external to the vehicle are responsible for approximately 10% of all driving incidents (Sisiopiku et al. 2013). Larue's simulation study implicated that the difference of signs combination potentially had a negative effect on driving safety (Filtness 2017). The result showed that the usage of the multi-boards directional road signs on highway distracted more drivers' attention and increased the time spent on reading the information. Drivers' fixation time has been extended due to the combination of two or more road signs. According to the result of Klauer's study, drivers who did not monitor the traffic environment for more than two seconds had a higher risk of accidents (Klauer et al. 2006). Hummer's experiment found that the signs with more panes decreased the participants' reading performance and greatly intensified their mental workload (Hummer 2008). Filtness also claimed that the combination of signs may increase the mental workload and cause more stress (Filtness et al. 2017).

Metz found that if drivers could use effective reading strategies to obtain the necessary information, the combination of road signs wouldn't have negative impacts on driving performance (Metz and Krüger 2014). Wu's paper focused on the impact of combination of directional road signs on drivers' driving performance and mental workload, the road sign design in the experiment is based on Chinese traffic rules (Yang 2020).

2.2 Road Sign Language

Road signs communicate upcoming changes to drivers' immediate environment. When understood correctly, they allow for effective decision making. Recently, several cross-culture driving studies had been conducted. Shinar has examined the cross-cultural understanding of road signs and revealed low comprehension scores for non-local signs and misinterpretation of road signs rules (Shinar et al. 2003). Wu conducted a driving simulator experiment to explore the impact of unfamiliar street language format on drivers' driving behavior (Wu et al. 2013). With the increasing unfamiliarity, the higher workload of drivers was found. Compared to the familiar language road signs, drivers had shorter glance duration when they encountered the unfamiliar language road signs. The study also proved that there was no significant main effect on maintaining lane position.

According to these studies, issues of driving safety for foreigners have received much attention and studies on cross-culture driving behaviors are expected.

2.3 Mental Workload

Driving has been described as a task that involves extremely fluctuating mental workload (Baldwin et al. 2004). Completing the observation of the road signs while driving is even more demanding on the mental workload. Especially, with the widespread usage of multi-board directional signs, there is more information displayed to drivers at one time, which increased the difficulty of the detection. With the increasing information on directional road sign, drivers had to sacrified more time to search for the target information, which increased the task processing demand and led to higher workload (Edquist et al. 2012). Previous studies have also mentioned that differences in mental workload can lead to significant changes in driving performance (Zhao et al. 2021; Liu et al. 2021). Therefore, the study that focuses on the influence of multi-board road signs on drivers' mental workload is necessary.

The advantage of fNIRS is that it can be used to monitor long-term cortical activity and the cognitive load without interruption (Fishburn et al. 2014). Compared to the self-reporting schemes, fNIRS excludes subjectivity because it does not rely on participants' recall of the study. In comparison to EEG, the fNIRS measurement equipment has a lower sense of existence for participants during the experiment, and it is easier to eliminate external interference. In recent years, fNIRS technology has been applied in various experimental scenarios related to cognitive activities and provides reliable experimental data (McKendrick et al. 2016). In particular, it provides unique advantages for the evaluation of cognitive activities in simulated driving experiments (Balters and Steinert 2015).

3 Methodology

3.1 Participants

Eight licensed drivers (four males; four females) completed this study as volunteers. The average age of the participants was 29.5, and the standard deviation was 4.74. Participants reported having normal or corrected-to-normal visual acuity, and all participants proved to have never taken stimulant and depressant drugs 24 h before the experiment. Participants must surrender their cellphones, smartwatch, and any other potentially distracting device and wouldn't be informed about the length of the drive to avoid the time-related motivational strategies.

3.2 Apparatus

A STISIM Drive TM driving simulator (32100) equipped with a Logitech G27 steering wheel, floor-mounted pedals, and an ergonomic chair was used in this study experiment. The STISIM simulator was installed on a Dell Workstation (Alienware Area-51 R2, Intel Core i7-5820K, 6-Core Processor) with 4 GB NVIDIA GeForce GTX 980 graphic card, and Sound Blaster Recon3Di system. The driving scenario was presented on three 23" LED monitors (Dell; 1920X1080) displayed driving scenes with a 135o horizontal field of view. The eye tracker was a Tobii Pro Glasses 2 (developed by Tobii Technology AB, Danderyd, Sweden) with a 100 Hz sampling rate. A NIRSport (NIRx, Germany) system was used to record hemodynamic responses with 8 LED illumination sources and 8 silicon sensors. As the Fig. 1 is shown, 8 sources and 7 detectors were applied in this experiment.

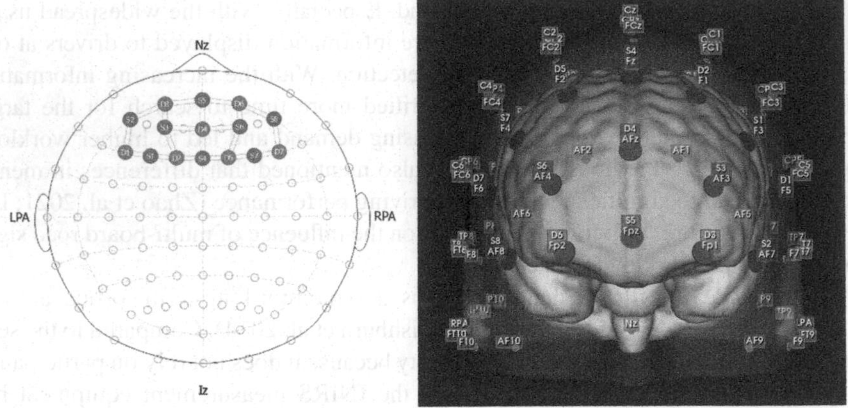

Fig. 1. Channels selected in fNIRS.

3.3 Experiment Design

There were two independent variables: Signs language (English and Spanish) and signs combination (1 and 3 boards). They were combined factorially to create 4 conditions. The cities (Houston, Austin, Dallas, Waco, Katy, Amarillo) were selected to create the English directional road signs. And the cities (Algeciras, Almería, Málaga, Melilla, Guadix, Granada, Guernica) were selected to create the Spanish directional road signs. Figures 2 and 3 shown the examples of different combinations of directional road signs in English and Spanish respectively.

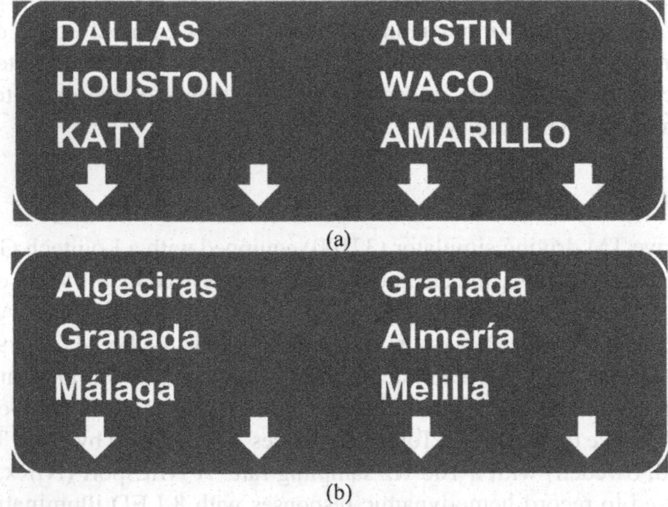

Fig. 2. (a) An example of the one board directional road sign design in English. (b) An example of the one board directional road sign design in Spanish.

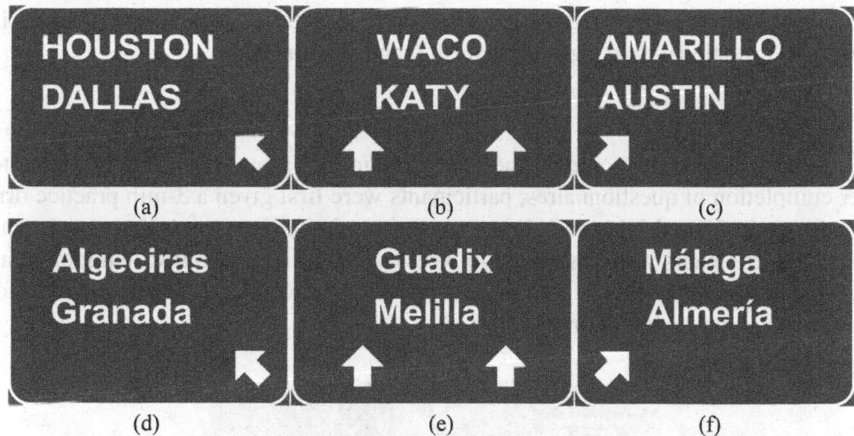

Fig. 3. (a) An example of the left part of three-board directional road sign design in English. (b) An example of the middle part of three-board directional road sign design in English. (c) An example of the right part of three-board directional road sign design in English. (d) An example of the left part of three-board directional road sign design in Spanish. (e) An example of the middle part of three-board directional road sign design in Spanish. (f) An example of the right part of three-board directional road sign design in Spanish.

There were five dependent variables:

1. Speed standard deviation. The average of speed standard deviation when drivers saw the direction sign until the lane change is completed.
2. Acceleration standard deviation. The average of acceleration standard deviation from drivers saw the direction sign until the lane change is completed.
3. Accuracy. Whether participants drove in the right lane. Changing the lane when it is not needed and keeping the lane when it needs to be changed are both considered wrong positions.
4. Gaze time. The time of drivers stared at each directional road sign.
5. Brain activity. The density of oxygen hemoglobin of cerebral cortex.

3.4 Task

Before the start of the experiment, the destination name was notified, participants were instructed to drive to the destination according to the overhead directional traffic signs information. Participants traveled on a straight, eight-lane, interstate freeway with driving a simulated vehicle and the traffic density was around 1400 vehicles per hour. Participants were required to monitor road signs and maintain their lane position until the directional road sign instructs them to change lanes. Each 30-min drive contained 16 overhead directional road signs. The number of each kind of directional road sign is 8, and the sequence of different kinds of road sign was random. In all conditions, 75% of road signs would need the drivers to change their lane, and 25% of road signs would ask the drivers to maintain their own lane. Changing the lane when it is not needed and keeping the lane when it needs to be changed are both considered wrong positions. To avoid the learning effect, participants were told to drive to another destination after passing through 12 directional road signs in Spanish language condition.

3.5 Procedure

Participants were asked to complete the demographic once seated in the driving simulator. After completion of questionnaires, participants were first given a 3-min practice drive and informed of the driving task in the meantime. Upon beginning the experimental trials, the participants were instructed to wear eye-tracking and fNIRS equipment and began the full drive as Fig. 3. Participants answered a workload questionnaire before and after finishing each section drive.

Fig. 4. Experiment with eye-tracking system and fNIRS system.

4 Result

4.1 Speed Standard Deviation

The result showed a significant main effect of language familiarity on speed standard deviation ($F1,7 = 11.83, p = 0.0108$). The mean of speed deviation in English condition ($M = 6.52, SD = 1.65$) was significantly smaller than that in Spanish condition ($M = 7.34, SD = 2.22$).

The result didn't show any significant main effect of signs combination ($F1,7 = 1.24, p = 0.3026$) or significant interaction effect between language familiarity and signs combination ($F1,7 = 0.39, p = 0.5530$) on speed standard deviation.

4.2 Acceleration Standard Deviation

The result showed a significant main effect of language familiarity on acceleration standard deviation ($F_{1,7} = 11.57, p = 0.0114$). The mean of acceleration standard deviation in English condition ($M = 0.073, SD = 0.030$) was significantly smaller than that in Spanish condition ($M = 0.076, SD = 0.030$).

The result didn't show any significant main effect of signs combination ($F_{1,7} = 0.30$, $p = 0.6023$) or significant interaction effect between language familiarity and signs combination ($F_{1,7} = 0.92, p = 0.3702$) on acceleration standard deviation.

4.3 Accuracy

The result did not show any significant main effect of language familiarity ($F_{1,7} = 0.29$, $p = 0.6060$), signs combination ($F_{1,7} = 2.64$, $p = 0.1480$) or significant interaction effect between language familiarity and signs combination ($F_{1,7} = 0.17$, $p = 0.6943$) on accuracy.

4.4 Gaze Time

Due to one participant's eye-tracking data missing, the result included only seven participants. The result did not show any significant main effect of language familiarity ($F_{1,6} = 0.36$, $p = 0.5692$), signs combination ($F_{1,6} = 0.05$, $p = 0.8304$) or significant interaction effect between language familiarity and signs combination ($F_{1,6} = 1.60$, $p = 0.2534$) on gaze time.

Fig. 5. An example of eye-tracking heatmap.

4.5 Brain Activity

Due to one participant's fNIRS data missing, the result included only seven participants. The result did not show any significant main effect of language familiarity ($F_{1,6} = 0.09$, $p = 0.7720$), signs combination ($F_{1,6} = 1.23$, $p = 0.3107$) or significant interaction effect between language familiarity and signs combination ($F_{1,6} = 0.78$, $p = 0.4113$) on brain activity (Fig. 6).

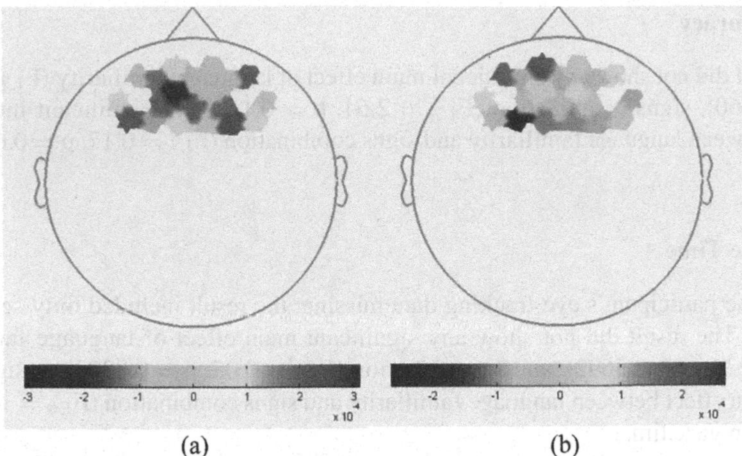

Fig. 6. (a) An example of fNIRS heatmap in English condition. (b) an example of FNIRS heatmap in Spanish condition.

5 Discussion

5.1 Language Familiarity

Different from previous research which found that there was no a significant main effect of language familiarity on driving speed (Wu et al. 2013), this study found that language familiarity significantly increased the standard deviation of speed. Due to the language unfamiliarity, drivers had to decelerate more to detect the information of destination, and then accelerated back to the normal speed. These driving behaviors resulted in the change of speed deviation. What's more, consistent with previous research (Yang 2020), this study found that language unfamiliarity significantly increased the acceleration standard deviation. The higher acceleration standard deviation in unfamiliar language condition proved that drivers had to brake harder than in familiar language condition to acquire the information of destination. The result indicated that the language unfamiliarity not only deteriorated drivers' driving performance, but also affect drivers' driving habits.

Although the result did not show significant effect of language familiarity on gaze time, the result showed that, drivers spent more time in Spanish directional road signs ($M = 3.25$, $SD = 1.38$) than in English directional road signs ($M = 2.90$, $SD = 1.19$). Figure 4 shown an example of eye-tracking heatmap when the driver encountered the three boards directional road sign. The result hinted that the participants still spent more time on unfamiliar road signs. The accuracy of English condition (86.72%) and the accuracy of Spanish condition (83.81%) are similar. On the one hand, the result implied that the difficulty of the task may be too easy for participants. On the other hand, the dissimilarity between English and Spanish is limited. Therefore, the difference of accuracy in two language conditions is not obvious enough.

Although language familiarity did not show a significant main effect on fNIRS result, the average density of oxygen-hemoglobin is higher in familiar language condition than in unfamiliar condition as Fig. 5 shown. The prefrontal cortex is theorized to be responsible for working memory and attention (Baldwin et al. 2004). In familiar language condition, the familiarity with the language mobilizes the drivers' memory storage resulted in the higher density of oxygen-hemoglobin of the prefrontal cortex. On the contrary, due to the language unfamiliarity, the Spanish directional road signs cannot stimulate the drivers' memory storage, which led to lower density of oxygen-hemoglobin.

5.2 Combination of Directional Road Signs

Different from previous research (Yang 2020), the road signs combination did not show a significant main effect on the standard deviation of speed and acceleration. Drivers maintained the same reaction when encountering road signs with different combination. No matter what road signs are encountered, the driver's driving behavior and driving habits had not significantly changed. Although there was not a significant main effect on accuracy, the mean accuracy of 3 boards road signs (M = 0.81, SD = 0.17) is less than the mean accuracy of one board signs (M = 0.90, SD = 0.26). When the driver faces the information given by multiple boards, it would be more difficult to process in a short time. The results of fNIRS further confirmed this conclusion.

The combination of directional road signs did not have a significant main effect on the driver's driving behavior and gaze time. Different drivers had different performance when facing different combinations of direction signs. This result can be proved by the post-test questionnaire. Participants who supported the one board directional signs claimed that the information of one board directional road sign is more concentrated, which is convenient to detect. On the other hand, participants who liked three boards directional road signs indicated that there is less information in the same list of three boards directional road signs, which is clearer for drivers and decrease the detection time greatly, especially in unfamiliar language conditions.

According to the fNIRS result, the density of oxygen-hemoglobin is highest when drivers encountered the three boards signs. The density of oxygen-hemoglobin is lowest when drivers encountered the one board signs. Oxygen-hemoglobin increased as the number of boards increased, which proved that increasing the number of boards may increase the drivers' workload.

6 Conclusion

In this study, a simulated driving experiment was conducted to explore the impact of language familiarity and the combination of directional road signs on driving performance and mental workload. The results showed a significant main effect of language familiarity on driving performance. In the next phase of our study, more participants will be assessed, and more kinds of eye-tracking data are considered to be analyzed.

Acknowledgements. This research was partially supported by the Center for Advances in Port Management (CAPM) at Lamar University. Any opinions, findings, and conclusions or recommendations expressed in this material are those of the authors and do not necessarily reflect the views of the CAPM.

References

Baldwin, C.L., Freeman, F.G., Coyne, J.T.: Mental workload as a function of road type and visibility: comparison of neurophysiological, behavioral, and subjective indices. PsycEXTRA Dataset (2004). https://doi.org/10.1037/e577202012-022

Balters, S., Steinert, M.: Capturing emotion reactivity through physiology measurement as a foundation for affective engineering in engineering design science and engineering practices. J. Intell. Manuf. **28**(7), 1585–1607 (2015). https://doi.org/10.1007/s10845-015-1145-2

Dissanayake, S., Lu, J.J.: Traffic control device comprehension. IATSS Res. **25**(2), 80–87 (2001). https://doi.org/10.1016/s0386-1112(14)60072-8

Edquist, J., Rudin-Brown, C.M., Lenné, M.G.: The effects of on street parking and road environment visual complexity on travel speed and reaction time. Accid. Anal. Prev. **45**, 759–765 (2012). https://doi.org/10.1016/j.aap.2011.10.001

Filtness, A., et al.: Safety implications of co-locating road signs: a driving simulator investigation. Transp. Res. F: Traffic Psychol. Behav. **47**, 187–198 (2017). https://doi.org/10.1016/j.trf.2017.04.007

Fishburn, F.A., Norr, M.E., Medvedev, A.V., Vaidya, C.J.: Sensitivity of fNIRS to cognitive state and load. Front. Hum. Neurosci. **8** (2014). https://doi.org/10.3389/fnhum.2014.00076

Sisiopiku, V., Hester, D., Gan, A., Stavrinos, D., Sullivan, A.: Digital roadside advertising and traffic safety (2013). http://nctspm.gatech.edu/sites/default/files/u60/Sisiopiku%20et%20al%20April%202013.pdf. Accessed 2 Apr 2021

Hummer, J.E., Maripalli, U.K.: Laboratory test of driver responses to nine-panel logo signs. J. Transp. Res. Board **2056**(1), 52–59 (2008). https://doi.org/10.3141/2056-07

Klauer, S.G., Dingus, T.A., Neale, V.L., Sudweeks, J.D., Ramsey, D.J.: The impact of driver inattention on near-crash/crash risk: an analysis using the 100-car naturalistic driving study data. PsycEXTRA Dataset (2006). https://doi.org/10.1037/e729262011-001

Liu, Y., Zhao, R., Li, T., Li, Y.: An investigation of the impact of autonomous driving on driving behavior in traffic jam. In: IIE Annual Conference, pp. 986–991. Norcross (2021)

McKendrick, R., et al.: Into the wild: neuroergonomic differentiation of hand-held and augmented reality wearable displays during outdoor navigation with functional near infrared spectroscopy. Front. Hum. Neurosci. **10** (2016). https://doi.org/10.3389/fnhum.2016.00216

Metz, B., Krüger, H.: Do supplementary signs distract the driver? Transp. Res. F: Traffic Psychol. Behav. **23**, 1–14 (2014). https://doi.org/10.1016/j.trf.2013.12.012

Shinar, D., Dewar, R.E., Summala, H., Zakowska, L.: Traffic sign symbol comprehension: a cross-cultural study. Ergonomics **46**(15), 1549–1565 (2003). https://doi.org/10.1080/0014013032000121615

Wu, C., Zhao, G., Lin, B., Lee, J.: Navigating a car in an unfamiliar country using an internet map: effects of street language formats, map orientation consistency, and gender on driver performance, workload and multitasking strategy. Behav. Inf. Technol. **32**(5), 425–437 (2013). https://doi.org/10.1080/0144929x.2011.566941

Yang, Y., Chen, Y., Wu, C., Easa, S.M., Lin, W., Zheng, X.: Effect of highway directional signs on driver mental workload and behavior using eye movement and brain wave. Accid. Anal. Prev. **146**, 105705 (2020). https://doi.org/10.1016/j.aap.2020.105705

Yannis, G., Golias, J., Papadimitriou, E.: Accident risk of foreign drivers in various road environments. J. Saf. Res. **38**(4), 471–480 (2007). https://doi.org/10.1016/j.jsr.2007.01.014

Zhao, R., Liu, Y., Li, Y., Tokgoz, B.: An investigation of resilience in human driving and automatic driving in freight transportation system. In: IIE Annual Conference, pp. 974–979. Norcross (2021)

Towards a Customizable Usage Requirements Cycle

Cindy Mayas(✉)

u.works GmbH, 98693 Ilmenau, Germany

mayas@uworks.de

Abstract. Usage orientation is an essential success factor in development processes. Especially in the mobility sector, development processes concern product combinations of software, hardware and services. These processes require interdisciplinary teams, but both the procedure and the results are shaped by the respective disciplines, such as software development, product design or marketing, and are difficult to access for outsiders. Thus, the flexible application of user-oriented methods remains difficult. The aim of this paper is a scalable process model that flexibly supports the integration of user-oriented methods in development processes and is oriented towards the needs of interdisciplinary development teams. The findings conclude in a concept of a usage requirements cycle supporting the integration of usage requirements especially in the mobility sector.

Keywords: Usage requirements · User-oriented development

1 Objectives

User-oriented methods in development processes optimize development times and results [1]. Furthermore, reduced usage errors and increased satisfaction of the users reduce future costs for training and support of the users [2]. Therefore, user orientation is an important success factor also for development processes in the mobility sector, in that user errors have critical effects on the achievement of goals and even safety aspects. But heterogeneous user groups, interdisciplinary developments teams and diverse product subsystems increase the complexity of the process models [3]. These challenges result in a potentiation of the possibilities for using and combining different user-oriented methods [4]. This makes it more difficult to efficiently locate and link the methods within a development process and to effectively utilize the results.

Successful user-oriented development cannot be guaranteed by the isolated use of user-oriented methods in the development process [3]. For example, a usability evaluation is more inefficient if it is conducted without incorporating the findings into the design process. Only the targeted combination and systematic integration of user-oriented methods supports development progress. This paper therefore focuses on a more flexible process model enabling especially interdisciplinary teams to integrate usage requirements effectively and efficiently into existing work steps and to optimize their use.

H. Krömker (Ed.): HCII 2022, LNCS 13335, pp. 205–217, 2022.
https://doi.org/10.1007/978-3-031-04987-3_14

2 Usage Requirements in Development Processes

The terms "User Requirements" and "Usage Requirements" are described in ISO/IEC TR 25060 standard as "requirements for use that provide the basis for design and evaluation of interactive systems to meet identified user needs" [5]. However, user requirements imply from the word meaning only the consideration of requirements, which consider the abilities and needs of the users. In order to capture the entirety of the usage context, the broader term of usage requirements is used in this work.

HEISEL and KRÖMKER emphasize that requirements from the perspective of users and the context of use describe how users want to perform certain operations [6]. In their call for usability standards, THEOFANOS and STANTON use a user requirements specification throughout the entire development process, which is not only based on the needs of the users and the context of use, but also takes ergonomic criteria and usability goals into account [7]. DIN EN ISO 9241-210 introduces a specialized work step for specifying the user requirements. Accordingly, user and usage requirements can be summarized as statements derived from the characteristics of the users, their tasks and usage environment as well as the relevant findings on ergonomics about a characteristic to be fulfilled or a service to be provided by a product or a process to meet the needs of the users [8].

Existing process models for user-orientation originate primarily from the discipline of usability engineering. An established process model is described in DIN EN ISO 9241-210. A key feature here is planning, which is carried out in advance of the process. The further steps of understanding, defining, developing and evaluating are then repeated until the design solution fulfills the specified usage requirements [8]. Other process models of usability engineering confirm this division into the four development phases of analysis, design, implementation and evaluation, which are also carried out iteratively [9, 10]. Agile versions of usability engineering try to integrate the methods flexibly and with little effort into existing agile development processes [11]. These procedure models focus on a similar structuring of development phases and the employment of specific methods. However, this anchoring of the process models to development phases or methods reduces the flexible applicability within existing processes.

The gaps in the individual development processes are also addressed in the literature and filled with approaches from various disciplines. For example, FOLMER et al. show how usability criteria can be included in the development of software architecture [12]. Despite all progress in the disciplines, KASHFI et al. emphasize the still existing challenges to integrate aspects of usability and user experience in companies [13].

3 Study Design

3.1 Literature Analysis

As a theoretical basis for the different elements of product combinations, 30 established development processes in the scientific disciplines of systems engineering, software engineering, service engineering as well as requirements engineering and usability engineering are analyzed. The focus of the analysis is on technically developing, so-called "engineering" processes, in order to consider above all the controllable and repeatable processes with reliable result quality. The goal of this theoretical analysis is to identify typical methods and activities, that are suitable for dealing with usage requirements, across disciplines.

Sample Selection. For the selection of the development processes, the first step is a search in "Google Scholar", where 90% of engineering publications after 1990 are indexed [14]. The respective scientific discipline, such as "service engineering", in combination with the terms "process", "development" and "design" are used as terms for the search to focus on development processes. The five hits with the highest number of citations that meet the following criteria are selected:

- Description of at least one complete development process,
- Description of the specific process flow,
- At least exemplary mention of methods within the process,
- Only the most highly cited work of an author will be selected.

In a second selection step, these results are supplemented with one industry standard of each discipline. This addition should mainly compensate for the neglect of standards in "Google Scholar". The 30 publication, which are chosen for the analysis, are presented in Table 1.

Content Analysis. The literature analysis is conducted as a reconstructive content analysis according to GLÄSER and LAUDEL, in which the category system is developed from the extracted content elements [15]. The method allows the combination of deductively derived categories with categories that are inductively derived from the material. In addition, the extractive method reduces the number of coding passes required, which, significantly increases efficiency. This results in the following steps of the content analysis:

1. Extraction of method mentions,
2. Dichotomous evaluation of method suitability for usage requirements,
3. Categorization of the methods,
4. Unification of the categorization to the category system.

The criterion of suitability of a method for the integration of usage requirements means the possibility to integrate references to the usage idea or usage situation into a method. It is not necessary that usage requirements are explicitly mentioned as an application area of this method in the process description. The method can also be integrated in the process for another purpose. In this way, this analysis can reveal a broad basis for the possible use of the method.

3.2 Expert Interviews

The research and development projects in mobility sector are analyzed in expert interviews with one or two members of the project team who have worked on the integration

Table 1. Selected literature

Authors	Titel (year)	Selection criteria
Blanchard, Fabrycky	Systems engineering and analysis (2011)	Citations: 3.545
Kossiakoff, Sweet	Systems engineering (2011)	Citations: 1.175
Weilkiens	Systems engineering with SysML/UML (2007)	Citations: 796
Martin	Systems engineering guidebook (1998)	Citations: 389
Haberfellner et al.	Systems engineering (2018)	Citations: 312
ISO	ISO 15288: systems and software engineering (2015)	Industry standard
Scheuing, Johnson	A proposed model for new service development (1989)	Citations: 694
Sakao, Shimomura	Service engineering (2007)	Citations: 463
Morelli	Designing product/service systems (2002)	Citations: 438
Bullinger, Schreiner	Service engineering (2005)	Citations: 229
Karwowski et al.	Introduction to service-engineering (2009)	Citations: 92
DIN	DIN-Fachbericht 75. Service engineering (1998)	Industry standard
Pressman	Software engineering: a practitioner's approach (2004)	Citations: 19.743
Schwaber, Beedle	Agile software development with scrum (2002)	Citations: 4.776
Pfleeger, Atlee	Software engineering: theory and practice (2010)	Citations: 2.254
Ghezzi et al.	Fundamentals of software engineering (2002)	Citations: 1.851
Bruegge, Dutoit	Object-oriented software engineering (2010)	Citations: 1.164
Bourque, Fairley	Software engineering body of knowledge (2014)	Industry standard
Nuseibeh, Easterbrook	Requirements engineering (2000)	Citations: 2.733
Kotonya, Sommerville	Requirements engineering (1998)	Citations: 2.707
Van Lamsweerde	Goal-oriented requirements engineering (2001)	Citations: 2.341
Dick et al.	Requirements engineering (2017)	Citations: 1.219
Macaulay	Requirements engineering (2012)	Citations: 554
Pohl, Rupp	Basiswissen requirements engineering (2021)	Industry standard
Nielsen	Usability engineering (1994)	Citations 21.164
Beyer, Holtzblatt	Contextual design (1998)	Citations 5.043

(*continued*)

Table 1. (*continued*)

Authors	Titel (year)	Selection criteria
Cooper et al.	About face (2014)	Citations: 2.118
Rosson, Carroll	Usability engineering (2002)	Citations: 1.887
Mayhew	The usability engineering lifecycle (1999)	Citations 1.877
ISO	ISO 9241-210: ergonomics of human-system interaction (2019)	Industry standard

of usage requirements. The advantage of this method is the possibility to question in detail [15] the benefit, the effort and the function of a method in the project. In this way the results of the projects are used in order to specify the general results of the literature analysis for the mobility sector.

Sample Selection. The expert interviews of the research projects comprise five projects, as shown in Table 2. The projects are selected from research projects in which the Media Production Group at Technische Universität Ilmenau in Germany is involved. All of the interviewed persons work directly on usage-oriented topics in their research projects.

Table 2. Analyzed development projects in the area of mobility

Name	Description	Resources
IP-Kom-ÖV	Standardization of interfaces for passenger information systems	42 months, 16 industry and research partners
Move@ÖV	Increasing the flexibility of public transport through electro mobility	36 months, 4 industry and research partners
Dynapsys	Development of a dynamic agenda planning system	45 months, 6 industry and research partners
ESIMAS	Development of an expert system for operators in tunnels	36 months, 7 industry and research partners
DIMO-OMP	Standardization of interfaces for open mobility platforms	21 months, 7 industry and research partners

Interview Method. An interview guideline was developed for conducting the expert interviews. At the beginning of the interview, general, easy-to-remember information about the goals, duration and phases of the project is asked. Then, the specific methods used in the project are collected on cards according to the project phases and their interrelationships are documented by grouping and moving the cards. For projects with a longer project duration, result and milestone reports are additionally used to support the interviewees' memorization of all methods used. Finally, the mentioned methods are explained individually based on their function in the project, and the benefits and effort are evaluated based on them. This selection is based on the decision criteria for system design "function", "benefit" and "effort", which are particularly suitable for evaluating the use of methods from a holistic system perspective [4].

4 Results

4.1 Set of Activities

The analysis revealed a total of 1268 method mentions, that as suitable for integrating usage requirements. Hence, a four-level categorization system is developed, in order to structure the multi-layered nature and complexity of the method mentions. The categorization results in the following distinctions:

- 3 content types: survey activities, analyze activities, concept activities;
- 16 activity types: e.g. questioning and testing, systematizing and describing, modeling and visualizing, all activity types are described in Table 3.
- 76 method types: e.g., interview and usability test, statistical analysis and scenario, use case, and low-fidelity prototyping;
- Mentioned method techniques: e.g., focused interview and thinking aloud, cross tabulation and use scenario, UML use case diagram and mock-up.

Across disciplines, the trend can be described that an increasing differentiation of methods makes the selection and application of methods more difficult, especially for interdisciplinary development teams. Some more informal method types, such as presentations or internal text notices, are not mentioned in literature, but often mentioned in the interviews. In addition, survey, analysis, and concept activities are distributed throughout the entire development cycle in all of the disciplines analyzed. For example, concept activities such as use cases and prototypes are often recommended for design but also for requirements analysis, and survey methods such as interviews and reviews are often recommended for requirements analysis but also for evaluations after implementation.

4.2 Activity Relations

An analysis of the input-output relationships is carried out at the level of the activity types, in order to be able to derive more generic conclusions. Based on the card sorting in the interviews, for each method mentioned its successor method is recorded, which indicates the activity that continues to work directly with the result of a method. An additional recording of the predecessor activity is not necessary, since these create duplicates of the same relations.

A total of 143 output relationships are recorded from the interviews. The analysis shows that many survey and analyze activities are not adequately transformed into other forms of documentation for further use. This results in abbreviations in the process, which for example derive descriptions of the situation of use from the recording of a survey without systematic analysis of the results. Due to these inaccuracies in the

Table 3. Activities for dealing with usage requirements.

Activity type	Description	Method types
Survey activities: integrate people or information outside the development team, relate to the usage situation and focus on open information collection		
Observing	Targeted viewing of the utilization situation in the natural utilization environment	Field observation, participant observation
Questioning	Targeted communication with persons who are familiar with the usage situation	Interview, questionnaire, user diary, group discussion, customer feedback
Testing	Application of a test object under use-oriented objectives or actions	Usability test, field test, demonstration
Checking	Analysis of a test object with regard to use-oriented criteria or action sequences	Review, heuristic evaluation, walkthrough
Informing	Collection of internal and external information related to the situation of use	Document research, market study, stakeholder input, literature research
Recording	Direct mapping and storage of collected data without manipulation or interpretation	Log file, recording, protocol, transcription
Analyze activities: integrate comparable analysis criteria, relate to the usage situation, focus on systematic information processing		
Extracting	Reduction of the recorded material to particularly relevant use-oriented aspects	Content Analysis, Critical Incidents
Systematizing	Revealing quantity relationships, interrelationships and structures of the utilization situation	Formal Analysis, Grouping Technique, Statistical Analysis, Tree Diagram, Data Visualization
Rating	Interpretation and prioritization of the various aspects of the usage situation	Weighting technique, discussion, classification
Tracking	Linking the information with its sources and conclusions	Referencing, decision table, fulfillment control, attribution
Describing	Solution-independent documentation of the usage situation and associated conditions and goals	Goals, scenario, user, task, usage environment, application knowledge, stakeholder, organizational conditions
Summarizing	Bundling and interpretation of information on the usage situation into solution-independent requirements and transfer documents	Requirements from usage perspective, report of results, context of usage, free documentation

(continued)

Table 3. (*continued*)

Activity type	Description	Method types
Concept activities: integrate existing knowledge about the usage situation, relate to the interaction with the users of the system, focus on interaction or information design		
Inspiring	Generation of solution ideas and approaches	Creativity technique, work-shop, standards and guidelines, creation of variants, practical examples
Modeling	Development of a solution structure for the system with regard to use-oriented aspects	Flow model, use case, functional model, interaction model, deduction and induction, modeling language
Visualizing	Transformation of the solution idea to a product illustration	Low-fidelity prototyping, high-fidelity prototyping, simulation, operation guide, storyboard, blue printing, physical prototypes, product status
Specifying	Documentation of the solution-dependent requirements and concepts with reference to the usage situation	Requirements from system point of view, concept, user interface design, system specification, evaluation design

practical procedure, only those relationships that explain more than 20.0% of the follow-up relationships of an activity are included in further considerations. In this way, Fig. 1 shows the most established relationships in practice and exceptions are excluded.

The generalized processes shown in Fig. 1 also reveal typical transitional activities between the colored content categories:

- The activity of recording represents the only link between the turquoise-colored, survey methods and the orange-colored, analyzing methods.
- The activities of describing, summarizing, and some methods of tracking provide links between the orange analyze activities and the concept activities in yellow.
- The activities of specifying as well as some methods of visualizing provide the links between the yellow depicted, conceptualizing methods and the turquoise-colored survey methods.

4.3 Usage Requirements Cycle

Based on these results, the activities and methods are transferred into a concept of the customizable Usage Requirements Cycle, as shown in Fig. 2. The Usage Requirements Cycle is designed as a scalable process model for the integration of usage requirements. The iterative character is oriented towards the development of requirements documents [16]. The concept focuses on the information flow of usage requirements between survey, analyze and concept activities [17] and on the perspective of the description forms [4, 18]. Simple and memorable terms for the activity categories are introduced, in order

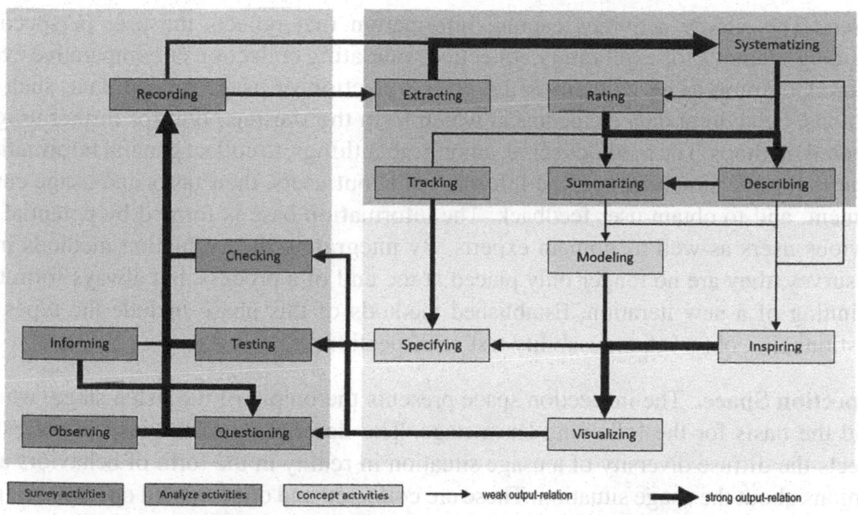

Fig. 1. Flow model of output relations between activity types

to support the intelligibility for interdisciplinary teams. Furthermore, a color coding is developed that emphasizes the content relationships. The descriptive forms thus also form the visual link, so that a holistic flow of information is created.

With the help of the iterative circular character of the process model, several loops for the integration of usage requirements can be performed within a development. The characteristics of the individual phases can be flexibly adapted to the current development challenges. As a quality factor for the application of the process model, a complete run-through of the process model within an iteration is recommended. Only the systematic combination of open data collection, independent data analysis and solution design based on this creates a comprehensible and repeatable quality of the results.

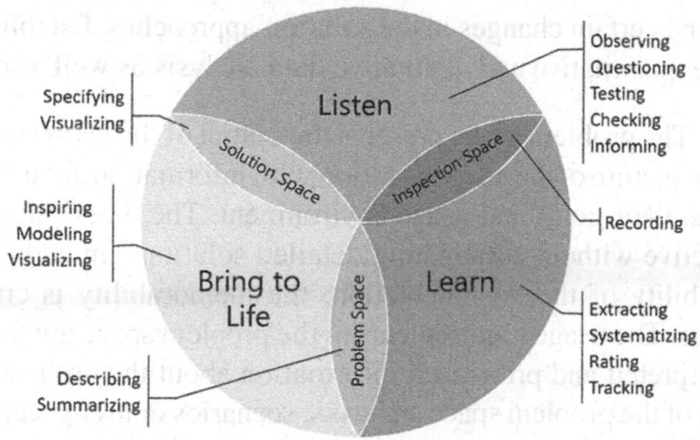

Fig. 2. Usage requirements cycle with activities

Listen. The survey activities capture information that reflects the user perspective including methods for exploratory collection, validating collection or comparative evaluation. Common to all of them is the open collection of usage-related data, such as opinions, behavioral data or feedback, which form the starting point for further usage-centered methods. The methods serve, among other things, to collect general information about the usage situation, specific information about users, their tasks and usage environment, and to obtain user feedback. The information base is formed by potential or previous users as well as domain experts. By integrating the evaluation methods into the survey, they are no longer only placed at the end of a process, but always form the beginning of a new iteration. Established methods of this phase include the types of questionnaire, observation, usability test or inspection.

Inspection Space. The inspection space presents the output of the listen stage, which build the basis for the following learn stage. The description of the inspection space reflects the diffuse diversity of a usage situation in reality in the form of behaviors and opinions about the usage situation. These are collected and documented openly and free of interpretations in order to preserve the holistic nature of the usage situation and not to anticipate results that are shaped by individual assessments of the development team. The resulting information can be very heterogeneous or even contradictory. Accordingly, the usage requirements of the inspection space are open to solution and free of interpretation. These are results of the recording activities including methods as natural language of quotations in transcripts, or customer specifications, as well as video and audio sequences of highlight scenes.

Learn. The analyze activities structure, evaluate and interpret the collected information about the usage situation systematically. The goal is to understand and prioritize the information relevant for the usage idea of a system in order to describe the problem area as solution-independently as possible. Especially in early phases of a development, this analysis is an essential prerequisite for a holistic understanding of the usage situation. But also in the case of user feedback that already refers to existing solution approaches, the analysis of the collected information aims at their systematization and interpretation without anticipating certain changes in the solution approaches. Established methods of this phase include quantitative and qualitative data analysis as well as ranking analysis.

Problem Space. The problem space presents the output of the learn stage and conveys a holistic, consistent picture of the usage situation with information about the users relevant for the usage idea, their goals and usage environment. The description is written from the user's perspective without anticipating detailed solutions. In addition to the clarity and comprehensibility of the documentation, the memorability is crucial for further conception process. The usage requirements in the problem space are therefore solution-independent, interpreted and prioritized information about the usage situation. Typical description forms of the problem space are tasks, scenarios or user groups. These method types are assigned to the describing, summarizing or tracking activities.

Bring to Life. Solution ideas are elaborated, adapted or improved with the goal of a human-system interaction, that is as usable as possible, in concept activities. The steps depend on the type of project and the progress of the development process. While in early phases user interfaces can still be worked out in brainstorming and visualized with simple paper prototypes in several variants, more complex functional adaptations to prototypes or even products have to be planned and implemented in later development phases. Established methods of the inspiring, modeling and visualizing activities include creativity techniques, prototyping or pattern analysis.

Solution Space. The solution space presents the output of the bring to life stage and concretizes possible solution alternatives for the usage idea. The description form of the resulting solution-dependent usage requirements is unambiguous and free of contradictions. The degree of detail of the solution idea depends on the application in early or late phases of a development process and leaves little or no room for interpretation. This form of description thus forms the basis for the implementation of the product. The challenge in this step is primarily to preserve the intent of the usage requirements in the specification. The usage requirements in the solution space are therefore solution-dependent information about the solution idea that is prepared consistently and without contradiction. Typical methods cover the areas of modeling diagrams, design principles and usability recommendations, but also prototypes. These method types originate from the visualizing and specifying activities.

5 Discussion

The selection of literature represents a snapshot of the variety of methods in dealing with usage requirements, which is constantly evolving. However, the category system with the superordinate content and activity types offers a consistent, flexible framework to classify the further developments in the disciplines.

The completeness of the methodological analysis is limited primarily by sampling. While the theoretical analysis is representative by integrating mostly cited works and industry standards, the sample of the empirical research and industry projects is limited to a narrow circle of influence that can be reached by the author. Due to the heterogeneous practical processes and corporate cultures, the practical study can only provide a spotlight on a small sample of projects. A larger intercultural project diversity would be recommendable for further empirical studies, but is hampered by the very limited accessibility to internal company processes.

Hardly any process runs ideally in practice. In addition, practices on which the process model is based can evolve. These adaptations make the specific delimitation and assignment of methods more difficult and require room for interpretation in the choice of methods. The Usage Requirements Cycle therefore does not represent an unambiguous, rigid process model, but is rather a flexible mental framework that depicts the relationships between the required activities for the integration of usage requirements.

6 Conclusion

The main added value of the Usage Requirements Cycle compared to the state of the art is the optimization of the transitions between the methods to reduce information loss and redundant work steps in the development process in the mobility sector. The descriptions of the usage requirements define these transitions between the application of several methods as the output of the previous phase and the input of the subsequent phase. Thus, the Usage Requirements Cycle offers a flexible basis for each user-oriented work step in the development process in mobility sector and supports in particular the efficient further utilization of the results.

To implement and maintain the Usage Requirements Cycle, a sustainable concept for a web-based information platform including methods und description is being developed. The Usage Requirements Cycle is intended to provide both a practical application for in-service training and a freely accessible point of contact for personal, self-directed information on user orientation.

As a next step, long-term studies on the use of the Usage Requirements Cycle in real practical projects are recommended. In addition, more analysis in the areas of education, medicine and entertainment, which are also typical for combination of products and services.

References

1. Bias, R.G., Karat, M.-C.: Justifying cost-justifying usability. In: Bias, R.G., Mayhew, D.J. (eds.) Cost-Justifying Usability, pp. 1–16. Morgan Kaufmann, San Francisco (2005)
2. Marcus, A.: User Interface Design's Return on Investment. In: Bias, R.G., Mayhew, D.J. (eds.) Cost-Justifying Usability, pp. 17–39. Morgan Kaufmann, San Francisco (2005)
3. Zowghi, D., da Rimini, F., Bano, M.: Problems and challenges of user involvement in software development. In: EASE 2015, pp. 1–10. ACM, New York (2015)
4. Haberfellner, R., de Weck, O., Fricke, E., Vössner, S.: Systems Engineering: Grundlagen und Anwendung. Orell Füssli Verlag, Zürich (2018)
5. International Organization for Standardization: ISO/IEC TR 25060:2010-07, System und Software-Engineering. Beuth, Berlin (2010)
6. Heisel, M., Krömker, H.: Logische Modellierung von Anwendungswelten aus Benutzersicht. In: NET.OBJECT Days 2002, pp. 649–656. tranSIT, Ilmenau (2002)
7. Theofanos, M.F., Stanton, B.C.: Usability standards across the development lifecycle. In: Kurosu, M. (ed.) HCD 2011. LNCS, vol. 6776, pp. 130–137. Springer, Heidelberg (2011). https://doi.org/10.1007/978-3-642-21753-1_15
8. Deutsches Institut für Normung e. V.: DIN EN ISO 9241-210:2020-03, Ergonomie der Mensch-System-Interaktion – Teil 210. Beuth, Berlin (2020)
9. Mayhew, D.J.: Usability Engineering Lifecycle. Morgan Kaufmann, San Francisco (1999)
10. Sarodnick, F., Brau, H.: Methoden der Usability Evaluation. Hogrefe, Bundesstadt (2006)
11. Gundelsweiler, F., Memmel, T., Reiterer, H.: Agile usability engineering. In: M&C 2004, pp.33–42. Oldenbourg Verlag, München (2004)
12. Folmer, E., van Gurp, J., Bosch, J.: Software architecture analysis of usability. In: Bastide, R., Palanque, P., Roth, J. (eds.) DSV-IS 2004. LNCS, vol. 3425, pp. 38–58. Springer, Heidelberg (2005). https://doi.org/10.1007/11431879_3
13. Kashfi, P., Feldt, R., Nilsson, A.: Integrating UX principles and practices into software development organizations. J. Syst. Softw. **154**, 37–58 (2019)
14. Meier, J.J., Conkling, T.W.: Google scholar's coverage of the engineering literature. J. Acad. Librariansh. **34**(3), 196–201 (2008)
15. Gläser, J., Laudel, G.: Experteninterviews und Qualitative Inhaltsanalyse. VS Verlag, Wiesbaden (2010)

16. Kotonya, G., Sommerville, I.: Requirements Engineering. Wiley, New York (1998)
17. Nuseibeh, B., Easterbrook, S.: Requirements engineering. In: ICSE 2000, pp. 35–46. ACM, New York (2000)
18. Fernandes, J.M., Machado, R.J.: Requirements in Engineering Projects. Springer, Berlin (2016). https://doi.org/10.1007/978-3-319-18597-2

Understanding Drivers' Physiological Responses in Different Road Conditions

Sara Mostowfi and Jung Hyup Kim(✉)

Industrial and Manufacturing Systems Engineering Department, University of Missouri, Columbia, MO, USA
sara.mostowfi@mail.missouri.edu, kijung@missouri.edu

Abstract. Although the driver's emotion has been studied in the different driving environments (such as city and highway), understanding what eye metrics and facial expressions correspond to specific emotion and behavior based on subjective and biosensor data to study emotion in depth is not well researched in previous studies. Using an eye-integrated human-in-the-loop (HTIL) simulation experiment, we studied how drivers' facial expressions and ocular measurements relate to emotions. We found that the driving environment could significantly affect drivers' emotions, which is evident in their facial expressions and eye metrics data. In addition, such outcomes provide knowledge to human-computer-interaction (HCI) practitioners on designing emotion recognition systems in cars to have a robust understanding of the drivers' emotions and help progress multimodal emotion recognition.

Keywords: Psychological conditions · Driving behavior · Eye tracking · Facial expression

1 Introduction

Internal and external variables such as traffic congestion, roadside infrastructure, and in-cabin situations are all factors that affect the driver's mental, cognitive, and attention states. Drivers' behavior and emotions could be influenced by both internal and external influences [1, 2]. A subjective experience, a physiological response, and a behavioral response are the three components of measuring emotional changes. However, no clear taxonomy of emotions serves as a standard foundation of driving studies, because many subjective emotional data might be inconsistent and unreliable compared to physiological responses [3].

Although emotion is based on subjective experience, adopting objective responses associated with emotional experiences could advance our understanding of emotion. Researchers in affective computing frequently create algorithms that turn internal emotional states into objective, visible data such as heart rate, skin conductivity, pupil dilation, and visual and auditory inputs and outputs. Combining scientifically recorded signals with subjective measurements makes it possible to detect internal emotional states. Combining scientifically recorded signals with subjective measurements makes it possible

H. Krömker (Ed.): HCII 2022, LNCS 13335, pp. 218–230, 2022.
https://doi.org/10.1007/978-3-031-04987-3_15

to detect internal emotional states [4]. Knowing these correlations will replace subjective emotion with objective, measurable measures like physiological signals, facial pictures, and so on. Indeed, Picard and Klein [5] observed that one of the most challenging inverse-problems is detecting emotion from visual signals because emotion is experienced through subjective sensations, which she regards as an "enigma" beyond the grasp of science. Cohn [6] also claims that "efforts at emotion detection… are intrinsically faulty unless one realizes that emotion-intents, action inclinations, evaluations, and other cognitions, physiological and neuromuscular changes, and sensations – is not observable". Self-report and physiological signals are the only ways to infer mood from context [7]. Objective approaches (facial expression recognition, physiological signals recognition, speech signals variation, and text semantics) cannot account for all subjective experiences. Recognizing emotions by facial expressions is one of the best ways to analyze the characteristics of emotions and technical aspects of the content [8]. Biosensors record physiological signals and kinesthetic data to make in-depth inferences regarding people's mental states [9]. People transmit their emotions through their facial expressions, voices, body posture, and physiological changes. In recognizing of drivers' emotions, various methods have been used in the literature, such as Behavioral measurements (e.g., facial expression analysis, speech analysis, driving behavior), physiological signal measurements (e.g., skin electrical activity, respiration), or self-reported scales (e.g., self-assessment manikin) [10].

Visual perception is another way to gather sensory information while driving. The majority of vehicle accidents are caused by inattention and inefficient information processing rather than a lack of capacity to respond to information (Diamond 2020). The majority of prior research in the psychological analysis of transportation has employed facial expression recognition to track the emotional condition of the driver. There has also been a great deal of research done on interpreting drivers' emotions by their eye movements and facial expressions. For example, [11] presented a system that learns which objects are most likely to be the driver's fixation object. Baujon et al. [12] have also investigated the driver's visual perception behavior using real car testing in corners and tangents. Using dynamic fixation behavior analysis, Brackstone and Waterson [13] have investigated how drivers' attention varies at different locations such as at the entrance and within highway tunnels. Increased eye movements and a shorter average fixation period are both the signs of increasing complex visual field. On rural roads, drivers use more conscious attention than on city roads, implying that the visual picture in the city traffic environment is more complicated. Driver eye behavior within and outside of a tunnel also revealed that, driver fixation's time was low as soon as they entered the tunnel, and the number of fixations outside was significantly higher than within [14]. The visual complexity may also explain the striking differences in eye-tracking patterns between participants seeing images of nature and urban surroundings. Natural settings have a modest amount of intricacy, which draws our attention and inspires a sense of gentle curiosity. Alternatively, the constructed environment may be highly complicated, making it challenging to hold our attention [15].

Therefore, knowing what specific driving' behavior is in a particular environment might be essential to provide a more accurate understanding of factors affecting outwardly expressed emotions. We also believe that knowing what facial expressions and eye metrics are associated with emotions will help researchers develop better emotion's multimodal systems. There is a direct link between driving ability and emotional content (negative or positive) [16]. When distracted by negative emotions, it has been found that lateral control was decreased and driving speed was lowered, impairing the capacity to drive safely [17, 18]. Positive valence has enhanced takeover quality by lowering the maximum resultant acceleration and reducing the maximum resultant jerk. On the other hand, high arousal did not result in a quicker takeover time [19]. Distraction also happens when the driver's attention is temporarily diverted by anything else (an item, a person, or a telecommunications device) [20]. There has also been a great deal of research done on interpreting participants' emotions by their eye movements and facial expressions. In this study, we conducted a study in an eye-integrated human-in-the-loop (HTIL) simulation, as shown in Fig. 1.

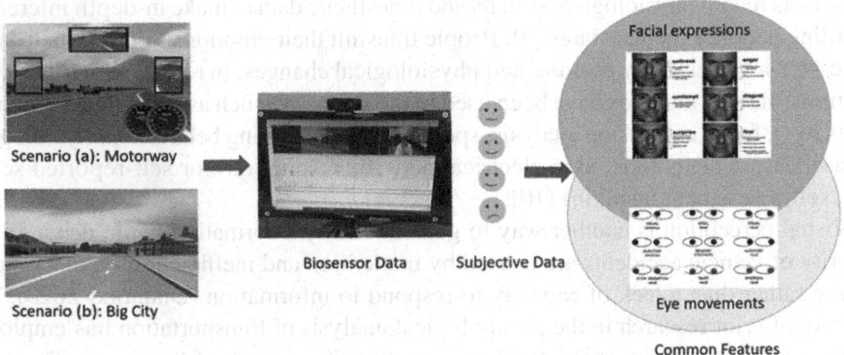

Fig. 1. Drivers reported the motorway scenario as stressful and the big city scenario as fatigue which is also evident from their eye and facial expressions data

This study investigated the effect of different driving environments corresponding to the participants' emotions by analyzing their eye movement data and facial expressions (Hypothesis: the environment differences between the driving scenarios (*Big city* and *Motorway*) will lead to significant emotional differences and facial expression & eye movements.

2 Method

2.1 Participants

Forty participants with normal eyesight (18–30 years in age) (Mean: 26.48, and SD: 3.89) participated in the experiment. Consent was obtained from participants before starting the experiment.

2.2 Apparatus

Eye-tracking has been used as a reliable technique to monitor eye movements for decades. Eye-tracking systems track the user's eye location, eye movement, and pupil size to identify zones of interest at any given time. Movement, position, numerosity, and latency measures are some of the visual behavior metrics that eye trackers provide for understanding the interpretative process [21]. We captured eye movements using an eye tracker (EyeTech VT3 Mini) with a 60 Hz sampling rate. Table 1 explain the eye metric measures extracted from eye tracking device.

Table 1. Eye metric's explanation

Metric	Detailed description	Unit
Interpolated distance	Estimated distance between the eye-tracker and the eyes, with missing values interpolated. Average of the eye tracker's distance to the left and right eye. Linear interpolation from the last sample before the gap until the first sample after the gap	Millimeters (mm)
Gaze velocity	Angular velocity of the gaze at the current sample point, i.e., how fast the eyes are moving at this point in time. Computation is based on a time window around the current sample. Distance between the first and last sample of this window is divided by the time lapse between them	Degrees per second (°/s)
Gaze acceleration	Angular acceleration of the gaze at the current sample point, i.e., how much the eyes increased in speed at the current sample. Computed as the difference in velocity between the current and previous sample	Degrees per second squared (°/s^2)
Fixation duration	Duration of the fixation, calculated as the time difference between fixation's start and end times	Milliseconds (ms)
Saccade duration	Duration of the saccade, calculated as the time difference between saccade's start and end times	Milliseconds (ms)
Saccade amplitude	Amplitude of the saccade, i.e., angular distance that the eyes travelled from start point to end point	Degrees (°)

(continued)

Table 1. (*continued*)

Metric	Detailed description	Unit
Saccade peak velocity	Peak velocity of the saccade, i.e., the maximal speed of the eyes during this saccade	Degrees per second (°/s)
Saccade peak acceleration	Peak acceleration of the saccade, i.e., the maximal increase in speed of the eyes during this saccade	Degrees per second squared (°/s^2)
Saccade direction	Direction of the saccade from it is start point to end point, indicated as clockwise angles: 0° mean a horizontal saccade from left to right, 90° a vertical saccade from top to bottom	Degrees (°)

2.3 Facial Expression Analysis

Face Action Coding System (FACS) [22], is a guideline that has been designed to assist in deciphering any physically possible facial movement and expression. Facial expressions in iMotion are measured with a 30% chance of being evaluated by a human to be analyzed, according to the AFFDEX algorithm. Furthermore, this threshold was chosen because it corresponded to the iMotions program's default settings for detecting tiny changes in facial expressions caused by any stimuli.

2.4 Multi-dimensionnel Mood Questionnaire (MDMQ)

The Multidimensional Mood State Questionnaire (MDMQ) is the English version of the "Multidimensional Mood State Questionnaire". The MDMQ is a well-established instrument for evaluating current mood through self-report questionnaires with excellent psychometric features [23]. It is especially well-suited for repeated assessments at short intervals because it is quick and easy to administer. Each dimension, good to bad (GB), awake to tired (AT), and calm to agitated (CA) has a score range of 4 to 24. High scores indicate good emotion attention and serenity depending on the dimension. Individuals took the MDMQ once before the actual session. This scale is divided into three sub-scales: good-bad, calm-nervous, and awake-tired. For each dimension, participants were given eight adjectives. Each participant was given a 6-point Likert scale, one being "absolutely not" and six being "extremely" and "Negativity" was scored in reverse: A high number indicated that the person was in a positive mood (pleasant or calm), while the number of negative items indicated that the person was in an unfriendly mood (angry) or apprehensive [24, 25].

2.5 Emotion Recognition Through Kansei Engineering (KE)

The Kansei engineering (KE) approach is an empirical tool for identifying and modeling relationships between design elements and emotive meaning assessments. The major goal of this method is to evaluate customer sentiments about products through emotional research, create correlations to physical product features, and translate those feelings into design requirements [26, 27]. In this study, among different methods KE was chosen by allowing people to convey their opinions about the designs even if they are not aware, as a result, Kansei aims to establish quantifiable relationships between subjective responses and design aspects [28]. Figure 2 shows the developed Kansei questionnaire for this study by authors for analyzing evoked emotions while driving.

Emotional
Very much ○ ○ ○ ○ ○ Not very much
Simple
Very much ○ ○ ○ ○ ○ Not very much
Spiritual
Very much ○ ○ ○ ○ ○ Not very much
Nostalgic
Very much ○ ○ ○ ○ ○ Not very much
Boring
Very much ○ ○ ○ ○ ○ Not very much
Modern
Very much ○ ○ ○ ○ ○ Not very much
Systematic
Very much ○ ○ ○ ○ ○ Not very much
Beautiful
Very much ○ ○ ○ ○ ○ Not very much
Artistic
Very much ○ ○ ○ ○ ○ Not very much
Enlivening
Very much ○ ○ ○ ○ ○ Not very much
Public
Very much ○ ○ ○ ○ ○ Not very much
Luxurious
Very much ○ ○ ○ ○ ○ Not very much
Regular
Very much ○ ○ ○ ○ ○ Not very much
Rhythmic
Very much ○ ○ ○ ○ ○ Not very much

Sedative
Very much ○ ○ ○ ○ ○ Not very much
Noisy
Very much ○ ○ ○ ○ ○ Not very much
Tired
Very much ○ ○ ○ ○ ○ Not very much
Concentration
Very much ○ ○ ○ ○ ○ Not very much
Rough
Very much ○ ○ ○ ○ ○ Not very much
Stressful
Very much ○ ○ ○ ○ ○ Not very much
Creative
Very much ○ ○ ○ ○ ○ Not very much
Gloomy
Very much ○ ○ ○ ○ ○ Not very much
Bright
Very much ○ ○ ○ ○ ○ Not very much
Lively
Very much ○ ○ ○ ○ ○ Not very much
Classic
Very much ○ ○ ○ ○ ○ Not very much
Dreamy
Very much ○ ○ ○ ○ ○ Not very much
Friendly
Very much ○ ○ ○ ○ ○ Not very much

Fig. 2. Kansei engineering questionnaire

3 Design Procedure

The study was conducted in one day for two different scenarios (Motorway and Big city). Each scenario lasted about 6–8 min in the simulator. In both scenarios (Motorway and Big city), the realistic traffic conditions that resemble the everyday traffic are included to extract the natural driving behavior of participants. After signing the consent form, the overall procedure was explained to each participant through a PowerPoint file. Then they filled out the MDMQ questionnaire to check their mood before the experiment. Then, participants sat on a chair with fixed legs behind a table with a PC screen fitted with a Logitech G920 steering wheel, brake, and gas pedal. Approximately 60–50 cm separates the eye from the screen. Each participant got 3–5 min to adjust to the eye tracker after the 9-point calibration. When eye tracker calibration was completed, then after a short break, the actual experiment started by driving one of the scenarios. During the test drive, participants could drive a car as usual in any direction and follow the traffic signs (which instructed them to change driving lanes). The first scenario is called "Big city" and the second one is called "Motorway". After they executed the first driving scenario, the participants completed the Kansei (KE) questionnaire. Then, another scenario was executed. Everyone had to fill out a Kansei (KE) questionnaire following the driving scenario, the same as before. When all the scenarios and questionnaires were done, the experiment was over. The estimated duration for this section is about 30 min per person upon arrival (Fig. 3).

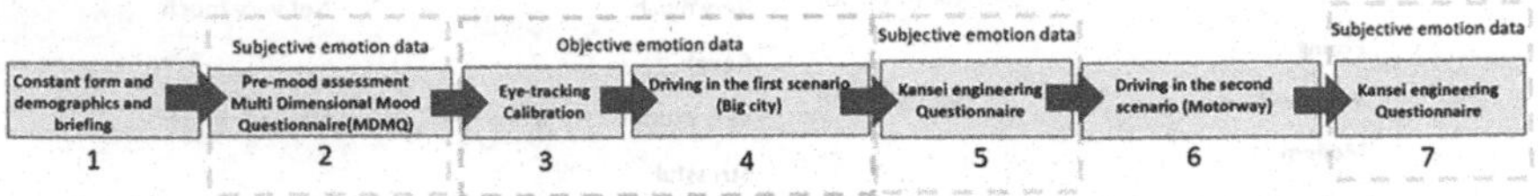

Fig. 3. The overall experiment protocols

4 Results

4.1 Comparing the Extracted Data from Kansei Engineering Metric (Perceived Emotion) in Both Scenarios

Among various Kansei engineering metrics, "Tired" and "Stressful" emotions were significantly different between two scenarios (Table 2).

Table 2. Statistical results of perceived emotions between two scenarios

Perceived emotion	Scenario	N	Mean	SD	SE mean	T-value	P-value
Tired	Big city	40	3.42	1.20	0.19	2.25	**0.027**
	Motorway	40	2.80	1.29	0.20		
Stressful	Big city	40	3.17	1.36	0.21	−2.42	**0.018**
	Motorway	40	3.88	1.22	0.19		

4.2 Comparing the Extracted Data from Facial Expression and Eye Tracking Between Both Scenario

We did the T-Test to analyze the data specifically the evoked emotions collected by iMotions and found drivers' emotion differences between the two scenarios (Motorway and Big city). The results (see Table 3) confirmed that both scenarios were significantly different in terms of facial expression on neutral and attention.

Table 3. Statistical results of extracted facial expressions between two scenarios

Facial expression	Scenario	N	Mean	SD	SE mean	T-value	P-value
Neutral	Big city	40	86.97	13.07	2.07	2.25	**0.027**
	Motorway	40	91.14	11.20	1.77		
Attention	Big city	40	90.70	14.04	0.067	−2.42	**0.018**
	Motorway	40	96.30	7.31	0.279		

For the eye-tracking data, the results showed significant difference in saccade peak acceleration between the two scenarios. There was not significant difference in other eye tracing metrics between the two scenarios.

Table 4. Statistical results of eye metrics between two scenarios

Eye metrics	Scenario	N	Mean	SD	SE mean	T-value	P-value
Saccade peak acceleration	Big city	40	15499	11240	1777	−2.53	**0.014**
	Motorway	40	24460	19364	3062		

4.3 Correlations Between Perceived Emotion and Facial Expression

According to the Pearson correlation, no correlation was found between the perceived emotion and facial expression in the big city scenario. However, a positive correlation exists between tired & stressful emotions and eye closure.

On the other hand, in the motorway scenario, a positive correlation exists between subjective feeling tired and neutral facial expression. It implies that every positive change in the unit of neutral expression is related to increased tired variable experience. There is also a positive correlation between stressful emotion and facial expression related to attention that indicates each positive difference in the unit of attention facial expression will result in increased driver's perceived stress.

Table 5. Correlations between perceived emotion and facial expression in Big city

Perceived emotions	Eye closure
Tired	**0.343** **P = 0.032**
Stressful	**0.321** **P = 0.046**

Table 6. Correlations between perceived emotions and facial expressions in motorway

Perceived emotion	Facial expression	
	Neutral	Attention
Tired	**0.326** **P = 0.043**	−0.078 P = 0.639
Stressful	0.075 P = 0.650	**0.410** **P = 0.010**

5 Discussion

This study investigates how different driving conditions affect drivers' emotions and facial expressions by analyzing drivers' physiological responses. The participants were driving in the motorway and big city scenarios for about 5 min with no hint about where they should go. Their eye, facial expressions, and behaviors were compared statistically and visually to answer the main research hypothesis: the environmental differences between the driving scenarios (*Big city* and *Motorway*) will lead to significant emotional differences and facial expression & eye movements.

According to the mood analysis (MDMQ), all participants were in a positive mood. The study results showed significant differences between driver facial and eye metrics in both scenarios. The results indicated that both scenarios are significantly different regarding the following facial expressions: neutral and attention level. ("neutral" (86.97 < 91.14) and the "attention level" (96.30 > 90.70)). Both facial expressions were calculated from the time percentage data extracted in the iMotions platform. The time percentage investigates which facial regions (the entire face, the eyes, and the lips) make correct detection simpler for each expression. Among different facial expressions, the neutral expression (the facial features are neutrally positioned, suggesting a lack of intense emotion) is the simplest to detect from the eyes and the easiest of all emotions to recognize from the mouth [29]. The respondents were significantly different in terms of being neutral. It means that the participants might have a significantly different amount of time being neutral between the two driving scenarios. The key features for identifying facial expressions are largely found in significant areas, including the eyes, nose, and mouth. By raising the weights of these critical features, the attention mechanism aids in improving expression recognition outcomes [30].

The subject perceived emotion results also revealed that the adjective means in the big city scenario is high for tired and the motorway scenario for stressful. Comparing the result of facial expressions with perceived emotions indicates that their high attention in the motorway scenario was related to their stress levels. Emotions like stress are very likely to occur while driving, as it is in all other activities that need mental energy [31]. As a result of negative person-environment interaction, stress generates unpleasant sensations. On the other hand, effective person-environment interactions may contribute to an individual's happiness and lead to a good sentiment [32]. Orientation of the head can also be used as a measure of attention. According to the facial expression results in Table 3, the mean for attention in the motorway scenario is higher than in the big city scenario (96.30 > 90.70). The 1–2-degree high-resolution center field represents overt attention, which is measured by the eyes. We use covert attention, also known as mental attention, in addition to overt attention. As the name implies, covert attention is difficult to measure since it involves our brain's attentional spotlight without the use of our eyes. As a result, our visual behavior is largely determined by a balance of covert and overt attention [6].

Among various eye metrics we tested in this study, saccade peak acceleration was the only one that showed a significant difference between the two driving scenarios (see Table 4). Saccade peak acceleration was higher when the participants drove the motorway scenario compared to the big city scenario. It is the maximal speed of the eyes during the saccade (degrees per second squared (°/2)) [33]. In the big city scenario, the participants felt that the scenario was tiring based on their feedback. Drowsy driving occurs when the driver is tired or exhausted, resulting in impaired concentration and coordination, a delayed response time, and poor judgment [34].

The correlations between perceived emotions and facial expressions imply that some of the facial expressions could be used to monitor the driver's emotional state (see Tables 5 and 6). Emotions are subjective and personal, and computers must balance that with the objective representations of emotions necessary for computers to work correctly. According to the result in Table 5, the subjective measure of fatigue was correlated to the facial expression "Eye closure" in the big city scenario. It means that the driver's fatigue level can be detected by the facial expression "Eye closure". Many prior studies have primarily focused on eye closure rather than other facial expressions to detect fatigue. However, those correlations were not found in the motorway scenario. The road design might significantly influence those correlations in the motorway scenario. This result will require further investigation.

In recent years, some studies have begun to look at various facial movements other than eye closure for detecting attentiveness, such as brow raise, yawning, and head or eye position orientation [35]. More studies are needed to systematically detect and categorize facial activities in developing drowsiness detection systems based on facial expressions. There is a psychological conflict between the desire to drive and the need to drive when it comes to driving. Possible consequences include an inability to concentrate on the activities necessary for safe driving [36]. The observed behavior in eye, face, and emotion can be explained by different factors in the driving environment, such as events, road design, and elements on the roadside.

6 Conclusion

Overall, this study shows that biosensor data could capture certain emotions induced in a motorist by surrounding road environments and road geometry as viewed from the vehicle cab. The hypothesis test revealed the relations between perceived emotion and facial expression corresponding to the road design, roadside elements, and road geometry. The findings of this study will advance our understanding of how emotions can be recognized through facial expressions and eye metrics to have an accurate judgment of the driving environment and its effect on driving behavior. These results would benefit engineers, HCI developers, and transportation municipalities.

References

1. Tavakoli, A., Balali, V., Heydarian, A.: A Multimodal Approach for Monitoring Driving Behavior and Emotions (2020)
2. Kleinginna, P.R., Kleinginna, A.M.: A categorized list of motivation definitions, with a suggestion for a consensual definition. Motiv. Emot. **5**(3), 263–291 (1981). https://doi.org/10.1007/BF00993889
3. Pittermann, J., Pittermann, A., Minker, W.: Emotion recognition and adaptation in spoken dialogue systems. Int. J. Speech Technol. **13**(1), 49–60 (2010). https://doi.org/10.1007/s10772-010-9068-y
4. Leahu, L., Schwenk, S., Sengers, P.: Subjective objectivity: negotiating emotional meaning. In: Proceedings of the 7th ACM Conference on Designing Interactive Systems, pp. 425–434 (2008)
5. Picard, R.W., Klein, J.: Computers that recognise and respond to user emotion: theoretical and practical implications. Interact. Comput. **14**(2), 141–169 (2002)
6. Cohn, J.F.: Foundations of human computing: facial expression and emotion. In: Proceedings of the 8th International Conference on Multimodal Interfaces, pp. 233–238 (2006)
7. Martis, J.E.: Effective emotion recognition of expressions from facial features. **5**(06), 4–7 (2017)
8. Geiger, A., Brandenburg, E., Stark, R.: Natural virtual reality user interface to define assembly sequences for digital human models. Appl. Syst. Innov. **3**(1), 15 (2020)
9. Sedenberg, E., Wong, R., Chuang, J.: A window into the soul: biosensing in public. arXiv preprint arXiv:1702.04235 (2017)
10. Liu, L., et al.: Deep learning for generic object detection: a survey. arXiv 2018. arXiv preprint arXiv:1809.02165 (2019)
11. Martinez-Conde, S., Macknik, S.L., Hubel, D.H.: The role of fixational eye movements in visual perception. Nat. Rev. Neurosci. **5**(3), 229–240 (2004)
12. Baujon, J., Basset, M., Gissinger, G.L.: Visual behaviour analysis and driver cognitive model. In: Proceedings of the 3rd IFAC Workshop on Advances in Automotive Control, Karlsruhe, Germany, pp. 47–52 (2001)
13. Brackstone, M., Waterson, B.: Are we looking where we are going? An exploratory examination of eye movement in high-speed driving. In: Proceedings of the 83rd Transportation Research Board Annual Meeting, vol. 2, p. 602 (2004)
14. Yan, Y., Yuan, H., Wang, X., Xu, T., Liu, H.: Study on driver's fixation variation at entrance and inside sections of tunnel on highway. Adv. Mech. Eng. **7**(1), 273427 (2015)
15. Nadal, M., Munar, E., Marty, G., Cela-Conde, C.J.: Visual complexity and beauty appreciation: explaining the divergence of results. Empirical Stud. Arts **28**(2), 173–191 (2010)

16. Chan, M., Singhal, A.: Emotion matters: Implications for distracted driving. Saf. Sci. **72**, 302–309 (2015)
17. Zhang, W., Zhang, X., Feng, Z., Liu, J., Zhou, M., Wang, K.: The fitness-to-drive of shift-work taxi drivers with obstructive sleep apnea: an investigation of self-reported driver behavior and skill. Transp. Res. Part F: Traffic Psychol. Behav. **59**, 545–554 (2018)
18. Eherenfreund-Hager, A., Taubman-Ben-Ari, O., Toledo, T., Farah, H.: The effect of positive and negative emotions on young drivers a simulator study. Transp. Res. Part F: Traffic Psychol. Behav. **49**, 236–243 (2017)
19. Du, N., et al.: Examining the effects of emotional valence and arousal on takeover performance in conditionally automated driving. Transp. Res. Part C: Emerg. Technol. **112**, 78–87 (2020)
20. Hedlund, J., Simpson, H.M., Mayhew, D.R.: Summary of proceedings and recommendations. In: International Conference on Distracted Driving. The Traffic Injury Research Foundation, The Canadian Automobile Association, Ottawa (2006)
21. Nyström, M., Holmqvist, K.: An adaptive algorithm for fixation, saccade, and glissade detection in eyetracking data. Behav. Res. Methods **42**(1), 188–204 (2010). https://doi.org/10.3758/BRM.42.1.188
22. Ekman, P., Friesen, W.V.: Facial Action Coding System: Investigator's Guide. Consulting Psychologists Press, Palo Alto (1978)
23. Steyer, R., Schwenkmezger, P., Notz, P., Eid, M.: MDMQ questionnaire (English version of MDBF). Jena: Friedrich-Schiller-Universität Jena, Institut für Psychologie, Lehrstuhl für Methodenlehre und Evaluationsforschung (2014). https://www.metheval.uni-jena.de/mdbf.php. Accessed 4 Apr 2016
24. Meinlschmidt, G., et al.: Smartphone-based psychotherapeutic micro-interventions to improve mood in a real-world setting. Front. Psychol. **7**, 1112 (2016)
25. Hinz, A., Daig, I., Petrowski, K., Brähler, E.: Die stimmung in der deutschen bevölkerung: referenzwerte für den mehrdimensionalen befindlichkeitsfragebogen MDBF. PPmP-Psychother. Psychosom. Med. Psychol. **62**(02), 52–57 (2012)
26. Park, J., Abdel-Aty, M., Yina, W., Mattei, I.: Enhancing in-vehicle driving assistance information under connected vehicle environment. IEEE Trans. Intell. Transp. Syst. **20**(9), 3558–3567 (2018)
27. Lynch, B.K.: Designing qualitative research by catherine marshall an Gretchen B. Rossman. Issues Appl. Linguist. **1**(2), 1–9 (1990)
28. Schutte, N.S., Malouff, J.M., Thorsteinsson, E.B., Bhullar, N., Rooke, S.E.: A meta-analytic investigation of the relationship between emotional intelligence and health. Pers. Individ. Differ. **42**(6), 921–933 (2007)
29. Guarnera, M., Hichy, Z., Cascio, M.I., Carrubba, S.: Facial expressions and ability to recognize emotions from eyes or mouth in children. Eur. J. Psychol. **11**(2), 183 (2015)
30. Li, J., Jin, K., Zhou, D., Kubota, N., Zhaojie, J.: Attention mechanism-based CNN for facial expression recognition. Neurocomputing **411**, 340–350 (2020)
31. Hassib, M., Braun, M., Pfleging, B., Alt, F.: Detecting and influencing driver emotions using psycho-physiological sensors and ambient light. In: Lamas, D., Loizides, F., Nacke, L., Petrie, H., Winckler, M., Zaphiris, P. (eds.) Human-Computer Interaction – INTERACT 2019, vol. 11746, pp. 721–742. Springer, Cham (2019). https://doi.org/10.1007/978-3-030-29381-9_43
32. Mesken, J.: Determinants and consequences of drivers' emotions. Stichting Wetenschappelijk Onderzoek Verkeersveiligheid SWOV (2006)
33. Remington, R.W.: Attention and saccadic eye movements. J. Exp. Psychol.: Hum. Percept. Perform. **6**(4), 726 (1980)
34. Murphy-Chutorian, E., Trivedi, M.M.: Head pose estimation and augmented reality tracking: an integrated system and evaluation for monitoring driver awareness. IEEE Trans. Intell. Transp. Syst. **11**(2), 300–311 (2010)

35. Sahayadhas, A., Sundaraj, K., Murugappan, M.: Detecting driver drowsiness based on sensors: a review. Sensors **12**(12), 16937–16953 (2012)
36. Mashko, A.: Subjective methods for assessment of driver drowsiness. Acta Polytech. CTU Proc. **12**, 64–67 (2017)

Co-designing the Next Generation Automatic Driving Vehicle HMI Interface with Lead-Users

Ning Zhang[1] and Ao Jiang[2](✉)

[1] Guangzhou City University of Technology, Guangzhou 510800, GD, People's Republic of China
[2] Imperial College London, University of Leeds, Leeds, UK
aojohn928@gmail.com

Abstract. The automatic driving vehicle mounted system is an important direction for future development of automobile industry. At present, there are relative few user studies on autopilot HMI. Therefore, from the user's point of view, this study aims to survey users' preferences for HMI information function, operation mode and the development vision of the next generation of HMI interface for autopilot, and guides the HMI design of automatic driving car is really meeting the needs of users. In this study, 10% of potential users selected were invited. We studied the HMI interface through separate interviews, and used cards with HMI interface elements and topics to cooperate with the interviews. Through the co-design with users, we build an easy-to-use, and safe of HMI interface to meet the needs of users. The user's behavior and choice, the user interface and the design of principles may provide some references for the design of HMI interface of the autopilot car, and lay the foundation for future theory and practice.

Keywords: Conceptual design and planning · Human machine interface

1 Introduction

The automotive industry is changing on the basis of the innovation of automatic driving, and the ongoing development of technology makes the level of automatic driving increasingly high. Although highly automated vehicles will not be commercially available in the short term, the driving experience is being changed by extensive technical support during the transition period. The control theory has a history of more than 100 years and it has developed from "classical control theory" to "modern control theory" and has entered "large scale system theory" and "intelligent control theory" With the development of the technology [1], the man-computer interaction system is not only constantly upgraded, but also occupies an important position in the car [2]. The environmental atmosphere created by the human-computer interaction system subtly affects people's performance, emotions and feelings [3]. In the mechanical period, the interactive function of the automobile dashboard is very simple, which can only meet the basic driving needs. Influenced by the aircraft instrument, people imitate it on the automobile instrument and make all kinds of instruments. These instruments have scattered functions

H. Krömker (Ed.): HCII 2022, LNCS 13335, pp. 231–243, 2022.
https://doi.org/10.1007/978-3-031-04987-3_16

and little intelligence. Such interactive design is very unfriendly to the driver, just like being in the virgin forest. By the late 1990s, the central console had integrated many functions, however, because the technology of the display screen was not mature, the dense keys made the operation very painful. With the explosion of vehicle embedded electronic products, the demand for platform development and modular development of vehicle operating system has increased significantly. In the following decades, the newly added function is only to increase the physical interaction such as keys and driving lever. More and more densely distributed physical interaction devices make the cockpit of vehicles more and more like the cockpit of aircraft. In the model year 2001, BMW 7 series models launched the first generation iDrive on-board interactive system, which integrates complex on-board functions into a simple HMI interface for the first time. A reasonable visual design of the centralized control cabin can provide operators with a good vision and a pleasant environment, which will help them to give full play to their work efficiency [4].

Since 2019, General Motors, Google and other companies in the United States have successively invested much research into intelligent vehicles and automatic driving [5]. Traditional automobile enterprises have cooperated with Internet enterprises to accelerate the research and development of automatic driving. With the wide application of computer technology in the field of transportation and the continuous development of network technology in vehicle information technology, revolutionary changes are taking place in the internal space, man-machine interface, operation and interaction of vehicles [6]. In other words, cars have gradually developed from traditional vehicles to complex human-computer interaction systems. The electrical system and mechanical control system of the automobile are developing in the direction of digitization. At present, a prominent phenomenon is that there are a large number of information systems, such as on-board information system, on-board entertainment system, smart phone and other on-board applications and software are constantly injected into the car. It has become the norm for drivers to drive vehicles while interacting with various devices and applications. When driving, drivers browse or send text messages, operate the navigation system, etc. are some common behaviors. These functions not only bring convenience to drive, but also increase the risk of driving [7].

Due to the increasing operating functions, the car has become a space, Integrating information acquisition, social networking, media consumption and personal entertainment [8]. Because the increasing number of cars leads to the decline of traffic efficiency, the time people spend on cars is also gradually increasing. This makes the car has gradually go beyond the concept of its own vehicle and become a personal space [9]. Because most of the technologies that bring about such a transformation is digital and networked, the personal space in the car goes beyond the office and home and becomes a representative digital space, which brings a good stage for human-computer interaction [10].

Theoretically, the internal information model of automobile has gradually developed from a single driving and the vehicle condition model for a complex information interaction system such as vehicle to vehicle (V2V), vehicle to infrastructure (V2I) [11]. Under such a system, drivers not only complete the main driving tasks such as controlling vehicles, keeping lanes and monitoring road conditions, but also perform a large number of in-vehicle secondary task [12]. It directly determines the human eye's ability to discern details and has an important impact on visual ergonomics and the efficiency of receiving visual in-formation [13]. These tasks occupy the driver's visual, cognitive and action resources to varying degrees, distract the driver's attention, and generate a high cognitive load [14]. And more than 90% of the information received by human beings is obtained through vision. Therefore, the visual environment of the central control cabin directly affects the crew's information reception and the work efficiency of the central control cabin [15].

When driving, the driver must be able to effectively identify the operation area of the system and intervene appropriately. Many studies believe that it is difficult for ordinary people to continuously monitor driving, especially automatic driving [16]. Because when users monitor automatic driving instead of driving by themselves, the cognitive demand is more intensive. Therefore, it is crucial to ensure that the driver can use the autopilot system safely. These systems will be responsible for ensuring the safety of vehicle members and other road users in the future [17]. Therefore, it is essential to make sure that the driver can safely operate the autopilot system. Proper consideration of these factors in the design can well improve people's psychological identity and stimulate work efficiency [18].

Some studies believe that there will be mixed traffic of automatic driving and non-automatic driving on the road in the next few years [19]. In mixed traffic, autopilot cannot correctly understand the behavior of other vehicles and react, especially when the traffic density is high [20]. Co driving with other road users will be necessary, because driving by the autopilot is more defensive [21]. Therefore, in the case of left turn or parallel road, the automatic driving system relies on the cooperative actions of other road users to make appropriate responses. Besides, vehicle to vehicle (V2V) communicate is of practical significance to support the information exchange between drivers [22]. Car socializing can bring great benefits and better affect drivers' driving behavior [23]. This information exchange can enable drivers to adopt better and more environmentally friendly driving habits, reduce drivers' aggression against social driving behavior, and reduce young people's risky driving behavior [24].

Although the automobile human-computer interaction system is facing the problems of rapidly increasing driving complexity and driving safety risks, a large number of human-computer interaction systems continue to enter the automobile driving space. The search for complexity is the epitome of human demand for the functionality and experience of the product. The key to the problem is not to simply reduce the complexity of human-computer interaction system, but to manage the complexity through well-designed system and provide users with complex and easy-to-use human-computer interaction system [25]. The complexity of human-computer interaction system is caused by the driver's pursuit of more driving experience and information functions. Therefore, in the complex information situation, the key problem of HMI interface design is how to meet the needs of drivers and ensure driving safety, efficiency, and experience in the design of human-computer interaction interface and information system [26].

Due to the complexity and peculiarity of the car usage scenario, the HMI interface is quite different from the man-computer interaction interface of the traditional desktop system and the mobile device system. The method has been found suitable for addressing problems, identifying opportunities, and developing forecasts in general and technological forecasts in particular [27, 28]. The tools, methods and experience of modeling, design and evaluation of the interaction interface of the current desktop system and mobile device system are difficult to be directly transferred to the automotive human-computer interaction system. The traditional automobile development cycle is generally 2–5 years, while the fastest development cycle of internet interactive products can be only one week. Different development models lead to different development cycles, especially the Internet "online first and then improved" model, which is difficult to imagine in the automotive industry. Due to the huge differences in the development mode and cycle of the system, the design of automotive HMI is also full of great challenges and opportunities.

2 Methods

2.1 Objectives

In this study, a new highly innovative HMI interface will be developed, which uses the co-creation method with users to build a user-satisfying HMI interface. It uses a group of 10 users, including three truck drivers, five white-collar workers and two drivers who often round trip between two cities. They all have more than ten years of driving experience. This group not only has a high awareness of driving safety, but also has long-term experience and their own views in deploying and designing some technologies (such as the display and distribution of HUD interface elements). After a week of interviews and discussions, the research group met, the method of co-creating with users, and conducted a large-scale participatory design, focusing on the HMI interface of the next generation of autopilot. The content of this discussion forms the subject of Sects. 2.3 and 2.4. These studies represent a pioneering approach to the HMI design of the next generation of autopilot cars, as well as upgrades of the functional defects and information defects of the original HMI interface. These similar, user-focused and comprehensive methods, as well as various theories and methods found in the area of human factors, have not been strongly reflected in other broader literature. The broad goal of this article is to provide useful insights when these user-centered methods are used.

2.2 Materials

This article is based on the participatory design method to ensure that users can participate in the design, and become the Creator with users, to shape the next generation of HMI interface. During the week of this study, the author and participants studied the HMI interface through individual interviews, centralized discussion and voting. Use cards with instrument screen elements, central control screen elements and topics to cooperate with the interview. After analyzing and sorting out all the solutions discussed with participants, let users vote to choose the best solution and solve. In the form of seminars, the purpose is to discuss with participants and inspire participants to associate with the next generation autopilot HMI interface, providing a foreshadowing for HMI design.

2.3 Procedure

There are four steps to participatory design, which are described in detail below. The test process is shown in Fig. 1.

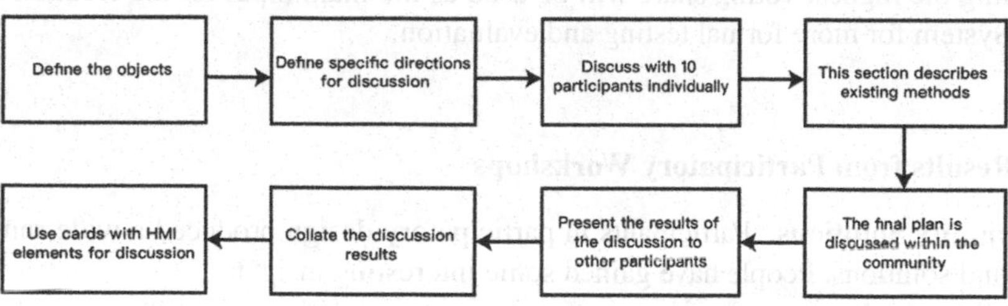

Fig. 1. Test process

Step 1: Define the Objects to be Concerned. During the discussion with participants, it is necessary to determine the specific content of the discussion and to ensure that there are specific outcomes after the discussion. At the pre-discussion meeting, participants and participants again identify topics of concern, which is communicated to participants at the beginning of the workshop. There are three specific directions for discussion. 1. Which basic functions should the self-driving car have? 2. What additional functions should the next generation of self-driving cars provide? 3. How should the HMI interface of the next generation of autopilot be distributed so that the HMI interface can be operated more conveniently? Participants can ask the research group for explanations of specific questions for better understanding and more efficient discussion.

Step 2: Discuss Solutions. The research team discussed with each participant the way to solve key problems and the trend of future technology. The research group introduced some existing methods to deal with key issues, and deliberately selected various methods to promote the discussion. For example, cards with HMI interface elements are made to cause topics and cooperate with interviews. The research team produced posters containing pictures and text descriptions of these existing methods, showing participants the details of each scheme, including the application environment and conditions. Participants can ask questions to ensure a clear understanding of each existing scheme. At the end of the meeting, the research team will resort out the results discussed with each participant. The research group will guide participants to think deeply and pave the way for joint discussion in step 3.

Step 3: Introduce the Results Discussed with Each Participant. This is a form of collective discussion, which gathers all participants to introduce their ideas and concepts to others and explain their opinions. They can also comment on the project based on their own or other people's concepts. Finally, the results of the discussion will be recorded and the data will be visualized.

Step 4: The Community Selects the Best Solution. Sort out the results of the group discussion in step 3, and the participants will vote. Participants were asked to consider all concepts, including concepts and solutions generated during the discussion. Use triangle, square and circle to express likes, dislike and ignore respectively. The first round of voting will screen out the concepts of dislike and neglect. The second round of voting will select several favorite concepts, and the results will be graded. The idea of obtaining the highest voting share will be used as the main input for the creation of an HMI System for more formal testing and evaluation.

2.4 Results from Participatory Workshops

Community Solutions. Participants in participatory design produced a wide range of ideas and solutions. People have gained some interesting insights.

1. *Overall design*
   The overall design idea of HMI interface should be to make the vehicle control more convenient, and the driver does not need to be distracted by many considerations of the operating mode of the central control system. At the same time, the information display of reminder instructions to the driver must be easy to obtain and understand. The HMI interface of the car is to make driving safer and more comfortable. Therefore, in the design, the safety of driving must be ensured, and the driver will not be distracted by complex functions.
2. *Design principles*
   From the perspective of driving safety, the ultra-wide integrated screen should be used. When driving, the driver's line of sight needs to observe the surrounding road conditions for a long time and should not divert attention frequently. The ultra-wide integrated screen can enable the driver to obtain the required information with less distraction. Ear-listening has obvious advantages in information input. Therefore, from the perspective of convenient driver operation, the way of information presentation and expression is mainly visual and auditory.

Moreover, voice control is widely regarded by participants as one of the user interfaces of the next generation HMI system. The cognitive ability, perceptual ability and spatial interaction ability of voice control can ensure the blind operation of drivers in the process of driving, and it will feed back information in time. It greatly reduces the distraction of the driver when interacting with an HMI system during driving, and ensures the safety of the driver. Furthermore, multimodal interaction is also a topic of interest to participants. New interaction channels such as sight, voice and gesture can naturally interact with HMI system, so as to accurately capture the driver's intention and improve the naturalness and efficiency of human-computer interaction. However, participants believed that in terms of practicability, the recognition of gesture interaction is not very mature, which will increase the distraction of drivers when driving.

Ranking and Priority. Ten participants put forward a HUD layout, a dashboard layout and a structured central control screen layout, as well as the important information of the instrument and the central control screen. After the participants scored, the important information level table of instrument and central control panel (Table 1) and the utilization rate level table of instrument and central control panel (Table 2). (Grades from A to D are important to unimportant) According to the two registration forms, it is obvious that for the information of the instrument, participants pay more attention to the display of instantaneous speed, fuel (electricity), light and gear, which are the most important for participants, but not so important for adaptive cruise assisted driving. For the important information on the central control screen, participants pay more attention to Bluetooth music, car play, air conditioning and panoramic image.

Table 1. The important information level table of instrument and central control panel

Information	Score
Air conditioner	9
Panoramic images	9
The bluetooth music	9
CarPlay	9
The parking lot	8
Navigation	8
Gas station	8
Bluetooth phone	8
The weather	6
Atmosphere lamp	6
The radio	6
The leisure entertainment	5
Information	Score
The instantaneous speed	9
Oil quantity (electricity)	9
The light	8
Gear	8
Range	8
Navigation	7
Adaptive cruise	7
Time	6
The average fuel consumption	6
The temperature	6

Final Jointly Created HMI Design. At the system level, the ultra-wide integrated screen should be used to maximize the speed and efficiency of information acquisition.

Table 2. The utilization rate level table of instrument and central control panel

Information	Score
Air conditioner	9
The bluetooth music	9
Panoramic images	8
Navigation	8
CarPlay	8
The parking lot	7
Bluetooth phone	7
Gas station	6
The weather	6
Atmosphere lamp	6
The radio	5
The leisure entertainment	4
Information	Score
The instantaneous speed	9
Navigation	8
The light	7
Gear	7
Oil quantity (electricity)	7
Range	6
Time	6
The average fuel consumption	6
Adaptive cruise	6
The outside temperature	5

Reasonably designed instrument display screen. (Fig. 2) Add head up display (HUD). (Fig. 3) Project important driving information onto the windshield in front of the driver, so that the driver can see important information such as speed and navigation without looking down or turning around. The central control screen is moved up so that the driver's line of sight can take into account the road conditions as much as possible when operating the screen. When there is important information, it should be displayed at the top of the system, so that the driver can get the relevant information first and respond.

When the central control screen provides the driver with driving convenience, it cannot threaten the driver's safety or trouble the driver's operation. Consequently, the interface is divided into three frameworks.

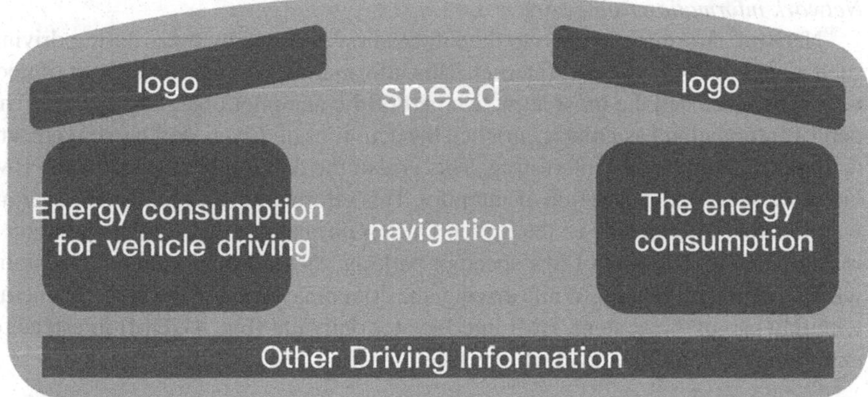

Fig. 2. The instrument display screen

Fig. 3. Head up display

1. *Scenario information framework*

   Situational information refers to the real-time information obtained by the driver in different situations during driving. In order to ensure the safety of driving, the position of this frame on the screen is relatively fixed, which is convenient for the driver to obtain information by scanning with his impression. Physical keys can also be set on the steering wheel or within reach to facilitate the blind operation of the driver.
2. *Status information framework*

   Status information refers to the information of vehicle driving status. In this framework, important elements can also allow the driver to customize the display position. The deeply customized interface offers users better control and comfortable and personalized user experience.

3. *Network information framework*

Network information refers to the information obtained by users during driving, such as call, information and Internet. This information is an important part of good user experience and the most attractive part of the autopilot operating system. This part of information has greatly enriched the activities of drivers and passengers, and is more entertaining and interesting. This is also the development trend of the HMI interface of the next generation of autopilot. This information is organized in a certain way to avoid interference to the driver. During normal driving, this information is insignificant. In the state of low speed or parking, the information about this frame will increase significantly. While driving, the driver may also use the voice to interact with that part of the content. HMI interface for daily life (Fig. 4), HMI interface for entertainment (Fig. 5), and HMI interface for office (Fig. 6).

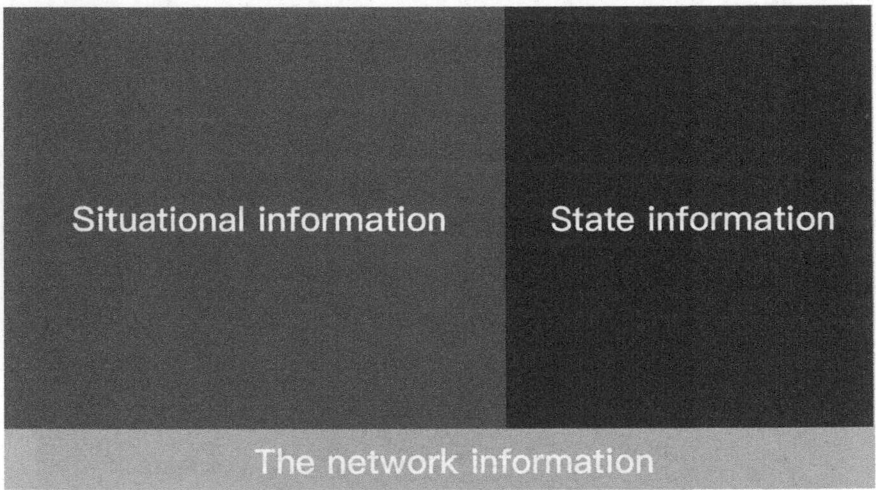

Fig. 4. HMI interface for daily life

In different life situations, the display of HMI interface will be slightly different. The participants divided the diversified scenes of pedestrian and vehicle space into three directions: daily life, entertainment and office. In daily life, HMI interface shall meet the personalized needs of different users as much as possible. With the scenes of office and entertainment, the function of HMI begins to extend. Drivers and passengers can expand car functions as needed, such as reading, business information processing, video conference, computer office, etc.

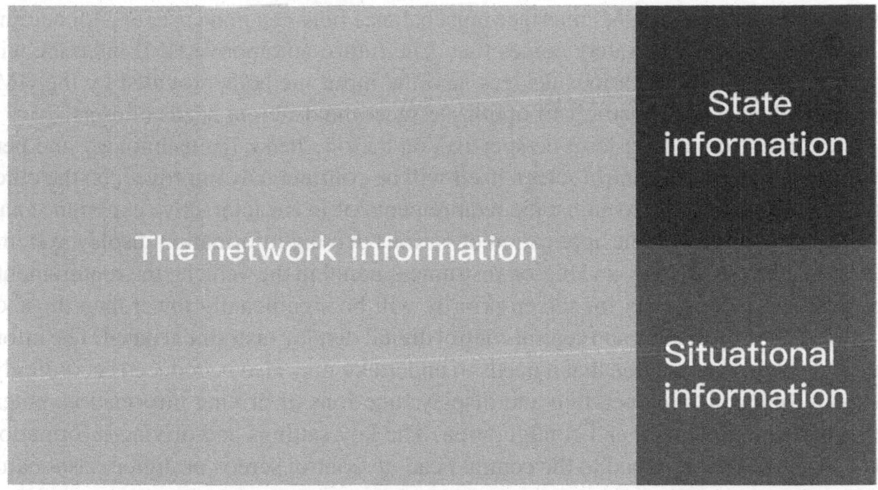

Fig. 5. HMI interface for entertainment

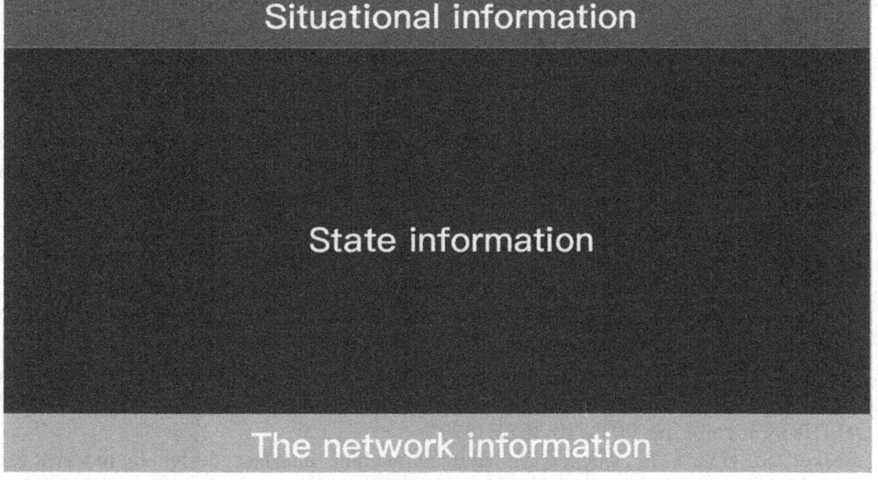

Fig. 6. HMI interface for office

3 Conclusion

This paper, based on the design of a concept and interaction design principle created by users, looking forward to the HMI interface of the next generation of automatic driving vehicles with users, and designs the basic layout. The interface is humanized and smart, allowing the driver to enjoy a comfortable driving experience.

The main highlight of the next generation of autopilot is the development and design of HMI interface. Its ultimate goal is to provide a good driving experience and pay more attention to safety and convenience in driving. This also makes the development and design of the automobile HMI interface must balance between good user experience and safety. To a large extent, safety comes first. The future automotive HMI interface will have seamless access to various devices, and the input methods provided by the HMI interface will also have a variety of options to meet the different needs of users.

Therefore, from a long-term perspective, on the one hand, the technology and performance of the central control screen itself will be continuously improved, on the other hand, it is also important to adjust the requirements of in car interactive experience and interface priority. Under the application of various driving information display systems such as heading up display and digital instrument panel in the vehicle, the requirements of digital instrument panel for screen priority will be significantly lower than those of traditional head up display and central control digital display instrument panel, The information displays the function that it needs to undertake may also be reduced accordingly, The main functions are operation and display functions of driving information, entertainment, communication and configuration. The key settings and driving information data can be directly returned to the central head up control screen or digital dashboard.

References

1. Jiang, A., Yao, X., Zhou, J.: Research on path planning of real-time obstacle avoidance of mechanical arm based on genetic algorithm. J. Eng. **2018**(16), 1579–1586 (2018)
2. Carsten, O., Martens, M.H.: How can humans understand their automated cars? HMI principles, problems and solutions. Cogn. Technol. Work **21**(1), 3–20 (2018). https://doi.org/10.1007/s10111-018-0484-0
3. Lu, S., et al.: The effect on subjective alertness and fatigue of three colour temperatures in the spacecraft crew cabin. In: Stanton, N. (ed.) Advances in Human Aspects of Transportation, vol. 270, pp. 632–639. Springer, Cham (2021). https://doi.org/10.1007/978-3-030-80012-3_58
4. Yu, K., Jiang, A., Wang, J., Zeng, X., Yao, X., Chen, Y.: Construction of crew visual behaviour mechanism in ship centralized control cabin. In: Stanton, N. (ed.) Advances in Human Aspects of Transportation, vol. 270, pp. 503–510. Springer, Cham (2021). https://doi.org/10.1007/978-3-030-80012-3_58
5. Gangyan, L., Pei, X., Mingzhong, Y.: Research on car central intelligent control system based on rules. In: 1997 IEEE International Conference on Intelligent Processing Systems (Cat. No. 97TH8335), vol. 1, pp. 707–710. IEEE (1997)
6. Becker, S., Hanna, P., Wagner, V.: Human machine interface design in modern vehicles. Encycl. Autom. Eng. 1–16 (2014)
7. McDonnell, A., Imberger, K., Poulter, C., Cooper, J.: The power and sensitivity of four core driver workload measures for benchmarking the distraction potential of new driver vehicle interfaces. Transp. Res. F: Traffic Psychol. Behav. **83**, 99–117 (2021)
8. Park, J., Nam, C., Kim, H.: Exploring the key services and players in the smart car market. Telecommun. Policy **43**(10), 101819 (2019)
9. Jeon, M.: i-PASSION": a concept car user interface case study from the perspective of user experience design. In: Proceedings of the 2nd International Conference on Automotive User Interfaces and Vehicular Applications (AutomotiveUI 2010) (2010)
10. Faas, S., Mathis, L., Baumann, M.: External HMI for self-driving vehicles: which information shall be displayed? Transp. Res. F: Traffic Psychol. Behav. **68**, 171–186 (2020)
11. Vaezipour, A., Rakotonirainy, A., Haworth, N., Delhomme, P.: A simulator evaluation of in-vehicle human machine interfaces for eco-safe driving. Transp. Res. Part A: Policy Pract. **118**, 696–713 (2018)

12. Debernard, S., Chauvin, C., Pokam, R., Langlois, S.: Designing human-machine interface for autonomous vehicles. IFAC-PapersOnLine **49**(19), 609–614 (2016)
13. Lu, S., et al.: Effects and challenges of operational lighting illuminance in spacecraft on human visual acuity. In: Stanton, N. (ed.) Advances in Human Aspects of Transportation, vol. 270, pp. 582–588. Springer, Cham (2021). https://doi.org/10.1007/978-3-030-80012-3_67
14. Xing, Y., Lv, C., Cao, D., Hang, P.: Toward human-vehicle collaboration: review and perspectives on human-centered collaborative automated driving. Transp. Res. Part C: Emerg. Technol. **128**, 103199 (2021)
15. Yu, K., Jiang, A., Zeng, X., Wang, J., Yao, X., Chen, Y.: Colour design method of ship centralized control cabin. In: Stanton, N. (ed.) Advances in Human Aspects of Transportation, vol. 270, pp. 495–502. Springer, Cham (2021). https://doi.org/10.1007/978-3-030-80012-3_57
16. François, M., Osiurak, F., Fort, A., Crave, P., Navarro, J.: Usability and acceptance of truck dashboards designed by drivers: two participatory design approaches compared to a user-centered design. Int. J. Ind. Ergon. **81**, 103073 (2021)
17. Götze, M., Ruff, F., Bengler, K.: Optimal information output in urban traffic scenarios: an evaluation of different HMI concepts. Procedia Manuf. **3**, 739–746 (2015)
18. Jiang, A., Yao, X., Schlacht, I.L., Musso, G., Tang, T., Westland, S.: Habitability study on space station colour design. In: Stanton, N. (ed.) Advances in Human Aspects of Transportation, vol. 1212, pp. 507–514. Springer, Cham (2020). https://doi.org/10.1007/978-3-030-50943-9_64
19. Ma, J., Gong, Z., Tan, J., Zhang, Q., Zuo, Y.: Assessing the driving distraction effect of vehicle HMI displays using data mining techniques. Transp. Res. F: Traffic Psychol. Behav. **69**, 235–250 (2020)
20. Li, X., Vaezipour, A., Rakotonirainy, A., Demmel, S., Oviedo-Trespalacios, O.: Exploring drivers' mental workload and visual demand while using an in-vehicle HMI for eco-safe driving. Accid. Anal. Prev. **146**, 105756 (2020)
21. Kraft, A., Maag, C., Baumann, M.: How to support cooperative driving by HMI design? Transp. Res. Interdisc. Perspect. **3**, 100064 (2019)
22. Papakostopoulos, V., Nathanael, D., Portouli, E., Amditis, A.: Effect of external HMI for automated vehicles (AVs) on drivers' ability to infer the AV motion intention: a field experiment. Transp. Res. F: Traffic Psychol. Behav. **82**, 32–42 (2021)
23. François, M., Osiurak, F., Fort, A., Crave, P., Navarro, J.: Automotive HMI design and participatory user involvement: review and perspectives. Ergonomics **60**(4), 541–552 (2017)
24. Li, S., et al.: Evaluation of the effects of age-friendly human-machine interfaces on the driver's takeover performance in highly automated vehicles. Transp. Res. F: Traffic Psychol. Behav. **67**, 78–100 (2019)
25. Prabhakar, G., Biswas, P.: A brief survey on interactive automotive UI. Transp. Eng. **6**, 100089 (2021)
26. Ulahannan, A., et al.: User expectations of partial driving automation capabilities and their effect on information design preferences in the vehicle. Appl. Ergon. **82**, 102969 (2020)
27. Jiang, A., Foing, B.H., Schlacht, I.L., Yao, X., Cheung, V., Rhodes, P.A.: Colour schemes to reduce stress response in the hygiene area of a space station: a Delphi study. Appl. Ergon. **98**, 103573 (2022)
28. Jiang, A., Yao, X., Hemingray, C., Westland, S.: Young people's colour preference and the arousal level of small apartments. Color Res. Appl. (2021)

Driver Information and Assistance Systems

Driving Experiment System Using HMDs to Measure Drivers' Proficiency and Difficulty of Various Road Conditions

Yukina Funazaki[1(✉)], Noboru Seto[1], Kota Ninomiya[1], Kazuyuki Hikawa[1], Satoshi Nakamura[1], and Shota Yamanaka[2]

[1] Meiji University, 4-21-1 Nakano, Nakano-ku, Tokyo, Japan
yukina.funazaki@gmail.com
[2] Yahoo Japan Corporation, Chiyoda-ku, Tokyo, Japan

Abstract. Car navigation systems typically calculate recommended routes on the basis of geographical factors and status of congestion. Such systems do not account for the user's driving skill or the difficulty of certain maneuvers (e.g., turning) or driving on different types of roads (e.g., narrow roads). This may result in problems for drivers, particularly beginners, when driving on a route recommended by the system. To develop a navigation system that takes these factors into account, we apply a performance model of GUI operation to driving operations and investigate a method of modeling driving difficulty, such as road conditions. In this study, we implemented an HMD-based driving experiment system to model drivers' behaviors. We also conducted an experiment to clarify the usefulness of our system and showed that our system could judge the driver's proficiency using the steering wheel operation in the driving trajectory of curves.

Keywords: Driving · HMD-based driving simulator · Experimen system · Driving Proficiency · Level of difficulty

1 Introduction

Advancements in GPS have led to the widespread use of car navigation systems. These systems recommend several routes and estimate the arrival time using environmental factors such as road preference, distance, and congestion. Driving skills vary greatly from driver to driver. For example, beginner drivers may have more difficulties with turns, curves, and narrow roads. To ensure safe driving and prevent accidents, it should be possible to change the route recommended by the system depending on the driver's skill, rather than prioritize shortest possible time. However, to our knowledge, no such system exists which can suggest routes on the basis of the driver's skills, characteristics, and mood. We aim to develop such a personalized navigation system in the near future.

The personalized navigation system must be able to determine the driver's proficiency level and the difficulty of driving on certain roads. To develop this system, it is necessary to create several models for environmental factors and drivers' characteristics. The models analyze the drivers' behaviors during operation on graphical user interfaces.

H. Krömker (Ed.): HCII 2022, LNCS 13335, pp. 247–257, 2022.
https://doi.org/10.1007/978-3-031-04987-3_17

The law of steering was proposed to model the act of drawing strokes, such as drawing a line or a task to pass through a path [1]. A few studies have applied the law of steering to driving. For example, Defazio et al. [2] conducted an experiment to examine a vehicle's steering model. However, this test was limited to narrow roads for safety reasons. Zhai et al. [3] investigated the human actions law by conducting steering tasks to drive on a VR route. The results of this study were not suitable for actual driving because participants were required to drive as fast as possible. These results led us to believe that it should be possible to apply the laws of steering to real-world driving in addition to virtual reality.

For our purposes, it is not appropriate to conduct experiments on real roads where the road conditions change between the number of trials and the subjects to control the experimental conditions. In addition, conventional driving simulators are not suitable for conducting experiments with the law of steering because these simulators cannot randomly generate controlled courses for individual driving trials.

Thus, as a preliminary modeling step, we develop an HMD-based driving experiment system that can reproduce multiple geographical conditions in a three-dimensional space. Our system generates multiple trials under selected conditions close to actual driving without changing the environmental conditions. In this study, we implemented a prototype of the system. Previous studies [4, 5] clarified that there was a difference in the driving trajectory of curves between novice (beginner) and advanced drivers. Therefore, we examined the difference in the driving activity of curve roads between between beginner driver and advanced driver to check the usefulness of our system as an experimental system.

The contributions of our paper are as follows:

- We developed an HMD-based driving experiment system that randomly generates various controlled road conditions, making it possible to conduct experimental driving tests easily and monitor participants' behaviors.
- We showed that our system could judge the driver's proficiency using the steering wheel operation in the driving trajectory of curves.

2 Implementation of Driving Experiment System

In the experiment for modeling driving, changes in difficulty level due to external factors such as time, weather, traffic, should be avoided from participant to participant. Driving simulators, particularly HMD-based driving simulators, have been developed in several studies [6], and companies have produced driving games as well. However, they are not suitable for modeling driving because the modeling system has to generate various patterns to instantly check the aforementioned external factors and collect information to analyze human factors. Therefore, we implement an HMD-based driving experiment system for modeling in a three-dimensional virtual space. In the standard HMD-based experimental design, observers cannot check what a participant was seeing or doing because the display only exists in the HMD. For this reason, to conduct the experiment correctly, the subject's behavior must be known to the experimenter.

The requirements for the HMD-based driving experiment system are as follows:

- Varying road conditions should be generated automatically in each experiment configuration, e.g., road width, length, angle of the curve, etc.
- Participants must be able to drive each generated road.
- An observer must be able to to set the experiment configuration remotely and monitor the experiment's progress, what participants see and do, and any trouble that may occur.
- Participants should not be restrained by cables.

We implemented our prototype system using Unity on the basis of these requirements. Our prototype system consists of two separated systems. One is for experiment observer and the other is for participants (see Fig. 1). Here, we used a PC (Microsoft Surface Book 2) for observers and the all-in-one VR headset (Oculus Quest) for participants (drivers) in this prototype system. The two were connected via a wireless network. In addition, we used the Thrustmaster T150 PRO force feedback racing wheel as the handle controller. We implemented a module that acquires information from the steering wheel controller and transmits the driving data to the HMD (Oculus Quest) via the network by using UDP because the Oculus Quest could not be directly connected to the steering wheel controller. In addition, we implemented another module that broadcasts the driving information and the participant's view to the observer's PC.

In this system, an observer first configures the experimental conditions such as the road width, curve angle, curve radius, total length of the course, and curve length, as shown in Fig. 2. The observer can also control other conditions such as switching between daytime (see Fig. 3) and night modes (see Fig. 4), showing guardrails, trees, buildings, etc. Then the system automatically generates a course from the given experimental conditions, as shown in Fig. 5.

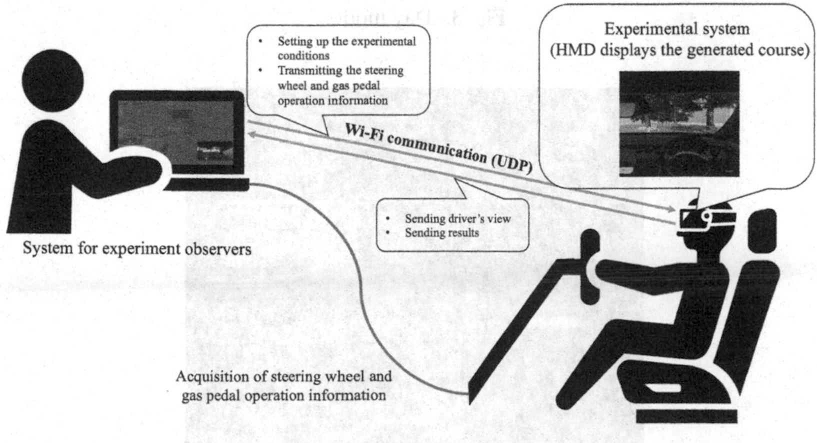

Fig. 1. Proposed method.

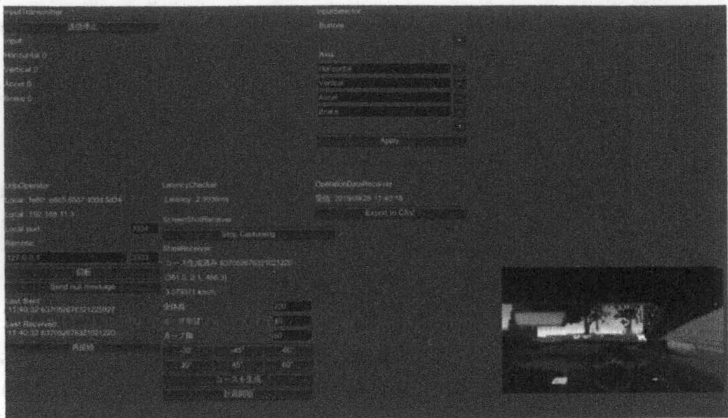

Fig. 2. Configuring and monitoring system for HMD.

Fig. 3. Day mode.

Fig. 4. Night mode.

Fig. 5. Course generated by proposed system.

Fig. 6. Screenshot of prototype system.

Fig. 7. A photograph of our experimental setup. The observer monitors the experiment progress and the participant's view.

Participants drive the car in the virtual space while wearing the HMD. Figure 6 shows an example of the particpant's view. The courses are regenerated repeatedly. While driving, the steering wheel on the screen rotates with the actual steering wheel. In addition, our system collects information on time, speed, the car's position, the number of times the participant steps on the accelerator, and the amount of steering wheel rotation about 33 times per second for the entire duration of each experiment.

The observer can check the participant's screen in real time (bottom right of Fig. 2) while wearing the HMD (see Fig. 7). By using this screen, the observer can check the progress of the experiment and even stop it when the participant's driving does not resemble actual driving.

3 Driving Experiment

We conducted an experiment to verify the usefulness of our implemented prototype system and to clarify the characteristics of the drivers' proficiency and driving difficulty of roads. We hypothesized that beginner drivers would turn and steer in curves more frequently as the difficulty of the road conditions increased. We set the angle of the curve to 0° (straight line) and prepared four types of right turns (30°, 60°, 90°, and 120°) and four types of left turns (30°, 60°, 90°, and 120°) for the experiment, as shown in Fig. 8. One-way roads were selected for the experiment to remove factors such as the possibility of the car protruding from the center line.

In the experiment, we instructed the participants to drive at a reasonable speed and avoid contact with guardrails. In addition, the participants could stop the test if they felt VR sickness. They were also told that the experiment was not a race and that they should begin driving as soon as the starting countdown was over. The participants completed five trials, took a five-minute break, and then completed another five trials. In each trial,

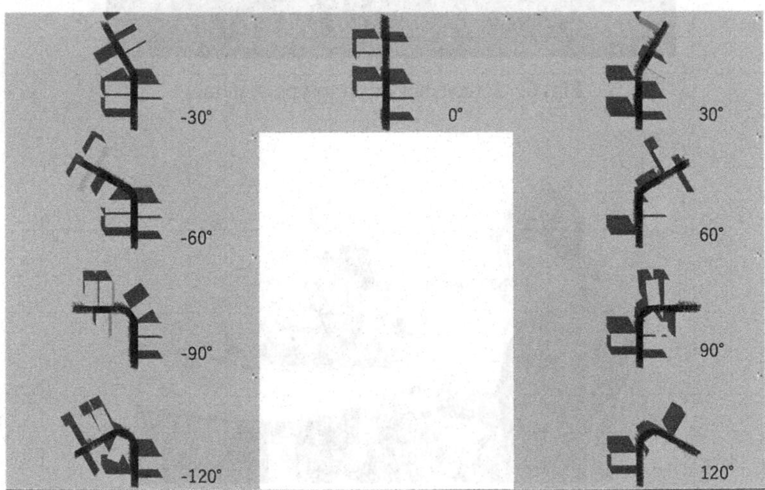

Fig. 8. Nine courses automatically generated by proposed system.

nine different angles were presented at random. Each participant drove 90 courses in total (nine angle conditions × ten trials).

After their trials, we asked the participants to answer a questionnaire about usability. Each course began with a countdown. If the car hit the guardrails located on the left and right sides of the road, it was considered an error, and the same course was presented again at the end of the trial. The entire test was approximately one hour long.

We recruited 18 university students (13 male and 5 female) as participants for this experiment. All of them had their driver's license. Participants who had been driving for three years or more and drove regularly were designated as advanced drivers, and the other participants were designated as beginners. Five participants were advanced drivers, and 13 were beginners.

4 Results and Discussion

Figure 9 shows the error rates of the experimental trials. The first trial, which had a high error rate of 13.1% compared to the other trials, was excluded from the analysis. Figure 10 shows the average error rate for each turn angle. The results indicate that turning left is more complex than turning right, with the 120° left turn resulting in the highest error rate. The graph of the left turn 120°, which had the highest error rate in this study, is shown as part of the analysis results. Figure 11 shows the steering wheel operation at each angle for both levels of drivers. The vertical axis shows the amount of steering wheel operation rotated during the curve, and the horizontal axis shows the angle. The results showed that the advanced drivers could rotate the steering wheel appropriately at each angle, while the beginner drivers moved the steering wheel several times to adjust the car's position. Figure 12 shows the results of the average time taken by the drivers for each angle. While the skilled drivers' times did not change at any angle, the the beginner drivers' time increased as the curve became larger, indicating that they could not turn precisely due to unnecessary steering. To clarify the difference between advanced and beginner drivers, we selected one advanced driver and one beginner driver and compared their 120° left turns. Figure 13 shows the steering wheel movement in each trial with respect to the driving distance, and Fig. 14 shows the driving speed in each trial. The left figures are the results of the advanced driver, and the right figures are the results of the beginner. We found that the beginner driver turned the wheel more frequently than the advanced driver. In addition, the advanced driver sped up in the middle of a curve. In contrast, the beginner driver slowed down from the start of a curve to the end. This suggests that beginner drivers turn and steer more frequently in curves and that the difficulty of driving increases as the curve angle increases.

In summary, the steering wheel operation was an accurate indicator of the driver's driving proficiency and could also be a possible indicator for road difficulty for beginners. However, in this experiment, we only changed the angle of the curve, and the radius was fixed. Therefore, we will consider conducting experiments with curves of varying radii in the future.

In the questionnaire regarding the system's usability, several respondents stated that the weight of the accelerator pedal was different from that of an actual car, making it difficult to drive. Since the accelerator pedal used in the experiment was made for a

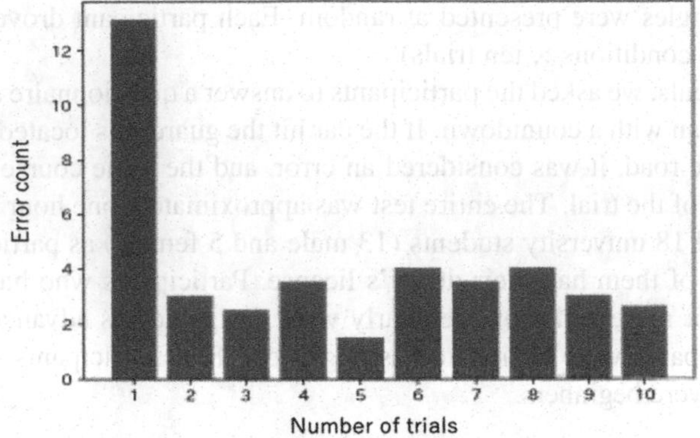

Fig. 9. Average error rate in each driving trial.

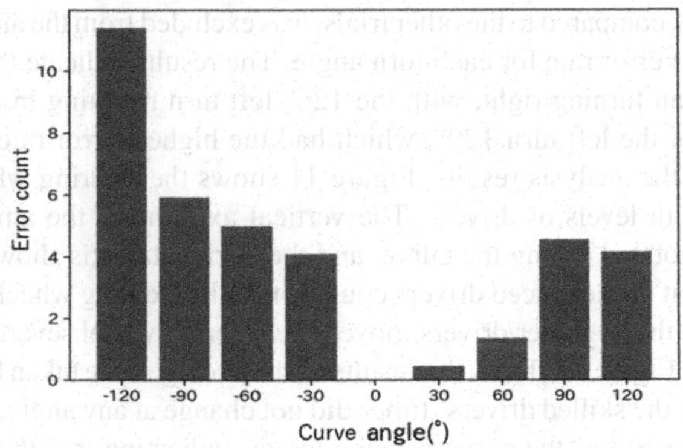

Fig. 10. Average error rate for each angle.

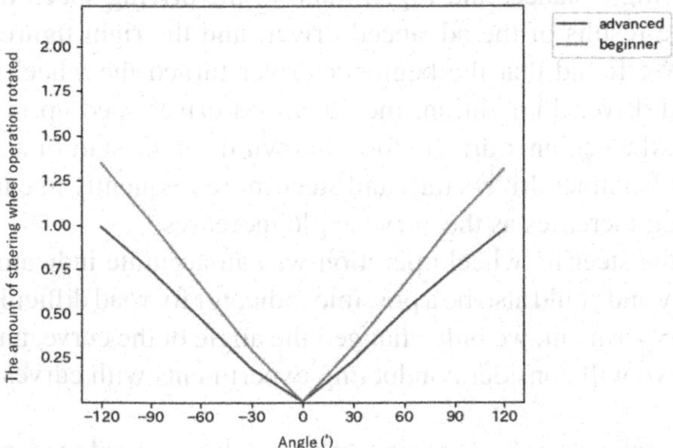

Fig. 11. Average amount of steering wheel movement at each angle.

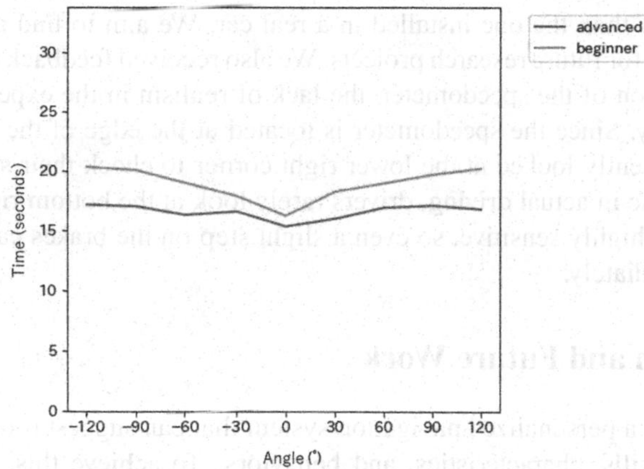

Fig. 12. Average time taken for each angle.

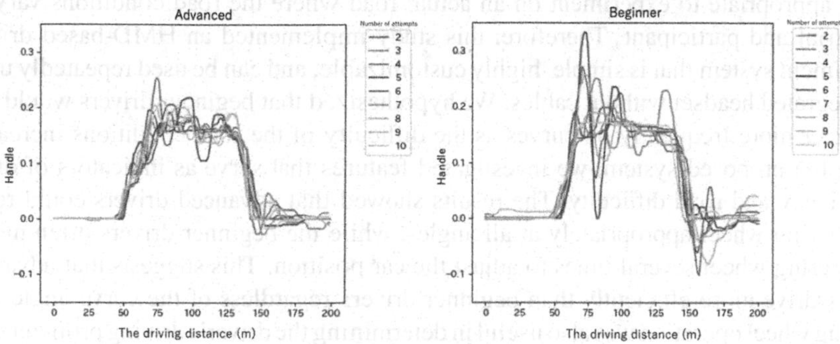

Fig. 13. Amount of steering wheel movement in each trial over distance in 120° left turn. Left: advanced driver. Right: beginner driver.

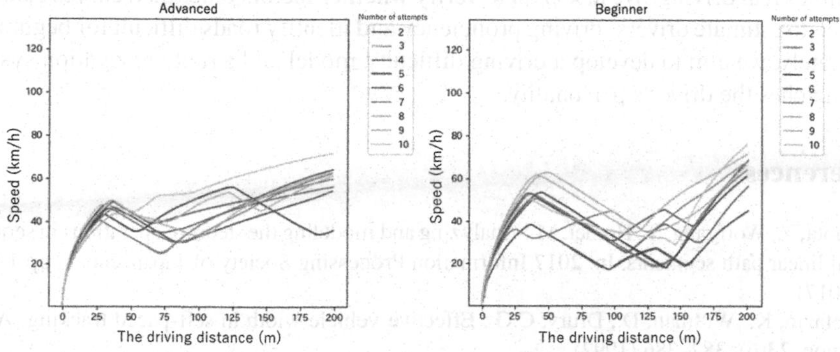

Fig. 14. Driving speed in each trial over distance in 120° left turn. Left: advanced driver. Right: beginner driver.

game, it is lighter than the one installed in a real car. We aim to find a more suitable driving controller for future research projects. We also received feedback on other issues, such as the location of the speedometer, the lack of realism in the experience, and the brakes' sensitivity. Since the speedometer is located at the edge of the field of vision, participants frequently looked at the lower right corner to check their speed. This was unrealistic because in actual driving, drivers rarely look at the bottom right corner. The brakes were also highly sensitive, so even a slight step on the brakes caused the car to slow down immediately.

5 Conclusion and Future Work

We aim to devlop a personalized navigation system that can suggest routes on the basis of the driver's skills, characteristics, and behaviors. To achieve this, it is necessary first to identify the driver's proficiency level, clarify the difficulty of driving certain roads, and create multiple models for environmental factors and driver characteristics to enable personalized navigation. However, to control the experimental conditions, it is not appropriate to experiment on an actual road where the road conditions vary for each trial and participant. Therefore, this study implemented an HMD-based driving experiment system that is simple, highly customizable, and can be used repeatedly using an integrated headset without cables. We hypothesized that beginner drivers would turn and steer more frequently on curves as the difficulty of the road conditions increased. Using the proposed system, we investigated features that serve as indicators of driver proficiency and road difficulty. The results showed that advanced drivers could rotate the steering wheel appropriately at all angles, while the beginner drivers often moved the steering wheel several times to adjust the car position. This suggests that advanced drivers drive more efficiently than beginner drivers regardless of the curve angle. The steering wheel operation was also useful in determining the driver's driving proficiency as the results differed significantly between the advanced and beginner drivers, suggesting that the difficulty of driving may increase with the amount of necessary steering wheel movement.

In the future, we intend to improve the experimental system so that it more closely resembles real driving. We also plan to verify whether factors other than curves can also be used to estimate drivers' driving proficiency and identify roads difficult for beginners. Ultimately, we aim to develop a driving difficulty model and a route navigation system that matches the driver's personality.

References

1. Shota, Y., Wolfgang, S., Homei, M.: Analyzing and modeling the steering operations in sequential linear path segments. In: 2017 Information Processing Society of Japan, Japan, pp.17–26 (2017)
2. Defazio, K., Wittman, D., Drury, C.G.: Effective vehicle width in self-paced tracking. Appl. Ergon. **23**(6), 382–386 (1992)
3. Zhai, S., Accot, J., Woltjer, R.: Human action laws in electronic virtual worlds: an empirical study of path steering performance in VR. Teleoperators Virtual Environ. **13**(2), 113–127 (2004)

4. Yukio, K.: Driving characteristics of novice and experienced drivers -part 1: characteristics of visual search. Rep. Transp. Nat. Res. Inst. Police Sci. **28**(2), 73–78 (1997)
5. Yukio, K., Masao, N.: Driving characteristics of novice and experienced drivers -2nd report, speed and directional controls on sharp curves. Rep. Transp. Nat. Res. Inst. Police Sci. **29**(2), 121–126 (1998)
6. Mourant, R.R., Schultheis, M.T.: A HMD-based virtual reality driving simulator. In: Proceedings of the First International Driving Symposium on Human Factors in Driver Assessment, Training and Vehicle Design, Colorado, pp. 300–304 (2001)

Inspection of In-Vehicle Touchscreen Infotainment Display for Different Screen Locations, Menu Types, and Positions

Saumil Patel(✉), Yi Liu, Ruobing Zhao, Xinyu Liu, and Yueqing Li

Lamar University, Beaumont, TX 77705, USA
spatel74@lamar.edu

Abstract. There has been a rapid increase in 'In-vehicle touchscreens' usage over the last decade, particularly for information and entertainment functions. And because of the dynamic interface functionality, the touchscreen becomes a major attraction for the automobile industry. As a result, today most car manufacturer uses touchscreen instead of static push buttons. For display screen locations, there have been two legacy display locations in the car. One is a 'Head-up display' and 'Head-down display'. The head-up display is similar to jet plans mounted on top of the instrument panel board and head-down display - located on the car console. However, the HUD position won't work for touchscreen devices since the touchscreen required direct touch input from the driver for which the HUD location either blocks the road view or is out of the driver's reach. Besides, there are numbers of possibilities for HDD locations to enhance driver's interaction and driving experience.

In the research study, we are evaluating 8 different possible "in-vehicle touchscreen designs". (2 HDD locations for touch screen display- Top & Middle, 2 different main menu layouts- Horizontal & Vertical, 2 screen mount positions- Fixed screen vs Tilted screen according to user preference). The study focused on assessing possibilities for different HDD locations within proximity of the driver. This experiment aims to find the most effective and efficient touchscreen position with the least possible discomfort and distraction. Participants were instructed to perform a series of different Music, A/C, Seat control tasks on the developed In-vehicle infotainment prototype in the experiment. The experiment tasks were focused on controlled and real-life task-based scenarios.

Keywords: In-vehicle touch screen display · Human machine interface · Automotive user interfaces · Touch screen display locations · Menu types

1 Introduction

1.1 What is IVIS? and History

IVIS – In-vehicle infotainment System. As the name indicates, it is a computer system that provides live information about vehicle conditions using sensors and cameras and allows drivers to access various entertainment options and vehicle information while

H. Krömker (Ed.): HCII 2022, LNCS 13335, pp. 258–279, 2022.
https://doi.org/10.1007/978-3-031-04987-3_18

driving. IVIS is a system specially designed for drivers to make the driving experience safer and more pleasurable.

In recent years human society evolved from the "industrial society age" and transitioned into the "knowledge society age." Therefore, the advancement of Human Machine Interfaces (HMI) is a tough, interdisciplinary test. Other than the technical aspect, the improvement was likewise tested by the need to adhere to the cognitive & psychological principle shown in the need to pick interaction designs that fit the user's mental model. Ex: Seat-belt sign design, window switch design, tire pressure on-screen, entertainment options.

The first automotive IVIS was mechanical. Their primary purpose and implemented functionalities planned to inform the driver with relevant information about the vehicle speed, gas level, break current status.

The MG T type was the first kind of manual car information system has been built in 1937. As time progresses, designers started developing more functionalities. Later on, displaying only this information was not sufficient anymore. The drivers also wanted to be entertained while driving. Therefore, entertainment functions like radios were progressively integrated into the car, leading to increased complexity. A system that combines vehicle condition information with entertainment functions is called an infotainment system [3]. However, in 2010 GPRS introduced a small screen in cars. It opens up a new way of communicating with the system using the dashboard. Before that, functionality was more mechanical buttons instead of digital screens and touchpads.

Moreover, the type of information introduced to the Driver has also evolved and changed over time. Today, standard functionalities of HMIs encompass the display of vehicle-related information, advanced driver assistance functionalities, and entertainment components like radio, media player.

Due to the increased complexity of the HMI, which consists of various input and output interfaces, its usability has become a significant quality factor [2]. Modern HMIs consists of a graphical user interface, a control unit, speech dialog systems, and gesture-based systems like touch interfaces. Furthermore, the application of up-to-date hardware and software components enables a steadily rising number of use cases. The specialized acknowledgment is liable for the sufficient execution of the simplicity of creating car HMIs numerous regular decades prior. Looking at the present and future developments, the primary difference to past developments is 'information processing' and 'entertainment options'. The types and the complexity of car IVIS have quickly changed in recent decades, corresponding to computer frameworks' improvement: from simple order line interfaces to a wide assortment of graphical UIs, discourse exchange frameworks, and motion-based frameworks like touch interfaces.

2 Literature

This thesis aims to evaluate the location and layout design of the In-vehicle infotainment system. The purpose of the study is to create the most effective and efficient interaction solution between the In-vehicle infotainment system (machine) and the Driver (human) with the least possible distractions and discomforts.

The literature section includes some of the previous studies about automotive display locations and layout designs on driving performance. The first section reviews the general introduction. The second section focuses on the effect of display location on driving performance. The third section reviews research on Interface design, mainly on Icons and display layout. The last section explains the limitations of previous studies and research questions.

Determinants of Automotive Infotainment Display-Based Applications: Operating vehicle driving is primarily characterized as a primary task. However, driving tasks include other necessary eyes off-road task activities such as mirror glances or speed checks. When a secondary task (entertainment system, car information system, navigation, cellphone use) comes into play, attention on the road is substantially reduced. Thus, an ongoing switch between the primary task(driving) and the secondary task increases safety risk.

The availability of various input devices and interaction methods makes interaction more engaging, practical, and complex at the same time. There have been several experiments were conducted to evaluate input devices and input methods [4, 37, 38, 43].With the rapid development of touchscreen display devices, IVIS dashboard displays have become the most chosen interaction device in the automotive industry. Besides, next-generation EV vehicles come with a larger screen display on the dashboard panel.

However, a significant disadvantage of IVIS is that drivers must look at the display while accessing it. At the same time, the IVIS display has various application benefits by commanding attention [44] which lies within the Driver's immediate field of view.

2.1 Device Locations

Several studies have been conducted on Head-up and Head-down device locations searching for the most effective device location for cars [47, 51, 30, 51]. The prior study divided device location into HUD – Head-Up Display and HDD – Head Down Display.

A HUD or heads-up display, also known as a HUD. According to the definition, an Automotive HUD is a transparent display that presents data in an automobile without requiring users to look away from the road. Originally HUDs were pioneered for fighter jets in the early 70s and later for low-flying military helicopter pilots, for whom information overload was a significant issue, and for whom changing their view to look at the aircraft's instruments could be a fatal distraction [28].

According to prior research, the Head-up display location is the most preferred and practical location for a display screen device [44, 5]. Since driving, attention relies on ambient/peripheral visual resources. If the device location is closer to the driver's focal/central vision while driving, it's easier for the driver to maintain eyes on the road. Head-up display close to windshield location makes it quite effortless for the driver to maintain their eyes on the road compared to any other location [26]. In addition, HUD's location next to the windshield makes glance distance comparatively low, resulting in lower subjective load, faster responses to hazards [22, 12].

However, the HUD cannot thoroughly replace the HDD display types (CID and DCD). Besides, for some applications (e.g., displaying the detailed navigation map or long lists), the HUD is not fully developed from a visualization technology and usability perspective 1.

HDD stands for Head down display location. And as the name indicates, the HDD display location required a driver to move his head down from the "driving environment." So, HDD is mostly placed on or attached to the car's console.

Head-down displays (HDD) were divided into two types the driver-centered display (DCD) for displaying speed and car status information and a central information display (CID) for entertainment options and car functions1.

From the first built automotive, all of the Automotive uses HDD: either driver-centered display (DCD) or central information display (CID) to display necessary driving information. HDD is considered to be the most effective location for displaying detailed information such as maps, driving safety/maintenance alerts, entertainment options in automotive [1]. Nowadays, as the modern automotive infotainment system became more interactive, HDD is considered the preferable position [27].

A study conducted by Normark [41] Liu [30] found no significant difference between HUD and HDD task performance. A comparison study performed by Ablassmeier1 using an eye gaze study indicates no secondary task performance difference between HUD and DCD (driver-centered display). On the contrary, participants' lane-keeping performance fluctuates for HUD compared to HDD. Another study conducted to measure the performance cost of digital HUD displays used three different locations: 2 HUD and 1 HDD location. 1st HUD location called digital HUD, located 5° below the horizon and 10° to the left of the center of the front screen, and another HUD location called analog HUD was centered relative to digital location subtended 10° both vertically and horizontal. HDD location was located on the car dashboard. According to experiment data, participants performed worse at maintaining their lane position for digital HUD compared to the analog HUD and HDD conditions [19] similar to the experiment conducted by Ablassmeier1. A study conducted on "The clutter effect of HUD" reveals no difference in lane-keeping data for HUD and HDD. Since driving performance relies on ambient/peripheral visual resources(surrounding) and secondary tasks rely on focal visual resources [42, 52].The possibility that device location angle from central vision matters more compared to HUD and HDD location difference. Similarly, as focal vision becomes a priority during hazard detection, HUD performs better compared to HDD because of HUD's closest location to the driving environment area [22].

According to prior research, HDD's distant location appeared more restrictive than HUD [47]. However, not all research studies are in favor of HUD [1, 19].

Besides the number of comparison studies that have been conducted on display locations [1, 19, 47], there were no conclusive results regarding the suitability of one location over another. Additionally, the majority of the prior research gave importance to comparisons between HUD and HDD display location, ignoring the importance of task type and input interaction.

Prior research lacks study on touch-screen device location. The majority of prior studies have considered a windshield or similar positions as HUD locations. However, similar locations could only work for display-only tasks (navigation, lane change); it won't work for tasks requiring user input. Besides, accessing any information/function that required some input from the driver causes similar or greater distraction since accessing any task required to glance at display and input device [8]. The majority of functions required some input from the driver. And for input interaction, the touchscreen is considered to be the most effective and efficient device [27].

None of the prior studies considered the possibility of different HDD positions. However, today number of automotive manufacturers are using different HDD locations. There are numerous possibilities for HDD location, which might be most suitable for secondary tasks with input. Besides, suppose the device is used for the HUD location. In that case, it will be blocking the driving view area unless the device is transparent or holographic. However, HUD visual technology is still not there yet. It certainly cannot completely replace HDD1. Moreover, besides accessing HUD touchscreen can cause driving discomfort. Finding the most suitable device location for touch screen devices with the least discomfort will be a key research finding.

2.2 Navigation Menu

The following section represents prior research on navigation menu design.

The user interface design has been a long-term interest in HCI research, and there has been considerable general research done on it. However, very few research papers have tried to explore the relation between 'task in hand' and 'human performance' with the possibility of different Navigation menu designs. The navigation menu is nothing but a group of buttons, where buttons contain graphical/text icons organized and grouped to work as the accessibility path of the system's functionality. The traditional Navigation menu design is mainly contained buttons: button location, button design, shape, space between buttons, icon type in the buttons, icon design [8, 9, 20, 21]. However, modern navigation menu design includes touch gesture functionality (tapping, flicking, panning), visual or haptic feedback [4, 37]. Besides, today users are getting more aware of visual perception.

Since driving tasks required eyes on the road, an in-vehicle touchscreen is considered a major visual distraction. The majority of the previous work considered touchscreen display as a greater distraction for driving tasks. Because of visual processing constraints, it is hard to grasp all visual layout elements at once glance [18, 31, 39], instead of focusing only on layout elements that come under the user's foveal vision. It reveals that even if the entire layout is represented in front of the user, the user cannot visually process all of its menu options, buttons, icons, fields, and other elements. As a result, the graphical layout becomes the problem of precise attention deployment [25]: How to present information effectively and efficiently?

Since we cannot ignore the use of IVIS while driving, we are focusing on designing and evaluating the most effective and efficient position for the navigation menu on the in-vehicle touchscreen.

Navigation Menu visual design can be divided into three groups:

Layout position: Horizontal vs. vertical, top vs. bottom.

Layout element design: buttons, button location, button design, shape, space between buttons, icon type in the buttons, icon design [8, 9, 20, 21].

Layout shape: linear, pie [7], circular, rectangle, triangle.

Navigation Menu Types. There has been a rapid increase in in-vehicle touchscreens over the last decade, particularly for information and entertainment functions. In comparison, traditional vehicle controls are limited to static design and cannot update once designed. With the touchscreen's dynamic control option, functions and layout can be altered and added as functionality evolves [32].

However, traditional static buttons are located on the car console to access it, unlike the touchscreen's dynamic control functionality. As Driving is considered a highly visual task where the driver "monitors a continuous stream of information through which the vehicle is traveling" [34] touchscreen becomes a major visual distraction. One of the major limitations of using in-vehicle displays is the poor design of the navigation menu, deep menu selections, excessive information presented at once, and similar-looking buttons that result in elevated visual distraction. It will result in longer task completion times, extending the frequency and duration of glances away from the road [11]. The more drivers glance away from the road and the further away they have to look, the more likely it will be for safety-critical information related to the driving environment to be missed [22]. As shown in the figure, a number of auto manufacturers use control penal as a replacement for traditional static functions. As technology evolves, the use of touch screens will gain more popularity. However, none of the prior research explores the effect of navigation menu types on the screen relative to screen position and type of button interactions (Fig. 1).

Fig. 1. Static buttons: (I) Push buttons, (II). Toyota A/C rotary controller, (III). Models 3 touch screen display (Images by Saumil (June 2021))

There have been studies investigating all manner of aspects to do with navigation menu type on-screen [17, 36]. However, the majority of the study included a website menu as a primary task. Very few studies explore the menu type effect with driving tasks [6, 13].

Navigation Menu Type in Websites. A study conducted by Burrell and Sodan [6] focused on the position of menus. The study included six different menu types. They experimented with a menu located on top and bottom, top, top tabbed, and left and top and right of the screen. In conclusion, no significant difference in performance besides the user preferred the top tabbed menu the most.

In 2011 Faulkner and Hayton [15] evaluated left, and right-side placed menu for an e-commerce website. Experiment tasks included searching and purchase of Christmas products. There was no significant difference in the time taken to perform the experiment task.

A study performed by Murano and Oenga [36] on menu design includes vertical and horizontal menus. The study was performed on an E-commerce website using the left side as vertical and topside as a horizontal menu. There were no major performance differences in both designs. However, later assumed that reason for no performance difference could have been less demanding experiment tasks [36]. Murano and Lomas conducted another experiment on four different menu types (left, right, top, and bottom of the screen). Where participant's performance was measured by mouse clicks and the number of errors, unlike previous experiments by Murano [36], tasks were designed to be more demanding and difficult. As a result, Top and left side menus required fewer clicks and the least number of errors [35]. According to a UX study performed by Nelson Norman group web users spends 80% of their time viewing the left side of the page and 20% viewing the right half [16].

Besides, several studies were conducted on vertical and horizontal menu typing. There are no conclusive results. On the contrary, the number of experiment study results have been diluted by the type of experiment task and task complexity [14, 29, 35].

Visual Attention for In-Vehicle Touch Screen Device. For an In-vehicle infotainment system driver has to perform secondary tasks without losing sight of the road. There are two menu elements for a vehicle information system: one is the navigation menu, and the second is static control functions. The static control function's location on the screen does play a vital role in limiting visual distraction.

According to an experiment conducted by Eren, Burnett, & Large on visual distraction, participants required greater attention and several visual glances to perform operations on the middle section of the screen and lower glances at the screen's corners [13]. Besides, the screen's top right corner was more in line with the driver's sight (depending on the side of the drive), resulted in fewer glances.

A study conducted by Vilchez on traffic signs and their effect on trajectory movement reveals that visual distraction location can influence lane-keeping performance [49]. In the experiment, the traffic sign was presented on the roadside, and participants were told to acknowledge the sign while conducting a driving task. According to the experiment data, the participant's lane-keeping performance was heavily influenced by the sign's side. In the experiment, participants' vehicles moved from the centerline to the side where a traffic sign was presented as they tried to look and lean towards that side. This study can be applied to IVIS's menu type design for its location on the screen.

Previous research indicated that the driver's side position and corner of the screen required the least glance to operate [13]. The majority of applications with a navigation menu preferred vertical position. However, the vertical menu consumes more space compared to the horizontal counterpart. As a result, in the era of desktop-based applications, the horizontal menu has become more popular. As Jakob's law of the internet user experience states, 'users spend most of the time on other sites.' In other words, users prefer your site to work the same way as all the other sites they already know [40]. Following the similar navigation approach means following the existing mental model, allowing users to apply their knowledge from previous experiences.

For menu typed at different corners increases the distance between menus, and as Fitts's Law states, the amount of time required for a person to move to a target area is a function of the distance to the target divided by the target's size. Thus, the longer the distance and the smaller the target's size, the longer it takes [17].

Besides, prior research didn't explore the relationship between different touch screen locations and menu types on user performance. For example, for the device's lower car console position, the top layout position is the nearest location to the driver; however, the device's upper console position bottom layout is the nearest location to the driver. With the complexity of diverse functions and tasks in hand, visual attention deployment becomes more important.

Despite the opinions and numerous studies around this subject, there are still unanswered questions regarding which menu type or design might be optimal in terms of performance and user preference.

2.3 Limitations of Previous Research

IVIS (In-vehicle infotainment system) display is the most enchanting invention in the automobile industry in the last decade. It brings driving experience to the next level by introducing hands in control to drivers and by providing real-time information, such as vehicle speed, entertainment options, map navigation, maintenance warning indicator signs, and fuel indicator signs while driving. However, IVIS creates a visual distraction for a driving task. As a part of the solution, the number of elements in the IVIS device location and layout design can be altered and manipulated to increase safety and driving experience.

Considerable research has been done on the IVIS display design. Much of the research has been introduced in the literature of this thesis. The thesis literature review explores many studies that have been examined and evaluated the effect of head-down and head-up display locations on users associated with different task types. The majority of research studies have been using display devices for IVIS instead of the touch screen; there is a significant lack of research for touch screens as IVIS devices. Besides all this research conducted, there are no conclusive results regarding the suitability of one display type location over the other.

Most importantly, most studies performed a comparison between head-down display and windshield as head-up displays; however, a similar position won't work for a touch screen display. Previous research didn't explore the possibility of different HDD device locations. Besides, several of the research studies have examined the display location experiment using IVIS functional task; however, most experiments have been completed with one specific task design or completely neglected effect of real driving scenario.

Research done in layout design is mostly limited and subjective. Prior layout research didn't explore the relationship between device location and layout location on driving performance. However, it does provide some insight into button design and driving performance, but it lacks a clear explanation for one over another.

Reviews studies highlighted some issues with simulation software and hardware capabilities rendering the information projection on the screen location and distance and capability with the IVIS device. Besides, existing research shows a comprehensive study covering the effect of an environmental factor on driving performance. Simultaneously, the secondary operation device (IVIS) has not included all the factors necessary to claim if the daytime or nighttime driving period performed better. Furthermore, the study of interior feature light effect, including screen layout design, affects driving performance and secondary task completion time, including distraction gaze time in the nighttime.

Finally, research studies in this literature explain independent study on device location, layout, and icons' effect on driving and secondary task performance. However, the research community fails to test all three independent factors combined and cross-functional impact in a single experiment.

3 Methodology

3.1 Participants

Eleven healthy participants, with ages ranging between 22 to 35 years, volunteered to participate in the study. An online general demographic questionnaire session was held to gather the data of participants' age, gender, education, years of driving experience, years of experience using phone, tablets, or any other touch display devices, years of experience with IVIS display (HUD, HDD), neck discomfort and eye stress while using different displays, comfortability using driving simulator, comfortability using a computer application.

Once participants were done with the general demographic questionary, a Secondary "In-vehicle infotainment system" survey questionnaire session was held online, continuing the first one; the purpose of the survey is to gather participant's opinions on IVIS usage and preference. Their understanding of what IVIS can do and design preference.

Participants have to obtain their post-experiment information and subjective comments once they finish the IVIS experiment task. Post-experiment information includes participants' feedback, subjective comments, suggestion, or preference they have any. Participants were provided with a written, informed consent form. The study was reviewed and approved by the Institutional Review Board of Lamar University.

3.2 Material

Driving Simulator. All experiment testing took place using STISIM Drive, a fixed-based driving simulator based at the Lamar University. A STISIM Drive driving simulator can help to improve basic driving skills by offering virtual training in diverse driving scenarios such as urban, rural, and metro city routes. A driving simulator accurately simulates random crossing pedestrians, unexpected lanes changing of the vehicles, and sudden break of the lead vehicle on the road.

The three 32 in., high-definition LED monitors provided drivers with a 135-degree field-of-view. A set of full-size driving controls, including the accelerator, brake pedal, steering wheel, and turn signals, were used to provide real-time feedback for speed control and lane maintenance. Wang [50] have used similar simulator setups for driving simulator experiments in terms of the real-world driving environment (Fig. 2).

Fig. 2. Simulator screens with 135-degree field of view (Image by Saumil (Jul 2021))

Driving Environment: The driving environment created in a loop way consisted of 4 different scenarios connecting with each other, starting from city area 2–3 lanes road to one-lane bidirectional ruler area road connecting to industrial zone and directed towards city residential area to the highway.

City area driving scenario was 2 miles long, consisting of two- and three-way lanes. Traffic in the city driving scenario was high. At various points throughout this drive, the participants encountered critical events (instant braking, pedestrian on the street, front car instant braking), which required an overt response maneuver in order to avoid a collision.

Interstate highway consisted of single lanes, with a posted speed limit of 70 mph. The highway scenario was 1 mile long. Highway included one-lane bidirectional roads. These roads included large amounts and varying degrees of curvature as well as frequent elevation changes and two crossroads. Traffic on highways varies from low to high, and high at the city to the interstate highway and low at the industrial roadway connecting to the highway. Interstate highway was connected with the city and industrial area.

The industrial roadway scenario included one-lane bidirectional rural roads. These roads included two crossroads. The industrial roadway was 2 miles long (traveling at the posted 55mph speed limit). There was limited traffic in the driver's lane; however, in the oncoming lane of traffic, there was a high level of traffic.

Residential area scenario included 2 miles long 1 and 2 lanes driveway, with a posted speed limit of 20 mph at school zone and 35 at residential zone. Traffic difficulty in the residential area was greater. Residential driving scenarios include critical static lane obstacles such as pedestrian crossing lanes, truck sudden lane change, a car passing in one way surrounded by parking vehicles.

Lane obstacles: Throughout the drive, there were 5–6 different types of obstacles were planted on different driving scenarios. At various points during the drive, a static and moving obstacle appeared in the driver's lane or Oncoming Lane Drift Periodically in the driver's lane. Drivers were allowed approximately 2 s to 3 s to recognize the hazard and initiate a safe response maneuver. Participants were initiated to perform secondary tasks approximately 1 s–3 s before obstacles become visible. Because implant of the secondary task before obstacles provide an opportunity to measure and analyze the subsequent effect of participants driving and lateral control performance.

Response times for lane obstacle events were measured from the moment the obstacle was visible until the driver made a measurable response. After obstacle appearance Back to drive time for these events was recorded until the beginning of the steering wheel deflection.

Braking responses were recorded as soon as the pedal was depressed 5%.

Experiment Setup. The experiment was conducted in the daytime at the 'Human Factor and Ergonomics Lab' at Lamar University. "F-GT Simulator Cockpit" was used for cockpit setup with touch screen device stand, surrounded by 3 XX-inch LCD screen in 135 Degree angle. Setup was designed to provide a realistic driving experience.

3.3 Independent Variables

- Device locations
- Menu types
- Device positions

Device Locations

1. Top Location: In the top location, the touch screen is mounted on the top of the car console and parallel to the steering wheel position. Location: Screen is located approximately 35° diagonally offset from the center of the horizon line, 25 cm to right from the staring wheel center, and 72 cm up from the bottom.
2. Middle location: As shown in the figure touchscreen is mounted at the middle down position of the car console. This position required a driver to head down every time he performs the task. Location: The screen is located approximately 35° diagonally offset from the center of the horizon line, 25 cm to right from the staring wheel center, and 55 cm up from the bottom.

Menu Types

1. Vertical menu: In the vertical menu, the navigation menu is aligned vertically on the interface at the driver's side. The touch screen is either mounted on top or middle car console location.
2. Horizontal menu: In the horizontal menu, the navigation menu is aligned horizontally on the interface at the top of the screen (Fig. 3).

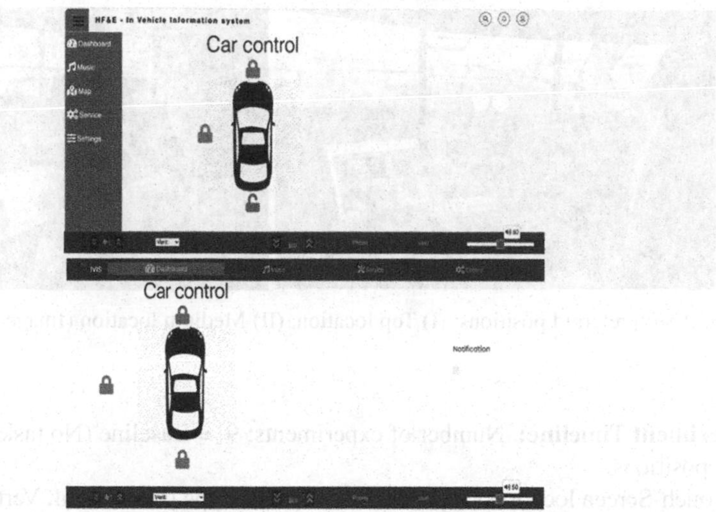

Fig. 3. (I) Vertical menu type (ii) Horizontal menu type (Prototype Screenshot by Saumil (May 2021))

Device Positions. In geometry, the touch-screen position, angular position, attitude, or direction of an object such as a line, plane, or rigid body is part of the description of how it is placed in the space it occupies. It refers to the rotation that is needed to move the object from a reference placement to its current placement.

1. Fixed Position: Touch screen is mounted at the top or middle car console position. The fixed position is used as a reference point for screen location (Fig. 4).

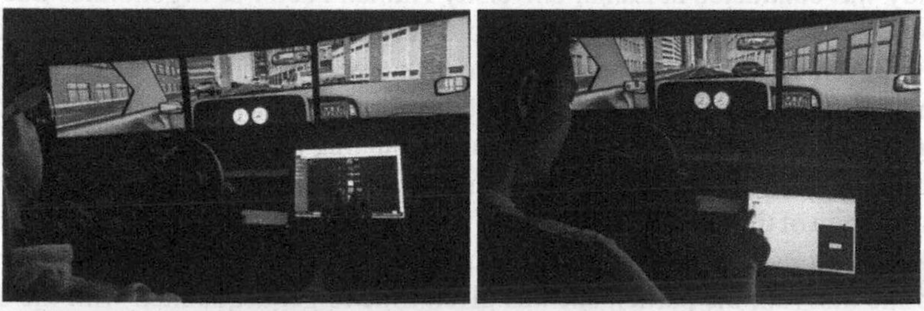

Fig. 4. Fixed positions: (I) Top location, (II) Medium location (Image by Saumil (July 2021))

2. User preferred Positions: Touch screen is mounted at the top or middle car console. Touch-screen position is angularly tilted towards the driver's side as per the driver's preference from a fixed reference position (Fig. 5).

Fig. 5. User preferred positions: (I) Top location, (II) Medium location (Image by Saumil (July 2021))

Experiment Timeline: Number of experiments: 9 = Baseline (No task) + 8 different IVIS positions.

Touch-Screen location (Top, Middle) x Menu type (Horizontal, Vertical) x Origination type (Fixed, user-preferred).

Total experiment time = Number of experiments x single experiment time = 9 x 8 – 12 min + 20 min (break & questionary) = 92 min – 128 min.

Single Experiment Timeline: Total distance in the single experiment: 3miles.

Total time is taken to perform a single experiment: 8–10 min (3miles driving).

Total driving scenarios: 3 (Metro, Industrial, Residential).

Number of tasks conducted in a single experiment: 6 tasks.

Number of tasks conducted in a single scenario: 2 tasks.

3.4 Procedure

The study was conducted at Lamar university Human Factor & Ergonomics Lab in the daytime. The participants were allowed to take a break and have some food if they want. However, all the experiment activities have been recorded in order to measure learnability, efficiency, error rate, memorability, and satisfaction rate. They were also instructed to have a good night sleep just prior to taking part in the study.

Before the start of the experiment, a general description of the experimental procedure and the aim of the study was read aloud to each participant. After that, the participant was asked to fill in a demographic survey questionnaire and a pre-study questionnaire. Prior to the first run, the participant was given time to get acquainted with the driving simulator and the display. There were given a 5 min–10 min trial drive.

In total, 9 (1 baseline (No secondary task) × 2 HDD locations × 2 Navigation menu layout × 2 screen position) trials were conducted in this study.

In every experiment trial, the participants were instructed to perform prescribed IVIS tasks. The prescribed tasks (see Table) were instructed by the facilitator using recorded audio instructions. The task sets were presented in a random order for both HDD locations, positions, and Navigation menu layouts sequences. The instructions for each task were read to the participant by recorded audio by the facilitator; If the participants were failed to follow the secondary task instruction, he or she required to say repeat or replay, and the facilitator will replay particular secondary task instruction.

The secondary tasks were video recorded by the facilitator using iPhone 6s. During all this time, the participant was asked to drive the vehicle normally and obey the traffic rules.

At the end of every trial, the participants were asked to fill in NASA TLX and post-survey questionnaires concerning the user experience with the simulator and the visual interaction display.

4 Results

In this experiment, 3 * 6 analysis of variance (ANOVA) was performed to analyze the effect of touchscreen device 2 different display locations, 2 menu types, and two orientation positions on participants' driving and secondary task performance.

4.1 Driving Task Performance

The results showed a significant main effect of orientation on the participant's total number of collisions ($F_{1,10} = 5.08$, $p = 0.0479$). The post hoc test showed that the mean number of collisions was significantly higher in fixed position (Mean = 1.2045, Std Dev = 1.5638) than in user preferred position (Mean = 0.7272, Std Dev = 0.8453) (Figure no. - 31). However, the results didn't show any significant main effect of location ($F_{1,10} = 0.01$, $p = 0.9321$), or layout ($F_{1,10} = 0.31$, $p = 0.5884$) on number of collisions. No interaction effect between location and layout ($F_{1,10} = 0.83$, $p = 0.3828$), location and orientation ($F_{1,10} = 2.73$, $p = 0.1296$) or layout and orientation ($F_{1,10} = 0.95$, $p = 0.3531$) was found either (Fig. 6).

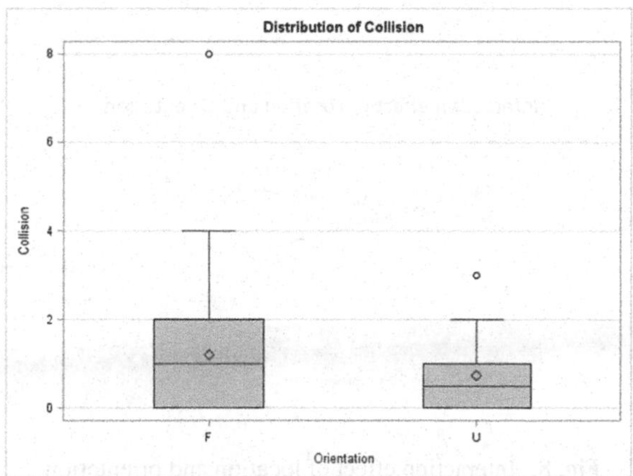

Fig. 6. Distribution of Collision graph

The results showed a significant interaction effect of layout and orientation on the participant's total number of centerline crossings ($F_{1,10} = 18.22$, $p = 0.0016$). When the orientation changes from fixed to user-preferred, the total number of centerline crossings will decrease in horizontal layout but increase in a vertical layout (Figure no. - 35) (Fig. 7).

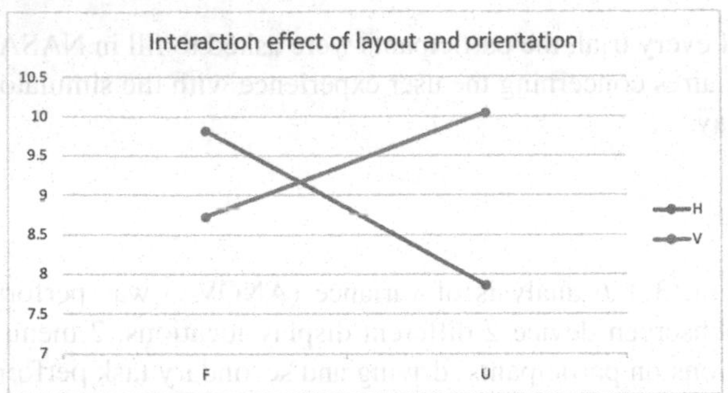

Fig. 7. Interaction effect of layout and orientation

However, the results didn't show any significant main effect of location ($F_{1,10} = 1.86$, $p = 0.2025$), layout ($F_{1,10} = 0.71$, $p = 0.4192$), and orientation ($F_{1,10} = 0.22$, $p = 0.6527$) on number of centerline crossings.

No interaction effect between location and layout ($F_{1,10} = 0.05$, $p = 0.8292$), or location and orientation ($F_{1,10} = 0.56$, $p = 0.4705$) was found either.

The results showed a significant interaction effect of location and orientation on the total number of stops sign tickets ($F_{1,10} = 5.20$, $p = 0.0457$). When the orientation changes from fixed to user-preferred for top location, the total number of stops sign tickets will increase. On the contrary, when orientation changes from fixed to user-preferred for the middle location, the total number of stops sign tickets will decrease (Fig. 8).

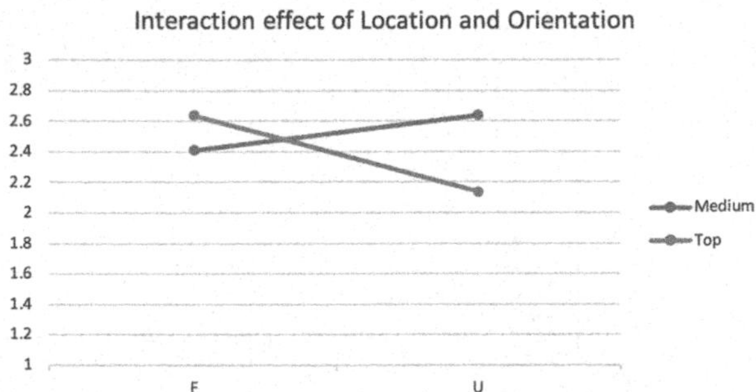

Fig. 8. Interaction effect of location and orientation

However, the results didn't show any significant main effect of location ($F_{1,10} = 0.34$, $p = 0.5737$), layout ($F_{1,10} = 3.20$, $p = 0.1039$), and orientation ($F_{1,10} = 1.00$, $p = 0.3409$) on number of stops sign tickets.

No interaction effect between location and layout (F1,10 = 0. 39, p = 0. 5482), or layout and orientation (F1,10 = 0.48, p = 0. 5059) was found either.

4.2 Secondary Task Performance

Secondary task performance was measured using the total time it took to perform the secondary task, the total number of crashes while performing the secondary task (total number of crashes), and the total number of secondary task errors (Total number of errors).

The results showed a significant main effect of layout type on the participant's total secondary task completion time (F1,10 = 5.39, p = 0.0427). The post hoc test showed that the mean number of secondary task completion time was significantly higher for horizontal menu (Mean = 109.2484, Std Dev = 47.784) compare to vertical menu (Mean = 99.438, Std Dev = 43.345). However, the result didn't show any significant main effect of location (F1,10 = 1.20, p = 0.2985), or orientation (F1,10 = 3.89, p = 0.0769) on secondary task completion time. No interaction effect between location and layout (F1,10 = 0.01, p = 0. 9313), location and orientation (F1,10 = 0.30, p = 0. 5930) or layout and orientation (F1,10 = 2.30, p = 0. 1600) was found either. The results showed a significant main effect of orientation on the total number of crashes (F1,10 = 5.11, p = 0.0473). The post hoc test showed that the mean number of crashes were significantly higher for fixed position (Mean = 0.8409, Std Dev = 1.098) compared to user preferred position (Mean = 0.4090, Std Dev = 0.6927) (Figure no. - 34). However, the results didn't show any significant main effect of location (F1,10 = 0.11, p = 0.7499), or layout (F1,10 = 1.81, p = 0.2077) on number of crashes. No interaction effect between location and layout (F1,10 = 0.03, p = 0. 8628), location and orientation (F1,10 = 0.02, p = 0. 8943) or layout and orientation (F1,10 = 0. 03, p = 0. 8713) was found either. The results showed a significant main effect of layout type on the participant's number of secondary task errors (F1,10 = 6.92, p = 0.0251). The post hoc test showed that the mean number of secondary task errors was significantly higher for horizontal menu type (Mean = 1.250, Std Dev = 1.586) compared to vertical menu type (Mean = 0.4318, Std Dev = 0.899) (Figure no. - 35).

However, the result didn't show any significant main effect of location (F1,10 = 0.02, p = 0.8909), or orientation (F1,10 = 0.19, p = 0.6761) on number of secondary task errors. No interaction effect between location and layout (F1,10 = 0.13, p = 0.7290), location and orientation (F1,10 = 0.05, p = 0. 8351) or layout and orientation (F1,10 = 0.21, p = 0.6595) was found either.

5 Discussion

Several studies were conducted to identify the best location for an In-vehicle infotainment display [30, 47, 48]. According to previous experiment results by Normark [41] and Liu [30] there is no significant difference between HUD and HDD task performance. Including Ablassmeier's eye gaze study indicates no secondary task performance difference between HUD and DCD (driver-centered display).

However, operating the vehicle is characterized as a primary task. When attention is not centered on the road, it would be a distraction and safety concern; the eyes-off-the-road time is still basically coordinated to essential undertaking exercises. For example, side mirror check, blank spot check, reflect looks, or speed/sign checks. And safe vehicle control can be reasonably maintained using peripheral/ambient vision. With an increase in the vehicle's speed, eyesight becomes narrow. In the meantime, it is unsafe to pay attention to the secondary activity, especially when the task is not in your focal visual field, according to the study conducted by Horrey, Wickens, & Alexander. The top location performs better than the middle location because the top location is closest to the driving environment area [24].

This experiment aimed to find the most suitable location for the 'In-vehicle infotainment system' with different menu types and orientation positions. For example, according to previous research, it is expected that HDD location is a significant distraction for driving. However, the top location distance becomes closer to the driving area for two HDD positions and becomes a preferable position for the IVIS screen. But if menu type and orientation position are included with booth location, comparison becomes more difficult. For example, with the horizontal menu on the top screen, accessing the menu becomes difficult. According to participants' reviews, 'accessing the last options on the horizontal menu was more challenging to reach.' Since the horizontal menu is in the top position, the eyesight distance between the previous options or edge of the screen becomes hard to reach and more restrictive; however, if you applied horizontal menu type on the middle location, accessibility between driver and screen increases.

From the post, questionary data majority of participants preferred top position compared to middle positions. According to one of the participants, 'Top position match the eye level with driving area', another participant described the top position as visually comfortable and easy to reach. This study compared two menu positions for IVIS. According to the results, menu types had a significant effect on secondary task completion time, the number of secondary task errors, and a significant interaction effect on the number of centerline crossings with orientation positions. However, the result did not significantly impact the number of crashes, the total number of road edge excursions, and Overspeed. Several studies were conducted to identify the best menu type for In-vehicle infotainment [15, 35, 36].

With excessive data accessibility, route menus become fundamentally crucial for fast and exact access. Because of visual preparing imperatives, the driver doesn't ordinarily see all visible format components immediately look exhaustively [18, 31, 39]. Instead of concentrating just on design components that go under the client's foveal vision. It uncovers that regardless of whether the whole format is addressed before the client, the client can't outwardly handle the entirety of its menu alternatives, catches, symbols, fields, and different components. Subsequently, the graphical design turns into the issue of precise attention deployment [25]. According to a study conducted by Burrell and Sodan [6] on six different menu types, the top tabbed menu appeared to be most significant. Similarly, a study conducted by Murano and Oenga [36] on horizontal and vertical menu design found no significant difference in performance. Another analysis directed by Murano and Lomas on four different menu types (left, right, top, and lower part of the screen), in contrast to past explore by Murano [36], tasks designed to be more demanding and challenging. As a result, the Top and left side menus required fewer clicks and the least number of errors [35].

According to a UX study performed by Nelson Norman group web users spends 80% of their time viewing the left side of the page and 20% viewing the right half [16]. With left positioned vertical menu, accessing the navigation menu becomes more effortless, and with the vertical menu, the easy option to slide for excessive options becomes more vital. Today the majority of applications with a navigation menu preferred vertical position. As Jakob's law of the internet user experience states, 'users spend most of the time on other sites.' In other words, users prefer your site to work the same way as all the other sites they already know [40]. Following the similar navigation approach means following the existing mental model, allowing users to apply their knowledge from previous experiences.

For menu located at distant corners increases the distance between user and button. As Fitts's Law states, the amount of time required for a person to move to a target area is a function of the distance to the target divided by the target's size. Thus, the longer the distance and the smaller the target's size, the longer it takes [17]. Besides, layout analysis for various IVIS menu screens was performed by different analytical techniques as their usability evolve. Analysis methods contain similar grouping functions and arrange these groups' layout according to three factors: 1. frequency, 2. importance, and 3. sequence of use [46]. The most efficient GUI design will be the ideal trade between these three factors regarding the task on hand. For numerous options in a menu, it required an efficient content organization method. One approach for organizing menu content is a hierarchy that includes "depth and breadth."

However, the vertical menu consumes fixed and more space compared to the horizontal counterpart. As a result, sometimes, it can be challenging to look at the detail moved on the right side—however, its where complete application layout, usability comes into focus.

Overall left side navigation menu reduces glance distance for drivers (for right-side drive countries) compare to any other menu position.

This experiment included eight combined positions. Majority of the previous studies considered each location menu type individually. However, there are possible combinations for better performance. For example, in most data analyses, the top location appeared to be the best performing compared to the medium location. However, medium location with horizontal and user preferred positions is more effective than the top location with horizontal menu and fixed position or top location with horizontal menu and fixed position. In orientation position, users can adjust according to their needs. As a result, gaze distance decreases, and the screen appeared to be more accessible.

6 Conclusion

This research study investigated the combined effect of 2 locations: Top and middle, 2 menu types: Horizontal and vertical, and 2 positions: fixed and user preferred position on driving task and secondary task performance, number of errors, and number of collisions using 8 different combinations. However, results revealed no main effect of location on driving performance.

For THU (Top location-horizontal menu-user preferred position) the least number of crashes were recorded and for TVF (Top location-vertical menu-fixed position) and MVF (Middle location-vertical menu-fixed position) positions, the highest number of crashes were recorded. Participants conducted the least number of task errors on the TVU location. Top positions are ideal for screen display because of their location close to the windshield area. However, according to a few participants, a Medium location for screen mounting is preferable over the top. According to participants' comments, the screen's top location blocks the driving view, and screen light reflation creates visual distraction and discomfort. According to participants' reviews, the vertical menu type is preferable over the horizontal. As per one finding, the horizontal menu positions the top location is in line with the driving view area, causing most minor distraction and neck discomfort. However, performance did not show a significant difference.

Based on results, the user preferred(orientation) position is the most preferable and significantly affected secondary task performance. Freedom of screen adjustment provides greater flexibility.

6.1 Research Limitation and Future Work

This section explains some of the limitations of studies. The research was conducted on F-GT Simulator Cockpit, a patented design for the GT racing position. Racing car seats tend to be more grounded than SUVs, which might be why SUV car seat results might differ.

In the future, as vehicles become more personalized and loaded with screens. User-preferred screen position will be in more focus, especially for the driver position.

References

1. Ablassmeier, M., Poitschke, T., Wallhoff, F., Bengler , K., Rigoll, G.: Eye Gaze studies comparing head-up and head-down displays in vehicles. In: IEEE International Conference on Multimedia and Expo, vol. 1, pp. 2250—2252. IEEE, Piscataway (2007)
2. Ariza, M., Zato, J.G., Naranjo, J.E.: HMI design in vehicles based in usability and accessibility concepts. In: 12th International Workshop on Computer Aided Systems Theory, EUROCAST 2009. Archivo Digital UPM, Madrid (2009)
3. Buhmann, A., Hellmueller, L.: Pervasive entertainment, ubiquitous entertainment. centre for the study of communication and culture. Santa Clara: A Quarterly Review of Communication Research (2009)
4. Burnett, G., Crossland, A., Large, D.R., Harvey, C.: The impact of interaction mechanisms with in- vehicle touch screens on task performance. In: Conference: Ergonomics & Human Factors. Stratford-upon-Avon, UK (2019)
5. Burnett, G., Lawson, G., Millen, L., Pickering, C.: Designing touchpad user-interfaces for vehicles: which tasks are most suitable? Behav. Inf. Technol. **30**(3), 403–414 (2011)
6. Burrell, A., Sodan, A.: Web interface navigation design: which style of navigation-link menus do users prefer? In: International Conference on Data Engineering Workshops, Atlanta, GA, USA, pp. 3–7. IEEE Computer Society (2006)
7. Callahan, J., Hopkins, D., Weiser, M., Shneiderman, B.: An empirical comparison of pie vs. linear menus. In: Proceedings of the SIGCHI Conference on Human Factors in Computing Systems, pp. 95–100. Association for Computing Machinery, Washington, D.C., USA (1988)

8. Card, S.: User perceptual mechanisms in the search of computer command menus. In: Proceedings of Human Factors in Computer Systems, pp. 190–196. ACM, New York (1982)
9. Card, S.K., Moran, T.P., Newell, A.: The Psychology of Human-Computer Interaction. Lawrence Erlbaum Associates Publishers, Hillsdale (1983)
10. Chiang, I.: Usability Testing Basics. Techsmith (2015). https://www.techsmith.com/
11. Chisholm, S.L., Caird, J.K., Lockhart, J., Fern, L.: Driving Performance while engaged in MP-3 player interaction: effects of practice and task difficulty on PRT and eye movements. In: 4th International Driving Symposium on Human Factors in Driver Assessment, Training, and Vehicle Design, pp. 238–245. Driving Assessment (2007)
12. Conley, C., Gabbard, J., Smith, M.: ead-Up vs. Head-down displays: examining traditional methods of display assessment while driving. In: Proceedings of the 8th International Conference on Automotive User Interfaces and Interactive Vehicular Applications, pp. 185–192, New York, NY, USA. Automotive'UI 2016 (2016)
13. Eren, A., Burnett, G., Large, D.R.: Can in-vehicle touchscreens be operated with zero visual demand? An exploratory driving simulator study. In: International Conference on Driver Distraction and Inattention. Sydney, New South Wales, Australia (2015)
14. Fang, X., Holsapple, C.W.: An empirical study of web site navigation structures' impacts on web site usability. Decis. Supp. Syst. **43**(2), 476–491 (2007)
15. Faulkner, X., Hayton, C.: When left might not be right. J. Usability Stud. **6**(4), 245–256 (2011)
16. Fessenden, T.: Nelson Norman group. www.nngroup.com. https://www.nngroup.com/articles/horizontal-attention-leans-left/. Accessed 22 Oct 2017
17. Fitts, P.M.: The information capacity of the human motor system in controlling the amplitude of movement. J. Exp. Psychol. **47**(6), 381–391 (1954)
18. Green, P.: The 15-second rule for driver information systems. In: America Conference Proceedings (CD) (standard (J2364)), pp. 1–9 (1999)
19. Hagen, L., Herdman, C., Brown, M.: The Perfomance consts of digital head-up displays. In: International Symposium on Aviation Psychology, pp. 244–246, Dayton, Ohio (2007)
20. Hemenway, K.: Psychological issues in the use of icons in command menus. In: Proceedings of the Conference on Human Factors in Computing Systems, pp. 20–23. ACM, New York (1982)
21. Hodgson, G., Ruth, S.R.: The use of menus in the design of on-line sytems: a retrospective view. ACM SIGCHI Bull. **17**(1), 16–22 (1985)
22. Horrey, W.J., Wickens, C.D., Alexander, A.L.: The effects of head-up display clutter and in-vehicle display separation on concurrent driving performance. In: Proceedings of the Human Factors and Ergonomics Society Annual Meeting, vol. 47, no. 16, pp. 1880–1884 (2003)
23. Horrey, W.J., Wickens, C.D., Consalus, K.P.: Modeling drivers' visual attention allocation while interacting with in-vehicle technologies. J. Exp. Psychol. Appl. **12**(2), 67–78 (2006)
24. Horrey, W., Alexander, A., Wickens, C.D.: Does workload modulate the effects of in-vehicle display location on concurrent driving and side task performance. In: Proceedings of the Driving Simulation Conference, vol. 217, pp. 1–20. Dearborn, Michigan (2003)
25. Jokinen, J.P., Wang, Z., Sarcar, S., Oulasvirta, A., Ren, X.: Adaptive feature guidance: modelling visual search with graphical layouts. Int. J. Hum. Comput. Stud. **136**, 1–22 (2020)
26. Jose, R., Lee, G., Billinghurst, M.: A comparative study of simulated augmented reality displays for vehicle navigation. In: Proceedings of the 28th Australian Conference on Computer-Human Interaction, pp. 40–48 (2016)
27. Large, D.R., Burnett, G., Crundall, E., Lawson, G.: Twist it, touch it, push it, swipe it: evaluating secondary input devices for use with an automotive touchscreen HMI. In: Automotive'UI 2016 Proceedings of the 8th International Conference on Automotive User Interfaces and Interactive Vehicular Applications, pp. 161–168. ACM, Ann Arbor (2016)

28. Lawrence, J., Risser, M., Prinzel: Head-Up Displays and Attention Capture. NASA, Man/System Technology and Life Support. NASA Langley Research Center Hampton, VA, United States. NTRS (2004)
29. Leuthold, S., Schmutz, P., Bargas-Avila, J., Tuch, A.N., Opwis, K.: Vertical versus dynamic menus on the world wide web: eye tracking study measuring the influence of menu design and task complexity on user performance and subjective preference. Comput. Hum. Behav. **27**, 459–472 (2011)
30. Liu, Y.-C., Wen, M.-H.: Comparison of head-up display (HUD) vs. head-down display (HDD): driving performance of commercial vehicle operators in Taiwan. Int. J. Hum.-Comput. Stud. **61**(5), 679–697 (2004)
31. Manufacturers, A.: Statement of principles, criteria and verification procedures on driver interactions with advanced in-vehicle information and communication systems. Draft Version 3.0, Alliance of Automobile Manufactures, Washington, DC, USA (2003)
32. McGookin, D., Brewster, S., Jiang, W.: Investigating touchscreen accessibility for people with visual impairments. In: Proceedings of the 5th Nordic Conference on Human-Computer Interaction: Building Bridges, Lund, Sweden, pp. 298–307. Association for Computing Machinery (2008)
33. Molich, R., Hornbaek, K., Krug, S., Johnson, J., Scott, J.: Usability and Accessibility (7.4) (2008). www.techsmith.com
34. Mourant, R.R., Rockwell, T.H.: Mapping eye-movement patterns to the visual scene in driving: an exploratory study. Hum. Fact. 12(1), 81–87 (1970)
35. Murano, P., Lomas, T.: Menu positioning on web pages. Does it matter? Int. J. Adv. Comput. Sci. Appl. **6**(4) (2015)
36. Murano, P., Oenga, K.: The impact on effectiveness and user satisfaction of menu positioning on web pages. Int. J. Adv. Comput. Sci. Appl. 3–9 (2012)
37. Louveton, N., McCall, R.: Driving while using a smartphone-based mobility application: evaluating the impact of three multi-choice user interfaces on visual- manual distraction. Appl. Ergon. **54**, 196–204 (2016)
38. Ng, A., Brewster, S.: An evaluation of touch and pressure-based scrolling and haptic feedback for in-car touchscreens. Automotive User Interfaces and Interactive Vehicular Applications, pp. 11–20. Oldenburg, Germany. ACM (2017)
39. NHTSA: Visual-Manual NHTSA Driver Distraction Guidelines for Portable and Aftermarket Devices. National Highway Traffic Safety Administration (NHTSA), Washington, DC (2016)
40. Nielsen, J.: End of Web Design. Nielsen Norman Group. https://www.nngroup.com/articles/end-of-web-design. Accessed 22 July 2000
41. Normark , C., Tretten, P., Gärling, A.: Do redundant head-up and head-down display configurations cause distractions? In: Driving Assessment Conference, pp. 398–404. Big Sky, Montana, USA (2009)
42. Previc, F.: The neuropsychology of 3-D space. Psychol. Bull. **124**(2), 123–164 (1998)
43. Purucker, C., Naujoks, F., Prill, A., Neukum, A.: Evaluating distraction of in-vehicle information systems while driving by predicting total eyes-off-road times with keystroke level modeling. Appl. Ergon. (n.d.)
44. Rydstrom, A., Brostrom, R., Bengtsson, P.: A comparison of two contemporary types of in-car multifunctional interfaces. Appl. Ergon. (43), 507–514 (2012)
45. Santos, J., Merat, N., Mouta, S., Brookhuis, K.W.: The interaction between driving and in-vehicle information systems: comparison of results from laboratory, simulator and real-world studies. Transp. Res. Part F: Traffic Psychol. Behav. **8**(2), 135–146 (2005)
46. Stanton, N., Hedge, A., Brookhuis, K., Salas, E., Hendrick, H.: Handbook of Human Factors and Ergonomics Methods. Taylor & Francis (2005)

47. Topliss, B., Harvey, C., Burnett, G.: How long can a driver look? Exploring time thresholds to evaluate head-up display imagery. In: 12th International Conference on Automotive User Interfaces and Interactive Vehicular Applications, pp. 9–18, New York, NY, USA: Association for Computing Machinery (2020)
48. Tretten, P., Gärling, A., Nilsson, R., Larsson, T.: An on-road study of head-up display: preferred location and acceptance levels. In: Proceedings of the Human Factors and Ergonomics Society Annual Meeting, vol. 55, pp. 1914–1918. SAGE Journals (2011)
49. Vilchez, J.: Representativity and univocity of traffic signs and their effect on trajectory movement in a driving-simulation task: regulatory signs. J. Safety Res. **66**, 101–111 (2018)
50. Wang, Y., Mehler, B., Reimer, B., Lammers, V., D'Ambrosio, L.A., Coughlin, J.F.: The validity of driving simulation for assessing differences between in-vehicle informational interfaces: a comparison with field testing. Ergonomics **53**(3), 404–420 (2010)
51. Weinberg, G., Harsham, B., Forlines, C., Medenica, Z.: Contextual push-to-talk: shortening voice dialogs to improve driving performance. In: International Conference on Human-Computer Interaction with Mobile Devices and Services, pp. 113–122 (2010)
52. Wickens, C.: Multiple resources and performance prediction. Theor. Issues Ergon. Sci. **3**(2), 159–177 (2002)

Ergonomics Evaluation of In-Vehicle HMI Based on Meander of Finger Trajectory

Qiuyang Tang[1,2(✉)], Qiang Zhang[2], and Gang Guo[3]

[1] Department of Post-Doctoral Research Station China Automotive Engineering Research Institute Co., Ltd., Chongqing, China
Tangqiuyang@caeri.com.cn
[2] China Automotive Engineering Research Institute Co., Ltd., Chongqing, China
[3] College of Automotive Engineering, Chongqing University, Chongqing, China

Abstract. The driver usually touches the central control screen several times to complete specific vehicle settings. This series of touch points can be connected into a trajectory. The meander of trajectory will affect the efficiency, load and satisfaction of HMI. The objective of this study was to investigate the influence of trajectory meander on HMI from the perspective of ergonomics. To achieve the research objective, three touch paths with different meandering degrees (0°, 90°, 180°) are designed and user experiment was conducted. The independent variables were the finger movement velocity, task load and satisfaction. The results indicated that clicking in the vertical direction will cause a large workload, and the click path in the horizontal direction should not be designed too long. Horizontal turn back clicking in a small range may be a scheme with high efficiency and low load.

Keywords: Finger movement · HMI evaluation · Trajectory meander

1 Introduction

With the rapid development of intelligent cockpit, more and more screens were embedded in the vehicle, which has allowed manufacturers to provide consumers with sophisticated in-vehicle functionalities [1]. Nowadays, the driver can even complete all vehicle settings on the central control screen. However, sophisticated functions make it possible for more interaction steps, which will increase the driver's load and reduce the user experience. Consumer-centered philosophy has been accepted by the vast majority of manufacturers, Kansei engineering has become an important tool for intelligent cockpit design [2]. The evaluation of human-computer interaction interface is of great significance to improve the quality of HMI [3].

In the process of interaction, gestures and screen angle are related to usability [4]. The interface layout will also have an impact on driving safety and availability [5]. Kim investigate the effect of touch-key size on usability of In-Vehicle Information Systems during simulated driving, the results revealed that both the driving safety and the usability increased while the touch-key size increased up to 17.5 mm [6]. Square-shaped keypad were considered to be better availability, and the combination of edge and color has a

H. Krömker (Ed.): HCII 2022, LNCS 13335, pp. 280–288, 2022.
https://doi.org/10.1007/978-3-031-04987-3_19

positive effect on the user satisfaction [7]. Touchscreen gestures' type and direction were also found to have an impact the input performance and subjective feeling [8].

There are many factors affecting HMI availability, and even age is often taken into account [9]. Therefore, the evaluation methods of HMI are also diverse. NASA-TLX was adopted to evaluate the work load during the interactive process[10]. Completion time, success rate Fitt's Law value, error times were usually used to evaluate the usability of HMI [4, 11]. In addition, subjective evaluation is also the main evaluation dimension of HMI [12]. However, the evaluation method based on finger trajectory is rarely studied. A variety of evaluation indexes can be extracted from the finger trajectory formed in the interaction process, such as finger velocity, angular velocity, distance [13]. In addition, meander of finger trajectory is also a valuable evaluation index. Because complex interactions require more touches, a curve could be formed by connecting these touch points. Complex finger trajectories may reduce the efficiency and increase the load of interaction.

The objective of this study is to investigate whether the meander of the trajectory has an effect on the efficiency, load and satisfaction of in-vehicle HMI. The average finger movement velocity was used to evaluate the interaction efficiency; NASA-TLX was used to evaluate the work load; Subjective evaluation was measured by a modified After-Scenario Questionnaire [14]. Two items on a 7-point Likert scale investigated the ease of operation (1point: extremely easy; 7point: extremely difficult) and satisfaction (1point: extremely satisfied; 7point: extremely unsatisfied) with the completion time.

2 Method

2.1 Experimental Design

A tapping task was adopted in this experiment. We designed three interactive interfaces. Each interface contains 5 keys, but the key layout was different from interface to interface which represented different trajectory meander. In the first interface, 5 keys were arranged in a horizontal line (0°, Fig. 1a). In the second interface, the five keys were arranged at a right angle (90°, Fig. 1b). In the third interface, the fourth and fifth keys coincide with the second and first keys (180°, Fig. 1c). The arrangements of the keys represent the different trajectory meanders. The key was a square with a side length of 2.5 cm, the distance between keys is also 2.5 cm.

Participants were required to complete the interaction with these three interfaces. They were asked to tap keys from 1 to 5 in turn, and repeated the task 5 times for each interface. For each participant, the order in which the three interfaces appear was random. At the same time, the movement of finger was recorded. The index of average finger movement speed could be calculated based on the data of finger movement. After the tapping task, participants will report their work load and subjective satisfaction based on NASA-TLX and After-Scenario Questionnaire.

2.2 Participants

Fourteen participants (11 men, 3 women) were recruited for the study, and the experience in using In Vehicle Information System (IVIS) must be more than 3 years. The age ranged

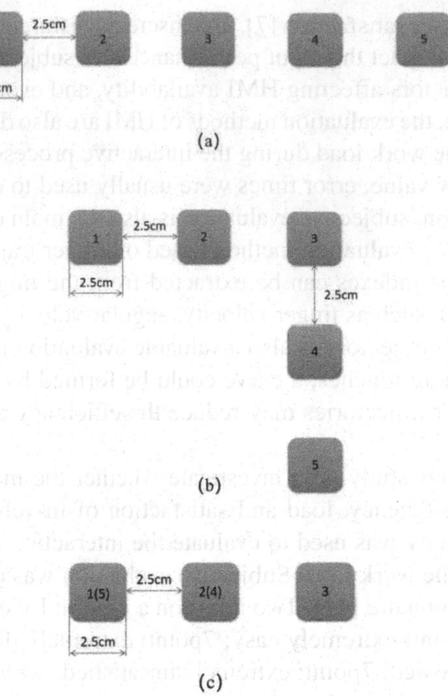

Fig. 1. The keys layout of interactive interfaces. (a) Horizontal arrangement. (b) 90° arrangement. (c) Turn back arrangement.

from 22 to 28 years (M = 24.6, SD = 1.8). The mean driving experience of participants was 5.1 years (SD = 2.7). Participants had no injuries or discomfort to their index finger and upper limbs, and no vision problems. Participants received monetary compensation for taking part in the experiment.

2.3 Apparatus

A fixed-base driving simulator was used to establish cabin environment, and the interactive interface was in the position of central control. Participants were asked to complete interactive tasks in the driver's seat. The experiment scene was shown in Fig. 2.

Ethovision XT 11.5 was adopted to measure the two-dimensional motion of the index finger on the screen. A marker that distinguishes the color from the environment was attached to the index finger nail, and the movement of the marker represented the movement of the index finger. A camera will record the movement of the finger, and the speed of finger movement will be calculated from the video.

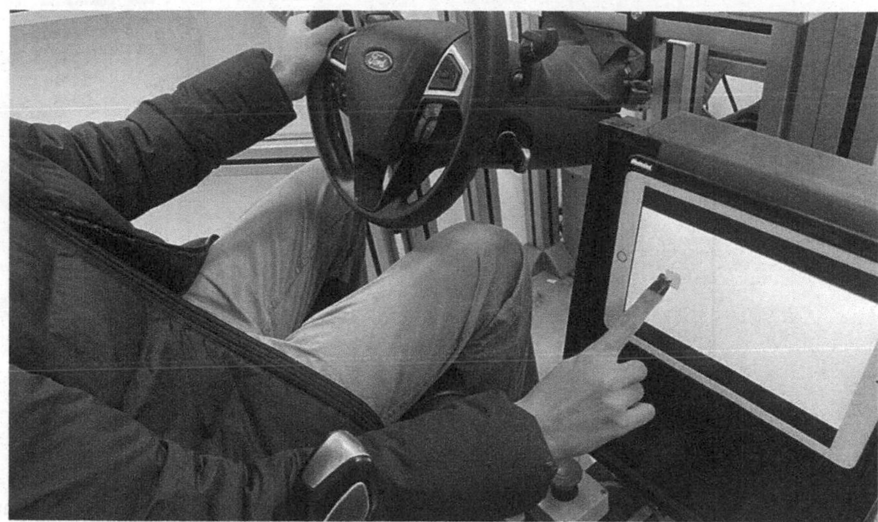

Fig. 2. Experiment sense of the tapping task.

2.4 Data Analysis

In order to test the influence of finger trajectory meander, a one-factor ANOVA was conducted on the index finger movement velocity, NASA-TLX, and subjective satisfaction. Bonferroni correction were performed as post-hoc tests. Statistical significance was noted when p-values were less than 0.05.

3 Result

3.1 Finger Movement Velocity

The result of finger movement velocity was shown in Fig. 3. There was a significant difference between the three interfaces ($F(2, 41) = 4.084$, $p = 0.025$). The post-hoc tests shown that the finger velocity of keys arrangement at 180° was significantly higher than keys arrangement at 0° ($p = 0.027$). However, no significant differences were found between 0°and 90° ($p = 1.000$) and no significant differences were found between 90°and 180° ($p = 0.146$).

3.2 Modified After-Scenario Questionnaire

The result of easy of operation was shown in Fig. 4. The result of one-factor ANOVA shown that there was no significant difference between the three interfaces ($F(2, 41) = 1.439$, $p = 0.249$). Although there was no significant difference, the keys arranged at 0° was still perceived to be more easy to operation. In addition, significant difference was also not founded in completion time between the three interfaces ($F(2, 41) = 0.147$, $p = 0.864$).

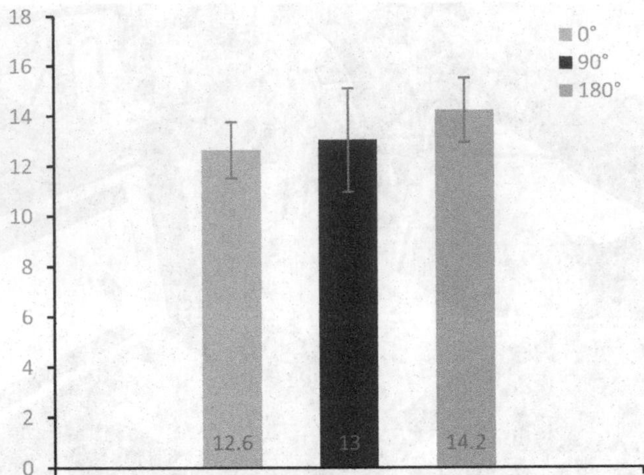

Fig. 3. Finger movement velocity while operating the three interfaces (0°, 90°, and 180°). Bars represent means, error bars represent standard deviations.

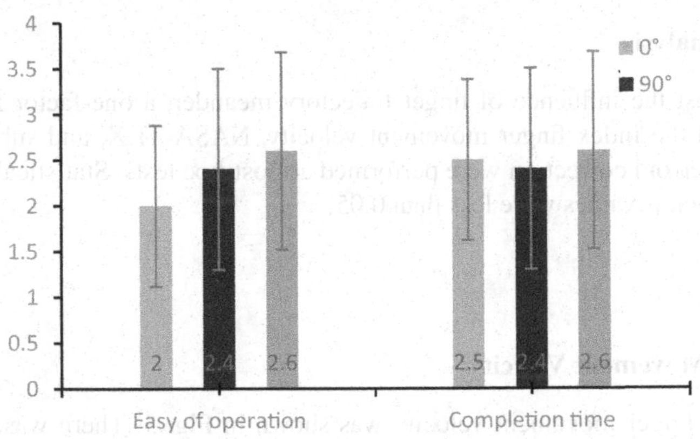

Fig. 4. Subjective evaluation of easy of operation and completion time while operating the three interfaces (0°, 90°, and 180°). Bars represent means, error bars represent standard deviations.

3.3 NASA-TLX

An ergonomics expert completed the pairwise comparisons of NASA-TLX to determine the weighs of the six factors Fig. 5. The results indicated that the physical demand was the most important factor with weight of 5. Complete results of the weighted score was shown in Fig. 6. The results of one-factor ANOVA shown that the NASA-TLX while operating the three interfaces were significantly different ($F(2, 41) = 9.927$, $p < 0.000$). The post-hoc tests shown that the workload of keys arranged at 90° was significantly higher than 0° ($p = 0.47$) and 180° ($p < 0.000$). However, no significant difference was found between 0°and 180° ($p = 0.189$).

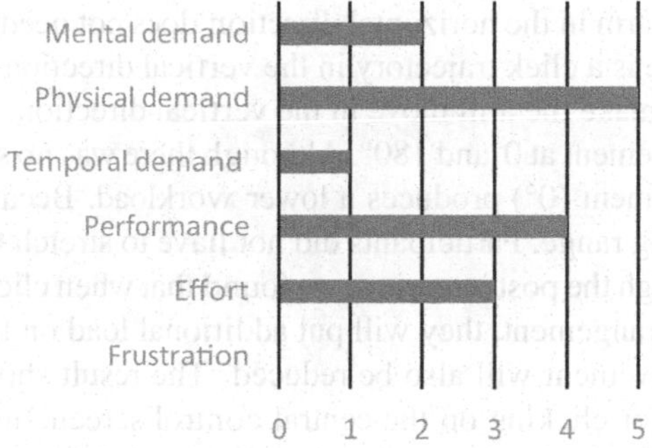

Fig. 5. Factors weights of **NASA-TLX** while operating the three interfaces (0°, 90°, and 180°).

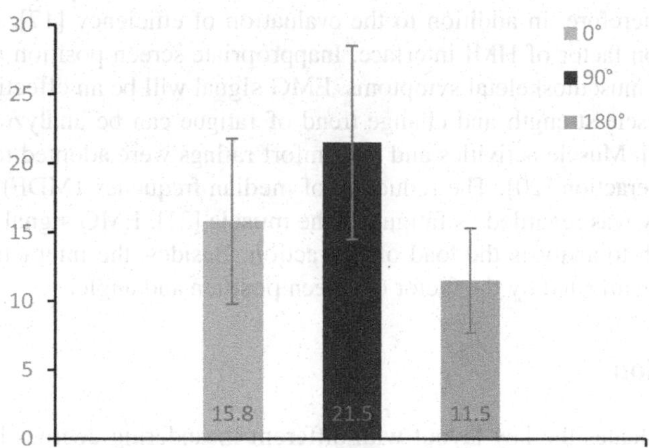

Fig. 6. Weighted score of **NASA-TLX** while operating the three interfaces (0°, 90°, and 180°). Bars represent means, error bars represent standard deviations.

4 Discussion

The efficiency of interaction is an important factor affecting user preferences. Finger movement speed can be used as an evaluation index of interaction efficiency [15]. Because the click task designed in this paper is relatively simple, participants can complete the click tasks of the three interfaces at a relatively fast speed. Therefore, no significant difference was found in objective finger movement speed and subjective completion time. Although the difference is not very significant, it will also affect users' preferences for products of HMI imperceptibly. In terms of ease of operation, although no significant difference was found, participants believed that it was relatively easy to operate while keys were arranged at 0°. However, the results of NASA TLX showed different conclusions. Interfaces with keys arrangement at 180° obtained a lower workload rating, The workload of keys arrangement at 90° was higher than the other two interfaces. As for keys arrangement at 90°, participants' arms will move in a vertical direction. In order to click the button accurately, participants had to overcome the gravity of their arms.

The movement of the arm in the horizontal direction does not need to overcome gravity. Therefore, when there is a click trajectory in the vertical direction, the user will always make extra efforts to make the arm move in the vertical direction.

As for keys arrangement at 0°and 180°. Although there was no significant difference, the turn back arrangement (0°) produces a lower workload. Because this arrangement has a smaller operating range. Participants did not have to stretch their arms to click on distant buttons. Through the post interview, we found that when click the last two buttons of interface with 0°arrangement, they will put additional load on the shoulder muscles. The speed of arm movement will also be reduced. The result shows that there will be a most suitable area for clicking on the central control screen, and the area is located on the side close to the driver. As for the specific size and location of the area, more in-depth research is needed to determine. According to a study on mobile touch screen device, not specially designed HMI may induce musculoskeletal symptoms and visual health [16]. Therefore, in addition to the evaluation of efficiency [17], health is also a key evaluation factor of HMI interface. Inappropriate screen position and excessive use may cause musculoskeletal symptoms. EMG signal will be an effective evaluation index. The muscle strength and change trend of fatigue can be analyzed from EMG signals [18, 19]. Muscle activities and discomfort ratings were adopted to evaluate the usability of interaction [20]. The reduction of median frequency (MDF) of the power spectral density was regarded as fatigue of the muscle [21]. EMG signal is needed for further research to analysis the load of interaction. Besides, the interaction efficiency and load will be affected by the factor of screen position and angle.

5 Conclusion

This paper evaluates the key layout with different meandering degrees by combining subjective and objective data. However, this field has not been deeply studied. Meandering degrees of the keys layout was studied as a variable for the first time in this study. To achieve the research purpose, a tapping task experiment in cockpit was designed. The results show that the three layouts have no significant difference in interaction efficiency. Clicking vertically causes a higher workload. At the same time, the length of horizontal click should not be too long. Clicking keys far away will cause greater load on the shoulder. The results of this paper can be used as a reference for automotive HMI design. The result of the study also helps to improve the user experience of HMI. We expect that the results of the study would be helpful to improve operational efficiency of In-vehicle HMI. Furthermore, this method can be used to investigate keys layout with various meander of finger trajectory and establish a database of comfortable and efficient click areas, like the idea of establishing driving emotion database and regulation method [22, 23]. In summary, in-vehicle HMI designers can make targeted optimization according to the results.

6 Limitation

Although this study has been carefully designed and controlled in a laboratory-based setting, there are some limitations. First, the position of the screen is not adjusted for users with different heights. The position of the screen is an important factor affecting the interaction. The influence of screen position on interaction efficiency and load should be considered in subsequent research. Second, EMG signal is not used to analyze the interactive load in this paper. EMG signal may get more accurate results than NASA TLX.

References

1. Zaidi, F., Bastien, C., Chalandon, X., Moiselet, L., Thianche, E.: The research-practice gap: an explanatory factor for automotive HMI customers' complaints?. In: Bagnara, S., Tartaglia, R., Albolino, S., Alexander, T., Fujita, Y. (eds) IEA 2018. Advances in Intelligent Systems and Computing, vol. 824, pp. 744–755. Springer, Cham (2019). https://doi.org/10.1007/978-3-319-96071-5_78
2. Vieira, J., et al.: Kansei engineering as a tool for the design of in-vehicle rubber keypads. Appl. Ergon. **61**, 1–11 (2017)
3. Gonzalez-Calleros, J., et al.: Automated UI evaluation based on a cognitive architecture and UsiXML. Sci. Comput. Program. **86**, 43–57 (2014)
4. Kim, H., Song, H.: Evaluation of the safety and usability of touch gestures in operating in-vehicle information systems with visual occlusion. Appl. Ergon. **45**(3), 789–798 (2014)
5. Li, R., et al.: Effects of interface layout on the usability of In-Vehicle Information Systems and driving safety. Displays **49**, 124–132 (2017)
6. Kim, H., et al.: The effect of touch-key size on the usability of In-Vehicle Information Systems and driving safety during simulated driving. Appl. Ergon. **45**(3), 379–388 (2014)
7. Jung, S., et al.: Effect of touch button interface on in-vehicle information systems usability. Int. J. Hum.-Comput. Inter. **37**(15), 1404–1422 (2021)
8. Jeong, H., Liu, Y.: Effects of touchscreen gesture's type and direction on finger-touch input performance and subjective ratings. Ergonomics **60**(11), 1528–1539 (2017)
9. Chen, R., Huang, J., Zhou. J.: Skeuomorphic or flat icons for an efficient visual search by younger and older adults?. Appl. Ergon. **85**, 103073 (2020)
10. Akyeampong, J., et al.: Evaluation of hydraulic excavator Human-Machine Interface concepts using NASA TLX. Int. J. Ind. Ergon. **44**(3), 374–382 (2014)
11. Tsai, T., Tseng, K.C., Chang, Y.: Testing the usability of smartphone surface gestures on different sizes of smartphones by different age groups of users. Comput. Hum. Behav. **75**, 103–116 (2017)
12. Lee, Y., et al.: Understanding the relationship between user's subjective feeling and the degree of side curvature in smartphone. Appl. Sci. **10**(9), 3320 (2017)
13. Xu, N., et al.: Usability study of two in-vehicle information systems using finger tracking and facial expression recognition technology. Int. J. Hum.-Comput. Interact. **34**(11), 1032–1044 (2018)
14. Lewis, J.R.: IBM computer usability satisfaction questionnaires: psychometric evaluation and instructions for use. Int. J. Hum.-Comput. Interact. **7**(1), 57–78 (1995)
15. Tang, Q., Guo, G. and Zhang, Q.: Empirical research on a driver's preference for onboard navigation or portable navigation. In: 2021 5th CAA International Conference on Vehicular Control and Intelligence (2021)
16. Toh, S.H., et al.: A prospective longitudinal study of mobile touch screen device use and musculoskeletal symptoms and visual health in adolescents. Appl. Ergon. **85**, 103028 (2020)
17. Xue, H., et al.: Ergonomics Evaluation of Cabin Human–Machine Interface Based on SHEL Model, pp. 623–629. Springer Singapore (2019)

18. Disselhorst-Klug, C., Schmitz-Rode, T., Rau, G: Surface electromyography and muscle force: limits in sEMG-force relationship and new approaches for applications. Clin. Biomech. **24**(3), 225–235 (2009)
19. González-Izal, M., Malanda, A., Gorostiaga, E., Izquierdo, M.: Electromyographic models to assess muscle fatigue. J. Electromyogr. Kinesiol. **22**(4), 501–512 (2012)
20. Chang, J., Choi, B., Tjolleng, A., Jung, K.: Effects of button position on a soft keyboard: muscle activity, touch time, and discomfort in two-thumb text entry. Appl. Ergon. **60**, 282–292 (2017)
21. Barszap, A.G., Skavhaug, I., Joshi, S.S.: Effects of muscle fatigue on the usability of a myoelectric human-computer interface. Hum. Mov. Sci. **49**, 225–238 (2016)
22. Li, W., et al.: A spontaneous driver emotion facial expression (DEFE) dataset for intelligent vehicles: emotions triggered by video-audio clips in driving scenarios. IEEE Trans. Affect. Comput. **1** (2021)
23. Li, W., et al.: Visual-attribute-based emotion regulation of angry driving behaviours. IEEE Intell. Transp. Syst. Mag. **1** (2021)

Face2Statistics: User-Friendly, Low-Cost and Effective Alternative to In-vehicle Sensors/Monitors for Drivers

Zeyu Xiong, Jiahao Wang, Wangkai Jin, Junyu Liu, Yicun Duan, Zilin Song, and Xiangjun Peng(✉)

User-Centric Computing Group, University of Nottingham, Ningbo, China
scyzx2@nottingham.edu.cn, shiangjunpeng@gmail.com
https://unnc-ucc.github.io

Abstract. We present **Face2Statistics**, a comprehensive roadmap to deliver user-friendly, low-cost and effective alternatives for extracting drivers' statistics. **Face2Statistics** is motivated by the growing importance of multi-modal statistics for Human-Vehicle Interaction, but existing approaches are user-unfriendly, impractical and cost-ineffective. To this end, we leverage **Face2Statistics** to build a series of Deep-Neural-Network-driven predictors of multi-modal statistics, by taking facial expressions as input only. We address two outstanding issues of the current design, and then (1) leverage HSV color space; and (2) Conditional Random Field to improve the robustness of **Face2Statistics** in terms of prediction accuracy and degree of customization. Our evaluations show that, **Face2Statistics** can be effective alternatives to sensors/monitors for Heart Rate, Skin Conductivity and Vehicle Speed. We also perform the breakdown analysis to justify the effectiveness of our optimizations. Both source codes and trained models of **Face2Statistics** are online at https://github.com/unnc-ucc/Face2Statistics.

Keywords: Human-Vehicle interaction · Vision computing · Image processing · Deep neural networks

1 Introduction

Modern Human-Vehicle Interaction systems leverage comprehensive statistics of drivers, to perform complex decision-making procedures for personalized Human-Vehicle Interactions. Particularly, the importance of in-vehicle drivers' statistics grows significantly, with the emerging trends of Autonomous Vehicles. To this end, developing mechanisms to provide user-friendly, low-cost and effective methods to extract in-vehicle drivers' statistics, is essential. However, existing methods, for extracting in-vehicle statistics of drivers, directly integrate either respective sensors (e.g. Heart Rate) or vehicle monitors (e.g. Vehicle Speed), which imposes two major challenges in practice.

H. Krömker (Ed.): HCII 2022, LNCS 13335, pp. 289–308, 2022.
https://doi.org/10.1007/978-3-031-04987-3_20

First, driver experiences would be endangered, if sensors/monitors are directly equipped or deployed for in-vehicle drivers. Existing mechanisms extract drivers' statistics by equipping or deploying sensors/monitors within vehicles. Though such methods are straightforward and easy-to-deploy, there are huge risks to degrade drivers' feelings regard to comforts, satisfaction and etc. For instance, to monitor drivers' Heart Rate, a Heart Rate sensor needs to be equipped with the driver along the way. However, such arrangements require physical-contact deployments, and this would indeed cause side effects on driving experiences. Furthermore, such side effects can grow exponentially with the number of sensors/monitors, if there are multiple types of statistics to be monitored.

Second, the costs and overheads of directly integrating sensors or monitors for in-vehicle drivers are unexpectedly high. Existing mechanisms require additional data transfer between sensors/monitors and in-vehicle computers, so that Human-Vehicle Interaction systems can take advantage of these statistics. Hence, there are two major issues for the adaptions. One is that extra data transfer, obtained from equipped sensors/monitors, can lead to huge performance degradation in terms of latency, which further affects Quality-of-Services; The other is that re-routing statistics of vehicle statuses, retrieved from in-vehicle monitors, can cause extra costs since internal modifications of vehicle structures might be required.

Therefore, it's apparent that user-friendly, low-cost and effective alternatives, for extracting drivers' statistics, are needed. **Our goal** is to present a comprehensive road-map on how to deliver a series of such alternatives, so that they can **obtain drivers' statistics via an unobtrusive manner**. We make the **key observation** that recent advances of Computer Vision techniques (e.g. by applying Deep Neural Networks for image classifications) can potentially serve as suitable alternatives in such purposes. Such techniques can leverage a large volume of historical data to train models, and then predict future statistics via these models by using only a subset of types from the historical data.

Based on such characteristics, we can choose a unified and unobtrusive source as the input streams, and leverage it to derive different types of drivers' statistics. To this end, we introduce **Face2Statistics**, a series of user-friendly, low-cost and effective alternatives for extracting drivers' statistics. The **key idea** of **Face2Statistics** is leveraging each frame of facial expressions, to predict instant status of in-vehicle drivers. Such prediction is powered by sophisticated, customized and pre-trained Deep Neural Network models, and we achieve this by exploring and examining various types of state-of-the-art Deep Neural Network models. We also design a comprehensive execution pipeline of **Face2Statistics**, so that **Face2Statistics** can be easily visualized/exported/integrated with other sub-systems for Human-Vehicle Interactions, as the sources of drivers' statistics.

Moreover, we address two major inefficiencies of **Face2Statistics** in practice, and provide viable solutions to them: (1) one problem of **Face2Statistics** is the effects of illuminance, which incurs variations of different models in terms of effectiveness; and (2) the other problem of **Face2Statistics** is that different drivers might have distinctive facial features during driving procedures, which substantially degrades the robustness of **Face2Statistics** if we apply the same model for every driver. To strengthen the robustness of **Face2Statistics**, we introduce two novel optimizations of **Face2Statistics**: (1) to mitigate the effects of illuminance, we leverage HSV encoding instead of commonly-used RGB encoding, for each frame of video captures; and (2) to take advantage of differences across individual drivers, we provide customization supports through *Conditional Random Field*, so that different models can have personalized customization, according to drivers' variations.

We quantitatively examine the performance and robustness of **Face2Statistics** over a state-of-the-art open-sourced data set for Human-Vehicle Interaction. The experimental results demonstrate significant benefits of our approach. Averaged across all drivers, the best of **Face2Statistics** achieves up to 58.44%, 72.68% and 70.25% accuracy in terms of Heart Rate, Skin Conductivity and Vehicle Speed predictions. Compared with two other models, the best of **Face2Statistics** improve the accuracy by 4.52%, 2.68% and 1.41% in terms of Heart Rate, Skin Conductivity and Speed predictions. We also perform the breakdown analysis to illustrate how our proposed optimizations improve the robustness of **Face2Statistics**. We show that both techniques can significantly improve the robustness of **Face2Statistics**. We believe both our proposal and related optimizations are essential in practice.

We make the following three contributions in this paper:

- We propose **Face2Statistics**, a comprehensive road-map to deliver user-friendly, low-cost and effective alternatives for extracting drivers' statistics. We also provide a comprehensive execution pipeline of **Face2Statistics**, for ease of visualization/exportation/integration with other sub-systems for Human-Vehicle Interactions, as the sources of drivers' statistics.
- We address two major issues of **Face2Statistics** for robustness, and introduce two techniques to mitigate them accordingly. We first leverage HSV encoding, rather than RGB, for better robustness against the effects of illuminance; and then we add *Conditional Random Field* to achieve customization supports for different individuals, to improve the robustness as well.
- We quantitatively examine the performance and robustness of **Face2Statistics**, and the results demonstrate significant benefits of our approach. **Face2Statistics** can achieve highly accurate predictions, in terms of Skin Conductivity, Heart Rate and Vehicle Speed. We also demonstrate that our optimizations can greatly enhance the robustness of **Face2Statistics**.

The rest of this paper is organized as follow. Section 2 introduces the background of **Face2Statistics**. Section 3 gives an overview of **Face2Statistics** and elaborates each component one-by-one. Section 4 elaborates key optimizations of **Face2Statistics** to enhance the robustness. Section 5 presents the experimental methodology to evaluate **Face2Statistics**. Section 6 provides the results and detailed analysis of our experiments. Section 7 gives the discussion in terms of experimental results, model limitation and driver's privacy issues. Section 8 introduces the related works and summary of **Face2Statistics**.

2 Background

In-vehicle drivers' statistics play a significant role in the designs and implementations of modern Human-Vehicle Interaction Systems. In the past two decades, there has been a large volume of research efforts being paid to leverage drivers' statistics, to obtain a better understanding of driving behaviors for personalized Human-Vehicle Interactions [9]. These statistics can be used for various purposes and we only list several examples hereby. In-vehicle drivers' statistics can be used for but not limited to the following: (1) Indicating the safety of road trips [37], (2) Classifying the driving styles and behaviors [18,36], (3) Classifying the health conditions for old drivers [27], (4) Validating the accuracy of self-reporting properties [30], (5) Detecting driving distraction [28], (6) Detecting road surface and hazard [19]. Therefore, to enhance the driving experience, In-vehicle drivers' statistics are considered essential building blocks in various example usages, and we envision they are becoming more important in the near future of Autonomous Vehicles.

The collection of in-vehicle data is therefore particularly important. For different types of in-vehicle data, researchers have used a variety of measurement methods, which can be classified into two main types: (1) Integrating/deploying specific devices, sensors, and monitors for certain statistics, (2) Re-routing statistics based on a vehicle's internal makeup. For the first type, an example application is heart rate/skin conductivity data collection by applying biosensors. However, wearing biosensors can often be distracting to drivers while driving, which is user-unfriendly and impractical. For the second type, rerouting data (e.g. vehicle speed) from dashboard to human-vehicle interaction system (in digital format) is not cost-effective. We introduce the related works in detail in Sect. 8. In summary, existing methods for the extraction of In-vehicle Drivers' Statistics are user-unfriendly, impractical and cost-ineffective. Therefore, providing user-friendly, low-cost and effective alternatives to sensors/monitors becomes essential for Human-Vehicle Interaction systems in practice. Our goal is to present a comprehensive road-map on how to deliver a series of such alternatives, so that they can derive drivers' statistics via an unobtrusive manner.

3 Face2Statistics: An Overview

In this section, we give an overview of the designs and implementations of **Face2Statistics**. We elaborate details regarding key components of **Face2Statistics**, including: (1) Image Processing (Sect. 3.1); (2) Neural Network Models (Sect. 3.2); and (3) Visualization/Integration Supports (Sect. 3.3). Particularly, we illustrate multiple attempts to obtain the best prediction models, by exploiting different state-of-the-art Deep Neural Network models (Sect. 3.2) (Fig. 1).

3.1 Component 1: Facial Expressions from Video Streams

The first component of **Face2Statistics** is a pre-processing component. The reason why we need to pre-process is that: raw video streams, obtained from an

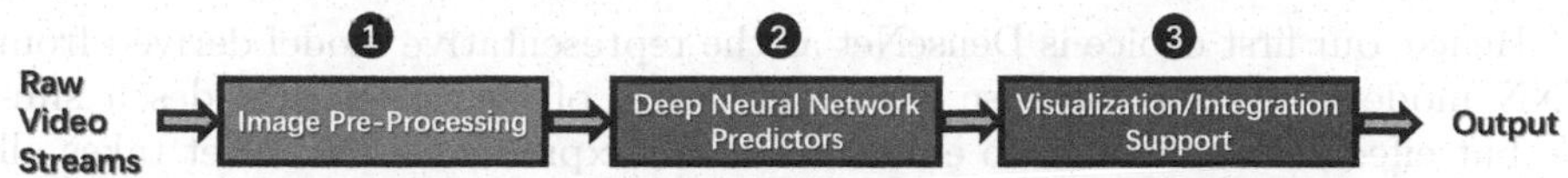

Fig. 1. Execution pipeline and components of **Face2Statistics**.

unobtrusive camera, contain many noisy pixels in addition to facial expressions. Therefore, the pre-processing component needs to support two functionalities. First, the pre-processing component needs to retrieve only the facial expressions rather than all pixels within a frame; and second, the pre-processing component may need other techniques to enhance the performance of **Face2Statistics**, such as adjusting encoding schemes of images, varying the size of images, etc.

We implement this component leveraging OpenCV library [5], which is a state-of-the-art image processing library. In total, we achieve three functionalities in our current prototypes: (1) we normalize image color channels to 32×32 pixels of matrix, as recommended by mainstream Computer Vision datasets (e.g. CIFAR-10 [22]) and the-state-of-the-art models (e.g. [21]); (2) we implement a facial detector to crop facial expressions, so that we can only retrieve relevant pixels; and (3) we implement a transformation tool of color matrices, so that we can represent frames in different encoding schemes (e.g. RGB, HSV and etc.)[1].

3.2 Component 2: Deep Neural Network-Driven Predictors

The core component of **Face2Statistics** is the Deep Neural Network-driven predictors. The models are the key to achieve accurate predictions of relevant statistics, via only facial expressions. Therefore, it's critical to determine which models fit the best in our scenarios. Hereby, we perform an in-depth comparison across different kinds of models shown in this section, where our comparisons are backed up by our quantitative evaluations (i.e. Sect. 6.1).

3.2.1 First Attempt: Convolution Neural Networks (CNNs)

Convolution Neural Networks (CNNs) achieve great performance in image classification, and representative examples include ResNet [11], DenseNet [14], SENet [13], etc. Though these models are well-suited for image classifications, there is still a gap to determine which one is better in our scenarios. By analyzing relevant data streams, we observe that In-Vehicle Drivers' Statistics (i.e. sequential data) exhibit a high volume of noises and they are potentially misguidance during the inference procedure. Therefore, we believe a model, which can enhance the weights of the particular features, is the best choice among all CNN models.

[1] We use this functionality to investigate how we can enhance the robustness of **Face2Statistics**, as described in Sect. 4.

Hence, our first choice is DenseNet as the representative model derived from CNN models[2]. This is because the architecture of DenseNet provides a simple but effective mechanism to enhance feature expressions: DenseNet takes all inputs from the early layers, merges them and feeds them into the next layer as inputs. More specifically, if the model has N layers in total, a conventional CNN architecture has only N connections, while DenseNet has $\frac{N(N+1)}{2}$ connections. This optimization strengthens the effects of feature extraction from previous layers, mitigates the gradient-vanishing issues, promotes feature reuse, emboldens feature reproduction and significantly reduces the number of parameters.

3.2.2 Second Attempt: Long Short-Term Memory (LSTM) Recurrent Neural Network (RNN)

Our second choice is Long-Short-Term Memory Recurrent Neural Network model (LSTM-RNN). This is motivated by the fact that, In-vehicle drivers' statistics are sequential in a continuous timeline. Therefore, Recurrent Neural Networks (RNN) might be a good fit since the design of RNN emphasizes the effects of sequential data streams. To better speculate long-term impacts, Long Short-Term Memory RNN (LSTM-RNN) architecture is proposed to address this challenge [12]. LSTM-RNN mitigates the issues of long-term memory dependency, and the key idea of LSTM-RNN is to selectively determine whether a state shall be kept or forgotten, instead of only considering the most recent states (i.e. as previous RNN models). This provides a more appropriate usage to predict sequential data streams.

3.2.3 Third Attempt: Bidirectional Long-Short-Term Memory (BiLSTM) Recurrent Neural Network (RNN)

Our third choice is Bidirectional Long-Short-Term Memory Recurrent Neural Network (BiLSTM-RNN). This is motivated by the fact that, LSTM-RNN is unable to encode information flow from front to back, in the sequence of data streams. To optimize LSTM-RNN, Bidirectional LSTM-RNN (BiLSTM-RNN) is proposed to address such challenges [10]. The key idea of BiLSTM-RNN is to enable both forward and backward across the flow of all layers, so that the learning procedure can be enhanced significantly.

3.3 Component 3: Visualization/Exportation of Predicted Results

The final component of **Face2Statistics** is to provide efficient visualization/exportation of predicted results. Since all previous components of **Face2Statistics** are within the in-vehicle systems, there is no need for extra data transfer or re-rountine. Therefore, we consider three parts of this component: (1) we provide a basic data-processing component for reorganizing/streaming results into flat files, to serve as system logs/records; (2) we provide a high-level API so

[2] A prior work showcases that DenseNet is effective in this scenario [15], and an exhaustive study [1] demonstrates the benefits via comparisons between this design and others.

that other systems can directly deploy **Face2Statistics** via a simple function call; and (3) we also build a visualization example using the API, to justify the feasibility of visualizations.

4 Customizing Face2Statistics for Different Individuals

In this section, we introduce two optimization methods for **Face2Statistics** to enhance its robustness in practice. We first elaborate the problem of illumination effects and our solution to this issue (Sect. 4.1), and then we identify the issues of individual variations and introduce a novel method to customize **Face2Statistics** for different individuals (Sect. 4.2). Figure 2 shows the pipeline of the detailed optimization.

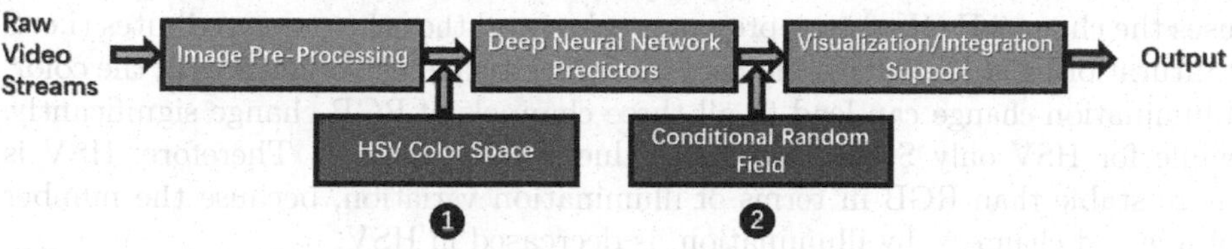

Fig. 2. Pipeline: detailed optimization.

4.1 Optimization 1: Mitigating the Effects of Illumination

During our empirical studies, we observe that the effects of illumination can significantly impact the performance of **Face2Statistics**. This is because the environmental factors of driving procedures can have significant variations in different scenarios, and the illumination is an outstanding example. In this section, we elaborate this issue via a concrete example (Sect. 4.1.1), and provide a viable solution to it (Sect. 4.1.2). This optimization is backed up by our quantitative evaluations (i.e. Sect. 6.2).

4.1.1 Issue: The Curse of Illumination

Illumination has significant impacts on the quality of facial expressions, as one of the most important environmental factors during the driving procedure. Considering a video stream (i.e. which consists of a sequence of frames/images), the evaluation of facial expression can be highly unstable. This is realistic since there are multiple driving scenarios causing illumination impacts (e.g. weather, daylight, tunnels and etc.). Therefore, the cause of illumination can be highly diverse and such a complicated situation is very hard to be resolved. Therefore, it is critical to provide a robust version of **Face2Statistics** to mitigate the side effects of illumination. To this end, we make the key observation that the impacts of illumination directly reflect on the values from the Color Matrix (i.e. the digital representation of each frame/image). Therefore, we conjecture that it might be possible to mitigate the issues of illumination by using a more stable and robust encoding scheme of frames/images.

4.1.2 Key Idea: Use HSV Color Space, Instead of RGB

The conventional representation of frames/images is to leverage "Red, Green and Blue" (RGB) channels, to visualize the images in a digital manner. Though this approach provides chromatic visualizations of frames/images, the impacts of illumination are also significant in this case. This is because that the illumination can significantly vary the values of each channel in RGB, and substantially lead to the degradation of the robustness in terms of **Face2Statistics** since the values are unstable.

Therefore, we propose to leverage "Hue, Saturation, Value" (HSV), instead of RGB, as the color space for **Face2Statistics**. The details of HSV are as follow. HSV color space is represented as a circular cylinder, where a color is defined in cylinder's coordinates [3]. Unlike RGB color space (i.e. using all three color channels to represent colors for each pixel in an image), HSV color space only uses the channel H (Hue) to represent a color, and the other two attributes (i.e. S (Saturation) and V (Value)) indicate the intensity and the brightness of the color. Illumination change can lead to all three channels of RGB change significantly, while for HSV only Saturation and Value will be affected. Therefore, HSV is more stable than RGB in terms of illumination variation, because the number of affected channels, by illumination, is decreased in HSV.

4.1.3 A Comparative Example Between RGB and HSV

We use a comparative example, by visualizing the scenarios using both RGB and HSV, to give a more straightforward comparison between two approaches. We consider a scenario as follow. A driver is driving to enter a tunnel, where we choose two timespots at "before entering the tunnel" and "after entering the tunnel". In the pair of these timespots, we visualize the captured frames/images using RGB and HSV respectively, and then compare these two pairs to justify the impacts of illumination. Figure 3 presents the visualized frames/images for this example. It's evident that, RGB encoding can be significantly impacted by the illumination since the light is lowered, but HSV has a more robust visualization in this case.

Fig. 3. A comparative example between RGB (left) and HSV (right): the visualized frames/images "before entering the tunnel" and "after entering the tunnel".

Therefore, in this case, HSV color space reduces the variance of illumination among different pixels. The reason behind it can be elaborated into two aspects.

1. If illumination of one color changes, for RGB color space pixel value in all three channels may change in a considerable range, while for HSV color space only saturation and value changes, fluctuation on hue channel has been minimized.
2. HSV color space can better represent the difference between two colors, while color difference in RGB martix may not distinctive.

4.2 Optimization2: Customizing Face2Statistics for Different Individuals

4.2.1 Issue: One Face2Statistics for Everyone is Impractical

The core component of **Face2Statistics** is the Neural Network model, and it's clear that a single model can not achieve the best performance for all individuals. This is because the facial expressions of different individuals vary significantly due to their distinctive inborn facial features. To this end, we make the key observation that personalized parameters are deployed successfully in other use cases, such as estimation of self-reported intensity of pains [26], the prediction of driving states with joint time series [41], the prediction of driving behaviors in lane changes [6] and etc. Therefore, we envision that it might also be important to provide customization/personalization supports for **Face2Statistics** as well.

4.2.2 Key Idea 1: Customization via Conditional Random Field

Conditional Random Field (CRF) is a conditional probability distribution model, by assuming the output distribution constituting a Markov random field [43]. More specifically, under the condition of the specific parameter (i.e. quantified by corresponding metrics), the output would be constrained based on the probabilistic distribution. Leveraging Hammersley Clifford theorem [38], the joint probability distribution, represented by linear chain CRF, can be expressed as the function of adjacent nodes. Therefore, CRF provides the constraints to ensure that the final prediction results are valid. These constraints can be automatically learned by the CRF when training the models.

Since existing Neural Network models don't have relevant constraints, based on different individuals while performing the inference. Therefore, we propose to leverage CRF for customizing different models. The key insight here is that, if we can measure the differences of the individuals quantitatively, we can feed these quantified values into CRF. Then the models can be adjusted during the training procedure, and they are customized according to these quantifications. In our case, we consider a standard pairwise CRF model, as shown in Eq. 1[3].

[3] In Eq. 1, A_μ is the association (observation matching) potential for modeling dependencies between the class label m_μ and the set of all observations μ. x_μ is the real-valued SVM response on the pixel (or node) μ. N_μ is the neighborhoods of pixels μ (a subset of the full spatial coordinate system S from above). $I_{\mu\nu}$ is the interaction (local-consistency) potential for modeling dependencies between the levels of neighboring elements. Z is the partition function: a normalization coefficient (sums over possible labels).

$$p(m|x) = \frac{1}{Z}\exp\left(\sum_{\mu\in S} A_u(m_\mu, x_\mu) + \sum_{\mu\in S}\sum_{\nu\in N_\mu} I_{\mu\nu}(m_\mu, m_\nu, x_\mu)\right), \quad (1)$$

4.2.3 Example: Models W/out CRF or W/CRF

Figure 4 provides a comparative example between model structures with/without CRF supports. In Fig. 4, W_1, . . ., W_n represent the input values, which can be regarded as different attributes respectively. Figure 4-(A) demonstrates the workflow of existing model prediction (i.e. models without CRF supports). There are three steps. ❶ all input values $W_{1..n}$ are passed into all models; ❷ the models perform the inference to generate a matrix of attributes; and ❸ the generated matrix of attributes are considered as results, and they might be inappropriate since the aggregations from all models may produce an unreasonable sequence.

On the contrary, to validate the output sequence, CRF provides the constraints to adjust the results. Figure 4-(B) demonstrates the workflow of CRF-integrated model prediction (i.e. models with CRF supports). There are four steps. ❶ all input values $W_{1..n}$ are passed into all models; ❷ the models perform the inference to generate a matrixes of attributes; ❸ the generated matrix of attributes are adjusted via CRF, and such adjustments rely on an assigned parameter (i.e. we denoted it as the personalized parameter); and ❹ the adjusted matrix of attributes are considered as results. Therefore, based on the personalized parameter, we can adjust the output tags to ensure the order of the tag results more reasonable, which achieves the customization/personalization of **Face2Statistics**.

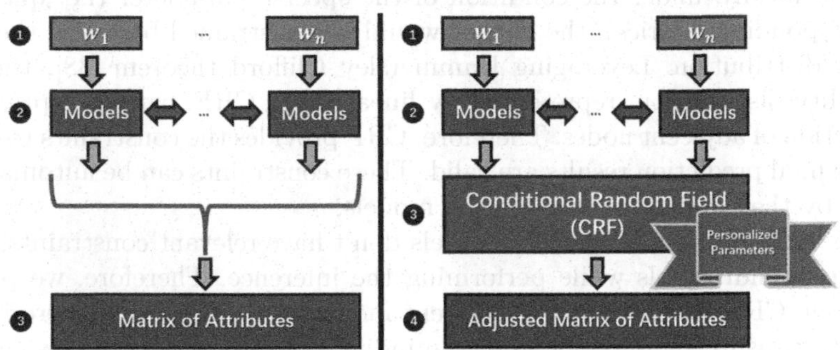

Fig. 4. A comparative example of model workflow, between (A) models without CRF and (B) models with CRF.

4.2.4 Key Idea 2: Measuring Personalized Parameters via Pearson Correlation Coefficients

Since CRF requires the personalized parameter to guide the adjustments, it's important to decide how to quantitatively measure the differences between individuals' facial expressions. To provide a quantitative examination of personalized parameters, we choose Pearson Correlation Coefficients (PCC) as the metric. PCC examines the correlation between two matrices, and it scales well when the data consists of more dimensions [20].

We elaborate how to use PCC in this case. Assuming a pair of data sets, X and Y, the distance is represented by the difference between targeted matrices, and the attributes are pixels from difference image matrices respectively. Therefore, we construct the examination of the two-dimensional correlation, and the values of the correlation range from –1 to 1. Equation 2 shows the detailed formulation of PCC, where X_i is a sample in set X, Y_i is a sample in set Y, $\overline{X}$ is the average value of set X, $\overline{Y}$ is the average value of set Y.

$$PCC = \frac{\sum_{i=1}^{n}(X_i - \overline{X})(Y_i - \overline{Y})}{\sqrt{\sum_{i=1}^{n}(X_i - \overline{X})^2}\sqrt{\sum_{i=1}^{n}(Y_i - \overline{Y})^2}}. \tag{2}$$

5 Experimental Methodology

In this section, we introduce details about our experimental methodology. We first cover the details of our implementations (Sect. 5.1), and then we elaborate details with regard to datasets and models (Sect. 5.2).

5.1 Implementation Details

We implement **Face2Statistics** using: (1) OpenCV library for data preprocessing; and (2) Tensorflow for all different Neural Network Models and the CRF model. We use these to ensure the practicality of **Face2Statistics** prototype. We evaluate different variants of **Face2Statistics** using a machine with Intel multi-core i9-9700 CPU and an AMD Radeon PRO 5600 GPU.

5.2 Dataset and Neural Network Models

We use the BROOK dataset [16, 29], an open-sourced and multi-modal dataset with facial videos for adaptive and personalized Human-Vehicle Interaction designs, to evaluate **Face2Statistics**. BROOK contains 11 dimensions of data, covering drivers' physiological statistics and vehicle status, which are collected from 34 drivers in a 20-minute driving process. We choose three dimensions of data streams: Vehicle Speed, Skin Conductivity and Heart Rate, with drivers' facial images as the input. Skin Conductivity and Heart Rate are representative data to monitor drivers' physiological status (e.g. stress, distraction), and Vehicle Speed is an intuitive data type to reflect the instantaneous driving context in different time spots. Note that any type of data streams can be used in **Face2Statistics**, as long as there are historical information to train the models. We cover all models, as described in Sect. 3.2, during our experiments.

6 Experimental Results

In this section, we present the experimental results and the analysis. Our evaluations aim to answer three questions: ❶ which Neural Network models, for **Face2Statistics**, has the best performance for different types of data streams? (Sect. 6.1) ❷ how our optimization, using HSV instead of RGB, would benefit **Face2Statistics**? (Sect. 6.2) ❸ how our optimization, adding CRF supports, would benefit **Face2Statistics**? (Sect. 6.3).

6.1 Comparisons Among Different Neural Network Models

Figure 5 reports the results of training and validation accuracy, in terms of DenseNet, LSTM and BiLSTM. We make three key observations. First, BiLSTM, LSTM and DenseNet achieve the best validation accuracy, in terms of Skin Conductivity, Heart Rate and Vehicle Speed respectively. This is because different types of data streams exhibit different symptoms, and the choices of models may vary as well. Second, the trend of training accuracy mostly correlates with the trends of validation accuracy. The only exception occurs when using BiLSTM for Skin Conductivity. This is because Skin Conductivity has a high frequency of occurrence in the time series, and BiLSTM has an advantage in terms of such structure. Third, all models achieve an extremely high training accuracy, across all types of data streams. The lowest precision of training accuracy occurs, when applying LSTM for Heart Rate prediction (i.e. 96.8%).

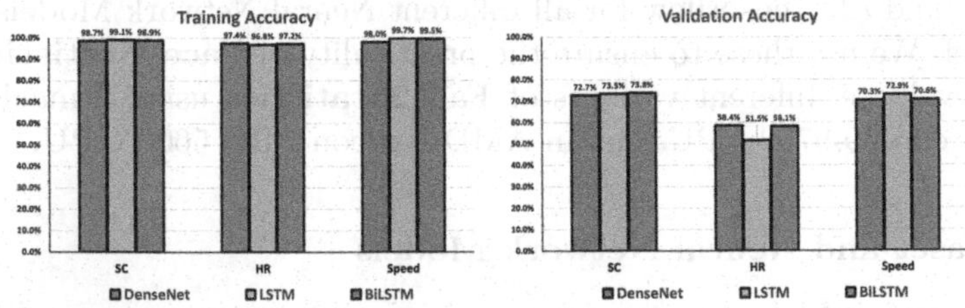

Fig. 5. Training (left) and Validation Accuracy (right) of all models, for Skin Conductivity (SC), Heart Rate (HR) & Vehicle Speed (Speed).

6.2 Comparisons Between HSV and RGB

Figure 6 reports the results of training and validation accuracy, in terms of applying HSV and RGB on BiLSTM. We make two key observations. First, BiLSTM, using HSV, achieves better validation accuracy in terms of all types of data streams (i.e. Skin Conductivity, Heart Rate and Vehicle Speed), compared with BiLSTM using RGB. More specifically, BiLSTM, using HSV, improves the validation accuracy by 1.0%, 4.9% and 1.1% for the predictions of Skin Conductivity, Heart Rate and Vehicle Speed. This is because HSV provides more robust representation in terms of illumination, and this provides consistent benefits in prediction. Second, the trends of training accuracy can't reflect the trends of validation accuracy. More specifically, for the predictions of Heart Rate, the validation accuracy are positively correlated with the training accuracy. However, for the predictions of Skin Conductivity, the validation accuracy is negatively correlated with the training accuracy. We believe this research direction for further characterizations deserves more efforts.

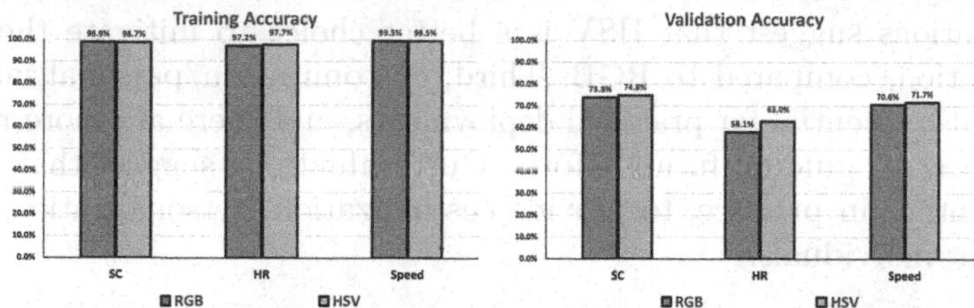

Fig. 6. Training (left) and Validation Accuracy (right) of BiLSTM using RGB or HSV, for Skin Conductivity (SC), Heart Rate (HR) & Vehicle Speed (Speed).

6.3 Comparisons Between Models W/ or W/out CRF

Figure 7 shows the comparative validation accuracy of BiLSTM w/ and w/out CRF support for four different drivers. The improvement of validation accuracy in all the cases proves the effectiveness of CRF for customization support. We notice that the prediction accuracy of the model with CRF is higher than that without CRF for all attributes. More specifically, BiLSTM, with CRF, increases the average validation accuracy by 0.95%, 0.44%, and 0.82% of Skin Conductivity, Heart Rate and Speed. This is because CRF provides customization/personalization of **Face2Statistics**, and this enables **Face2Statistics** to adapt different individuals accordingly.

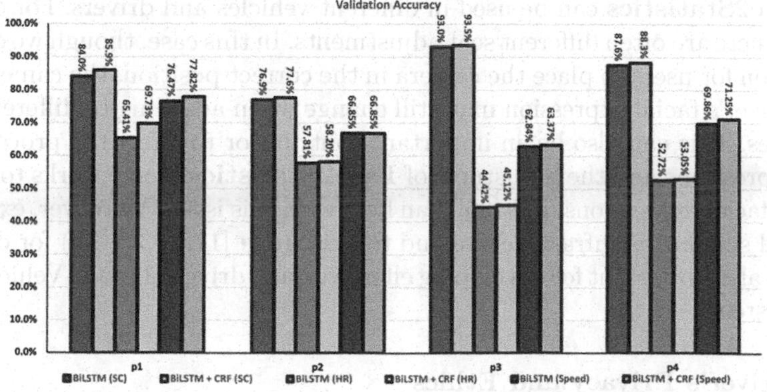

Fig. 7. Validation accuracy of BiLSTM w/ and w/out CRF for different individuals.

6.4 Takeaways from Experimental Results

We discuss our findings from the experimental studies. First, there is no one-size-fits-all solutions to all types of data streams, in terms of Neural Network model selections. Our evaluations show that both feature-reuse (i.e. DenseNet) and sequence-awareness (i.e. LSTM and BiLSTM) are important in particular cases. Second, image representation can have great impacts in terms of validation accuracy, and it's essential to consider a suitable one in driving scenarios. Our evaluations suggest that HSV is a better choice to mitigate the impacts of illumination, compared to RGB. Third, customization/personalization supports are also essential for practical deployments, and there are more rationales to be formed for guiding future efforts. Our evaluations suggest that CRF has great potentials in practice, to provide customization/personalization supports for different individuals.

7 Discussion

7.1 Model Limitations

To address the limitations of the current models, we optimize **Face2Statistics** by utilizing HSV color space to mitigate the effects of illumination, and using CRF to customize for different individuals. Beyond the optimizations described in our paper, we believe there are still an extensive amount of opportunities to explore in the future. There are mainly two aspects. First, it's potential to exploit *Adaptation in different driving scenarios.* Currently we only consider general driving scenarios in the context, we can add more information to **Face2Statistics** (e.g. weather, road congestion, etc.) in the future. Furthermore, these information can also make **Face2Statistics** to assist other contexts in Human-Vechile Interaction (e.g. User Trust [34], Driving Styles [42], etc.) Therefore, **Face2Statistics** can be much more personalised for training and prediction. Consequently, this requires a high degree of adaptation of the data set for re-collection and more robust deep neural networks to classify multiple attributes. Second, enabling *Adaptation in different angles of facial expression video streams* is also promising for future works. In practice, **Face2Statistics** can be used in different vehicles and drivers. For different drivers, there are often different seat adjustments. In this case, though we can set a instruction for users to place the camera in the correct position, the camera angle of the driver's facial expression may still change when adapting to different types of vehicles. This can also be an important contributor to affect the processing of facial expressions and the robustness of **Face2Statistics**. Some works to explore detailed facial expressions (e.g. [39]) can help with this issue. Moreover, exploiting advanced simulation infrastructure and toolkits (e.g. [17,32,33,40]) for data collection is also important for developing effective data-driven Human-Vehicle Interactive systems.

7.2 Driver's Privacy and Ethics

Privacy and ethical issues of **Face2Statistics** can be considered as general problems in the context of Human-Vehicle Interaction. For users, before data collection, **Face2Statistics** demands the approval from drivers (e.g. sign terms-of-use) and guarantees that there are no abuse of all collected data for other purposes. For systems, to achieve the real-time prediction, **Face2Statistics** needs to capture driver's facial expression, and transfers raw data to the back-end. There are two types of back-ends: (1) online servers and (2) local machines. For an online server, the data transmission procedure can incur potential issues of privacy protection. This is because both facial expression images and corresponding attributes may be vulnerable to leakage. A potential solution is to encode the driver's facial data by blurring before the data transformation, and decode when the data has been received by the server. Some works to explore advanced privacy protection to address this issue (e.g. [23–25]). As for a local machine, avoiding data transmission provides a natural guarantee for data isolation, but this requires more computational power on the local machine to facilitate with the needs of local computation. Therefore, enabling data protection in the context of privacy and ethical issues for Human-Vehicle Interaction systems like **Face2Statistics** is an interesting direction to balance the tradeoffs, and there are already some works starting to explore this part (e.g. [8]).

8 Related Works

In this section, we give an overview related works of **Face2Statistics**. We firstly introduce existing methods for extracting drivers' statistics (Sect. 8.1). Next, we compare existing methods and identify key limitations of them in practice (Sect. 8.2). Finally, we compare existing methods with **Face2Statistics** to justify the novelty of our work (Sect. 8.3).

8.1 Existing Methods for Extracting Drivers' Statistics

In order to collect In-vehicle drivers' statistics, existing methods can be grouped into two approaches. One approach is to directly integrate/deploy particular devices for specific types of statistics (e.g. Heart Rate Monitor); and the other approach is to re-routine statistics from internal compositions of a vehicle (e.g. Vehicle Speed). In the following, we discuss these two approaches in details.

1. *Integrating/Deploying particular devices/sensors/monitors for specific types of statistics.* Previous efforts (as covered in Sect. 2) show personal statistics of In-Vehicle Drivers are important to explore a large design space. To obtain personal statistics of In-Vehicle Drivers, existing solutions directly integrate/deploy particular devices/sensors/monitors to retrieve specific types of statistics. We use commonly-used types of statistics to elaborate, including Heart Rate, Skin Conductivity and Eye-Tracking. (1) to supply Heart Rate/Skin Conductivity statistics, drivers need to equip these bio-sensors for data collections [2,7,35]; and (2) to supply Eye-Tracking statistics, both drivers and vehicles need to equip parts of the Eye-Tracking system for data collection [31].

2. *Re-routing statistics from internal compositions of a vehicle.* Previous efforts also demonstrate the importance of vehicle statuses, while a particular driver is driving. To obtain vehicle statistics from a specific driver, existing solutions directly re-routine statistics from internal composition of a vehicle. For instance, to supply Vehicle Speed statistics, existing methods need to re-routine the information (i.e. displayed in dash board) to digital formats for Human-Vehicle Interaction systems.

8.2 Limitations of the Existing Methods

Existing methods are sufficient to leverage In-Vehicle Drivers' Statistics, to explore the design space of their usages. However, there are three major issues to adapt these methods: (1) user-unfriendliness of equipping devices while driving; (2) practical challenges of integrating/deploying devices; and (3) extra costs of vehicle design and manufacture. Note that these issues can further endanger the practicality of more designs, which consider In-Vehicle Drivers' Statistics as the source of data inputs. Hereby, we identify these issues and discuss them in details.

1. *User-unfriendliness of equipping devices while driving.* Existing approaches can lead to user-unfriendliness when collecting In-Vehicle Drivers' Statistics. As covered in Sect. 8.1, the collection of personal statistics requires drivers to equip multiple devices/sensors/monitors. Though it's acceptable for in-lab simulations/filed studies, it's not user-friendly for the majority of drivers in practice (e.g. equipping Heart Rate/Skin Conductivity monitors). Moreover, such integration/deployments might lead to more serious issues. For instance, the deployments of Eye-Tracking devices might affect the driver's field of vision, which incurs risks of driving safety in practice [4].
2. *Practical challenges of integrating/deploying devices.* Existing approaches have significant challenges of integrating/deploying devices in practice. As covered in Sect. 8.1, the collection of both personal and vehicle statistics demands a massive amount of extra data transfer across individual systems. Such transfer can incur large overheads in supplying statistics for Human-Vehicle Interaction systems. Though it might be applicable for off-line analysis during in-lab/field studies, this design choice is very difficult to deliver a high level of Quality-of-Services in practice.
3. *Extra costs of vehicle design and manufacture.* The only way to ensure a high-level of Quality-of-Services, is to incorporate the methods as parts of vehicle designs and manufactures. However, this is very challenging and can incur extra costs. For currently available devices/sensors/monitors, merging them into one single vehicle demand significant efforts in both hardware and software. As for in-vehicle statistics, the digitization of relevant statistics (e.g. Vehicle Speed, etc.) might also require extra efforts and costs in production.

Therefore, we can summarize the above three limitations as (1) user-unfriendly in practice; (2) impractical in production; and (3) not cost-effective. These limitations can further endanger the practicality of advanced Human-Vehicle Interaction designs, which relies on In-vehicle Drivers' Statistics.

8.3 Novelty of Our Approach

mechanism addresses all limitations mentioned above. Firstly, taking facial expressions only as input is **user-friendly**, as drivers do not need to equip bio-sensors which distracts them while driving. Next, with regard to data transfer, **Face2Statistics** only requires a video stream of the user's facial expressions and all in-vehicle data is handled via model prediction, which can significantly **reduce the cost** of data transfer and the subsequent risks of data leakage. Second the ease of use of **Face2Statistics** makes it a great **advantage in terms of vehicle designs and manufactures. Face2Statistics** can predict drivers' statistics in real time by simply installing a video recorder in the vehicle. Third, **Face2Statistics** enables personalised models for different drivers and eliminates the effects of illumination on facil expressions.

9 Conclusions

We propose, optimize and evaluate **Face2Statistics. Face2Statistics** provides a comprehensive road-map to deliver user-friendly, low-cost and effective alternatives for extracting drivers' statistics. Using **Face2Statistics**, in-vehicle drivers are not required to equip sensors/monitors for extracting relevant statistics, which improves the user-friendliness, practicality and efficiency. **Face2Statistics** takes facial expressions as the only input, and provides effective predictions of relevant statistics. We identify two major issues in terms of robustness, and provide viable solutions to optimize **Face2Statistics**. Our evaluations confirm the effectiveness of **Face2Statistics** in representative data types, and justify the benefits of our proposed optimizations. We release both source codes and trained models of **Face2Statistics** online at https://github.com/unnc-ucc/Face2Statistics.

Acknowledgements. We thank anonymous reviewers in HCI'22 and AutomotiveUI'21 for their valuable feedback. We thank for all members of User-Centric Computing Group at University of Nottingham Ningbo China for the stimulating environment. An earlier version of this work is at [15].

References

1. Abbas, Q., Alsheddy, A.: A methodological review on prediction of multi-stage hypovigilance detection systems using multimodal features. IEEE Access **9**, 47530–47564 (2021). https://doi.org/10.1109/ACCESS.2021.3068343
2. Asada, H.H., Shaltis, P., Reisner, A., Rhee, S., Hutchinson, R.C.: Mobile monitoring with wearable photoplethysmographic biosensors. IEEE Eng. Med. Biol. Mag. **22**(3), 28–40 (2003)
3. Berk, T., Brownston, L., Kaufman, A.: A new color-namiing system for graphics languages. IEEE Ann. Hist. Comput. **2**(03), 37–44 (1982)

4. Blignaut, P.J., Beelders, T.R.: Trackstick: a data quality measuring tool for tobii eye trackers. In: Morimoto, C.H., Istance, H.O., Spencer, S.N., Mulligan, J.B., Qvarfordt, P. (eds.) Proceedings of the 2012 Symposium on Eye-Tracking Research and Applications, ETRA 2012, Santa Barbara, CA, USA, 28–30 March 2012, pp. 293–296. ACM (2012). https://doi.org/10.1145/2168556.2168619
5. Bradski, G., Kaehler, A.: Learning OpenCV: Computer Vision with the OpenCV Library. O'Reilly Media, Inc., Sebastopol (2008)
6. Butakov, V.A., Ioannou, P.: Personalized driver/vehicle lane change models for adas. IEEE Trans. Veh. Technol. **64**(10), 4422–4431 (2014)
7. Dao, D., et al.: A robust motion artifact detection algorithm for accurate detection of heart rates from photoplethysmographic signals using time-frequency spectral features. IEEE J. Biomed. Health Inform. **21**(5), 1242–1253 (2016)
8. Duan, Y., Liu, J., Jin, W., Peng, X.: Characterizing differentially-private techniques in the era of internet-of-vehicles. Technical report-Feb-03 at User-Centric Computing Group, University of Nottingham Ningbo China (2022)
9. Erzin, E., Yemez, Y., Tekalp, A.M., Erçil, A., Erdogan, H., Abut, H.: Multimodal person recognition for human-vehicle interaction. IEEE Multimedia **13**(2), 18–31 (2006)
10. Graves, A., Mohamed, A.R., Hinton, G.: Speech recognition with deep recurrent neural networks. In: 2013 IEEE International Conference on Acoustics, Speech and Signal Processing, pp. 6645–6649. IEEE (2013)
11. He, K., Zhang, X., Ren, S., Sun, J.: Deep residual learning for image recognition. In: Proceedings of the IEEE Conference on Computer Vision and Pattern Recognition, pp. 770–778 (2016)
12. Hochreiter, S., Schmidhuber, J.: Long short-term memory. Neural Comput. **9**(8), 1735–1780 (1997)
13. Hu, J., Shen, L., Sun, G.: Squeeze-and-excitation networks. In: Proceedings of the IEEE Conference on Computer Vision and Pattern Recognition, pp. 7132–7141 (2018)
14. Huang, G., Liu, Z., Van Der Maaten, L., Weinberger, K.Q.: Densely connected convolutional networks. In: Proceedings of the IEEE Conference on Computer Vision and Pattern Recognition, pp. 4700–4708 (2017)
15. Huang, Z., et al.: Face2multi-modal: in-vehicle multi-modal predictors via facial expressions. In: 12th International Conference on Automotive User Interfaces and Interactive Vehicular Applications, pp. 30–33. AutomotiveUI 2020, Association for Computing Machinery, New York, NY, USA (2020). https://doi.org/10.1145/3409251.3411716
16. Jin, W., Duan, Y., Liu, J., Huang, S., Xiong, Z., Peng, X.: BROOK dataset: a playground for exploiting data-driven techniques in human-vehicle interactive designs. Technical report-Feb-01 at User-Centric Computing Group, University of Nottingham Ningbo China (2022)
17. Jin, W., Ming, X., Song, Z., Xiong, Z., Peng, X.: Towards emulating internet-of-vehicles on a single machine. In: AutomotiveUI 2021: 13th International Conference on Automotive User Interfaces and Interactive Vehicular Applications, Leeds, United Kingdom, 9–14 September 2021-Adjunct Proceedings, pp. 112–114. ACM (2021). https://doi.org/10.1145/3473682.3480275
18. Khodairy, M.A., Abosamra, G.: Driving behavior classification based on oversampled signals of smartphone embedded sensors using an optimized stacked-lstm neural networks. IEEE Access **9**, 4957–4972 (2021)

19. Kortmann, F., et al.: Creating value from in-vehicle data: detecting road surfaces and road hazards. In: 23rd IEEE International Conference on Intelligent Transportation Systems, ITSC 2020, Rhodes, Greece, 20–23 September 2020, pp. 1–6. IEEE (2020). https://doi.org/10.1109/ITSC45102.2020.9294684
20. Kosov, S., Shirahama, K., Grzegorzek, M.: Labeling of partially occluded regions via the multi-layer crf. Multimed. Tools Appl. **78**(2), 2551–2569 (2019)
21. Krizhevsky, A., Hinton, G.: Convolutional deep belief networks on cifar-10. Unpublished manuscript **40**(7), 1–9 (2010)
22. Krizhevsky, A., Hinton, G., et al.: Learning multiple layers of features from tiny images (2009)
23. Liu, J., Jin, W., He, Z., Ming, X., Duan, Y., Xiong, Z., Peng, X.: HUT: enabling high-UTility, batched queries under differential privacy protection for internet-of-vehicles. Technical report-Feb-02 at User-Centric Computing Group, University of Nottingham Ningbo China (2022)
24. Martin, S., Tawari, A., Trivedi, M.M.: Balancing privacy and safety: protecting driver identity in naturalistic driving video data. In: Boyle, L.N., Burnett, G.E., Fröhlich, P., Iqbal, S.T., Miller, E., Wu, Y. (eds.) Proceedings of the 6th International Conference on Automotive User Interfaces and Interactive Vehicular Applications, Seattle, WA, USA, 17–19 September 2014, pp. 17:1–17:7. ACM (2014). https://doi.org/10.1145/2667317.2667325
25. Martin, S., Tawari, A., Trivedi, M.M.: Toward privacy-protecting safety systems for naturalistic driving videos. IEEE Trans. Intell. Transp. Syst. **15**(4), 1811–1822 (2014)
26. Martinez, D.L., Rudovic, O., Picard, R.: Personalized automatic estimation of self-reported pain intensity from facial expressions. In: 2017 IEEE Conference on Computer Vision and Pattern Recognition Workshops (CVPRW), pp. 2318–2327. IEEE (2017)
27. Nishiuchi, H., Park, K., Hamada, S.: The relationship between driving behavior and the health condition of elderly drivers. Int. J. Intell. Transp. Syst. Res. **19**(1), 264–272 (2021)
28. Omerustaoglu, F., Sakar, C.O., Kar, G.: Distracted driver detection by combining in-vehicle and image data using deep learning. Appl. Soft Comput. **96**, 106657 (2020)
29. Peng, X., Huang, Z., Sun, X.: Building BROOK: a multi-modal and facial video database for human-vehicle interaction research, pp. 1–9 (2020). https://arxiv.org/abs/2005.08637
30. Porter, M.M., et al.: Older driver estimates of driving exposure compared to in-vehicle data in the candrive ii study. Traffic Inj. Prev. **16**(1), 24–27 (2015)
31. Silva, N., et al.: Eye tracking support for visual analytics systems: foundations, current applications, and research challenges. In: Krejtz, K., Sharif, B. (eds.) Proceedings of the 11th ACM Symposium on Eye Tracking Research & Applications, ETRA 2019, Denver, CO, USA, 25–28 June 2019, pp. 11:1–11:10. ACM (2019). https://doi.org/10.1145/3314111.3319919
32. Song, Z., Wang, S., Kong, W., Peng, X., Sun, X.: First attempt to build realistic driving scenes using video-to-video synthesis in OpenDS framework. In: Adjunct Proceedings of the 11th International Conference on Automotive User Interfaces and Interactive Vehicular Applications, AutomotiveUI 2019, Utrecht, The Netherlands, 21–25 September 2019, pp. 387–391. ACM (2019). https://doi.org/10.1145/3349263.3351497

33. Song, Z., Duan, Y., Jin, W., Huang, S., Wang, S., Peng, X.: Omniverse-OpenDS: enabling agile developments for complex driving scenarios via reconfigurable abstractions. In: International Conference on Human-Computer Interaction (2022)
34. Sun, X., et al.: Exploring personalised autonomous vehicles to influence user trust. Cogn. Comput. **12**(6), 1170–1186 (2020)
35. Tamura, T., Maeda, Y., Sekine, M., Yoshida, M.: Wearable photoplethysmographic sensors-past and present. Electronics **3**(2), 282–302 (2014)
36. Toledo, T., Lotan, T.: In-vehicle data recorder for evaluation of driving behavior and safety. Transp. Res. Rec. **1953**(1), 112–119 (2006)
37. Toledo, T., Musicant, O., Lotan, T.: In-vehicle data recorders for monitoring and feedback on drivers' behavior. Transp. Res. Part C Emerg. Technol. **16**(3), 320–331 (2008)
38. Wallach, H.M.: Conditional random fields: an introduction. Technical reports (CIS), p. 22 (2004)
39. Wang, J., Xiong, Z., Duan, Y., Liu, J., Song, Z., Peng, X.: The importance distribution of drivers' facial expressions varies over time!, pp. 148–151. Association for Computing Machinery, New York, NY, USA (2021). https://doi.org/10.1145/3473682.3480283
40. Wang, S., Liu, J., Sun, H., Ming, X., Jin, W., Song, Z., Peng, X.: Oneiros-OpenDS: an interactive and extensible toolkit for agile and automated developments of complicated driving scenes. In: International Conference on Human-Computer Interaction (2022)
41. Xing, Y., Lv, C., Cao, D., Lu, C.: Energy oriented driving behavior analysis and personalized prediction of vehicle states with joint time series modeling. Appl. Energy **261**, 114471 (2020)
42. Zhang, Y., Jin, W., Xiong, Z., Li, Z., Liu, Y., Peng, X.: Demystifying interactions between driving behaviors and styles through self-clustering algorithms. In: Krömker, H. (ed.) International Conference on Human-Computer Interaction (2021). https://doi.org/10.1007/978-3-030-78358-7_23
43. Zheng, S., et al.: Conditional random fields as recurrent neural networks. In: Proceedings of the IEEE International Conference on Computer Vision, pp. 1529–1537 (2015)

User-Centered Information Architecture of Vehicle AR-HUD Interface

Han Zhang[1], Zhefan Yu[1], Cen Zhang[1], Ruotian Zhang[1], Yuyang Liu[1], and Seung Hee Lee[2](✉)

[1] Graduate School of Comprehensive Human Sciences, University of Tsukuba, 1-1-1 Tenno-dai, Tsukuba-shi, Ibaraki 305-3577, Japan
{s2036050,s2121642}@s.tsukuba.ac.jp

[2] University of Tsukuba, 1-1-1 Tennodai, Tsukuba-shi, Ibaraki 305-3577, Japan
lee.seunghee.gn@u.tsukuba.ac.jp

Abstract. Augmented reality head-up display (AR-HUD) presents a more natural way to process images with breakthroughs in optics. The technology also become the primary development trend of automobile human-machine interface (HMI). However, too much virtual information might interfere with drivers' attention to their surroundings and affect their driving judgments. To effectively manage the complexity of vehicle information systems while further improving driving safety, this study aims to establish the information architecture of two driver groups (beginner drivers and skilled drivers) in different road environments. We developed a priority classification model and recruited 60 university students to participate in a card sorting experiment based on the criteria of beginner and skilled drivers. The cluster analysis findings were used to determine the AR-HUD information's grouping structure and hierarchical connection for the two driving user groups. Additionally, we investigated the impact of common road types and driving experience on the diversity of information architecture. The findings of this study constructed a user-centered information architecture and provided a theoretical foundation and role for the automobile industry in managing AR-HUD information and interface design.

Keywords: AR-HUD · Information architecture · Navigation · Card sort

1 Introduction

The architecture of information classification has an important role in the usability of automobile human-machine interaction (HMI) systems [1]. With the increasing maturity of advanced driver assistance systems (ADAS) and augmented reality (AR) technologies [2], future AR-HUDs will allow for a field of view (FOV) of 10° or more overlay images directly onto the actual environment [3]. This enables the driver to get more information at the same time. However, superimposing too much virtual information on the actual traffic environment can lead to driver distraction, annoyance, or masking other road users [4–6]. In particular, the AR impacts the allocation of visual attention more strongly during the decision-making phase [7]. Consequently, before AR-HUD can be

H. Krömker (Ed.): HCII 2022, LNCS 13335, pp. 309–325, 2022.
https://doi.org/10.1007/978-3-031-04987-3_21

used in production vehicles, one more challenge must be overcome: how to manage the complexity of in-vehicle information systems efficiently while also improving driving safety.

In terms of AR-HUD design improvements, the most widespread use of HUD is in luxury automobiles manufactured by BMW, Mercedes-Benz, Lexus, and Audi [8]. Currently, mainstream AR-HUD contain the following information features: current speed, adaptive cruise control, driver assistance, distance warning, lane change warning, ambient pedestrian warning, lane departure warning, and vehicle ahead warning. In the actual driving process, while each company uses different visual communication methods for information display, the information is mainly divided into driving information, vehicle status information and driver assistance information. The application's present design is constrained by technological constraints and may deliver far less information than the conceptual design provided by technology companies. However, independent of the automobiles manufacturer or technology company, most of their HUD designs have only one mode, resulting in customers with varying driving experiences receiving too much or too little information.

Additionally, manufacturers often provide a deactivation option for driver assistance information to limit visual distractions in AR-HUD information display settings. However, these designs underestimate the fact that the driver's familiarity with driving directly affects the amount of information required. For example, whether navigation may require and how much information is needed. In the existing AR-HUD interface design process, the estimating architecture used in information database does not provide a comprehensive view of the effects of driving experiences. Additionally, it implies that all drivers with comparable experience driving on the road are capable of capacity assessment. The road traffic accidents caused by beginner drivers who have few practical experience and cannot make accurate judgments and responses facing changing traffic conditions is much higher than that of skilled drivers [9]. With automotive manufacturers confronted with the problem of integrating AR-HUD functionalities into mid-segment vehicles, further study is required to determine whether driving experience influences information requests.

Moreover, the current studies have focused on the development a system that offered driving-safety information to the driver through various modalities in the technical parts [10]. Numerous researchers claimed that prototypes of in-vehicle AR-HUD project information about detected pedestrians, vehicles, and traffic signals directly into the driver's forward perspective [5, 11]. There is a shortage of study on the information architecture of AR-HUD interface in a variety of road environments with different navigation instruments.

In this paper we developed a priority classification model and recruited 60 university students to participate in a card sorting experiment based on the criteria of beginner and skilled drivers. The purpose of this study is to compare the information requirements of beginner and skilled drivers in various road environments. Additionally, it determines whether different driving experiences influence the amount and priority classification architecture of information requirements for identical navigation directions.

2 Information Architecture of AR-HUD Interface

Information architecture is the fundamental part of the visual and display design of the automobile HMI interface [12]. HMI in automobiles needs to face various dangerous driving situations [13], there is a large amount of interface information required. Also, the information provided by the system must ensure that it does not interfere with the normal driving task of the driver and cause additional driving distractions [14]. As a result, when designing the AR-HUD human-computer interaction interface, the layout of the interface and amount of information should be reasonable [15]. Designers must capture and guide the driver's attention while minimizing distractions from the driving landscape.

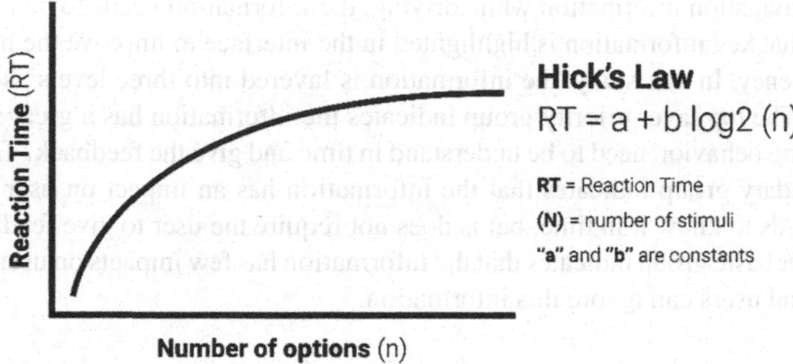

Fig. 1. Hick's Law Graph, "RT" is the reaction time. "(n)" is the number of stimuli (choices). "a" and "b" are constants, depending on the task and condition.

In the HMI design, Hick's Law is commonly used to determine how the information is organized in the user interface. The Hick-Hyman law describes a linear increase in reaction time (RT) as a function of the information entropy of response selection, which is computed as the binary logarithm of number of response alternatives [16]. The Hick's law formula defines this principle as Fig. 1 shown: $RT = a + b \log2 (n)$.

Figure 1 showed the relationship between the number of choices presented in the interface and the user's reaction time to decide on these choices. Increasing the number of choices will increase the reaction time for people to decide. If too much information is distributed, attention will be disturbed while the cognitive burden will increase.

During the driving judgment phase, AR has a greater effect on the allocation of visual attention. When the AR-HUD presents information relevant to the driving task, it enhances driving behavior. On the other hand, a non-driving task AR-HUD reduces visual attention allocation and instead causes distractions in the driver's decision making. As a result, a good AR-HUD system should display only the most important or prioritized information required to construct that driving activity.

2.1 Priority Classification of AR-HUD Interface Information

According to the user mental model derived in current work, we find out that users' expectations and needs for the AR-HUD interface are as follows: (i) Real-time understand of various types of status information of the vehicle; (ii) Real-time understanding of navigation information to make driving decisions; and (iii) to be reminded of potential hazards in the driving environment in time.

However, there is a limit to the amount of information that can be displayed on a single interface. If too much information is displayed at once, it can cause confusion and distraction to the driver's decision making. This can easily lead to driving errors and even traffic accidents. Considering these requirements, the information architecture of the AR-HUD needs to do the following: (i) Prioritize the information that affects the driver's driving decisions by placing it at the highest level; and (ii) improve cognitive efficiency and reduce the cognitive burden on the user. Information needs to be summarized and streamlined. Prevent the user from being overloaded with too much information at once.

To ensure that the user spends as little effort as possible in mastering driving conditions and navigation information while driving, the information needs to be prioritized. To ensure that key information is highlighted in the interface to improve the user's cognitive efficiency. In this study, the information is layered into three levels as shown in the Fig. 2. The top layer priority group indicates the information has a great impact on user's driving behavior, need to be understand in time and give the feedback. The second layer secondary group indicates that the information has an impact on user behavior, the user needs to know it in time, but is does not require the user to give feedback. The bottom layer basic group indicates that the information has few impacts on users' driving behavior, and users can ignore this information.

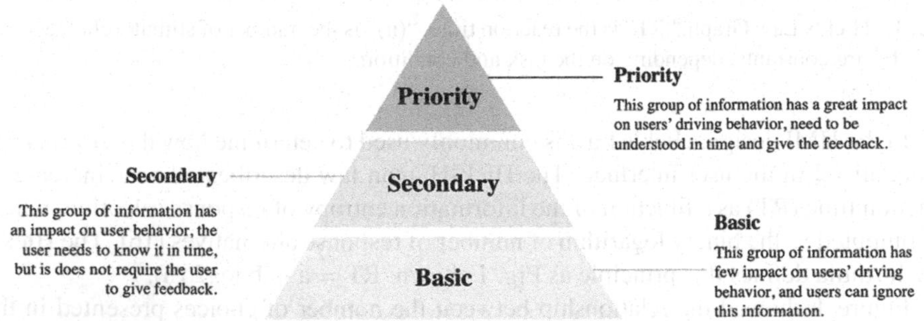

Fig. 2. Priority classification model of AR-HUD interface information

The information architecture of AR-HUD interface should be straightforward and uncomplicated, with clear information priorities and no extraneous information displayed. Presenting the most critical information on the interface in real time and without interfering with the environment's integration is the optimal design approach for increasing the efficiency of the driver's information access.

Cognitive economic theory shows that a clearly partitioned modular information interface can effectively reduce the occupation of users' attention resources and improve their cognitive efficiency and accuracy of information.

Consequently, the basic group's information is inappropriate for display in the AR-HUD. Whereas as the lower area is more compatible with the visual flow and properties of the human eye-viewing, the second group's information may be shown as the HUD interface in the area that the driver can scan at 30°. Additionally, priority information

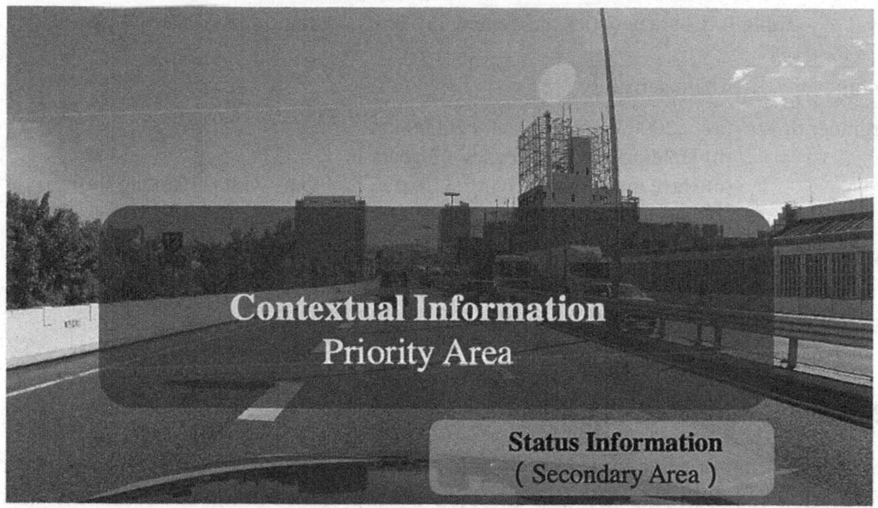

Fig. 3. Layout of AR-HUD interface

should be presented in real time on the actual road through augmented reality presentation to assist the driver in making judgments (see Fig. 3). The contextual information in priority area that affects users' driving decisions is integrated with the driving context of the front windshield to provide driving assistance and warnings to the driver.

Based on this model, we used card sorting experiments to classify the information requirements database obtained in current work into three groups according to different road environments.

3 Card Sorting Experiments

Card sorting is an established method for understanding users' mental models of information architecture. It is used frequently in software development, evaluation and human-computer interaction design, to understand the clustering of information and relationships between information from the users' perspective [17].

In this study, the card sorting method can be used to grasp the changes in user requirements for the interface in different driving scenarios, which allows the information architecture of the AR-HUD interface to be constructed on this basis. The processing of the results of the card sorting method usually uses cluster analysis to define different values [18] for the information classification results in each road environment, thereby structuring and integrating this information based on the values of the ratings.

3.1 Participants

Participants conducting card sorting experiments need to meet the criteria of the target users of the design. A total of 60 participants, 30 in each group were recruited for the experiments according to the definitions of beginners and skilled drivers (see Table 1).

Table 1. Characteristics of beginner driver group and skilled driver group

Group	Characteristics
Beginner driver	(a) <2000 km/year, total <20000 km (b) Holding driving licenses <3 years (c) Have inadequate driving skills and problems with perceiving traffic conditions
Skilled driver	(a) >5000 km/year, total > 50000 km (b) Holding driving licenses > 5 years (c) Sufficient driving skills and environmental adaptability

3.2 Road Environment Condition

Driving in different road environments such as highways and urban roads, the driver's information requirements are also affected by the surrounding environment, which affects the related driving operations. As a result, card analysis experiments for information stratification need to be conducted based on different road environment conditions. In the experiment, there were four different road environment conditions used: urban road, highway, residential and countryside road.

Urban road that are Urban in nature will generally be characterized by low to moderate posted speeds, frequent entrances, and moderate to heavy residential or commercial development. Curbed sections with closed drainage will generally be prevalent, although open drainage sections may be interspersed. Intersections, sidewalks, and on-street parking are often characteristic of Urban roadways.

Highway that are two or more lanes in each intersection. They have double solid lines to separate high-speed traffic. Driving on the highway with long distances between cars, high speeds, simple information about road conditions and single driving operations.

Residential road in residential areas with narrow roads, difficult to see turn offs, and pedestrian bicyclists and cars on the same lane.

Countryside road that are few traffic values and often lack pavements, should be mindful of pedestrians, cyclists and riders passing either side of car while driving on the road.

Depending on the characteristics of each road environment, different traffic conditions and driving situations can also occur. This experiment sets the same driving instructions to compare the variability of information priority in each environment (see Fig. 4).

Fig. 4. Four road environments and navigation commands

3.3 Design Cards

When designing the cards, the appropriate number of cards will ensure the accuracy of the experiment. When the number of cards is less than 30, the experimental results cannot fully reflect the correlation between the information of each card: when the number of information is greater than 100, it is easy to cause stress to the subjects and affect the accuracy of the experimental results [19]. In this experiment, the 36 items of information from the beginner mode and the 30 items of information from the skilled driver mode derived in current study were used as the card base for classification (see Table 2).

Table 2. Information card of the two groups

Beginner driver group (n = 36)	
Navigation information	Start notification, turn instructions, U-turn instructions, the current lane of the car, lane change instructions, driving route, distance from destination, change route reminder, keep straight, destination, distance reminder (turn right after 300 m), park instructions, arrival notification, time to destination
Vehicle status information	Speed, remaining battery, air conditioning operating status, light status, whether the system is abnormal, **milage, gear position, door switch status, seat belt status**

(*continued*)

Table 2. (*continued*)

Driving assistance information	Direction visualization, departure warning, safe distance reminder, speed reminder, parking assist, speed limit information, road restrictions, traffic condition ahead, **pedestrian's information, obstacles around the vehicle, other vehicles, turn path visualization, overtaking assist**
Skilled driver group (n = 30)	
Navigation information	Start notification, turn instructions, U-turn instructions, the current lane of the car, lane change instructions, driving route, distance from destination, change route reminder, keep straight, destination, distance reminder (turn right after 300m), park instructions, arrival notification, time to destination
Vehicle status information	Speed, light status, door switch status, air condition status
Driving assistance information	Direction visualization, departure warning, safe distance reminder, speed reminder, traffic condition ahead, speed limit information, road restrictions, **vehicle service (gas station nearby)**
Entertainment information	**SMS reminder, music information, nearby restaurants information, building introduction**

3.4 Experimental Procedure

This experiment is in the form of a closed classification. We defined the number of groups and names of the card categories in advance and laid out the experimental interface according to the four driving environments.

As shown in the Fig. 5, according to the situation of the navigation instructions, the participants were asked to divide the cards into two groups: priority group, secondary group (see Fig. 2) using Google jam-board. Also mentioned that the remaining information would be classified as basic group, and only three or less cards can be selected to be placed in the priority area. The number of cards in each area is determined by the participants' own judgment. In the end, explain the reason for grouping. We interacted with the participants in real time and recorded the whole experiment on screen.

3.5 Cluster Analysis

At the end of the experiment, the experimental results of each group were analyzed by using the cluster analysis method. The procedure is shown in Fig. 6.

To perform cluster analysis, the first step is to create a matrix with the same number of rows and columns as the number of cards. For example, for the beginner group, matrix chart of 36 × 36 and set the 36 cards are set as horizontal and vertical coordinates. Using the matrix chart to record the results of the above classification of the participant's selected cards, assign a value of 1 to the position of the matrix icon with coordinates (m, n) if card M and card N are placed in the same group. While card M and card N are not in the same group, they are assigned a value of 0 at the location of the matrix

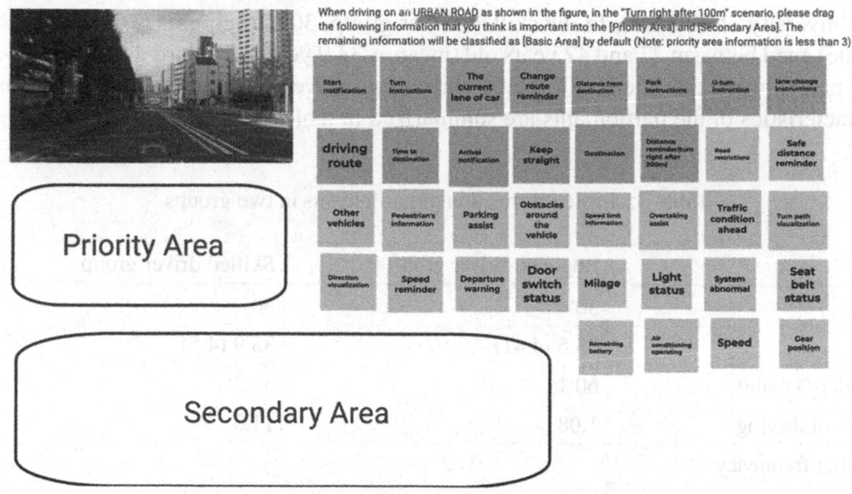

Fig. 5. Jam board interface for card sorting experiments

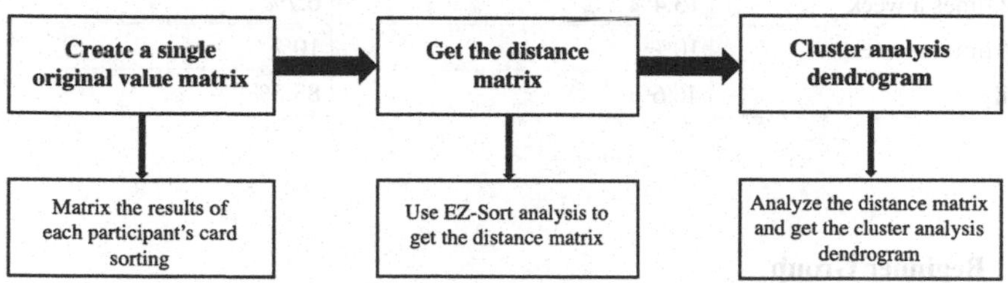

Fig. 6. Flow chart of cluster analysis method

icon coordinate (m, n) [20]. Using this principle, a single-trials original value matrix is created for each participant.

When the first step is accomplished, the single-participant original value matrix for each test subject was entered into the card classification cluster analysis software EZSort, and cluster analysis was performed to derive the distance matrix. The generated distance matrix is analyzed using EZSort software. EZSort is a software tool that simplifies both the card sorting exercise procedure and the interpretation of the resulting trees [21]. Researcher can use the EZCalc package to manage card sort data generated by USort and perform cluster analyses. EZCale generates tree diagrams that allow direct adjustment of the cluster thresholds. At the end, analyze the distance matrix and get the cluster analysis deprogram for each group in different environment and driving conditions.

4 Results

In the beginner group, 30 participants (18 male and 12 female) aged between 20 and 29 years old (mean = 23.5 years, standard deviation = 4.41) took part in this experiment. Participants are all undergraduate and graduate students from different departments of the University of Tsukuba. In the skilled driver group, 30 participants (16 male and 14 female) aged between 27 and 42 years old (mean = 33.9 years, standard deviation = 4.5) took part in this experiment. All the 60 participants have the Japanese driving license. Characteristics of the participants are summarized in table 3.

Table 3. Basic information of participants in two groups

	Beginner driver group	Skilled driver group
N	30	30
Age	23.5 (4.41)	33.9 (4.5)
Gender(%male)	60%	53.3%
Years of driving	1.08	11.3
Driving frequency		
do not use it much	10%	0%
monthly	20%	0%
1–2 times a week	13.4%	6.7%
3–4 times a week	10%	10%
Daily	46.6%	83.3%

4.1 Beginner Group

The cluster analysis tree diagram illustrating the cluster analysis between each card contents in terms of information priority grouping is obtained in this experiment, as shown in Fig. 7. The top orange section contains the most essential information, the middle blue section has the basic information, and the bottom light-yellow section contains the second group. When drivers are making a left turn choice in an urban road setting, the most important information they want to receive is speed, distance, and turn The top orange section contains the most essential information, the middle blue section has the basic information, and the bottom light yellow section contains the second group. When drivers are making a left turn choice in an urban road setting, the most important information they want to receive is speed, distance, and turn direction indication. direction indication.

Based on the cluster analysis findings, it is possible to describe the grouping architecture and hierarchical linkages between the data included in the AR-HUD interface. The information classification architecture for the beginning group is shown in Table 4. For the information requirements of beginner drivers, there was a significant difference between each environment in the driving instruction "go straight" "turn left" "turn right" ($p < 0.01$). For example, under the driving instruction "go straight", the three-priority information on urban roads and highways are: speed, departure warning and distance reminder. However, on countryside roads, the priority information "distance reminder"

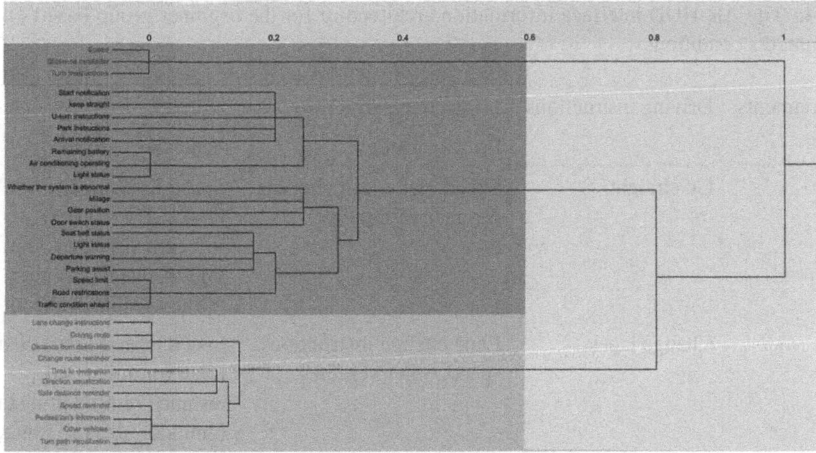

Fig. 7. Information prioritization card sort EZSort cluster analysis tree diagram (turn left in Urban Road)

is changed to "traffic condition ahead"; and on residential roads, the priority information "departure warning" became "pedestrian's information". Differences in information requirements are impacted by route features, such as shown on residential roads, where pedestrians and vehicles use the same lane and must maintain a vigilant look out for other road users.

4.2 Skilled driver Group

We also construct the skilled driver's AR-HUD information architecture using the 30 information needs collected in current work based on the findings of the cluster analysis and our evaluation of the card information of the 30 participants. It depicts the grouping structure and hierarchical relationship between the information needs in each environment, as shown in Table 5.

For the information requirements of skilled drivers, there was no significant difference between each environment in the same driving instruction ($p > 0.01$). Skilled drivers are most concerned with directional navigation information during driving. Additionally, it is emphasized that direction visualization is a priority information for both beginner driver group and skilled driver group on residential roads. The spaces between houses on Japanese residential roads are quite narrow, making it difficult to instantly locate the intersection at which need to turn, resulting in missed important intersections. When driving on unfamiliar roads, both beginner drivers and skilled drivers place a priority on direction visualization.

5 Discussion and Conclusions

Visual communication is the combination of visual organization and perception, and its goal is to represent the content and function of a product in the best form for user experience [22]. In this study, the research purpose is to minimize the use of user attention

Table 4. The AR-HUD interface information architecture for the beginner group based on four environments conditions

Environments	Driving instructions	Information structure	
		Priority group	Secondary group
Urban	Go straight	Speed, departure warning, distance reminder	Speed limit, pedestrian's information, other vehicles, driving route, safe distance reminder, traffic condition ahead
	Change lanes	Lane change instructions, speed, other vehicles	Speed, speed limit, change route reminder, safe distance reminder, distance reminder, driving route, turn path visualization
	Turn left	Turn instructions, speed, distance reminder	Lane change instructions, driving route, distance from destination, change route reminder, time to destination, direction visualization, safe distance reminder, speed reminder, pedestrian's information, other vehicles, turn path visualization
	Overtaking	Other vehicles, speed, lane change instructions	Distance reminder, driving route, change lane reminder, safe distance reminder, speed reminder
	Turn right	Change route reminder, turn instructions, speed	Distance reminder, lane change instructions, driving route, other vehicle, pedestrian's information, direction visualization
Countryside	Go straight	Speed, departure warning, traffic condition ahead	Speed limit, other vehicles, driving route, safe distance reminder, distance reminder

(*continued*)

Table 4. (*continued*)

Environments	Driving instructions	Information structure	
		Priority group	Secondary group
	Change lanes	Lane change instructions, speed, change route reminder	Speed, speed limit, other vehicles, safe distance reminder, distance reminder, driving route, turn path visualization
	Turn left	Turn instructions, speed, pedestrian's information	Distance reminder, lane change instructions, driving route, distance from destination, change route reminder, time to destination, direction visualization, safe distance reminder, speed reminder, other vehicles, turn path visualization
	Overtaking	Other vehicles, speed, lane change instructions	Distance reminder, driving route, change lane reminder, safe distance reminder, speed reminder
	Turn right	Change route reminder, direction visualization, speed	Turn instructions, distance reminder, lane change instructions, driving route, other vehicle, pedestrian's information, direction visualization
Highway	Go straight	Speed, departure warning, distance reminder	Speed limit, other vehicles, driving route, safe distance reminder, distance reminder
	Change lanes	Speed, lane change instructions, change route reminder	Speed limit, other vehicles, driving route, safe distance reminder, distance reminder

(*continued*)

Table 4. (*continued*)

Environments	Driving instructions	Information structure	
		Priority group	Secondary group
	Overtaking	Distance reminder, speed, other vehicle	Driving route, change lane reminder, safe distance reminder, speed reminder
	Convergence	Other vehicle, driving route, speed	Speed limit, other vehicles, safe distance reminder,
Residential	Go straight	Speed, distance reminder, Pedestrian's information	Other vehicle, speed limit, road restrications
	Turn left	Turn instruction, direction visualization, pedestrian's information	Speed, distance reminder, other vehicle, road restrications
	Turn right	Turn instruction, direction visualization, pedestrian's information	Speed, distance reminder, road restrications

resources while communicating timely information related to driving decisions. Since the interface information of AR-HUD system is closely related to the driving environment and user driving behavior. The design of the AR-HUD interface should meet the principles of human-computer interaction design on the one hand and the requirements of improving the driver's driving distraction and cognitive load during driving on the other hand. At the same time, the driving experience has a significant impact on the efficiency of extracting information during driving [23]. In contrast to the single information basis used by present AR-HUD systems, we suggest it is necessary to developing a composite information base based on differing driving experiences for improve driving safety.

In this study, card sorting experiments and cluster analysis were used to categorize information into three groups based on the priority classification model by the target user group while driving. The target user group's mental model for the AR-HUD interface's information architecture was collected and analyzed. Simultaneously, the information architecture was created utilizing four typical Japanese road types as environmental stimuli. The resulting AR-HUD interface information architecture and information priority classification provide an important basic framework for the subsequent design work. At the same time, it provides a reference for the layout design of the AR-HUD interface and the visual element design.

Additionally, we identified that different environments had an influence on the group of beginner drivers' information prioritization choices. They would adjust their information requirements based on the road environment. It indicates that the variety of the driving experience cannot be overlooked when designing AR-HUDs and should be enhanced and varied in future design development.

Table 5. The AR-HUD interface information architecture for the skilled driver group based on four environments conditions

Environments	Driving instructions	Information structure	
		Priority group	Secondary group
Urban	Go straight	Speed, time to destination, distance reminder	Speed limit, nearby convenience store, traffic condition ahead
	Change lanes	Lane change instructions, speed, other vehicles	Speed, speed limit, change route reminder
	Turn left	Turn instructions, speed, distance reminder	Pedestrian's information, other vehicles, turn path visualization
	Overtaking	Speed	Safe distance reminder, speed reminder
	Turn right	Turn instructions, speed	Distance reminder, direction visualization
Countryside	Go straight	Speed, traffic condition ahead, distance reminder,	Vehicle service, nearby convenience store
	Change lanes	Lane change instructions, speed	Speed limit, other vehicles, distance reminder
	Turn left	Turn instructions, speed, distance reminder,	Distance reminder, pedestrian's information
	Overtaking	Speed	Distance reminder, speed reminder
	Turn right	Direction visualization, speed	Turn instructions, distance reminder
Highway	Go straight	Speed, distance reminder	Speed limit, vehicle service
	Change lanes	Speed, lane change instructions	Speed limit, change route reminder
	Overtaking	Speed, other vehicle	driving route, speed reminder
	Convergence	Other vehicle, speed	Speed limit, other vehicles, safe distance reminder
Residential	Go straight	Speed, distance reminder, warning	Other vehicle, speed limit,
	Turn left	Turn instruction, direction visualization	Speed, distance reminder,

(continued)

Table 5. (*continued*)

Environments	Driving instructions	Information structure	
		Priority group	Secondary group
	Turn right	Turn instruction, direction visualization	Speed, distance reminder, other vehicle

The findings of this study constructed a user-centered information architecture and provided a theoretical foundation and role for the automobile industry in managing AR-HUD information and interface design. Contribute original thoughts for constructing a vehicle customized AR-HUD interface that provides driving safety information.

References

1. Daimler: Safety first for automated driving. White Pap. Differ. car manufacutres suppliers, pp. 1–157 (2019). https://www.press.bmwgroup.com/global/article/attachment/T0298103EN/434404
2. Robb, E.R., Cashen, D.: Augmented reality human-machine interface: defining future AR System Technology. In: 2014 Veh. Displays Interfaces …, October 2015 (2017)
3. Firth, M.: Introduction to automotive augmented reality head-up displays using TI DLP ® technology (2019)
4. Gabbard, J.L., Fitch, G.M., Kim, H.: Behind the glass: Driver challenges and opportunities for AR automotive applications. Proc. IEEE **102**(2), 124–136 (2014). https://doi.org/10.1109/JPROC.2013.2294642
5. Schneider, M., Bruder, A., Necker, M., Schluesener, T., Henze, N., Wolff, C.: A real-world driving experiment to collect expert knowledge for the design of AR HUD navigation that covers less. Mensch und Comput. 2019 - Work, 410–420 (2019). https://dl.gi.de/handle/20.500.12116/25230
6. Jurklies, B., Heiligenhaus, A., Steuhl, K.P., Wessing, A.: Electrophysiological evaluation in intermediate uveitis. Investig. Ophthalmol. Vis. Sci.**37**(3) (2016)
7. Abdi, L., Meddeb, A.: In-vehicle augmented reality system to provide driving safety information. J. Vis. **21**(1), 163–184 (2017). https://doi.org/10.1007/s12650-017-0442-6
8. Maroto, M., Caño, E., Gonzálezz, P., Villegas, D.: Head-up Displays (HUD) in driving, 1 (2018). http://arxiv.org/abs/1803.08383
9. Yang, L., Zhang, X., Zhu, X., Luo, Y., Luo, Y.: Research on risky driving behavior of novice drivers. Sustainability **11**(20), 1–20 (2019). https://doi.org/10.3390/su11205556
10. Merenda, C., et al.: Augmented reality interface design approaches for goal-directed and stimulus-driven driving tasks. IEEE Trans. Vis. Comput. Graph. **24**(11), 2875–2885 (2018). https://doi.org/10.1109/TVCG.2018.2868531
11. Zhang, M.: Optimization analysis of AR-HUD technology application in automobile industry. J. Phys. Conf. Ser. **1746**(1) (2021). https://doi.org/10.1088/1742-6596/1746/1/012062
12. Weber, J.B.: Applying Visual Basic for Human Machine Interface Applications (1999)
13. Amditis, A., et al.: Towards the automotive HMI of the future: overview of the AIDE - integrated project results. IEEE Trans. Intell. Transp. Syst. **11**(3), 567–578 (2010). https://doi.org/10.1109/TITS.2010.2048751
14. Campbell, J.L., et al.: Human factors design principles for level 2 and level 3 automated driving concepts. Highw. Traffic Saf. Adm. Natl. Dep. Transp. 122 (2018). www.ntis.gov

15. Valverde, R.: Principles of human computer interaction design. Lambert Acad. Books, 1–113 (2011). https://www.researchgate.net/publication/280689716_Principles_of_Human_Computer_Interaction_Design
16. Wu, C., Yu, D., Doherty, A., Zhang, T., Kust, L., Luo, G.: An investigation of perceived vehicle speed from a driver's perspective. PLoS ONE **12**(10), 1–11 (2017). https://doi.org/10.1371/journal.pone.0185347
17. Nawaz, A.: A comparison of card-sorting analysis methods. In: Proceedings of 10th Asia Pacific Conference on Computer Human Interaction, pp. 583–592 (2012). http://openarchive.cbs.dk/handle/10398/8587
18. Strategy, A.D., Behavior, H., Young, I., Veen, J.: Aligning Design Strategy with Human Behavior How to Use this Book (2008)
19. Volkamer, M., Renaud, K.: Mental models – general introduction and review of their application to human-centred security. In: Fischlin, M., Katzenbeisser, S. (eds.) Number Theory and Cryptography. LNCS, vol. 8260, pp. 255–280. Springer, Heidelberg (2013). https://doi.org/10.1007/978-3-642-42001-6_18
20. Mohamedally, D., Zaphiris, P., Petrie, H.: A web based tool for HCI-orientated massive asynchronous linear card sorting. In: Proceedings of British HCI Conference, (Volume 2), vol. 2, pp. 99–103 (2003)
21. Dong, J., Martin, S., Waldo, P.: A user input and analysis tool for information architecture. In: Conference on Human Factors in Computing Systems - Proceedings, pp. 23–24 (2001). https://doi.org/10.1145/634067.634085
22. Boström, A., Ramström, F.: Head-up display for enhanced user experience department of applied information technology (2014)
23. Drummond, A.E.: An overview of novice driver performance issues, p. 55 (1989)

Emotional Design for In-Vehicle Infotainment Systems: An Exploratory Co-design Study

Siyuan Zhou[1], Ruiheng Lan[1], Xu Sun[1,2](✉), Jiming Bai[1], Yaorun Zhang[1], and Xiaowu Jiang[3]

[1] Faculty of Science and Engineering, University of Nottingham Ningbo China, 199 Taikang East Road, Ningbo 315100, China
{siyuan.zhou,xu.sun,jiming.bai,yaorun.zhang}@nottingham.edu.cn

[2] Nottingham Ningbo China Beacons of Excellence Research and Innovation Institute, 211 Xingguang Road, Ningbo 315101, China

[3] Ningbo Weizhi Digital Information Technology Co., Ltd., Building E, 655 Xueshi Road, Ningbo 315194, China
jxw@weizhiai.cn

Abstract. As increasingly complex in-vehicle infotainment systems (IVIS) are available in the automotive marketplace, there is a growing tendency to move from usability to user experience, the latter emphasizing more strongly the importance of users' emotions during system design. Emotions have long been recognized as cognitive processes that affect decision making, perception, and attention. Recent literature reveals that design based on emotions can influence the overall user experience of interacting with IVIS. Therefore, this paper presents an exploratory co-design study aimed at identifying the emotional needs of car occupants (particularly for passengers inside the vehicle) and potential directions for the design of future passenger targeted IVIS. 16 participants were invited to participate in the co-design process, which mainly included the sessions of brainstorming and concept generation. The results showed that emotional design plays a vital role in user engagement with IVIS. In line with Norman's emotional design model, a thematic network was constructed to illustrate how the visceral, behavioral, and reflective levels of mental processing can be supported and enhanced by the appropriate emotional design of passenger targeted IVIS.

Keywords: In-vehicle infotainment systems · Emotional design · Interfaces

1 Introduction

In-vehicle infotainment systems (IVIS) constitute an important part of automotive human-machine interfaces (HMIs) that serve to offer a range of information and entertainment services (e.g., navigation, media, and radio) to occupants inside the vehicle [1]. Since the driver is often the primary user of the vehicle, most of the existing IVIS is driver-targeted and designed with driving safety as a foremost consideration, whereas neglecting the needs and interests of front and rear-seat passengers [2, 3]. Only certain

H. Krömker (Ed.): HCII 2022, LNCS 13335, pp. 326–336, 2022.
https://doi.org/10.1007/978-3-031-04987-3_22

types of luxury cars (e.g., BMW 7 series) are equipped with dedicated rear-seat infotainment systems for delivering tailored information and entertainment content to backseat passengers [2]. As the car of the near future will assume the role of a digital companion rather than merely a means of transportation, there has been a growing interest in recent years in enhancing the in-car interaction from the passenger perspective among designers, researchers, and car manufacturers worldwide [1–3]. For instance, a study by Sen and Sener [1] used virtual reality (VR) as an experience prototyping tool to investigate how the IVIS design can potentially empower front-seat passengers during their luxury car journeys. They also identified several design recommendations based on *why*, *what*, and *how* levels of interactions to further address user concerns and expectations. Additionally, Berger, et al. [3] proposed a new design concept of a car door that can present essential information (e.g., points of interest) on the sidecar window and door panel through the use of augmented reality (AR) technology. This concept helps to improve the user experience (UX) of rear-seat passengers by engaging them more fully with their surroundings. Although these studies provide valuable insights into possible strategies for enriching the in-car experience for passengers, the emotional design aspects of IVIS interfaces have not yet been adequately considered.

Design based on emotions is vital for shaping the overall passenger experience of interacting with IVIS because emotions have the power to influence decision making, perception, and attention [4, 5]. In general, the emotional design includes a range of pleasant or engaging features that help evoke and amplify pleasure, while also considering the need to sense and respond to the emotional states of users [5]. A well-recognized model describing how the principles of emotional psychology can be applied to the design of innovative products and technologies is the emotional design theory by Norman [6], which comprises three different but interconnected levels of mental processing, namely visceral, behavioral, and reflective. The visceral level performs ingrained and automatic determination of responses that are primarily biologically oriented [7]. Secondly, the behavioral level emphasizes the controlled aspects of human action in response to patterns of information [6]. Regarding the highest layer of the brain, the reflective level is viewed as "the home of reflection, of conscious thought, of the learning of new concepts and generalizations about the world" (p. 23) [6]. These three levels are closely linked and influence each other.

In line with Norman's theoretical model, the design of passenger targeted IVIS should carefully consider the visceral, behavioral, and reflective levels of emotional processing to elicit positive experiences for car occupants (particularly for front and rear-seat passengers). On this basis, the current study attempts to focus on the emotional aspects of IVIS design and adopt a user-centered approach to exploring the emotional needs of users, as well as envisioning how the future IVIS might look like.

2 Methods

Co-design was employed in this study due to its advantages in improving idea generation and innovation, as well as facilitating multi-disciplinary cooperation [8]. The workshop intended to bring together the insights of participants to inspire the design process for better understanding the emotional needs of car occupants (particularly from the perspective of passengers) that may be overlooked in the current IVIS design and exploring their design preferences. There were two major activities in the co-design process. The first session was brainstorming, in which different ideas and thoughts related to the emotional needs of potential IVIS users were generated and collected both individually and by the group. The second step was concept generation, where all participants were asked to choose from among the creative ideas of themselves and others and to identify several possible directions for the design of future passenger targeted IVIS at the emotional level.

2.1 Participants

The study consisted of 16 participants (10 male, 6 female) ranging in age from 21 to 45 years (M = 27.50 years, SD = 7.57 years) with different backgrounds, such as engineering, computer science, design, and human factors. The study population was relatively young as it mainly recruited university students in China as participants due to the effect of the Covid-19 pandemic. This study was approved by the Research Ethics Committee at the University of Nottingham Ningbo China. Written informed consent was completed by each participant before taking part in the co-design activities.

2.2 Procedure

An overview of the study procedure is given in Fig. 1. First, participants were welcomed by the researcher and briefly informed about the aim and protocol of the study. Then we explained to the participants how Norman's three levels of emotional processing work. All participants signed an informed consent form and filled out a demographic questionnaire. In the second stage, participants were directed to recall their experiences as car occupants either in the front or rear seat, with an emphasis on the link between IVIS design and emotions at the visceral, behavioral, and reflective levels. A total of 16 participants were then evenly divided into four groups and asked to brainstorm possible strategies to support their emotional well-being during car journeys in small groups by following Norman's theory. Furthermore, we instructed participants to think divergently and generate as many ideas as possible (mainly in textual form) without judgement according to their personal experience and knowledge. This allows for the gathering of a great variety of thoughts and ideas about the user-preferred design of future IVIS from three different layers of emotional responses. The next activity was concept generation. Participants were encouraged to discuss and share their insights on the emotional design of IVIS with group members, and then chose one or several preferred ideas from a set of proposed design solutions for further concept development. Lastly, after identifying potential design directions by the group, we required each participant to create a design concept for future passenger targeted IVIS.

2.3 Data Analysis

Thematic network analysis was employed for data interpretation in this study. This method helps to recognize patterns and summarize the main themes in textual data [9]. Firstly, visual information (e.g., a rough sketch of the design concept) collected

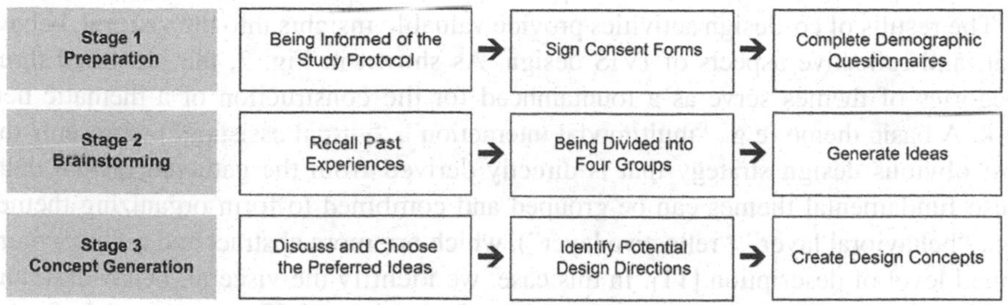

Fig. 1. Overview of the study procedure

from the brainstorming and concept generation sessions were transformed into textual data, such as by using keywords to describe its major design features. Then all text information gathered from 16 participants was dissected into meaningful text segments. We attempted to interpret and organize these text segments into three categories of themes as guided by the principles of thematic analysis: (i) basic theme; (ii) organizing theme; iii) global theme [10]. The literature was also reviewed to provide theoretical support for the rationale behind each theme.

3 Results and Discussion

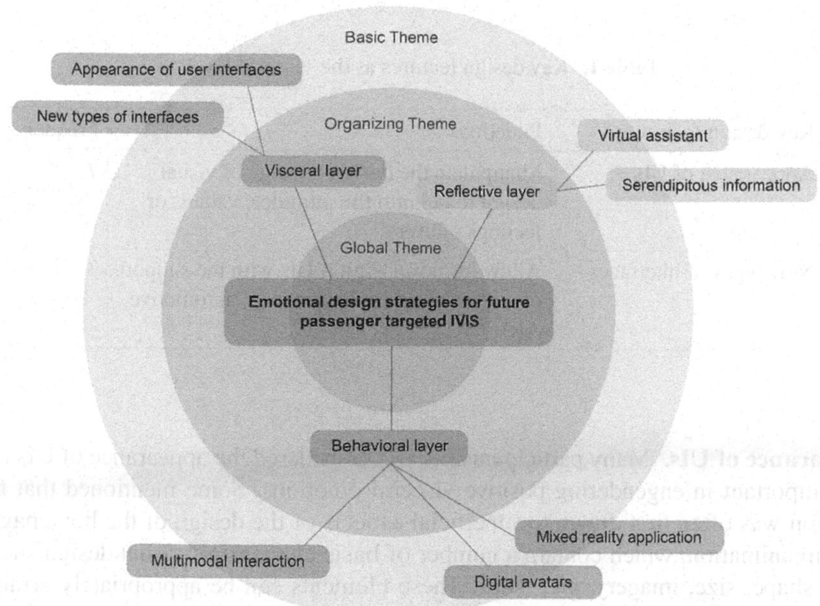

Fig. 2. A thematic network of emotional design strategies for IVIS

The results of co-design activities provide valuable insights into the visceral, behavioral, and reflective aspects of IVIS design. As shown in Fig. 2, the identified three categories of themes serve as a fountainhead for the construction of a thematic network. A basic theme (e.g., "multimodal interaction", "virtual assistant") represents the most obvious design strategy that is directly derived from the gathered textual data. These fundamental themes can be grouped and combined to form organizing themes (e.g., "behavioral layer", "reflective layer"), which are more abstract and reflect a more refined level of description [11]. In this case, we identify the visceral, behavioral, and reflective levels of design as organizing themes in accord with Norman's model of emotions [6]. Lastly, the global theme (e.g., "emotional design strategies for future passenger targeted IVIS") condenses the overarching point of the text into a single statement, and it also functions as the core of this thematic network [10].

3.1 Visceral Design

The visceral layer of emotional design is typically governed by the perceptible qualities of IVIS interfaces, such as their physical features and appearance [6]. It is capable of triggering immediate emotional impact so that IVIS users are likely to experience certain types of visceral emotions based on what they have seen at first glance [7]. In this sense, effective visceral design should be pleasant and attractive to car occupants before their first interaction with IVIS. The findings revealed that the appearance of user interfaces (UIs) and new types of interfaces are two crucial design features at the visceral level (see Table 1).

Table 1. Key design features at the visceral level.

	Key design features	Functions	Frequency
1	Appearance of UIs	Manipulate the basic elements of visual design to tap into the attitudes, values, or feelings of users	7
2	New types of interfaces	Allow for novel digital UIs with the support of advanced technologies (e.g., automotive AR)	3

Appearance of UIs. Many participants (n = 7) considered the appearance of UIs to be very important in engendering positive visceral emotions. Some mentioned that their attention was often first drawn to superficial aspects of the design of the homepage or start-up animation, which contain a number of basic elements of visual design such as color, shape, size, imagery, and icons. These elements can be appropriately arranged and adjusted to tap into the attitudes, values, or feelings of IVIS users, thus eliciting specific types of emotional responses [5]. For instance, this may be achieved by using warm colors (e.g., red and orange) to evoke positive emotions (e.g., joy and hope), or using pictures of nature to bring a sense of relaxation and calmness [6]. Furthermore, some of the visual design elements (e.g., color and imagery) in IVIS interfaces are also expected to be able to change automatically along with the shifts in the emotional states of car occupants.

New Types of Interfaces. It was found that the visceral responses of IVIS users may also be motivated by new types of interfaces, such as using holographic projection, or AR technologies. Three participants pointed out the role of novel HMIs in their first impression of the appeal of IVIS. As stated by a participated student, the provision of immersive 3D continuous depth displays inside the vehicle could engage him more actively, as well as encourage greater enthusiasm and interest in the use of IVIS in comparison with the traditional 2D screens. Additionally, recent studies highlighted the potential of adopting AR head-up displays (HUDs) and windshield displays (WSDs) in the design of future IVIS [12, 13]. It is worth noting that as in-vehicle interfaces become increasingly digital, there will be a transition away from hardware-intensive UIs (including buttons and sliders) toward novel tailored virtual UIs, which may greatly change driver and passenger experiences [12].

3.2 Behavioral Design

Design at the behavioral level focuses on the pleasure and effectiveness of use in the interaction with IVIS [6]. Designers should be particularly aware of how users perceive and respond to the usability and functionality of the system in this layer [6]. For instance, behavioral design may attempt to address how quickly and effectively users can complete tasks, and how well they can achieve desired goals [14]. According to the results gained from the co-design practices, three new and interesting design features deserve attention in the behavioral level of emotional design: multimodal interaction, digital avatars, and mixed reality (MR) application (see Table 2).

Multimodal Interaction. The IVIS featuring multimodal interfaces is reported as an essential element for emotional design at the behavioral level. Half of the participants (n = 8) shared their desire to use multimodal interaction (e.g., gesture recognition, and possibly gaze awareness) in their future journeys. Some of them explained that multiple modalities will enable a more natural and effective interaction, thus allowing them to process information via IVIS with less conscious effort. The literature also suggests a number of benefits associated with multimodal interaction, such as permitting more flexible use of input modes [15, 16], as well as accommodating a broader range of users, tasks, and contexts [17]. Car occupants should typically experience positive emotions when their goals can be better accomplished by multimodal systems. However, there may be a concern that certain alternative modalities have the potential to increase the cognitive load of passengers in use [16]. The issues related to cognitive load in multimodal in-car interaction deserve to be further considered in the IVIS design.

Digital Avatars. Passengers are likely to feel more engaged, as mentioned by several participants (n = 6) in this study if they can create digital avatars that highly resemble their likeness in IVIS. Avatars are seen as visual representations of the car occupants themselves in virtual communities [18]. It is noteworthy that younger generations often

Table 2. Key design features at the behavioral level.

	Key design features	Functions	Frequency
1	Multimodal interaction	Facilitate a more natural and effective interaction, as well as reducing the conscious effort needed to process information	8
2	Digital avatars	Enable the visual representations of car occupants in virtual environments for social communication	6
		Visualize the real-time emotions of car occupants on the interfaces	3
		Inform the front-seat passenger about the changing emotional state of the vulnerable individual in the rear seat for better caring	1
3	MR application	Allow for immersive gaming and entertainment experiences	10
		Help build a personal and private virtual space	2

prefer the avatar representation and perceive it as a digital approach to expressing themselves authentically and freely online [19]. A potential future scenario is, therefore, envisioned in which passengers may appear as digital avatars and socially connect with people who can provide assistance or company in the so-called *Metaverse* virtual world during the car journey. Previous studies [20, 21] have shown evidence that the use of avatars is able to facilitate interaction and communication in online environments.

Another anticipated advantage of IVIS is the capability to recognize and visualize the real-time emotions of car occupants on interfaces. Figure 3 provides an example of the visual representation of affective states by facial expressions of digital avatars. This means that the virtual avatars on the screen will mimic the emotions of car occupants and show the corresponding facial expressions once the system accurately detects their emotions. Furthermore, when there are vulnerable groups of people (e.g., the elderly or children) sitting in the rear seat of a vehicle, one participant highlighted the need to inform the front-seat passenger about the changing emotional state of the backseat passenger for caring purposes. As illustrated in Fig. 4, for example, the anxiety of a child in the rear seat is detected and recognized, then this information will be delivered to the front-seat passenger, such as by adjusting the facial expression of the avatar to indicate her anxious emotional state on the HMI.

MR Application. Since MR technology allows a smooth blend of the physical and digital environments, the integration of MR into the IVIS design (e.g., through the use of MR headsets) can potentially add value to the in-car experience [22]. As anticipated by a majority of participants (n = 10) in this workshop, on the one hand, MR will enable immersive gaming and entertainment during their everyday travel. On the other hand, two participants also indicated that MR experiences may help create a personal and

Fig. 3. The visual representation of emotional states by facial expression of avatars

Fig. 4. The avatar representation of the anxious emotional state of a rear-seat passenger

private virtual space that is not penetrated by others in the car journey. These benefits offered by MR are considered important for the emotional wellbeing of passengers, such as its contribution to stress reduction outside the workplace [23]. Nevertheless, there are still many challenges associated with the adoption and usage of MR in the automotive context, including the problems of motion sickness, inattentional blindness, and technological limitations [22]. These challenges should be carefully managed to take full advantage of MR applications in the IVIS design.

3.3 Reflective Design

The third level is reflective, which represents the conscious thought layer [6]. It suggests that users tend to interact with and interpret IVIS design based on their reasoning process (e.g., placing multiple meanings and values on design features) at this stage [14]. Because the overall impact of a system usually comes through reflection on direct experience (i.e., in retrospective memory and reassessment) [6], the reflective level is highly important for the appeal of IVIS and occupies the paramount position in Norman's emotional design model. Two main design characteristics have been identified in this layer: virtual assistant and serendipitous information (see Table 3).

Table 3. Key design features at the reflective level.

	Key design features	Functions	Frequency
1	Virtual assistant	Act as a human companion capable of understanding and reacting appropriately to the emotional needs of IVIS users	5
2	Serendipitous information	Provide users with a wide range of novel, relevant, and unexpected content based on their personal interests and preferences	12

Virtual Assistant. A number of participants (n = 5) viewed the inclusion of the virtual in-vehicle assistant as a promising strategy to enhance their reflective aspects of emotional experience. The virtual assistant in the future is envisioned as a human companion capable of understanding and reacting properly to the emotional needs of car occupants, rather than merely as a technical assistant. For instance, the communication style and content of a virtual assistant may be tailored more flexibly to the different emotional needs of IVIS users. Moreover, in a recent study by Strohmann, et al. [24], the authors shed light on the need for the in-vehicle virtual assistant to perform proactive behaviors (e.g., using context-aware technology to determine when and how to communicate) to prevent users from unpleasant circumstances during the interaction phase. These features are likely to help cultivate a long-term friendly relationship between IVIS and its users [24].

Serendipitous Information. Design for serendipity in digital information environments was desired by most participants (n = 12) in our study. This means that the process of information acquisition via IVIS should emphasize more on serendipitous encountering. For example, a future infotainment system is expected to be capable of recommending novel, relevant, and unexpected content (e.g., about music, videos, or point of interests) that takes into account the individual preferences of car occupants (especially for front and rear-seat passengers) to avoid repetition and boredom during the journey [25, 26]. Past research has demonstrated that serendipitous suggestions play a significant role in improving user engagement with the system [25, 27]. Given that some positive emotions (e.g., joy and interest) do not last long and may disappear after the first several encounters with IVIS, it is essential to promote serendipity in recommendations, thereby allowing IVIS users to have positive emotional experiences for longer periods [5].

4 Conclusion

In conclusion, this paper presented an exploratory co-design study to identify user needs and possible design directions for future passenger targeted IVIS. By following the emotional design theory of Norman [6], we constructed a thematic network consisting of basic, organizing, and global themes to demonstrate how the emotional experiences of car occupants (particularly for passengers in the car) can be improved at the visceral, behavioral, and reflective levels. The functionalities and content offered by the proposed design strategies are primarily for information, entertainment, and communication purposes. Despite the relatively small sample size, the outcome of this study still provides interesting insights to both automotive manufacturers and researchers for further understanding the emotional needs and design preferences of potential IVIS users. Future studies may extend this research by including a more diverse and larger sample (e.g., considering the views of car occupants with different demographics in terms of age, occupation, and education) to allow for greater generalizability of the results.

Furthermore, the findings of this study may also have implications for the future passenger experience in highly and fully automated vehicles. Since the role of human drivers will shift from an operator to a front-seat passenger with the introduction of automated driving systems, most of the gained insights associated with the emotional needs of passengers are still applicable in the context of automated vehicles. However, some features of IVIS design may require to be modified and adapted to automated driving scenarios, such as the need to support the take-over process for passengers in emotional terms, particularly when they engage in non-driving secondary tasks.

References

1. Sen, G., Sener, B.: Design for luxury front-seat passenger infotainment systems with experience prototyping through VR. Int. J. Hum.-Comput. Interact. **36**(18), 1714–1733 (2020)
2. Berger, M., Bernhaupt., R., Pfleging, B.: A tactile interaction concept for in-car passenger infotainment systems. In: Proceedings of the 11th International Conference on Automotive User Interfaces and Interactive Vehicular Applications, pp. 109–114. ACM Press, Utrecht, Netherlands (2019)
3. Berger, M., Dandekar, A., Bernhaupt, R., Pfleging, B.: An AR-enabled interactive car door to extend in-car infotainment systems for rear seat passengers. In: Extended Abstracts of the 2021 CHI Conference on Human Factors in Computing Systems, pp. 1–6. ACM Press, Yokohama, Japan (2021)
4. Van Gorp, T., Adams, E.: Design for Emotion. Elsevier, Waltham (2012)
5. Triberti, S., Chirico, A., La Rocca, G., Riva, G.: Developing emotional design: emotions as cognitive processes and their role in the design of interactive technologies. Front. Psychol. **8**, 1773 (2017)
6. Norman, D.A.: Emotional Design: Why We Love (or Hate) Everyday Things. Basic Books, New York (2004)

7. Norman, D.A.: Emotion and design: attractive things work better. Interact. Mag. **9**(4), 36–42 (2002)
8. Steen, M., Manschot, M., De Koning, N.: Benefits of co-design in service design projects. Int. J. Des. **5**(2), 53–60 (2011)
9. Melo, C.D.O., Cruzes, D.S., Kon, F., Conradi, R.: Interpretative case studies on agile team productivity and management. Inf. Softw. Technol. **55**(2), 412–427 (2013)
10. Hanington, B., Martin, B.: Universal Methods of Design. Rockport Publishers, Beverly (2012)
11. Attride-Stirling, J.: Thematic networks: an analytic tool for qualitative research. Qual. Res. **1**(3), 385–405 (2001)
12. Riegler, A., Riener, A., Holzmann, C.: Augmented reality for future mobility: insights from a literature review and HCI workshop. I-com **20**(3), 295–318 (2021)
13. Murali, P.K., Kaboli, M., Dahiya, R.: Intelligent in-vehicle interaction technologies. Adv. Intell. Syst. (2021)
14. Zolkifly, N.H., Baharom, S.N.: Selling cars through visual merchandising: proposing emotional design approach. Procedia Econ. Financ. **37**, 412–417 (2016)
15. Lee, G., Kim, S., Choe, J., Jung, E.S.: The effects of multi-modality on the use of smart phones. J. Ergon. Soc. Korea **33**(3), 241–253 (2014)
16. Turk, M.: Multimodal interaction: a review. Pattern Recognit. Lett. **36**, 189–195 (2014)
17. Schnelle-Walka, D., McGee, D.R., Pfleging, B.: Multimodal interaction in automotive applications. J. Multimodal User Interf. **13**(2), 53–54 (2019). https://doi.org/10.1007/s12193-019-00295-x
18. Oh, S.Y., Bailenson, J., Krämer, N., Li, B.: Let the avatar brighten your smile: effects of enhancing facial expressions in virtual environments. PloS One **11**(9), e0161794 (2016)
19. Choi, T.R., Sung, Y.: Instagram versus Snapchat: self-expression and privacy concern on social media. Telemat. Inform. **35**(8), 2289–2298 (2018)
20. Hart, J.D., Piumsomboon, T., Lee, G.A., Smith, R.T., Billinghurst, M.: Manipulating avatars for enhanced communication in extended reality. In: 2021 IEEE International Conference on Intelligent Reality, pp. 9–16. IEEE, virtual event (2021)
21. Messinger, P.R., Ge, X., Smirnov, K., Stroulia, E., Lyons, K.: Reflections of the extended self: visual self-representation in avatar-mediated environments. J. Bus. Res. **100**, 531–546 (2019)
22. Riegler, A., Riener, A., Holzmann, C.: A research agenda for mixed reality in automated vehicles. In: 19th International Conference on Mobile and Ubiquitous Multimedia, pp.119–131. ACM Press, Essen, Germany (2020)
23. McGill, M., Williamson, J., Ng, A., Pollick, F., Brewster, S.: Challenges in passenger user of mixed reality headsets in cars and other transportation. Virtual Real. **24**(4), 583–603 (2020)
24. Strohmann, T., Siemon, D., Robra-Bissantz, S.: Designing virtual in-vehicle assistants: design guidelines for creating a convincing user experience. AIS Trans. Hum.-Comput. Interact. **11**(2), 54–78 (2019)
25. Kotkov, D., Wang, S., Veijalainen, J.: A survey of serendipity in recommender systems. Knowl. Based Syst. **111**, 180–192 (2016)
26. Sun, X., Sharples, S., Makri, S.: A user-centered mobile diary study approach to understanding serendipity in information research. Inf. Res. **16**(3), 1–22 (2011)
27. Oh, J., Sudarshan, S., Lee, J.A., Yu, N.: Serendipity enhances user engagement and sociality perception: the combinatory effect of serendipitous movie suggestions and user motivations. Behav. Inf. Technol. (2021). https://doi.org/10.1080/0144929X.2021.1921027

Studies on Automated Driving

Watch Out Car, He's Drunk! How Passengers of Vehicles Perceive Risky Crossing Situations Based on Situational Parameters

Valeria Bopp-Bertenbreiter[1](✉), Sabina Bähr[1], Simon Albrecht[2], Thomas Freudenmann[3], Mohanad El-Haji[3], Manuel Martin[4], Natalya Anh[5], and Stephan Rauber[5]

[1] University of Stuttgart, Nobelstr. 12, 70569 Stuttgart, Germany
valeria.bopp-bertenbreiter@iat.uni-stuttgart.de

[2] Fraunhofer IAO, Nobelstr. 12, 70569 Stuttgart, Germany

[3] EDI GmbH – Engineering Data Intelligence, Wöschbacherstr. 73, 76327 Karlsruhe, Germany

[4] Fraunhofer IOSB, Fraunhoferstr. 1, 76131 Karlsruhe, Germany

[5] IPG Automotive GmbH, Bannwaldallee 60, 76185 Karlsruhe, Germany

Abstract. Automated vehicles promise enhanced road safety for their passengers, other vehicles, and vulnerable road user (VRU). To do so, automated vehicles must be designed to reliably detect potentially critical situations [1]. Humans can detect such situations using context cues. Context cues allow humans drivers to anticipate unexpected crossings, e.g., of intoxicated night owls in a street full of bars and clubs on a Friday night and, consequently, to decelerate in advance to prevent critical incidents [2].

We used the "Incident Detector" to identify possible context cues that human drivers might use to assess the criticality of traffic situations in which a car encounters a VRU [3]. Investigated potential predictors include VRUs' mode of transport, VRUs' speed, VRUs' age, VRUs' predictability of behavior, and visibility obstruction of VRUs by parked cars.

In an online study, 133 participants watched videos of potentially risky crossing situations with VRUs from the driver's point of view. In addition, the participants' age, gender, status of driver's license, sense of presence, and driving style were queried.

The results show that perceived risk correlates significantly with age, speed, and predictability of VRUs behavior, as well as with visibility obstruction and participants' age. We will use the results to include detected influence factors on perceived subjective risk into virtual test scenarios. Automated vehicles will need to pass these virtual test scenarios to be deemed acceptable regarding objective and subjective risk. These test scenarios can support road safety and thus, greater acceptance of automated vehicles.

Keywords: Driver behavior modeling · Realistic traffic flow simulation · Active safety systems · Autonomous driving and ADAS algorithms · Dynamic Risk Management · Safety Cushion Time

H. Krömker (Ed.): HCII 2022, LNCS 13335, pp. 339–354, 2022.
https://doi.org/10.1007/978-3-031-04987-3_23

1 Introduction

Automated driving provides a promising approach to increase road safety (e.g., see Vision Zero [4]). Pedestrians and cyclists (vulnerable road users; VRU) might profit in particular, as VRUs are currently at increased risk of accidents in urban areas where they share road space with motor vehicles [5]: Pedestrians make up about 17% and cyclists about 6% of all traffic fatalities in the EU, although distribution varies widely between countries [5]. Human error is the common cause of accidents and is responsible for 88.4% of all traffic accidents with personal injury in Germany [6], e.g., due to excessive speed or distraction. Automated vehicles (AV) can make a decisive contribution here, as even low levels of automation can reduce traffic fatalities [7].

To develop towards fully AV, an integrated approach must consider the interaction of humans, environment, and vehicles [8]. AV must be able to detect potentially critical situations, especially situations involving VRU [1, 2]. In addition, AV must adopt context-based and expectation-compliant driving behaviors [2], giving people both an objective and subjective sense of safety [1]. Experienced human drivers use cues from infrastructure and behavior of VRUs to assess the criticality of a potentially risky situation. This is called "hazard-anticipatory driving" [3]. Therefore, this work investigates which influence factors human drivers currently use to assess the criticality of a situation involving crossing VRUs. We aim to use this study's results to design test scenarios involving VRUs. AV need to pass these test scenarios to be considered safe [2]. The aim of this study is to analyze which parameters increase perceived risk of a situation involving a crossing VRU from the driver's perspective.

2 Related Work

2.1 Objective and Subjective Risk in Traffic

Any mobility in road traffic involves risks [9]. While different sciences interpret the concept of risk differently; risk is generally distinguished into two perspectives: the objective and the subjective risk [10].

The quantitative, objective, and technical view, defines risk as the product of the probability of occurrence of an event and the amount of damage [11]. In real-world driving situations, collision risk assessment is often performed using the Time-to-Collision (TTC) approach [12]. Haywards defines TTC as the time until a collisions occurs if two vehicles continue on the same course without changes in speed [13]. Another approach for the dynamic assessment of risk in traffic situations is the Safety Cushion Time. The Safety Cushion Time includes current vehicle-VRU distance, vehicle speed, and system reaction time [1].

In the second, more psychosocial, subjective view, risk and the associated risk perception focus on values, personal attitudes, and social, political, and cultural influences [10]. Literature assesses subjective risk using statements on perceived safety in combination with Likert-scales [14], answers to open questions on risk assessment [14], qualitative data derived from interview responses [15] or numeric scales [16]. In traffic, subjective and objective safety may not coincide naturally [17].

Regarding the future mobility of AVs current research rather focuses on the technical development of AVs than on the interaction of vehicles and VRUs [8]. While this may enhance objective safety, AV users and other road users must feel safe subjectively, too [18]. For example, an experienced, considerate driver passing by a kindergarten in the morning might slow down, anticipating children could cross the street based on time and place. The driver carries out a dynamic risk assessment [1, 3]. The driver estimates the probability of a possible unpleasant scenario and takes measures to prevent a possible critical situation, for example by reducing vehicle speed or acceleration [3]. This context-based anticipation, and associated dynamic risk assessment, is a skill AVs must master to be acceptable. Test procedures to certify AVs function safety should therefore audit this skill [2, 3].

2.2 Towards Virtual Test Scenarios for Automated Vehicles

To test whether autonomous driving functions react correctly and safely to critical situations, the project "RELAI – Risk Estimation with a Learning AI" was founded in which the following study is integrated [2]. It aims at generating virtual safety test scenarios for AVs which incorporate the expectations of both passengers and VRU [2]. RELAI uses Machine Learning, namely the "Incident Detector", to find situations that led to intense braking of human drivers (see Fig. 1). We thus assume that human drivers assessed these situations as risky [2].

Fig. 1. Crossing situation involving a child, from driver's point of view.

We used data from the Near-Miss Incident Data Base to train the Incident Detector. The Near-Miss Incident Data Base includes data on risky situations in traffic (video sequences, vehicle dynamics and position, and driver interventions from tachographs in more than 200 cabs in Japan [1]). Whenever the longitudinal acceleration of these cabs exceeded a certain threshold, a dashcam recorded the situation.

Trained raters from the Tokyo University of Agriculture and Technology labeled the data regarding general conditions and driving context, and rated the criticality of the event manually [1].

We used the Incident Detector to make first assumptions about which contextual cues human drivers use to rate situations as risky. The video snippets only comprise of snapshots in time and do not cover drivers' reasoning for subjective risk assessment. To contribute to the state of the art, this work investigates which of the following potential influence factors affect perceived subjective risk assessment in an encounter of a crossing VRU.

2.3 Potential Influence Factors on Perceived Risk of Crossing Situations

Based on the empirical data provided by the Incident Detector and the TUAT data, we assume that the following factors may have an influence on risk perception:

Age of VRUs. The age of VRUs appears to play a critical factor in subjective risk perception. Several studies have showed that children behave differently from adults due to their not yet fully developed cognitive and motor skills as well as visual and acoustic perception [19, 20]. Divided and selective attention develops gradually during childhood. Therefore, the ability of children to distinguish safe from dangerous traffic situations enhances with age [21]. We assume that experienced drivers are aware of these behavioral patterns and include them in their risk assessment.

Visibility of Traffic Situation. Traffic accidents involving pedestrians and bicyclists occur due to limited visibility [22]. Particularly at intersections and junctions, visibility of the oncoming traffic situation is limited. Another obstruction of visibility for road users results from parked vehicles on the side of the road. Thus, the vehicle user might see children and smaller adults intending to cross the road between parked vehicles rather poorly or late [23]. Unfavorable weather and lighting conditions also influence the frequency of accidents, which increases the potential risk [24].

Predictability of Behavior. Unpredictable behavior of children may result in more accidents [20]. Predicting the behavior of other road users is also crucial for road safety and for crash free coexistence. If a pedestrian is distracted (e.g., by using a smartphone), their attention and situational awareness for the traffic situation are reduced [25]. Distracted pedestrians often change their walking direction [26]. At the same time, anticipating the VRUs behavior may become more difficult, which can lead to a potentially risky situation.

Speed of VRUs. A variety of factors determine the speed of VRU. According to Tian et al. [27], when vehicles have the right of way or when the vehicle is approaching, pedestrians tend to cross the street at a higher walking speed.

Older pedestrians tend to walk slower [28] and female pedestrians cross the street more slowly than males [28, 29]. Pedestrians in larger groups walk slower when crossing a road [28, 30], and road conditions also affect pedestrians' speed [28].

2.4 Hypotheses

The following hypotheses investigate the research question *"Which potential contextual triggers affect subjective risk assessment of a crossing situation from the driver's point of view?"*. This work investigates the following hypotheses based on potential influence factors on subjective risk assessment described above:

1. H1: Traffic situations in which a child crosses the road are perceived as more dangerous than when an adult person crosses the road.
2. H2: Traffic situations in which a VRU appears between parked cars are perceived as more dangerous than situations in which visibility on approaching VRU is not blocked.
3. H3: The lower the predictability of the VRUs behavior, the higher the perceived subjective risk.

Furthermore, in an exploratory approach, the following research questions are investigated:

- Exploratory question 1: Is the speed of the pedestrian or cyclist related to a higher risk perception?
- Exploratory question 2: Is there a significant difference between risk perception in traffic situations involving a bicyclist compared to situations involving a pedestrian?
- Exploratory question 3: Are children emerging from behind parked cars seen later by the driver than adults?

3 Method

The following sections describe the user study in detail, including the design, the preparation of the scenarios assessed in the study as well as the procedure of conducting the study and its statistical analysis.

3.1 Study Design

This study uses a between-subjects design investigate hypotheses and to allow for an appropriate duration of the test runs. We conducted the study as online study, in which participants assess several scenarios in the form of videos. Online studies allow to reach a variety of participants in a time efficient manner [31] and are safe to conduct in times of a pandemic.

The study investigates the following *predictor variables* (see Table 1):

Table 1. Predictors varied for the videos of scenarios of a crossing situation between automated vehicle and vulnerable road user.

Means of Transport	Age Group	Speed of VRU	Predictability of VRU	Cars at the Roadside
Pedestrian	Child	Middle (5,4 km/h)	Low	Yes
Cyclist	Adult	High (10,8 km/h)	Medium	No
			High	

The combination of predictor manifestations results in $2 \times 2 \times 2 \times 3 \times 2 = 48$ possible scenarios. As *outcome variable*, participants assessed the perceived risk of the respective situation on a scale from 0 (*not dangerous at all*) to 10 (*extremely dangerous*). The participants also rated control variables as described in the materials section.

3.2 Materials

The following section describes the materials utilized in the study and how we prepared and selected these materials.

Preparation: How to Create and Vary Videos Based on Real-World Traffic Data. This section describes how we derived scenarios from real-world traffic data, transferred them into simulated scenarios, varied the manifestations of the predictor variables, validated the scenarios, and then used the scenarios in an online study.

First of all, we assessed the TUAT data from Japanese cab drivers that experienced risky situations using the Incident Detector algorithm of project RELAI [1, 3]. This allowed us to identify the most critical situations in traffic involving VRU and these scenarios' infrastructural setting as well as potential influence factors.

We then selected a test field for autonomous driving in Germany ("Testfeld Autonomes Fahren") for transfer of the situations into virtual test scenarios. We manually coded data from publicly available map data such as OpenStreetMap[1] and Google Maps[2] to assess the risk level in the test field based on infrastructural parameters. We inspected the test field by foot to fill in missing data, e.g., on crosswalks, turn lanes, and bicycle lanes, and to ensure that data were current.

Based on this assessment, we selected a route where infrastructure would allow the three most common critical incidents derived from the TUAT to happen. These situations primarily related to interactions between vehicles and VRUs, such as pedestrians or cyclists. Thus, we chose a route where encounters of vehicles and VRUs were likely due to infrastructure (e.g., restaurants, bicycle lanes) and where variation were probable

[1] https://www.openstreetmap.org/#map=5/51.330/10.453, last checked on 08 February 2022.

[2] https://www.google.de/maps, last checked on 08 February 2022.

(e.g., due to number of persons walking by and parking spaces). We then searched for infrastructure matching the three most relevant basic scenarios in the test field using Google Maps. Project partners familiar to the locations confirmed the match.

We transferred the resulting basic scenarios into the driving simulation software SILAB 6.5 [32] using bird's eye view pictures of the locations, by manually replicating the locations in the scenario editor of the simulation software (see Fig. 2). We choose one scenario for the online study, because occurrence of cyclists and pedestrians seemed most natural in this situation. We then varied and implemented predictor variables. In a last step, we validated the scenarios with experts who had seen various videos of critical situations from TUAT data to ensure realistic variations of parameters. We then created videos of the scenarios to enable systematic testing in the online study.

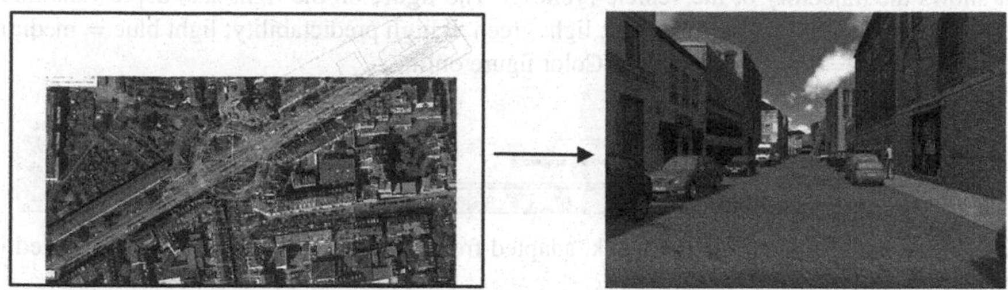

Fig. 2. Replication of a real-world location from Testfeld Autonomes Fahren, Germany (2a, left) that provided infrastructure for a potentially critical situation in simulation software SILAB 6.5 (2b, right).

Creation of the Videos of Different Scenarios. All videos depict the same traffic infrastructure. We then inserted the relevant vehicles and VRUs into the scenario and varied their trajectories (see Fig. 3). As the study investigates how human drivers use cues from context, particularly VRU, we captured the videos from the driver's perspective (Fig. 2b). In each video, the vehicle turned right into a two-lane road, where a VRU moved onto the road from the sidewalk (see Fig. 1). Two control videos showed no VRU crossing the road. The speed of the vehicle after cornering was 25,2 km/h. Vehicle speed and deceleration profile was the same for all videos to provide a constant basis for assessment. Weather conditions also remained stable. An accident never occurred. Each video lasted about 14 s and contained no sound.

Questionnaire. We created the questionnaire using LimeSurvey software, version 5.2.8 + 220103 [33]. The questionnaire contained the following constructs:

Risk Perception. After viewing each video, participants rated subjective risk of the respective situation, from 0 (not dangerous at all) to 10 (extremely dangerous). We gave the option "No person in the video" (for control videos). We adapted the scale from Neukum and Krüger [34], see Fig. 4. After the scale, a free text field allowed participants to describe the reason for their assessment.

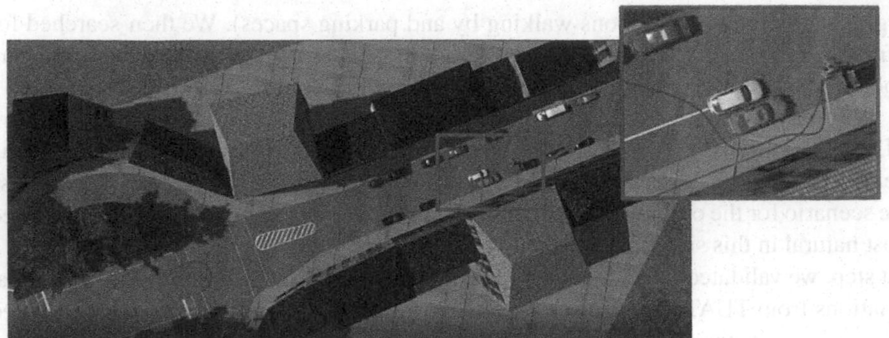

Fig. 3. Example of a scenario situation, shown from bird's eye view. The figure on the upper right shows the trajectory of the vehicle (yellow). The figure on the right also depicts the three levels of predictability of VRU behavior: light green = high predictability; light blue = medium predictability; red = low predictability. (Color figure online)

Not dangerous at all	Harmless			Moderately dangerous			Dangerous			Extremely dangerous	No person in the video
0	1	2	3	4	5	6	7	8	9	10	

Fig. 4. Scale for assessing perceived risk, adapted from Neukum and Krüger [34] (presented in English translation).

Control Variable Predictability. We used the control variable perceived predictability of the VRU's behavior to assess whether operationalized predictability levels corresponded to participants' perception. Participants rated perceived predictability on a 11-point scale with verbal categories: 0 (very predictable), 1–3 (well predictable), 4–6 (moderately predictable), 7–9 (not very predictable), 10 (not predictable at all).

Visibility. We introduce these questions to determine when the respondent first spotted the VRU. We introduced several verbal answers categories, e.g., "when the VRU left the intersection" or "when the VRU entered the road directly in front of the moving car". In the last question for every video, the participants were free to write an individual text about their impressions.

Sociodemographic Data. Participants stated gender, age, and status of driver's license. We asked participants to state personal driving style to investigate a possible influence of driving style on perceived risk. In literature, driving style is often classified into two basic types: "defensive, quiet, and fuel-efficient driving" and "offensive, aggressive and sporty driving with high fuel consumption" [35–37].

Feeling of Presence. We used items from the Igroup Presence Questionnaire[3] [38] to evaluate the sense of presence experienced in the virtual environment (= videos).We only used items suitable for assessment of presence of videos, which mostly represent spatial presence and experienced realism. The items used a 5-point Likert scale from 1 (fully disagree/not real at all) to 5 (fully agree/completely real).

[3] http://igroup.org/pq/ipq/index.php.

Division of Participants into Groups. We divided the 48 videos into six groups to ensure a reasonable duration of one run of the study. At the beginning of each run, the LimeSurvey software assigned participants to a group randomly. We balanced the groups regarding videos to ensure that in each group, participants would see four videos with a pedestrian/four with a cyclist, four videos with a child/four with an adult, and four videos with/four without parked vehicles at the side of the road. We added two control videos without any VRU per group to check whether participant really watched the videos before assessment. Thus, each participant saw a total of ten videos.

3.3 Sample

133 participants (82 female) fully completed the survey. The main age group was 25–34 years (67 participants). 92% of participants held a driver's license. 49 participants reported a neutral driving style, 23 participants indicated a defensive, restrained, and 4 participants a sporty, offensive driving style. Other participants rated their driving style as somewhere in between. All participants voluntarily participated in the survey. We recruited the participants through social networks. Participants did not receive any incentives. Any person of legal age could participate in the study.

3.4 Procedure

Participants required a computer or mobile device with a stable internet connection to conduct the study. First, participants read the instruction and gave informed consent. The LimeSurvey software then randomly assigned participants to a group. Participants then saw the first video of a crossing situation between a vehicle and a VRU. Afterwards, participants rated the presented situation regarding perceived risk and visibility of VRU. We also randomized the order of videos per group to avoid sequence effects (see Fig. 5). The end of the study contained questions on sociodemographic data and a clarification of the objective of the study.

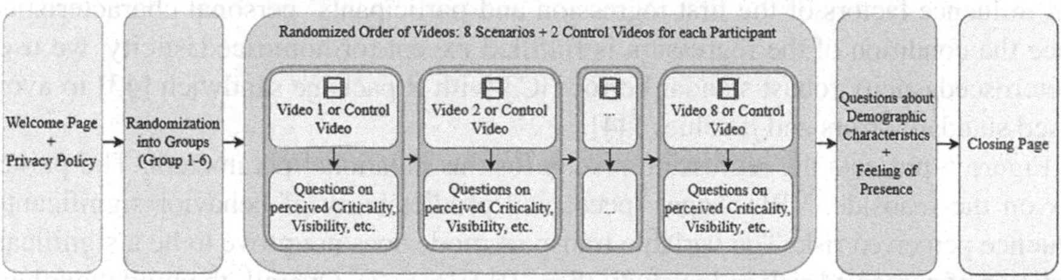

Fig. 5. Survey procedure for each participant.

3.5 Preparation for Data Analysis

For analysis, we first checked data for plausibility and completeness. We removed data if subjective criticality for control videos (without a crossing VRU) exceeded 5, as this strongly suggests that the participant did not watch the video, or if questionnaires were not fully completed.

4 Results

We executed analysis using RStudio (version 1.4.1717) [39], which is the graphical user interface for the open-source statistical software R (version 4.1.0) [40].

We divided analysis into two sections: Correlation analyses for control and other study variables and multiple regression analyses to determine the influence of the predictors on perceived risk. We evaluate the correlation coefficients according Cohen's standard: Cohen considers values between .1 and .29 as weak, values between .3 and .49 as medium and values above .5 as strong correlation [41].

4.1 Operationalization of VRUs' Predictability

First, we calculated correlation for the control variable predictability of VRU behavior. We used Spearman's correlation to examine whether participants perceived the rank-based predictor levels of VRU behavior as operationalized. The analysis revealed a weak positive correlation with $\rho = .11, p < .001$.

Furthermore, we used a biserial rank correlation to investigate whether parked cars at the roadside have a significant influence on the visibility of the crossing VRU. The biserial rank correlation was highly significant, $r_{s(bis)} = .13, p < .01$, such that participants see the VRU significantly later when cars are parked on the side of the road.

Furthermore, the study examined whether participants see children later than adults, if they emerge from behind parked cars. The examination by means of biserial rank correlation showed a positive highly significant correlation ($r_{s(bis)} = .24, p < .001$).

4.2 Influence of Manipulated Predictors on Perceived Risk

Next, we checked the preconditions for multiple regression. We performed the analysis using the R package lmtest [42]. The first multiple regression only considered predictors varied in the videos (see Table 1). The second multiple regression considered significant influence factors of the first regression and participants' personal characteristics. Since the condition of the regression is fulfilled except for homoscedasticity, we used a heteroscedasticity robust standard error HC3 with R package sandwich [43] to avoid biased standard errors and *p*-values [44].

Figure 6 presents the regression results for the situational parameters. The parked cars on the roadside, VRUs' age, speed, and predictability of behavior significantly influence perceived risk. The variable transport mode does not prove to be a significant predictor of perceived risk in the study ($\beta = .011; p = .7$). Overall, the model explains $R^2 = 6{,}8\%$ and $R^2{}_{adj} = 6{,}4\%$ of the variance in perceived risk. The largest explanatory contribution to the variance share is provided by the variable "Cars on roadside" with 4,4%.

	Dependent variable: Perceived risk		
	Unstandardized Coefficients B + standard error (SE)		Standardized Coefficients β + (SE)
	default	robust	
Transport mode	0.050	0,050	.011
	(0.130)	(0.130)	(.03)
Age group	0.297**	0.297**	.068**
	(0.130)	(0.130)	(.030)
Cars on roadside	0.914***	0.914***	.209***
	(0.130)	(0.131)	(.030)
Speed	0.472***	0.472***	0,108***
	(0.130)	(0.130)	(0,030)
Predictability of behavior	0.229***	0.229***	0,085***
	(0.080)	(0.080)	(0,030)
Constant	3.698***	3.698***	-0,000
	(0.424)	(0.439)	(0,030)
Observations	1,064	1,064	1,064
R^2	.068	.068	.068
Adjusted R^2	.064	.064	.064
Residual Std. Error (df = 1058)	2.119	2,119	0,968
F Statistic (df = 5; 1058)	15.519***	15.519***	15,519***
Significance level			*p < .1; **p < .05; ***p < .01

Fig. 6. Regression results of predictors on perceived risk, made with R package stargazer [45]

4.3 Influence of Participants' Characteristics on Perceived Risk

To assess the influence of personal characteristics on perceived risk, we performed another multiple regression to include the factors of participants' age, gender, and sense of presence. We excluded the factor possession of a driver's license from the regression due to insufficient difference. We considered personal driving style in a separate correlation analysis, since not all participants made a statement about their driving style. The missing data on driving style would have led to a reduction of data in the multiple regression. In this analysis, the participants' age is significantly associated with the perceived risk, where younger probands assessed the situations as riskier.

When we include participants' age and the four significant situation parameters into the regression model, variance resolution increases to $R^2 = 8.7\%$, $R^2_{adj} = 8.2\%$, (F(5, 1058) = 20.03, $p < .001$).

We found no significant influence for participants' gender ($\beta = -.042$; $p = .157$) and sense of presence ($\beta = -.04$; $p = .17$). Internal consistency of the sense of presence questionnaire was acceptable ($\alpha = .72$).

A Spearman correlation analysis revealed no relationship between the participants' driving style and perceived risk ($r = .06$, $p = .96$).

5 Discussion

5.1 Discussion of Results

This study investigates the research question "*Which potential contextual triggers affect subjective risk assessment of a crossing situation from the driver's point of view?*". Participants assessed the level of perceived risk via a questionnaire after they watched videos of traffic situations in which a VRU crossed the road in front of the ego vehicle.

The results show that perceived risk was significantly associated with poorer visibility of the VRU, higher VRU speed, poorer predictability of VRU behavior, and younger VRUs, but not with whether the VRU was a pedestrian or bicyclist. For personal characteristics, younger age was significantly associated with higher risk perception; nonsignificant predictors were participants gender, driving style, and sense of presence.

Regarding hypotheses, results showed that perceived risk was significantly higher when children crossed the street instead of adults (*H1: Traffic situations in which a child crosses the road are perceived as more dangerous than when an adult person crosses the road.*). We assumed that participants would perceive it as riskier when a child rather than an adult crosses the road. We based this assumption on the fact that children under 14 years of age (and adults 65 years of age and older) are the age groups most frequently affected by fatal pedestrian accidents [46]. Factors that can be blamed for the above-average risk of accidents are, on the one hand, the motor, visual, acoustic, and cognitive skills that children only learn over the years [19]. Furthermore, children are often seen later by drivers due to their smaller body size [23].

Regarding exploratory research question 3 *(Are children emerging from behind parked cars seen later by the driver than adults?)*, participants indeed saw children who emerged from behind parked vehicles significantly later than adults.

With respect to H2 (*Traffic situations in which a VRU appears between parked cars are perceived as more dangerous than situations in which visibility on approaching VRU is not blocked.*), results show that participants rated traffic situation as riskier when visibility was obstructed by parked vehicles on the side of the road. This is not unusual, as visibility obstructions mean that VRU who emerge from between parked vehicles are generally seen later by motorists. Being seen later has a favorable effect on the occurrence of accidents according to Schüller et al. [23]. Our study also found a correlation between visual obstruction through parked cars and the time of the first sighting of the VRU.

Regarding H3 (*The lower the predictability of the VRUs behavior, the higher the perceived subjective risk.*), results show that unpredictable road user behavior led to a higher risk perception. This finding is in line with numerous studies [25, 47, 48], which have shown that road users who are distracted by a smartphone, for example, had lower situational awareness. Distracted road users were also more unpredictable to other road users, and more prone to traffic accidents. It can be assumed that the participants in this work were also aware of these potentially dangerous factors, which led to a higher assessment of the danger level.

Regarding exploratory question 1 (*Is the speed of the pedestrian or cyclist related to a higher risk perception?*), another finding of this study was that a higher speed of the VRU led to a significantly higher perceived risk. Based on the literature, no evidence could be found to confirm this relationship. For this reason, the authors consider making their own assumptions, which is based on two factors. On the one hand, we assumed that the moment of surprise for the vehicle driver might be greater when a VRU emerges from between parked vehicles at a high speed. On the other hand, the higher speed of the VRU leads a lower predictability about the VRUs exact position after a certain time. Therefore, further studies should investigate the reasons why a higher speed of VRUs is associated with a higher perceived risk.

Regarding exploratory question 2 (*Is there a significant difference between risk perception in traffic situations involving a bicyclist compared to situations involving a pedestrian?)*, no significant results emerged.

Furthermore, the results show that younger participants perceived situations as riskier than older participants. However, this finding is not in line with an earlier study: The accident risk of traffic situations requiring a high degree of driving reflexes were rated as less risky by young male drivers rated than by older male drivers [49]. The discrepancy between the two studies could be explained by the current sample's age. In this work, 82% of participants were under the age of 35. Due to the unequal frequency distributions in the age groups, this results in low statistical power.

Regarding the other sociodemographic factors, we found no significant correlation to perceived risk. However, as this is confirmed in numerous studies, we recommend to further consider participants' gender, driving style and their feeling of presence for future studies.

5.2 Discussion of Limitations

The sample size of this study was relatively small in relation to the number of test groups. Less predictors would have resulted in less videos per group, but valuable information explaining the variance in perceived risk would have been lost. Furthermore, gender and age distribution were unbalanced. To obtain a representative sample, older people would have to be specifically approached. Finally, limitations may include the creation of the scenarios: As VRUs always moved onto the road from the right side of the sidewalk, participants might have been primed to primarily watch the right sidewalk. Therefore, participants may have seen the crossing VRU earlier compared to scenarios where the VRU would cross the road from either side.

6 Conclusion

We used an online study to present videos of potentially risky traffic situations to participants. Participants saw situations in which a VRU crossed a street in front of the ego vehicle from the driver's point of view. Out of the 5 predictors, poorer visibility of the VRU, higher VRU speed, poorer predictability of VRU behavior, and younger VRU had a significant influence on perceived risk in a multiple regression analysis. Whether the crossing VRU was a pedestrian or bicyclist did not influence subjective risk assessment in our study. Participants' age did also significantly influence perceived risk, while we found no influence of gender, driving style, and sense of presence.

Influence factors with a significant influence on perceived risk will be implemented into the virtual test scenarios of our project RELAI. Thus, subjective risk assessment is included into virtual test scenarios for AVs. AVs passing the virtual test scenarios will not only drive safe objectively, but also comply to driver's expectations on subjective safety.

References

1. Inoue, H., El-Haji, M., Freudenmann, T., Zhang, H., Raksincharoensak, P., Saito, Y.: Validation methodology to establish safe autonomous driving algorithms with a high driver acceptance using a virtual environment (2019)
2. Freudenmann, T., Bopp-Bertenbreiter, V., El-Haji, M., Martin, M.: Project RELAI: risk assessment for automated driving based on multiple data sources. In: ITS World Congress, Hamburg, 11.-15.10 Ertico ITS Europe (2021)
3. Saito, Y., Raksincharoensak, P., Inoue, H., El-Haji, M., Freudenmann, T.: Context-sensitive hazard anticipation based on driver behavior analysis and cause-and-effect chain study. AVEC (2018)
4. European Commission. Directorate-General for Mobility and Transport: Next steps towards 'Vision Zero': EU road safety policy framework 2021-2030. Publications Office (2020)
5. SafetyNet: Pedestrians & Cyclists (2009)
6. Statistisches Bundesamt (Destatis): Verkehr. Verkehrsunfälle (2019). https://www.destatis.de/DE/Themen/Gesellschaft-Umwelt/Verkehrsunfaelle/Publikationen/Downloads-Verkehrsunfaelle/verkehrsunfaelle-jahr-2080700187004.pdf?__blob=publicationFile&v=2. Accessed 8 Feb 2022
7. Lindström, A., et al.: Safety through automation? Ensuring that automated and connected driving contribute to a safer transportation system. FERSI Position Paper – January 19, 2018. Forum of European Road Safety Research Institutes (FERSI) (2018). https://fersi.org/wp-content/uploads/2019/02/180202-Safety-through-automation-final.pdf. Accessed 10 Oct 2021
8. Deublein, M.: Automatisiertes Fahren. Mischverkehr, Bern (2020)
9. Schlag, B.: Risikoverhalten im Straßenverkehr. Wiss. Z. Tech. Univ. Dresden **55**, 35–40 (2006)
10. Timm, J.: Theorie der gesundheitlichen Risiken: Zwei Welten im Streit (Theory of health risks: dispute of disciplines). Bundesgesundheitsblatt, Gesundheitsforschung, Gesundheitsschutz **52**, 1122–1128 (2009). https://doi.org/10.1007/s00103-009-0968-4
11. Pfister, H.-R., Jungermann, H., Fischer, K.: Die Psychologie der Entscheidung. Springer, Heidelberg (2017)
12. Lee, D.N.: A theory of visual control of braking based on information about time-to-collision. Perception (1976). https://doi.org/10.1068/p050437
13. Hayward, J.C.: Near-miss determination through use of a scale of danger. Highway Research Record (1972)
14. Hensch, A.-C., Neumann, I., Beggiato, M., Halama, J., Krems, J.F.: How should automated vehicles communicate? – effects of a light-based communication approach in a Wizard-of-Oz study. In: Stanton, N. (ed.) AHFE 2019. AISC, vol. 964, pp. 79–91. Springer, Cham (2020). https://doi.org/10.1007/978-3-030-20503-4_8
15. Rothenbücher, D., Li, J., Sirkin, D., Mok, B., Ju, W.: Ghost driver: a field study investigating the interaction between pedestrians and driverless vehicles. In: 2016 25th IEEE International Symposium on Robot and Human Interactive Communication (RO-MAN), New York, NY, USA, 26–31 August 2016, pp. 795–802. IEEE (2016). https://doi.org/10.1109/ROMAN.2016.7745210

16. Kesharwani, A., Singh Bisht, S.: The impact of trust and perceived risk on internet banking adoption in India. Int. J. Bank Mark. (2012). https://doi.org/10.1108/02652321211236923
17. Furian, G., Kaiser, S., Senitschnig, N., Soteropoulos, A.: Subjective safety and risk perception. ESRA2 Thematic report Nr. 7, Vienna, Austria Austrian Road Safety Board KFV (2020)
18. Batsch, F., Kanarachos, S., Cheah, M., Ponticelli, R., Blundell, M.: A taxonomy of validation strategies to ensure the safe operation of highly automated vehicles. J. Intell. Transport. Syst. **26**, 14–33 (2022). https://doi.org/10.1080/15472450.2020.1738231
19. Schmidt, J., Funk, W.: Stand der Wissenschaft: Kinder im Straßenverkehr. Bergisch Gladbach (2021)
20. Schieber, R.A., Thompson, N.J.: Developmental risk factors for childhood pedestrian injuries. Injury Prevent. **2**, 228–236 (1996)
21. Tabibi, Z., Pfeffer, K.: Finding a safe place to cross the road: the effect of distractors and the role of attention in children's identification of safe and dangerous road-crossing sites. Infant Child Dev. **16**, 193–206 (2007)
22. Habibovic, A., Davidsson, J.: Requirements of a system to reduce car-to-vulnerable road user crashes in urban intersections. Accid. Anal. Prevent. **43**, 1570–1580 (2011). https://doi.org/10.1016/j.aap.2011.03.019
23. Schüller, H., et al. (eds.): Systematische Untersuchung sicherheitsrelevanten Fußgängerverhaltens. Berichte der Bundesanstalt für Straßenwesen: Mensch und Sicherheit, Heft 299. Fachverlag NW in Carl Schünemann Verlag GmbH, Bremen (2020)
24. Walter, E., Achermann Stürmer, Y., Scaramuzza, G., Cavegn, M., Niemann, S.: Fussverkehr, Bern (2013)
25. Pizzamiglio, S., Naeem, U., Réhman, S.U., Saeed Sharif, M., Abdalla, H., Turner, D.L.: A mutlimodal approach to measure the distraction levels of pedestrians using mobile sensing. Proc. Comput. Sci. **113**, 89–96 (2017). https://doi.org/10.1016/j.procs.2017.08.297
26. Rasouli, A., Tsotsos, J.K.: Autonomous vehicles that interact with pedestrians: a survey of theory and practice. IEEE Trans. Intell. Transp. Syst. **21**, 900–918 (2019)
27. Tian, R., et al.: Pilot study on pedestrian step frequency in naturalistic driving environment. In: 2013 IEEE Intelligent Vehicles Symposium (IV), Gold Coast City, Australia, 23–26 June 2013, pp. 1215–1220. IEEE (2013). https://doi.org/10.1109/IVS.2013.6629632
28. Willis, A., Gjersoe, N., Havard, C., Kerridge, J., Kukla, R.: Human movement behaviour in urban spaces: implications for the design and modelling of effective pedestrian environments. Environ. Plann. B Plann. Des. **31**, 805–828 (2004). https://doi.org/10.1068/b3060
29. Ishaque, M.M., Noland, R.B.: Behavioural issues in pedestrian speed choice and street crossing behaviour: a review. Transp. Rev. **28**, 61–85 (2008). https://doi.org/10.1080/01441640701365239
30. Dipietro, C.M., King, L.E.: Pedestrian gap-acceptance (1970)
31. Wright, K.B.: Researching internet-based populations: advantages and disadvantages of online survey research, online questionnaire authoring software packages, and web survey services. J. Comput.-Mediat. Commun. (2005). https://doi.org/10.1111/j.1083-6101.2005.tb00259.x
32. WIVW GmbH: SILAB
33. Limesurvey GmbH. / LimeSurvey: An Open Source survey tool/ LimeSurvey GmbH. Hamburg, Germany (2021)
34. Neukum, A., Krüger, H.: Fahrerreaktionen bei Lenksystemstörungen: Untersuchungsmethodik und Bewertungskriterien. VDI Bericht, pp. 297–318 (2003)
35. Marina Martinez, C., Heucke, M., Wang, F.-Y., Gao, B., Cao, D.: Driving style recognition for intelligent vehicle control and advanced driver assistance: a survey. IEEE Trans. Intell. Transport. Syst. **19**, 666–676 (2018). https://doi.org/10.1109/TITS.2017.2706978

36. Schulz, A., Fröming, R.: Analyse des Fahrerverhaltens zur Darstellung adaptiver Eingriffsstrategien von Assistenzsystemen. ATZ Automobiltech Z **110**, 1124–1131 (2008). https://doi.org/10.1007/BF03222040
37. Johnson, D.A., Trivedi, M.M.: Driving style recognition using a smartphone as a sensor platform. In: 2011 14th International IEEE Conference on Intelligent Transportation Systems (ITSC), Washington, DC, USA, 5–7 October 2011, pp. 1609–1615. IEEE (2011). https://doi.org/10.1109/ITSC.2011.6083078
38. Schubert, T., Friedmann, F., Regenbrecht, H.: The experience of presence: factor analytic insights. Presence Teleoper. Virtual Environ. **10**, 266–281 (2001). https://doi.org/10.1162/105474601300343603
39. RStudio Team: RStudio: Integrated Development for R. RStudio. PBC, Boston (2021)
40. R Core Team: R: A language and environment for statistical computing. R Foundation for Statistical Computing, Vienna (2021)
41. Cohen, J.: Statistical Power Analysis for the Behavioral Sciences, 2nd edn. (1988)
42. Zeileis, A., Hothorn, T.: Diagnostic checking in regression relationships. R News **2**, 7–10 (2002)
43. Zeileis, A., Köll, S., Graham, N.: Various versatile variances: an object-oriented implementation of clustered covariances in R. J. Stat. Soft. **95**, 1–36 (2020). https://doi.org/10.18637/jss.v095.i01
44. Hayes, A.F., Cai, L.: Using heteroskedasticity-consistent standard error estimators in OLS regression: an introduction and software implementation. Behav. Res. Methods **39**, 709–722 (2007). https://doi.org/10.3758/bf03192961
45. Hlavac, M.: stargazer. Well-Formatted Regression and Summary Statistics Tables (2018)
46. European Commission: Pedestrians and Cyclists. European Commission, Directorate General for Transport (2018)
47. Nasar, J., Hecht, P., Wener, R.: Mobile telephones, distracted attention, and pedestrian safety. Accid. Anal. Prevent. **40**, 69–75 (2008). https://doi.org/10.1016/j.aap.2007.04.005
48. Schwebel, D.C., Stavrinos, D., Byington, K.W., Davis, T., O'Neal, E.E., de Jong, D.: Distraction and pedestrian safety: how talking on the phone, texting, and listening to music impact crossing the street. Accid. Anal. Prevent. **45**, 266–271 (2012). https://doi.org/10.1016/j.aap.2011.07.011
49. Matthews, M.L., Moran, A.R.: Age differences in male drivers' perception of accident risk: the role of perceived driving ability. Accid. Anal. Prevent. **18**, 299–313 (1986). https://doi.org/10.1016/0001-4575(86)90044-8

Impacts of Autonomous Vehicle Driving Logics on Heterogenous Traffic and Evaluating Transport Interventions with Microsimulation Experiments

Robel Desta(✉) and János Tóth

Department of Transport Technology and Economics, Faculty of Transportation Engineering and Vehicle Engineering, Budapest University of Technology and Economics, Muegyetem rkp. 3, Budapest 1111, Hungary

robeldesta@edu.bme.hu, toth.janos@kjk.bme.hu

Abstract. Automated Vehicles (AVs) are predicted to have a substantial impact on safety, traffic congestion, energy consumption, and, eventually, urban space transformation. In the near future, the market penetration of AVs is likely to increase significantly. Until AVs become common reality on roadways, there will be an extended transition period during which different types of AVs with varied driving logics will coexist alongside human-driven vehicles. This study analyzes the range of potential impacts on traffic performance for various types of AV driving logics and physical interventions in heterogenous motorways using microscopic traffic simulation considering several hypothetical scenarios. The simulations clearly portrayed how network performance changes with physical modifications on the network elements and behavioral modifications with AV driving logics in PTV Vissim. Traffic performance results based on average delay, travel speed, vehicles arrived in the network, travel time and queue length depicted better results for most parameters with advanced driving logics and higher penetrations. The driving logics should evolve faster to progressive levels to balance the trade-off between the various safety and performance attributes. Overall, automation alone could not bring the expected improvements, others aspects such as AV-readiness of infrastructures and the change in driving behaviors of humans alongside AVs should be assessed in simulation environments parallel to the legal issues regarding deployment of AVs.

Keywords: Automated vehicles · Driving logics · Heterogenous traffic · Traffic performance · VISSIM

1 Introduction

Traffic congestion, increasing emissions, and recurrent traffic accidents are inescapable consequences of the continuing growth of traffic in urban areas. The introduction of Automated Vehicles (AVs) technology is expected to have a significant impact on safety, traffic congestion, energy consumption, and, eventually, the transformation of urban space. The deployment of AVs in transportation and mobility is a major turning point for road traffic

H. Krömker (Ed.): HCII 2022, LNCS 13335, pp. 355–370, 2022.
https://doi.org/10.1007/978-3-031-04987-3_24

and the automotive industry, where it is expected to play a critical role in addressing current and future transportation and environmental concerns. As AVs replace human drivers, the saved daily driving time could be redirected to other meaningful activities and AVs make transportation a resource that anybody can use at any moment [1, 2]. The use of microscopic traffic simulation allows for a better understanding and interpretation of the complicated traffic interactions, as well as the assessment of transportation solutions.

In the context of motorized vehicles, there are six stages of automated driving: no driving automation (Level 0), driver assistance (Level 1), partial driving automation (Level 2), conditional driving automation (Level 3), high driving automation (Level 4) and full driving automation (Level 5). Level 5 autonomous vehicles, if all goes well, will be safe and reliable by 2025. Testing and regulatory certification will take a few more years, but autonomous vehicles might be commercially available and allowed to operate in many locations by 2030 [3, 4]. The Connected and Autonomous Vehicle (CAV), which is considered a major agent of future transportation and the Cooperative Intelligent Transport System, is an AV with connectivity features. With their platoon-building ability, vehicle-to-vehicle (V2V) and vehicle-to-infrastructure (V2I) communications, AVs are likely to improve traffic performance, allowing for increased comfort on the motorway by reducing queue length at intersections and other locations. AVs must be proven safe before they can be allowed on public roads and at the deployment phase, they are expected to operate more cautiously than most human drivers [5, 6].

According to current trends, Level 5 autonomous vehicles, which can run without a driver, could be commercially accessible and legal to use in some jurisdictions by the late 2020s, but, presumably, they will be expensive and have limited performance at first. Some benefits, such as independent mobility for wealthy non-drivers, may begin in the 2030s. However, most impacts, such as reduced traffic and parking congestion, independent mobility for low-income people (and thus reduced need for public transportation), increased safety, energy conservation, and pollution reductions, will only be significant when autonomous vehicles become common and affordable, most likely in the 2040s to 2060s and certain advantages may necessitate dedicated AV lanes, raising questions about social equality [4]. Major accident injuries are more likely in metropolitan locations, with higher speed limits, signalized crossings, harsh topography, one-way roads, and during the day [7], which might be greatly decreased with AVs.

Because of their ease of use, flexibility to construct hypothetical models, and numerous scenario management possibilities, microscopic traffic simulators are being used all over the world to forecast and illustrate the features of AVs and CAVs. Changes in simulation models can be caused by differences in automation functions, sensor equipment, and driving logics. The extent of functionalities that vehicles can offer today or in the future is determined by microscopic traffic modeling approaches. However, because the models used in simulation tools were designed to represent human driving behaviors, they must be modified, extended, or replaced with new parameters in order to be utilized for automated driving. There are suggestions for how to enhance current modelling practice, but unless large-scale field data is available to validate them, any method will be surrounded by uncertainties [5, 8, 9].

The driving behavior parameters in any traffic simulator are critical in representing reality in simulation models. It's realistic to imagine that several generations of autonomous vehicles, each with its own set of capabilities and driving styles, will coexist on the road with human-driven vehicles in the near future. CoEXist is a European project that intends to prepare for the transition period when AVs and traditional vehicles coexist on city roads. Within the CoEXist project, many AV-related advancements and new features in PTV Vissim were implemented [8, 10]. The aim of this study is to evaluate the possible impacts on traffic performance for various types of AV driving logics and physical interventions in heterogenous motorways using microscopic traffic simulation by considering several hypothetical scenarios in PTV Vissim 2020.00-14.

2 Literature Review

AVs are self-driving vehicles that can drive themselves without the need for human intervention depending on the level of automation. Because there is a shortage of accurate data and knowledge about the new technology, articles in this subject contain speculations and opinions. Cooperative adaptive cruise control (CACC) and adaptive cruise control (ACC) are two critical technologies that must be deployed in the early stages of autonomous driving and connected vehicle development, according to the automobile industry. This has a direct impact on travelers' experiences, the logics of ACC and CACC can be utilized to successfully reflect the behavior of AVs and CAVs, respectively [6, 9, 11–13].

By 2045, AVs might account for up to half of new vehicle sales and 40% of vehicle trips [4]. Potential effects of AVs on traffic flow and performance can be investigated in several approaches: using vehicle throughput as principal performance measure to evaluate their coexistence with human-driven vehicles on heterogeneous motorways [5, 14, 15], investigate AVs influences on the capacity of urban freeway segments [2, 16, 17], and impacts of AVs on network performance parameters at 100% penetration [18]. According to the studies, AVs will alter traffic flows in a variety of ways, enhancing or deteriorating traffic performance. In simulation environments, the techniques adopted to mimic AVs or automated driving differ from study to study.

A quick way to model AV driving logics is to adjust based on the parameters of conventional automobile following or lane changing models as benchmarks. Models that are new or expanded could simulate AV sensors, control algorithms (importing developed driving logic algorithms to PTV Vissim or using AV driving behaviors offered by PTV Vissim), or safety features. However, calibration of the models is among the most challenging task due to the scarcity of precise data. As part of the CoEXist project, the three driving logics of cautious, normal, and aggressive/all-knowing are incorporated in PTV Vissim. In cautious driving logic, the car follows the rules of the road and behaves in a safe manner at all times. The features of enforce absolute braking distance and unsignalized intersections and lane changes are possible, but the vehicle will maintain substantial gaps. While in the normal driving logic, with its range of sensors, the vehicle acts like a human driver, with the added capability of measuring distances and speeds of nearby vehicles. All-knowing vehicles have a high level of awareness and prediction, resulting in lower gaps for all maneuvers and scenarios with anticipation cooperative behavior. The driving parameters to simulate automated vehicles are mainly based on Wiedemann 99, due to the availability of more choices for behavior control [8, 19].

As demand grows, more delays are seen for the AV mix of 100% cautious. The greater gaps required by cautious AVs could be preventing them from merging into the main flow [5]. Traffic simulation based on different levels of AV penetration and various behavioral characteristics such as platooning, V2V, and V2I communication has shown the potential to cut travel times by 11% and delays by more than 40% [10]. The positive effects of AV on roadways are especially emphasized when the network is in peak hour time based on simulation results. This is undoubtedly a positive development for the future of high-demand transportation networks. In the AV scenario, the average density of the study segment increased by 8.09% during peak hours, while the average travel speed increased by 8.48% [18]. However, the performance impacts of different driving logics at varied penetration rates were not considered in this study and the variation in driving logic would obviously influence the obtained results. A quantitative and qualitative analysis with a scenario building method depicted that in scenarios with large shared AV use, parking demand can be reduced (by about 83%), fleet size can be reduced, the kind of shared mode can be changed to various occupancies, and urban space repurposing has the highest potential [20, 21].

3 Materials and Methods

3.1 Characteristics of the Studied Junction

In this study, a typical signalized junction in Budapest is considered, which is characterized by dedicated two-way median Public Transport (PuT) lane (various tram types and buses), dedicated cycle lanes on curbsides, on-street parking facilities, lanes for the general traffic, active pedestrian flow and coordinated fixed time signal system (for pedestrians, PuT lines and general traffic). Therefore, each element of the junction along with specific arrival schedules of PuT systems were modeled in VISSIM 2020.00-14 (see Fig. 1). Among the studied scenarios in this paper, the behavioral modification focusses on the automation features in Private Transport (PrT) mode, while the PuT characteristics are mainly considered for the Physical adjustment scenario.

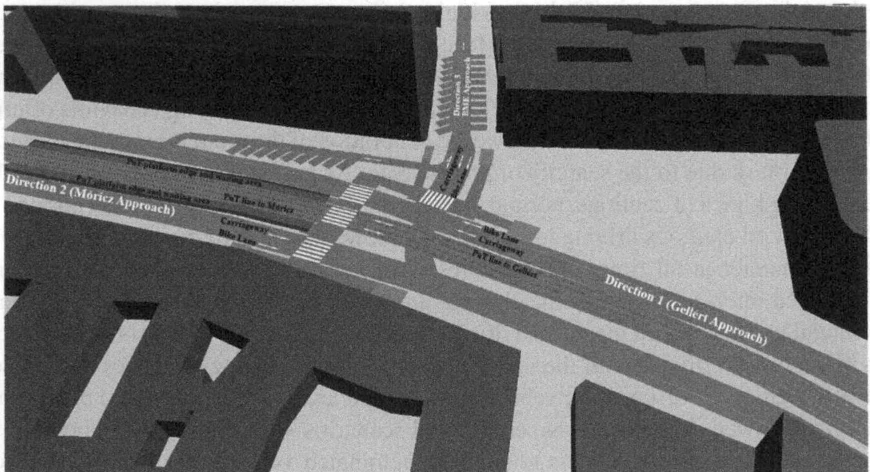

Fig. 1. Snapshot of the geometric layout and approaches at Gardonyi junction (Budapest, Hungary) in 3D display

3.2 Data Preparation

The main categories of the collected data include traffic data (traffic volume, queue length, and time headway), PuT data (tram and bus types/geometries, PuT volumes, and tram and bus stops/schedules) and traffic signal data (pedestrian, general traffic, and PuT). The collected data were fed in VISSIM to give codes and develop the model on the OpenStreetMap of the study location as shown in Table 1.

Table 1. Collected data sets for model development and their corresponding attribute

Collected data type	Model development use case in VISSIM environment
Traffic volume at each leg of the junction by vehicle type (major and minor roads)	Generates realistic vehicle inputs, types, compositions, 2D/3D model distributions and vehicle routing decisions based on field data
Queue length and Time headways based on statistical requirements	To verify the validity on the developed model by calculating the percentage change in errors with the simulated average value
Tram and bus types or geometries	To create a realistic PuT input based on the different typologies/sizes of trams and buses in the section (accurate 2D/3D model distributions)
PuT frequency	Generates realistic volumes of the various trams and buses with genuine arrival patterns in the simulation environment
Tram and bus stops/schedules	To create PuT stops, platform edges, waiting areas and generate departure times/arrival rate
Traffic signal data	Creates coordinated traffic flow on each direction based on fixed time signal data for pedestrians, PuT lines and general traffic
Pedestrian data and information of driving behaviors and/or vehicular behaviors	To create realistic VisWALK elements (pedestrian routes, pedestrian inputs, pedestrian walkable areas etc.). Then, to calibrate the model based on vehicular behaviors (functions and distributions) and driver behaviors (car following, lane changing and, gap acceptance principles)

3.3 Creating the Base Model, Calibration, and Validation

Developing a realistic base model is a critical step before any scenario development and intervention analysis. In this study, a scenario management was initiated after ensuring the reliability of the base model, which involves creating the model based on field data, calibration, and validation processes. After developing a reliable base model, the studied scenarios in this research are the physical/geometric modification and behavioral intervention by injecting various percentages of autonomous vehicles (10%, 20%, 30%, 40%, 60%, 80% and 100%).

In the physical/geometric modification, the left turners from the minor road are forced to use the side lane, which make the central lanes in the major road as fully dedicated PuT lines. Therefore, the impact of such intervention was investigated in relation to the base scenario ('do nothing'). The behavioral intervention involves the penetration of progressive percentages of autonomous vehicles with various driving logics (cautious, normal autonomous, and aggressive/all-knowing) into the traffic stream.

The approach in creating the VISSIM model (see Fig. 2) involves creating several network elements (defining conflict areas/priority rules, establishing reduced speed areas, setting vehicle 2D/3D distributions, defining vehicle types and compositions, setting vehicle inputs, and routing decisions, and defining changes to desired speed for all vehicle types), establishing the signal controller, defining PuT lines/routes, setting PuT stops (platform edges, waiting areas etc.), and adjust VisWALK elements (pedestrian routes, pedestrian inputs, pedestrian walkable areas etc.).

The base model ensures the capability of the traffic simulation model in representing the existing conditions in field. According to [22, 23], recommended simulation settings for VISSIM were adopted in this study (resolution = 10, initial random seed = 40, increment = 3, number of runs = 10). Therefore, before running the base model simulation in VISSIM, such adjustments were made to produce results for an average of 10 simulation runs. The generated outputs were extracted from the VISSIM interface and results directory for the given volume of traffic.

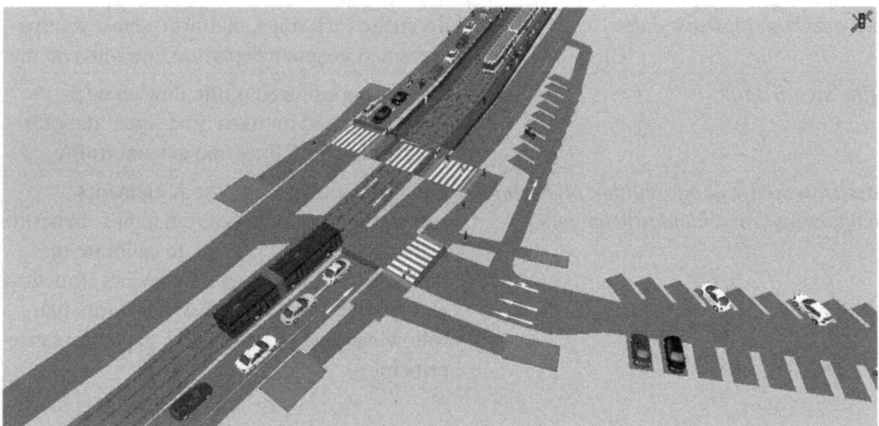

Fig. 2. Snapshot of developed base model during the simulation run

The ability of Traffic simulation models in capturing the local area traffic behavior, geometry and drivers' behaviors lies in the processes of model calibration and validation, which needs to be conducted before evaluating any given scenario [23–25]. The model calibration in this paper involves adjustment of different vehicle and driver behaviors in

VISSIM based on parametric field data in the study area. In the vehicle behaviors, for each vehicle type, the desired speed distribution and acceleration-deceleration behaviors were adjusted. For the driver's behaviors, the adjusted parameters include the driving behavior when following other cars, the adopted Wiedemann 74 car following model parameters for each vehicle category, the lane change behaviors, lateral distance (desired position at free flow, overtaking behaviors, diamond queueing etc.), drivers' behaviors at signal control, autonomous driving parameters (suitable for base models that include AVs in the future) and drivers' errors.

Following the adjustment of the calibration parameters and running the simulation model with aforementioned simulation settings, the validation process was then conducted. "The validation process entails comparing the model and its behavior to the real system. In general, if two sets of output data compare "favorably", then the model of the existing system is considered to be "valid". For any validation to be accurate, the error obtained between the simulated and the real data should not be greater than 10%" [26, 27].

Selected traffic parameters from the simulation results were summarized to match the corresponding measures of effectiveness in field. The validation process at the intersection was performed by comparing parameters like average queue length, average time headway and average volume, which are conducted at randomly chosen approaches of the intersection as summarized in Table 2.

Table 2. Calculated errors between field and simulated averages for selected traffic performance parameters

Validation criteria (Traffic parameter)	Simulation result (average of 10 simulation)	Field result for statistical samples	Average percentage change in error (%)
Average queue length (Direction 1 as in Fig. 1) in meters	16.14	17.28	6.60
Average queue length (Direction 2 as in Fig. 1) in meters	9.59	10.17	5.70
Average time headway (Direction 1) in seconds	5.79	5.28	9.66
Average volume (Direction 1) in veh/hr	622	646	3.72

Therefore, calculated percentage in errors for the selected traffic performance parameters at the intersection were all under 10%, which affirms that the base model was an acceptable representation of the real traffic behavior in the field. Provided that the developed model was an accurate representation of the real traffic characteristics. Therefore, it can be used for further evaluation of various traffic planning strategies, like the physical intervention and impact of progressive percentage penetration of autonomous vehicle driving logics in this study.

3.4 Scenario Definition and Development

Physical Intervention. In normal situation, the intersection at Gardonyi, have left turners from the minor road, which pass through the PuT Lane at the major road. The goal of this intervention to avoid crossing the PuT Lane for PuT priority. Therefore, the modification in this scenario was preventing the left turns from the minor road and assign them to the side lane so that the central lanes on the major road could be dedicated PuT lines (see Fig. 3). This scenario is expected to improve the Level of Service (LoS) of the junction and ensure more green time for the mass transit operations with respect to the base scenario, where left turners are allowed from the neighboring minor street.

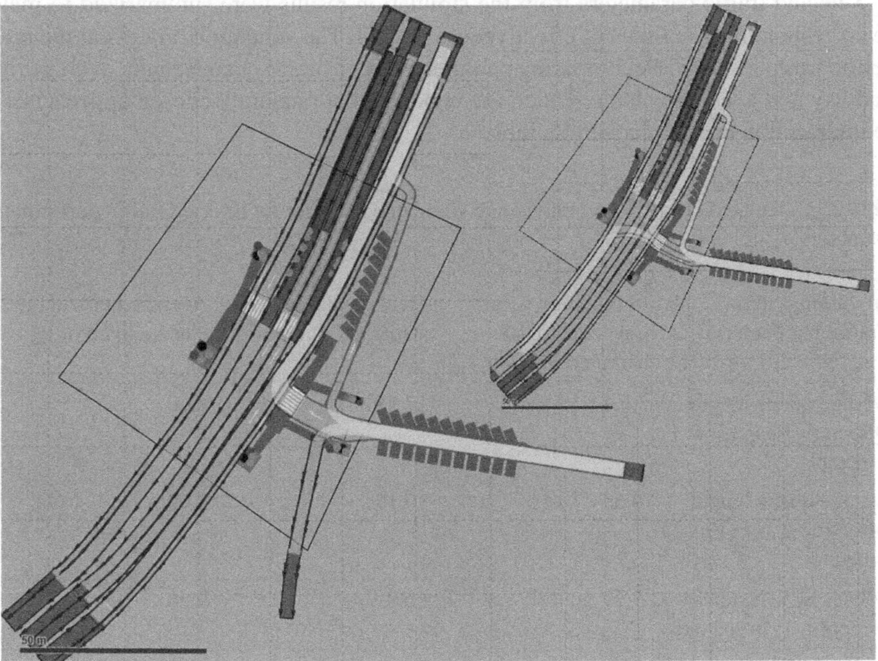

Fig. 3. Snapshot of the modified vehicle routing decision (left) relative to the base scenario (right)

As exhibited in Fig. 3, the new rearrangements were assigned in the modified scenario, including the new routing decision, reorganization of signal head locations, development of new links and connectors, definitions of new conflict areas and so on.

Behavioral Intervention. This scenario is developed in the base model with no physical modification, except for the penetration of different levels of autonomous vehicle driving logics in to the heterogenous motorway (10%, 20%, 30%, 40%, 60%, 80% and 100%). In the scenario management of this study, the various compositions of autonomous vehicle driving logics were adopted with close increment at lower penetrations.

The important predefined parameters for simulating AVs were imported from VISSIM base network file by selecting important attributes from the network object options. This procedure populates new driving behaviors with recommended settings for the AV driving logics. In this study, the driving behavior for the loaded AVs applies in all links, this can also be further tested by assigning specific driving behavior in specific links with various mixture of driving logics. The penetration rates were assigned as different scenario modifications by splitting the regular vehicle composition with the percentages of AVs.

4 Results and Discussions

4.1 Results of the Physical Intervention Scenario

The physical intervention scenario depicted a significant improvement in traffic performance parameters, mainly in the major traffic line (Direction 1), which moves traffic to the city center locations. For instance, the queue length in Direction 1 is reduced by nearly 7.2% compared to the base scenario, while there is no significant difference in Direction 2 as the traffic volume is not very significant. Moreover, the delay on Direction 1 considerably reduced and the travel speed has increased by an amount of 18.2% and 5.7% respectively (see Fig. 4).

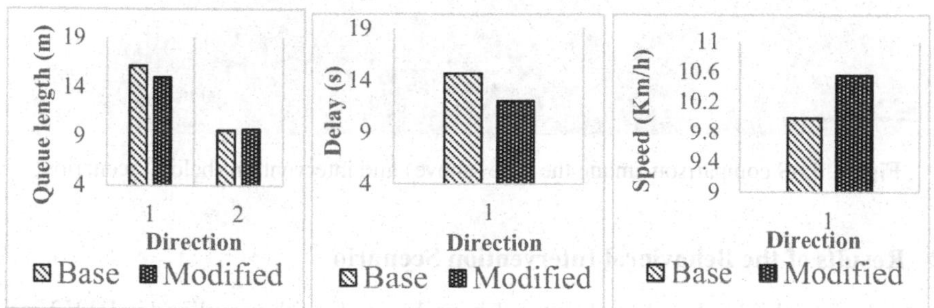

Fig. 4. Relative comparison of queue length, delay and speed between the base and physical intervention scenario.

The junction Level of Service (LoS) in the modified scenario has also improved due to the prohibition of the left turners (see Fig. 5). The LoS for the left turners got improved to LoS 'A', since the left turners will not have conflict due to the modification. The minimum LoS on each lane of Link 2/Direction 2 become 'B' and more lane freedom is achieved at Link 1/Direction 1. The LoS for the right turning lane from the minor road has improved considerably from LoS 'C' to 'A', which is attributed to the early departing of the left turners to the side lane by leaving more space to the right turners to use.

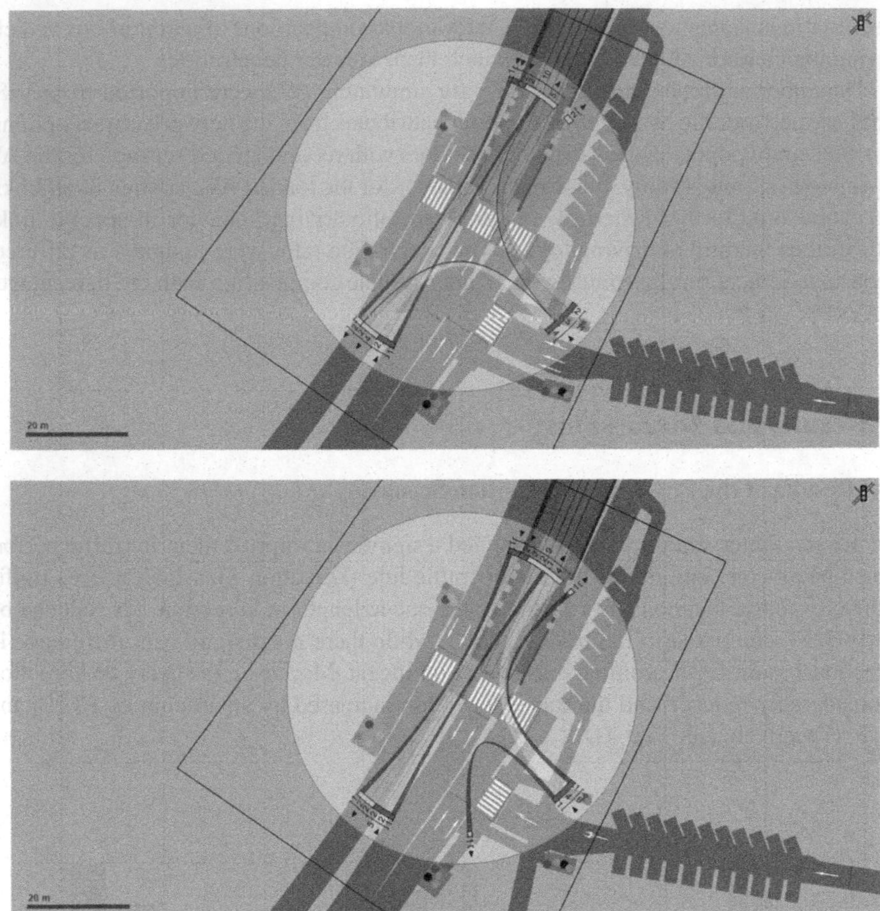

Fig. 5. LoS comparison among the base (above) and intervention (below) scenarios

4.2 Results of the Behavioral Intervention Scenario

The analysis in this study is based on the driving logic algorithm outlined in PTV Vissim environment based on the CoEXist project. The values of driving parameters in PTV Vissim are considered based on empirical studies, collated data and several assumptions (mainly based on Wiedemann 99 model due to its flexibility for automated vehicles).

Network Evaluation Based on Traffic Performance Parameters. The simulation was conducted at lower penetration increment rate as the actual deployment is expected to be applied with progressive rates. Therefore, to visualize how the different driving logics of automated vehicles coexist with human-driven vehicles, a 10%, 20%, 30%, 40%, 60%, 80% and 100% penetration rates are considered for each driving logics (cautious, normal and aggressive/all-knowing autonomous driving logics). Accordingly, the delay results depicted that at lower penetration rates of 10%, the delay has increased by an average of 47.8% for all driving logics as compared to the base condition with

0% penetration. However, as the penetration rate increases to 100%, the communication between the vehicles and the environment increases, which has significantly reduced the delay by 19.7%, 30.25% and 33.58% for cautious, normal and aggressive respectively (see Fig. 6). Considering the trend of the simulation results, the higher delay reduction Aggressive driving logic could further be increased by improving the AV-readiness of the infrastructure, synchronizing the legal issues on the interaction between human-driven and automated vehicles or by advancing the AV driving logic algorithms considered by the automotive industry.

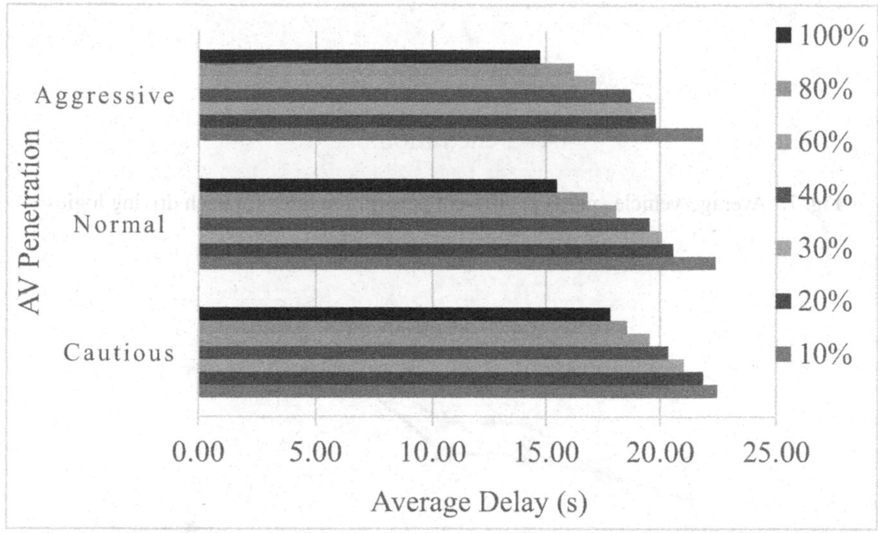

Fig. 6. Average vehicle delays at different penetration rates for each driving logics

The average speed for each of the simulated scenarios depicted an average of nearly 1km/h speed reduction for all driving logics between the 10% penetration and the base condition with 0% penetration (see Fig. 7). With the current infrastructure and under mixed traffic flow condition, the junction speed has increased by 1.47%, 4.72% and 5.95% with increased AV penetration to 100% for cautious, normal and aggressive respectively.

The results of total number of vehicles, which have already reached their destination and have left the network before the end of the simulation depicted an overall change at each penetration of the driving logics to be less than 1% (see Fig. 8). Therefore, all vehicles reasonably reached their destination with insignificant differences among the driving logics. This result could meaningfully differ in locations with congested road links.

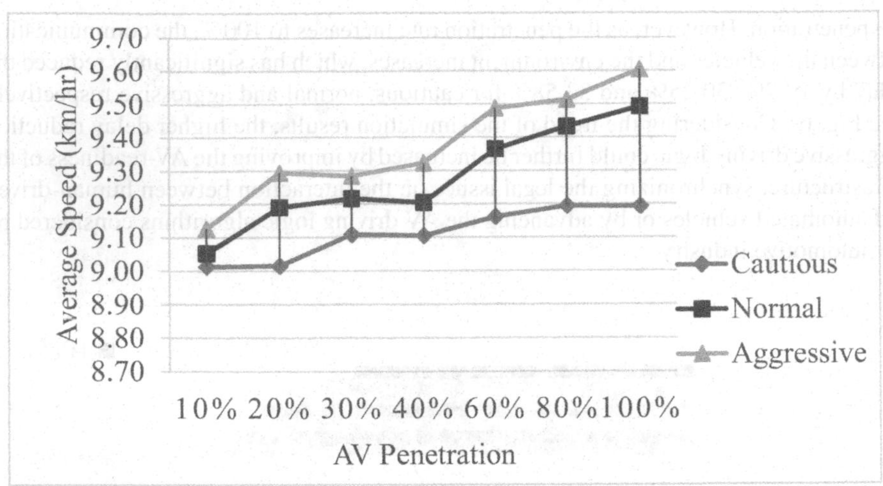

Fig. 7. Average vehicle speeds at different penetration rates for each driving logics

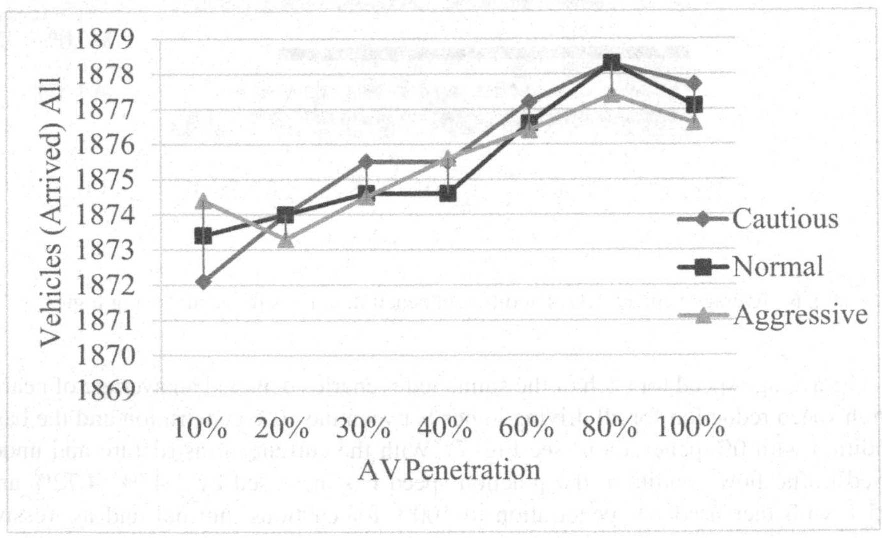

Fig. 8. Average vehicles arrived on the network (all vehicle categories) at different penetration rates for each driving logics

With the current infrastructure setup, AV driving logics have a favorable outcome at very high penetration rates and advanced driving logics. The results portrayed that at lesser penetration rate (10%), the queue length has increased by an average of 47.58% for all driving logics as compared to the base condition with 0% penetration. Nevertheless, as the penetration rate increases to 100%, the queue length has significantly reduced by 16.1%, 44.39% and 53.10% for cautious, normal and aggressive driving behaviors respectively (see Fig. 9). The progression trend depicted that unlike the shallow queue changes in Cautious driving logic, much more proportional improvement are observed with increasing penetration rates for Normal and Aggressive driving behaviors.

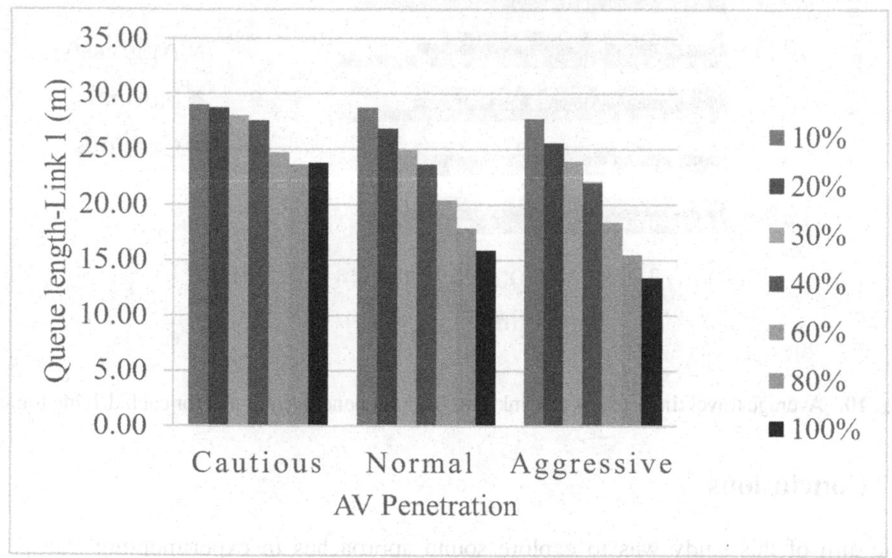

Fig. 9. Average queue length results on Link 1 at different penetration rates for each driving logics

Vehicle travel time data collection points were defined for each simulation runs considering a 150 m road segment, which starts before the intersection and ends after crossing the junction. The results depicted that the travel time for crossing the junction in the defined section has generally increased despite slight decrease with increased penetration rates for the cautious driving logic. However, a small reduction in vehicle travel times were perceived as the driving logics advance to normal and aggressive types at higher penetration rates (see Fig. 10). Based on the progression of the penetration trend on the travel time, Cautious driving logic has slightly increased the travel time with increase in penetration rate, but vice versa for the other logics, which showed much better travel time reduction with increasing rate of AV penetration.

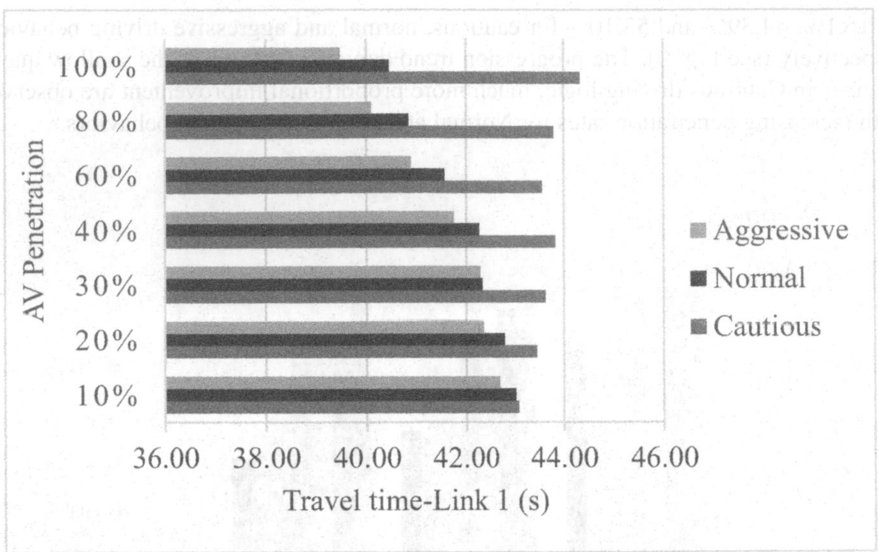

Fig. 10. Average travel time results on Link 1 at different penetration rates for each driving logics

5 Conclusions

The aim of this study was to explore sound approaches in experimenting transport interventions in microsimulation environment and investigate the traffic performance impacts of autonomous vehicle driving logics on heterogenous motorways with PTV Vissim. Based on current trends, it will be normal to see autonomous vehicles regularly in the near future, which may coexist with conventional vehicles for some periods. The real deployment may initially commence with shared vehicles in controlled/AV-ready institutional setups like airports with cautious driving logics before normal and aggressive types for safety reasons, then the vehicles may join the regular heterogenous motorways with progressive penetration. Therefore, with consideration of various traffic performance parameters, this paper portrays the impacts at different AV penetration rates based on cautious, normal and aggressive driving logics.

Carefully developed microsimulation experiments (with proper calibration and validation) render crucial insight on possible transport solutions for policy makers. In this study, the solution of reliving the PuT lines from the conflict with the left turners from the minor road greatly improved the junction performance as well as the overall level of service. These aspects could further be used to evaluate microscopic impacts AV-ready infrastructure types with various prudently designed scenarios for testing the physical interaction characteristics of autonomous vehicles with the infrastructure.

The summarized results of the scenario management in this study clearly demonstrated the potential directions with the corresponding policy decisions in introducing autonomous vehicles with varying driving logics. Despite the practicality in injecting more safer AV driving logics like cautious type in the initial phase to ensure smooth coexistence with regular human-driven vehicles, such driving logics have negative impacts on traffic performance. The driving logics should evolve faster to advanced levels to balance the trade-off between the various attributes. However, the AV-readiness of the infrastructure also plays a crucial role in affecting the performance of AVs in motorway networks.

The traffic performance results based on average delay and travel speed clearly indicated that better results on those parameters can be achieved with higher penetration with much favorable results for aggressive driving logics, then followed by normal and cautious. Based on the average vehicles arrived on the network, no significant volume change was observed amongst the driving behavior scenarios, except for small outlier values. One of the promising results was the reduction on queue length, which has significantly reduced by very high percentages for cautious, normal and aggressive driving behaviors progressively. Regarding the vehicle travel time, as the driving logics progress to normal and aggressive types with larger penetration rates, a slight reduction in vehicle travel durations was seen. However, for cautious driving logic, the travel time has generally increased despite slight decrease with increased penetration rates.

Overall, the progression of AV driving logics should advance as quicky as possible to get the best results on traffic performance. This study investigated the impact of AVs based on the different driving logics when they coexist with human driven vehicles and the change in the driving behavior of humans in the presence of AVs should also be investigated deeply to make the transition smoother along with hypothetical practical scenarios of AV-ready infrastructures.

Acknowledgments. The research reported in this paper and carried out at the Budapest University of Technology and Economics has been supported by the Hungarian Government and co-financed by the European Social Fund through the project "Talent management in autonomous vehicle control technologies" (EFOP-3.6.3-VEKOP-16-2017-00001).

Conflict of Interest. The authors declare that they have no competing interest.

References

1. Anderson, J.M., Nidhi, K., Stanley, K.D., Sorensen, P., Samaras, C., Oluwatola, O.A.: Autonomous Vehicle Technology: A Guide for Policymakers. RAND Corporation, Santa Monica (2016)
2. Olia, A., Razavi, S., Abdulhai, B., Abdelgawad, H.: Traffic capacity implications of automated vehicles mixed with regular vehicles. J. Intell. Transp. Syst. **22**(3), 244–262 (2018)
3. SAE International: Taxonomy and definitions for terms related to driving automation systems for on-road motor vehicles. ISO/SAE International, Washington (2021)
4. Litman, T.: Autonomous vehicle implementation predictions: implications for transport planning. Victoria Transport Policy Institute, Canada (2021)
5. Postigo, I., Olstam, J., Rydergren, C.: Effects on traffic performance due to heterogeneity of automated vehicles on motorways: a microscopic simulation study. In: Proceeding of the 7th VEHITS International Conference, pp. 142–151. Scitepress, Portugal (2021)
6. Makridis, M., Mattas, K., Ciuffo, B., Raposo, M.A., Toledo, T., Thiel, C.: Connected and automated vehicles on a freeway scenario. Effect on traffic congestion and network capacity. In: 7th Transport Research Arena. p. 13, TRA, Austria (2018)

7. Jaber, A., Juhász, J., Csonka, B.: An analysis of factors affecting the severity of cycling crashes using binary regression model. Sustainability **13**(12), 6945 (2021)
8. Sukennik, P.: D2.5 Micro-Simulation Guide for Automated Vehicles—Final. PTV Group, Karlsruhe, Germany (2018)
9. He, S., Guo, X., Ding, F., Qi, Y., Chen, T.: Freeway traffic speed estimation of mixed traffic using data from connected and autonomous vehicles with a low penetration rate. J. Adv. Transp. **2020**(1) (2020)
10. Evanson, A.: Connected autonomous vehicle (CAV) simulation using PTV Vissim. In: 2017 Winter Simulation Conference (WSC), p. 4420. IEEE (2017)
11. Zhong, Z., Lee, E.E., Nejad, M., Lee, J.: Influence of CAV clustering strategies on mixed traffic flow characteristics: an analysis of vehicle trajectory data. Transp. Res. Part C: Emerg. Technol. **115**, 102611 (2020)
12. Beza, A.D., Zefreh, M.M.: Potential effects of automated vehicles on road transportation: a literature review. Transp. Telecommun. **20**(3), 269–278 (2019)
13. Bohm, F., Häger, K.: Introduction of autonomous vehicles in the Swedish traffic system: effects and changes due to the new self-driving car technology (2015)
14. Talebpour, A., Mahmassani, H.S.: Influence of connected and autonomous vehicles on traffic flow stability and throughput. Transp. Res. Part C: Emerg. Technol. **71**, 143–163 (2016)
15. Ye, L., Yamamoto, T.: Impact of dedicated lanes for connected and autonomous vehicle on traffic flow throughput. Physica A **15**(512), 588–597 (2018)
16. Tilg, G., Yang, K., Menendez, M.: Evaluating the effects of automated vehicle technology on the capacity of freeway weaving sections. Transp. Res. Part C: Emerg. Technol. **96**, 3–21 (2018)
17. Lu, Q., Tettamanti, T., Hörcher, D., Varga, I.: The impact of autonomous vehicles on urban traffic network capacity: an experimental analysis by microscopic traffic simulation. Transp. Lett. **12**(8), 540–549 (2020)
18. Aria, E., Olstam, J., Schwietering, C.: Investigation of automated vehicle effects on driver's behavior and traffic performance. Transp. Res. Procedia **15**, 761–770 (2016)
19. Ahmed, H.U., Huang, Y., Lu, P.: A review of car-following models and modeling tools for human and autonomous-ready driving behaviors in micro-simulation. Smart Cities **1**, 314–335 (2021)
20. Silva, D., Földes, D., Csiszár, C.: Autonomous vehicle use and urban space transformation: A scenario building and analysing method. Sustainability **13**(6), 3008 (2021)
21. Silva, D.S., Csiszár, C., Földes, D.: Autonomous vehicles and urban space management. Sci. J. Silesian Univ. Technol. Ser. Transp, **110**, 13 (2021)
22. Zheng, Y., Hua, X., Wang, W., Xiao, J., Li, D.: Analysis of a signalized intersection with dynamic use of the left-turn lane for opposite through traffic. Sustainability **12**(18), 7530 (2020)
23. Desta, R., Tesfaye, D., Tóth, J.: Microscopic traffic characterization of light rail transit systems at level crossings. Adv. Civ. Eng. **2021**, 1–11 (2021)
24. Maheshwary, P., Bhattacharyya, K., Maitra, B., Boltze, M.: A methodology for calibration of traffic micro-simulator for urban heterogeneous traffic operations. J. Traffic Transp. Eng. (Engl. Ed.) **7**(4), 507–519 (2020)
25. Desta, R., Dubale, T., Tóth, T.: Transit performance evaluation at signalized intersections of bus rapid transit corridors. In: Proceedings of the 7th VEHITS International Conference, pp. 618–625. Scitepress, Portugal (2021)
26. Desta, R., Tóth, T.: Simulating the performance of integrated bus priority setups with microscopic traffic mockup experiments. Sci. African **11**(2021), 1–11 (2021)
27. Vedagiri, P., Jain, J.: Simulating performance impacts of bus priority measures. ACEE Int. J. Transp. Urban Dev. **2**(1), 15–19 (2012)

HAVIT: A VR-Based Platform to Support Human-Autonomous Vehicle Interaction Study

Xiaolei Guo[1], Dayu Wan[1], Dongfang Liu[2], Christos Mousas[1], and Yingjie Chen[1](✉)

[1] Department of Computer Graphics Technology, Purdue University, West Lafayette, IN, USA
{guo579,wand,cmousas,victorchen}@purdue.edu

[2] Department of Computer Engineering, Rochester Institute of Technology, Rochester, NY, USA
dongfang.liu@rit.edu

Abstract. We propose the Human-Autonomous Vehicle Interaction Testbed (HAVIT), a VR-based platform that enables researchers and designers to quickly configure AV-pedestrian interaction scenarios and evaluate their design concepts during the design process in a holistic and consistent manner. The HAVIT presents an efficient workflow that combines the Scenario Configuration, Experimental Setting, and Batch Configuration. Our workflow enables researchers to quickly and flexibly configure motion behaviors of AVs and external human-machine interfaces (eHMIs) through visual panels and direct manipulation; complete experimental setting through Data Collection component and Testing Instruction component; and immediately enact and immersively experience them to reasonable iterate and generate virtual scenarios for testing. We conducted an usability testing with domain experts and designers to test the effectiveness of how HAVIT can support AVs-pedestrian interaction design process.

Keywords: Human-autonomous vehicles interaction · Virtual reality testbed · eHMI

1 Introduction

Autonomous vehicle (AV)-pedestrian interactions directly impact pedestrian safety, etiquette, and overall acceptance of AV technology [1]. It is vital to fully explore this emerging interaction type to address potential ambiguities and conflicts in the future of transportation. However, designing and evaluating communication techniques for AV-pedestrian interactions is a challenging task due to the unavailability of AVs for experiments and the potential harms involved in physical field tests. As such, within these circumstances, virtual reality (VR)-based methods have received considerable attention from the research

H. Krömker (Ed.): HCII 2022, LNCS 13335, pp. 371–390, 2022.
https://doi.org/10.1007/978-3-031-04987-3_25

community and are increasingly being used to investigate pedestrians' behavior in relation to AVs and to understand different interaction solutions [2]. Compared with other methods (e.g., the Wizard-of-Oz [3,4] and video-based [5–7] methods), VR-based approach offers a number of benefits for examination of the simulated scenarios and to conduct AV-pedestrians interaction evaluation. An immersive environment enables improved spatial perception ability that can facilitate realistic judgment of the speed and distance of AVs [8]. Furthermore, greater flexibility in parameter manipulation and environmental control can be easily achieved [9].

While VR-based approaches are becoming increasingly powerful and popular, they can involve difficulties in achieving consistency and reproducibility in AV-pedestrian interaction design and testing [10]. The root cause of these issues is that the design concepts in existing studies are usually evaluated in different virtual environments or applications, leading to varying levels of fidelity in terms of traffic scenarios, communication interface prototypes, system settings, etc. [11]. Therefore, it is hard for designers and researchers to evaluate their design and compare the results across different scenarios and reach a consensus about the knowledge gained.

At the same time, to create virtual scenarios for evaluation, researchers and designers are limited to expert tools for the design of VR environments, which requires considerable effort. Even with expertise on such tools, it is time-consuming and labor-intensive to perform the process of design iteration, and evaluation of the testing scenarios [10], and this issue will become more serious when multiple testing scenarios are required. As a result, new tools and methods need to be developed to overcome the methodological and process issues raised above, which impeding knowledge development in the research community.

To this end, we propose the Human-Autonomous Vehicle Interaction Testbed (HAVIT), a VR-based platform, as a possible solution for enhancing the consistency and efficiency of AV-pedestrian interaction design and study process. To implement our testbed, (1) we were inspired by previous studies to develop the components of the key parameters of the HAVIT in terms of Physical Context, Vehicle Behavior, and External Human-Machine Interface (eHMI) Behavior, which can be adapted to address the factors critical to future AV-pedestrian interaction and interface design; (2) In addition, corresponding structured visual panels in the HAVIT allow users to easily manipulate those parameters for intuitiveness interaction scenarios creation; (3) Finally, the HAVIT provides a coherent and iterative workflow to facilitate the efficiency of formative study towards the eHMI concepts, starting with the Scenario Configuration, moving to Experimental Setting, and ending with Batch Exportation, which enables a rapid examination and generation of virtual testing scenarios.

2 Related Work

We classify the related work into two categories: (1) AV-pedestrian interaction studies and (2) VR simulation for AV-pedestrian interaction research.

2.1 Interaction Between AVs and Pedestrians

Many factors have been explored and proven to influence the decision-making processes of pedestrians. Rasouli and Tsotsos [12] provided a comprehensive summary of the factors influencing pedestrian behavior through a review of the related literature. These factors can be divided into two main categories: environmental factors and pedestrian factors. Environmental factors include traffic characteristics (e.g., vehicle appearance and traffic flow), dynamic factors (e.g., vehicle speed and spacing), and the physical environment (e.g., road structure, traffic signs, and weather), while pedestrian factors include demographics, status (pedestrians' physical status includes attention, walking pattern, speed, and trajectory), ability, characteristics (features that define how pedestrians' think and behave, including culture, past experience, and faith), and social factors. It is worth noting that the above influences are often interrelated in real-life traffic scenarios, and they combine to influence road users' perceptions and understandings of the state and intent of AVs [11]. Studying the interaction between these influences is essential to understand traffic situations' complexity and to facilitate safer AV-pedestrian interactions.

eHMI is an important aspect of AV-pedestrian interactions, which is the form of communication external to an AV that is typically used to communicate the AV's current state and future behavior to pedestrians; it can help in overcoming AV trust issues and improving the effectiveness and experience of AV-pedestrian communication [13]. Various eHMI concepts have been proposed and tested, such as text [8,14], symbols [5,15], street projections [16], light animations [17,18], and information from mobile devices [19]. However, researchers have not yet reached a consensus about how different eHMIs should be used [9]. More and more research is now focusing on details related to the implementation of eHMIs to achieve the best interactions in terms of usability, security, and efficiency. For example, many eHMI studies have started to explore in-depth the dimensions of communication perspectives [20,21], communication subjects [22], and covered states [7]. Other studies have analyzed the design of the interactive elements of a particular type of eHMI, such as color [23,24], placement location [17,21], and display mode [6].

The scalability of eHMIs is another aspect that needs to be explored in the long term [10,25]. Most eHMIs have been tested in relatively simple and unrealistic situations, which has led to many eHMI concepts becoming viable options. The problem, however, is that the results of these studies often only show that the eHMIs improve simple interactions; most studies do not provide insights into using eHMIs in more complex traffic scenarios [1]. Therefore, more evaluations of interactions between pedestrians and eHMIs in diverse traffic scenarios–such as those involving multiple pedestrians [27] or different weather conditions–are needed in the future [11].

Most of the previous research has focused on common traffic scenarios and strategies for communicating the status or intent of AVs to the normal road user. However, research on AV-pedestrian interactions are equally critical in special cases and situations [28], such as sensor failure, a lack of system action, or action errors. As such, future research should include evaluations of (1) how pedestrians should be informed and instructed to act depending on the type of malfunction occurring, (2) how to optimize safe interactions between eHMIs and pedestrians in special scenarios, and (3) how to conduct interactions in a way that ensures the public acceptance and trust of AVs [6]. In addition, while people with disabilities are among the most vulnerable road users in traffic, only a few studies have been done on forms of external communication for people with disabilities (e.g., physical, visual, or hearing impairment) [29–31]. When conducting studies on these specific conditions, a method with high degree of flexibility in manipulating the vehicles behaviors is required.

Many dimensions of AV-pedestrian interaction have not yet been adequately studied, and research on each dimension is indispensable. More importantly, the complexity of the study of AV-pedestrian interaction will increase with the number of studies being conducted and the aspects being studied, making many traditional research methods infeasible. In the face of such challenges, a VR-based method can provide more flexible, scalable approaches that can support more aspects of AV-pedestrian interaction research. This was one of the critical motivations behind the development of HAVIT.

2.2 VR Simulation for AV-Pedestrian Interaction Design and Study

VR simulation has been widely used to study AV-pedestrian interactions. Compared to traditional, non-immersive virtual environments (e.g., paper-based [26], video-based [6,7,32], or real-world-based [3] environments), the VR-based method combines the advantages of the above approaches to allow for flexible environmental control and simulations under highly realistic conditions. For example, Chang et al. [33] designed and evaluated an eHMI concept using the "eyes on the front of the car" eHMI; specifically, they developed two VR scenarios, each including five components: the environment, the user (i.e., a three-dimensional computer-generated pedestrian model), the car, the eHMI, and the car movement route (i.e., a straight line). Doric et al. [34] implemented a VR-based simulation that includes a simple, uncontrolled pedestrian crossing scenario in which virtual vehicles are continuously generated at regular intervals. de Clercq et al. [14] used VR simulation to evaluate the impact of four interface concepts on pedestrian crossing intentions. Specifically, VR was used to simulate the vehicle behavior (e.g., giving way or not giving way), vehicle size, eHMI (four types), and display time of the eHMI (i.e., early, middle, and late). Studies have also begun to evaluate sound interfaces using VR simulations [30]. To evaluate auditory concepts for people with visual impairments, VR-simulated scenarios have included background noise (e.g., a mixture of human voices and engine sounds) and have given participants the ability to control the direction and location of the sounds so that testers can immerse themselves in a realistic sound experience. The closest related work to ours describes the On-Foot [1], a VR-based simulator that aims to simulate mixed traffic scenarios. It provides users with a set of control modules that can be modified by coding. In this case, VR showed a higher degree of control over the simulation of diverse AV-pedestrian interaction conditions.

Furthermore, one of the essential reasons VR-based simulation have produced convincing evidence is that they primarily utilize objective measures [9], such as reaction time, duration, and accuracy. In addition, VR can capture information about the test taker's body movement. For example, Schmidt et al. [35] used an immersive VR environment to explore the intricate social cues that underlie the non-verbal communication involved in pedestrians' crossing decisions. They collected motion trajectories generated by moving the body, legs, arms, and head of each subject in the physical and virtual world.

3 Design Principles

Our primary aim with the HAVIT was to create a VR-based research tool that could improve the consistency and efficiency of AV-pedestrian interaction design studies. To achieve this, we identified three key design principles (DPs) from the literature review and the interview with domain designers and experts.

DP1: Customizable and Flexible. Most VR simulations are unable to support setting and modifying the factors that influence pedestrians' decision to cross the street [10] and are limited in their flexibility to fulfill requirements of diverse AV-pedestrian interaction scenarios creation. The HAVIT builds upon the previous works, sythsized a set of key parameter components to address the factors critical to future AV-pedestrian interaction and interface design.

DP2: Easy to Use. The implementation of virtual AV-pedestrian interaction scenarios often requires researchers to set various factors by coding [15,25]. Our goal was to achieve an intuitive configuration process of virtual testing scenarios that easy-to-use for designers.

DP3: Efficient and Iterative. HAVIT aimed to present an iterative workflow that enables researchers and designers to modify and generate multiple virtual scenarios simultaneously. Besides, HAVIT supports the set up of experiments in the virtual testing scenarios and the collect of data within the developed scenarios; thus, achieving the quick exploration and iteration of design concepts.

4 The HAVIT System

This section presents the HAVIT, providing descriptions of the user interface (UI), the main process it enables, and the relevant components. As Fig. 1 shows, the HAVIT supports three processes at the highest level: Scenario Configuration, Experimental Setting, and Batch Exportation. Each process can be configured via user panels and scripts provided by the HAVIT.

Scenario Configuration. We organized the key parameters into three user panels—Physical Context, Vehicle Behavior, and eHMI Behavior—to guide users to create the scenario. The HAVIT also allows users to quickly add and remove objects from the scenario by interacting directly with them. In addition, users can preview the current scenario at any time during the configuration process.

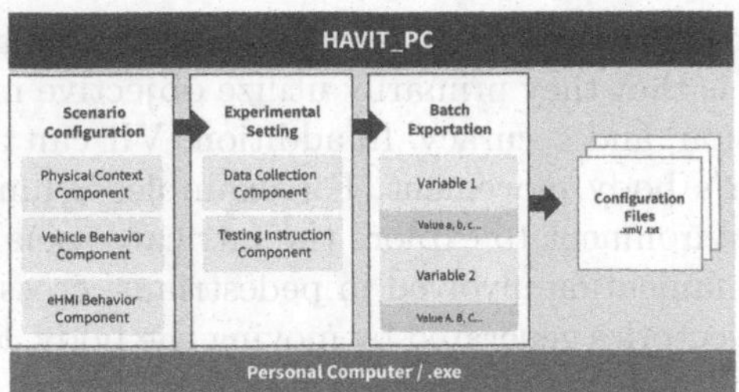

Fig. 1. The main processes of the HAVIT.

Experimental Setting. The HAVIT enables the rapid setup of experiments by providing a Data Collection component and a Testing Instruction component. The Data Collection component allows researchers to collect assigned quantitative data (e.g., the start/end time of crossing behavior, time required for decision-making, distance traveled, and average speed) and qualitative data (i.e., the participants' subjective experiences). The Testing Instruction component provides a set of adjustable panels that will be displayed in the VR environment to enable the guidance of participants during the testing.

Batch Exportation. Studies often involve manipulating a group of variables and, thus, generate a set or several sets of trials for an experiment. Repetitive manual configuration reduces the development efficiency and increases the risk of human error when many test scenarios are required. The HAVIT allows users to add variables and values according to the experimental requirements and generate multiple scenarios simultaneously to enhance testing scenarios' development efficiency.

The HAVIT is a Unity-based desktop program that can easily be used on a personal computer at the system level. With the HAVIT, users can configure interaction scenarios and export configuration files according to their needs. These configuration files can then be read easily by a VR device, such as an Oculus, and loaded with the appropriate environment and parameters to generate scenarios for testing. Below, we detail the parameter components, UI, and design of each system component.

4.1 Parameter Components

The design of the key parameters of HAVIT was inspired by previous literature, mainly refers to the important factor aspects of AV-pedestrian interaction that need to be explored in-depth in the future (see Sect. 2.1 of the literature review). Figure 2 shows the key parameter components of the HAVIT, which are (1) Physical context component, (2) Vehicle behavior component, and (3) eHMI behavior component. Each parameter component is consisted of several key classes. Specifically, a `ScenarioController` manages the road structure, and the natural conditions show the corresponding scenario to the user and contain several `RouteControllers`. A `RouteController` controls a specific route in the current scenario, as well as the set of vehicles driving on this route. In addition to a vehicle's appearance and behavior information, a `Vehicle` can display several `eHMIs` when interacting with pedestrians. Also, the `eHMI` class has two child classes: `Visual eHMI` and `Sound eHMI`. Each child class has different properties to control the display behavior of the eHMI. The `PedestrianTaskController` and `DataCollectionController` manage the testing task and the data to collect in the VR experiment. The `ExportationController` contains several variables, each of which points to a specific parameter and has multiple values.

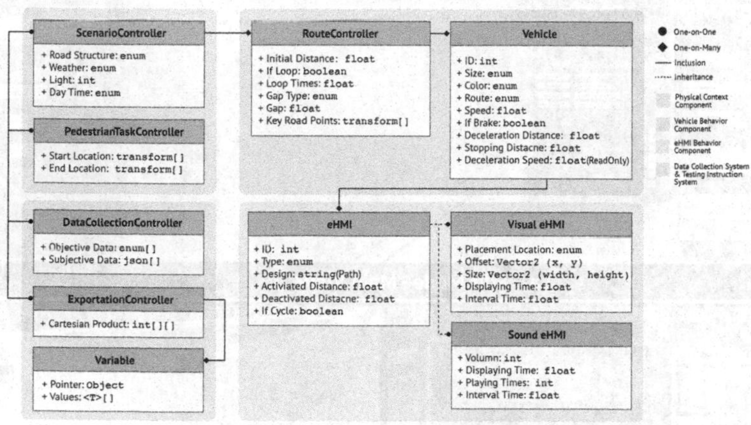

Fig. 2. Summary of the parameter components and key classes of the HAVIT.

4.2 User Interface

As Fig. 3 shows, the HAVIT consists of three UI components: the Main View, user panels, and Mini-Map. The Main View allows users to inspect the entire scenario two modes: (1) Edit Mode, in which users can directly interact with objects within the scenario, such as turning the vehicle to move in a different direction or moving the position, and (2) Preview Mode, in which users can check the effect of the scenario in the current configuration conditions. Users can also freely move the camera to change the viewing angle. Next, the key parameter components and functionalities are implemented and presented to users through the user panels, of which there are five: the Physical Context Panel (Fig. 3a [U1]), Vehicle Behavior Panel (Fig. 3a [U2 and U3]), and eHMI Behavior Panel (Fig. 3a [U4]), which are used to manipulate the parameters for creating scenarios; the Experimental Setting Panel (Fig. 3a [U5]), which is used to set up the collected data and the testing instructions in the VR environment; and the Batch Exportation Panel (Fig. 3b [U6]), which is used to generate multiple scenarios at the same time. Last, the Mini-Map (Fig. 3a [M]) is used to provide an overview of the current scenario. Also, location markers and vehicle routes are displayed on the Mini-Map to allow for quick checks.

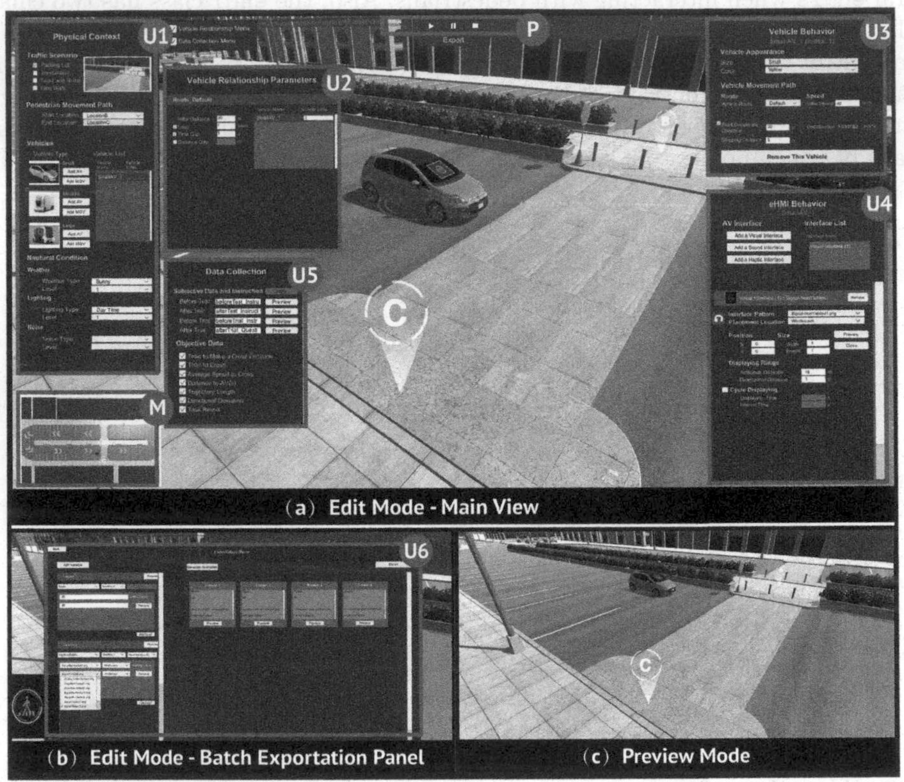

Fig. 3. The UI of the HAVIT. (a) Edit Mode - Main View, (b) Edit Mode - Batch Exportation Panel, and (c) Preview Mode. The panels and interactive components are marked with red borders in the image.

4.3 Scenario Configuration

The first main process enabled by the HAVIT is scenario configuration. Users can quickly and easily configure various AV-pedestrian interaction scenarios using a set of user panels.

Physical Context. The Physical Context parameter allows users to define the road structure, the participant's movement path, the test vehicles, and the natural conditions. These elements are discussed in greater detail in this section.

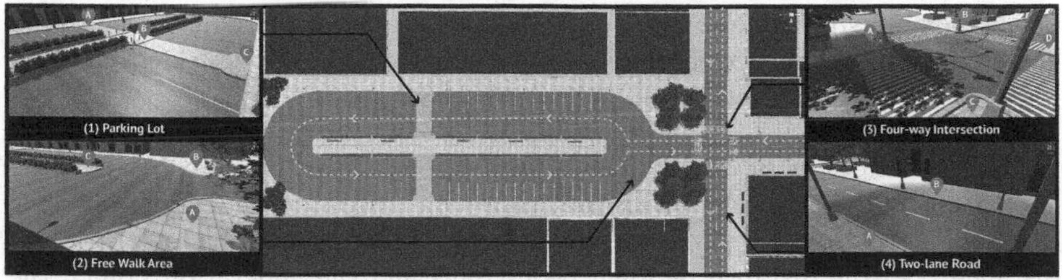

Fig. 4. Road structures in the HAVIT. The aerial-view map of the HAVIT is shown in the middle. The yellow dotted lines represent the routes on which a vehicle can move. The four road-structure scenarios are visualized on either side of the aerial-view map: (1) Parking Lot, (2) Free Walk Area, (3) Four-Way Intersection, and (4) Two-Lane Road. The blue markers with capital letters represent the optional locations that are used to specify the pedestrian movement path in each scenario.

Road Structure. The HAVIT contains a street map showing an area of 396 × 561 square feet (as shown in Fig. 4) that includes four road structure types: (1) Parking Lot, (2) Free Walk Area (i.e., the entrance/exit area of a parking lot), (3) Four-Way Intersection, and (4) Two-Lane Road. All of these are locations where AVs and pedestrians frequently interact in daily traffic. Each road structure has a predetermined travel route for vehicles. The initial settings do not include traffic signals, and users can add traffic signals (e.g., traffic lights, crosswalks, and stop signs) to the scenarios as needed.

Pedestrian (Participant) Movement Path. Once the road structure scenario has been decided on, the user needs to assign the movement path for the participants in the testing scenario. Users can determine the path by specifying the start location and end location, which are dynamically generated according to the road structure selected by the user.

Vehicles. The HAVIT provides three vehicle model sizes: Large (i.e., buses and trucks), Medium (i.e., vans), and Small (i.e., passenger cars). This is because prior works showed that vehicle size leads to differences in the subjective risk perception and objective distance perception of pedestrians [13].

Natural Conditions. The natural condition parameters supported by HAVIT include Weather Condition, Lighting Condition, and Noise. Currently proposed external communication interfaces mainly rely on visual cues and auditory cues. Lighting and weather factors are critical to examining the visibility and interactive performance of visual-based interface concepts. In addition, noise is an important consideration when designing auditory-based interfaces, which are effective solutions for visually impaired people [6].

Vehicle Behavior. One of the critical features of the HAVIT is the ability to provide the flexible control of vehicle behavior. There are two control modes offered for users to achieve this: controlling the behavior of vehicle groups and controlling the behavior of individual vehicles. These act on vehicle groups and on specific vehicles within the scenario, respectively.

Vehicle Relationship Behavior. The HAVIT allows users to control the vehicle behavior for multiple vehicles at the same time based on the vehicles' travel routes. The controllable parameters include the sequence of vehicles, the initial distance (i.e., the distance between pedestrians and the generation point), the number of travel loops, and the generation gap (i.e., the time gap or distance gap) between vehicles.

Individual Vehicle Behavior. The HAVIT also allows users to configure parameters for each vehicle in a scenario. This control mode is useful when the vehicles in the scenario all have different behaviors or when more complex changes in vehicle behavior need to be simulated. Specifically, the HAVIT supports the initial speed (in km/h) of the vehicle, the acceleration/deceleration distance (i.e., the distance at which the vehicle starts to decelerate, in meters) of the vehicle, and the stopping distance of the vehicle (i.e., the distance to pedestrians, in meters). When the user selects the above three parameters, the acceleration/deceleration speed is calculated and shown on the user panel.

The eHMI Behavior. The HAVIT supports the import of user-defined interfaces. Further, the HAVIT allows the simultaneous placement of multiple eHMIs on an AV to evaluate the effects of multiple eHMI combinations. To enable the exploration of the functional details of these interaction concepts, we also provided controllable parameters related to visual and auditory eHMIs and ensured that the parameters of each added eHMI could be adjusted independently. The HAVIT's parameters are as follows:

- **Placement Location (Only for Visual eHMIs):** This refers to the placement area of an eHMI on an AV, which can be the windshield, bumper, roof, side windows, front road, or front cover of the vehicle.
- **Display Position (Only for Visual eHMIs):** This refers to the specific position of an eHMI in the placement area, controlled by the offsets in the horizontal and vertical coordinates based on the center of this area.
- **Display Size (Only for Visual eHMIs):** This refers to the exact size of an eHMI, controlled by width and height.
- **Activate and Deactivate Distance (for Both):** This refers to the distance to pedestrians from where an eHMI starts to appear and disappears on the AV.
- **Cycle Display (for Both):** This refers to whether an eHMI is displayed periodically or not. It can be controlled by setting the displaying time and the interval time.
- **Play Volume (Only for Auditory eHMIs):** This refers to the sound volume of an auditory eHMI.

4.4 Experimental Setting

Data Collection Component. Considering data collection is an indispensable part of the experimental process, we implemented a Data Collection component in the HAVIT to allow users to collect the data generated by tests. We classified the types of data collected by the HAVIT, based on previous research, as subjective data and objective data.

Objective Data. One of the key reasons that VR-based approaches can produce convincing results is the use of objective measurements. The HAVIT provides a variety of pedestrian task-related metrics that can be automatically activated through the provided scripts. When the task is completed for each scenario, the tracking component automatically reports data information for the corresponding metric. The metrics currently covered by the HAVIT are the time to make a cross decision, time to cross, trajectory length, average speed to cross, distance to AV(s), directional deviation, and task result.

Subjective Data. To improve the validity of subjective data collection, we utilized InVRQs [37], an existing VR questionnaire toolkit, as a complement to the HAVIT. This toolkit was useful, as it provided the questionnaire structure and question types. The HAVIT allows the user to determine where the questionnaire panel appears in the VR scenario.

Testing Instruction Component. The Testing Instruction component is provided to display experimental instructions for participants in VR testing scenarios, which rely on a set of panels inside the VR that are shown to the participants. Four display timings are provided: before the test, after the test, and before and after each trial—all of which support the customization of the questionnaire or text presentation.

4.5 Batch Exportation

To reduce the repetitive manual configuration process, the HAVIT provides a Batch Exportation component. Specifically, after configuring one testing scenario, the user can specify one or more variables (i.e., parameters in the HAVIT) required for batch configuration and assign specific values accordingly through the user panel. After the user specifies all the variables and their values, the system will create a set for each of them and perform the Cartesian product operation on these sets. The HAVIT also provides a scenario list to allow users to preview the generated scenarios. When a user previews a specific scenario, the system will modify the values of each involved parameter according to the corresponding combination. Also, when exporting batch scenarios, the system will iterate through all combinations and export the corresponding configuration file for each combination.

4.6 Preview Mode

To allow users to check the effect of the configured scenario, the HAVIT supports Preview Mode. Specifically, the system refers to the Unity game engine's Play Mode and provides three buttons in game Game window: Play, Pause, and Stop. The user can click the Play button to preview, click again or click the Stop button to exit.

5 Implementation

The HAVIT was developed in the Unity game engine (v. 2020.1.9f1), with all related scripts written in `C#`. The project has been packaged to the Windows platform to work independently from the engine. After testing on an HP OMEN Gaming Laptop with a GTX 1650 graphics processing unit (GPU), the HAVIT was found to have a guaranteed a framerate 60 Hz (default setting) when 20 vehicles are running simultaneously.

6 Evaluation

This work presents the first version of HAVIT. Therefore, we primarily focused on its overall usability in this evaluation, i.e., whether the designed system and features of HAVIT are understandable and easy to use for our intended users. Specifically, we conducted a formative user study with professionals. We were interested in the participants' performance when using the testbed and the qualitative impressions of their experience.

6.1 Participants

We relied on the intended users of the HAVIT to gain insights from their workflows, and we expect that this initial feedback will help distill the strengths and areas for improvement of the HAVIT for the future. As such, we recruited professionals in fields related to human-computer interaction (HCI; $n = 8$; 3 females), including VR experience researchers (P2, P3, P4, and P5), intelligent systems researchers (P6 and P8), and user experience designers (P1 and P7). None of the users had prior experiences with our testbed.

6.2 Procedure

The participants were first introduced to the HAVIT, and they then were instructed to configure a set of testing scenarios for an AV-pedestrian study that featured a within-subject study design, 2 independent variables, and a total of 9 (3×3) testing scenarios (trials). We chose this study topic because its complexity allowed us to demonstrate and test many of the HAVIT's features. The participants then completed questionnaires evaluating the HAVIT's main features and answered interview questions from the researchers. The testing process lasted about 50 min. One researcher took observational field notes, which were analyzed and used to help interpret the results from our survey data.

*Introduction and Training (*15 min*).* Following the signing of informed consent forms and obtaining recording permission, the participants were provided with some background knowledge about the AV-pedestrian interaction study and all the features of the HAVIT system. They were then guided through configuring a simple scenario and allowed to explore freely.

*Tasks (*25 min*).* In this part, the participants configured a set of testing scenarios using the HAVIT, following specific instructions. They were provided with a Study Method document that included the study goal and the experimental design (i.e., independent variables, dependent variables, pedestrian tasks, and experimental setup). We took care to ensure that the content was as short and concise as possible. The instructions were as follows: (1) Manual Configuration (Task 1): Configure 1 of the 9 testing scenarios (a total of 15 parameters need to be set); and (2) Batch Configuration (Task 2): Generate the 9 required testing scenarios at the same time (a total of 6 parameters need to be set). We emphasized that there was no correct order for the configuration of the scenarios and that they could complete the task according to their understanding of it. The participants were asked to verbally report, "I'm done" after completing the first task. The researcher checked the configuration results and informed the participants to make adjustments if necessary, after which they continued with the second task. The participants were also told to complete the tasks as quickly and accurately as possible. The whole process was screen recorded.

*Questionnaire (*5 min*).* After the two configuration tasks were completed, each participant was then asked to answer Likert-type questions related to the system features. Each Likert-type item was graded by users from 1 to 5 in relation to the usefulness of the feature and their level of agreement with the item. Our questions were inspired by the "first-use study" in Exemplar [38].

*Semi-Structured Interview (*5 min*).* Finally, we conducted a semi-structured interview with each participant, which addressed the following: (1) the ease of configuration with the HAVIT, (2) its usefulness, (3) the scenario results achieved and the participant's satisfaction with those, and (4) the potential for the future use of the add-on. The interviews were all audio recorded.

6.3 Measurements

To test this first version of the HAVIT, we defined two basic metrics for analysis: (1) completion time, which refers to how much time the participants required to complete each task (the timing started when the participants verbally reported, "I'm ready" and ended when they stated, "I'm done"); and (2) task success result, which refers to whether the task was completed successfully (i.e., if all parameters were set up correctly) or was failed. A thematic analysis of the participants' opinions was conducted; these opinions were collected during the semi-structured interviews. The themes also stemmed from the observations of the participants' behavior during the tasks and the observer's debriefing after the VR testing scenario configuration session.

6.4 Results

Objective Data. Table 1 shows a summary of the participants' completion times and task success. In general, the participants were able to understand the features provided by the HAVIT. All participants completed both tasks. In Task 1 (T1, Manual Configuration), all participants except P1 and P7 finished in approximately 10 min (mean [M] = 9.02). P1 and P7 had less quantitative experimental experience and spent extra time on reading the study method document. Four participants (P1, P3, P7, and P8) were unsuccessful in completing T1, and the errors they made are shown in Table 1. In Task 2 (T2, Batch Configuration), 7 out of the 8 participants completed the task successfully, and P4 was unsuccessful because of one omission error. The average completion time of T2 was 4.22 min.

Table 1. Summary of the participants' task-completion times (T1 and T2) and success results.

Participants	Task 1 (Minutes)	Task 1 (Success & Accuracy Score)	Task 1 (Error Type & Number)	Task 2 (Minutes)	Task 2 (Success & Accuracy Score)
P1	12:05	Fail (14/15)	Input error: 1	4:41	Success (6/6)
P2	7:56	Success (15/15)	None	3:28	Success (6/6)
P3	8:32	Fail (13/15)	Input error: 1 Omission error: 1	4:24	Success (6/6)
P4	5:24	Success (15/15)	None	5:37	Fail (5/6)
P5	6:18	Success (15/15)	None	3:43	Success (6/6)
P6	6:35	Success (15/15)	None	3:35	Success (6/6)
P7	17:46	Fail (14/15)	Omission error: 1	5:17	Success (6/6)
P8	9:43	Fail (14/15)	Omission error: 1	4:58	Success (6/6)

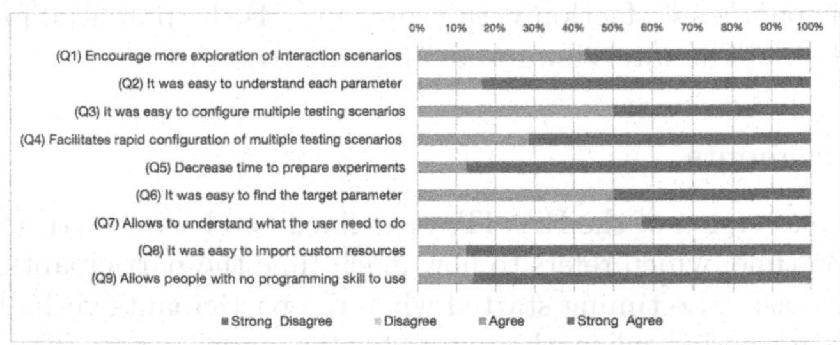

Fig. 5. System feature-related Likert-type question results ($n = 8$).

Subjective Data. Here, we report the results from the Likert-scale questions, in terms of mean (M), median (m), and standard deviation (SD). Most participants reported that the HAVIT enabled them to quickly understand a wide range of impact factors related to AV-pedestrian interaction and that it encouraged exploration (Q1: $M = 4.38$, $m = 4.50$, $SD = .74$). Likewise, 7 participants held positive views about the HAVIT's ability to reduce the time needed to prepare for an experiment (Q5: $M = 4.75$, $m = 5.00$, $SD = .71$). For the Batch Exportation process, most participants reported that the HAVIT could help decrease the time needed to configure multiple scenarios (Q4: $M = 4.50$, $m = 5.00$, $SD = .76$), and the Batch Configuration method is easy to understand (Q3: $M = 4.00$, $m = 4.00$, $SD = .93$). Further, the participants were generally confident about uploading their self-defined interface to the HAVIT (Q8: $M = 4.88$, $m = 5.00$, $SD = .35$) and ranked it highly in relation to the statement that the HAVIT "allows people with no programming skill to use it" (Q9: $M = 4.63$, $m = 5.00$, $SD = .74$). Several participants also agreed that the parameters are intuitive and easy to understand (Q2: $M = 4.38$, $m = 5.00$, $SD = .91$), but they would like some video illustrations and more detailed information. Several participants suggested that better user panels for managing related parameters could help improve the "time to configure the scenario" and "rapid modification" (Q6: $M = 3.75$, $m = 3.50$, $SD = .89$). Finally, the HAVIT's workflow received positive feedback from the participants (Q7: $M = 4.25$, $m = 4.00$, $SD = .71$). Across all questions, the median ratings were at or above 4 on a 5-point Likert scale (5 = best; see Fig. 5).

7 Discussion

7.1 Effectiveness at Facilitating Efficient Exploration Process

This work presented the HAVIT as a promising solution for facilitating the efficiency of the AV-pedestrian interaction design and study process. From the feedback from the questionnaire and interviews, we found that the promotion of efficiency mainly comes from three key features of the HAVIT.

The category-based user panel design was found to guide researchers and designers to explore more AV-pedestrian interaction scenarios, even if they have limited knowledge about this field. P2 and P6 mentioned that the HAVIT provided a framework to improve the efficiency of gaining an understanding of this research topic. For example, P2 explained, "The panels are organized logically, with the relevant parameters all together, which gives me a quick idea of which types of the factors to focus on".

The flexible workflow—such as being able to preview the scenarios at any time during the configuration process—not only helped users explore ideas directly but also helped them focus more on the pedestrians and the potential interactions. P5 explained the main benefit of the HAVIT as being that it "Immediately gets you into a headspace for thinking of spatially instead of having to extrapolate in a text document". P4 also explained that previewing the generated scenarios enabled a quick assessment of the reasonableness of the parameter settings by comparing the effects of multiple scenarios.

The HAVIT combines the authoring phase and evaluating phase in a coherent workflow by implementing the Batch Configuration, Data Collection, and Testing Instruction components. P4 mentioned that quickly generating multiple testing scenarios was helpful for avoiding the repetitive configuration process, which might have discouraged exploration and led to thought fixation. P3 and P6 said that being able to collect data and provide instruction tools in the VR environment was a significant advantage, explaining, "the design of these features is reasonable; they fit the needs of the VR-based experiment process and are very convenient for researchers". P5 added, "I like how fast it is from planning the task to acting it out; it encourages me to try more".

7.2 The Ease of Use of the Scenario Configuration

The participants' questionnaire responses were mainly positive and encouraging. Still, from the performance data and researchers' observations, we identified some key usability aspects that needed to be improved during the configuration process. First, all our participants were able to complete the configuration task in a relatively short period. However, 4 of them made a few errors (1–2 omission errors or input errors) in the first task. Two participants reported that "it would not be easy to find a specific parameter and adjust it when many parameters are involved." P2 added, "Sometimes I don't realize that I have adjusted this parameter, so I don't check if its value is correct". Although the participants who made these errors reported that they were confident in the configuration process and believed that they would not make similar errors if they used the HAVIT one or two more times. This issue could be circumvented by either providing highlight cues or by implementing a panel to show the parameters that have been set by the user.

In addition, the current user panel features a hierarchy that shows less information, which aimed to improve the efficiency of information access for users. While most users appreciated the usefulness of the user panels in terms of gaining a quick understanding and overview of the information, five of the eight participants mentioned in one way or another that the user panels occasionally became obtrusive and distracting: "There are too many user panels in front of me when I am trying to see and set up parameters" (P5). This feedback emerged after the users became familiar with the system when they started to feel as though they did not need the user panels to be displayed all the time. This finding raises an important question when designing such systems: how can we strike a balance between an intuitive parameter structure and a clear user view while providing both to the user? We believe a further comparative evaluation study with two groups of participants who are given different experiences might help in understanding this phenomenon and identifying a well-balanced solution.

7.3 Prospective Applications of the HAVIT

Based on our investigation of the HAVIT, we see a flexible platform and relatively strong generative power for AV-pedestrian interaction studies. Here, we discuss the potential applications made possible by the HAVIT: (1) Scalability studies of interface concepts related to AVs, which need to evaluate the ability of eHMI concepts to be used in various scenarios with different numbers and types of vehicles, different road structures, etc. (2) The HAVIT can be used to investigate the finer details of the implementation of eHMI concepts, which need to explore how to use and organize interactive elements (e.g., display location, time pattern, and color) in design to communicate crucial messages. (3) Finally, HAVIT can be used to explore pedestrian responses under extreme situations, such as when sensor failures and interface display errors. The above applications are critical to the universality and standardization of AV interaction technology, and they are also significant challenges facing AV-pedestrian interaction research at present.

8 Limitation and Future Work

There are some limitations related to the parameter components of the HAVIT. First, although our testbed is based on generic parameters applicable to AV-pedestrian interaction studies, it provides a limited choice of some parameters. This is because we recognized that some aspects of AV-pedestrian interaction scenarios and influencing factors cannot be fully predicted in advance. We envisioned the HAVIT to be based on core processes and critical functions rather than an all-encompassing solution. To improve the universality of the HAVIT, future versions could include additional road scene types, pedestrian interaction methods, and eHMI interaction prototypes.

Second, the current version of the HAVIT does not support the exploration of interactions among pedestrians. To address this limitation in the future, an initial step could be utilizing characteristically controllable (e.g., in terms of gender, age, moving speed, and group size) virtual pedestrians. Furthermore, we would like to allow multiple participants to be present and tested simultaneously in a scenario. By embedding additional sensory input and body tracking to capture critical features in a user's motion, the HAVIT can support a more realistic, accurate investigation of the effects of interactions between pedestrians. In addition, the HAVIT provides a Preview Mode designed to allow users to preview the final effect of a scenario; however, this preview is based on a two-dimensional (2D) display of the 3D scenario, so there are still some differences in immersion and fidelity between the preview and the final VR scenario.

For the evaluation method, considering the different levels of familiarity of the recruited participants with this research topic, giving them the freedom to construct simulation scenarios may have led to significant differences in the difficulty of the final scenario configuration. Therefore, we assigned them configuration tasks that needed to be completed. However, this causes the experimental results to be in a constrained situation. Further validation is essential to establishing the HAVIT as a research tool. We plan to conduct additional evaluations to benchmark the HAVIT in relation to existing simulation tools. Besides, an end-users (experts in AV-pedestrian interaction domain) goal-driven use case study will be considered in the near future to examine if HAVIT can facilitate their requirements.

9 Conclusion

In this work, we introduced HAVIT, a VR-based platform aimed to facilitate the design process of AV-pedestrian interactions. In this line of work, we structured the key parameter components in a set of panels that users can easily select and modify to create virtual interaction scenarios, with a focus on rich, spatiotemporal interaction between the AVs and pedestrians. We also proposed an efficient workflow with three phases to further ease the creation, iteration, and generation cycles of virtual scenarios. To evaluate the usefulness of HAVIT, we conducted a formative user study with intended professional users. Our evaluation received positive results, indicating that the workflow of the HAVIT is usable and easy to understand. We believe that our workflow can increase the flexibility and efficiency of concept exploration of possible interactions in the early design stage.

References

1. Mahadevan, K., Sanoubari, E., Somanath, S., Young, J.E., Sharlin, E.: AV-Pedestrian interaction design using a pedestrian mixed traffic simulator. In: Proceedings of the 2019 on Designing Interactive Systems Conference, pp. 475–486 (2019)
2. Deb, S., Carruth, D.W., Sween, R., Strawderman, L., Garrison, T.M.: Efficacy of virtual reality in pedestrian safety research. Appl. Ergon. **65**, 449–460 (2017)
3. Habibovic, A., et al.: Communicating intent of automated vehicles to pedestrians. Front. Psychol. 1336 (2018)
4. Rothenbücher, D., Li, J., Sirkin, D., Mok, B., Ju, W.: Ghost driver: a field study investigating the interaction between pedestrians and driverless vehicles. In: 2016 25th IEEE International Symposium on Robot and Human Interactive Communication (RO-MAN), pp. 795–802. IEEE (2016)
5. Ackermann, C., Beggiato, M., Schubert, S., Krems, J.F.: An experimental study to investigate design and assessment criteria: what is important for communication between pedestrians and automated vehicles? Appl. Ergon. **75**, 272–282 (2019)
6. Dey, D., et al.: Distance-dependent eHMIs for the interaction between automated vehicles and pedestrians. In 12th International Conference on Automotive User Interfaces and Interactive Vehicular Applications, pp. 192–204, September 2020
7. Fridman, L., Mehler, B., Xia, L., Yang, Y., Facusse, L.Y., Reimer, B.: To walk or not to walk: crowdsourced assessment of external vehicle-to-pedestrian displays. arXiv preprint arXiv:1707.02698 (2017)
8. Kemeny, A., Panerai, F.: Evaluating perception in driving simulation experiments. Trends Cogn. Sci. **7**(1), 31–37 (2003)
9. Rouchitsas, A., Alm, H.: External human-machine interfaces for autonomous vehicle-to-pedestrian communication: a review of empirical work. Front. Psychol. 2757 (2019)

10. Colley, M., Walch, M., Rukzio, E.: Unveiling the lack of scalability in research on external communication of autonomous vehicles. In Extended Abstracts of the 2020 CHI Conference on Human Factors in Computing Systems, pp. 1–9 (2020)
11. Dey, D., et al.: Taming the eHMI jungle: a classification taxonomy to guide, compare, and assess the design principles of automated vehicles' external human-machine interfaces. Transp. Res. Interdisc. Perspect. **7**, 100174 (2020)
12. Rasouli, A., Tsotsos, J.K.: Autonomous vehicles that interact with pedestrians: a survey of theory and practice. IEEE Trans. Intell. Transp. Syst. **21**(3), 900–918 (2019)
13. Faas, S. M.: What pedestrians want from autonomous vehicles-Mercedes cooperative car (2018)
14. De Clercq, K., Dietrich, A., Núñez Velasco, J.P., De Winter, J., Happee, R.: External human-machine interfaces on automated vehicles: effects on pedestrian crossing decisions. Hum. Factors **61**(8), 1353–1370 (2019)
15. Holländer, K., Wintersberger, P., Butz, A.: Overtrust in external cues of automated vehicles: an experimental investigation. In: Proceedings of the 11th International Conference on Automotive User Interfaces and Interactive Vehicular Applications, pp. 211–221 (2019)
16. Nguyen, T. T., Holländer, K., Hoggenmueller, M., Parker, C., Tomitsch, M.: Designing for projection-based communication between autonomous vehicles and pedestrians. In: Proceedings of the 11th International Conference on Automotive User Interfaces and Interactive Vehicular Applications, pp. 284–294 (2019)
17. Bazilinskyy, P., Kooijman, L., Dodou, D., De Winter, J.C.F.: How should external human-machine interfaces behave? Examining the effects of colour, position, message, activation distance, vehicle yielding, and visual distraction among 1,434 participants. Appl. Ergon. **95**, 103450 (2021)
18. Deb, S., Strawderman, L.J., Carruth, D.W.: Investigating pedestrian suggestions for external features on fully autonomous vehicles: a virtual reality experiment. Transport. Res. F: Traffic Psychol. Behav. **59**, 135–149 (2018)
19. Hussein, A., Garcia, F., Armingol, J.M., Olaverri-Monreal, C.: P2V and V2P communication for pedestrian warning on the basis of autonomous vehicles. In: 2016 IEEE 19th International Conference on Intelligent Transportation Systems (ITSC), pp. 2034–2039. IEEE (2016)
20. Dey, D., Martens, M., Wang, C., Ros, F., Terken, J. : Interface concepts for intent communication from autonomous vehicles to vulnerable road users. In: Adjunct Proceedings of the 10th International Conference on Automotive User Interfaces and Interactive Vehicular Applications, pp. 82–86 (2018)
21. Eisma, Y.B., Reiff, A., Kooijman, L., Dodou, D., De Winter, J.C.F.: External human-machine interfaces: effects of message perspective. Transport. Res. F: Traffic Psychol. Behav. **78**, 30–41 (2021)
22. Dey, D., Matviienko, A., Berger, M., Pfleging, B., Martens, M., Terken, J.: Communicating the intention of an automated vehicle to pedestrians: the contributions of eHMI and vehicle behavior. IT-Inf. Technol. **63**(2), 123–141 (2021)
23. Rettenmaier, M., Schulze, J., Bengler, K.: How much space is required? Effect of distance, content, and color on external human-machine interface size. Information **11**(7), 346 (2020)
24. Werner, A.: New colours for autonomous driving: An evaluation of chromaticities for the external lighting equipment of autonomous vehicles. Colour Turn 1 (2018)
25. Löcken, A., Golling, C., Riener, A.: How should automated vehicles interact with pedestrians? A comparative analysis of interaction concepts in virtual reality. In

Proceedings of the 11th International Conference on Automotive User Interfaces and Interactive Vehicular Applications, pp. 262–274 (2019)
26. Matthews, M., Chowdhary, G., Kieson, E.: Intent communication between autonomous vehicles and pedestrians. arXiv preprint arXiv:1708.07123 (2017)
27. van Vastenhoven, A.: The effect of distance-dependent eHMIs on the interaction between automated vehicles and two pedestrians. Doctoral dissertation, Master' thesis. Eindhoven University of Technology (2020)
28. Kyriakidis, M., et al.: A human factors perspective on automated driving. Theor. Issues Ergon. Sci. **20**(3), 223–249 (2019)
29. Asha, A.Z., Smith, C., Oehlberg, L., Somanath, S., Sharlin, E.: Views from the wheelchair: understanding interaction between autonomous vehicle and pedestrians with reduced mobility. In: Extended Abstracts of the 2020 CHI Conference on Human Factors in Computing Systems, pp. 1–8 (2020)
30. Colley, M., Walch, M., Gugenheimer, J., Askari, A., Rukzio, E.: Towards inclusive external communication of autonomous vehicles for pedestrians with vision impairments. In Proceedings of the 2020 CHI Conference on Human Factors in Computing Systems, pp. 1–14 (2020)
31. Colley, M., Walch, M., Gugenheimer, J., Rukzio, E.: Including people with impairments from the start: external communication of autonomous vehicles. In: Proceedings of the 11th International Conference on Automotive User Interfaces and Interactive Vehicular Applications: Adjunct Proceedings, pp. 307–314 (2019)
32. Bhagavathula, R., Williams, B., Owens, J., Gibbons, R.: The reality of virtual reality: a comparison of pedestrian behavior in real and virtual environments. In: Proceedings of the Human Factors and Ergonomics Society Annual Meeting, vol. 62, no. 1, pp. 2056–2060. SAGE Publications, Los Angeles (2018)
33. Chang, C.M., Toda, K., Sakamoto, D., Igarashi, T.: Eyes on a car: an interface design for communication between an autonomous car and a pedestrian. In: Proceedings of the 9th International Conference on Automotive User Interfaces and Interactive Vehicular Applications, pp. 65–73 (2017)
34. Doric, I., et al.: A novel approach for researching crossing behavior and risk acceptance: the pedestrian simulator. In: Adjunct Proceedings of the 8th International Conference on Automotive User Interfaces and Interactive Vehicular Applications, pp. 39–44 (2016)
35. Schmidt, H., Terwilliger, J., AlAdawy, D., Fridman, L.: Hacking nonverbal communication between pedestrians and vehicles in virtual reality. arXiv preprint arXiv:1904.01931 (2019)
36. Kooijman, L., Happee, R., de Winter, J.C.: How do eHMIs affect pedestrians' crossing behavior? A study using a head-mounted display combined with a motion suit. Information **10**(12), 386 (2019)
37. Feick, M., Kleer, N., Tang, A., Krüger, A: The virtual reality questionnaire toolkit. In Adjunct Publication of the 33rd Annual ACM Symposium on User Interface Software and Technology, pp. 68–69 (2020)
38. Hartmann, B., Abdulla, L., Mittal, M., Klemmer, S.R.: Authoring sensor-based interactions by demonstration with direct manipulation and pattern recognition. In: Proceedings of CHI 2007, pp. 145–154. ACM (2007)

Visualization Analysis on Literature Maps of Chinese Intelligent Vehicle Design Based on Citespace

Ying Li and Yangshuo Zheng(✉)

Wuhan University of Technology, Wuhan 430000, China
zhengyangshuo@163.com

Abstract. This study adopts the scientific metrology method, selects the relevant documents of intelligent vehicles in CNKI database from 2001 to 2021 as the data basis, and analyzes the atlas of Chinese intelligent vehicle design research papers with the help of CiteSpace software. The research shows that: (1) the number of documents issued has increased year by year, especially after 2017, which has gone through the stages of concept germination, technology exploration and market-oriented transition; (2) several closcly related interdisciplinary research teams have been formed, and there are also a large number of independent research forms; (3) the topics and research perspectives of papers related to intelligent vehicles are obviously diversified, with a total of 12 cluster labels, 408 keyword nodes and 701 connections, forming a cross domain, open, high complexity and high-level design and research ecology; (4) research hotspots mainly focus on three categories: driving automation, information networking and energy electrification.

Keywords: Intelligent vehicle · Knowledge map · Automatic driving

1 Concept of Intelligent Vehicle

1.1 Definition of Intelligent Vehicle

Pursuant to the definition in the "*intelligent vehicle innovation and development strategy*" issued by the national development and Reform Commission in February 2020, "intelligent vehicle" refers to a new generation of vehicle gradually becoming an intelligent mobile space and application terminal with automatic driving function by carrying advanced sensors and other devices and using new technologies such as artificial intelligence, usually referred to as "automatic driving vehicle", "intelligent networked car" and so on. With the rapid rise of new energy industry and the continuous maturity of transportation infrastructure construction, cloud server construction, artificial intelligence technology and fifth generation information and communication technology, single vehicle autonomous driving (AV) and networked vehicle (CV) are gradually integrated, and a new intelligent vehicle product architecture has been constructed. In the development process of intelligent vehicle, it has experienced the process of continuously improving the ability of intelligence and automation from radio remote control,

H. Krömker (Ed.): HCII 2022, LNCS 13335, pp. 391–401, 2022.
https://doi.org/10.1007/978-3-031-04987-3_26

computing control system, "lidar" and other technologies. The research of intelligent vehicle focuses on whether the vehicle itself can improve the degree of intelligence, in order to assist the driver to complete the driving task more safely and reliably. Intelligent cars have not only been limited to the role of simple transportation vehicles, but also gradually extended into mobile entertainment, communication and workspace. As a critical component of intelligent transportation system in smart city, intelligent vehicle will have a profound impact on the ode of human production, travel pattern, and connection form with the external environment.

1.2 Evolution of Intelligent Vehicles

The exploration of intelligent vehicles can be traced back to the early 20th century. In his book "*Unmanned systems of World Wars I and II*", HR Everett recorded the first radio-controlled ground tricycle manufactured in 1904, which was used by the army to transport and detonate gunpowder during World War I. In 1925, Francis P. Houdina, the founder of Houdina radio control company, invented a car operated by radio remote control, and later named the car as "American wonder". John McCarthy, a pioneer of artificial intelligence, wrote in the article (1968) "*Computer Controlled Cars*" that "The user enters the destination with a keyboard, and the car drives him there. Other commands include change destination, stop at that rest room or restaurant, go slow, go at emergency speed." which laid a foundation for the follow-up research on driverless cars in developed countries and regions such as the United States and Europe. In 1989, Dean Pomerleau of Carnegie Mellon University built a self-driving vehicle named ALVINN (Autonomous Land Vehicle in A Neural Network) based on deep learning algorithm. It can acquire data through camera and laser rangefinder and control the vehicle according to the result of neural network. In the 21st century, many developed countries have successively introduced the development strategy of intelligent vehicles, and accelerated the improvement of relevant policies, regulations and technology roadmap. Google Corporation of the United States started the test of driverless vehicle project in 2010 [1]. In 2014, it announced the completely independently designed self-driving intelligent vehicle, thus starting the intellectualization of the traditional automobile industry. Since 2019, US General Motors, Google and other enterprises have postponed the commercial landing time of high-level autopilot function. Although Tesla president Elon Musk announced that L5 automatic driving function will be launched in some areas in 2021, but from the frequent occurrence of automatic driving safety accidents, The actual landing of automatic driving still faces many technical problems and regulatory bottlenecks. From the present to a considerable period of time, the automatic driving vehicle will always be in the development stage from "L2.5 to L4".

China's research in the field of intelligent vehicles started late than other countries. In the 1980s, the "Remote Controlled Anti-Nuclear Reconnaissance Vehicle" project, which was cooperated by the National University of Defense Technology and Harbin Institute of Technology and Shenyang Institute of automation, marked the official launch of China's driverless research. In 1992, Qian Xuesen elaborated the rationality and necessity of studying new energy vehicles in a letter to Vice Premier Zou Jiahua of the State Council. Since 2009, the China intelligent vehicle future challenge series organized by the National Natural Science Foundation of China has greatly promoted the rapid development of smart car related technologies. In 2012, the PLA Academy of military communications successfully developed China's first officially certified high-speed test autonomous intelligent vehicle. In December 2015, Baidu's refitted intelligent vehicle completed the high-speed section test in Beijing; announced the Apollo program in April 2017 subsequently, which triggered an upsurge of intelligent vehicle manufacturing in China. In recent years, the Ministry of industry and information technology has successively launched a number of policies, such as *"the smart car innovation and development strategy"*, *"the guide for the construction of the national Internet of vehicles industry standard system"*, and *"the key points for the standardization of smart Internet connected vehicles in 2020"*, which not only accelerated the upgrading and transformation of the traditional automobile industry, but also gave birth to "new forces" automobile enterprises such as NIO, Xpeng and Li Auto. The construction of a new ecosystem through the cooperation between traditional manufacturing industry and external service ecology has injected more vitality into the intelligent automobile industry and promoted the gradual maturity of China's intelligent automobile industry.

Overall, the development of intelligent vehicle industry around the world is in the primary stage, especially in the maturity of automatic driving technology, and there is still a lot of room to be studied in terms of comfort, handling and safety of internal cockpit. With the acceleration of the development of intelligent vehicle industry and the increasing attention of the society to the field of intelligent vehicles, literature research and theoretical combing on the design status of intelligent vehicles have certain research value.

2 Research Design

2.1 Research Methods

This study intends to use the mapping knowledge domain method to analyze the literature in the field of intelligent vehicle design. "Knowledge map" is widely used to detect the development process and structural relationship of subject knowledge field, and show the implicit complex relationship among knowledge units, such as network, structure, interaction, intersection, evolution and derivation [2]. CiteSpace citation space software is selected to visually analyze the academic literature in the field of intelligent vehicle design in China, to reveal the evolution logic and research trend in the field of intelligent vehicle design in the past two decades, which is intended to provide some references for researchers in the field of intelligent vehicles.

2.2 Research Dimension

In order to make a reasonable analysis of the design and research status and trend of intelligent vehicles in China, this paper tends to rely on two dimensions of automation and networking.

From the perspective of automation, single vehicle automatic driving refers to a mechanical vehicle that uses sensors to ensure a safe distance between itself and other vehicles, other people and objects. According to the degree to which the automatic driving system can perform dynamic driving tasks, role assignment and condition restrictions in driving tasks, the Ministry of industry and information technology of China divides it into six levels in the classification of automobile driving automation: L0 emergency assistance; L1 partial driving assistance; L2 combined driving assistance; L3 conditional automatic driving; L4 highly automatic driving, L5 fully automatic driving. On April 30, 2021, cooperating with ISO international organization for standardization, SAE issued a new version of SAE J3016 ™ "Recommended Practice: Taxonomy and Definitions for Terms Related to Driving Automation Systems for On-Road Motor Vehicles", in which the L1 and L2 automatic driving system is named "Driver Support Systems", corresponding to SAE definition L3 - L5 level as "Automatic Driving System".

From the perspective of networking, intelligent connected vehicle (ICV) [3] integrates modern communication technology, vehicle networking and other technologies, realizes the functions of real-time online communication and intelligent information exchange between vehicles, people, terminals and the Internet, innovates the tradition-al travel experience, and is the organic integration of mobile tools and living space. In 2018, McKinsey Center for Future Mobility(MCFM) developed a hierarchical framework for car networking and user experience, that is, the Mckinsey Connected Car Customer Experience, C3X (as shown in Fig. 1), which summarizes the car networking and user experience from the most basic to extremely complex, and covers five levels: Level 1 Basic vehicle monitoring; Level 2 Link to driver's digital ecosystem; Level 3 Personalization for all occupants; Level 4 Multisensory interactions for all occupants; Level 5 Intelligent decision making and Seamless link to environment.

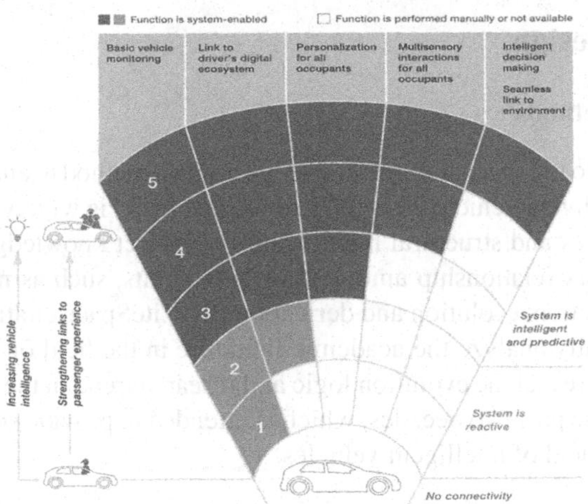

Fig. 1. Mckinsey Connected Car Customer Experience, C3X

2.3 Data Sources

In order to accurately grasp the research progress and trend in the field of intelligent vehicles and ensure the authenticity of data and analysis quality, this paper takes CNKI database as the source, limits the scope to Chinese academic journals, sets the time interval from 2001 to 2021, and defines intelligent vehicles according to CNKI advanced retrieval rules and the definition of Intelligent vehicles in the "Innovation and Development Strategy of Intelligent Vehicles". The search term is limited to (subject = intelligent vehicle + driverless vehicle + new energy vehicle + intelligent network connected vehicle) and (title = Design). The search time is August 2021, totally 1176 literatures were obtained, and 981 representative literatures were selected as the data sample source of this paper.

3 Research Progress and Trend Analysis of Intelligent Vehicle Design

3.1 Number and Annual Distribution of Documents

Overall, the annual number of documents issued by China's intelligent vehicle design and research shows an upward trend year by year. Taking 2007 and 2017 as turning points, it can be roughly divided into three stages (as shown in Fig. 2): 2001–2007 is the initial exploration stage, with a small number of papers, with an annual average of about 2.5; The period from 2008 to 2016 is a steady-state development stage, with an annual average of about 40.4 articles; The period from 2017 to 2020 is a research breakthrough stage, with a rapid growth in the number of articles, with an annual average of about 175.7 articles (except 2021). The increasing number of articles reflects the gradual expansion of the scale of relevant research and has become an important design research hotspot.

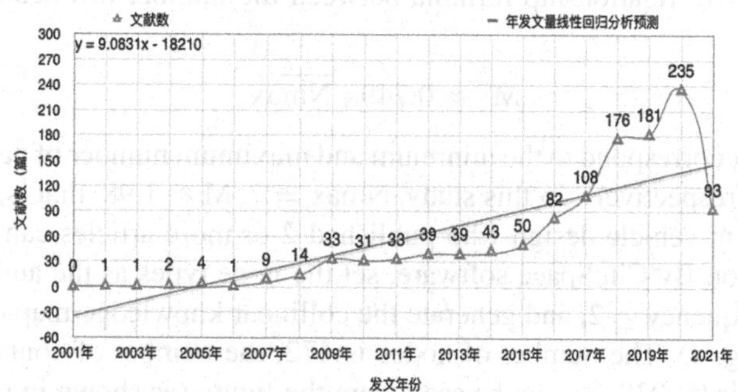

Fig. 2. Annual statistics of intelligent vehicle design and research literature in China

3.2 Collinear Network Analysis of the Author

The law of distribution of authors of scientific papers, also known as Lotka's law, was proposed by American statistician Lotka in 1926 [4]. In a relatively mature research field, the number of authors publishing n papers is about 1/n2 of the number of authors publishing 1 paper, and the number of authors publishing 1 paper is about 60% of the total number of authors. The study included 472 authors, and 307 authors published 1 paper, which was about 86.22% of the total, much higher than the theoretical value of Lotka's law by 60%; The number of authors who wrote 2, 3, 4 and 7 papers was 147, 9, 3 and 2, accounting for about 47%, 3.9%, 0.9% and 0.6% respectively. On the whole, the ratio is far lower than the theoretical value of Lotka's Law (1/4, 1/9, 1/16 and 1/49), indicating that the research on intelligent vehicle design in China has begun to take shape, but it is not completely mature.

Fig. 3. Collinear knowledge map of Chinese intelligent vehicle design literature authors

According to the quantitative relationship between the number of documents and scientists at different ability levels proposed by American Metrological scientist Price [5], the quantitative relationship formula between the number of documents and core authors is

$$M \approx 0.749\sqrt{Nmax}.$$

M and Nmax correspond to the minimum and maximum number of papers published by core authors respectively. In this study, Nmax = 7, M ≈ 1.98, that is, authors in the field of intelligent vehicle design who published 2 or more articles can be recognized as the core author. By CiteSpace software, set the node types as the author, screen the authors with frequency ≥ 2, and generate the collinear knowledge map of core authors (as shown in Fig. 4). The number of nodes is 472, the number of connections is 417, and the density is 0.0038. As can be seen from the figure (as shown in Fig. 3), most of the author nodes in the central area have a certain degree of collinear relationship, and a small number of authors have a strong collinear relationship, indicating that China's intelligent vehicle design and research has formed several closely related research teams. Scholars with weak collinearity or no collinearity in the edge area of the map indicate that many scholars are still taking the form of independent research. On the whole China's intelligent vehicle design has formed a certain number of closely cooperated research teams, and there are certain cross team cooperation and exchanges, but there is still a lack of mature, stable and core scholars with outstanding contributions.

3.3 Research Progress and Time Zone Distribution

According to the keyword time zone map generated by CiteSpace software, the stage characteristics, evolution dynamics and evolution logic of intelligent vehicle design field can be explained. From figure 2001-2001 keyword time zone map (as shown in Fig. 4), the evolution trend of intelligent vehicle design can be divided into three stages: concept germination period, technology exploration period and market-oriented transition period.

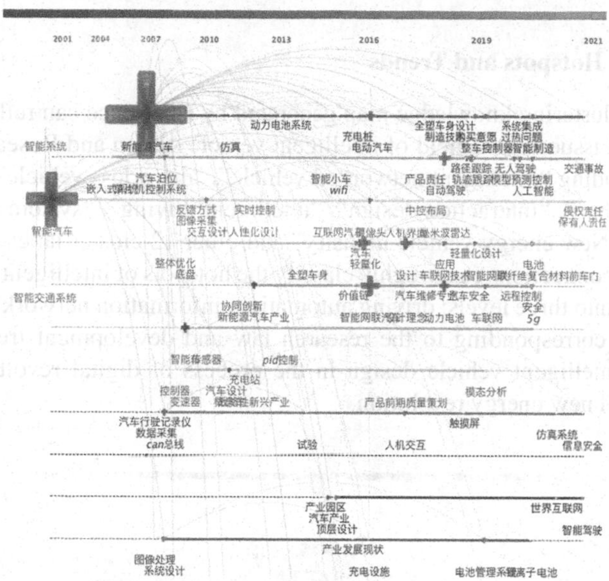

Fig. 4. Time zone distribution map of key words for intelligent vehicle design in China

In the early stage (2000–2007), the research on intelligent vehicle is in the embryonic stage. The concepts of "intelligent vehicle", "intelligent transportation system" and "new energy vehicle" have been preliminarily studied at this stage. They are in the exploration period of intelligent vehicle development. The research progress is slow and there is no research upsurge; From 2008 to 2016, relevant research has gradually become a large-scale stage, which is a centralized exploration stage of intelligent vehicle technology. As shown in the figure, "data acquisition", "real-time control", "interaction design", "system design", "sensor", "feedback mode", "all plastic body", "power battery" and other keywords reflect a certain breakthrough in the technical efficiency of intelligent vehicles, promoting the steady growth and gradual deepening of research in this field; Since 2017, there has been an explosive growth in relevant research. The research mainly focuses on keywords such as "Internet of vehicles", "human-computer interaction", "charging facilities", "central control layout", "human-computer interface", "tort liability", "simulation system", "intelligent driving" and "battery management system". The boundary of the research is gradually extended, and the intelligent vehicle technology is gradually maturing, during the time window of disruptive changes. It is changing from the technology led research and development stage to the market-oriented transition stage for user needs, from manually operated machinery to intelligent terminal products controlled by information system. Among them, the design perspective gradually focuses on the micro level design popularized to users. The research content changes from the design of physical products to the interconnection service, experience reconstruction and utility gain between virtual environments. And interdisciplinary and interdisciplinary system design methods will be used to comprehensively explore the complex practical problems such as "safety", "responsibility", "ethics" that will be brought about by the industrialization and marketization of intelligent vehicles.

3.4 Research Hotspots and Trends

The keyword clustering knowledge map generated by CiteSpace can reflect the current situation of hot issues in the field of intelligent vehicle design and Research (as shown in Fig. 5), including "intelligent networked vehicle", "driverless vehicle", "new energy vehicle", "can bus", "interaction design", "intelligent driving", "system design", "concept vehicle" "New energy vehicle industry" and other 12 cluster labels, 408 keyword nodes and 701 connections can roughly classify the hotspots of intelligent vehicle design trend research into three levels: driving automation, information networking and energy electrification, corresponding to the research law and development trend of China's assistance in intelligent vehicle design in the process of digital revolution, artificial intelligence and new energy revolution.

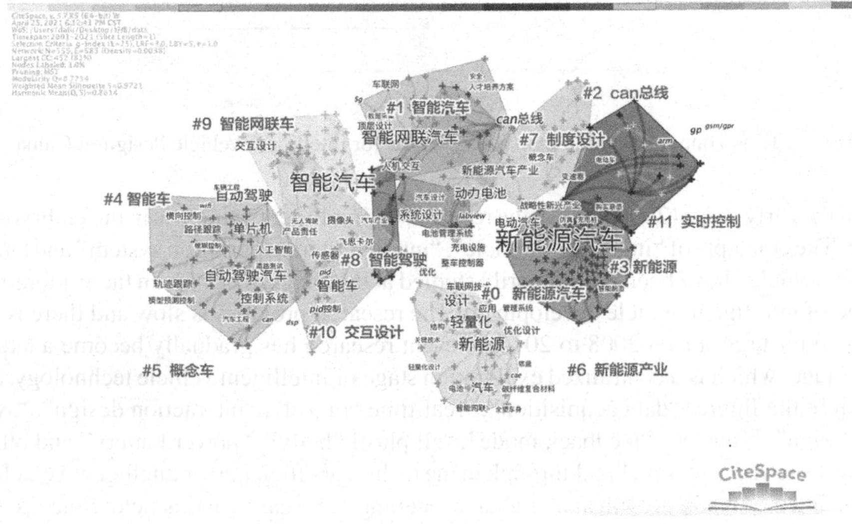

Fig. 5. Clustering map of Chinese intelligent vehicle design keywords

First, the design and research related to driving automation is the continuous research hotspots in the field of intelligent vehicles, including co-occurrence words: automatic driving, intelligent driving, artificial intelligence, control system, driving assistance, single chip microcomputer, sensor, road test, product responsibility, etc. and most of the co-occurrence words focus on "automatic driving technology". Professor Yuan Zengren of Tsinghua University made the earliest academic definition of intelligent vehicle in China in 1982. He believed that "intelligent vehicle can be regarded as a mobile robot with high movement speed and need to identify more complex road environment" and pointing out the core position of automatic driving technology in the field of intelligent vehicle research. Today, how to realize driving automation is still the core content of research in the field of intelligent vehicle design in China, including driving assistance function based on the primary stage of driving automation, on-board HMI, vehicle operating system, on-board application design, etc., as well as the research on the correlation of human-computer task redistribution scene in the highly automated stage. It fully reflects the research characteristics of "technical progress promotes design development" at the level of driving automation; At the same time, the examination and exploration of technical standards, driving safety, digital safety, responsibility definition [7], infrastructure and other practical problems extended by automatic driving are also covered. In order to adapt to the development trend of the dynamic travel transportation system composed of urban infrastructure, energy environment, urban services and human society, the systematic research on automobile road safety, Internet connected automobile data security, ethics and responsibility has far-reaching research significance, which is waiting for a sustained and long-term discussion.

Second, the research on the related design of information networking is the research hotspot with the characteristics of the digital age, including co-occurrence words: intelligent networked vehicle, can bus, vehicle networking, system design, interaction design, data acquisition, human-computer interaction, 5G, concept vehicle, etc. Based on the gradual improvement of the maturity of driving automation technology, the research of information networking is also in line with the trend of digital construction. The resulting new "Travel + service" design paradigm has a direct impact on the whole vehicle design and development process in the field of intelligent vehicles. Firstly, the research object is gradually transitioning from the past vehicle modeling design to the information-based intelligent mobile terminal design, that is, the physical product design based on technology development is extended to the information transmission and interactive terminal design in the virtual environment, in which the intelligent cockpit is the primary medium for the interaction between users and vehicles and a vital link in the future extension and innovation of automobile interior decoration and a breakthrough point in realizing the intellectualization of automobile products. Secondly, the research scope continues to expand, paying more attention to the Scenario based Internet service and personalized travel experience built by Intelligent Connected Vehicle, forming the system design direction of the integration of human-computer interaction and business ecology. The research focuses upgrading from the development of automotive engineering technology to the "human-vehicle relationship" based on intelligent interconnection technology. Through the humanized design of user data, combined with advanced sensors, biometrics, intelligent computing platform and other technologies, the intelligent vehicle has become a new intelligent subject with certain active perception ability, and establishes benign interaction with human through multi-modal three-dimensional interaction system. It reconstructs the coupling relationship among human, vehicle and environment, which is expected to become a representative design to explore how human and intelligent life coexist harmoniously in the future. In addition, from the perspective of discipline integration, the research on intelligent vehicle information networking integrates the relevant professional knowledge of mechanical design, information science, transportation, psychology, human factors engineering, urban planning, industrial design and so on, showing the obvious characteristics of multi-disciplinary, multi field and multi perspective systematicness and complexity.

Third, the design research related to energy electrification is an inevitable research trend driven by the new energy revolution, which injects new kinetic energy into the development of intelligent vehicle industry. The co-occurrence words include new energy vehicles, electric vehicles, strategic emerging industries, lightweight design, power batteries, charging facilities, battery management system, top-level design, man-machine environment, etc. In order to build an energy supply system for sustainable intelligent vehicles. Some studies have carried out orderly exploration with new energy vehicles as the core, covering macro top-level design such as industrial layout and strategic planning, as well as specific supporting measures such as charging facilities, battery management and lightweight design at the micro level. Particularly, it makes a new interpretation of the relationship between smart cars and natural resources. Based on the application of technical achievements such as information technology and new energy technology, it focuses on building a harmonious, dynamic and efficient relationship between man and nature. The design concept of "people-oriented" is gradually transformed into a sustainable design with "protection and respect for natural resources as the core". In terms of design method, under the trend of technological transformation of energy electrification, the traditional automobile production and R & D mode is about to usher in reconstruction, and the lean design of smart, fast and cheap will become the mainstream in the subsequent mass production and large-scale application stage of intelligent vehicles, including optimized design, lightweight design and modular assembly has become a design method to help automobile enterprises accelerate technological upgrading and transformation to adapt to the digital networked automobile ecology. In addition, some documents demonstrate that the design practice of intelligent vehicle closely combined with industrial development and the practical application oriented to the goal of green, low-carbon and recyclable development have further promoted the in-depth intersection and integration innovation of interdisciplinary fields. Electrification of energy has become an important engine to promote the coordinated, open and sustainable development of intelligent vehicle industry.

4 Research Conclusion

By combing the development context of intelligent vehicle design in China and analyzing the knowledge map of relevant literature in recent 20 years, the relevant research conclusions are as follows.

First, China's intelligent vehicle design and research progress is obvious and has begun to take shape. It has shown an explosive trend since 2017, but not fully mature on the whole. Scholars from various regions have formed a few research teams with very close exchanges and cooperation, and a number of scholars have adopted the form of independent research. The mobility and flexibility of research results are conducive to multiple linkage and collaborative innovation of academic related groups, with a view to more paper results with important academic contribution value in the future.

Second, Chinese intelligent vehicle design and research has experienced three stages: concept germination period, technology exploration period and market-oriented transition period, and gradually presents a systematic and scientific trend. The research perspective is more diversified, from macro top-level design to micro specific measures. The research boundary has constantly broken through traditional disciplines, including mechanical design, transportation, vehicle engineering, urban planning, industrial design, art and human factors engineering, and has formed an interdisciplinary, interdisciplinary, open, highly complex and high-level design and research ecology; The research topics are rich and point to reality. From the research on design principles and methods to the practice of intelligent vehicle design scheme jointly promoted by government, industry, University and research.

Third, combined with the background of China's digital transformation, new energy revolution and the development of artificial intelligence technology, the trend can be summarized into three aspects: driving automation, information networking and energy electrification. Among them, the research on driving automation is the continuous focus and core driving force, and the challenges such as safety, responsibility and infrastructure brought by the renewal of automatic driving technology will continue to drive the relevant research in-depth. The research on information networking aims to build the constituent elements of user ecosystem and external interconnection environment. With the continuous upgrading of intelligent transportation system in smart city, it will produce a new design paradigm and redefine the relationship between people and vehicles for the future. The research on energy electrification is not only a new driving force to promote the green development of intelligent vehicles, but also an inevitable trend under the national implementation of the goal of sustainable development of ecological civilization. In order to promote the automotive industry to achieve the national strategic goal of carbon peaking and carbon neutralization, the relevant research with the theme of new energy vehicles will promote the in-depth innovative development of China's intelligent vehicle industry.

References

1. 张新钰, 高洪波, 赵建辉, 周沫. 基于深度学习的自动驾驶技术综述. 清华大学学报(自然科学版) **58**(04), 438–444 (2018)
2. 曾建勋: 基于海量数字资源的科研关系网络构建探究. 情报学报 **32**(09), 929–935 (2013)
3. 李克强,戴一凡,李升波,边明远:智能网联汽车 (ICV) 技术的发展现状及趋势. 汽车安全与节能学报 **8**(01), 1–14 (2017)
4. Lotka, A.J.: The frequency distribution of scientific productivity. J. Wash. Acad. Sci. **16**(12), 317–323 (1926)
5. Price, D.J.: The exponential curve of science. Discovery **17**(6), 240–243 (1956)
6. 和鸿鹏: 无人驾驶汽车的伦理困境、成因及对策分析. 自然辩证法研究 **33**(11), 58–62 (2017)
7. 崔明阳, 黄荷叶, 许庆, 王建强, Sekiguchi, T.: 耿璐,李克强:智能网联汽车架构、功能与应用关键技术.清华大学学报(自然科学版) 1–16 [2021-08-17]. https://doi.org/10.16511/j.cnki.qhdxxb.2021.26.026

Social Acceptability of Autonomous Vehicles: Unveiling Correlation of Passenger Trust and Emotional Response

Corey Park and Mehrdad Nojoumian(✉)

Department of Electrical Engineering and Computer Science, Florida Atlantic University, Boca Raton, FL 33431, USA
{cpark7,mnojoumian}@fau.edu

Abstract. Social acceptability of fully autonomous systems, such as self-driving cars (SDC), is a prominent challenge that academic communities as well as industries are now facing. Despite advances being made in the technical abilities of SDCs, recent studies indicate that people are negatively predisposed toward utilizing SDCs. To bridge the gap between consumer skepticism and adoption of SDCs, research is needed to better understand the evolution of trust between humans and growing autonomous technologies. In this paper, the question of mainstream acceptance and requisite trust is scrutinized through integration of virtual reality (VR) SDC simulator, an electroencephalographic (EEG) recorder, and a new approach for real-time trust measurement between passengers and SDCs. An experiment on fifty (50) subjects was conducted where participants were exposed to driving scenarios designed to induce positive and negative emotional responses, as sub-dimensions of trust. Emotions were picked up by EEG signals from a certain area of the brain, and simultaneously, trust was measured based on a 5-point Likert scale. The results of our experiment unveiled that there is a direct correlation between passengers' real-time trust in SDCs and their emotional responses. In other words, the trust level and trust rebuild after faulty behaviors depend on the driving style as well as reaction of the SDC to passengers' emotions. Our results therefore illustrate that trust in SDCs, and accordingly, social acceptability can be achieved if SDCs become responsive to emotional responses, e.g., by selecting proper operation modes.

Keywords: Real-time trust measurement · Trust in self-driving cars · EEG signals · VR-based simulator · Human-autonomy interaction

1 Introduction

Trust can be conceptualized as a belief that an entity will act with benevolence, integrity, predictability, or competence [14]. Recent studies indicate that people have negative attitudes toward utilizing autonomous platforms [7,11]. With the growth and the increase in the complexity of autonomous systems in the 21st

H. Krömker (Ed.): HCII 2022, LNCS 13335, pp. 402–415, 2022.
https://doi.org/10.1007/978-3-031-04987-3_27

century, managing the trust of users in such systems has become an important concept when designing new autonomous systems [18,19]. Numerous studies in the domain of trust and AI have suggested that the management and the constant improvement of this mutual trust between autonomous systems and their users will be one of the primary challenges the industry professionals will face when trying to popularize the use of fully autonomous systems [3,4,9]. These discoveries highlight the necessity and urgency of conducting research to better understand the evolution of trust between humans and growing autonomous technologies, and to provide technologies that are responsive to human trust.

Google-Waymo, Tesla, Mercedes-Benz, and others have been developing semi or fully-autonomous vehicles, and they predict this technology will be deployed in the near future [23]. It is known that the widespread adoption of autonomous technologies depends on consumers experiencing and maintaining positive emotional responses in autonomy.

We therefore aim at this problem using Electroencephalography (EEG) signals. The EEG signal analysis is a methodology that researchers use to monitor brain activities and relate those signals to emotional states [6,12,15,25,26]. In our experimental study, the emotional responses of fifty (50) human subjects are evaluated through EEG analysis while they are in a SDC simulator. The simulator is utilized to elicit negative emotions in order to evaluate the level of passenger fear, stress, and anxiety in response to actions of the SDC. In fact, this information can be used to develop controllers for SDCs so that they become responsive to passengers' emotional states, and accordingly, adjust their behaviors whenever it's needed [18].

1.1 Motivation, Novelty and Contribution

The uniqueness of our experiment lies in the immersiveness of the SDC simulator, its sequential-and-structured data collection approach, and the way it correlates basic emotions such as fear, stress and anxiety to real-time trust. Prior research works have not implemented a VR environment with real videos from roads and highways, not computer-generated or animated videos, along with a motion chair to create a SDC simulation while monitoring basic emotions by EEG and measuring real-time trust by an objective approach. This work builds on prior work from [21]. Our earlier work [24] illustrated that our simulator is highly effective for collecting real-time data from subjects. The previous work only required subjects to self-report their trust levels, while the usage of an additional EEG brainwave monitor has potential to provide meaningful data to validate the self-report metrics.

In fact, the way that our research correlates basic emotions to real-time trust through objective as well as subjective data collections is unique. Basic emotions such as fear, stress, anxiety, sadness, happiness and excitement are well-studied. There are known brain's activities and/or hormones, e.g., oxytocin, cortisol and serotonin, associated with these basic emotions. They usually emerge in real-time with visible signs and gestures. However, human factors such as trust/distrust or satisfaction/frustration [1,2] are shaped over time, and often with invisible signs. I.e., there are no obvious connections between these human factors and brain's activities and/or hormones although there are prior studies that show indirect connections, e.g., oxytocin increases trust in humans [10]. Our results showed that the elements of basic emotions collected in real-time by an EEG headset were consistently associated with real-time trust measures collected by our objective data collection approach. Indeed, we studied sub-dimensions of trust by triggering elements of basic emotions that could affect trust when observed.

The results of our experiment unveiled that there is a direct correlation between the real-time trust in SDCs and emotional responses. In other words, the trust level and trust rebuild after faulty behaviors depend on the driving style as well as reaction of the SDC to passengers' emotions. Using the mean EEG beta/alpha wave band power, i.e., quantification of the emotional state, as an indicator of feeling stress and anxious in a SDC appears to be effective when the stress inducing event is dramatic and strong within a small time interval, but becomes more difficult to obtain meaningful data when the incident does no elicit a very strong response or the time interval is long.

Our results therefore illustrate that trust in SDCs, and accordingly, social acceptability can be achieved if SDCs become responsive to emotional responses by using proper operation modes, e.g., normal, cautious, and alert modes. For instance, the SDC can avoid busy roads or highways, drive on the right-hand-side lane with a speed lower than the speed limit, or avoid overpassing other cars when it's in the cautious mode. Our results are expected to inform the design and operation of a control module that monitors the emotional state of passengers, using computational models [17,20], and adjusts the AI control parameters accordingly in semi or fully-autonomous vehicles [18]. Moreover, these results can be utilized to better understand passengers' expectations from semi or fully-autonomous vehicles [5,19].

2 Self-driving Car Simulator Setup

The SDC Simulator is a safe platform to expose human subjects to a variety of driving scenarios. It is built by fusion of an Oculus Rift headset with an Atomic A3 Full Motion Simulator and offers a combination of complete visual, audio, and motion immersion that creates a convincingly realistic simulation. This platform allows for participants to safely be exposed to unique driving situations that would otherwise offer potential risk to passengers if performed with real vehicles. Figure 1 shows a participant in our VR SDC simulator.

Our driving scenarios were randomly recorded using the GoPro Fusion Camera and edited using the GoPro Fusion Studio to produce 360° video[1]. The videos of driving scenarios were exported from Fusion Studio at 4k resolution as MP4s along with 360° MP3 audio files. The Oculus Rift headset outputs 1080×1200 resolution per eye, at 90 Hz refresh rate, a 110° field of view, and has headphones which output a 3D audio effect. Our human subjects could freely

[1] gopro.com.

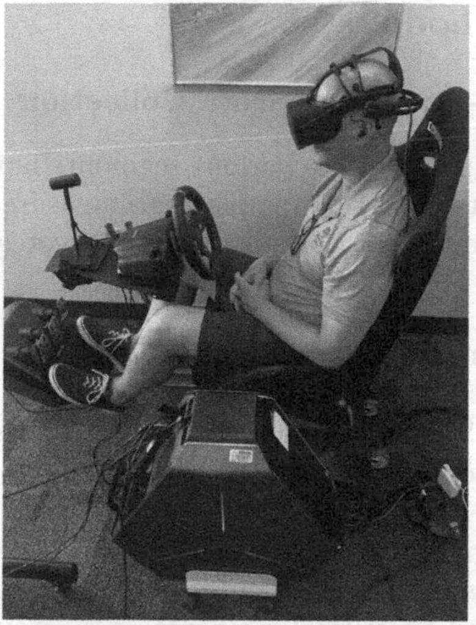

Fig. 1. Participant using the SDC simulator.

move their heads 360° to see the complete scene while using the Oculus Rift VR headset. See Fig. 2 for the view inside the simulator.

Fig. 2. View from the simulation. Each frame represents the participant's view as they turn their head to look around, illustrating the 360° view inside the simulator.

Our motion simulator could move up to 71° per second across a full 27° dual-axis movement range[2]. The Atomic A3 Motion simulator has been used previously by NASA to create realistic moon rover simulations[3]. The combination of complete visual, audio, and movement immersion provides a convincingly realistic simulation.

2 atomicmotionsystems.com.

3 talonsimulations.com/clients.html.

3 Research Methodology

3.1 Sequential-and-Structured Data Collection

The exposure of participants to the various segments builds on prior work from [16]. Two structured data collection templates to measure trust with autonomous systems were used in the present work. Segments are categorized into five distinct groups, as shown below.

1. **Initial Trust:** Segments that capture the initial trust of the passengers in the first few minutes of the interaction.
2. **Trust Escalation:** Segments where the subject's trust is increased: Involves smooth and predictable driving by the SDC without any complications.
3. **Trust Reduction:** Segments where the human subject's trust is decreased: Involves the SDC driving aggressively.
4. **Trust Mutation:** A sequence of mild incidents (e.g., a rapid lane change by the SDC) followed by critical incidents (e.g., stop-sign violation or near collision with another car) and vice versa, can be negative/positive incidents.
5. **Re-Building Trust:** Segments designed to rebuild trust between the passenger and the SDC. Involves the SDC driving predictably and calmly after trust-damaging incidents.

3.2 Experimental Design

Participants were randomly placed in one of two possible SDC simulation scenarios that were based on templates from prior work in [16]. Each scenario is made up of 5 segments. Specific scenario-segment pairs are denoted with a two letter abbreviation followed by the scenario and segment numbers, e.g., TR_{I-II} denotes trust reduction segment 2 of scenario 1, shown in Tables 1 and 2.

Table 1. Simulation Scenario 1.

IT_{I-I}	Initial Trust
TR_{I-II}	Trust Reduction
TR_{I-III}	Further Trust Reduction
NM_{I-IV}	Negative Trust Mutation
RT_{I-V}	Rebuild Trust

Table 2. Simulation Scenario 2.

IT_{II-I}	Initial Trust
TE_{II-II}	Trust Escalation
TR_{II-III}	Trust Reduction
NM_{II-IV}	Negative Trust Mutation
RT_{II-V}	Rebuild Trust

Once the participant is in the SDC simulator, the EPOC+ EEG is attached to the participant. An initial 1 min baseline is taken of the participant's brainwaves with no visual, audio, or motion stimulus. After the baseline, the scenario begins, and the EEG records the participant's brainwaves for each segment. Each segment is an exposure to an approximately 2 min SDC driving simulation. After each segment, the participant is presented with a Likert Scale that appears inside the Oculus Rift. The participant selects their response by focusing their gaze on the desired answer for five seconds while wearing the Oculus Rift.

During the response interval, the participant responds to the question "*On a scale of 1–5 with 1 being the lowest and 5 being the highest, after this simulation, what is your level of trust in the self-driving car?*". After the participant responds, the application moves on to the next segment until the simulation scenario is complete. Tables 1 and 2 define the scenario and segment pairings.

An initial trust/trust escalation segment involved the SDC moving slowly and predictably while adhering to the rules of the road. A trust reduction segment involved the SDC along with Human-Driving Cars (HDC) moving erratically and unpredictably, breaking rules of the road including speeding, tailgating, and sudden lane changes. In the NM_{I-IV} segment, the SDC ran through a non-visible stop sign and nearly collided with another car and then proceeded to drive through a residential neighborhood. In the NM_{II-IV} segment, the SDC ran through a stop sign unexpectedly and detected a pedestrian and a bicyclist crossing a crosswalk and abruptly came to a stop. A rebuild trust segment involved the SDC driving defensively and adhering to rules of the road. Note that HDCs were involved in all scenarios.

In reality, it takes months and even years to be able to repair/rebuild damaged trust. In the case of minor issues, it may take several months to rebuild trust. In critical situations, it may take years. If the concentration of the project was on repairing trust between human-and-human, we probably could execute a multi-year clinical study to conduct this research. However, to rebuild trust between human-and-SDC, it would be challenging to run similar studies. For that reason, we made it clear that, after the trust-damaging incident in segment-4, the human subject should assume that the behavior of the car in segment-5 will be repeated for months and months.

It is predicted that after the initial trust/trust escalation segments, the participants will respond with high levels of trust in the SDC, and after trust reduction segments, the participant will respond with low levels of trust in the SDC. It is also predicted that after the negative trust mutation segment, the participant will report a drastic decrease in trust. For EEG response, it is predicted that when trust damaging events occur in the simulation a high beta/alpha ratio will be observed in participants, indicating negative emotional response, and loss of trust. In trust building segments, it is expected that a low beta/alpha ratio will be observed in participants, indicating positive emotional response, calmness, and trust in the SDC simulator. It is also expected that spikes in the power of the beta/alpha ratio will correlate in time to when negative incidents occur inside the SDC simulator, e.g., in segment NM_{I-IV} when the SDC does not stop at an intersection and is nearly in a devastating car accident.

4 Experiment and Technical Results

Fifty (50) human subjects were recruited to participate in the 11-minute VR autonomous driving simulation[4]. Subjects were each given \$25 gift cards. Each subject was randomly placed in either Scenario 1 or Scenario 2.

[4] IRBNET ID #: 1187756-1.

4.1 Participant's Response

Scenario 1. Figure 3 shows subjects response to *"On a scale of 1–5 with 1 being the lowest and 5 being the highest, after this simulation, what is your level of trust in the SDC?"* after each segment in Scenario 1. The green box shows the quartiles of the dataset. The yellow whiskers extend to show the whole distribution, except for points that are determined to be outliers using a method that is a function of the inter-quartile range. Pink lines are the median response.

In the initial trust segment ($\text{IT}_{\text{I-I}}$), participants responded with a mean score of 4.68 ± 0.47, followed by a mean score of 3.72 ± 0.96 in the first trust reduction segment ($\text{TR}_{\text{I-II}}$). After exposure to the further trust reduction segment ($\text{TR}_{\text{I-III}}$), the score decreased slightly to 3.68 ± 1.25, followed by a large decline to 1.92 ± 0.84 when exposed to the negative trust mutation segment ($\text{NM}_{\text{I-IV}}$). Finally, trust levels increased to 3.96 ± 0.92 in the rebuild trust segment ($\text{RT}_{\text{I-V}}$). The largest change across segments was between the negative trust mutation ($\text{NM}_{\text{I-IV}}$) and the initial trust segment ($\text{IT}_{\text{I-I}}$), consistent with the expectation that erratic driving has the potential to severely reduce trust.

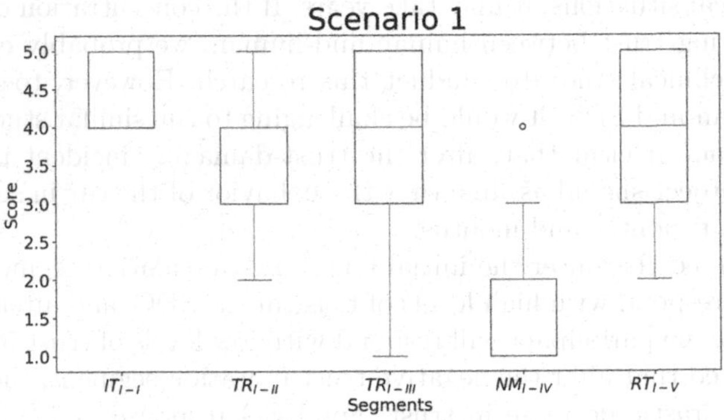

Fig. 3. Subjects reported trust level in the SDC.

Scenario 1 performed as expected. Participants scored the initial-trust and rebuild-trust segments with high levels of trust. Participants scored the trust reduction segments with lower levels of trust, and the negative trust mutation segment with the lowest level of trust. As expected, the negative trust mutation had the lowest trust levels and was significantly lower than all other segments.

An interesting result is the difference between the initial trust segment and the final segment designed to rebuild trust. While participants scored their level of trust after $\text{RT}_{\text{I-V}}$ at 3.96 ± 0.92, a high value, it is significantly lower than the initial trust value (4.68 ± 0.47), representing a 15% decrease. This seems to indicate that participants trusted the SDC less after being exposed to trust-damaging segments.

Segment (NM_{I-IV}) was the most drastic portrayal of a malfunction in a SDC. In segment (NM_{I-IV}) the SDC runs through a stop sign, and comes within inches of colliding with another vehicle. The view from the participant's perspective of this incident can be seen in Fig. 4.

Fig. 4. During the (NM_{I-IV}) segment an incident occurs where the SDC does not stop at an intersection and nearly collides with another vehicle. The frames from top to bottom show the progression of the incident from the perspective of the participant.

Scenario 2. Figure 5 shows subjects response to "*On a scale of 1–5 with 1 being the lowest and 5 being the highest, after this simulation, what is your level of trust in the SDC?*" after each segment in Scenario 2. The green box shows the quartiles of the dataset. The yellow whiskers extend to show the rest of the distribution, except for points that are determined to be outliers using a method that is a function of the inter-quartile range. Pink lines are the median response.

In the initial trust segment (IT_{II-I}), participants responded with a mean score of 4.40 ± 0.69, followed by a mean score of 4.64 ± 0.68 in the first trust escalation segment (TE_{II-II}). After exposure to trust reduction (TR_{II-III}), the score decreased to 3.68 ± 1.12, followed by a further decline to 3.64 ± 1.13 when exposed to the negative trust mutation (NM_{II-IV}). Finally, trust levels increased to 4.04 ± 1.11 in the Rebuild Trust segment (RT_{II-V}).

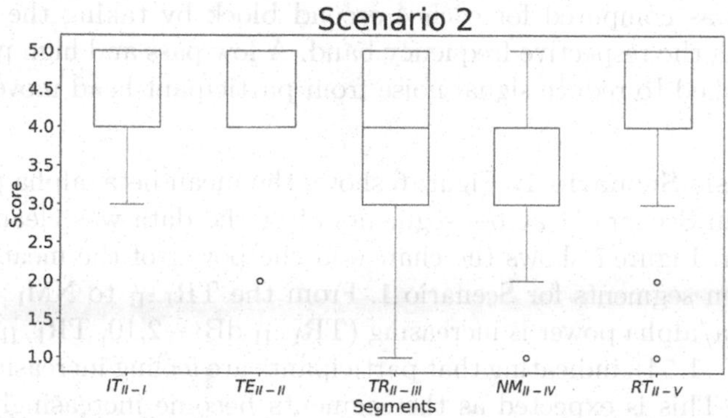

Fig. 5. Subjects reported trust level in the SDC.

In (NM_{II-IV}), the SDC approaches a crosswalk and stops for a pedestrian to cross the street. This was the only segment that involved the SDC interacting near a pedestrian. Participants reported low levels of trust after this segment and commented that they especially did not trust the SDC near pedestrians. In Scenario 2, while participants score their level of trust after RT_{II-V} at 4.04 ± 1.11, a high value, it is significantly lower than the initial trust segment (4.40 ± 0.69), representing a 8% decrease. This seems to indicate that participants trusted the SDC less after being exposed to trust-damaging segments.

The results of the experiment were generally consistent with our expectations. The participants reported higher trust levels after experiencing initial trust and trust escalation segments and reported distrust after the trust reduction segments, as well as high distrust after the negative trust mutation segment. Participants did not trust the SDC around pedestrians. Finally, participants in both groups were able to relatively rebuild their trust after the trust damaging Negative Trust Mutation segments.

4.2 EEG Response and Data Cleaning

Based on prior research [8,22,26] the ratio of the average power between the beta and alpha waves was used as the main feature to determine emotional state. A high beta/alpha power ratio indicates negative emotional response. A low beta/alpha ratio indicates positive emotional response. The average power in the delta (0.5–4 Hz), theta (4–8 Hz), alpha (8–12 Hz), and beta (12–30 Hz) is computed from the PSD of the raw EEG data.

Since Wang et al. [26] found that the features with the most information on emotional response were mainly on right occipital lobe and parietal lobe in alpha band, the parietal lobe and temporal lobe in beta band, the P7, T7 and O1 electrodes were the channels used for the signal processing and data analysis. In the future, more channels and interaction between channels will be analyzed.

The power spectral density of raw EEG data sampled 128 Hz was computed in 4 second blocks using Welch's method with a 50% overlap. The beta to alpha power ratio was computed for each 4 second block by taking the ratio of the mean power in the respective frequency band. A low pass and high pass variance filter was applied to reduce signal noise from participant head movement.

EEG Analysis Scenario 1. Figure 6 shows the mean beta/alpha power for all participants in Scenario 1 across segments after the data was cleaned with the variance filter. Figure 7 shows the change in the power of the mean beta/alpha power between segments for Scenario 1. From the TR_{I-II} to NM_{I-IV} segments the mean beta/alpha power is increasing (TR_{I-II} dB: −2.10, TR_{I-III} dB: −1.78, NM_{I-IV}, dB: −1.54), indicating that participants are feeling increasingly stressed and anxious. This is expected as the segments become increasingly stress-full, and this matches the subjects ratings of their mean trust in the SDC (TR_{I-II} Mean Trust Score: 3.72 ± 0.68, TR_{I-III} Mean Trust Score: 3.68 ± 1.25, NM_{I-IV} Mean Trust Score: 1.92 ± 0.84).

As predicted, NM_{I-IV} segment had the lowest mean beta/alpha power (−1.54 dB) for all participants, matching the lowest mean reported trust score of

1.92 ± 0.84. In the RT_{I-V} a large increase in the mean beta/alpha power across participants is observed. An interesting observation is that the largest change in the beta/alpha power between segments occurs from NM_{I-IV} to RT_{I-V}. The largest change in how participants rated their trust levels also occurred between these two segments (NM_{I-IV} 1.92 ± 0.84 to RT_{I-V} 3.96 ± 0.92).

The only segment in Scenario 1 that deviated from expectation was the IT_{I-I} segment that had a mean beta/alpha power (−1.59 dB) that was higher than the TR_{I-II} −2.10 dB and TR_{I-III} −1.78 dB segments. It would be expected that the IT_{I-I} segment would have low beta/alpha power since subjects reported having high levels of trust in the SDC in this segment IT_{I-I} 4.68 ± 0.47. The IT_{I-I} segment was the subjects' first experience in the simulator and there may have been increased stress due to becoming acclimated with the simulator.

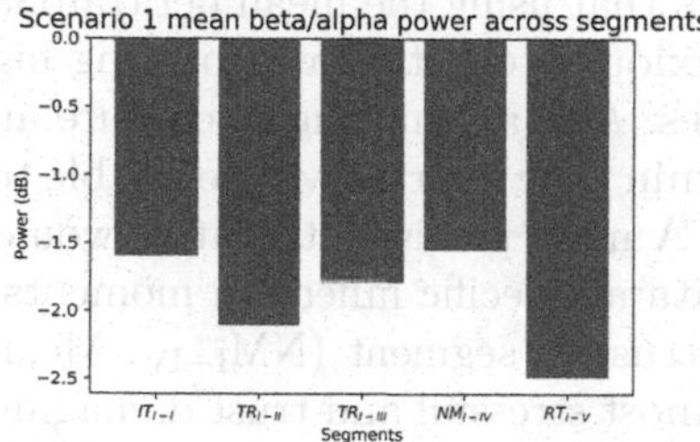

Fig. 6. The β/α mean power across segments.

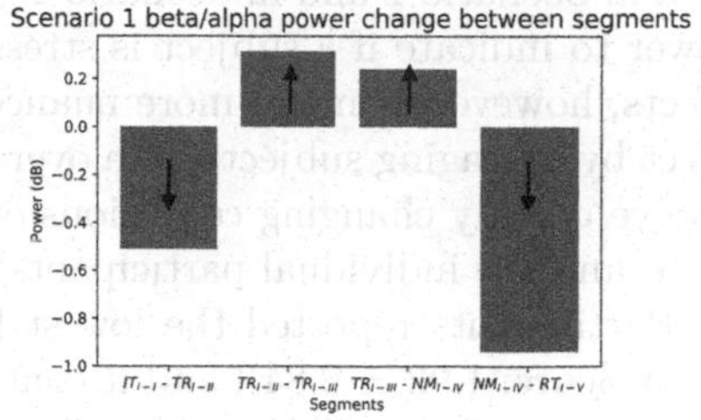

Fig. 7. Change in β/α power across segments.

EEG Analysis Scenario 2. Figure 8 shows the mean beta/alpha power for all participants in Scenario 2 across segments after the data was cleaned with the variance filter. Figure 9 shows the change in the power of the mean beta/alpha power between segments for Scenario 2. Scenario 2 did not perform as expected. It was predicted that in segments that did not induce stress or anxiety and that participants rated with high levels of trust in the SDC, IT_{II-I} 4.40 ± 0.69, TE_{II-II} 4.64 ± 0.68 and RT_{II-V} 4.04 ± 1.11, a lower mean beta/alpha power would be observed, and in segments that elicit stress and anxiety and that participants rated with low levels of trust in the SDC, TR_{II-III} 3.68 ± 1.12 and NM_{II-IV} 3.64 ± 1.13, a higher mean beta/alpha power would be observed. This was not the case as segments IT_{II-I} −0.46 dB and TE_{II-II} −0.37 dB had relatively higher mean beta/alpha power compared to TR_{II-III} −0.83 dB and NM_{II-IV} −1.01 dB.

However, the anticipated effect of a decrease of mean beta/alpha power from a stressful to non-stressful segment was observed between segments NM_{II-IV} −1.01 dB and RT_{II-V} −2.47 dB. Between segments of Scenario 2 participants self-reported the largest change in trust levels to be between segments NM_{II-IV} 3.64 ± 1.13 and RT_{II-V} 4.04 ± 1.11, and it was found that the EEG is able to capture the strongest effect between segments.

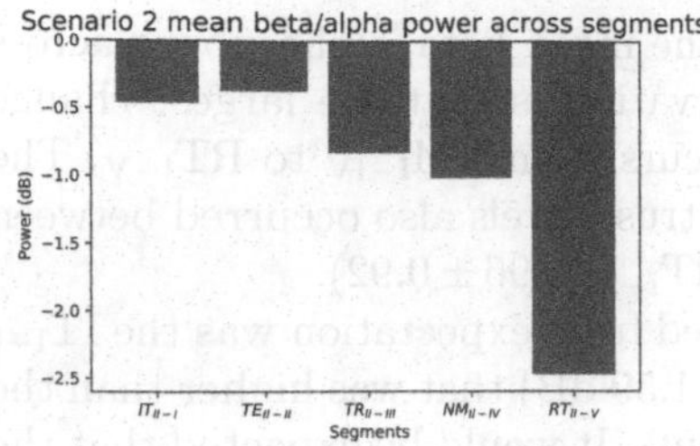

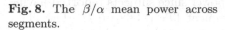

Fig. 8. The β/α mean power across segments.

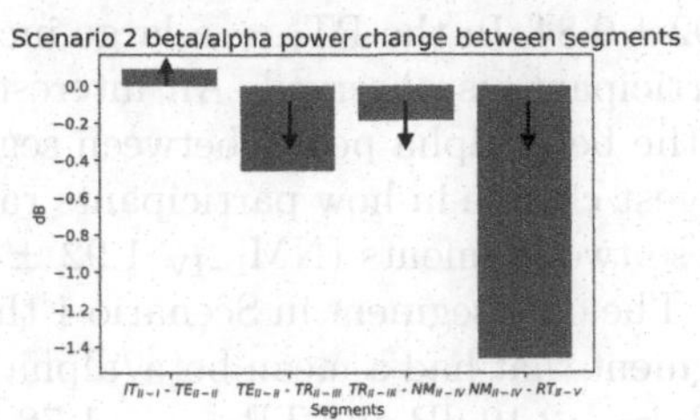

Fig. 9. Change in β/α power across segments.

EEG Analysis at Moment of Near Collision. From the analysis of the EEG data in Scenario 1 and in Scenario 2, it appears that using the mean beta/alpha power to indicate if a subject is stressed or anxious is effective at capturing big effects, however it misses more nuanced changes. Also attempting to capture an effect by averaging subjects data over a long 2 min time interval will be unable to resolve quickly changing conditions or events. A more precise alternative would be to analyze individual participants' EEG data at specific inflection moments.

Participants reported the lowest levels of trust in segment ($\text{NM}_{\text{I}-\text{IV}}$, Mean Trust Score: 1.92 ± 0.84), and it contains the most stressful and trust damaging incident were the SDC malfunctions and nearly causes a car accident at an intersection. The incident is outlined in Fig. 4. Since Participant 50 had the cleanest EEG signal, due to having a shaved head and limited head movement, this single participant's mean beta/alpha power during the stressful incident of nearly experiencing a car crash is plotted in Fig. 10. A much shorter time interval of 16 s is used to analyze the EEG data.

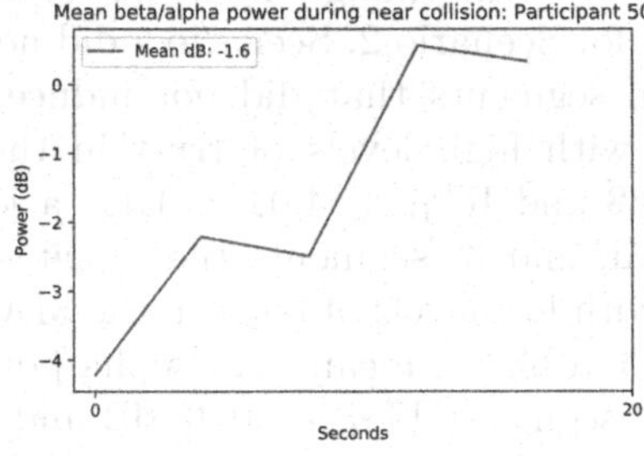

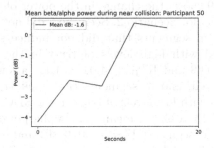

Fig. 10. Beta/alpha power change at point of near collision inside the SDC simulator.

As expected, a large increase in the mean beta/alpha power is observed during the small time window that coincides with the near car accident. Analyzing subjects individually at specific moments using small time intervals allows for more meaningful information retrieval. It is worth noting that being able to selectively evaluate subjects with clean EEG signals (having less interference due to hair and limited head movement) makes it easier to gain meaningful results.

5 Conclusion and Future Work

As stated earlier, social acceptability of autonomous vehicles is a prominent challenge that academic communities and industries are now facing. Therefore, research is needed to better understand the evolution of trust between humans and growing autonomous technologies. In this paper, an experiment on fifty (50) subjects was conducted where participants were exposed to driving scenarios designed to induce positive and negative emotional responses, as sub-dimensions of trust. Emotions were picked up by EEG signals from a certain area of the brain, and simultaneously, trust was measured based on a 5-point Likert scale.

The results of our experiment unveiled that there is a direct correlation between passengers' real-time trust in SDCs and their emotional responses. In other words, the trust level and trust rebuild after faulty behaviors depend on the driving style as well as reaction of the SDC to passengers' emotions. In our experiment, the participants reported higher trust levels after experiencing initial trust and trust escalation segments and reported distrust after the trust reduction segments, as well as high distrust after the negative trust mutation segment. A notable observation was that participants especially did not trust the SDC around pedestrians. Interestingly, all these objective observations were fully consistent with emotional responses picked up by the EEG signals.

We utilized signal processing parameters for power spectral density estimates and the resultant EEG beta/alpha wave band power ratios based on a limited investigation of spectral processing methods, windows and overlaps. However, it may be that better results can be obtained by optimizing the signal processing parameters, and it is likely that parameters best suited for responsive detection of emotional changes in short intervals will differ from those that work best for longer-term emotional states.

The EEG data has a low signal to noise ratio. Therefore, it would be challenging to manually classify a data set, making the usage of a Machine Learning (ML) based classifier necessary for large data sets. Prior research works have illustrated that Linear Support Vector Machine (LSVM) and multilayer perceptron (MLP) neural networks are possible candidates to classify EEG data [13]. Other physiological sensors (heart rate, skin perspiration, etc.) will be used in future work to detect stress. Perhaps EEG in combination with other physiological sensors will create a more robust system of detecting stress and anxiety in participants. Also future work will dedicate more time to analyzing the interaction of EEG signals with various electrode positioning.

Our results therefore illustrate that trust in SDCs, and accordingly, social acceptability can be achieved if SDCs become responsive to emotional responses, e.g., by using proper operation modes such as normal, cautious, and alert modes. Future work will utilize ML classifiers to determine the human subjects' emotional state based on a combination of sensors. As stated earlier, our results are expected to inform the design and operation of a control module that monitors the emotional state of passengers and adjusts the AI control parameters accordingly in semi or fully-autonomous vehicles [18].

References

1. Abd, M.A., Gonzalez, I., Ades, C., Nojoumian, M., Engeberg, E.D.: Simulated robotic device malfunctions resembling malicious cyberattacks impact human perception of trust, satisfaction, and frustration. Int. J. Adv. Robot. Syst. (IJARS) **16**(5), 1–16 (2019)
2. Abd, M.A., Gonzalez, I., Nojoumian, M., Engeberg, E.D.: Trust, satisfaction and frustration measurements during human-robot interaction. In: 30th Florida Conference on Recent Advances in Robotics (FCRAR), pp. 89–93 (2017)
3. Beer, J., Fisk, A.D., Rogers, W.A.: Toward a framework for levels of robot autonomy in human-robot interaction. J. Hum.-Rob. Interact. **3**(2), 74 (2014)
4. Choi, J.K., Ji, Y.G.: Investigating the importance of trust on adopting an autonomous vehicle. Int. J. Hum.-Comput. Interact. **31**(10), 692–702 (2015)
5. Craig, J., Nojoumian, M.: Should self-driving cars mimic human driving behaviors? In: Krömker, H. (ed.) HCII 2021. LNCS, vol. 12791, pp. 213–225. Springer, Cham (2021). https://doi.org/10.1007/978-3-030-78358-7_14
6. Haak, M., Bos, S., Panic, S., Rothkrantz, L.: Detecting stress using eye blinks and brain activity from EEG signals. In: Proceeding of the 1st Driver Car Interaction and Interface (DCII 2008), pp. 35–60 (2009)
7. Hancock, P.A., Billings, D.R., Schaefer, K.E., Chen, J.Y., De Visser, E.J., Parasuraman, R.: A meta-analysis of factors affecting trust in human-robot interaction. J. Hum. Factors Ergon. Soc. **53**(5), 517–527 (2011)
8. Jun, G., Smitha, K.G.: EEG based stress level identification. In: IEEE International Conference on Systems, Man, and Cybernetics (SMC), pp. 003270–003274, October 2016
9. Koo, J., Kwac, J., Ju, W., Steinert, M., Leifer, L., Nass, C.: Why did my car just do that? Explaining semi-autonomous driving actions to improve driver understanding, trust, and performance. Int. J. Interact. Design Manuf. (IJIDeM) **9**(4), 269–275 (2015)
10. Kosfeld, M., Heinrichs, M., Zak, P.J., Fischbacher, U., Fehr, E.: Oxytocin increases trust in humans. Nature **435**(7042), 673–676 (2005)
11. Kyriakidis, M., Happee, R., De Winter, J.: Public opinion on automated driving: results of an international questionnaire among 5000 respondents. Transp. Res. F: Traffic Psychol. Behav. **32**, 127–140 (2015)
12. Lin, Y.P., et al.: EEG-based emotion recognition in music listening. IEEE Trans. Biomed. Eng. **57**(7), 1798–1806 (2010)
13. Lotte, F., Congedo, M., Lécuyer, A., Lamarche, F., Arnaldi, B.: A review of classification algorithms for EEG-based brain-computer interfaces. J. Neural Eng. **4**(2), R1 (2007)
14. Harrison McKnight, D., Chervany, N.L.: Trust and distrust definitions: one bite at a time. In: Falcone, R., Singh, M., Tan, Y.-H. (eds.) Trust in Cyber-societies. LNCS (LNAI), vol. 2246, pp. 27–54. Springer, Heidelberg (2001). https://doi.org/10.1007/3-540-45547-7_3
15. Nie, D., Wang, X.W., Shi, L.C., Lu, B.L.: EEG-based emotion recognition during watching movies. In: 5th International IEEE/EMBS Conference on Neural Engineering, pp. 667–670 (2011)

16. Nojoumian, M.: Trust, influence and reputation management based on human reasoning. In: 4th AAAI Workshop on Incentives and Trust in E-Communities (WIT-EC), pp. 21–24 (2015)
17. Nojoumian, M.: Rational trust modeling. In: Bushnell, L., Poovendran, R., Başar, T. (eds.) GameSec 2018. LNCS, vol. 11199, pp. 418–431. Springer, Cham (2018). https://doi.org/10.1007/978-3-030-01554-1_24
18. Nojoumian, M.: Adaptive mood control in semi or fully autonomous vehicles. US Patent 10,981,563 (2021)
19. Nojoumian, M.: Adaptive driving mode in semi or fully autonomous vehicles. US Patent 11,221,623 (2022)
20. Nojoumian, M., Lethbridge, T.C.: A new approach for the trust calculation in social networks. In: Filipe, J., Obaidat, M.S. (eds.) ICETE 2006. CCIS, vol. 9, pp. 64–77. Springer, Heidelberg (2008). https://doi.org/10.1007/978-3-540-70760-8_6
21. Park, C., Shahrdar, S., Nojoumian, M.: EEG-based classification of emotional state using an autonomous vehicle simulator. In: 10th Sensor Array and Multichannel Signal Processing Workshop (SAM), pp. 297–300. IEEE (2018)
22. Putman, P., van Peer, J., Maimari, I., van der Werff, S.: EEG theta/beta ratio in relation to fear-modulated response-inhibition, attentional control, and affective traits. Biol. Psychol. **83**(2), 73–78 (2010)
23. Shahrdar, S., Menezes, L., Nojoumian, M.: A survey on trust in autonomous systems. In: Arai, K., Kapoor, S., Bhatia, R. (eds.) SAI 2018. AISC, vol. 857, pp. 368–386. Springer, Cham (2019). https://doi.org/10.1007/978-3-030-01177-2_27
24. Shahrdar, S., Park, C., Nojoumian, M.: Human trust measurement using an immersive virtual reality autonomous vehicle simulator. In: 2nd AAAI/ACM Conference on Artificial Intelligence, Ethics, and Society (AIES), pp. 515–520. ACM (2019)
25. Tong, J., et al.: EEG-based emotion recognition using nonlinear feature. In: IEEE 8th International Conference on Awareness Science and Technology (iCAST), pp. 55–59 (2017)
26. Wang, X.W., Nie, D., Lu, B.L.: Emotional state classification from EEG data using machine learning approach. Neurocomputing **129**, 94–106 (2014)

Beyond SAE J3016: New Design Spaces for Human-Centered Driving Automation

Lorenz Steckhan[1](✉), Wolfgang Spiessl[2], Nils Quetschlich[2], and Klaus Bengler[1]

[1] Chair of Ergonomics, Technical University of Munich, Garching, Germany
lorenz.steckhan@tum.de
[2] BMW Group, Munich, Germany

Abstract. The SAE International plays a major role in shaping research and development in the field of automated driving through its SAE J3016 automation taxonomy. Although the taxonomy contributed significantly to classification and development of automated driving, it has certain limitations. SAE J3016 implies an "all or nothing" approach for the human operation of the driving task. Within this paper, we describe the potential of moving considerations regarding automated driving beyond the SAE J3016. To this end, we have taken a structured look at the system consisting of the human driver and the automated vehicle. This paper presents an abstraction hierarchy based on a literature review. The focus lies particularly on the functional purpose of the system under consideration. In particular, optional parts of the functional purpose like driver satisfaction are introduced as a main part of the target function. We extend the classification into optional and mandatory aspects to the lower levels of abstraction within the developed hierarchy. Especially the decisions on movement and dynamics in terms of driving parameters and driving maneuvers offer a so far underestimated design space for (optional) driver interventions. This paper reveals that the SAE J3016 lacks a consideration of these kind of interventions. The identified design space does not replace the SAE J3016, it does however broaden the perspective provided by this important taxonomy.

Keywords: Automated driving · Driving experience · Interfaces for cooperative driving · User interaction · Driver satisfaction · Abstraction hierarchy · Design spaces · Taxonomy

1 Introduction

There are many positive effects anticipated with the introduction of automated driving. In particular, research focuses on increasing safety, reducing driver workload, and more flexible use of driving time. The SAE International (Society of Automotive Engineers) plays a major role in shaping research and development in the field of automated driving through its SAE J3016 automation taxonomy [1]. This taxonomy defines six levels of driving automation ranging from no automation to fully autonomous driving. For this classification, the taxonomy divides the dynamic driving task into "sustained lateral and

H. Krömker (Ed.): HCII 2022, LNCS 13335, pp. 416–434, 2022.
https://doi.org/10.1007/978-3-031-04987-3_28

longitudinal vehicle motion control" and "object and event detection and response". In addition, the responsibility to act as fallback for the driving task and the operational design domain of the automation are used as criteria for the classification. Although the taxonomy has made a valuable contribution to the classification and development of automated driving, it has certain limitations.

The numerical levels are often understood as incremental steps of development [2], even though in recent revisions the taxonomy clarifies that the levels are nominally and not ordinally scaled [1]. Among others, this misunderstanding leads the development towards a complete replacement of the human being in control of the driving task [2]. Humans are often seen as the single source of potential failures, ignoring the fact that in many situations humans provide an important layer of safety [3]. Reducing solution space to a few discrete levels can lead to missing out on opportunities. For example, a missing or wrong definition of a level of the SAE taxonomy has already been described [4]. Levels 1 to 4 can sometimes lead to user confusion [5]. This is aggravated by the various names given to equivalent functions by different manufacturers, which can result in false user expectations [6]. These expectations are linked to the user's mental model, in which less than six levels of driving automation were identified [7, 8].

The limited consideration of user interventions within the six levels implies an "all or nothing" approach for human control. This supports the misconception of a full replacement of the human being in automated driving as the final goal. Existing literature describes interaction concepts for automated vehicles that cannot be adequately categorized by this taxonomy e.g., maneuver control or haptic shared control [9]. However, more recent revisions of SAE J3016 provide a first starting point for describing user interventions across different levels using a definition of the term features [1]. Hence, there are some levels of cooperation between humans and driving automation for which the six levels of the SAE J3016 are not suitable.

Human control in driving automation is not necessarily a negative aspect. Next to the additional safety layer, manual driving control enables users to perceive an optimized driving experience (DX) through self-determined driving behavior. Today, automated vehicles offer only limited inputs during automated driving modes. Therefore, an individual user-centered adaptation of the journey cannot be achieved in these modes. It is necessary to understand the drivers with their purpose and goals of actions to find new design spaces for cooperative interaction concepts. Such concepts have the potential to transfer the advantages of manual driving to automated driving without removing the benefits of automated driving functions. This can lead to improved user experience of automated driving.

2 Methods

We aim to identify design spaces for novel driving control concepts that go beyond the implied "all or nothing" approach of the SAE J3016. The main focus of this paper lies on DX during an automated drive. To this end, we have taken a structured look at the system consisting of a driver and an automated vehicle. Following Rasmussen's method of abstraction hierarchy (AH) from the field of work domain analysis [10], the focus lies particularly on the functional purpose of the system under consideration. This method is part of the cognitive work analysis framework, which is suitable for the design of innovative user interfaces [11].

AH as a method has been applied widely in the context of driving [11–16]. However, the scope of investigation was mostly manual driving. Unlike previous studies, we consider humans as part of the overall system. This allows for the description of non-driving-related tasks (NDRT) to be a functionality of the system. An AH divides the functional properties of a system into several layers of abstraction. Based on the functional purpose as the top level of the AH, abstract and concrete functions are arranged in multiple levels [17]. Typically, the AH is composed of five levels connected by means-end relations. Rasmussen's original definition of these five levels was later generalized for a broader range of applications [18]. The top-level presents the functional purpose, followed by values and priority measures on the second layer. This layer shows metrics that help to evaluate the fulfillment of the functional purpose. The third layer consists of purpose-related functions and the fourth one shows object-related functions. These levels construct a connection between the upper levels and the basic resources and objects on the lowest level of abstraction. By considering all connections of one node to the level above, it is possible to identify the reason for its existence [11]. The connections to the lower level show what is needed to fulfill the node's purpose [11]. All connections can be used to validate the AH. This involves checking the described structure and coherence for each node's connections [11, 19].

The AH developed uses existing literature as its foundation, which is shortly presented in the respective sub-chapters. The definition of layers and the structure of connections provided by the general method has been used to structure the process of identification of relevant literature. In addition, existing applications of this method within the context of driving [11–16] were used as a starting point. The developed AH has been verified using the described method of validating each node based on its connections to other nodes.

AH as a method has limitations concerning automated control systems [20]. Therefore, we considered monitoring failures as another function of the system next to the inclusion of the human operator. For this purpose, we also looked at generic cases of failures based on a simplistic model of information processing and reaction.

By using the aforementioned method, design spaces for new interaction concepts have been identified. This paper provides an overview of the most relevant aspects of the described analysis and provides insights into used literature. We also describe proposed simplifications and the proposed design spaces.

3 Abstraction Hierarchy

In the following sub-chapters, the AH of the system consisting of the human operator and the automated car is described. For the sake of clarity, a generalized and simplified version of the developed AH is shown in Fig. 1. Therefore, some of the functions and objects identified were combined into logical groups. For each group, solely a selection of the influencing factors is shown. The relevance of the connections between the individual elements can vary. The numerous connections show the multilayered and complex interrelations existing between the elements of the AH.

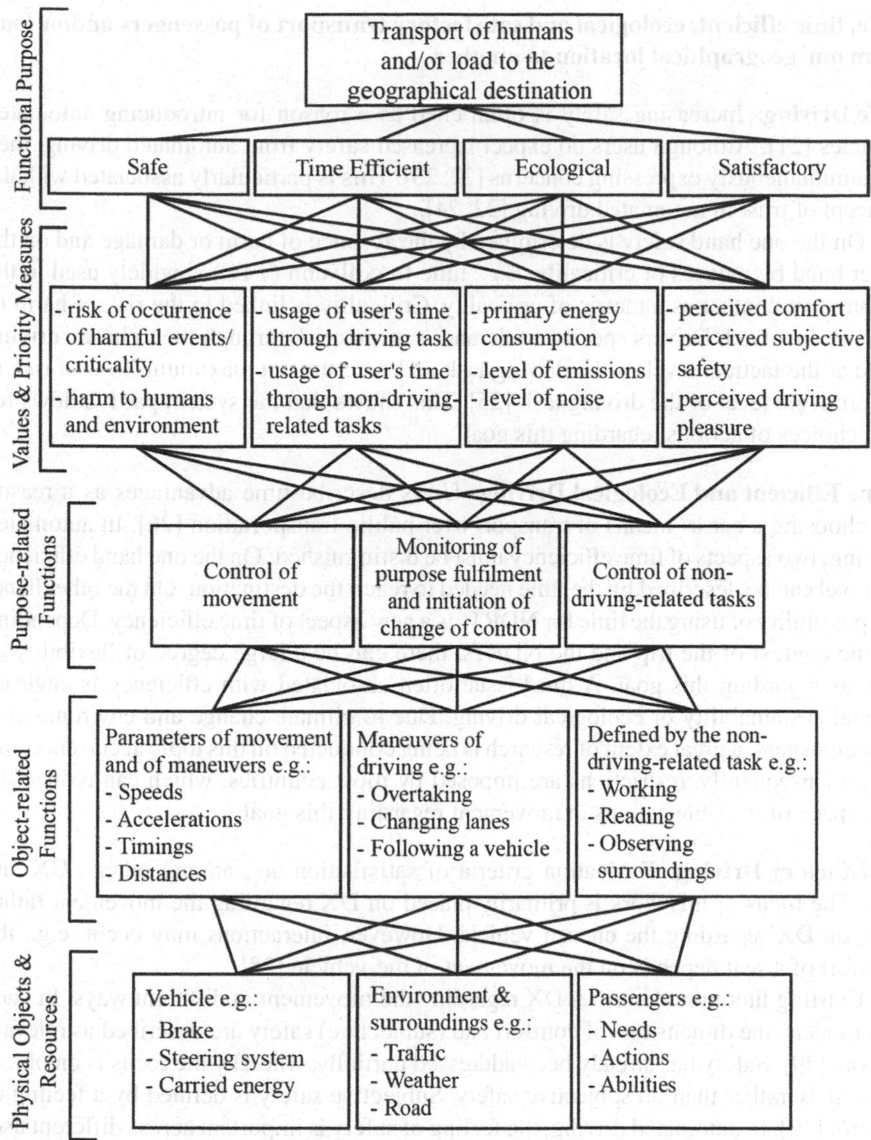

Fig. 1. Generalized and simplified abstraction hierarchy of the heterogeneous task system consisting of a driver and an automated vehicle

3.1 Purpose and Goal Structure

In contrast to a distinct purpose, a goal defines a direction for the considered actions. However, goals and purpose are not always clearly separable. In current literature, identical aspects of driving are partly described as goals and partly as purposes of driving. We define an overall purpose-goal-structure of the system in this section, which is described as:

Safe, time efficient, ecological and satisfactory transport of passengers and/or load from one geographical location to another.

Safe Driving. Increasing safety is often cited as a reason for introducing automated vehicles [21]. Although users do expect increased safety from automated driving, they are simultaneously expressing concerns [22, 23]. This is particularly associated with the concept of trust in automated driving [22, 24].

On the one hand safety is determined by the absence of harm or damage and on the other hand by metrics of criticality. E.g., time-to-collision (TTC) is widely used in the automotive context as a metric of criticality. Criticality is linked to the risk of harm or damage involved. Drivers specify a tolerance towards risk through their chosen driving style at the tactical level of the driving task and determine a maximum level of risk at the strategic level of the driving task [25]. This shows that the system partly allows for free choices of actions regarding this goal.

Time Efficient and Ecological Driving. Users describe time advantages as a reason for choosing a car as means of transport over public transportation [26]. In automated driving, two aspects of time efficiency must be distinguished: On the one hand efficiency of travel can be described by the time needed to reach the destination. On the other hand, the possibility of using the time for NDRTs is a new aspect of time efficiency. Depending on the context of the trip and the NDRTs, there can be a large degree of flexibility of actions regarding this goal. A third issue often associated with efficiency is environmental sustainability or ecological driving. Due to climate change and environmental consciousness, a great extent of research is being conducted on this topic at current times [27]. Consequently, restrictions are imposed by most countries, which can reduce the free space of possible actions in movement regarding this goal.

Satisfactory Driving. Evaluation criteria of satisfaction are, among others, UX and DX. The focus of this work is primarily placed on DX regarding the movement rather than on DX regarding the chosen vehicle. However, interactions may occur, e.g., the comfort of a seat depends on the movement of the vehicle [28].

Existing literature describes DX regarding the movement in different ways. In various models, the dimensions of comfort and (subjective) safety are described as relevant factors [29]. Safety has already been addressed partially, whereby the focus is on objective safety rather than on subjective safety. Subjective safety is defined by a feeling of control [30]. In automated driving, the feeling of safety is important across different user groups [31]. Perceived feeling of control is expected to be lower [32] and perceived safety is expected to be higher [33] in automated driving compared to manual driving. This correlates with trust in its functionality [34]. In addition to safety, perceived efficiency can also influence DX.

In the literature, different expected changes of perceived comfort are described, depending on the automation's characteristics, the scenarios considered, and the individual user [22, 23]. Hartwich et al. [22] describe a dependency of perceived comfort on users' trust. According to Engeln and Vratil [35], the dimension of comfort can be divided into action comfort, action enjoyment, usage comfort, and usage enjoyment.

Enjoyment is characterized by the occurrence of situations driven by intrinsic motivation, while comfort is determined by situations driven by extrinsic motivation [35]. In the case of enjoyment, the action itself creates pleasure, while in the case of comfort, the result of the action creates pleasure [35]. The term driving fun is also often used to describe this. Automated vehicles are expected to cause a positive influence on comfort and a negative influence on driving fun [22, 23, 32]. For some user groups, driving fun can be identified as a crucial factor affecting the selection of automobiles as a preferred means of transportation compared to other options [36]. In addition, emerging boredom at automated driving and fun at manual driving are partly reasons for switching off automated driving functions [37]. Users also rate perceived driving pleasure differently when riding along with a human driver compared to automated driving [22].

The described aspects of driver satisfaction are often related to control or perceived control which are basic psychological needs of the user. Satisfaction allows a higher flexibility in choosing actions compared to other goals. Satisfaction is more difficult to measure than other goals. For example, an assessment of emotions based on camera footage is possible.

Goal Prioritization and Target Function. The different aspects of the presented purpose-goal-structure can be prioritized. We propose that the objective elements of the goals of transportation and safety are to be considered as mandatory criteria for the overall goal fulfillment. A larger optional freedom of action with acceptance tolerance can be defined regarding the subjective goals. This means, for example, efficiency does not necessarily have to be optimized to the maximum. There are possible situations in which users purposefully want to drive inefficiently to increase satisfaction (e.g., a winding mountain road with a beautiful view instead of the faster motorway). The proposed concept of prioritization and categorization into optional and mandatory goals can be transferred to the lower levels of abstraction through the means-end relations of the AH to identify concrete spaces for interactions. The emerging concept of optional and mandatory behavior overlaps with general social behavior theories. For example following Rosenstiel [38], the behavioral determinants of willing, allowing, intending, and situational enabling could be used in a modified form to further specify freedom of action in (automated) driving regarding the control of movement and the control of non-driving-related tasks.

The prioritization of goals can change over time. This happens e.g., to ecological goals, as laws concerning environmental compatibility are constantly being tightened in some countries, which can reduce flexibility in choosing actions. For simplification, we propose to combine all sub-goals to an overall target function with adaptable weights for the criteria of the second level of the AH.

3.2 Control of Movement

General Driving Task. Control of movement is represented by the driving task. Driving is a necessary task in order to fulfill the general purpose of transport. The individual style of driving influences the different sub-goals. According to Donges [39], the driving task is divided into navigation, guidance and stabilization. Navigation involves route planning, which can be automated by using a navigation system. There are possibilities for user interventions on this layer to adapt the route to the individual target function of the user via a selection of various alternative routes. To fulfill the navigation task, suitable driving maneuvers must be selected at guidance level. The guidance level also includes the selection of trajectories and parameters of driving. Implementation of any change in movement always takes place at the level of stabilization. Normally, a high degree of control over the movement is available here.

There are different driving styles that can be chosen to reach a destination. Multiple types of driving styles can be distinguished based on the choice of maneuvers and driving parameters [e.g., 40, 41]. In automated driving, the manufacturer usually defines the car's driving style. Numerous studies can be found in the literature in which optimal specifications for maneuvers and parameters in automated driving are defined [e.g., 42]. Here, metrics of the second level of our AH are usually used as design criteria [cf. 42]. Among drivers the preferred driving style varies based on their personal characteristics and habits [43]. It may also vary depending on the driving environment [44]. In automated driving, there may be different driving styles preferred than in manual driving [45]. Driving maneuvers, trajectories and driving parameters represent the object-related functions of motion control in the proposed AH. As object-related functions, these aspects in the AH stand above basic objects and resources, which are combined into the three basic groups: passengers, vehicle, and environment.

Driving Maneuvers. Maneuvers provide a rough scheme of movement. There is a distinction made between implicit and explicit maneuvers. Explicit maneuvers are those operation units of the guidance task that are complete on their own (e.g., "changing lanes"), while implicit maneuvers are not [46, 47]. Implicit maneuvers are only completed by the initiation of explicit maneuvers or the end of the journey (e.g., "following lane") [46]. In some cases, there exists optional freedom of choice in the selection of explicit maneuvers. A change of lanes on the motorway, for example, can be considered as an optional action in terms of purpose, which solely influences efficiency and satisfaction. However, there are other situations in which a change of lanes is mandatory e.g., to take the correct exit to reach the determined destination. Implicit maneuvers are mandatory and can be interrupted by explicit optional maneuvers.

Parameters of Driving. Maneuvers on their own are not sufficient to fully define the movement of a vehicle. Further parameters must be set to define the exact movement. This coincides with the driving styles that have been mentioned afore. A maneuver usually defines the reference systems for relevant driving parameters. In particular, the lane, other road users and environmental factors are possible references. Dynamic references (e.g., a vehicle in front) require a continuous flow of information to control the connected parameters. Primarily velocity, acceleration, distance, and time parameters can be described. Especially for distance parameters, a multitude of alternatives can be described based on varying references. The start or end time of a maneuver or a parameter change is a specific time parameter. Depending on the reference system, the chosen lane on a multi-lane road or the chosen parking space at a parking area, for example, can also be described as parameters of the current maneuver.

At least one alternative of possible parameters can usually be identified as highly relevant by the current maneuver. We propose to categorize parameters into maneuver parameters and movement parameters. For example, steering angle is a basic movement parameter and eccentricity between lane markings is a maneuver parameter for following the course of a road. On a free field, however, steering angle can become the maneuver parameter, as there are no reference points defined for the transverse guidance by the maneuver.

The optional space for choosing parameters varies depending on the driving situation. For example, in the case of following a free lane, the optional space of action regarding the velocity is larger than in the case of following another vehicle. Therefore, the choice of parameters usually offers optional freedom that is restricted by mandatory limits.

3.3 Control of Non-Driving-Related Tasks

If the automation allows users to perform NDRTs (level 3 or higher of SAE J3016), the driver is usually free to choose which tasks to perform. Activities such as reading, eating and watching a movie are possible tasks that users could perform [48]. The completion of some NDRTs may be mandatory for the user (e.g., work tasks). By completing mandatory NDRTs, overall time efficiency increases. Optional NDRTs can be considered as an influence on user satisfaction. For this reason, controlling NDRTs is considered a purpose-related function in this paper. The actual NDRT is the object-related function or defines the object-related function that utilizes the basic resources.

Each NDRT can require different resources of the driver. Although this may cause a distraction from the driving task, users will usually continue to perceive parts of the movement (e.g., through vestibular perception). During the NDRT observing surroundings [49], perception of the movement will be extensive.

The automation can intervene in NDRTs if these take place in controllable areas, e.g., on in-vehicle screens. Otherwise, the automation could only interact with the user via sensory cues (e.g., auditive or visual cues).

3.4 Monitoring, Failures, and Changes in Control

Monitoring Task. The monitoring of automation by humans is described as a task for the fulfillment of safety goals in case of an automation failure [1]. Monitoring of the human by automation usually means observing the driver's status to make sure the driver complies with his or hers monitoring task [1]. In addition to monitoring the interaction partner, an agent can also perform self-monitoring. This is mandatory for an automation of level 3 of SAE J3016 or above. Self-monitoring can take place, for example, through redundant system design or plausibility checks using stored knowledge.

For the monitoring task, all relevant information must be accessible by the monitoring agent. If an action with negative effects on the target function is detected, a change in control over the corresponding subtask should be initiated. Based on the prioritization of goals, we also propose to divide the monitoring task into mandatory and optional parts. This adjustment leads to mandatory and optional interventions in case of failures in the mandatory and optional action spaces.

Failures and Interventions. To avoid failures, the acting agent (human and/or automation) must be fully aware of the overall target function. Within user-centered design, the target function from the user's point of view should be the criterion used for optimization. The automation must perceive this since the target function varies depending on user and situation. However, the user's wishes and needs are currently not well measurable and therefore represent the first source of possible failures, which particularly affects the optional goal components.

Despite complete knowledge of the target function, failures can occur for both agents and in each step of information processing and reaction. Therefore, we combined basic information processing models by Parasuraman et al. [50] and Endsley and Kaber [51] in connection with the previous insights. Figure 2 shows the combined process model.

Failures can occur in all steps of the model. In addition to failures, self-monitoring can lead to uncertainty in the execution of a processing step. For example, this could be the case when several layers of the previous step serve as an input and contradict each other. Uncertainties can be treated like (possible) failures, where an active involvement of the interaction partner is possible.

Failures are transmitted through the process model to the following processing steps and only become effective at execution level. Consequently, the user's target function is influenced only in the last step of the process (cf. Fig. 2). A transmission of failures to the following steps can be prevented by intervening in every process step in which the failure or consequential failures occur. To do this, failures must be identified via monitoring and appropriate correction must be initiated.

A distinction must be made between transitions and interventions. Transitions are defined as changing between two different driving states of automated driving [52]. Driving states are usually understood as levels of SAE J3016. Transitions often cause a change of roles. Interventions, on the other hand, only describe a conscious active flow of information from the user towards the automation. An intervention can either require a transition or be necessary at the current driving state. The term takeover is often used in this context.

On decision level, failures can affect the mandatory reduction of action space and/or the decision in the remaining optional solution space (cf. Fig. 2). In addition, failures can occur on maneuver level and/or on parameter level. For example, the optimal maneuver may be known, but the parameterization, e.g., of the start time, may be erroneous.

If a decision is actively not being taken due to uncertainty regarding expected effects on mandatory goals, the resulting effect can have a negative influence on optional goals. If, for example, an overtaking maneuver is not initiated due to safety concerns, this only negatively affects optional goals like efficiency, as no action is being taken.

In research, the most critical failures are often considered because the focus is on safety goals. When viewing the system holistically, different types of failures can be distinguished. This is especially important for failures in the optional action space. Based on the conducted literature review and previous insights, we propose the following dimensions of description:

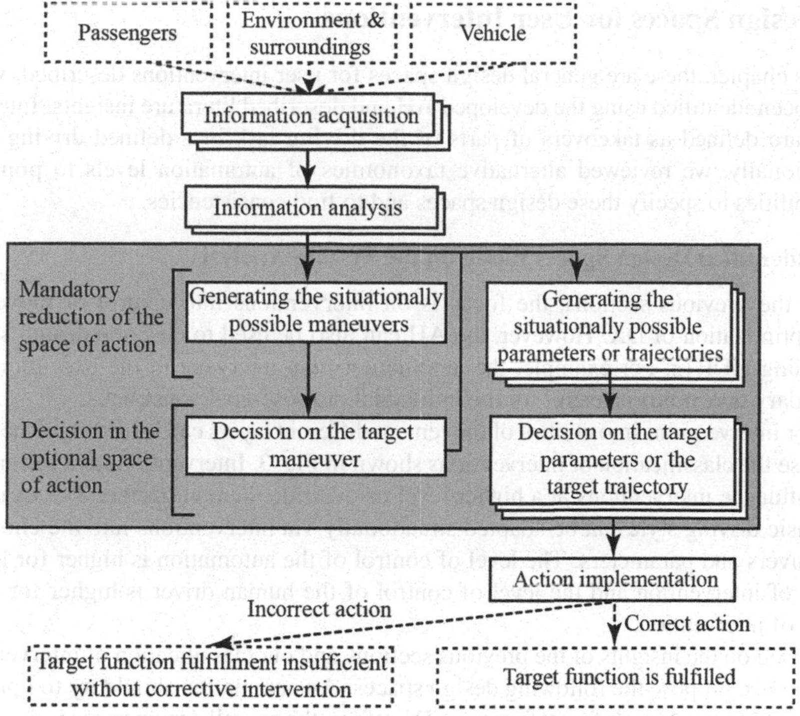

Fig. 2. Simplified process of information acquisition and reaction of driving a car

- **Time budget for failure correction:** How much time remains before a corrective intervention must be made to be able to correct the failure without causing avoidable secondary failures?
- **Information requirements for failure correction:** Does the automation require a static or a continuous flow of information from the user to correct the failure?
- **Effect of failure on user target function:** Does the uncorrected state of driving has a negative effect on optional and/or mandatory parts of the overall target function from the driver's point of view?
- **Initiator of failure correction:** Does the human or the automation start the interaction for failure correction through a first active action?

These dimensions partly overlap with descriptions of transitions from Lu et al. [52]. Similar distinctions to dimensions three and four are also mentioned by Lu et al. [52] but are defined more broadly here. Additionally, in this work, an intervention is considered as initiated by the automation if the automation asks the user to perform an action. This is described differently by Lu et al. [52].

4 Design Spaces for User Interventions

In this chapter, there are general design spaces for user interventions described, which have been identified using the developed AH and described literature insights. Interventions are defined as takeovers of parts of the driving task in a defined driving state. Additionally, we reviewed alternative taxonomies of automation levels to point out possibilities to specify these design spaces and to find consistencies.

4.1 Identified Design Spaces Based on the System Analysis

As in the previous sections, the focus is on interventions into control of movement and optimization of DX. However, the AH can also be used to describe design spaces regarding NDRTs. For example, the automation may intervene in the execution of a secondary task if this is useful for the individual purpose-goal construct.

For interventions into control of movement different layers can be distinguished. We propose the classification of interventions shown in Fig. 3. Interventions at a lower level can influence interventions at a higher level or override them altogether. For example, the basic driving style can be adapted situationally via interventions into the choice of maneuvers and parameters. The level of control of the automation is higher for higher levels of intervention and the level of control of the human driver is higher for lower levels of intervention.

Based on the insights of the previous sections and our classification of interventions (Fig. 3), we propose the following design spaces. An automation should try to optimize movement to the driver's target function. Therefore, the overall design space is described as follows.

1. The automation should model the driver's overall target function as closely as possible to be able to make decisions based on these. This should include individual optional components of the target function of the current user.

It cannot be expected that vehicles will be able to reproduce the target function completely in the near future. Intrinsically motivated optional actions are likely to be problematic. Therefore, design space two emerges.

2. The user should be able to adapt the basic target function used by the automation to individual needs.

Normally the maneuver in execution defines a dominant set of maneuver parameters, which is most relevant for the current situation. For some parameters it is possible to define alternatives. Maneuver parameters are often connected to a dynamic reference target e.g., distance to another moving vehicle. This design space can be used for a correction of failures in the optional and the mandatory action space, as long as reference targets are perceived correctly by the automation.

Timing parameters open up another space for interaction concepts for an improved DX, which is described by design space three.

3. The time between a decision to perform an action and the point of necessary execution can be used for interactions with the user.

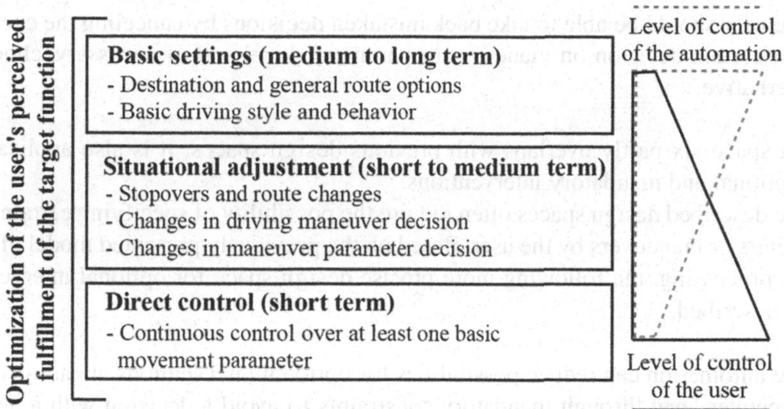

Fig. 3. Layers of user interventions in automated driving

This design space can be used for optional and mandatory interventions as well. The time span to be used can vary between situations. Optional interventions might often offer longer time spans than mandatory interventions. In case of a fallible automation (level 2 and 3 of SAE J3016), we propose two generic automation behaviors regarding the use of the optional action spaces.

- **Defensive optional decision behavior:** The automation avoids optional actions to produce as few mandatory interventions as possible. This tends to make the optional components of the target function less well served or users may have to take advantage of these opportunities on their own.
- **Offensive optional decision behavior:** The vehicle tends to provoke mandatory interventions through the execution of optional actions. This results in a tendency to serve the optional target components more often, but simultaneously in a tendency to produce more mandatory interventions.

The actual decision behavior might be a combination of both types. However, the types illustrate the connection between optional and mandatory interventions. Both types can be optimized through partial interventions into maneuver and parameter decisions.

4. If the automation anticipates a (potentially) failure, it can actively request the user to intervene in the intended action on parameter or maneuver level.

This design space is usable for optional and mandatory actions. If interventions are considered in such a way as described here, the sources of (possible) failures could be mapped onto their (possible) effects on specific maneuvers and parameters. Thus, automation can direct interventions to specific parameters or maneuvers and does not need to trigger a general takeover. One has to differentiate between the impact of a desired action and the impact of the (expected) failure onto the target function of the user.

In some situations, users or automations can take wrong decisions. For mistaken decisions, the following design space arises.

5. The user should be able to take back mistaken decisions by canceling the execution of a certain decision on maneuver or parameter level and, if necessary, choose an alternative.

Design space six partly overlaps with previous design spaces. It is also applicable to both optional and mandatory interventions.

The described design spaces often require the possibility of specifying certain target parameters or maneuvers by the user. Based on the previously presented model of information processing, the following more precise design space for optional interventions can be described.

6. The automation can reduce possibilities for optional interventions at parameter and maneuver level through mandatory constraints to avoid a decision with a negative impact on mandatory goals.

If the automation may cause failures during determining the mandatory constraints for this design space, this contradicts design spaces four and five.

For mandatory interventions, the various characteristics of failures based on the proposed dimensions of description can be used to optimize emerging operating concepts.

The lowest level of interventions of Fig. 3 describes direct and continuous interventions of the user via at least one basic movement parameter that is not dependent on surroundings. A basic parameter of movement is e.g., steering wheel angle. This level of intervention is useful if the automation is not able to identify maneuver parameters correctly. Also, in some maneuvers the defined basic movement parameters are the only option because there are no reference points to be used. Design solutions for this statement are e.g., haptic shared control concepts [56].

4.2 Specification Using Alternative Automation Taxonomies

The general design spaces described in the previous section can be transformed into different interaction concepts. We reviewed alternative taxonomies to the SAE J3016 to discover consistencies with our findings and to point out possibilities to specify these design spaces. This is only presented briefly in this paper as an extension. An overview of different alternative taxonomies is given by Vagia et al. [53]. In this paper we used the taxonomies of Sheridan [54, 55] and Endsley and Kaber [51]. Both taxonomies describe ten levels of human automation interaction. These levels offer various modes of cooperation between both agents. Based on this, we identified the following basic dimensions for the description of user interventions in interaction concepts for automated systems.

1. **Informing the user:** Is the user actively informed by the automation regarding an intervention?
2. **Decision selection by the user:** Does the user have to or can they choose one option out of a set of possible actions?

There are two concepts of decision selection. Either the user can choose from the full set of actions, or the automation reduces the solution space to a certain set.

3. **Decision reviewing by the user:** Does the automation present a concrete decision, which can or should be reviewed by the user?

If a decision is taken by the vehicle, a user intervention can be implemented using one of the following options.

- The user can cancel or reverse the decision taken by the automation during execution.
- The user is given a finite period of time to place a veto before the automated excution of the decision taken begins.
- The user has to agree to the decision taken by the automation before the automated execution will begin.

These three types differ only in the duration given to the user for a potential veto. It is less than or equal to zero in case of the cancellation concept and it is infinite in case of the approval concept.

4. **Implementation of user interventions:** How are user decisions implemented in relation to decisions taken by the automation?

The following three options show the possible range for this dimension.

- The decision taken by the human operator is only implemented if the automation agrees.
- A mixture between the decision taken by the automation and the one taken by the human is implemented.
- The human's decision is always implemented, even if the automation does not agree.

The first dimension (informing) is needed for all interventions initiated by the automation. In addition, users can be actively informed if a decision does not reach sufficient confidence and they should consequentially review it. This corresponds to design spaces four and five of the previous section. The second dimension overlaps with design spaces two, three and seven. In case of optional interventions, the automation can reduce the set of possible actions by the described mandatory constraints, if it recognizes them correctly. Dimension three corresponds with design space six of the previous section. Based on various possible situations in road traffic, a long time for an optional veto to be placed will not be applicable in every situation, which is why all of the described options of this dimension can be relevant. The dimension of implementation is primarily relevant for the lowest level of interventions as defined in Fig. 3, which is not considered in detail in this paper. Design solutions can be created by combining the different dimensions in their various forms. Not every combination is useful, but these descriptive dimensions of interventions can be used to create new design solutions based on the design spaces defined in the previous chapter.

5 Discussion and Limitations

This paper presents a system of design spaces for user interventions in automated driving. These design spaces derive from theoretical models and literature on human machine interaction and cognitive engineering. We define the safe, time efficient, ecological, and satisfying transport of human and/or load as the functional purpose of the system consisting of a driver and an automated vehicle. This definition leads to a large degree of complexity at its level of abstraction while it is still non-exhaustive.

AH as a method has limitations concerning automated control systems [20]. This article addresses this limitation by considering the user as part of the system and thus raising the analysis to a higher level of abstraction. We also included failures and the monitoring of failures into our analysis.

Since this is a theoretical approach, the most important limitation is the lack of applicable validation of the findings. Real world applications could lead to other findings, even if the current literature reveals a dependency between parameters, maneuvers and the functional purpose. Nevertheless, the results can be used to further structure future developments in this field. In addition, there are numerous statements in existing literature that fully or partially support our results. Also, in some studies, initial concepts for design spaces as described here have already been developed. For example, an option for adjusting driving style was recommended multiple times [42, 56, 57], which is in line with the findings of this work. Hecht et al. [58] describe alternative concepts for settings in route planning, which can also be understood as a concept to optimize the automated drive to the target function of the individual user.

First approaches of maneuver-based control have already been tested [9]. The focus was usually not on optional interventions. This paper reveals a potential in these kinds of interaction concepts for user-centered driving automation. As proposed, the maneuver defines dominant parameters in most cases. Applying these to user interventions is to be considered as a design space. However, it may make sense to partially switch to other parameters e.g., because an alternative parameter might be easier to track for the automation or to reduce the complexity of the interaction concept.

The described design spaces arise because of differences among user characteristics. In turn this also means that not every design space useful for every user.

Based on the findings of this work, the criticism towards SAE J3016 presented in the introduction can be expanded. SAE J3016 lacks a detailed description of interventions and of how they affect transitions between different levels. However, this does not argue against SAE J3016 itself, but shows the need of an extension of this taxonomy. It has become clear that focus must be shifted from safety as the main evaluation criterion to the overall target function of the individual user. Even if the system performs in an ideal way regarding safety, a positive value can be added for some user groups through optional interventions. Therefore, the driving task has to be disassembled into smaller units than currently done by SAE J3016. As described above, it is reasonable to look at the level of driving maneuvers and driving parameters.

With the identified design spaces implemented, complete takeovers of the driving task can potentially be reduced. With this approach, there could be automation created that integrates the driver in a situation-specific, proactive and user-centered manner to (partly) avoid mandatory failures and to achieve optimal DX. For mandatory takeovers, the entire spectrum of failures should be considered. In addition, the driver could exploit the optional space of action at any time, adapting to personal needs.

6 Conclusion

We have identified and described design spaces occurring beyond the scope of SAE J3016. Our findings broaden its perspective and should be used for an extension and not a replacement of the SAE J3016. Based on this, various alternative operating concepts can be developed for (partially) automated vehicles. A concrete implementation of these operating approaches and an evaluation of their real-world applicability is the reasonable next step. We propose that the aim of future driving automation should be a frequent, self-determined and variant-rich use of automation functions in order to fulfill users' individual and situational needs. Safety is more important than driver satisfaction, but it should not be the only criterion of evaluation. The option to adapt the automated drive to users' individual target functions via optional interventions can be used to improve the driving experience of at least some user groups at every level of driving automation described by SAE J3016.

Acknowledgement. This work was funded by the BMW Group.

References

1. SAE International: Taxonomy and Definitions for Terms Related to On-Road Motor Vehicle Automated Driving Systems: J3016_202104 (2021)
2. Stayton, E., Stilgoe, J.: It's time to rethink levels of automation for self-driving vehicles [opinion]. IEEE Technol. Soc. Mag. **39**(3), 13–19 (2020)
3. Bengler, K., Winner, H., Wachenfeld, W.: No human – no cry?. at – Automatisierungstechnik **65**, 471–476 (2017). https://doi.org/10.1515/auto-2017-0021
4. Inagaki, T., Sheridan, T.B.: A critique of the SAE conditional driving automation definition, and analyses of options for improvement. Cogn. Technol. Work **21**(4), 569–578 (2019). https://doi.org/10.1007/s10111-018-0471-5
5. Seppelt, B., Reimer, B., Russo, L., Mehler, B., Fisher, J., Friedman, D.: Consumer confusion with levels of vehicle automation. Driving Assess. Conf. **10**, 391–397 (2019)
6. Abraham, H., Seppelt, B., Mehler, B., Reimer, B.: What's in a name: vehicle technology branding & consumer expectations for automation. In: Boll, S., Pfleging, B., Donmez, B., Politis, I., Large, D. (eds.) Proceedings of the 9th International Conference on Automotive User Interfaces and Interactive Vehicular Applications. AutomotiveUI 2017, pp. 226–234. ACM (2017). https://doi.org/10.1145/3122986.3123018
7. Homans, H., Radlmayr, J., Bengler, K.: Levels of driving automation from a user's perspective: how are the levels represented in the user's mental model? In: Ahram, T., Taiar, R., Colson, S., Choplin, A. (eds.) IHIET 2019. AISC, vol. 1018, pp. 21–27. Springer, Cham (2020). https://doi.org/10.1007/978-3-030-25629-6_4
8. Zacherl, L., Radlmayr, J., Bengler, K.: Constructing a mental model of automation levels in the area of vehicle guidance. In: Ahram, T., Karwowski, W., Vergnano, A., Leali, F., Taiar, R. (eds.) IHSI 2020. AISC, vol. 1131, pp. 73–79. Springer, Cham (2020). https://doi.org/10.1007/978-3-030-39512-4_12

9. Flemisch, F.O., Bengler, K., Bubb, H., Winner, H., Bruder, R.: Towards cooperative guidance and control of highly automated vehicles: H-Mode and conduct-by-wire. Ergonomics **57**(3), 343–360 (2014). https://doi.org/10.1080/00140139.2013.869355
10. Rasmussen, J.: The role of hierarchical knowledge representation in decision making and system management. IEEE Trans. Syst. Man Cybern. **15**(2), 234–243 (1985). https://doi.org/10.1109/TSMC.1985.6313353
11. Allison, C.K., Stanton, N.A.: Constraining design: applying the insights of cognitive work analysis to the design of novel in-car interfaces to support eco-driving. Automot. Innov. **3**(1), 30–41 (2020). https://doi.org/10.1007/s42154-020-00090-5
12. Lee, S., Nam, T., Myung, R.: Work domain analysis (WDA) for ecological interface design (EID) of vehicle control display. In: ICAI 2008, pp. 387–392 (2008)
13. Li, M., Katrahmani, A., Kamaraj, A.V., Lee, J.D.: Defining a design space of the auto-mobile office: a computational abstraction hierarchy analysis. Proc. Hum. Factors Ergon. Soc. Ann. Meet. **64**(1), 293–297 (2020). https://doi.org/10.1177/1071181320641068
14. Stoner, H.A., Wiese, E.E., Lee, J.D.: Applying ecological interface design to the driving domain: the results of an abstraction hierarchy analysis. Proc. Hum. Factors Ergon. Soc. Ann. Meet. **47**(3), 444–448 (2003). https://doi.org/10.1177/154193120304700341
15. Birrell, S.A., Young, M.S., Jenkins, D.P., Stanton, N.A.: Cognitive work analysis for safe and efficient driving. Theor. Issues Ergon. Sci. **13**(4), 430–449 (2012). https://doi.org/10.1080/1463922X.2010.539285
16. Walker, G., et al.: Modelling driver decision-making at railway level crossings using the abstraction decomposition space. Cogn. Technol. Work **23**(2), 225–237 (2021). https://doi.org/10.1007/s10111-020-00659-4
17. Burns, C.M., Vicente, K.J.: Model-based approaches for analyzing cognitive work: a comparison of abstraction hierarchy, multilevel flow modeling, and decision ladder modeling. Int. J. Cogn. Ergon. **5**(3), 357–366 (2001). https://doi.org/10.1207/S15327566IJCE0503_13
18. Reising, D.V.C.: The abstraction hierarchy and its extension beyond process control. Proc. Hum. Factors Ergon. Soc. Ann. Meet. **44**(1), 194–197 (2000). https://doi.org/10.1177/154193120004400152
19. McIlroy, R.C., Stanton, N.A.: Getting past first base: going all the way with cognitive work analysis. Appl. Ergon. **42**(2), 358–370 (2011). https://doi.org/10.1016/j.apergo.2010.08.006
20. Lind, M.: Making sense of the abstraction hierarchy in the power plant domain. Cogn. Tech Work **5**, 67–81 (2003). https://doi.org/10.1007/s10111-002-0109-4
21. Chan, C.-Y.: Advancements, prospects, and impacts of automated driving systems. Int. J. Transp. Sci. Technol. **6**(3), 208–216 (2017). https://doi.org/10.1016/j.ijtst.2017.07.008
22. Hartwich, F., Schmidt, C., Gräfing, D., Krems, J.F.: In the passenger seat: differences in the perception of human vs. automated vehicle control and resulting HMI demands of users. In: Krömker, H. (ed.) HCII 2020. LNCS, vol. 12212, pp. 31–45. Springer, Cham (2020). https://doi.org/10.1007/978-3-030-50523-3_3
23. Simon, K., Jentsch, M., Bullinger, A.C., Schamber, G., Meincke, E.: Sicher aber langweilig? Auswirkungen vollautomatisierten Fahrens auf den erlebten Fahrspaß. Z. Arb. Wiss. **69**, 81–88 (2015). https://doi.org/10.1007/BF03373944
24. Mühl, K., Strauch, C., Grabmaier, C., Reithinger, S., Huckauf, A., Baumann, M.: Get ready for being chauffeured: passenger's preferences and trust while being driven by human and automation. Hum. Factors **62**(8), 1322–1338 (2020). https://doi.org/10.1177/0018720819872893
25. Zhang, Y., Angell, L., Bao, S.: A fallback mechanism or a commander? A discussion about the role and skill needs of future drivers within partially automated vehicles. Transp. Res. Interdiscip. Perspect. **9** (2021). https://doi.org/10.1016/j.trip.2021.100337

26. Gardner, B., Abraham, C.: What drives car use? A grounded theory analysis of commuters' reasons for driving. Transp. Res. F: Traffic Psychol. Behav. **10**(3), 187–200 (2007). https://doi.org/10.1016/j.trf.2006.09.004
27. Sciarretta, A., Vahidi, A.: Energy-Efficient Driving of Road Vehicles. Springer, Cham (2020). https://doi.org/10.1007/978-3-030-24127-8
28. Naddeo, A., Califano, R., Cappetti, N., Vallone, M.: The effect of external and environmental factors on perceived comfort: the car-seat experience. In: Proceedings of the Human Factors and Ergonomics Society Europe, pp. 291–308 (2016)
29. Eberl, T.X.: Charakterisierung und Gestaltung des Fahr-Erlebens der Längsführung von Elektrofahrzeugen. Dissertation, Technische Universität München (2014)
30. Klebelsberg, D.: Das Modell der subjektiven und objektiven Sicherheit. Schweizerische Zeitschrift für Psychologie und ihre Anwendungen, pp. 285–294 (1977)
31. Frison, A.-K., Wintersberger, P., Liu, T., Riener, A.: Why do you like to drive automated? In: Fu, W.-T., Pan, S., Brdiczka, O., Chau, P., Calvary, G. (eds.) Proceedings of the 24th International Conference on Intelligent User Interfaces, IUI 2019, pp. 528–537. ACM, New York (2019). https://doi.org/10.1145/3301275.3302331
32. Rödel, C., Stadler, S., Meschtscherjakov, A., Tscheligi, M.: Towards Autonomous Cars. In: Miller, E. (ed.) Proceedings of the 6th International Conference on Automotive User Interfaces and Interactive Vehicular Applications, AutomotiveUI 2014. ACM, New York (2014). https://doi.org/10.1145/2667317.2667330
33. Helgath, J., Braun, P., Pritschet, A., Schubert, M., Böhm, P., Isemann, D.: Investigating the effect of different autonomy levels on user acceptance and user experience in self-driving cars with a VR driving simulator. In: Marcus, A., Wang, W. (eds.) DUXU 2018. LNCS, vol. 10920, pp. 247–256. Springer, Cham (2018). https://doi.org/10.1007/978-3-319-91806-8_19
34. Hartwich, F., Beggiato, M., Krems, J.F.: Driving comfort, enjoyment and acceptance of automated driving - effects of drivers' age and driving style familiarity. Ergonomics **61**(8), 1017–1032 (2018). https://doi.org/10.1080/00140139.2018.1441448
35. Engeln, A., Vratil, B.: Fahrkomfort und Fahrgenuss durch den Einsatz von Fahrerassistenzsystemen. In: Schade, J., Engeln, A. (eds.) Fortschritte der Verkehrspsychologie. VS Verlag für Sozialwissenschaften, pp. 175–288 (2008)
36. Bier, L., Joisten, P., Abendroth, B.: Warum nutzt der Mensch bevorzugt das Auto als Verkehrsmittel? Eine Analyse zum erlebten Fahrspaß unterschiedlicher Verkehrsmittelnutzer. Z. Arb. Wiss. **73**, 58–68 (2019). https://doi.org/10.1007/s41449-018-00144-9
37. van Huysduynen, H.H., Terken, J., Eggen, B.: Why disable the autopilot? In: Proceedings of the 10th International Conference on Automotive User Interfaces and Interactive Vehicular Applications, AutomotiveUI 2018, pp. 247–257. ACM, New York (2018). https://doi.org/10.1145/3239060.3239063
38. von Rosenstiel, L.: Wertewandel und Kooperation. In: Spieß, E. (ed.) Formen der Kooperation. Bedingungen und Perspektiven. Schriftenreihe Wirtschaftspsychologie, pp. 279–294. Verlag für angewandte Psychologie, Göttingen (1998)
39. Donges, E.: Aspekte der aktiven Sicherheit bei der Führung von Personenkraftwagen. Automobil-Industrie **27**(2), 183–190 (1982)
40. Sagberg, F., Selpi, Piccinini, G.F., Engström, J.: A review of research on driving styles and road safety. Hum. Factors **57**(7), 1248–1275 (2015). https://doi.org/10.1177/0018720815591313
41. Colombo, T., Panzani, G., Savaresi, S.M., Paparo, P.: Absolute driving style estimation for ground vehicles. In: 2017 IEEE Conference on Control Technology and Applications. CCTA, pp. 2196–2201. IEEE (2017). https://doi.org/10.1109/CCTA.2017.8062777
42. Ossig, J., Cramer, S., Bengler, K.: Concept of an ontology for automated vehicle behavior in the context of human-centered research on automated driving styles. Information **12**(1), 21 (2021). https://doi.org/10.3390/info12010021

43. Chen, S.-W., Fang, C.-Y., Tien, C.-T.: Driving behaviour modelling system based on graph construction. Transp. Res. Part C: Emerg. Technol. **26**, 314–330 (2013). https://doi.org/10.1016/j.trc.2012.10.004
44. Han, W., Wang, W., Li, X., Xi, J.: Statistical-based approach for driving style recognition using Bayesian probability with kernel density estimation. IET Intell. Transp. Syst. **13**, 22–30 (2019). https://doi.org/10.1049/iet-its.2017.0379
45. Craig, J., Nojoumian, M.: Should self-driving cars mimic human driving behaviors? In: Krömker, H. (ed.) HCII 2021. LNCS, vol. 12791, pp. 213–225. Springer, Cham (2021). https://doi.org/10.1007/978-3-030-78358-7_14
46. Schreiber, M., Kauer, M., Schlesinger, D., Hakuli, S., Bruder, R.: Verification of a maneuver catalog for a maneuver-based vehicle guidance system. In: 2010 IEEE International Conference on Systems, Man and Cybernetics, SMC 2010, pp. 3683–3689 (2010). https://doi.org/10.1109/ICSMC.2010.5641862
47. Kauer, M., Schreiber, M., Bruder, R.: How to conduct a car? A design example for maneuver based driver-vehicle interaction. In: 2010 IEEE Intelligent Vehicles Symposium, pp. 1214–1221 (2010). https://doi.org/10.1109/IVS.2010.5548099
48. Naujoks, F., Befelein, D., Wiedemann, K., Neukum, A.: A review of non-driving-related tasks used in studies on automated driving. In: Stanton, N.A. (ed.) AHFE 2017. AISC, vol. 597, pp. 525–537. Springer, Cham (2018). https://doi.org/10.1007/978-3-319-60441-1_52
49. Pfleging, B., Rang, M., Broy, N.: Investigating user needs for non-driving-related activities during automated driving. In: Häkkila, J., Ojala, T. (eds.) Proceedings of the 15th International Conference on Mobile and Ubiquitous Multimedia, MUM 2016, pp. 91–99. ACM (2016). https://doi.org/10.1145/3012709.3012735
50. Parasuraman, R., Sheridan, T.B., Wickens, C.D.: A model for types and levels of human interaction with automation. IEEE Trans. Syst. Man Cybern. Part A Syst. Hum. **30**(3), 286–297 (2000). https://doi.org/10.1109/3468.844354
51. Endsley, M.R., Kaber, D.B.: Level of automation effects on performance, situation awareness and workload in a dynamic control task. Ergonomics **42**(3), 462–492 (1999). https://doi.org/10.1080/001401399185595
52. Lu, Z., Happee, R., Cabrall, C.D.D., Kyriakidis, M., de Winter, J.C.F.: Human factors of transitions in automated driving: a general framework and literature survey. Transp. Res. F: Traffic Psychol. Behav. **43**, 183–198 (2016). https://doi.org/10.1016/j.trf.2016.10.007
53. Vagia, M., Transeth, A.A., Fjerdingen, S.A.: A literature review on the levels of automation during the years. What are the different taxonomies that have been proposed? Appl. Ergon. **53**, 190–202 (2016). https://doi.org/10.1016/j.apergo.2015.09.013
54. Sheridan, T.B., Verplank, W.L.: Human and Computer Control of Undersea Teleoperators (1978)
55. Sheridan, T.B.: Telerobotics, Automation, and Human Supervisory Control. MIT Press, Cambridge (1992)
56. Festner, M., Eicher, A., Schramm, D.: Beeinflussung der Komfort- und Sicherheitswahrnehmung beim hochautomatisierten Fahren durch fahrfremde Tätigkeiten und Spurwechseldynamik. In: 11. Workshop Fahrerassistenzsysteme und automatisertes Fahren, pp. 63–73 (2017)
57. Beggiato, M., Hartwich, F., Krems, J.: Der Einfluss von Fahrermerkmalen auf den erlebten Fahrkomfort im hochautomatisierten Fahren. at – Automatisierungstechnik **65**(7), 512–521 (2017). https://doi.org/10.1515/auto-2016-0130
58. Hecht, T., Sievers, M., Bengler, K.: Investigating user needs for trip planning with limited availability of automated driving functions. In: Stephanidis, C., Antona, M. (eds.) HCII 2020. CCIS, vol. 1226, pp. 359–366. Springer, Cham (2020). https://doi.org/10.1007/978-3-030-50732-9_48

Study of the Hazard Perception Model for Automated Driving Systems

Yanbin Wang(✉) and Yatong Tian

Nanjing University of Aeronautics and Astronautics, Jiangsu 210016, China
{wangyanbin,yatongt}@nuaa.edu.cn

Abstract. Automated and human-driven vehicles will coexist for a long time. It would be helpful to improve user experience of automated vehicles by considering drivers' psychological model of hazard perception. This work attempts to build a hazard perception model of a typical traffic scenario for automated driving systems. Seventeen drivers were recruited as participants for the driving simulation experiment to investigate the effects of different road conditions on drivers' subjective assessment of danger level and risk acceptance. A nonlinear regression model of hazard perception was built based on the experimental results. A case study has shown that the model can effectively reflect the quantitative relationship between drivers' perceived danger level and the relevant road conditions. It will provide theoretical basis for the development of future automated driving systems for users with different risk preferences.

Keywords: Automated driving · Hazard perception · Driving simulation · Nonlinear regression

1 Introduction

With the development of technologies such as the Internet of Things (IoT), artificial intelligence, and computer vision, the research and application of automated vehicle technologies has developed rapidly in recent years. The United States, Japan, and Germany have gradually started legislation to regulate road testing of automated vehicles since 2016, and China also issued a management regulation for road testing of automated vehicles in 2018 [1]. It is believed that more and more human-driven vehicles will be replaced by automated vehicles in the near future.

An automated driving system can perceive the surroundings of the vehicle from various sensors, and control the steering and speed of the vehicle according to the road, vehicle position and obstacle information, so that the vehicle can drive on the road safely and reliably [1]. The research work in the field of automated driving mainly focuses on engineering issues such as the path planning method for obstacle avoidance [2], the traffic logic at intersections for automated vehicles [3], and the vehicle control model [4]. Such models or algorithms usually

H. Krömker (Ed.): HCII 2022, LNCS 13335, pp. 435–447, 2022.
https://doi.org/10.1007/978-3-031-04987-3_29

take traffic efficiency, cost, and safety as the optimization goals, and rarely consider the psychological needs of drivers and passengers. For example, there are two vehicles passing through an intersection at the same time. The automated driving system can make the vehicles pass through the intersection quickly and safely by calculating the vehicle driving data and applying coordination strategies. With automation in L4 or L5, vehicles are assumed to drive safely and independently, and thus the mental demand from human driver decreases significantly [5]. However, passenger' perception of danger should not be ignored. In other words, the road conditions deemed safe by the automated driving system may not necessarily be safe for the driver and passengers. Moreover, there are large differences in the perception of safety among different individuals. Although there have been significant advances in fully autonomous driving in recent years, it has not achieved the large-scale commercial applications due to a wide range of limitations such as social dilemma, high costs and public trust [6]. Human-driven vehicles will coexist with automated vehicles for a long time before being completely replaced. The solutions designed for fully automated driving scenarios are likely not suitable for the transition period [7]. Therefore, it is crucial for the development of automated driving to consider drivers' and passengers' psychological factors in system solutions at present and for a long time in the future.

Driving simulation is an effective method to carry out experimental research on traffic safety, with which various hazard scenarios can be created in virtual environments [8,9]. Participants' safety is guaranteed in driving simulation experiments. This study investigated drivers' behaviors and subjective assessment of danger level and risk acceptance under given traffic conditions. A hazard perception model was built based on the experimental results. The results and findings of this study will help to improve the driving behavior of automated vehicles, so that they will meet the safety expectations of their drivers and passengers as well as other road users.

2 Method

2.1 Participants

Seventeen participants were recruited for the experiment. All participants have (corrected to) normal vision. Those with vision correction needed to wear optical lenses during the experiment. Two participants quit the experiment due to virtual reality (VR) sickness, and 15 participants (10 males and 5 females, 22–27 years of age) completed the experiment.

2.2 Apparatus

The driving simulation application was developed based on Unity 3D and Steam VR. The virtual environment was rendered by Dell Precision 7820 Tower workstation (Intel Xeon Silver 4110, NVIDIA Quadro P4000). HTC Vive

(2160 × 1200@90 Hz) HMD was used for VR display. Betop steering wheel and pedals (BTP-3189K) were used as input devices. The virtual scene was a 1-km urban road with buildings and transportation facilities. The subject vehicle was on a two-way four-lane road with a lane width of 3.75 m, and there was an intersection 700 m ahead. Participants sat in the driver's seat to observe the road conditions in the virtual environment. The driving simulation system can provide sound effects, such as engine sound and ambient sound through earphone. Steering wheel, brake pedal and gas pedal can be used for driving control. Figure 1 shows the participant practicing the virtual driving operation.

Fig. 1. Experiment setting.

2.3 Scenarios

In order to fully understand different types of road traffic hazards and their mechanisms, a total of 208 collision video clips were collected from video websites including traffic surveillance videos and driving recorder videos. After screening and classifying the collision videos, a hazard scenario library consisting of 20 categories was obtained finally. A typical traffic scenario was chosen for experimental study, in which the subject vehicle is approaching to an intersection while the opposite vehicle is about to turn left through the intersection. As shown in Fig. 2, the white car is the subject vehicle and the traffic light is green, and the black car is in the opposite inner lane with the left turn signal flashing.

2.4 Experimental Design

This study investigated drivers' behavior and hazard perception in a specific traffic scenario. In vehicle collision accidents, the driving speed and the distance

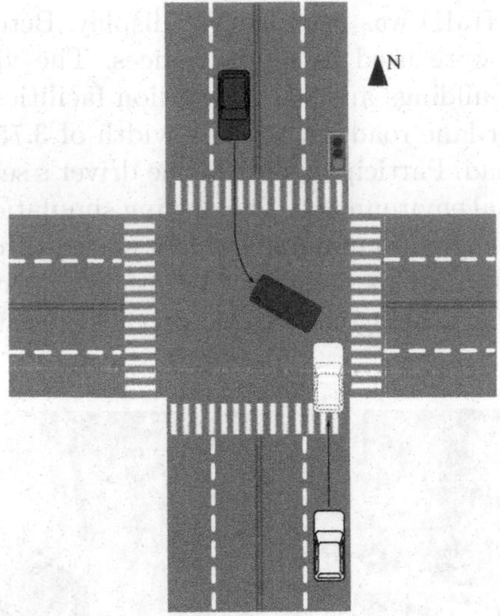

Fig. 2. Traffic scenario of the experiment. (Color figure online)

are two key factors, so speed of subject vehicle (SSV), speed of opposite vehicle (SOV), and travel distance between two vehicles when either one reached the intersection point (distance to collision) were selected as independent variables (Table 1). Both SSV and SOV had two levels, low speed and high speed. Considering the speed limit of urban roads and the speed limit of passing intersections required by the Road Safety Law of China, the low speed was set to 30 km/h, and the high speed was set to 60 km/h. As shown in Fig. 3, O is the intersection of the extension lines of the two vehicles' travel trajectories. There are three cases in the sequence of the two cars arriving at point O: the subject vehicle arrives at the intersection first, the two vehicles arrive at the same time, and the opposite vehicle arrives first.

In order to understand the relationship between hazard perception and distance to collision more accurately, it was subdivided. For the case of the subject vehicle arriving at O first, there must be a certain point A on the driving trajectory of the opposite vehicle, so that when the subject vehicle reaches O and the opposite vehicle has not yet reached A, the subject thinks that it is safe to pass through the intersection, while when the opposite vehicle has reached A, the subject thinks that it is dangerous. The driving distance from A to O is called the psychological safety distance. Due to individual differences in hazard perception, the psychological safety distance was determined through a pilot test including 5 participants. The participants drove straight through the intersection at a constant speed in the virtual environment and met with opposite vehicle turning into the intersection. Different safety distances were set for each test to allow the subjects to conduct safety assessments. Considering the influence of driving speed on hazard perception, low-speed and high-speed test conditions were used for both the subject vehicle and the opposite vehicle. The average value of the test results of the 5 participants was finally obtained, and the psychological safety distance AO was 14.73 m. The driving distance of AO was divided into 3 sections evenly, and the distances from B and C to O were obtained as 9.82 m and 4.91 m respectively (Fig. 3). Following the same way, the psychological safety distance GO was 21.00 m for the case of the opposite vehicle arriving at O first. The driving distance of the GO was divided into 4 sections evenly, and the distances from D, E, F to O were obtained as 5.25 m, 10.50 m, and 15.75 m respectively (Fig. 3).

Finally, the independent variable distance to collision had eight levels, namely the three positions A, B, C for the opposite vehicle, the four positions D, E, F, G for the subject vehicle and the intersection point O for the two vehicles arriving at the same time. A 2 SSVs $\times$ 2 SOVs $\times$ 8 distances within-group experimental design was adopted in this experiment. The order of the SSV and SOV conditions was counter-balanced and the order of the distance conditions was randomized to minimize the influence of the experimental sequence on the test results.

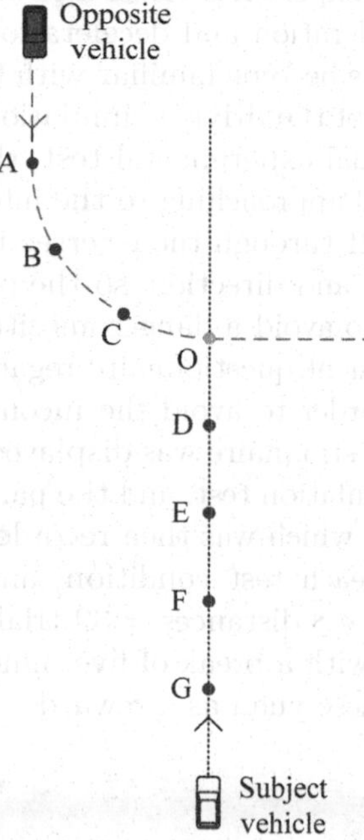

Fig. 3. Eight vehicle positions when the other one arriving at the intersection point. A, B, C is for the opposite vehicle and D, E, F, G is for the subject vehicle.

2.5 Procedure

The driving simulation experiment included two parts: warm-up practice and formal experimental test. The participants were briefed on the research objec-

Table 1. Independent variables.

Independent variables	Levels
Speed of subject vehicle (SSV)	Low: 30 km/h; High: 60 km/h
Speed of opposite vehicle (SOV)	Low: 30 km/h; High: 60 km/h
Distance to collision	A, B, C, O, D, E, F, G (Fig. 3)

tives and precautions. Afterwards, they provided their consent to the experimenter. The experimenter helped the myopic participants choose and install the optical lenses, and then the participants wore the HMD with the assistance of the experimenter. The interpupillary distance of the HMD was also adjusted for each participant if necessary. It was ensured that each participant wore the HDM comfortably and can see the virtual environment clearly.

All participants were asked to take a warm-up practice for at least 3 min before the formal experimental test. They can use the steering wheel, accelerator pedal and brake pedal to control the vehicle to drive in the virtual environment. They were required to experience visual and auditory feedback at different driving speeds through acceleration and deceleration operations. The warm-up practice can help participants become familiar with the virtual environment and the handling characteristics of the driving simulation system.

For each trial of the formal experimental test, the subject vehicle was driving at a predetermined speed approaching to the intersection while the opposite vehicle was about to turn left through the intersection. The subject vehicle can maintain the constant speed and direction, so the participant did not need any operation until he/she had to avoid a dangerous situation. The participant was asked to complete an assessment questionnaire regarding the scenario just experienced after each trial. In order to avoid the inconvenience caused by wearing the HMD repeatedly, the questionnaire was displayed in the virtual environment directly after the driving simulation test, and the participant simply said the rating option for each question, which was then recorded by the experimenter. One trial was performed under each test condition, and each participant need to complete 2 SSVs × 2 SOVs × 8 distances = 32 trials totally. The whole experiment took around an hour, with a break of five minutes every eight trials. Each participant received 50 Chinese yuan as a reward.

3 Results

3.1 Time to Intersection

In order to study the driving behavior of the subject vehicle when the opposite vehicle turned left through the intersection at different speeds and different timings, the experimental results were analyzed in three cases: the subject vehicle arrived at the intersection first, the two vehicles arrived at the same time, and the opposite vehicle arrived first. For the first case (A, B, C in Fig. 3), the time when the participant braked was recorded. The average time to reach the intersection was calculated for the two conditions of SSV and the two conditions of SOV correspondingly. As shown in Fig. 4(a), when the subject vehicle passed through the intersection at low speed, the participants reserved longer response time, and when the speed of the opposite vehicle was higher, the participants tended to reserve a longer response time as well. Figure 4(b) shows the result of the two vehicles arriving at the same time. The difference from the first case is that the subject vehicle would take hazard avoidance actions in advance when it passed through the intersection at high speed and found the opposite vehicle turning left slowly. The average time to reach the intersection is about 1.0 s. While for the last case, the subject vehicle tended to take hazard avoidance actions earlier than the first two cases when passing at low speed. If the subject vehicle was passing at high speed and encountered a high-speed vehicle turning left, the actions would be taken later (0.9 s) as shown in Fig. 4(c).

3.2 Danger Level Assessment

The danger level for each test scenario was rated on a 7-point Likert scale, with 1 to 7 representing from not at all dangerous to extremely dangerous. The results are shown in Table 2. Figure 5 shows the relationship between the perceived danger level and distance to collision when the subject vehicle and the opposite vehicle were driving at different speeds. The perceived danger level increased as the distance to collision decreased in general, no matter the subject vehicle passed first or the left-turning vehicle passed first. However, it is likely to be biased due to the influence of traffic rules. The subjective assessment of the danger level tended to be lower when participants were observing traffic rules, while it tended to be higher when the danger was caused by violating traffic rules by themselves.

When the speed difference between the two vehicles was large and they maintained a relatively large distance, the danger level perceived by the driver of the subject vehicle was low and did not change significantly with the distance, such as A, B, C under L/H speed condition and E, F, G under H/L speed condition. When comparing the left and right sides of point O of each curve, it is found that the left part is concave downward except for H/L. That means in the case where the subject vehicle passed first, the perceived danger level decreased rapidly with the increase of the distance to collision as long as no collisions occurred. The above psychological perception of danger is likely to be caused by the traffic rules for left-turning vehicles to yield to straight vehicles. The post-experiment interviews also confirmed this. The reason for the shape difference between H/L and other speed conditions on the left is probably due to the influence of violating the speed limit at an intersection. The right part of curve H/L is concave and lower than most of other speed conditions, which is determined by the participants' high controllability of the dangerous situation. Since the opposite vehicle turned through the intersection at low speed and the subject vehicle was driving at high speed, collision can be avoided by slowing down. Based on the observation of the highest danger level area as shown in the dotted circle in Fig. 5, there are two

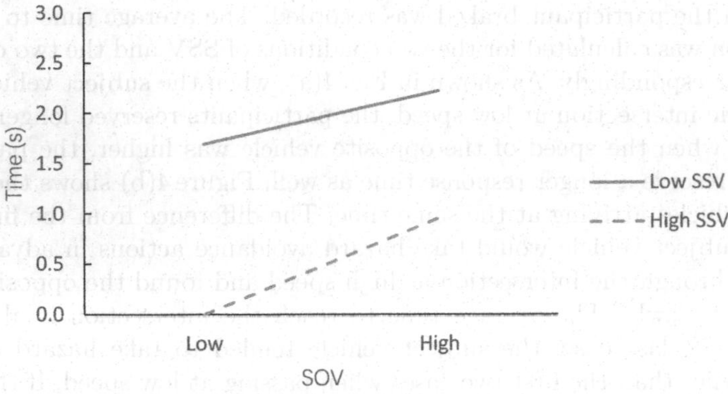

(a) Subject vehicle arrived first

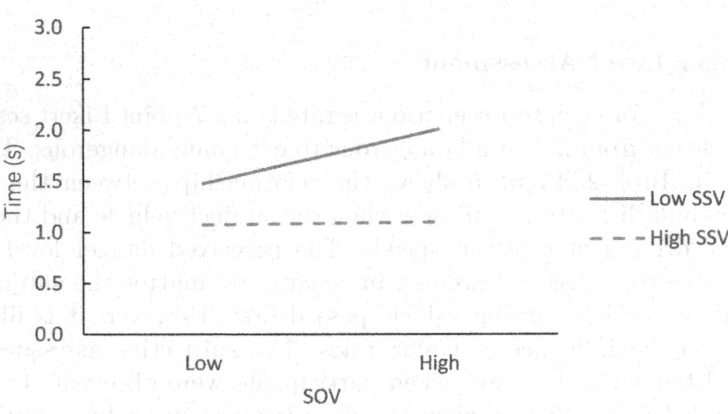

(b) Two vehicles arrived at the same time

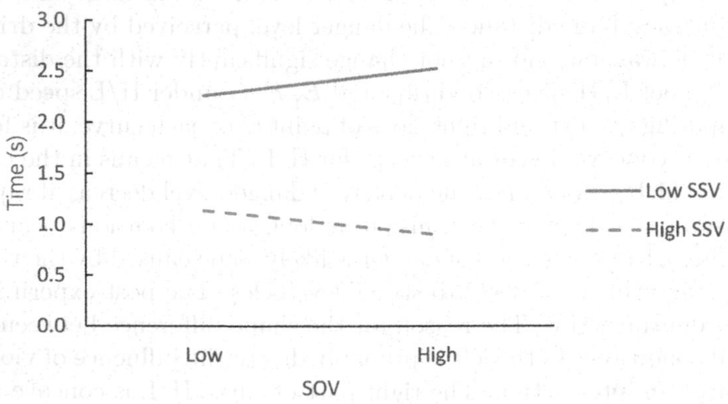

(c) Opposite vehicle arrived first

Fig. 4. The average time to reach the intersection point when the participants started braking.

types of situations in which participants perceive a higher risk except for the situation where the two vehicles arrived at the same time and collided. The first case is that the subject vehicle passed first at high speed, and the left-turning vehicle passed at low speed. The second case is that the subject vehicle passed behind, and it was at low speed or both vehicles were at high speed.

Table 2. The results of danger level assessment.

SSV/SOV		A	B	C	O	D	E	F	G
H/H	M	2.13	2.53	3.93	6.67	6.00	4.73	3.73	2.80
	SD	1.25	1.36	1.58	0.49	1.00	1.49	1.79	1.70
L/H	M	1.67	1.33	1.93	5.80	5.33	4.13	3.00	2.07
	SD	1.11	0.62	1.22	1.21	1.35	1.25	1.69	1.44
H/L	M	2.53	2.87	5.47	6.47	4.07	2.67	2.33	2.13
	SD	1.68	1.81	1.51	0.74	1.53	1.35	1.54	1.46
L/L	M	1.80	2.40	4.20	6.07	5.60	3.20	2.33	1.60
	SD	1.01	1.50	1.78	1.28	1.18	1.37	1.54	0.83

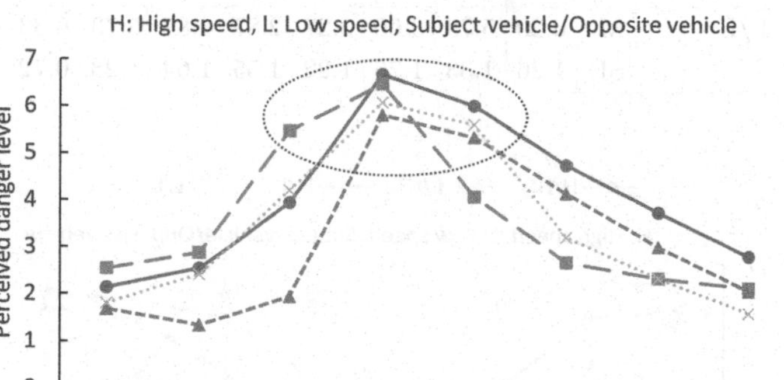

Fig. 5. The relationship between perceived danger level and distance to collision under different speed conditions.

3.3 Risk Acceptance

The risk acceptance for each test scenario was rated on a 7-point Likert scale, with 1 to 7 representing from totally unacceptable to perfectly acceptable. The results are shown in Table 3. Figure 6 shows the relationship between the risk acceptance and distance to collision when the subject vehicle and the opposite vehicle were driving at different speeds. It was found that risk acceptance and perceived danger level were roughly negatively correlated when comparing the corresponding curves in Fig. 6 and Fig. 5. That means drivers were less receptive to scenarios that feel dangerous and more receptive to scenarios that feel safe, which is consistent with common sense. However, there are exceptions as shown in Fig. 6. For example, D is the lowest point of curve L/H, which means that although the left-turning vehicle could pass the intersection at high speed before the subject vehicle, the small safe distance caused extreme discomfort to the subject vehicle. In addition, the risk acceptance changes of H/H and L/H at G were inconsistent with the danger level assessment, indicating the subject vehicle's low acceptance of the left-turning vehicle's behavior of rushing through the intersection at high speed.

Table 3. The results of risk acceptance assessment.

SSV/SOV		A	B	C	O	D	E	F	G
H/H	M	6.00	5.80	4.27	1.53	2.27	3.53	4.60	4.20
	SD	1.00	1.32	1.79	0.83	1.58	1.92	1.72	2.08
L/H	M	6.53	6.60	6.07	3.00	2.40	4.60	5.80	6.00
	SD	0.74	0.63	1.16	1.89	1.18	1.64	1.08	1.36
H/L	M	5.73	4.80	3.00	1.80	4.47	5.80	6.20	6.33
	SD	1.10	1.97	1.89	1.57	1.36	1.21	0.86	0.82
L/L	M	6.20	5.73	3.60	2.27	2.87	4.87	5.73	6.33
	SD	1.26	1.33	1.76	1.22	1.55	1.64	1.28	0.72

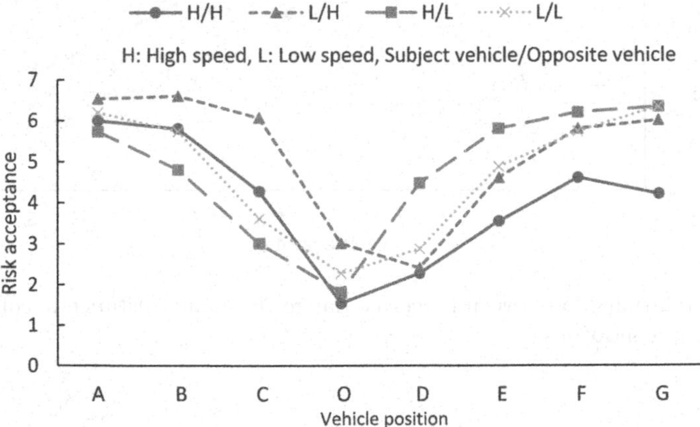

Fig. 6. The relationship between risk acceptance and distance to collision under different speed conditions.

4 Hazard Perception Model

4.1 Model Building

A hazard perception model for this traffic scenario was built to enable the experimental results to be applied in vehicle control of automated driving systems. Two cases were considered according to the order in which the two vehicles passed through the intersection: Case 1, the opposite vehicle passed first; Case 2, the subject vehicle passed first. For the first case, it was observed that the perceived danger level decreased with the increasing distance to collision (see Fig. 5, O to G). In addition, the perceived danger level should be zero when the distance is far enough according to common sense. Based on the observation and analysis of the danger level curves, the relationship between danger level and distance roughly conforms to the asymptotic regression model. The degree of curvature is mainly affected by SOV. Therefore, the model is represented as

$$r = \beta_1 + \beta_2 e^{\beta_3 \frac{d_1}{v_1}} \tag{1}$$

where r is the perceived danger level; d_1 is the distance between the two vehicles when the opposite vehicle is arriving at the intersection; and v_1 is the SOV. The experimental data of r were normalized before nonlinear regression analysis was performed. The parameter estimates, $\beta_1 = 0.117$, $\beta_2 = 0.801$ and $\beta_3 = -2.66$, were obtained ($R^2 = 0.910$). The model expression for Case 1 is

$$r = 0.117 + 0.801 e^{-2.66 \frac{d_1}{v_1}} \tag{2}$$

For the case of the subject vehicle passing first, the shape of the left part of the curve is similar to the right side. The curves H/H and L/L are very close. Based on the observation of the other two curves, the regression model expression for Case 2 is

$$r = \beta_1 + \beta_2 e^{\beta_3 \frac{v_1 d_2}{v_2}} \tag{3}$$

where r is the perceived danger level; d_2 is the distance between the two vehicles when the subject vehicle is arriving at the intersection; v_1 is the SOV; and v_2 is the SSV. The initial parameter estimates of nonlinear regression analysis were $\beta_1 = 0.193$, $\beta_2 = 0.712$ and $\beta_3 = -0.158$. The model was corrected considering the consistency of the two cases. The r values of the two equations should be the same when $d_1 = d_2 = 0$. The regression model for Case 2 is represented as the following equation after correction ($R^2 = 0.951$).

$$r = 0.193 + 0.725 e^{-0.161 \frac{v_1 d_2}{v_2}} \tag{4}$$

4.2 Model Application

The above model can reflect drivers' subjective perception of danger under different road conditions in that traffic scenario. Using this model in automated driving can help the vehicle control system to better understand the driver and passengers' psychological feelings of the hazard scenario, so that the automated driving behavior can not only meet the road safety needs, but also meet the users' psychological safety needs. In addition, it can also be customized according to different risk preferences of users. For example, an automated vehicle is going straight through the intersection at a speed of 30 km/h and meets an oncoming vehicle that is about to turn left at the intersection at a speed of 45 km/h. At this moment, the automated vehicle can determine the relationship between the perceived danger level and the relative position of the two vehicles based on the hazard perception model as shown in Fig. 7. The driving speed can be adjusted by comparing the perceived danger level with the user's risk preference. The customized automated driving system will be able to meet the psychological safety expectations of a specific user. This feature is particularly important in road traffic environments where automated vehicles and human-driven vehicles coexist, and can help improve the user experience of automated vehicles.

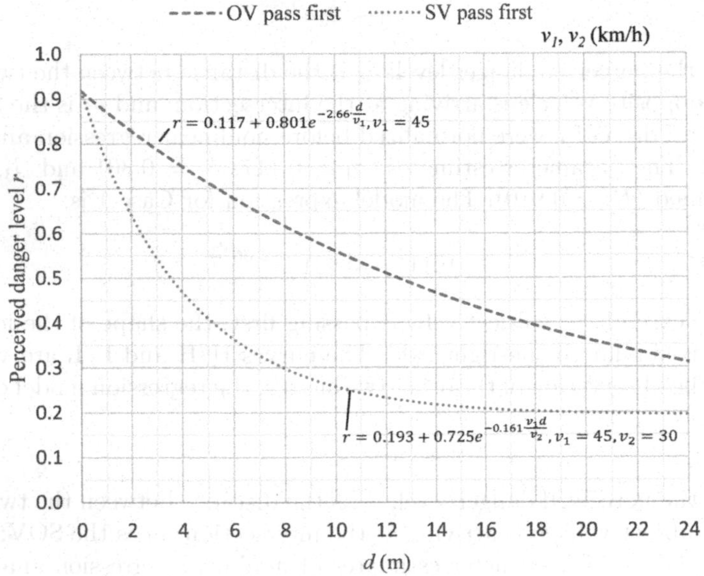

Fig. 7. The application of hazard perception model for the given traffic scenario. OV is short for opposite vehicle and SV is short for subject vehicle.

5 Conclusion

It is crucial to improve user experience of automated vehicles by considering drivers' psychological model of hazard perception. This work takes a typical traffic scenario where a straight vehicle encounters a left-turning vehicle in the opposite lane at an intersection as an example. The effects of the two vehicles' speeds and distance to collision on driving behaviors, perceived danger level, and risk acceptance were investigated through a driving simulation experiment. A regression model of driver hazard perception was built based on the experimental results. The regression model fit the data well, which can effectively reflect the quantitative relationship between perceived danger level and the relevant road condition parameters, so that the automated driving system can better understand users' psychological safety expectations. It makes the customized design based on user's risk preference become possible.

The hazard perception modeling method is also applicable to other types of hazard scenarios. Other hazard scenarios will be experimentally researched and modeled in future. In addition, only vehicle speed and distance to collision were considered as impact variables in the regression model. Drivers' perception of danger may also affected by their previous experience [10]. The sample size of this study is relatively small. Therefore, the influence of other factors will be further investigated with a bigger sample size to improve the accuracy of the model in future.

Acknowledgements. This work is supported by the Jiangsu "Mass Innovation and Entrepreneurship" Talent Programme.

References

1. Chen, Y.S., Wang, J.P.: Prospects for the driverless commercial vehicle market. Automob. Parts **18**, 43–47 (2020)
2. Liu, B., Lup, X., Zhu, J.: Research on simulation of planning obstacle avoidance path for automated vehicles. Comput. Simul. **35**(02), 105–110 (2018)
3. Mirheli, A., Hajibabai, L., Hajbabaie, A.: Development of a signal-head-free intersection control logic in a fully connected and autonomous vehicle environment. Transp. Res. Part C **92**, 412–425 (2018)
4. Wu, W., Liu, Y., Ma, W.J.: Intersection traffic control model for free-turning lane in connected and autonomous vehicle environment. China J. Highw. Transp. **32**(12), 25–35 (2019)
5. Flemisch, F.O., Bengler, K., Bubb, H., Winner, H., Bruder, R.: Towards cooperative guidance and control of highly automated vehicles: H-mode and conduct-by-wire. Ergonomics **57**(3), 343–360 (2014)
6. Hang, P., Lv, C., Xing, Y., Huang, C., Hu, Z.: Human-like decision making for autonomous driving: a noncooperative game theoretic approach. IEEE Trans. Intell. Transp. Syst. **22**(4), 2076–2087 (2021)
7. Cabri, G., Gherardini, L., Montangero, M., Muzzini, F.: About auction strategies for intersection management when human-driven and autonomous vehicles coexist. Multimed. Tools Appl. **80**(10), 15921–15936 (2021). https://doi.org/10.1007/s11042-020-10222-y
8. Wang, Y.B., Zhang, W., Salvendy, G.: Effects of a simulation-based training intervention on novice drivers' Hazard Handling Performance. Traffic Inj. Prev. **11**(1), 16–24 (2010)
9. Wang, Y.B., Zhang, W., Salvendy, G.: A comparative study of two hazard handling training methods for novice drivers. Traffic Inj. Prev. **11**(5), 483–491 (2010)
10. Xie, S., Chen, S., Zheng, J., Tomizuka, M., Zheng, N., Wang, J.: From human driving to automated driving: what do we know about drivers? IEEE Trans. Intell. Transp. Syst. (2021). https://doi.org/10.1109/TITS.2021.3084149

A Preliminary Evaluation of Driver's Workload in Partially Automated Vehicles

Ruobing Zhao, Yi Liu, Tianjian Li, and Yueqing Li(✉)

Department of Industrial and Systems Engineering, Lamar University, Beaumont, TX 77705, USA

{rzhao1,yueqing.li}@lamar.edu

Abstract. Driving could result in driver's overload if the demands of the tasks are beyond the attentional capacity of the driver, which is the main cause of poor driving performance and high car accident risks. As the use of automation is becoming increasingly common, it provides the potential to reduce such risks. However, when automation relieves the driver from continuous driving tasks, underload may occur. The study investigated driver's mental workload in partially automated vehicles and conventional vehicles under different traffic density conditions. Eight participants "drove" a simulated vehicle on a 10 mile straight, two-way rural interstate highway in 4 scenarios (2 (traffic density: Low, High) × 2 (vehicle type: Partially automated vehicle, Conventional vehicle) in random order. Data was recorded using a STISIM driving simulator, a Tobbi pro glasses 2 eye tracking device, and a NIRSport system. Workload was evaluated from subjective method (NASA-TLX questionnaire) and objective physiological methods (eye pupil diameter and oxygenated hemoglobin). The findings indicate the importance of combining different approaches to evaluate workload in driving.

Keywords: Automated driving · FNIRS · Eye tracking

1 Introduction

Driving is a complex task. It requires high cognitive demands as drivers need to remain situational awareness and perform tasks such as monitoring the environment and changing lanes. Because human working memory is a system with limited capacity, it can only hold a limited amount of information at a time. This amount varies between individuals and tasks. Therefore, driving may result in driver's mental overload. Overload occurs if the demands of a task are beyond the limited attentional capacity of the driver. Mental overload is a key cause of traffic accidents and poor driving performance. According to the National Highway Traffic Safety Administration (NHTSA), more than 90% of car accidents in the United States can be classified as caused by human error behind the steering wheel.

As automated vehicles are becoming increasingly common, the self-driving technology may fundamentally transform our transportation system. In SAE level 2 automation, lateral and longitudinal vehicle motion control is transferred from the driver to the vehicle, but the driver still needs to monitor the driving environment and be able to intervene

H. Krömker (Ed.): HCII 2022, LNCS 13335, pp. 448–458, 2022.
https://doi.org/10.1007/978-3-031-04987-3_30

when necessary (SAE International 2016). Previous research has shown that automated vehicles can reduce driver's mental workload (Zhao et al. 2021; Liu et al. 2021; Heikoop et al. 2019). However, reducing mental workload is not always a good thing. This raises the issue of mental underload, which can lead to a state of drowsiness, inattention, and slower reactions, and is consequently detrimental to driving performance. Therefore, it is vital to understand driver's workload. A comprehensive understanding of the driver's workload would be of great help to predicting driving risk, and to the design and implementation of automated vehicle safety systems.

2 Literature Review

2.1 Workload Assessment in Driving Contexts

Mental workload can be assessed using subjective measures, performance measures and physiological measures (Miller, S. Workload Measures—Literature Review; National Advanced Driving Simulator: Coralville, IA, USA, 2001). Subjective measurements are performed through self-evaluation by the drivers to reflect feelings in real time. Multidimensional assessment questionnaires such as NASA-Task Load Index (Hart 2006) and DALI (Driving Activity Load Index) (Pauzié 2008) are widely employed in driving research. The NASA Task Load Index uses six dimensions to assess workload: mental demand, physical demand, temporal demand, performance, effort, and frustration. Subjective measurement is easy and practical. However, it is not enough to rely solely on subjective measures. One drawback to subjective measures is that they do not provide a continuous form of measurement. People may forget the amount of workload they were feeling during a particular segment of the task if the delay is excessive, and the actual workload may not be reflected. More accurate methods are needed to meet different experimental environment and task requirements. Therefore, various objective assessment approaches are applied to measure workload in driving studies.

One objective way to evaluate workload is performance measurement (Paas and Vanmerrienboer 1993). Workload can be estimated by measuring the decrease in performance by either the primary or secondary tasks. In driving situations, tasks such as steering wheel movement, lane-keeping behavior and speed control are widely used to estimate workload (Wierwille and Eggemeier 1993). Recently, physiological measurements started to show its advantage in workload assessment. Workload is measured through heart rate, skin conductance response, blood pressure, eye measurement, brain activity, etc. (Engström et al. 2005). For example, a consistently increased pupil diameter during verbal secondary tasks during driving was shown (Recarte and Nunes 2003). The electroencephalogram (EEG) is one of the most studied and accepted form of workload measurement that uses brain activity. For example, Di Flumeri et al. used EEG to objectively assess the mental workload experienced by the driver in real traffic conditions (Di Flumeri 2018). A significantly higher sensitivity in discriminating the different impact of road complexity and traffic intensity on mental workload was shown. Although EEG is effective at detecting general physiological, its sensitivity to motion artifact due to muscle activity and long setup time may limit the experimental results. Another promising approach to assess workload is to measure brain activation with functional near-infrared spectroscopy (fNIRS).

2.2 FNIRS in Workload Assessment

FNIRS is an optical imaging hemodynamic technique to assess the functional activity in the human brain (Villringer 1997). It is able to measure the oxygenated and deoxygenated hemoglobin content in different cortical regions because of cerebral activity. Neuroimaging studies indicate that the prefrontal brain areas are involved in the processes required for working memory (D'Esposito 1999). Compared to EEG, FNIRS devices are characterized by lower presence during the experiment as well as easier removal of motion artifacts, therefore achieving higher spatial accuracy within collected data. It also has advantages because it's secure, portable and easy to implement. In recent studies, fNIRS has been used to evaluate driver's workload. Cortical activation was measured during on road driving and in realistic, simulated driving tasks. A significant change in HbO levels around the frontal eye field during speed changes were reported as compared to driving with constant speed (Yoshino et al. 2013).

FNIRS is also applied in automated driving research. Unni et al. assessed drivers working memory load with whole head, high density fNIRS (Unni et al. 2017). The results from those studies indicated fNIRS could be used as a useful tool to predict variations in cognitive workload in automation studies. Sibi et al. compared driver's cortical activity under different levels of vehicle automation. It was observed drivers of partially automated systems are as cognitively engaged as drivers of manually operated vehicles. In a recent study, low cognitive load was observed when participants were asked to monitor the driving of an autonomous car compared to when the same participants were asked to perform a secondary reading or video watching task (Sibi et al. 2016). However, no traffic considerations were involved in those studies. As increasing traffic densities may have an impact drivers mental demand (Jamson et al. 2013), it is necessary to include traffic density when evaluating driver's workload.

Therefore, a better approach to assess workload in both partially automated vehicles and conventional vehicles under more realistic environments is still required. This paper measured workload in partially automated vehicles and conventional vehicles in different traffic densities using fNIRS. Workload was measured using both subjective method (NASA-TLX questionnaire) and physiological method (brain activity and eye measurement).

3 Methodology

3.1 Participants

Eight participants (3 females, 5 males) completed this preliminary study as volunteers. The participants were required to hold a valid driver license. All participants reported having normal or corrected-to-normal visual acuity, and all participants proved never take stimulant and depressant drugs within 24 h before the experiment. The mean age of the drivers was 29.5 years (SD = 5.39), with a range from 25 to 42 years. The mean driving experience of the drivers was 5.875 years (SD = 5.11), with a range from 1 to 13 years. In the last week, the mean driving miles by participants was 50 miles (SD = 51.20), with a range from 0 to 150 miles. Three participants reported that they had no experience in automated driving vehicles.

3.2 Apparatus

This study was conducted in a driving simulator. As shown in Fig. 1, a STISIM Drive™ driving simulator (3.15.03) equipped with a Logitech G27 steering wheel, floor-mounted pedals, and an adjustable driver's seat was used. Three 23″ LED Dell monitors (1920 × 1080 resolution) with a 135° horizontal field of view were arranged in front of the driver's seat. A Tobbi pro glasses 2 eye tracking device was used to record eye tracking related information. The glasses were equipped with four cameras for locating pupil positions and an HD camera for recording the area in front of the participant.

Fig. 1. Apparatus used in this study.

A NIRSport (NIRx Medical Technologies LLC, Germany) system was used to record hemodynamic responses with 8 LED illumination sources and 8 silicon sensors. The emitters used optical signals of two wavelengths, 760 nm and 850 nm. The configuration was shown in Fig. 2.

3.3 Independent Variables

Two independent variables were used in this study: traffic density (low, high) and vehicle type (Level 2 partially automated vehicles and conventional vehicles). Traffic density was designed following the rules of LOS (Level of Service). Type A and E of traffic density were included, each of which includes 10 vehicles per mile per lane and 36 vehicles per mile per lane, respectively.

3.4 Dependent Variables

Three dependent variables were presented in this paper. 1. Pupil diameter. 2. Oxygenated hemoglobin. 3. NASA-TLX workload. Six subscales (mental demand, physical demand,

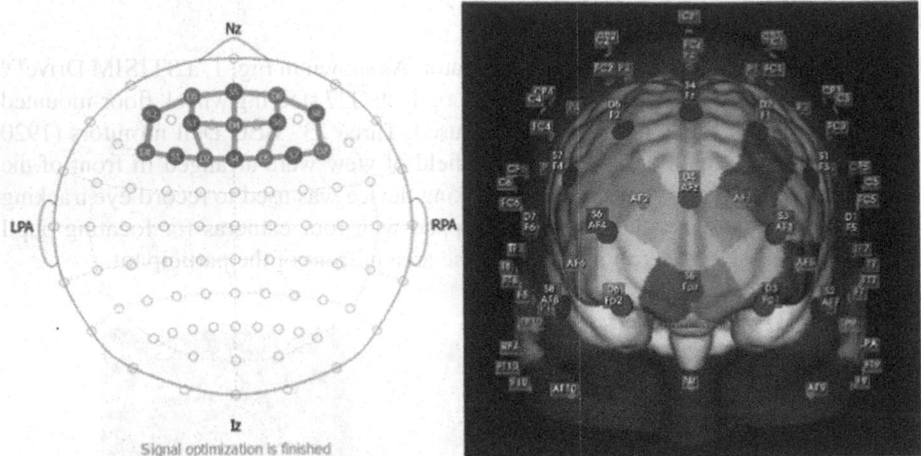

Fig. 2. FNIRS configuration.

temporal demand, frustration, effort and performance) were evaluated, with a scale from 0 to 10.

3.5 Task

A 10 mile straight, two-way rural interstate highway was designed in the driving simulator. The speed limit was set at 60 and 55 in each traffic density condition based on the rule of LOS. Participants were assigned to each scenario at random order. During each drive, participants were asked to perform lane change and overtaking when the vehicle ahead was moving at a speed much slower than the speed limit. A total of ten lane changing task were assigned in each scenario.

3.6 Procedure

The experiment was conducted in a quiet, dimly lit room. First, participants were asked to complete a pre-test questionnaire, which acquires demographic information such as age, gender, education level and driving experience. After that, a consent form was provided to each participant, which stated the objective, task, procedure, benefits, and risks of this study. The informed consent forms were signed and collected. Next, participants were given a 3-min practice drive to help them get familiar with the operation of the driving simulator. After that, participants started the full drive experiment. They were asked to drive like they do in daily life and follow traffic rules. After each scenario, participants were provided with a NASA-TLX questionnaire. After the entire experiment, participants were provided with a post-test questionnaire to evaluate their driving preferences and user experience as feedback.

4 Results

4.1 NASA-TLX

The result showed a significant main effect of vehicle type on NASA-TLX workload ($F_{1,7} = 7.43$, $p = 0.0295$). The post hoc test showed that the mean workload in conventional vehicles ($M = 5.42$, $SD = 1.56$) was significantly higher than that in automated vehicles ($M = 4.46$, $SD = 1.36$). Also, the result showed a significant main effect of traffic density on NASA-TLX workload ($F_{1,7} = 11.00$, $p = 0.0128$). The post hoc test showed that the mean workload in high traffic density ($M = 5.88$, $SD = 1.34$) was significantly higher than that in low traffic density ($M = 4.01$, $SD = 1.06$).

The result didn't show any significant interaction effect between traffic density and vehicle type ($F_{1,7} = 0.76$, $p = 0.4114$) on workload.

4.2 FNIRS Data

The raw data was pre-processed using the nirsLAB package (Xu et al. 2014). A band-pass filter was applied with cut off frequencies of 0.01 Hz and 0.2 Hz to reduce artifacts and

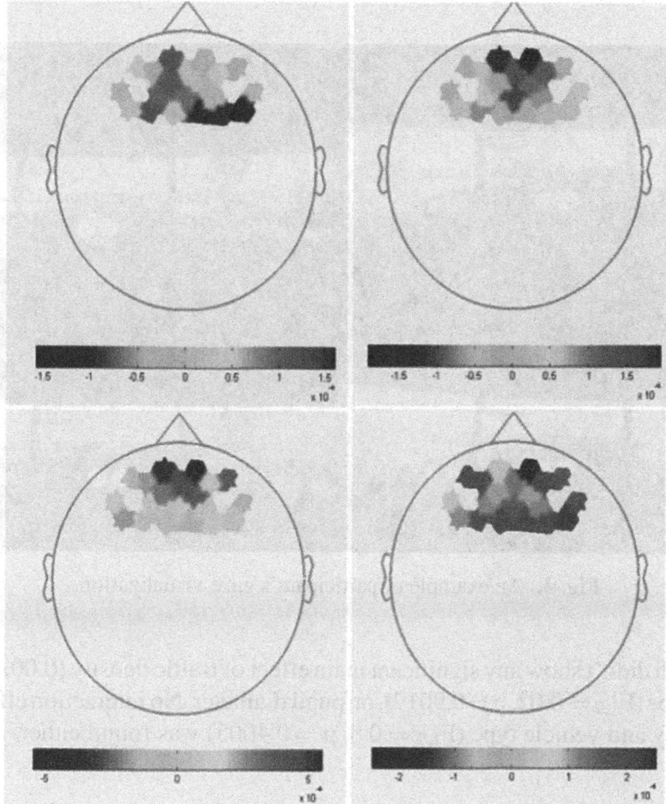

Fig. 3. An example of Oxy-Hb concentration mapping for all hemodynamic states under different scenarios.

machine noise. The modified Beer Lambert's law was then applied to convert the data from voltage to relative concentration change. An example of Oxy-Hb concentration mapping for all hemodynamic states at same frame in different scenarios is showed in Fig. 3. The upper part of the figure showed Oxy-Hb mapping for partially automated vehicles, with traffic density low and high (from left to right). Similarly, the lower part of the figure showed Oxy-Hb mapping for conventional vehicles, with traffic density low and high (from left to right).

A total of 20 channels were measured during the experiment. The results of each participant's average Oxy-Hb in channel 19 (s8-d6) from right lateral cortex were presented in this paper. The result didn't show any significant main effect of traffic density ($F_{1,7} = 0.42$, $p = 0.5399$) or vehicle type ($F_{1,7} = 0.68$, $p = 0.4380$), on Oxy-Hb. No interaction effect between traffic density and vehicle type ($F_{1,7} = 0.06$, $p = 0.8067$) was found either.

4.3 Eye Tracking Measurement

Figure 4 and Fig. 5 showed examples of participants' gazes and heatmap. The gaze path was dynamically visualized as a video scene throughout the timeline.

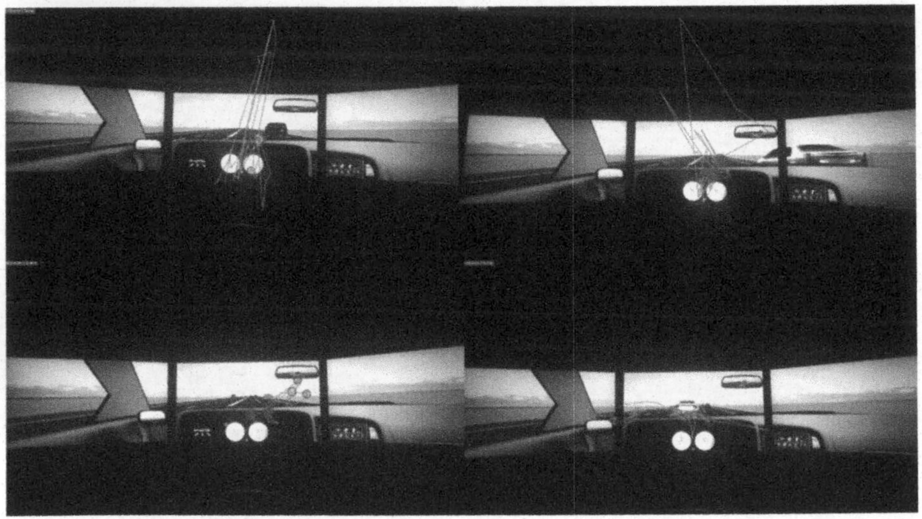

Fig. 4. An example of participant's gaze visualization.

The result didn't show any significant main effect of traffic density (0.00, $p = 0.9799$) or vehicle type ($F_{1,7} = 0.02$, $p = 0.9019$), on pupil diameter. No interaction effect between traffic density and vehicle type ($F_{1,7} = 0.8$, $p = 0.4005$) was found either.

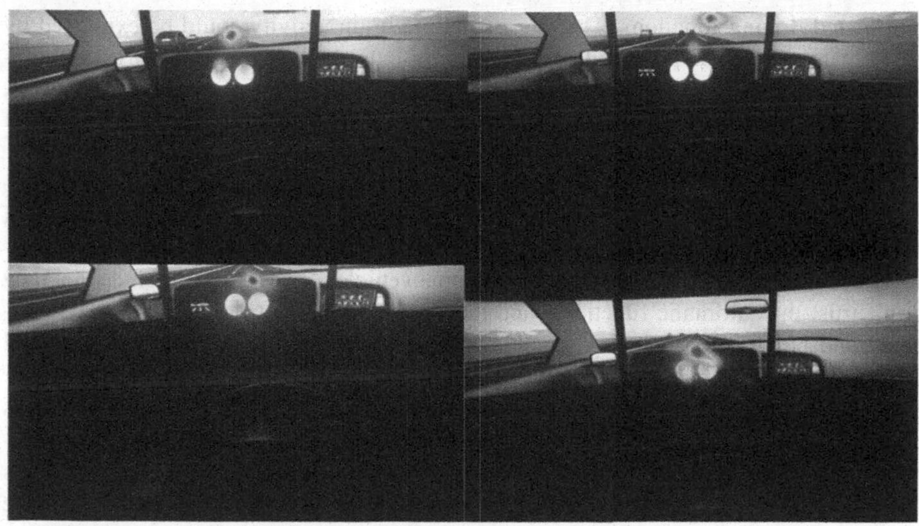

Fig. 5. An example of participant's heatmap.

5 Discussion

Results showed that vehicle type and traffic density had a significant effect on participants' workload based on the NASA-TLX questionnaire. This is consistent with previous research (Stapel et al. 2019). It indicated that participants felt different vehicle types and different traffic densities will have an impact on their workload, although it was not shown in their physiological measurements. The reasons could be, first, the workload was truly decreased under automated vehicle operation and low traffic density. Second, participants would be more inclined to feel that automated vehicles and low traffic density could save more effort. Therefore, it is not comprehensive to use only one method when assessing driver's workload. A combination of different approaches would be a better choice.

Unlike previous study (Palinko et al. 2010), the result didn't show any significant main effect of traffic density or vehicle type on pupil diameter. As average pupil diameter would decrease with drowsiness, and increase with cognitive load (Lohani et al. 2019), different driving feelings will have different impact on driver's workload, and consequently will have different influence on average pupil diameter. In addition, the tasks in this experiment may not be difficult enough to provide a significant change in pupil size. As a result, the average pupil diameter showed no significant difference under different scenarios.

It appears that traffic density and vehicle type does not provide a significant effect on Oxy-Hb from the results. This is consistent with previous research (Sibi et al. 2017). Participants dedicate as many cognitive resources during the operation of partially automated vehicles as they do during the operation of conventional vehicles when performing lane changes. But a more obvious change in Oxy-Hb was observed in partially automated vehicles when compared to conventional vehicles. As three of the participants had no experience in automated vehicles before, they may find it exciting and novel when using automated driving functions. The increase in the brain activity could be explained by participants getting familiar with automation system. And the degree of trust in automatic functions will also affect participants' cortical activity (Wilson et al. 2020). Also, as a preliminary study, only one channel from the fNIRS data was analyzed. It is not enough to show the overall changes in brain activity of the participants.

According to the post-test questionnaire, four participants preferred automated vehicles. They felt it was simple, easy to drive, effort saving and safer than conventional vehicles. Also, they reported a reduction in fatigue and stress during automated driving. While the other four preferred conventional vehicles. The reasons include that they don't trust the automatic functions, and they believe the electronic system is complicated and not 100% reliable. Also, although the participants were responsible for all driving controls, they felt more familiar with the operation of conventional vehicles. Some participants reported they are more confident in driving and prefer driving. This could be one of the explanations for no significant difference found in objective workload measurements. Another reason could be that the sample size is relatively small as a preliminary study. So, it may not be able to fully reflect the workload in objective measurements.

6 Conclusion

This study evaluated driver's workload with both subjective and physiological measurements under different traffic densities using partially automated vehicles and conventional vehicles. The study indicated the importance of combining both objective and subjective measurements to measure driver's workload. Several limitations of the present study were as follows. First, as a preliminary study, the number of the participants is very small. Workload may not be fully reflected using statistical analysis in this sample size. Second, most of the drivers in this study were young drivers, and the driving experience with automated vehicles vary from different participants. Familiarity of automation may have an impact on driver's workload. Studies regarding different ages and automation experiences need to be considered. For future studies, more participants will be recruited to conduct the experiment. Evaluation of driving performance such as wheel angle and lane position will also be included to assess workload. More physiological measurements such as eye fixation, Oxy-Hb and Deoxy-Hb of other brain regions will also be analyzed and compared.

Acknowledgements. This research was partially supported by the Center for Advances in Port Management (CAPM) at Lamar University. Any opinions, findings, and conclusions or recommendations expressed in this material are those of the authors and do not necessarily reflect the views of the CAPM.

References

D'Esposito, M., Postle, B.R., Jonides, J., Smith, E.E.: The neural substrate and temporal dynamics of interference effects in working memory as revealed by event-related functional MRI. Proc. Natl. Acad. Sci. **96**(13), 7514–7519 (1999). https://doi.org/10.1073/pnas.96.13.7514

Di Flumeri, G., et al.: EEG-based mental workload neurometric to evaluate the impact of different traffic and road conditions in real driving settings. Front. Hum. Neurosci. **12** (2018). https://doi.org/10.3389/fnhum.2018.00509
Engström, J., Johansson, E., Östlund, J.: Effects of visual and cognitive load in real and simulated motorway driving. Transp. Res. Part F: Traffic Psychol. Behav. **8**(2), 97–120 (2005). https://doi.org/10.1016/j.trf.2005.04.012
Hart, S. G.: NASA-task load index (NASA-TLX); 20 years later. PsycEXTRA Dataset (2006). https://doi.org/10.1037/e577632012-009
Heikoop, D.D., De Winter, J.C., Van Arem, B., Stanton, N.A.: Acclimatizing to automation: driver workload and stress during partially automated car following in real traffic. Transp. Res. Part F: Traffic Psychol. Behav. 65, 503–517 (2019). https://doi.org/10.1016/j.trf.2019.07.024
Jamson, A.H., Merat, N., Carsten, O.M., Lai, F.C.: Behavioural changes in drivers experiencing highly-automated vehicle control in varying traffic conditions. Transp. Res. Part C: Emerg. Technol. **30**, 116–125 (2013). https://doi.org/10.1016/j.trc.2013.02.008
Lohani, M., Payne, B.R., Strayer, D.L.: A review of psychophysiological measures to assess cognitive states in real-world driving. Front. Hum. Neurosci. **13** (2019). https://doi.org/10.3389/fnhum.2019.00057
Liu, Y., Zhao, R., Li, T., Li, Y.: An Investigation of the impact of autonomous driving on driving behavior in traffic jam. In: IIE Annual Conference, Norcross, pp. 986–991 (2021)
Paas, F., Vanmerrienboer, J.J.G.: The efficiency of instructional conditions – an approach to combine mental effort and performance-measures. Hum. Factors **35**(4), 737–743 (1993)
Palinko, O., Kun, A.L., Shyrokov, A., Heeman, P.: Estimating cognitive load using remote eye tracking in a driving simulator. In: Proceedings of the 2010 Symposium on Eye-Tracking Research & Applications - ETRA 2010 (2010). https://doi.org/10.1145/1743666.1743701
Pauzié, A.: A method to assess the driver mental workload: the Driving Activity Load Index (DALI). IET Intell. Transp. Syst. **2**(4), 315 (2008). https://doi.org/10.1049/iet-its:20080023
Recarte, M.A., Nunes, L.M.: Mental workload while driving: effects on visual search, discrimination, and decision making. J. Exp. Psychol. Appl. **9**(2), 119–137 (2003). https://doi.org/10.1037/1076-898x.9.2.119
SAE International (2016). Taxonomy and Definitions for Terms Related to On-road Motor Vehicle Automated Driving Systems (NoJ3016). https://doi.org/10.4271/J3016_201401
Sibi, S., Ayaz, H., Kuhns, D.P., Sirkin, D.M., Ju, W.: Monitoring driver cognitive load using functional near infrared spectroscopy in partially autonomous cars. In: 2016 IEEE Intelligent Vehicles Symposium (IV) (2016). https://doi.org/10.1109/ivs.2016.7535420
Sibi, S., Baiters, S., Mok, B., Steiner, M., Ju, W.: Assessing driver cortical activity under varying levels of automation with functional near infrared spectroscopy. In: 2017 IEEE Intelligent Vehicles Symposium (IV) (2017). https://doi.org/10.1109/ivs.2017.7995923
Stapel, J., Mullakkal-Babu, F.A., Happee, R.: Automated driving reduces perceived workload, but monitoring causes higher cognitive load than manual driving. Transp. Res. F: Traffic Psychol. Behav. **60**, 590–605 (2019). https://doi.org/10.1016/j.trf.2018.11.006
Unni, A., Ihme, K., Jipp, M., Rieger, J.W.: Assessing the driver's current level of working memory load with high density functional near-infrared spectroscopy: a realistic driving simulator study. Front. Hum. Neurosci. **11** (2017). https://doi.org/10.3389/fnhum.2017.00167
Villringer, A.: Non-invasive optical spectroscopy and imaging of human brain function. Trends Neurosci. **20**(10), 435–442 (1997). https://doi.org/10.1016/s0166-2236(97)01132-6
Wierwille, W.W., Eggemeier, F.T.: Recommendations for mental workload measurement in a test and evaluation environment. Hum. Factors: J. Hum. Factors Ergon. Soc. **35**(2), 263–281 (1993). https://doi.org/10.1177/001872089303500205
Wilson, K.M., Yang, S., Roady, T., Kuo, J., Lenné, M.G.: Driver trust & mode confusion in an on-road study of level-2 automated vehicle technology. Saf. Sci. **130**, 104845 (2020). https://doi.org/10.1016/j.ssci.2020.104845

Xu, Y., Graber, H.L., Barbour, R. L.: NirsLAB: a computing environment FOR FNIRS neuroimaging data analysis. Biomed. Opt. (2014). https://doi.org/10.1364/biomed.2014.bm3a.1
Yoshino, K., Oka, N., Yamamoto, K., Takahashi, H., Kato, T.: Functional brain imaging using near-infrared spectroscopy during actual driving on an expressway. Front. Hum. Neurosci. 7 (2013). https://doi.org/10.3389/fnhum.2013.00882
Zhao, R., Liu, Y., Li, Y., Tokgoz, B.: An investigation of resilience in human driving and automatic driving in freight transportation system. In: IIE Annual Conference, Norcross, pp. 974–979 (2021)

Testing Approach of HMI Designs for Vehicles with Automated Driving Systems: A Usability Test Case Based on the Driving Simulator

Hua Zhong[1](✉), Suzhen Hong[1], Chunbin Gao[1], Kai Liu[1], Xuning Wang[1], Qing Zhang[2], Kunxiong Zhu[2], Yue Wang[2], and Yaowen Guo[2]

[1] Baidu Apollo Design Center, Shenzhen 518000, China
zhonghua02@baidu.com

[2] Dongfeng Nissan User Experience Design, Guangzhou 510800, China
df-zhangqing@dfl.com.cn

Abstract. With the rapid development of Intelligent Vehicle, higher levels of automation (SAE level 3 and above; Society of Automotive Engineers [SAE] 2021) will be brought to the market in the next few years, and the corresponding in-car HMI will also usher in significant development and reform. However, the application of new technologies brings about more complex human-machine interfaces, longer development cycles and higher costs. Ensuring the safety and convenient interactive experience of in-car HMI becomes a greater challenge faced by designers. This paper investigates a driving simulator, which aims at achieving pre-launch experience assessment of a new in-car HMI design. Through the real-time linkage of virtual simulation HMI, virtual environment and cockpit hardware, the real restoration of users' driving scenes and in-car HMI experience can be realized, so that the evaluation can help the product team redesign or optimize HMI to improve its safety and availability. A set of automated driving system (SAE level 2&3) prototype was developed, and a usability study was performed on a driving simulator to evaluate the usability of the prototype. Fifteen participants were called upon to perform high-frequency common tasks base on two storylines while driving in the driving simulator. Their behavior and subjective feedback during driving were observed and recorded. After driving, semi-structured interviews were carried out. The results of the usability study helped us to improve HMI design solutions. According to this study, we have summarized the advantages and disadvantages of studying the usability of the driving simulator and provided reference suggestions for its subsequent development and improvement.

Keywords: Automated driving · Human-machine interface · Usability testing · Driving simulator · User experience

1 Introduction

With the emerging and rapid development of technologies such as deep learning and cloud computing, artificial intelligence [1] is focused on driving autonomous driving, including research, technology and economic development. The rapid development of

H. Krömker (Ed.): HCII 2022, LNCS 13335, pp. 459–471, 2022.
https://doi.org/10.1007/978-3-031-04987-3_31

smart cars has not only disrupted the traditional automotive industry, but has also profoundly affected and changed the relationship between drivers and pedestrians on the road and the car. Its recognition of the vehicle's surroundings and prediction of its behavior [2] requires timely feedback to the driver, which facilitates the driver's understanding and monitoring of the subsequent behavior of the smart car. Consequently, with the new technologies, more human-computer interaction paradigms have emerged that better handle the collaboration and interaction between human and vehicle.

In the SAE J3016 standard, there are six main stages in the process of moving a vehicle from fully manual operation to full automation. According to "Made in China 2025" (2015), China is officially encouraging the development and application of ADAS technology [3]. In particular, L3 technology is currently developing rapidly, which means that more vehicles in China will be equipped with L3 level autonomous driving technology in the future. However, how to better usability testing of the new technology and human-computer interaction paradigm has become an urgent issue to be addressed.

In the past, the more common methods of testing the usability of vehicles were static evaluation (vehicle, bench, real vehicle) and dynamic on-road evaluation of real vehicles. However, the static evaluation approach to defining L3 autonomous driving functions does not reflect the actual feedback from users in the vehicle's operational state, and the evaluation data is less reproducible. It is clear that this method cannot meet the needs of a complete L3 level of autonomous driving. The dynamic evaluation method requires a high degree of vehicle prototype development and cannot meet the needs of rapid testing of vehicle functions in the early stages of development, while there are significant safety risks in on-road testing and operation.

Therefore, it is necessary to adopt a new method of evaluating the autonomous driving function to realistically reproduce the real operating behavior and first reactions of drivers in various driving scenarios, while controlling costs and ensuring safety. This study adopts a dynamic evaluation method based on a highly driving simulator. This method allows the user to evaluate the human-machine interface design of high-level autonomous driving functions in the closest realistic driving conditions.

The aim of this study is to investigate suitable usability testing methods for highly automated vehicles in the process of open design for human-computer interaction. Through design and demonstration, feasible methods are identified to optimize current solutions and to explore how simulator evaluation can be further improved in the light of the rapid development of autonomous driving technology.

2 Method

The history of driving simulation has been motivated by advancements in technology, related to the various cueing systems including visual, auditory, and proprioceptive feedback, and the equations of motion or vehicle dynamics that translate driver control actions into vehicle motions.

As a practical matter, driving simulation development started in the 1960s using analog computers, electronic circuits, and various display technologies (Hutchinson, 1958; Sheridan, 1967; Rice, 1967; Sheridan, 1970; Weir & Wojcik, 1971; Kemmerer & Hulbert, 1975; Allen, Hogge, & Schwartz, 1977) [4–6]. The doubling of computing power every 18 months as specified by Moore's Law has lead to a dramatic increase in computing power and the associated capabilities of driving simulators over the last decades. However, with the rapid development of autonomous driving technology, the driving simulator is lagging behind and its use for testing advanced autonomous driving functions is still lacking.

In order to explore the usability of the human-machine interface for the newly developed L3 level autonomous driving function in a suitable manner, a driving simulator for this function was developed in this study. Specifically, participants were first randomly divided into two groups to experience the L3 level autonomous driving function under different driving routes to ensure that the evaluation of the function performance was not influenced by the route environment. Then, each group was given a simulated driving experience and each participant was asked to experience and evaluate the corresponding L3 level autonomous driving interaction prototype scenario to obtain the attitudes and preferences of each participant.

2.1 Experiment Environment

The combined hardware and software high-fidelity driving simulator once established in this study consisted of three steps to build a suitable experimental environment. Firstly, a Volkswagen had been modified as a simulated driving vehicle, providing a complete in-car information interaction channel through the addition of a triplex screen (Fig. 1). Then, the sensors of the steering wheel, brake, accelerator, doors and other body hardware were retrofitted and modified (Fig. 2) to achieve complete acquisition and input of driver control signals. The driver can turn on, off and adjust the L3 autonomous driving functions via physical buttons, and several physical buttons can be programmed to achieve customized interaction functions.

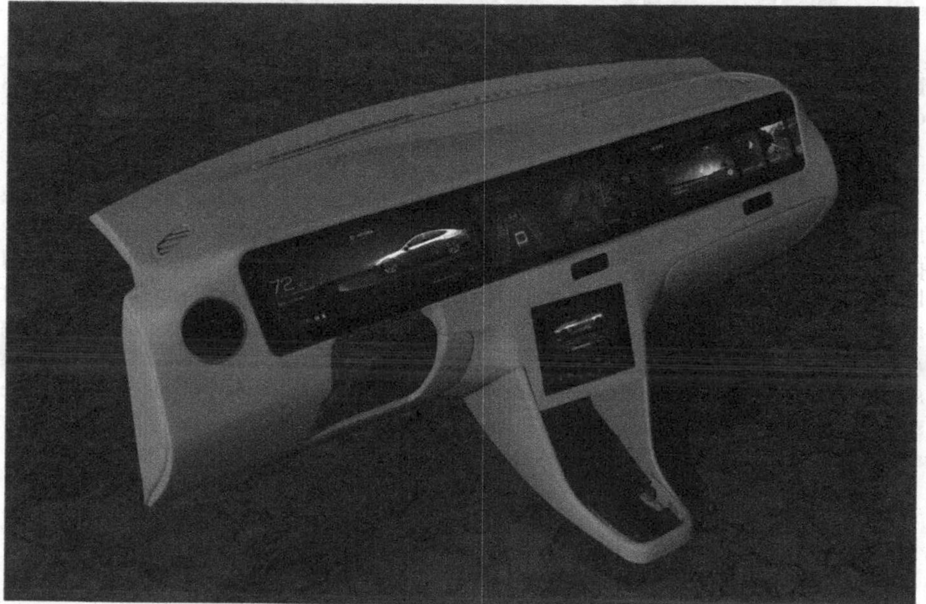

Fig. 1. Central control screen of driving simulator

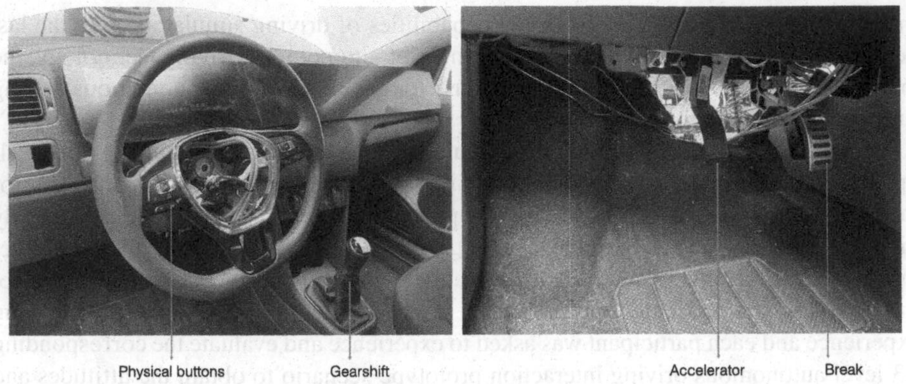

Fig. 2. Effect of relevant sensor modifications for the driving simulator

Secondly, based on the unity 3D engine software, we have built a simulated traffic environment with Chinese characteristics. The software tool was used to nest the L3 autonomous driving functions and develop the corresponding high-fidelity HMI dynamic prototype, thus realizing the L3 level autonomous driving functions in the simulated traffic environment (Fig. 3).

Fig. 3. Construction of simulation driving environment and nested development of autonomous driving function and HMI

At the same time, given that AR-HUD is highly intuitive to the driver, it can combine realistic road information with real-time AR images to more accurately and intuitively prompt and guide the driver, thus more effectively avoiding the information prompted by the vehicle to distract the driver while driving. This technology will play an important role in the future of high-level autonomous driving technology. However, the existing AR-HUD hardware technology is difficult to support the modification of the driving simulator, so we have ingeniously nested the AR-HUD information display into the simulated scenario and successfully achieved the visualization of its information by adjusting the appropriate display position (Fig. 4).

Fig. 4. Nested development of AR-HUD function

Finally, the joint debugging test of the 3D scene projected by the projector, the HMI and the driving simulator hardware were carried out (Fig. 5) to guarantee the simultaneous display of *information* from multiple ends. We have developed a virtual driving simulation system with an AR-HUD, a multi-screen IVI system and L3 level autonomous driving (Fig. 6).

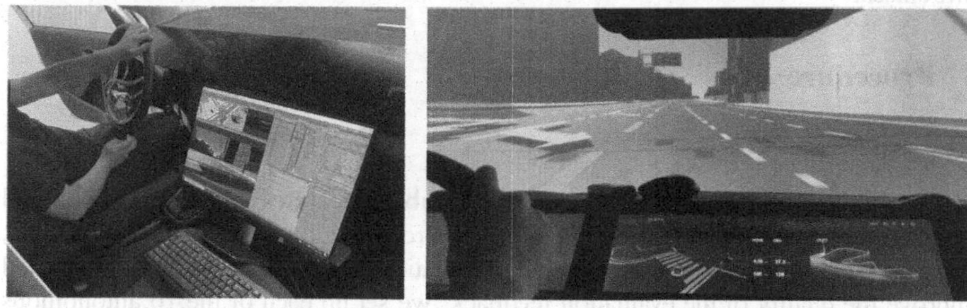

Fig. 5. Joint debugging test of 3D scene, HMI and driving simulator

2.2 Participants

A total of 15 participants were recruited for this study. Three main criteria were considered when recruiting participants: gender (male and female), driving experience (more than 3 years) and the type of vehicle used (cars with a high level of intelligence, such as Tesla model3, Lixiang one, Xiaopeng P7, etc.; cars with a low level of intelligence, such as Nissan Skyline, Volvo XC60, etc.). Each of the 15 participants had experienced 2 different driving routes. After the participants had experienced a full driving route (interacting with the modified driving simulator), they were briefly interviewed for the test. All participants successfully completed the experiment and, with the help of the facilitator, provided their subjective evaluation of each tested feature.

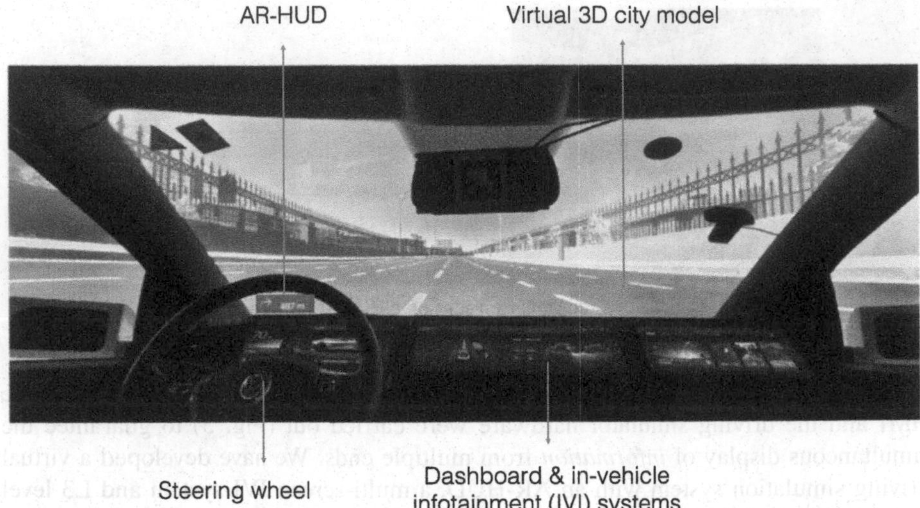

Fig. 6. Virtual driving simulation system with synchronous linkage of driver, vehicle and environment

3 Procedure

3.1 Experiment Process

here are limitations to this study, including the number of features to be tested, the limited number of participants and time constraints. In order to fully evaluate all the features, decrease the time spent on a single evaluation, reduce the fatigue of the participants and improve the quality of the evaluation feedback, we set up each of the 16 autonomous driving features to be tested on a different driving route based on people's usual driving habits and the characteristics of each autonomous driving feature. Story line 1 was an urban road and story line 2 was a highway (Fig. 7 and Table 1). Both lines were pre-programmed in the unity software in the form of navigation so that participants could experience all the features smoothly on the right roads and at the right time.

Step 1 – Familiar with Vehicle Operation. Before starting the experiment, each participant was asked to adjust the seat to their proper driving position. The vehicle was then started and driven freely for 2 min to familiarize themselves with the operation of the vehicle, including the sensitivity of the steering wheel, accelerator and brakes, so that the further driving experience could run smoothly and reduce subsequent simulator sickness.

Step 2 – Simulated Driving Experience. Once participants have familiarized themselves with the vehicle, they will be asked to undertake a formal driving simulation experience. For the first short part of the story line, participants will be expected to drive the vehicle autonomously according to a preset navigation. When the vehicle reaches a predetermined location, the driver will be prompted to turn on Autopilot, which will then put the vehicle into autonomous driving mode. With Autopilot on, participants will not have to steer the vehicle but simply pay attention to the road.

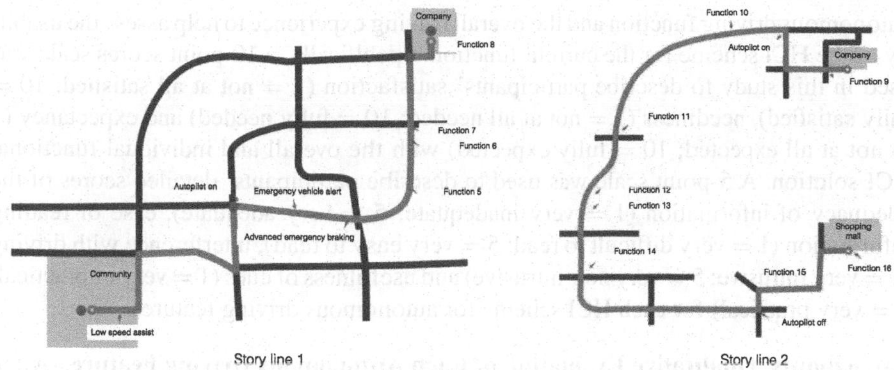

Fig. 7. Two different test routes of autonomous driving

Table 1. Terminologies and brief explanations used in the study

Terminology	Brief explanation
Low speed assist	When the vehicle needs to pass at low speeds, the system will automatically trigger and use panoramic images and collision alerts to assist the driver to have full control of the vehicle's surroundings
Autopilot on	When the vehicle drives itself in a variety of complex road conditions or driving scenarios, the user only takes over when prompted to do so when the vehicle is out of control
Emergency vehicle alert	Monitoring the passage of emergency vehicles in the vicinity (e.g. emergency vehicles, fire engines, police cars, unexpected social vehicles, etc.) will warn the driver in advance
Advanced emergency braking	The vehicle will detect and indicate to the driver the potential risk of a collision and intervene differently based on the level of danger. Emergency braking is automatically triggered when the vehicle is in a high-risk scenario

Step 3 – Evaluation After Driving. After taking part in each round of the driving experience, all participants were invited to evaluate and score the interaction prototype solution and describe their feelings.

3.2 Measures

The measurement in this study focuses on two assessment dimensions to help determine the optimal HCI solution improvement, including subjective scores by participants (a 10-point scale and a 5-point scale) and a qualitative evaluation of each function.

Participant's Subjective Scores for Each Autonomous Driving Feature. At the end of the simulated driving experience, the interviewer required participants to score each autonomous driving function and the overall driving experience to help assess the usability of the HCI scheme for the current function. Specifically, a 10-point scores scale was used in this study to describe participants' satisfaction (1 = not at all satisfied; 10 = fully satisfied), neediness (1 = not at all needed; 10 = fully needed) and expectancy (1 = not at all expected; 10 = fully expected) with the overall and individual functional HCI solution. A 5-point scale was used to describe participants' detailed scores of the adequacy of information (1 = very inadequate; 5 = very adequate), ease of reading information (1 = very difficult to read; 5 = very easy to read), interference with driving (1 = very intrusive; 5 = very non-intrusive) and usefulness of cues (1 = very impractical; 5 = very practical) for each HCI scheme for autonomous driving features.

Participants' Qualitative Evaluation of Each Autonomous Driving Feature. After scoring each autonomous driving feature, participants participated in a quick in-depth interview to describe their feelings, preferences and suggestions for improvements to the interaction scheme. The interview outline is prepared in advance and the questions include an overall evaluation of the driving experience and a detailed evaluation of each Autopilot feature. The specific questions were further analyzed based on the participants' previous scoring.

Questions exploring the participants' overall evaluation of the programme were as follows.

1) What is your overall feeling about the overall human-computer interaction experience with the autonomous driving features?
2) What impressed you most/least satisfied? Why?

The questions that probed participants' evaluation of each autonomous driving feature were as follows.

1) Compared to your own vehicle or other features of the same type, what is it about the design of the feature that is more impressive and advantageous?
2) What are the reasons for the lower (<3 points)/higher (≥3 points) scores for information adequacy/information legibility/driving distractions/tip usefulness?

Finally, some open-ended questions were also asked. For example, "does the current HMI solution meet your usage needs? Do you have any other suggestions for the way information is prompted in the autopilot?".

4 Result

In this study, the participants' evaluation of the human-computer interaction design solutions for each autonomous driving function was summarized by analyzing the mean values of their scores. The results were divided into two parts: the overall evaluation of the scheme, and the evaluation of the individual autopilot functions.

As a whole, the current autonomous driving design solutions compare to the assisted driving features available on the market. The former solution performs better overall and better meets the driver's needs for vehicle information prompts under autonomous driving (Fig. 8). The advantages of the Autopilot design solution are specifically demonstrated by the functionality and the comprehensiveness of the system's information presentation and tips. Interestingly, even though the demand scores are high, participants scored relatively low on satisfaction and expectation. This may be due to the fact that the participants generally believe that the current design solution is able to meet their own needs and thus have a high demand score. However, there is still room for refinement in the details of individual features, and thus a slightly lower performance in satisfaction. In addition, given the implementation of the powerful autonomous driving technology, users feel that the corresponding vehicle experience performs in line with the development of the technology, but some of the current features do have detail issues that slightly reduce user expectations. This also helps us to confirm the reasonableness of the relevant feature set and the direction of improvement.

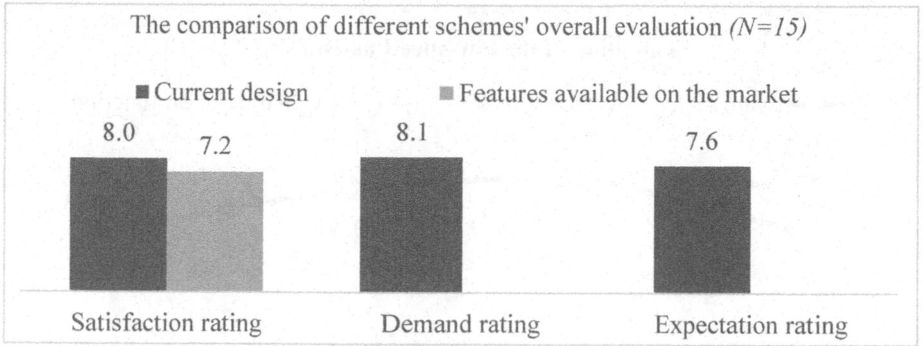

Fig. 8. Comparison of participants' evaluation differences on the overall design scheme and their vehicle system

The analysis of the scores for each specific autonomous driving function identifies the right direction for improvement of the design solution. Comparing the satisfaction scores for the different autonomous driving functions, we found that functions such as Low speed assist performed below average (Fig. 9). Due to copyright restrictions, only some of the results are shown. Low speed assist was measured by analyzing the performance of this feature in terms of information adequacy, information readability, driving distractions and usefulness of tips, and then comparing the average performance of all eight features in story line 1, combined with qualitative interview information. It was found that there is still a need to focus on improving this feature in terms of "information sufficiency" and "usefulness of cues", as the current design does not provide the information that participants need (Fig. 10).

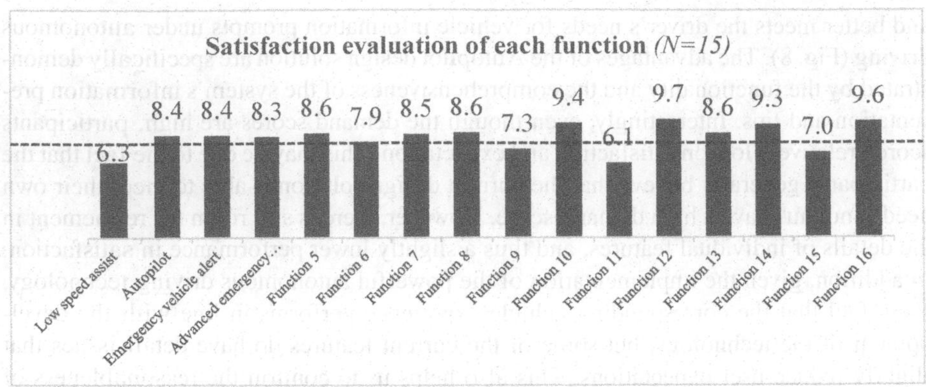

Fig. 9. Participants' satisfaction evaluation of each function

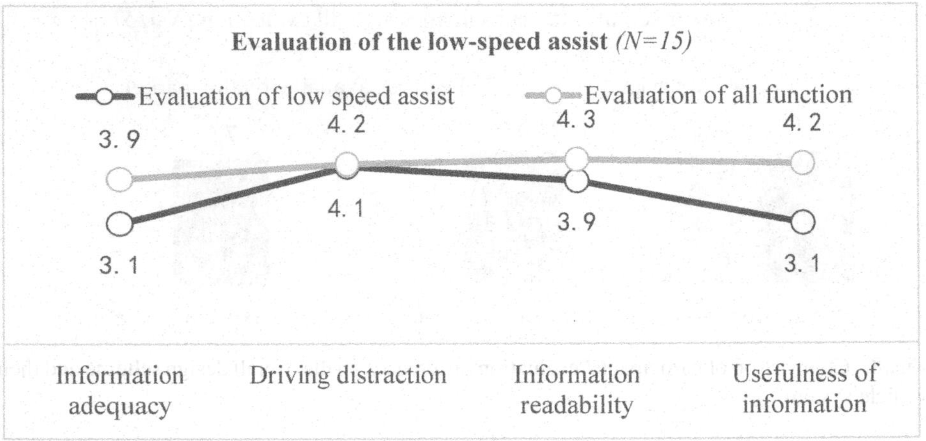

Fig. 10. Participants' experience detail evaluation of the low-speed assist

In addition to the quantitative evaluation of the various functions, a number of experiential issues were identified in our dynamic high-fidelity driving simulator using semi-structured interviews. The majority of participants felt that the layout of the AR-HUD in the scenario we presented was not in line with driving habits. For example, the graphics and text were displayed too far down to the left, which was not easy to view while driving and could easily distract the driver. We have revised and improved the design based on these findings, but the new solution cannot be disclosed in this article at this time due to copyright restrictions.

In combination with the scores for each function and the qualitative interview information, it can be seen that, even in autonomous driving situations, there is currently a high demand for drivers to be alerted to key road information, including emergency vehicles, congested roads and driver blind spots (Fig. 9). As autonomous driving is still in its early stages of development, drivers generally have not yet fully established their trust in the new technology and thus need the technology to provide sufficient information to assist drivers in making decisions to take over the vehicle at the appropriate time.

5 Conclusion

The results of the study show that drivers still have a strong demand for the timeliness and richness of information enhancement when the vehicle is in autonomous driving. Moreover, the interaction design of relevant functions should fully consider four experience levels including information adequacy, driving interference, information readability and prompt practicality to meet the driver's needs.

Through the practical application of the driving simulator, this study also concludes its relevance for usability testing of high-level autonomous driving functions. This includes the following five specific points.

1) Low cost: Compared to real vehicle development, a low development cost, high fidelity simulator can be competent for research during the development of autonomous driving functions and obtain customer insight input earlier.
2) High simulation: Highly simulated scenario modelling via Unity maximises the real driving environment and its evaluation results are closest to objective.
3) Anti-interference: Each participant experiences the developed and designed autonomous driving function under the same pre-set driving route and driving environment, eliminating the interference of environmental factors on the evaluation results.
4) Safety: Compared to real-world vehicle evaluation, it provides the user with an inherently safe environment in which the user is not actually exposed to any danger when the technology for the assisted driving function is not yet mature.
5) Versatility: virtual scenarios can be freely created to match the requirements of a particular evaluation scenario to the needs of the project, and can be configured more easily and economically.

When evaluating usability through driving simulator, care should be taken to reduce the incidence of simulator disorders in a sensible manner. For example, the hardware needs to have a fully simulated motion base to ensure consistent visual and body movement sensory information for the participants. Software needs to improve visual image stability, including higher pixels, faster screen refresh rates, smoother 3D scene changes, etc. Display Alignment cannot be ignored, as the simulator often requires multiple screens or projection devices to form a virtual driving scene around the driver. Therefore, images at the boundaries of different displays/projectors should be adequately aligned to avoid driver simulator illnesses caused by the visual focus not being able to converge.

This study confirms the effectiveness of driving simulators for usability testing of high-level autonomous driving, but also reveals some problems. For example, customized development modelling is still time consuming and cannot meet the needs of fast and agile testing. Future simulators could be developed in the direction of improving development efficiency, for example by providing modular development tools for HMI design, autonomous definition and setting of autonomous driving functions, etc.

6 Discussion

With the rapid advances in autonomous driving technology, relevant practitioners are beginning to think about how highly autonomous vehicles can communicate their driving intentions and information to drivers in complex road traffic environments in order to meet their needs for driving information in the new technological form. A rapid approach to usability testing is a key point in validating and correcting design solutions to better meet the needs of drivers. Through the practical application of the driver simulator, this study understands the driver's attitude and needs towards the vehicle HMI in an autonomous driving situation, refines the corresponding HMI design, and further explores the advantages and disadvantages of applying the simulator to autonomous driving technology and HMI development.

Given the time schedule of the project and the limitations of the simple experimental setting, the study has certain limitations and room for improvement. Firstly, there was a lack of physiological and behavioral data on the drivers. In this study, due to time constraints, physiological measurement equipment such as eye-tracking devices were not adequately used to fully obtain the behavioral parameters of the participants to help improve the accuracy of the experimental results. Secondly, due to technical reasons, the motion system was not fully integrated with the virtual scenario software, which prevented the vehicle motion simulation system from being sufficiently effective in this study, resulting in an increase in the reporting of driver simulator illnesses. Two of the participants in this experiment suffered from some degree of driver simulator illness, and although their symptoms were alleviated through interviews and breaks during the experience, they may not have been able to focus completely on the functional experience, affecting the accuracy of the results. Finally, the limited number of participants in this study due to project funding and time constraints, and the large number of HMI functions to be tested, prevented the participants from experiencing each and every function, reducing the comparability of the results to some extent.

In future research, we will first optimize the test equipment by further modifying the driving simulator to ensure that it is better suited to the evaluation. We will then try to apply the simulator to more human-vehicle interaction development projects for autonomous driving functions and pre-set up a more simulated experimental environment to explore more effective human-machine interface design solutions for advanced autonomous driving functions.

References

1. Liao, J., Hansen, P., Chai, C.: A framework of artificial intelligence augmented design support. Hum.-Comput. Interact. **35**(5–6), 511–544 (2020)
2. Ohn-Bar, E., Trivedi, M.M.: Looking at humans in the age of self-driving and highly automated vehicles. IEEE Trans. Intell. Veh. **1**(1), 90–104 (2016)
3. Made in China 2025. http://www.miit.gov.cn/n973401/n1234620/. Accessed 22 Jan 2020
4. Hutchinson, C.H.: Automobile driving simulator feasibility study. Cornell Aeronautical Laboratory, Incorporated of Cornell University (1958)

5. Sheridan, T.B.: Mathematical models and simulation of automobile driving. In: Conference Proceedings, Massachusetts Institute of Technology, Cambridge, Mass, USA (1967)
6. RICE, RS: Methods of improving point-light source techniques for application to automobile driving simulators (Point source techniques for automobile driving simulation) (1967)

Micro-mobility and Urban Mobility

Towards a Framework for Detecting Temporary Obstacles and Their Impact on Mobility for Diversely Disabled Users

Enka Blanchard[1,2,3(✉)], David Duvivier[1], Christophe Kolski[1], and Sophie Lepreux[1]

[1] Laboratoire d'Automatique, de Mécanique et d'Informatique industrielles et Humaines, UMR CNRS 8201, Université Polytechnique Hauts-de-France, Valenciennes, France
enka.blanchard@gmail.com

[2] Chaire d'Intelligence Spatiale, Université Polytechnique Hauts-de-France, Valenciennes, France

[3] Centre Internet et Société, UPR CNRS 2000, Paris, France

Abstract. While walking around a city, the temporary obstacles present on the sidewalk barely register in most people's minds. The reality for people with disabilities is quite different, whether it's a scooter left in the way, crowds that refuse to budge, or construction work loud enough to trigger somatic effects. While detecting permanent obstacles (e.g. wheelchair-inaccessible areas) is a relatively easy thing, detecting and addressing temporary obstacles is very difficult. The objective of this paper is to propose some first elements to build a framework aimed at detecting temporary obstacles for diversely disabled users. We point out several scientific and technical issues that pave the way to reach this goal and highlight the limits of existing approaches. We insist on three significant problems to overcome: incomplete models of the environment, limited availability of good-quality data, and absence of tailored algorithms . Taking inspiration from percolation theory, we propose some leads to solve the first two problems mentioned.

Keywords: Disabled mobilities · Percolation theory · Obstacles · Routing

1 Introduction and Problem Statement

If one is attentive while strolling around a city, one can notice a large variety of obstacles that don't initially come to mind: construction work with its loud noises and equipment left on the ground that we must sidestep, trash bins on the sidewalk, crowds and queues in front of pubs and shops... These obstacles (illustrated on Fig. 1) rarely register in the conscious mind of most pedestrians, as their impact is generally negligible. There is, however, one group on whom those obstacles can have a considerable impact: disabled people. To be precise,

H. Krömker (Ed.): HCII 2022, LNCS 13335, pp. 475–488, 2022.
https://doi.org/10.1007/978-3-031-04987-3_32

we are not using this term as shorthand for people with physical impairments or wheelchair users, who already have very varied approaches to mobility [19]. Instead we use it to denote anyone whose bodymind peculiarities[1] are not compatible with all environments, such as the following (non-exhaustive) list[2]:

- People with multiple chemical sensitivities, for whom various aerosols (smoke, perfumes, pollutants) can trigger intense short- and long-term adverse reactions [28].
- People with mobility impairments or lowered manoeuvrability for whom a physical obstacle can be impossible to go around (especially in a constrained environment like a sidewalk) [2].
- Blind people[3] who cannot generally perceive obstacles at a distance and plan their path, and who are especially at risk when it comes to floor irregularities [14,24].
- People with hyperacusis for whom loud noises can be painful, disorienting, and even act as a trigger for anxiety disorders [32].
- People with cognitive impairments who rely on specific landmarks and for whom a small change can prevent recognition and prevent them from reaching their destination [1,10,22].
- Agoraphobic and ochlophobic people for whom the presence of a crowd in a street can make it an impassable obstacle.

Previous work on disabled mobilities and spatialities has mostly focused on physical impairments and especially wheelchair users [2,7,13], albeit with some exceptions [10,24]. In all cases, however, a common finding is that many of the people concerned have restricted spatial habits (sometimes dependent on the availability of a companion). They tend to move in a discrete fashion, such as from home to workplace and back (with no stops in between), and rarely deviate from known routes to explore their environments (for example, one study on blind people found that 40% deviated from known routes less than once per week [24]).

There are many reasons for this reduced tendency to explore one's environments, including potentially higher intrinsic costs as well as safety considerations and stress factors. Intelligent Transportation Systems (ITS) can be of assistance in such contexts by providing accessible routes to one's destination for different transport modalities, sometimes with multiple routes [8,26]. However, most algorithms—whether online (during the trip) or offline (during the preparation phase)—rely on the assumption that the environment is known with reasonable

[1] The term *bodymind* is used in disability studies to accentuate the importance of corporeity (against an imagined detached mind). We choose to use peculiarities as the issues here are not always impairments, but rather incompatibilities between the bodymind and its environment. A classification of disabilities will not be attempted here as it is an endeavour fraught with difficulties [18].

[2] This list does not include the troubles caused by harassment and discrimination, which play a big role in disabled spatialities but are much harder to evaluate, and are thankfully not as frequent as the obstacles mentioned for most users [3,25].

[3] We use the term here as one chosen by the community to describe itself [20].

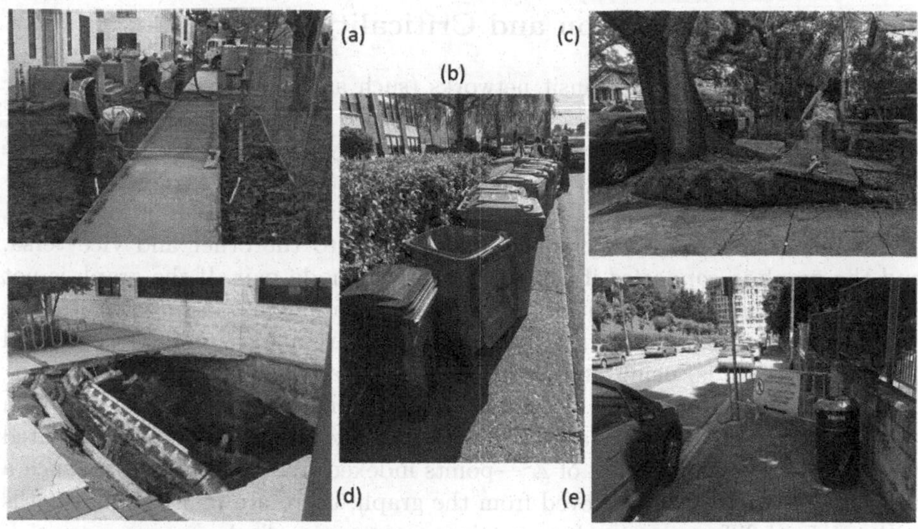

Fig. 1. Various kinds of temporary and semi-permanent obstacles. Images from Wikimedia Commons under CC-A licenses by the Oregon Department of Transportation (a and b), Bart Everson (c), En el nido (d), Eric Fischer (e).

accuracy. They might allow for rerouting in case of increased traffic, but are generally not optimised for cases where a significant proportion of the network can become suddenly unusable. This is where temporary obstacles create an issue, as their distributions—or even rough estimates—are generally not available, and require specific measurements methods, which we seek to address here. The main previous study that addressed some of the same issues did not take such temporary obstacles into account—and also collected limited data, based on questionnaires [33].

Using percolation theory [6] allows us to look at how the impact of temporary obstacles on disabled mobilities can differ from that of permanent obstacles and requires different solutions. If their density is high enough, moving around a city can become nigh-impossible, and this can be subject to threshold effects. Having good estimates of the prevalence and impact of temporary obstacles would be a useful tool, whether for informing policy-making or to evaluate spatial discriminations (or help disability advocacy groups). Knowing the obstacle distribution also makes it possible to use operations research tools to address path-planning with redundancies.

This paper is structured as follows. First, we give some background on the model and tools we use, before analysing why existing databases are not sufficient to get quantitative data. We then propose first ideas concerning a framework to measure and handle temporary obstacles, and finally discuss its limitations and potential extensions.

2 Graphs, Percolation and Criticality Effects

A common way to model transit networks (such as the ones in cities, whether they are road-based or rail-based) is to use graphs where each node is an intersection (or a terminus) and two nodes are joined by an edge if and only if there is a street between them (with no intersection in-between). The edges can potentially be weighted (to denote travel time, cost, or any other information). Then, two nodes are *connected* if one can go from one to the other and vice versa, and the graph is *connected* if this is true for any node pair. If the graph is not *connected*, then it can be split into a set of maximal *connected components* [15].

From a driving point of view, nearly all cities are made up of one connected component (that is, using one's car, one can go anywhere, even when taking into account one-way streets). Pedestrians can ignore one-way restrictions which simplifies matters. A pedestrian moving in a grid-like city can then be assimilated to a path between two nodes of $\mathbb{Z}^2$—points indexed by (x,y) integers. In such a case, even if one edge is removed from the graph, there are many similar paths with minimal differences (such as turning one street earlier).

Let's now consider a wheelchair user in San Francisco—which is mostly grid-like [4]. Unlike for most pedestrians, some streets are completely impassable (such as Greenwich Street which features stairs). Moreover, other streets can be impassable or too dangerous to be tried (such as Filbert street, with a slope of 31.5%). These, however, are permanent obstacles, and any frequent user (or anyone that prepares their trip) can plan to avoid the area. Moreover, they are sufficiently rare that they don't affect most trips in most cities.

Let's now add the constraint of temporary obstacles. As those cannot be known in advance (at least for now), a reasonable model is the one where each street has a constant probability of being impassable. Hence the following:

- take the graph G corresponding to the city;
- remove from the graph G any edges that are permanently impassable;
- for each remaining edge, keep it with probability p (or equivalently remove the edge from the graph with probability $1-p$, corresponding to the probability of adding an impassable obstacle).

This brings us to percolation theory, which is dedicated to the study of such structures, of their connected components, and of the probability of being able to go from one point to another) [5]. One result from this field is of particular interest to us:

- There is a critical threshold p_c for many classes of graph—such as $\mathbb{Z}^2$, but also more general graphs that could be better models for non-grid cities.
- If $p < p_c$, the connected component around the starting point is exponentially small (in $p_c - p$).
- If $p > p_c$, there is one major connected component that corresponds to a constant proportion of the graph (which depends on p).

For our considerations, this means that there is a critical value for p, above which users can safely explore nearly all their environment, and under which they are stuck in a finite and small neighbourhood. Moreover, as illustrated on Fig. 2, this type of model can also allow us to compute not only the probability of finding a path between two points, but also the expected additional cost of detours. Additionally, this model can have an impact on users' spatial habits. If p is known for a city (and for a person, as the type of impassable obstacle varies widely), and is sufficiently above p_c, then the user can be secure in the hope that nothing wrong will happen on their trips. Whereas if it is below (or close to p_c), the user would have to plan backup solutions. Some disabled users may have a personal estimate (obtained from experience) of such probabilities, but these are generally not transferable from one place to another, meaning that travelling disabled people might be forced to use very conservative estimates just in case (and unnecessarily limit their activities).

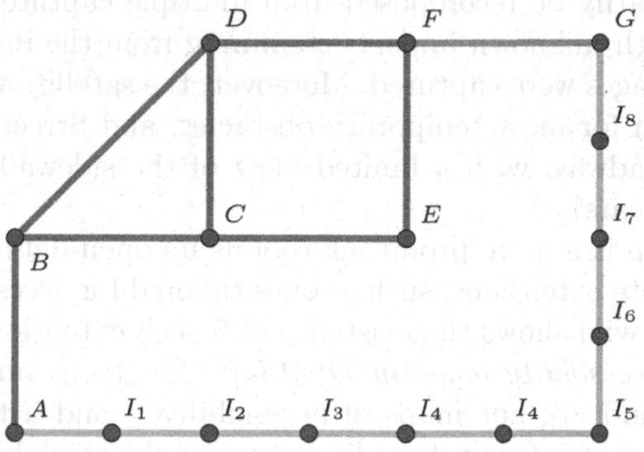

Fig. 2. An illustration of percolation in a small graph where we try to go from A to G. Let's assume that the red FG edge is often unavailable (for any reason) for a disabled user, with probability 0.5. Then a temporary obstacle on any orange edge is enough to prevent them from reaching our destination. Assuming that each non-red edge has a probability $p = 0.9$ of being usable, the probability of being stuck is 0.367 (a non-disabled user not affected by the red edge and with $p = 0.95$ would be stuck with probability 0.023). More importantly for the disabled user, no matter the path chosen, the probability of encountering an obstacle is at least 0.56, and in all but 1% of cases, this means having to take a long detour (more than two edges). This is a toy example as, due to the exponential nature of some of the behaviours, the difference is most visible on bigger graphs. (Color figure online)

Alas, as the next section shows, existing tools and databases are not sufficient to compute p. A central goal of the framework introduced in Sect. 4 is to create databases that can compute approximate values of p in various localities, while handling multiple models depending on the types of obstacles considered.

3 Existing Potential Solutions

Most of the potential sources for data on temporary obstacles come from intelligent transportation systems. Those sometimes integrate some rudimentary features for disabled mobilities (such as indicating the presence of elevators, or the accessibility of given public transit routes).However, this data is partial, and the objective functions that are used to compute or rank the paths are generally not able to take specificities of disabled users into consideration. Moreover, they can't be used directly to study the prevalence of temporary obstacles, as we will show below.

Google is the best-known provider and has two main services that could be useful in the measurement of temporary obstacles. The first is Google Maps in its satellite version, and the second is the Street View service, for which the coverage is not as complete, especially in the Global South [12]. A central concern in both sources is that due to their proprietary nature and limited transparency, it is not always feasible to get accurate metadata (temporally, the precision is at best at the month level). As such, it would be very hard to obtain a "snapshot" of a zone as it would necessarily be recomposed from multiple capture times (sometimes months apart), with unknown impacts stemming from the imprecision on when (time/day) the images were captured. Moreover, the satellite version is generally not precise enough for most temporary obstacles, and Street View is generally taken from the roadway, with a limited view of the sidewalk (especially when hidden by parked cars).

OpenStreetMap is a more promising tool as its open-database license allows users to easily create extensions, such as ones tailored for accessibility. As of January 2021, OSM's wiki shows the existence of 5 such extensions. Two of them—*GetThere* and *Accessibility layer in OSMS-WMS*—focus on making the map itself accessible (and are not maps of accessibility), and a third—*BiViMap*—is a map of points of interest for blind users, only available in German and mostly focused on German metropolitan areas. The last two—*Wheelmap* and *Wheelchair map*—are focused on wheelchair accessibility. They use existing OSM data plus additional user inputs to list accessible and inaccessible places. However, even a cursory visit to known locations (or comparisons with Google Street View history) show that some of the data has been obsolete for at least two years.

There have been attempts to create user-collected databases of obstacles, but they are a priori not able to address the problems of temporary obstacles. One central issue is the dynamic nature of the data collected. The obstacles can be either inherently ephemeral or require an intervention to be removed, and their temporal duration vary from minutes to weeks. Moreover, an obstacle is added when someone sees it, but might stay a long time before being removed from the database as users don't systematically report obstacles and no-one knows how many kilometres the user walked before reporting the obstacle (which would be needed to estimate the obstacle density). So if three obstacles are shown in one neighbourhood, it could correspond to three independent points reported over a week, each immediately reported and present for only a few hours, with no other obstacles ever being there. Or it could be a single person on a five-minute walk forced to deviate from their route three times. Collating dynamic data to have an idea of which percentage of the network is unavailable is not a priori solvable, even before getting into issues of manipulation, false-reporting and DoS attacks.

Some navigation software tools like Waze try to address temporary road obstacles such as accidents [23,31] by looking at slowdowns in the network, but they rely on a massive distributed sensor system (made up of all their users). They also rely on the relative simplicity of the data collected (location and speed) which is given with no direct cost to the user. Automatically identifying temporary obstacles might be at the edge of feasibility by detecting detours taken by certain people, but the system would need to guess the type of obstacle, and if it truly is an obstacle or if the user didn't simply cross the street to say hello to a friend. Moreover, there might not be the critical mass of users needed to obtain the information—even when discounting the fact that disabled users tend to go out less frequently.

Security camera networks and drones could be an eventual lead but their data is generally not made public, they are not available everywhere, and their use raises many privacy concerns and is often opposed by human-rights groups [30].

4 Proposal: A Framework for Detecting Temporary Obstacles in Mobility Contexts

The goal of this section is to provide a framework for the detection of temporary obstacles in mobility contexts. This type of detection has to be considered jointly with the detection of permanent obstacles. A central constraint is that we want an agnostic approach. That is, an approach which is not tailored to one disability but is as general as possible, to maximise the applicability and re-usability of the databases collected—although the characteristics of the eventual end-user will have to be taken into account to tailor the system to their needs. Figure 3 shows how a global view of how such systems could interact in the future, taking data from a variety of sources and feeding it into ITS.

In this approach, as suggested in Fig. 3, the bodymind peculiarities of the target user or group have to be defined and known by the support system. Indeed, they are necessary to identify the categories of obstacles to be detected; the obstacles are different, for instance, in the cases of agoraphobia, hyperacusis, or sensitivity to odours. One also has to keep in mind that many users have multiple categories of obstacles that affect them (e.g. hyperacusis and sensitivity to odours are often found together). This idea of groups reflects the fact that many disabled users are in many cases, for different personal, safety or health reasons, accompanied by one or several members of their social environment, which is sometimes referred to as the ecosystem [16,17]. This ecosystem is composed, for example, of family and/or professional caregivers, therapists, friends or colleagues, and this in relation to a set of activities to perform. It should be noted that the presence of one or more other people can in some cases help the person overcome certain types of obstacles, just as it can hinder in other situations.

The target user or group has in most cases objectives (e.g., go to a concert), habits (e.g., go through a park) and preferences (e.g., go through the main street rather than its parallel streets). Such characteristics have to be taken into account by the system with a view of personalisation/customisation [27,34].

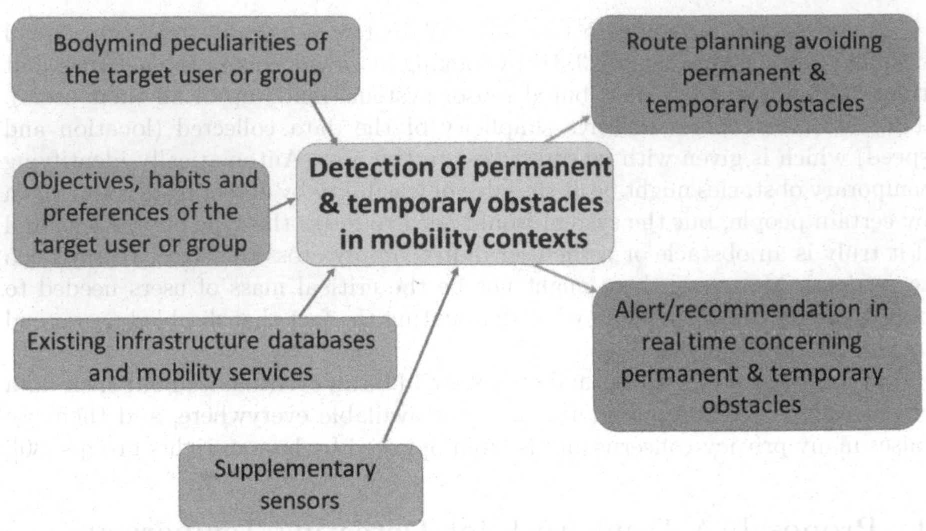

Fig. 3. Global view of the approach proposed allowing the detection of permanent and temporary obstacles, and its uses.

Concerning the obstacles to be detected, a specific work about how to categorise finely them into categories and sub-categories needs to be performed and may be object of further research. Globally speaking, they may be classified into two main categories:

- Permanent or semi-permanent obstacles, such as: broken elevators, missing curb cuts, illegally narrow sidewalks, high slopes, unmaintained pavement (or specific kinds of pavement), traffic lights not equipped with acoustic systems, street signs at head level...
- Temporary obstacles, such as: garbage cans or scooters on the sidewalks, invasive terraces (e.g. restaurant or bar terraces that extend in good weather), gatherings of people in the broadest sense (including queues spilling over onto the sidewalks, or groups of exuberant fans before or after games), animals leashed to posts on the sidewalk, loud roadworks—which can also emit MCS-triggering chemicals...

In order to model all the notions seen in this article, we wish to propose a class diagram in Fig. 4 that synthesises them and allows them to be related. In the model, the *Obstacle* element is linked to the detection mode. Thus it is possible to know by which means the obstacle is identified and thus to be able to associate a probability in time or to use machine learning on the prediction of this obstacle. The model shows two possible elements of detection, which are: information given by the user themself, or by automatic detection via sensors. As mentioned above, the obstacles are of two types. For example, a person who cannot walk on steep streets will set it as a constraint so steep streets will be considered a permanent obstacles and won't be offered during pathfinding.

This information is specific to them, it does not mean that it is an obstacle for other users. For this person, the obstacle is permanent. Another example concerning a person who often follows routine routes, with the same streets and the same sidewalks. In the case of work on the sidewalk or the installation of scaffolding, they would have to cross the road. For some of these users, this is very complicated and they might turn back. The system is there to help them in this difficult situation, either by anticipating and proposing another known route (link between *Recommendation* and *Trip*) or by assisting them in crossing the road (link between *Recommendation* and *Ecosystem*). This data-centric system could be complementary to the wayfinding-centric ones as [21].

Figure 3 leaves open the possibility of extracting data about possible ways and/or certain potential permanent, semi-permanent or temporary obstacles from existing databases and from mobility services. For instance, from entertainment, sport or transport databases, it is possible to deduce at what time there is a risk of gatherings of people in one or several streets and/or on a place. However, as said in Sect. 3, existing databases are not sufficient to obtain a working model that can optimise routing—in both route-planning and real-time recommendation—and provide guarantees.

A central missing element to feed these eventual models is the density of temporary obstacles—to obtain an approximate value for p. Before other approaches can be developed we can already imagine a rudimentary setup where one equips a device (such as a wheelchair) with a set of sensors and exhaustively covers a given locale, while registering all the obstacles they perceive (and capturing generic data to also allow later refinement and classification). Such a setup could potentially include:

- video capture, possibly from multiple angles (such as at wheel level to observe street quality);
- sound capture (or sound intensity measurement, for different frequencies);
- GPS to coordinate with map data;
- a manual clicker to add arbitrary points in the database, both for facilitating later classification and to add elements that are only perceived by the user operating the capture device;
- pollution or chemical sensors.

With such an apparatus, one could cover all streets of a neighbourhood at different times in a systematic way, thus avoiding the biases inherent in the options mentioned in Sect. 3. A practical implementation would still need to address multiple technical hurdles:

- There is the question of how the general database architecture should be organised to be most useful in different contexts. Just from the data-presentation side, there are advantages to having it as video, as a clickable map$\Longleftrightarrow$picture interface (as in Google Street View), or as a set of obstacle-events (viewable chronologically and geographically). With some work, all those formats should be convertible to each other (except potentially for the video source), but a first step before the practical realisation of any database

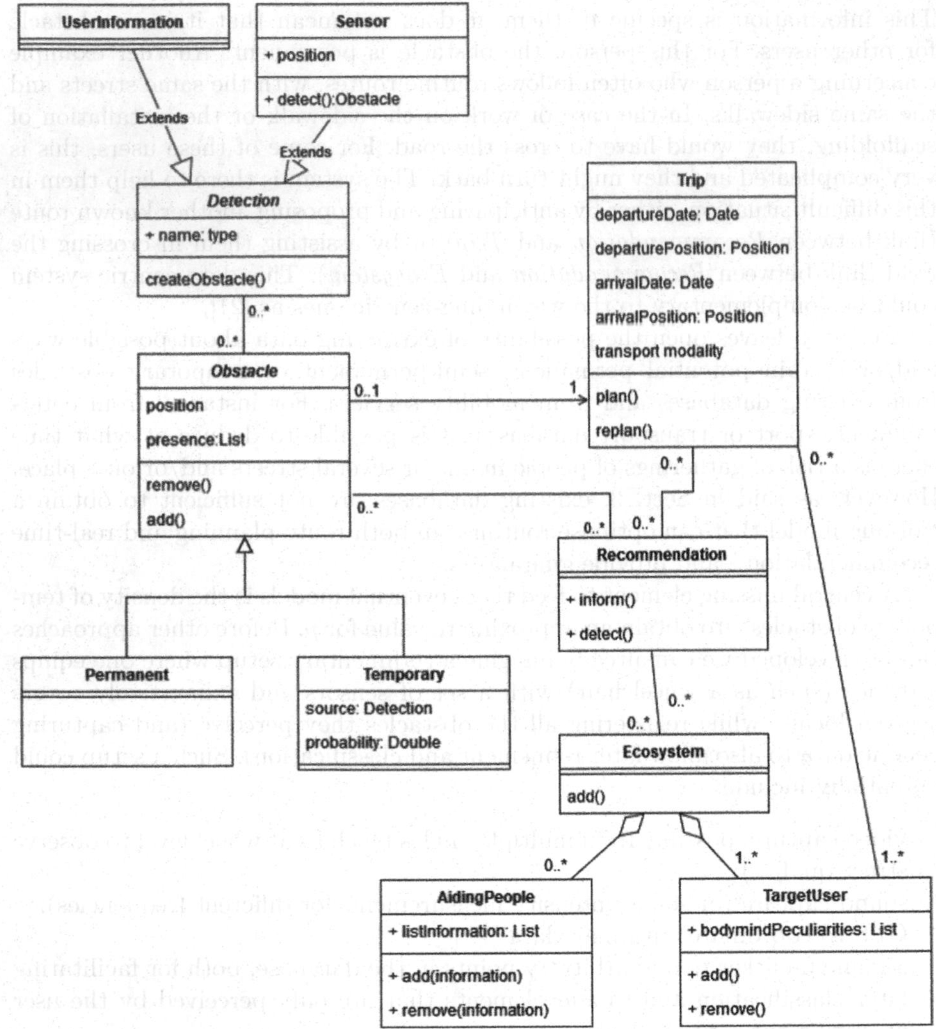

Fig. 4. UML classes diagram to model notions and the relations between them to provide the support system.

should be a reflection on the desired architecture (to privilege usability, interoperability, performance...).
- There is also, as mentioned above, the design of the obstacle classification system.
- Finally, the data collection procedure should alleviate privacy concerns, which are affected by various laws, and would be non-trivial, as previous work has shown [11].

5 Discussion

The proposal above gives a first lead as to how to determine the prevalence and cost of multiple kinds of temporary (and semi-temporary) obstacles. The goal is not to detect them in real-time for end-users but rather to integrate their statistical presence in our ways of thinking, especially for path-planning (although this work raises the question of how to best present these statistical obstacles to users and which interfaces to use to show alternative or redundant routes). We leave open multiple questions regarding both how to implement it and how to optimise it in practice.

A first subject concerns the temporal aspects of data gathering, with three questions arising. First, when capturing data for a single database, what would be the impact of the capture day and hour? For example, trash bins are often left outside and collected on given days. Similarly, electric scooters might be more frequently left on sidewalks in the evening, before they get picked up to get charged. Night-time capture (and corresponding temporary obstacles) nearly constitutes a different problem by itself. There are probably no good answers to this conundrum, but eventual data gathering endeavours will have to choose a temporal modality, and see how it affects the corresponding database. The second question is related, and concerns the weather and long-term temporal aspects, as certain obstacles are not the same in summer and winter—e.g. crowd behaviours on sidewalks or pavement quality when freezing. The third question is whether the database should include some repeated segments, to see the dynamic evolution of temporary obstacles. Ideally, each database would correspond to a single snapshot, which is made impossible due to the time necessary to capture the data. Although there are additional costs to capturing certain elements multiple times, it could also provide interesting data. How to best integrate such data and how to optimise the capture of the most interesting segments—for example, those with certain obstacles already present—is another complex question.

There are two technical elements worth looking into. First, if we assume that people in an area obtain information on the distribution of temporary obstacles, it would be useful to integrate the corresponding percolation models in routing algorithms. This would mean creating algorithms to handle multi-objective routing while maintaining a balance between the route redundancy, the length of eventual detours, and their probability (all depending on the users' constraints and risk profiles). Second, experience shows that a significant percentage of people working on improving accessibility are directly affected by various impairments. Most databases are not usable by blind users, especially visual ones (such as Google Street View), and the databases created in our context should be usable by all, which might require some new solutions.

There are also two questions on the social and geographical side. First, this article has introduced a framework for the study of temporary obstacles, and this could be useful for decision-making on urban questions. However, we did not address who should be the ones to implement such frameworks in practice (municipalities, NGOs, public advocacy associations), or how the framework, data and conclusions could be used (and whether they could have a negative impact). Moreover, the creation of such databases—with potentially semi-sensitive data on the privacy front—requires special considerations concerning both cybersecurity and updating/maintenance, with digital obsolescence being a growing concern [9,29], especially if undertaken by small NGOs without cyber-security expertise. Second, the framework shown above is more adequate for urban/suburban environments and urban policy-making. If one seeks to adapt it to rural areas, what changes would be necessary?

Finally, two main open problems also remain:

- The framework allows for the capture of data for chemical sensitivities—and allergies—but the manner of capture remains a problem, as most commercially available equipment only allows the measurement of some proxies (such as particulate air pollution). How then to measure the various sources of chemical obstacles?
- What would be necessary to obtain a system that deals with temporary obstacles in real-time (such as certain routing services do for both traffic and speed cameras)?

6 Conclusion

We have shown the importance of temporary obstacles to disabled mobilities, and the difficulties in both keeping track of these obstacles and simply estimating their prevalence, and introduced some concepts from percolation theory to model their impact on disabled users. We have also discussed the interest in using a disability-agnostic approach that does not focus in advance on a specific impairment but captures as much as possible to be reusable by all who could benefit from it—with the ITS optimising for the user's eventual impairments. We've introduced some initial ideas on how to build a framework to detect and handle such temporary obstacles. They require further study on multiple fronts, from the sensor systems that should be used to the questions of interoperability between databases and services and the problem of user privacy and respect of existing legislations (such as GDPR).

Acknowledgments. This work has been partially supported by PIA Accroche Active in particular Valmobile action and the SAMDI Project supported by the Region Hauts-de-France.

References

1. Antonakos, C.L., Giordani, B.J., Ashton-Miller, J.A.: Wayfinding with visuo-spatial impairment from stroke and traumatic brain injury. Disabil. Stud. Quart. **24**(3) (2004)
2. Blanchard, E.: Crip spatialities and temporalities I:discreet crips in a discrete world. EspacesTemps.net (2020). https://doi.org/10.26151/espacestemps.net-vmak-xq38. https://www.espacestemps.net/en/articles/discreet-crips-in-a-discrete-world-spatialities-and-temporalities-of-disability/

3. Blanchard, E.: Crip spatialities and temporalities II:a systematic typology of temporal taxes. EspacesTemps.net (2020). https://doi.org/10.26151/espacestemps.net-g7ca-v287. https://www.espacestemps.net/en/articles/crip-spatialities-and-temporalities-ii-a-systematic-typology-of-temporal-taxes/
4. Boeing, G.: Urban spatial order:street network orientation, configuration, and entropy. Appl. Netw. Sci. **4**(1), 1–19 (2019). https://doi.org/10.1007/s41109-019-0189-1
5. Borgs, C., Chayes, J.T., Kesten, H., Spencer, J.: The birth of the infinite cluster:finite-size scaling in percolation. Commun. Math. Phys. **224**(1), 153–204 (2001). https://doi.org/10.1007/s002200100521
6. Broadbent, S.R., Hammersley, J.M.: Percolation processes:I. Crystals and mazes. Math. Proc. Cambridge Philos. Soc. **53**(3), 629–641 (1957). https://doi.org/10.1017/S0305004100032680
7. Clarke, P., Ailshire, J.A., Bader, M., Morenoff, J.D., House, J.S.: Mobility disability and the urban built environment. Am. J. Epidemiol. **168**(5), 506–513 (2008)
8. Dimitrakopoulos, G.J., Uden, L., Varlamis, I.: The future of intelligent transport systems. Elsevier, Amsterdam (2020)
9. El Idrissi, B.: Long-term digital preservation:a preliminary study on software and format obsolescence. In: Proceedings of the ArabWIC 6th Annual International Conference Research Track, pp. 1–6 (2019)
10. Escuriet, M.: Comprendre les représentations mentales de l'espace des personnes en situation de handicap: vers une évaluation des dispositifs d'accompagnement mis en place par l'association LADAPT. Ph.D. thesis, Université Clermont Auvergne (2021)
11. Frome, A., et.al.: Large-scale privacy protection in google street view. In: 2009 IEEE 12th International Conference On Computer Vision, pp. 2373–2380. IEEE (2009)
12. Fry, D., Mooney, S.J., Rodríguez, D.A., Caiaffa, W.T., Lovasi, G.S.: Assessing google street view image availability in Latin American cities. J. Urban Health **97**(4), 552–560 (2020). https://doi.org/10.1007/s11524-019-00408-7
13. Gharebaghi, A., Mostafavi, M.A., Edwards, G., Fougeyrollas, P.: User-specific route planning for people with motor disabilities:a fuzzy approach. ISPRS Int. J. Geo-Inf. **10**(2), 65 (2021)
14. Giudice, N.A., Legge, G.E.: Blind navigation and the role of technology. Engi. Handb. Smart Techno. Aging, Disabil. Independence **8**, 479–500 (2008)
15. Gondran, M., Minoux, M., Vajda, S.: Graphs and Algorithms. Wiley, Hoboken (1984)
16. Guffroy, M., Guerrier, Y., Kolski, C., Vigouroux, N., Vella, F., Teutsch, P.: Adaptation of user-centered design approaches to abilities of people with disabilities. In: Miesenberger, K., Kouroupetroglou, G. (eds.) ICCHP 2018. LNCS, vol. 10896, pp. 462–465. Springer, Cham (2018). https://doi.org/10.1007/978-3-319-94277-3_71
17. Guffroy, M., Nadine, V., Kolski, C., Vella, F., Teutsch, P.: From human-centered design to disabled user & ecosystem centered design in case of assistive interactive systems. Int. J. Sociotechnol. Knowl. Dev. (IJSKD) **9**(4), 28–42 (2017)
18. Hammell, K.W.: Deviating from the norm:a sceptical interrogation of the classificatory practices of the ICF. Br. J. Occup. Ther. **67**(9), 408–411 (2004)
19. Inckle, K.: Disabled cyclists and the deficit model of disability. Disabil. Stud. Quart. **39**(4) (2019)
20. Jernigan, K.: The pitfalls of political correctness:euphemisms excoriated. Braille Monit. **52**(3) (1993)

21. Lakehal, A., Lepreux, S., Letalle, L., Kolski, C.: From wayfinding model to future context-based adaptation of HCL in urban mobility for pedestrians with active navigation needs. Int. J. Human-Comput. Interact. **37**(4), 378–389 (2021). https://doi.org/10.1080/10447318.2020.1860546
22. Letalle, L., et al.: Ontology for mobility of people with intellectual disability:building a basis of definitions for the development of navigation aid systems. In: Krömker, H. (ed.) HCII 2020. LNCS, vol. 12212, pp. 322–334. Springer, Cham (2020). https://doi.org/10.1007/978-3-030-50523-3_23
23. Li, X., Dadashova, B., Yu, S., Zhang, Z.: Rethinking highway safety analysis by leveraging crowdsourced waze data. Sustain. **12**(23), 10127 (2020)
24. Manduchi, R., Kurniawan, S.: Mobility-related accidents experienced by people with visual impairment. AER J. Res. Pract. Vis. Impairment Blindness **4**(2), 44–54 (2011)
25. Mason-Bish, H., Kavanagh, A.: Private places, public spaces (2019). https://privateplacespublicspaces.blog/about-the-project/
26. Mine, T., Fukuda, A., Ishida, S.: Intelligent Transport Systems for Everyone's Mobility. Springer, Singapore (2019). https://doi.org/10.1007/978-981-13-7434-0
27. Mourlas, C., Germanakos, P.: Intelligent user interfaces: adaptation and personalization systems and technologies:adaptation and personalization systems and technologies. IGI Global (2008)
28. Rossi, S., Pitidis, A.: Multiple chemical sensitivity: review of the state of the art in epidemiology, diagnosis, and future perspectives. J. Occup. Environ. Med. **60**(2), 138 (2018)
29. Sandborn, P.: Software obsolescence-complicating the part and technology obsolescence management problem. IEEE Trans. Compon. Packag. Technol. **30**(4), 886–888 (2007)
30. Schwartz, A.: Chicago's video surveillance cameras: a pervasive and poorly regulated threat to our privacy. Northwest. J. Technol. Intellect. Property **11**, ix (2012)
31. Silva, T.H., de Melo, P.O.S.V., Viana, A.C., Almeida, J.M., Salles, J., Loureiro, A.A.F.: Traffic condition is more than colored lines on a map:characterization of waze alerts. In: Jatowt, A., et al. (eds.) SocInfo 2013. LNCS, vol. 8238, pp. 309–318. Springer, Cham (2013). https://doi.org/10.1007/978-3-319-03260-3_27
32. Tyler, R.S., et al.: A review of hyperacusis and future directions: part i definitions and manifestations. Am. J. Audiol. **23**(4), 402–419 (2014)
33. Victor, N., Klein, O., Gerber, P.: Handicap de situation et accessibilité piétonne: reconcevoir l'espace urbain. Espace populations sociétés. Space populations societies (2016/2) (2016)
34. Zanker, M., Rook, L., Jannach, D.: Measuring the impact of online personalisation: past, present and future. Int. J. Human-Comput. Stud. **131**, 160–168 (2019)

Assistive Systems for Special Mobility Needs in the Coastal Smart City

René Chalon[1], Chuantao Yin[2], and Bertrand David[1](✉)

[1] Université de Lyon, CNRS, Ecole Centrale de Lyon, LIRIS, UMR5205, 69134 Lyon, France
{Rene.Chalon,Bertrand.David}@ec-lyon.fr

[2] Sino-French Engineer School, Beihang University, Beijing 100191, China
chuantao.yin@buaa.edu.cn

Abstract. The Smart City is an important evolution for cities of different sizes and contexts. Multifaceted proposals are made all around the world. Mobility support and its evolution is an important part of this issue. In this paper we propose to study a particular context, which is devoted to showing how a Coastal city can become a Coastal Smart City. We present our study and proposals based mainly on special mobility configurations, the role and functionalities of corresponding assistive systems, and the HCIs implemented in practice. Finally, we integrate all these aspects in the architecture of the assistive system managing them.

Keywords: Smart City · Mobility of people and goods · Assistive systems for mobility · Special needs · Tourism · On the beach · On the sea · Boat mobilities

1 Introduction

The Smart city originated in the media sector, which refers to integration of urban systems and services by using various information technologies or innovative concepts to improve the efficiency of resource utilization, optimize urban management, and improve the quality of life of citizens.

Today, countries world-wide realize in varying degrees the idea of smart cities and the different implementation efforts. However, there is no denying that in the 21st century, the age of smart is here.

The Smart City is not only the application of new information technologies, but also concerns the participation of citizens in the various activities of the city with the intelligence of humans, combined with Artificial Intelligence in different forms. A variety of classifications try to clarify this huge domain. One of these proposes six dimensions: environment, economy, living, mobility, people, and government with the following orientations: wireless city, smart home, smart transportation, smart public service and social management, smart urban management, smart medical treatment, green city and smart tourism [1].

It is also possible to examine whom these evolutions concern. By avoiding the generic "to everybody", we classify the answers by age: kids, teenagers, adults, seniors; by implication in the city: citizen, neighbor, student, worker, administrator, governor; without avoiding important orientation to all persons with deficiencies.

H. Krömker (Ed.): HCII 2022, LNCS 13335, pp. 489–506, 2022.
https://doi.org/10.1007/978-3-031-04987-3_33

We can also try to draw up a list of reasons for: better common welfare and neighborhood, energy, transportation of goods and passengers, information dissemination on culture, sports, social services, tourism, etc.

The Smart City is an area where all ICT possibilities can be used: data accessibility, data processing, information access exchange and manipulation in static and mobility situations, using wired or wireless networks, mainly in contextual situations. Multiple ICT technologies are used to solve these problems such as Internet, Internet of Things (IoT), Location-Based Services (LBS), Big Data and Open Data, as well as Artificial Intelligence with Machine and Deep Learning.

The presentation at this conference is steered towards mobility in the city, as well as towards HCI devices allowing propagation and collection of appropriate information to the users concerned.

The next sections of this paper are organized as follows. After a short state-of-the art in Sect. 2, we identify in Sect. 3 multiple aspects of our field of study which is a coastal city. We try to identify characteristic situations to consider, as well as corresponding activities and/or applications in order to manage them. Data collection, management, and evolution are studied in Sect. 4. The architecture of an assistive system and its role in the field are studied in Sect. 5 based on data exchanges with the ground and with users. Appropriate HCI supports and devices are presented and discussed at appropriate places in the paper.

2 State-of-the-Art

To carry out a complete state-of-the-art for the Smart City would appear to be totally impossible as the amount and diversity of work is large and diversified. It would be hard enough to establish a common definition and classification, and indeed this has not yet been achieved, while listing all approaches and contributions seems totally impossible. We thus propose that the reader consults our paper [2]. In relation to transportation aspects, a relevant reference is [3]. The Japanese view seems interesting [4], as is also Singapore's perception of emerging technologies [5]. The questions on the effectiveness of smart cities make for instructive reading [6], as does also the view presented to CIOs [7]. [8] directly relates to our approach. From the coastal city point of view, we shall now suggest two references [9, 10].

3 Coastal City Characterization and How It Becomes Smart

To show how a city evolves into a smart city, specifically in the case of a coastal city, we need first to characterize what a Coastal city is. Then, we identify progressively different dimensions of its evolution into a Smart City. We limit our work to the dimension of management of mobility and the assistive system, the role of which is to manage corresponding behaviors (Fig. 1).

Fig. 1. Coastal city with downtown, harbor, port, beaches, and boating industrial zone.

We start with the definition of a Coastal City: A Coastal City is a city that is located by the sea or the ocean. Its activities are related to the sea, i.e. fishing, boat transportation, boat and ship repairs, as well as possibly boat and ship construction. A large majority of coastal cities in France also have important tourist activities related to the proximity of more or less popular beaches. Swimming, diving, snorkeling, yachting, kitesurfing, and fishing are common practices.

This aspect of welcoming tourists is dominant in the organization of City life. It introduces the notion of the high and low seasons, mainly by the number of inhabitants that can vary considerably between these seasons (their number can be multiplied by 10 or more in summer). As such, the requirements of life organization are totally different. In the low season, a few inhabitants can live quietly without stress, noise or traffic jams. However, economically speaking, this period is a "waiting" period for a large majority of inhabitants who rely on their tourist businesses to live (retired people excluded), whether in the form of restaurants, shops, accommodation or recreation activities.

It seems natural to study the evolution of this kind of city into a smart city in the context of high season city life, while only later showing that in the low season it is possible to propose appropriate limited behaviors and city services adapted to this season and its inhabitants.

We begin our study with the general problem of circulation in a city with a large population density. We can inherit classical smart city solutions for different kinds of mobility: pedestrian, bike, scooter, motorbike, car, truck, and public transportation (bus and, for large cities, tram and subway). The solutions implemented are traffic reorganization with pedestrian zones, one-way streets and roads, prioritized lanes for public transportation, emergency services, and taxis, pedestrian and bike lanes. In coastal cities two evolutions can be considered: (1) organization of circulation between specific zones, i.e. park-and-ride and downtown, downtown and recreation areas and beaches, etc. and (2) new transportation modes such as boat taxis and individual boats, pedalo-boats. New protected lanes can also be created for automated shuttles between these zones.

It is also important to consider the dynamicity of these reorganizations, which can be permanent (available all the time) or evolve according to the time scale (each month, week, day, weekdays, weekend, morning, afternoon, evening, night, per hour or in unpredictable exceptions). As we will see later, signaling must be appropriate (static or with appropriate dynamicity), as must also be propagation of applicable rules to different users. The goal is evolution of the circulation map during the high season in order to optimize fluidity and preferential transportation. Creation of park-and-ride can be associated with public automated transport to the city, the harbor (port) and the beaches. Management of priority for several kinds of vehicles such as buses, delivery trucks, emergency vehicles, and vehicles for disabled people can also be considered.

3.1 Management of Circulation in the City, in the Harbor/port, and on the Sea

Let us now recall an approach to mobility devoted to **dynamic lane management** on which we worked [11]. Its objective was to create these lanes dynamically only when buses are present and to leave all lanes open to general traffic when buses are not present. This allows management of general traffic speed. The main technologies used are: a Location-Based Service integrating bus detection sensors; an intermediation platform collecting sensor information and determining dynamic bus section activation and deactivation; in-the-field infrastructure and/or embedded vehicle interface receiving instantaneous information on selected situations (Fig. 2). From the HCI point of view, it is important to indicate the present situation on in-the-field indicators, as well as on the screen in the vehicle.

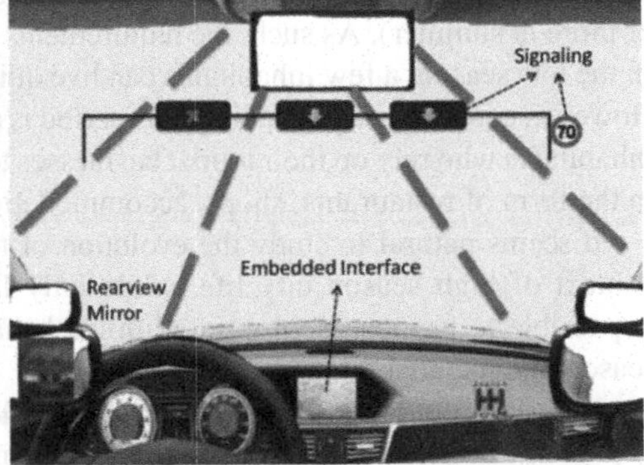

Fig. 2. Dynamic lane management [11].

Another non-coastal specific service is devoted to **better and easier parcel delivery to inhabitants or stores.** In this case, we proposed to create delivery areas which can be reserved as priority by delivery vehicles, in order to shorten delivery times [12]. In this context, the main data are: delivery addresses of parcels to be distributed and the geographical location of delivery areas to be reserved. An algorithm or interactive tool is used to create a delivery trip integrating the schedule of use delivery areas allowing transported parcels to be delivered to destination addresses. A mobile interaction tablet-based tool allows the driver to modify the trip if a traffic jam problem or other problems occur (Fig. 3).

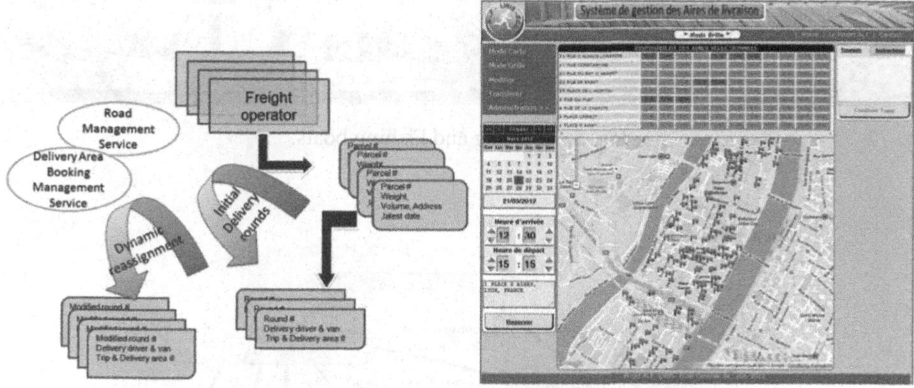

Fig. 3. Parcel distribution based on delivery area reservation [12].

Management of circulation in the commercial port/harbor is totally specific and has no relation to the touristic part of the city, in order to preserve appropriate working conditions in this part of the city and on the sea (Fig. 4).

In the context of the coastal city, a specific service is devoted to **management of circulation in the port,** taking into account weather conditions and the state of the sea, as well as access to different parts of the port (industrial, professional, sailing, and yachting). In this context, not only local mobility can be managed, but also all the activities of fishing boats and cruising boats (as we will see later). From the HCI point of view, integrated screens and mobile tablets will be used by the crew.

Fig. 4. Industrial coast and navigation zones.

This service can be generalized to the overall management and supervision of boats in the harbor and on the sea. The ecosystems for fishing and cruising boats (Fig. 5) are schematized in Figs. 6 and 7. The principle is to identify all concerned actors and situations and to indicate their behaviors, their interrelations and contributions to appropriate trip and work conditions. In the past we studied this kind of ecosystem for buses (e-bus) and trucks (e-truck) [13] and adapted them to these situations.

Fig. 5. Cruising and Fishing boats.

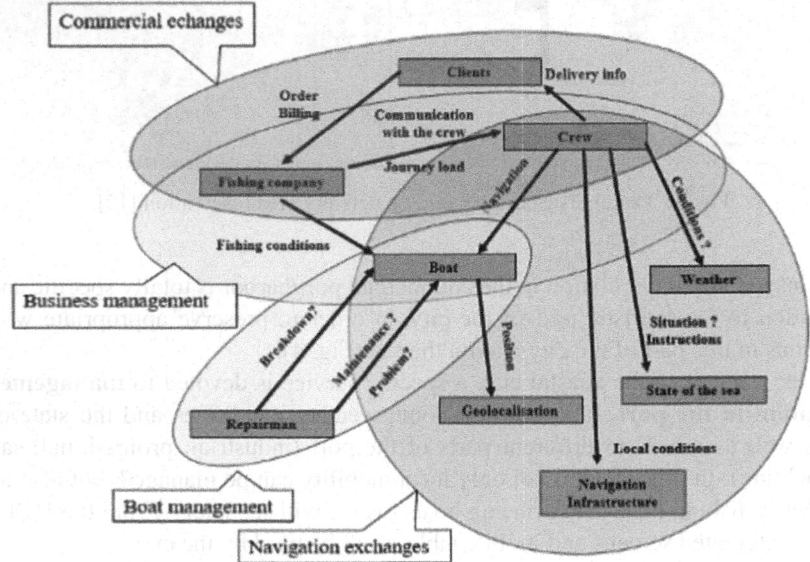

Fig. 6. Fishing boat information ecosystem.

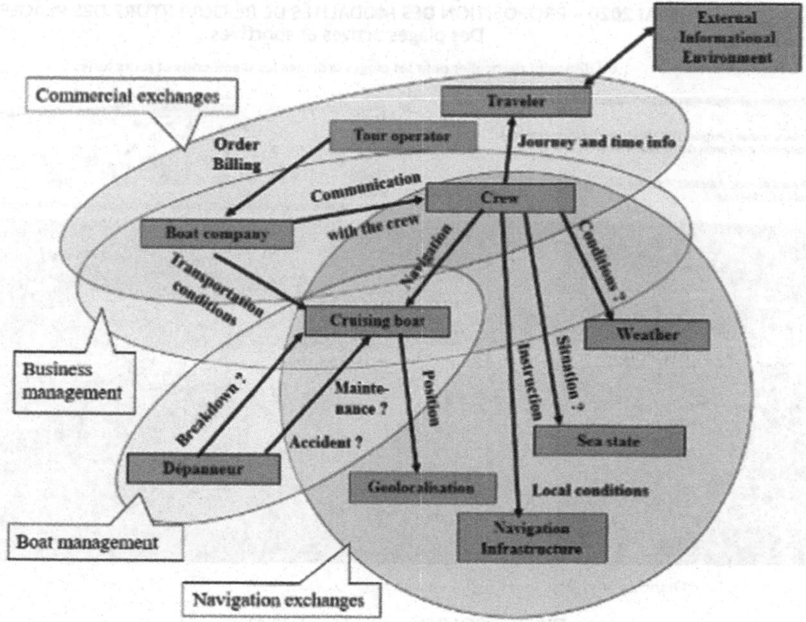

Fig. 7. Cruising Boat information ecosystem.

3.2 Beaches and Sea

Another important aspect for coastal cities is management of mobility on the beaches and on the sea. On the beach several activities are possible, more or less dynamic: sunbathing, walking along the seashore, carrying out various sports or family activities. In all cases, it is important to look out for other beach users, to avoid accidents and ensure you do not disturb them. In the recent COVID period, on many French beaches, city mayors at local level or, more globally, government authorities have determined several categories of rules: prohibit access to beaches, authorize only "dynamic use of the beach" (no sitting or sunbathing, only walking and running), respect of distances between groups of users, either natural or physically materialized zones, with the possibility of reserving them (Fig. 8 and 9).

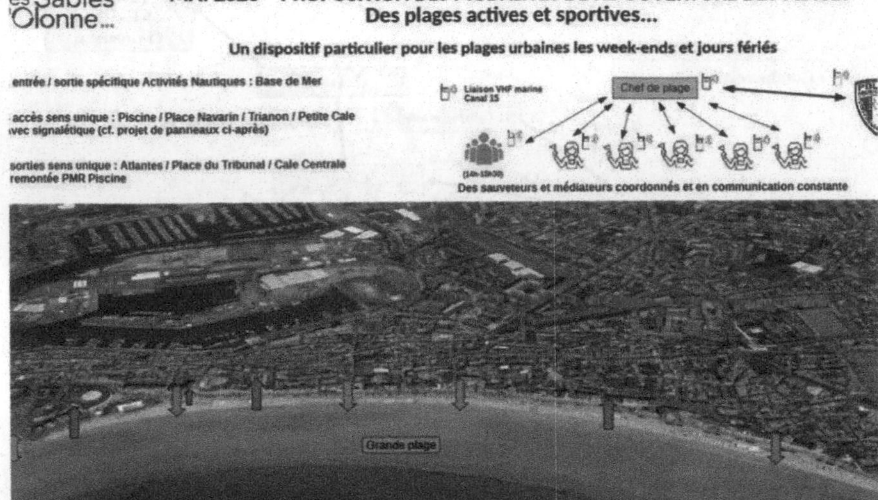

Fig. 8. COVID on the beach [14].

Fig. 9. COVID location management on the beach

On the sea (Fig. 10), the creation of activity zones is a common approach resulting in the creation of specific zones with supervised swimming, diving, and snorkeling activities, as well as sailing, yachting, surfing, kitesurfing, with either visual supervision, or more instrumented electronic monitoring. In this case, each actor (swimmer, sailor, kite surfer has at his/her disposal a connected watch, or more sophisticated devices able to communicate his/her position and related situation (OK, emergency call, etc.). On the beach, life guards are equipped with a receiver allowing them to monitor the situation and trigger the appropriate rescue actions.

Fig. 10. Beach and sea zone management, supervision and rescue organization.

Another service that can be used in downtown, near the parking area, on the harbor and near the beaches, is an information shelter. Its objective is to provide potential passengers and visitors with appropriate information on transportation lines and their schedules, using appropriate screens, as well as providing local, cultural and sports programs, commercial advertising, etc. (Fig. 11).

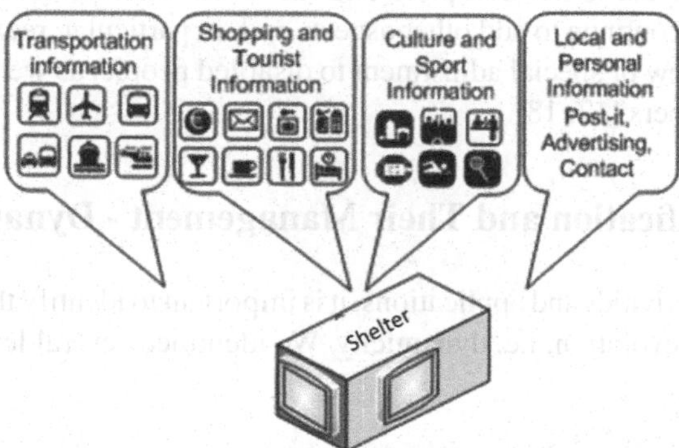

Fig. 11. Bus or Boat shelter for inhabitants' information.

Last but not least, a service we would like to mention is the **Pedestrian Drive,** the aim of which is to provide fresh food distribution based on box-lockers [15]. The idea is to convey fresh food to the beach instead of asking clients to go to a supermarket. The pedestrian drive is a variant of the concept of the supermarket drive, specially designed for pedestrians. Located as near as possible to client locations (beaches, sports arenas, etc.) and accessible 24 h a day, it allows ordered goods to be collected at any time. It is able to store not only ambient temperature products but also fresh and frozen goods. This fresh product box-locker can be either owned by a supermarket firm and totally integrated into the ordering, management and logistics process of the firm or can be managed independently. This case offers an interesting support system for the shared economy, as the role of the pedestrian drive manager is to manage such use for multiple providers. His/her role is to ensure Internet access for all provider offers and to organize the global supply chain with consumer information on availability of ordered goods in the box-locker. This makes it possible to support the circular economy as a short circuit of agricultural goods (Fig. 12).

Fig. 12. Box/Lockers for fresh and frozen food [16].

For all these identified activities, it is fundamental to define how to collect the data on which they are based and to determine their management and evolution. The following Sect. 4 is devoted to this issue.

Of course, this list is not complete and has been voluntarily limited to mobility aspects. We could continue to add other aspects and, in particular, reexamine our propositions from the view of special adjustment to disabled people, as we have already done in our previous papers [17, 18].

4 Data Identification and Their Management - Dynamicity

For all identified activities and applications, it is important to identify the data needed and to determine their evolution, i.e. dynamicity. We identified several levels and providers of data dynamicity.

4.1 Data Dynamicity

The first, basic, level, is totally static, which means not smart, but useful for a large majority of city users (on the whole or by category): physical panels, boards and signs, as well as circulation signs. A contextual example can be seen in Fig. 13.

The second level, with very low dynamicity, is based on boards with QR codes. In this case, in the field (city), the information indicator is static, and dynamicity is provided by the information sent to the user's smartphone from the website address encoded in the QR code. This approach is appropriate for optional information, which is accessed only by interested users and known only to them, in the form of historical information for example, but also for commercial and advertising purposes.

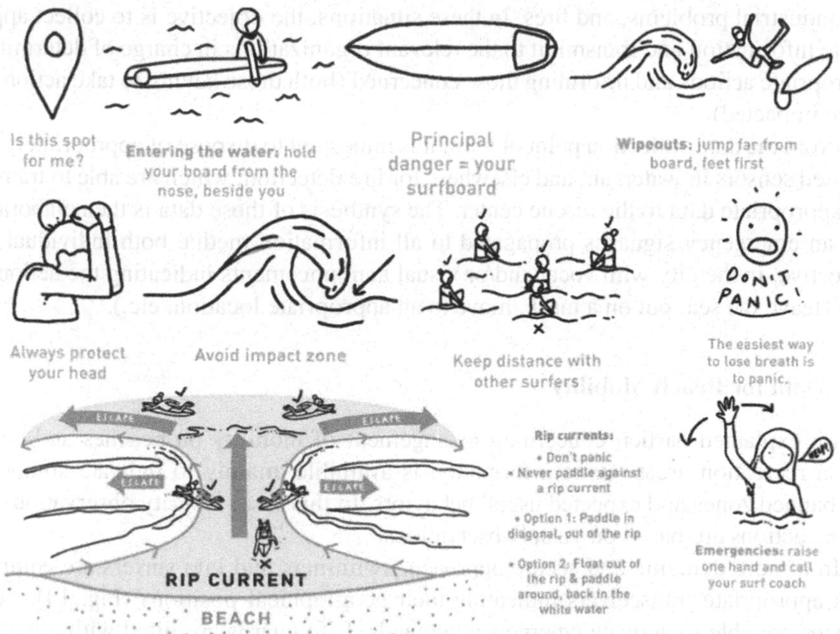

Fig. 13. Surf safety physical panel [19].

The third level of dynamicity is characterized by the need to propagate information that is of general interest and needs to be commonly known. The solution is to propagate it directly on users' smartphones or on GPS vehicle screens. Another solution is to use public active screens and information boards. This is the case for circulation information for dynamically managed circulation lanes such as we described earlier. This kind of dynamicity is usually determined by external decision centers working on collected or predefined data.

The fourth level of dynamicity is a contextual one, i.e. it is related to particular cases or situations that can be produced by an action on a local device, manually or automatically. A classic example is a sender located on a bus, which activates the opening of a barrier accessing a restricted portion of the road. This kind of sender (or remote control) can be either integrated on the vehicle (bike, car, bus, boat, etc.) or used manually by the user, often in emergency situations. These devices are attributed by the relevant authority. The actuator associated with the remote control can be either mono-located and mono-answer acting on a single door, barrier, etc. or integrated in a system assisting more sophisticated behaviors. Management of this dynamicity requires appropriate association between sender(s) and receiver(s) in order to organize the corresponding behaviors.

4.2 Emergency and Rescue Management

The highest level of dynamicity concerns emergency and rescue situations, mainly related to weather and environmental situations, such as floods, landslides, tsunamis, ecological and industrial problems, and fires. In these situations, the objective is to collect appropriate information and transmit it to the relevant organizations in charge of determining appropriate actions and informing those concerned (both those having to take action and those impacted).

From the data collection point of view, it is important to dispose of appropriately distributed sensors in water, air, and elsewhere for fire detection, which are able to transmit the appropriate data to the rescue center. The synthesis of these data is then elaborated, and an emergency signal is propagated to all information media, both individual and collective, in the city with vocal and/or visual announcements indicating the actions to take (leave the sea, put on a mask, move to an appropriate location, etc.).

4.3 Data for Beach Mobility

As we explained earlier, concerning management of mobility on beaches and on the sea in recreation areas, static information is available, mainly to indicate authorized and banned zones and expected users' behaviors. In this case, security observations and rescue actions are based on visual observations.

In a more dynamic and secure approach, swimmers and kite surfers are equipped with appropriate transceivers indicating their geographical positions (Fig. 14). These devices are able to activate emergency demands. Life guards are fitted with a receiver designed to observe the movements of everyone in the beach zones and beyond in order to observe users' behaviors and contact each one in order to clarify their situation. They can indicate inappropriate behaviors, such as use of an inappropriate zone or ask the swimmer for the reason for his/her emergency signal and trigger appropriate action.

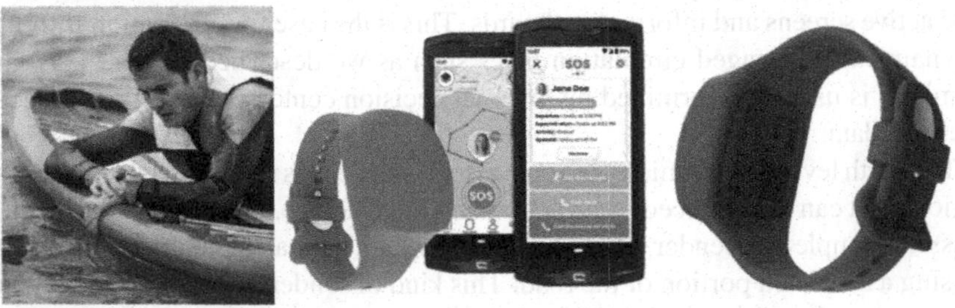

Fig. 14. The GPS wristband saving lives [20].

4.4 Data for Traffic Management

Organization of traffic is a very important aspect. Of course, in the low season, we can consider that static allocation of the circulation map is appropriate. However, in the high season, dynamicity aims at ensuring better traffic speed by introducing several restrictions during different periods of the day with authorized or prohibited vehicles. Circulation restrictions can vary frequently between buses, trucks, tourist vehicles, and so on. It is also important to take into account the main objective of each zone in the city. In tourist zones, such variation is natural. In industrial zones, mainly dedicated to boat construction and maintenance, priority must be given to the fluidity of this activity. Such dynamicity is either based on collected and preprocessed data (behavioral patterns) or on real-time data. This is then propagated to the assistive system and drivers in an appropriate manner, either by electronically driven signs and/or by propagation of corresponding information to the in-vehicle screens, smartphones, and GPS applications.

5 Data Collection and Elaboration

As analyzed in the previous section, data availability is the main problem in the provision of appropriate solutions. For the first levels of dynamicity, work can be elaborated progressively and be used relatively long-term. For greater levels of dynamicity, three different approaches can be used.

The first is totally related to the local context. The aim of local senders addressing local receivers is to obtain local and appropriate answers, such as opening of a read section that is managed.

A more general solution is to be able to share available data that are collected by communicating devices, namely senders and receivers, on site in the field, the city, and its neighborhood. This approach, which is called Open Data, constitutes major progress in general utilization of available data.

Another interesting approach is based on evolution of collected data by the acquisition of new, more recent data and their integration in the elaborated behavior model. This approach is based on a very active research field called Machine and Deep Learning. We decided to devote the next two sections to these last two approaches.

5.1 Open Data

One of the possible sources of information is access to open data published by different operators, such as municipalities, road operators, etc. These data can be either old data that are synthetized and give general trends or real-time data, indicating what is happening now or a few minutes ago.

Open Data [21] is the idea that some data should be freely available to everyone to use and republish as they wish, without restrictions from copyright, patents or other mechanisms of control [22]. The goals of the open-source data movement are similar to those of other "open(-source)" movements such as open-source software, hardware, open content, open specifications, open education, open educational resources, open government, open knowledge, open access, open science, and the open web. Paradoxically, the growth of the open data movement is paralleled by a rise in intellectual property rights [23]. The philosophy behind open data has been long established (for example in the Mertonian tradition of science), but the term "open data" itself is recent, gaining popularity with the rise of the Internet and World Wide Web and, especially, with the launch of open data government initiatives such as Data.gov, Data.gov.uk and Data.gov.in. INSPIRE (Infrastructure for Spatial Information in the European Community) is an EU initiative to establish an infrastructure for spatial information in Europe that is geared to help to make spatial or geographical information more accessible and interoperable for a wide range of purposes supporting sustainable development.

One of the most important forms of open data is open government data (OGD), which is a form of open data created by ruling government institutions. The importance of open government data is that it is a part of citizens' everyday lives, down to the most routine/mundane tasks that are seemingly far removed from government.

We give the following example [24]: Since January 1, 2015, the Metropolis of Lyon has grouped the missions of the Lyon Urban Community and the Rhône department into the 59 municipalities that make up the territory of Greater Lyon. The Metropolis of Lyon builds and preserves a pleasant living environment for its 1.3 million inhabitants by acting in broad areas: travel, mobility, knowledge, culture, environment, energy, solidarity, public health, childhood, family, city politics, habitat, housing, cleanliness, water, sanitation. It is in charge of major urban facilities and infrastructure, economic development, the attractiveness and influence of the territory. The Metropolis of Lyon is committed to opening up data to strengthen the innovation capacities of stakeholders on its territory and to invent the services and uses of the city of tomorrow.

5.2 Machine Learning and Deep Learning

Deep learning is hugely popular today. The past few decades have witnessed its tremendous success in many applications. Academia and industry alike have competed to apply deep learning to a wider range of applications due to its capability to solve many complex tasks while providing state-of-the-art results [25].

In some situations, it seems that deep learning can be used to analyze existing data and lead to interesting solutions. We can take intelligent navigation and travel planning as examples. For intelligent navigation, the intermediation platform considers the starting position and the destination position, combines the time information, meteorological information and other interfering factors, and finally provides the most appropriate one or more recommended paths. As for travel planning, the focus is to intelligently analyze the user's intention his/her behavior and finally make travel recommendations based on the tags that he/she is interested in and his/her browsing history.

Concerning the automated buses between park-and-ride and the main destinations (downtown, several beaches), it would be interesting to study the evolution of the trip trajectories, day-time periods, and the type of passengers. The objective is to determine the appropriate trip trajectory and timetable.

For goods transportation, it is important to start with a case-by-case study of the different destinations. We can then work progressively on these data that we capitalize in order to find main transportation trajectories and propose their evolution if necessary.

In practice, we can use the RNN (Recurrent Neural Network) structure in path planning, including intelligent navigation, travel for the disabled, parcel post and so on. The CNN (Convolutional Neural Network) model can be used for vehicle recognition to assist smart parking. For some scenarios with recommendation tasks, such as goods transportation and travel planning, we can use multilayer perceptron, LSTM (Long Short Term Memory networks), and other models [26].

Deep learning-based intermediation has proved very effective. However, the key problem for deep learning in different application scenarios is always data. Once data have been sufficiently collected and tagged, some deep learning-based solutions could be studied and applied.

6 Mobility Assistive System and Its Relationship with the Field

As we explained in the previous sections, the process consisting in transforming a city into a smart city usually starts by identifying the actors concerned, as well as the necessary services and associated data.

In practice, in order to organize and manage these aspects, we need a system that groups the different services and their applications, the data on which they work, and the relationship, if needed, between the field and the system. We call this system an Assistive System, the aim of which is to manage contextually all smart city applications. Its architecture is organized in 4 layers (Fig. 15) where:

Layer number 1 is devoted to applications, while layer number 2 is geared towards management of common data and proposing general services. The aim of the third layer is to work on what is called "Data Vitalization". The idea is to work on data and elaborate new constructions on them that can be used in new applications. An example of this need is to be able to collect and associate data in order to manage situations that were not predictable, such as several cases of rescue for not necessarily easily predictable situations.

The last (fourth) layer aims at acquiring and distributing the data needed for appropriate working of all applications concerning the coastal smart city. In order to take into account the evolution of this assistive system, an appropriate user interface, called the Supportive User Interface, is provided, allowing maintenance staff to provide the modifications requested easily.

Appropriate user interfaces, called Supportive User Interfaces, are provided to facilitate these evolutions. The "mashup" technique can be used for this purpose [29].

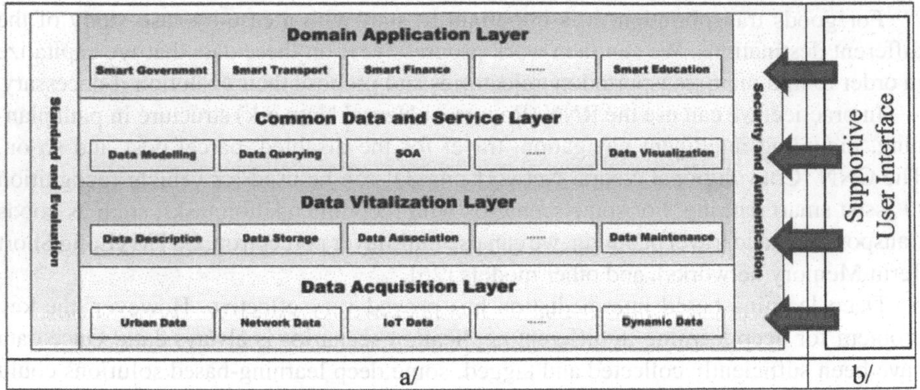

Fig. 15. a/ Architecture of an Intermediation platform with Data Vitalization [27], b/ Supportive User Interface [29].

7 Conclusion

In this paper we studied how a coastal city evolved to become a Smart Coastal City. The process was mainly based on the study of the actors concerned (inhabitants, tourists, workers, government authorities, etc.) and the corresponding services for each of them and globally. The specificity of a coastal city with activities related to the sea, industry, and tourism were the main instigators of this study. Our reasoning was based on the existence of two seasons (the high season – tourism-oriented - and the low season – inhabitant-oriented).

We proposed what we consider to be major transformations, either specific to the coastal city or adapted from the smart city in general. We identified expected services, associated data, corresponding user interfaces, individual or more common, and we described the links (passive or active) with the field (part of the city concerned) and the need for in-the-field indicators, senders and receivers. The dynamicity of the functional periods was also studied. We only briefly presented technological aspects (assistive system as an intermediation platform, open data use, and Machine and Deep Learning techniques), which we consider out of scope of this conference.

We also avoided the problem of assistance to disabled people, which we studied in our previous publications [17, 18], in which we presented several solutions applicable in Smart Cities and that can be transposed easily to this context. Of course, new solutions, specific to the coastal context (beaches, sea, harbor, boats) can be proposed. This is our objective in the near future, together with the discovery of other Coastal Smart City services and applications.

Acknowledgements. This study is partially supported as regards China by the National Key R&D Program of China (No. 2019YFB2102200) and the National Natural Science Foundation of China (No. 61977003). As regards France, the study was mainly supported by the French Ministry of Ecology (No. 09MTCV37 and PREDIT-G02 CHORUS 2100527197).

References

1. Caragliu, A., Del Bo, C., Nijkamp, P.: Smart cities in Europe. J. Urban Technol. **18**(2), 65–82 (2011)
2. Yin, C., Xiong, Z., Chen, H., Wang, J., Cooper, D., David, B.: A literature survey on smart cities. Sci. China Inf. Sci. **58**, 1–18 (2015). https://doi.org/10.1007/s11432-015-5397-4
3. Kolski, C.: Human-Computer Interactions in Transport. Wiley, Hoboken (2011)
4. Hosaka, T.A.: Japan Creating 'Smart City' of the Future. San Francisco Chronicle. Associated Press (2010)
5. Ng, P.T.: Embracing emerging technologies: the case of the Singapore intelligent nation 2015 vision. In: Ordóñez de Pablos, P., et al. (eds.) Regional Innovation Systems and Sustainable Development: Emerging Technologies IGI Global, pp. 115–123 (2011). https://doi.org/10.4018/978-1-61692-846-9.ch008
6. Giffinger, R., Gudrun, H.: Smart cities ranking: an effective instrument for the positioning of the cities? Arch. City Environ. **4**(12), 7–25 (2010)
7. Washburn, D., Sindhu, U.: Helping CIOs understand "smart city" initiatives. Forrester Res. (2010)
8. Nam, T., Pardo, T.A.: Conceptualizing smart city with dimensions of technology, people, and institutions. In: Proceedings of 12th Annual International Digital Government Research, College Park, 12–15, pp. 282–291 (2011)
9. Isla, F.I.: From touristic villages to coastal cities: the costs of the big step in Buenos Aires. In: Ocean & Coastal Management, vol. 77. Elsevier (2013). https://doi.org/10.1016/j.ocecoaman.2012.02.005
10. Chuai X., et al.: Land use and ecosystems services value changes and ecological land management in coastal Jiangsu, China. Habitat Int. **57** (2016). https://doi.org/10.1016/j.habitatint.2016.07.004
11. Wang, C., David, B., Chalon, R., Yin, C.: Dynamic road lane management study: a smart city application. Transp. Res. Part E Logist. Transp. Rev. **89**, 272–287 (2015). https://doi.org/10.1016/j.tre.2015.06.003
12. Patier, D., David, B., Deslandres, V., Chalon, R.: A new concept for urban logistics: delivery area Booking. In: Taniguchi, E., Thompson, R.G. (eds.) The Eighth International Conference on City Logistics, Indonesia, pp. 99–110. Elsevier. Proc. Soc. Behav. Sci. **125** (2014). ISSN 1877-0428
13. David, B., et al.: User-oriented System for Smart City approaches. In: The 12th IFAC/IFIP/IFORS/IEA Symposium on Analysis, Design, and Evaluation of Human-Machine Systems, 11–15 August 2013, Las Vegas, Nevada, USA, pp. 333–340. IFAC/Elsevier (2013). ISSN 1474-6670
14. https://france3-regions.francetvinfo.fr/pays-de-la-loire/coronavirus-plages-baule-pornichet-sables-olonne-nouveau-accessibles-1828366.html
15. David, B., Chalon, R.: Hotspot based mobile web communication and cooperation: ABRI+ Bus Shelter as a hotspot for mobile contextual transportation and social collaboration, SWWS 2010 (Semantic Web and Web Services) as part of WorldComp 2010 Conference, Las Vegas (2010)
16. David, B., Chalon, R.: Box/lockers' contribution to collaborative economy in the smart city. In: 2018 IEEE 22nd International Conference on Computer Supported Cooperative Work in Design (CSCWD 2018), 11 MAI 2018, Nanjing (Chine), pp. 802–807 (2018). https://doi.org/10.1109/CSCWD.2018.8465151
17. Yin, C., David, B., Chalon, R., Sheng, H.: Assistive systems for special needs in mobility in the smart city. In: Krömker, H. (ed.) HCII 2020. LNCS, vol. 12213, pp. 376–396. Springer, Cham (2020). https://doi.org/10.1007/978-3-030-50537-0_27

18. Li, Y., Yin, C., Xiong, Z., David, B., Chalon, R., Sheng, H.: Assistive systems for mobility in smart city: humans and goods. In: Krömker, H. (ed.) HCII 2021. LNCS, vol. 12791, pp. 89–104. Springer, Cham (2021). https://doi.org/10.1007/978-3-030-78358-7_6
19. https://barefootsurftravel.com/fr/livemore-magazine/aspects-de-securite-en-surf
20. https://www.dial.help/
21. Auer, S., Bizer, C., Kobilarov, G., Lehmann, J., Cyganiak, R., Ives, Z.: DBpedia: a nucleus for a web of open data. In: Aberer, K., et al. (eds.) ASWC/ISWC - 2007. LNCS, vol. 4825, pp. 722–735. Springer, Heidelberg (2007). https://doi.org/10.1007/978-3-540-76298-0_52
22. Kitchin, R.: The Data Revolution, p. 49. Sage, London (2014). ISBN 978-1-4462-8748-4
23. https://en.wikipedia.org/wiki/Open_data
24. https://www.data.gouv.fr/fr/organizations/grand-lyon/
25. He, X., Liao, L., Zhang, H., Nie, L., Hu, X., Chua, T.-S.: Neural collaborative filtering. In: Proceedings of WWW 2017 (World Wide Web conference), pp. 173–182 (2017)
26. Dziugaite, G.K., Roy, D.M.: Neural network matrix factorization. Human-Computer Interaction: Interaction Technologies - 17th International Conference, HCI International 2015, Los Angeles, CA, USA, 2–7 August 2015, Proceedings, Part II. Lecture Notes in Computer Science 9170. Springer (2015). arXiv preprint arXiv: 1511.06443
27. Liu, P., Peng, Z.: China's smart city pilots: a progress report. Computer **10**, 72–81 (2014)
28. Atrouche, A., Idoughi, D., David, B.: A mashup-based application for the smart city problematic. In: Kurosu, M. (ed.) HCI 2015. LNCS, vol. 9170, pp. 683–694. Springer, Cham (2015). https://doi.org/10.1007/978-3-319-20916-6_63
29. Grammel, L., Storey, M.: An end user perspective on mashup makers. University of Victoria Technical Report DCS-324-IR (2008)

Exploring Private Scooter Owners' Willingness to Introduce Their Own Scooter into Vehicle Sharing Services

Fei-Hui Huang(✉)

Asia Eastern University of Science and Technology, New Taipei City 220303, Taiwan R.O.C.
Fn009@mail.aeust.edu.tw

Abstract. Shared micro-mobility services enable travelers to have access to a collection of personal transportation vehicles. This study examines the willingness of introducing their own private scooter into scooter-sharing services by scooter owners and adapts the attitude, user experiences (UX), and behavioral intention to investigate the factors that may influence scooter owner acceptance of scooter sharing services. The data were collected from Taiwanese scooter owners' feedback on the questionnaire ($n = 266$). The results indicate that the model constructs of attitude toward scooters as a great means of transportation, UX with shared scooter service, and behavioral intention toward shared scooter services may positively affect private vehicle owners' willingness to introduce their own scooter into sharing services, while attitude toward scooters meeting the transportation needs may negatively affect their willingness. In light of the findings, recommendations for increasing the willingness of private vehicle owners to introduce their own vehicle into sharing services and a reference basis for the development of future shared vehicle services are provided.

Keywords: Shared micro-mobility · Scooter sharing service · Attitude · User experience

1 Introduction

With developments in ICT such as online social networks, GPS-enabled mobile devices, the Internet of Things (IoT), mobile payments, and cloud computing, economic models have emerged that are based on sharing or collaborative consumption of resources, called the sharing economy. This study focuses on shared micro-mobility, which is an innovative and sustainable transportation strategy. Shared micro-mobility provides station-based bike sharing (a bicycle picked up from and returned to any station) and dockless bike, scooter, or e-scooter sharing (a two-wheeler picked up and returned to any location). Such services enable travelers to have access to a collection of personal transportation vehicles, which can be accessed anytime (subject to vehicle availability) and between a large number of source and destination locations [1, 2]. This paper concerns scooter-sharing services in the context of Taiwan. Taiwan is an island country with the highest density of scooter commuters worldwide. The average scooter use is 5.2 days per week;

H. Krömker (Ed.): HCII 2022, LNCS 13335, pp. 507–516, 2022.
https://doi.org/10.1007/978-3-031-04987-3_34

of these days, the average riding time is 51.1 min [3]. This means that private-scooter/e-scooter efficiency is very low. This paper proposes an innovative shared-scooter service whereby scooter owners can authorize the rental of their scooters by others through a mobile service platform. It constitutes a public short-distance mobility service for travelers and increases the efficient utilization of each private scooter.

2 Literature Review

2.1 Scooter Sharing Service

Shared micro-mobility is an innovative and sustainable transportation strategy. Shared micro-mobility provides station-based bike-sharing and dockless bike, scooter, or e-scooter sharing. Dockless e-scooter sharing service that hailed as a convenient and inexpensive solution for to/from transit "last mile" (i.e., to/from transit) [4, 5]. E-scooter products are considered as environmentally-friendly [6]. Using e-scooters may reduce the problems caused by fuel gas-powered scooters, such as air pollution and noise [7] and caused by automobiles, such as greenhouse gas emissions and Traffic congestion [8]. E-scooters are generally popular or seen as providing a valuable service. The reasons for the travelers who choose shared-scooters for short-distance trips involve speed and reliability, fun, cost, convenience, and recreation [9, 10]. The number of charging stations and potential range to be driven with electric vehicles constitute driving forces for or against using electric vehicles [11, 12]. E-scooters are the main product in the Taiwanese shared scooter market, which is mainly based on 24-h dockless services. However, with more and more two-wheeler products on the road, road safety/injury risks issues and the interaction between e-scooters and other road users are important challenges. Apart from that, e-scooters' short lifespan may cause slightly more CO_2 emissions per kilometer than other modes of transportation [13].

Innovation is crucial for the functioning of a public transportation services. Especially for the steady growth of urban population combined with the increase of vehicle traffic volumes, environmental pollution, and fuel prices have driven government related units to experiment new systems for a sustainable mobility. The crucial innovation of e-scooter/scooter sharing system was the introduction of mobile app technology to book, pick up, lock, return, and pay for the scooters/e-scooters. Individual ownership of vehicles with combustion engines is associated with congestion in cities, loss of communal space, air pollution, CO_2 emissions, and residents' health problems [14]. Shared-vehicle services are feasible means to raise the efficiency of urban transportation and avoid the burden of private vehicle ownership [15]. Since shared-car services introduction as a commercial service in 2007, it has lowered the number of cars owned privately, reduced demand for parking space, vehicle mileage, and greenhouse gas emission levels [16–21]. To ensure large-scale uptake and to convince vehicle-owners to give up their private vehicles, low entry fees, easy access throughout the year and a sufficiently large fleet size are required [22–24]. The transportation innovations of vehicle sharing services hold the key to improving the quality of life while lowering greenhouse gas emissions, and form the key elements for a sustainable mobility system [25]. Sharing mobility has become a valid alternative to vehicle ownership and traditional public transport systems in urban cities in recent years.

2.2 Attitude and User Experience

Mobile technology has changed the traveler's attitude to transportation mode, mobility behavior, and further travel experiences.

Attitude is defined as a mental or neural state of readiness, organized through experience, exerting a directive or dynamic influence on the individual's response to all objects and situations to which it is related [26]. Attitude formation is a result of learning, modeling others, and individual's direct experiences with people and situations. Attitudes influence individual's decisions, guide individual's behavior, and impact what individual's selectively remember. Attitudes come in different strengths, and like most things that are learned or influenced through experience, they can be measured and they can be changed. To change an individual's attitude need to address the cognitive and emotional components. Attitude transformation takes time, effort, and determination, but it can be done [27]. Attitudes are formed over a lifetime through an individual's socialization process. An individual's socialization process includes his/her formation of values and beliefs during childhood years, influenced not only by family, religion, and culture but also by socioeconomic factors. This socialization process affects an individual's attitude toward related behavior [28]. The measure of attitudes toward vehicle ownership is one indicator related to general attitudes toward owning material goods. Several previous researches verified that attitudes play a role in influencing behavioral choices of transportation, such as Spears et al. [29], Domarchi et al. [30], and Kitamura et al. [31]. In addition, traveler with environmentally conscious are more likely to support environmentally-focused policies such as alternative energy [32] and mobility decisions [33].

User experience (UX) is defined as concentrates on a person's perceptions and responses resulting from the use or anticipated use of a product, system, or service [34]. Above mentioned perceptions and responses are considered psychological in nature. Consumer decision-making is increasingly driven by emotional factors rather than rational factors [35]. In other word, UX are integrating cognition, emotion, and motivation with perception and attention to be a set of psychological compartments that make an analysis of "person's perceptions and responses" relevant and valid in any given context. Naturally, our past experiences or memories and attitudes have an impact on this experiential process [36].

3 Methods

This study was conducted to examine a dockless scooter-sharing service located around the campus of Asia Eastern University of Science and Technology in New Taipei City, Taiwan, and to elicit users' subjective responses to shared scooter usage in order to understand how the service affects scooter owners' willingness to introduce their own scooter into the sharing service. The study recruited user who own a private scooter to ride on the shared scooters for short-distance mobility without payment. All participants were invited to fill out online questionnaire after their shared scooter usage. The Research Ethics Committee of National Tsing Hua University approved this study (IRB protocol number 10906EC065).

3.1 Measurements

The questionnaire contained the following four sections: (1) personal information, including three items designed to collect sociodemographic data on gender, age, and main means of transportation; (2) attitude, including six items designed to measure attitudes toward the scooter product, scooter information, scooter usage, and demand for private scooter; (3) UX, including two items designed to measure user's experience after using the shared scooters; and (4) behavioral intention, including four items designed to measure user's willingness to introduce his/her private scooter into sharing services.

3.2 Participants

Of 308 surveys, 42 involved material data omission, and the effective response rate was 86.3%. Two hundred and sixty six individuals (123 males and 143 females) used the shared scooters and completed questionnaire.

3.3 Data Analysis

Analyses were conducted using SPSS software, Version 22.0. Variables were assessed by factor analysis, reliability analysis, t-test, correlation analysis, and hierarchical multiple regression analysis. The two-tailed significance level was set at $p < 0.05$.

4 Results

In this study, the internal consistency of the attitude scores ($\alpha = .938$), UX scores ($\alpha = .807–.905$), and behavioral intention scores ($\alpha = .908–.960$) were high (see Table 1).

4.1 T-Test

The t-test results indicated that "spend a lot of time riding a scooter every day" ($F = 5.69, p < .05; t = 3.02, p < .01$), "I understand scooters well" ($t = 3.72, p < .001$), "Scooters are a great means of transportation" ($t = 4.19, p < .001$), and "I pay attention to scooter information a lots" ($t = 2.00, p < .05$) differed significantly by gender. Male respondents tended to have a higher agreement with the attitude items "spend a lot of time riding a scooter every day" (males $\overline{X} = 4.40$, $\sigma = 1.89$; females $\overline{X} = 3.65$, $\sigma = 2.16$), "I understand scooters well" (males $\overline{X} = 4.31$, $\sigma = 1.83$; females $\overline{X} = 3.46$, $\sigma = 1.88$), "Scooters are a great means of transportation" (males $\overline{X} = 4.20$, $\sigma = 1.95$; females $\overline{X} = 3.26$, $\sigma = 1.70$), and "I pay attention to scooter information a lots" (males $\overline{X} = 4.91$, $\sigma = 1.70$; females $\overline{X} = 4.47$, $\sigma = 1.89$) than females.

Table 1. Scale reliabilities for each construct of questionnaire.

Construct	Item	M	SD	∝
Attitude	I should have my own scooter	4.97	1.44	0.816
	I spend a lot of time riding a scooter every day	4.00	2.07	
	I understand scooters well	3.85	1.90	
	Scooters can meet my transportation needs	5.09	1.55	
	Scooters are a great means of transportation	3.69	1.87	
	I pay attention to scooter information a lots	4.67	1.82	
UX	I am satisfied with shared scooters	4.94	1.51	0.801
	The experience of riding shared scooters is great	4.50	1.65	
Behavioral intention	I am willing to introduce my private scooter into sharing services	3.73	1.87	0.902
	Introducing private scooter into sharing services is for earning rental fees	3.76	1.95	
	Introducing private scooter into sharing services is to have a professional managing my scooter	3.87	1.89	
	Shared scooters will replace private scooters	3.88	1.71	

4.2 Hierarchical Multiple Regression Analysis

Hierarchical multiple regression (a stepwise regression analysis) was used to predict behavioral intention toward introducing respondent's own scooter into scooter sharing services (YBI). Table 2 lists the main predictor variables (excluding interactions) for the YBI model. R2 was significant ($F(5, 260) = 123.23$, $p < 0.001$), accounting for 70.3% of the variance. The results indicated that "scooters can meet my transportation needs", "scooters are a great means of transportation", "the experience of riding shared scooters is great", "introducing private scooter into sharing services is for earning rental fees", and "introducing private scooter into sharing services is to have a professional managing my scooter" significantly influenced behavioral intention toward introducing individual's own scooter into sharing services.

Table 2. Hierarchical multiple regression results for Y_{BI}

Model		β	VIF	R^2	ΔR^2
Y_{BI}	Meet transportation needs	−0.139**	1.439	0.703	0.698**
	Great means of transportation	0.127**	1.468		
	The experience is great	0.149**	1.418		
	Earning rental fees	0.319***	4.544		
	Professional managing scooters	0.437***	4.571		

Notes: 1. *$p < 0.05$, **$p < 0.01$, ***$p < 0.001$
2. VIF (variance inflation factor).

5 Discussion

In this study, psychological measurements of attitude and UX were used to obtain shared scooter user acceptance of vehicle sharing service. Furthermore, hierarchical multiple regression was used to predict their behavioral intention toward introducing his/her own scooter into sharing service. Results revealed that the attitudes toward scooter usage have gender differences and the factors of attitude, UX, and behavioral intention may influencing user's willingness to introduce his/her own scooter into vehicle sharing services.

5.1 Attitude Toward Scooter Usage

The results showed that the respondents' attitudes toward scooter products is positive. Most of them agree with they should have their own scooter to satisfy their transportation needs. As Taiwanese scooter industries and related scooter infrastructures are mature, it is easier for the public to receive the information about scooter products and services. This may positively influencing respondents to pay more attention to the information about scooters and understand scooter products and services well. Finally, most of the scooters consider that the scooter is a great means of transportation; therefore, they may spend a lot of time to ride a scooter every day. Because of the long-term accumulated scooter usage habits, they have even more dependence on scooter commuting in their daily life.

In this study, gender difference has been found in the attitude item "spend a lot of time riding a scooter every day", "I understand scooters well", "Scooters are a great means of transportation", and "I pay attention to scooter information a lots". More specifically, male respondents perceived themselves have higher agreements with understanding scooter products/services, paying attention to scooter information a lots, spending a lot of time riding his own scooter, and considering scooter as a great means of transportation than females. Therefore, male scooter riders have more active attitudes toward scooter products/services than females had.

5.2 User Willingness to Introduce Scooter into Sharing Service

In this study, 59.7% of the respondents were willing to introduce their own scooter into scooter sharing services, and significant support was found for the Y_{BI} model, with goodness of fit. The model was successful in predicting behavioral intention toward introducing respondent's own scooter into vehicle sharing services. Five of Y_{BI}'s predicted relationships were supported, with "scooters are a great means of transportation", "the experience of riding shared scooters is great", "introducing private scooter into sharing services is for earning rental fees", and "introducing private scooter into sharing services is to have a professional managing my scooter" contributing uniquely and positively to behavioral intention, while "scooters can meet my transportation needs" contributing uniquely and negatively to behavioral intention. These results showed that attitudes, UX, and behavioral intention toward scooter sharing services had direct effect on behavioral intention toward introducing their own scooter into shared scooter services.

The item of behavioral intention "I will introduce my own private scooter into sharing services for having a professional managing the scooter" was the strongest predictor, suggesting that scooter owner-perceived scooter management quality regarding a scooter sharing service is the most important factor influencing behavioral intention to introduce his/her own scooter into the sharing service. It is not easy for the vehicle owners to manage a vehicle. The vehicle owners have to take the tasks that include refueling, vehicle maintenance and repair, vehicle parking location, risks of vehicle theft/damage, vehicle insurance, and so on. These tasks may accompanied by corresponding expenses. Regarding the cost of a vehicle, vehicle owners focus on one primary thing when purchasing a vehicle is the price. However, the cost of the vehicle is not that simple. One of the biggest reasons why it's expensive to own a vehicle is depreciation. Other costs on which vehicle owners should focus are insurance, maintenance/repairs, fuel, financing/interest, state and local taxes and fees, parking, tolls, car washes, and so on. These total costs are what make vehicles are expensive to own and operate. Therefore, for car owners, it is an important service to have a professional team to manage their won vehicles.

The item of behavioral intention "I will introduce my own private scooter into sharing services to earn rental fees" has a strong and direct impact on behavioral intention that highlights the importance of allowing individual vehicle owners to authorize the rental of their vehicles by others through a mobile service platform to earn rental fees during the vehicle's idle time. Providing opportunities to earn rental fees for the private vehicle owners may positively influence their willingness to introduce their own vehicle into shared services. This also means that how much revenue vehicle owner can get from the service is an important factor to influence the owner's behavioral intention to introduce vehicle into shared service. Related researches should be discussed in the near future.

Private vehicle owner perceived "scooters are a great means of transportation" and "the experience of riding shared scooters is great" have positive impact on behavioral intention, which suggests that owners' attitudes towards scooters and their experiences in riding shared scooters may influence their willingness toward introducing vehicle into shared services. The results indicated that vehicle owner considers scooter to be a great means of transportation. Once the shared vehicles may create user with a usage experiences as great as scooter usage, it may positively influence vehicle owner's intention to introduce vehicle into shared service.

Private vehicle owner's attitude "scooters can meet my transportation needs" has negative impact on behavioral intention, which suggests that owners' attitudes towards scooters that can meet their transportation needs may negatively influence their behavioral intention. It means that under the conditions of private vehicle owners believe that the vehicle can meet their transportation needs, they would not need the shared vehicle services. This may also cause the private vehicle owners unperceived the advantages and values of shared vehicle services. Furthermore, the possibility of introducing the private vehicle into sharing service for them may be reduced.

6 Conclusion

Subjective rating scales of attitude, UX, and behavioral intention were used to investigate the factors in the shared scooter usage context. Results showed the usefulness of subjective measurements for increasing our understanding of the factors contributing to user acceptance of scooter sharing service and user's willingness to introduce his/her private scooter into shared services. This study provided evidence that the attitudes toward scooter products/services, UX in shared scooter usage, and behavioral intention toward vehicle sharing service were important factors that predicted private vehicle owner's willingness to introduce his/her private vehicle into sharing service. Finally, directions for future research could include a study of the standards of shared vehicle management quality and a model for vehicle owners' revenue.

Acknowledgments. This research was funded by the Ministry of Science and Technology (Taiwan), grant number: MOST 109-2221-E-161-002.

References

1. Banerjee, S., Freund, D., Lykouris, T.: Pricing and optimization in shared vehicle systems: an approximation framework. arXiv preprint arXiv:1608.06819 (2016)
2. Fyhri, A., Fearnley, N.: Effects of e-bikes on bicycle use and mode share. Transp. Res. Part D: Transp. Environ. **36**, 45–52 (2015)
3. MOTC (Statistics Department of Taiwan's Ministry of Transportation and Communications): Motorcycle Usage Survey (2019). https://www.motc.gov.tw/ch/home.jsp?id=56&parentpath=0,6
4. National Association of City Transportation Officials (NACTO): Shared Micromobility in the U.S.: 2018 (2019). https://nacto.org/wp-content/uploads/2019/04/NACTO_Shared-Micromobility-in-2018_Web.pdf
5. Sandt, L., Harmon, K.: Dockless electric kick scooter systems: what we know and don't know. In: Presentation at the Transportation Research Board Annual Meeting, 14 January 2019
6. Che, M., Lum, K.M., Wong, Y.D.: Users' attitudes on electric scooter riding speed on shared footpath: A virtual reality study. Int. J. Sustain. Transp. **15**(2), 152–161 (2021). https://doi.org/10.1080/15568318.2020.1718252
7. Gössling, S.: Integrating e-scooters in urban transportation: Problems, policies, and the prospect of system change. Transp. Res. Part D Transp. Environ. **79**, 102230 (2020)
8. Allem, J.-P., Majmundar, A.: Are electric scooters promoted on social media with safety in mind? A case study on Bird's Instagram. Prev. Med. Reports **13**, 62–63 (2019)

9. Portland Bureau of Transportation (PBOT): 2018 E-Scooter Findings Report (2019). https://www.portlandoregon.gov/transportation/article/709719
10. Dill, J.: The e-scooter gender gap, 3 March 2019. https://jenniferdill.net/2019/02/01/the-e-scooter-gender-gap/
11. Cordera, R., dell'Olio, L., Ibeas, A., Ortúzar, J.D.: Demand for environmentally friendly vehicles: a review and new evidence. Int. J. Sustain. Transp. **13**, 210–223 (2019). https://doi.org/10.1080/15568318.2018.1459969
12. Haustein, S., Jensen, A.F.: Factors of electric vehicle adoption: a comparison of conventional and electric car users based on an extended theory of planned behavior. Int. J. Sustain. Transp. **12**, 484–496 (2018). https://doi.org/10.1080/15568318.2017.1398790
13. Moreau, H., de Jamblinne Meux, L., Zeller, V., D'Ans, P., Ruwet, C., Achten, W.M.J.: Dockless E-scooter: a green solution for mobility? Comparative case study between dockless E-scooters, displaced transport, and personal E-scooters. Sustainability **12**, 1803 (2020). https://doi.org/10.3390/su12051803
14. Thurner, T., Fursov, K., Nefedova, A.: Early adopters of new transportation technologies: attitudes of Russia's population towards car sharing, the electric car and autonomous driving. Transp. Res. Part A: Policy Pract. **155**, 403–417 (2022)
15. Tessum, C.W., et al.: Air pollution-related health and health equity effects of the united states economy: 1997–2015. In ISEE Conference Abstract, vol. 2018, no. 1 (2018)
16. Schreier et al.: (2018). https://www.cambio-carsharing.de/cms/downloads/d8d44462-f940-423c-8b0c-fc44d1f3bc39/tr_Endbericht_Bremen_.pdf
17. Baptista, P., Melo, S., Rolim, C.: Energy, environmental and mobility impacts of car-sharing systems. Empirical results from Lisbon, Portugal. Proc. Soc. Behav. Sci. **111**, 28–37 (2014)
18. De Luca, S., Di Pace, R.: Modelling users' behaviour in inter-urban carsharing program: a stated preference approach. Transp. Res. Part A: Policy Pract. **71**, 59–76 (2015)
19. Bert, J., Collie, B., Gerrits, M., Xu, G.: What's ahead for car sharing? The Boston Consulting Group Report, February 2016
20. Clewlow, R.: Carsharing and sustainable travel behavior: results from the San Francisco Bay Area. Transp. Policy **51**, 158–164 (2016)
21. Martin, E., Shaheen, S.A.: Assessing greenhouse gas emission impacts from carsharing in North America: theoretical and methodological design. In: 15th World Congress on Intelligent Transport Systems and ITS America's 2008 Annual Meeting ITS America ERTICOITS Japan Trans Core (2008)
22. Correia, G., Viegas, J.M.: Carpooling and carpool clubs: Clarifying concepts and assessing value enhancement possibilities through a Stated Preference web survey in Lisbon, Portugal. Transp. Res. Part A: Policy Pract. **45**(2), 81–90 (2011)
23. Firnkorn, J., Müller, M.: What will be the environmental effects of new free-floating car-sharing systems? The case of car2go in Ulm. Ecol. Econ. **70**(8), 1519–1528 (2011)
24. Zoepf, S., Keith, D.: User decision-making and technology choices in the US carsharing market. Transp. Policy **51**, 150–157 (2016)
25. Sperling, D.: Three Revolutions: Steering Automated, Shared, and Electric Vehicles to a Better Future. Island Press, Washington (2018)
26. Allport, G.W.: Attitudes. In: Murchison, C. (ed.) Handbook of Social Psychology, pp. 798–844. Clark University Press, Worcester (1935)
27. Moore, M.: How to improve staff morale using humor, appreciation and praise—Practical strategies to help you turn your workplace into a "Thank God it's Monday" type of organization (2003). www.motivationalplus.com
28. Pickens, J.: Attitudes and perceptions. Organiz. Behav. Health Care **4**(7), 43–76 (2005)
29. Spears, S., Houston, D., Boarnet, M.G.: Illuminating the unseen in transit use: a framework for examining the effect of attitudes and perceptions on travel behavior. Transp. Res. Part A Pol. Pract. **58**, 40–53 (2013). https://doi.org/10.1016/j.tra.2013.10.011

30. Domarchi, C., Tudela, A., González, A.: Effect of attitudes, habit and affective appraisal on mode choice: an application to university workers. Transportation **35**(5), 585–599 (2008). https://doi.org/10.1007/s11116-008-9168-6
31. Kitamura, R., Mokhtarian, P., Laidet, L.: A micro-analysis of land use and travel in five neighbourhoods in the San Francisco bay area. Transportation **24**(2), 125–158 (1997). https://doi.org/10.1023/a:1017959825565
32. Rainie, L., Funk, C.: Americans, politics and science issues. Washington, DC, Pew Research Center (2015). http://www.pewinternet.org/2015/07/01/americans-politics-and-science-issues/
33. Hopkins, D.: Can environmental awareness explain declining preference for car-based mobility amongst Generation Y? A qualitative examination of learn to drive behaviours. Transp. Res. Part A **94**(C), 149–163 (2016). https://doi.org/10.1016/j.tra.2016.08.028
34. ISO 9241-210:2008: Ergonomics of human system interaction – Part 210: Human-centered design for interactive systems (formerly known as 13407). International Standardization Organization (ISO) (2008)
35. Clarke, D.W., Perry, P., Denson, H.: The sensory retail environment of small fashion boutiques. J. Fash. Mark. Manag.: Int. J. **16**, 492–510 (2012)
36. Särkelä, H., Takatalo, J., Komulainen, J., Nyman, G., Häkkinen, J.: Attitudes to new technology and experiential dimensions of two different digital games. In: Proceedings of the Third Nordic Conference on Human-Computer Interaction, pp. 349–352, October 2004

Temporal Travel Demand Analysis of Irregular Bike-Sharing Users

Ahmed Jaber(✉) and Bálint Csonka

Department of Transport Technology and Economics, Faculty of Transportation Engineering and Vehicle, Engineering, Budapest University of Technology and Economics, 1111 Budapest, Hungary
ahjaber6@edu.bme.hu

Abstract. Visitors and occasional users represent a sizable portion of all bike-sharing users. This study focuses on how people travel in different weather and time conditions. Over the investigation process, it was discovered that users, bookings, and rentals all had constant percentages. Bicycle-sharing is more expensive for visitors than for occasional users. An exponential smoothing study was done for forecasting reasons. In Budapest, it is expected that bike-sharing services would be used more regularly during the next few months. The results showed that during the forecasted 5 months, the average number of bikes used could reach 3.3% increase after one year, and the trips per user could reach 20% increase for the same period of time. For irregular users, moderate temperatures, low humidity, precipitation, and wind speed are optimal weather conditions. The top ranked variables influencing trips and bookings, according to Random Forest techniques, are sun hours and temperature, with precipitation ranking last.

Keywords: Bike sharing · Random Forest · Travel demand · Exponential smoothing

1 Introduction

In the 1960s, the notion of "bike-sharing" was introduced in Amsterdam, the Netherlands, in response to rising use over owning bicycles. This development has resulted in a rapid spread of bike-sharing systems around the world [1, 2]. In recent years, there has been a rise in interest of eco-friendly transportation as a consequence of increase in traffic congestion and air pollution. Particularly, bike-sharing services provide an environmentally friendly alternative in urban areas [1, 3].

Furthermore, bike sharing have a positive impact on economic transportation, health, and improves rider safety by boosting driver awareness [4]. Bike-sharing services (BSS) became popular tourist attractions because people can use BSSs to explore and visit new locations [5]. As [6] found that there is a higher demand for shared bikes and tourism attractions on weekends. BSS gives inhabitants and visitors a low-cost alternative for short trips in cities [2]. [7] investigated that many visitors are cyclists who are unable to transfer their own vehicles to their destination and prefer public transportation or bike

H. Krömker (Ed.): HCII 2022, LNCS 13335, pp. 517–525, 2022.
https://doi.org/10.1007/978-3-031-04987-3_35

sharing. Visitors can benefit from bike sharing in a variety of ways. Thus, all bikers can use bike sharing to connect to public transit at a lower cost and with greater accessibility [8].

In Budapest, Hungary, several bike rental companies offer BSS and gained more attention because of cycling infrastructure development and positive side effect of the pandemic. Thus, bike-sharing is becoming a common mode of mobility. Visitors and occasional users form a significant percentage among all bike-sharing riders. The aim of this research is to analyze the temporal characteristics of bike-sharing use. The literature has considered all users as a single group. Accordingly, the main novelty of this study is the temporal characteristics analysis of irregular user groups.

Several review papers [1, 9], investigated factors affecting bike-sharing demand, such as weather, built environment [10], land use, public transportation, spatial aspects [11], socio-demographics [12], temporal factors, and safety. Research of bike user characteristics have several aspects. Moreover, [13] quantified the effect of weather conditions in the San Francisco Bay Area Bike Share System on the prediction of bike counts in the stations using the Random Forest. The results showed that the time-of-the-day, temperature, and humidity level are the most significant count predictors. In the same line, [14] discussed the hourly rental bike demand prediction in the Seoul Public Park for one year. Among the different weather variables such as: Temperature, Humidity, Wind, Visibility, Dew point, Solar radiation, Snowfall, Rainfall – Temperature was found as top ranked predictor. Moreover, [15] used the same method of random forest in addition to the linear regression for the Capital Bike share program in Washington, D.C. The findings indicated that the order of variables from the most having affecting is temperature, time, humidity, rain, and finally wind. In Europe, [16] developed a system providing short and long-term predictions of bikes and slots availabilities for bike sharing stations in real-time based on Random Forest algorithm and Convolutional Neural Networks. Again, temperature was the top, then wind, humidity and type of the day if it is weekday or weekend.

This research explores travel behavior under weather and temporal characteristics for irregular users who are not members or visitors. We are focusing on the trend of using bike-sharing systems over time. The series is five months starting from June and ending in October 2021.

2 Methodology

As research in this field increases; only a few studies consider bike-sharing-related issues in Central and Eastern Europe [7]. Thus, Budapest is taken as a case study. The dataset consist of a daily series of users, number of bookings, and number of trips, as well as weather conditions of precipitation, humidity, wind speed, and temperature.

Among more than three years of data, we have chosen the period after COVID 19 off restrictions to have similar behavior to the original situation. The series is five months starting from June and ending in October. In this study, visitors (people with foreign phone numbers and without membership) and occasional users (people with local phone numbers and without membership) were considered as irregular users. Temporal comparisons are conducted from day to day, as well as between weekdays and weekends.

Average of daily bookings is analyzed based on temperature, precipitation, humidity, and wind speed.

2.1 Exponential Smoothing

Exponential smoothing analysis was performed to forecast average number of trips and bikes used per user that predicts future values based on existing values that follow a seasonal pattern as a technique of time-series decomposition method. This function calculation depends on triple exponential smoothing. This is an algorithm that applies overall smoothing, trend smoothing, and seasonal smoothing [17]. Following that, a random forest analysis is conducted to find the top ranked weather variables that affecting both of trips and booking for the system, as presented in the next subsection.

2.2 Random Forest

The Random Forests (RF) approach is one of the top ensemble learning algorithms [18]. This methodology effectively handles the input data's enormous complexity as well as the general, characteristic non-linearity. In any event, Random forest algorithm is a very effective tool for reducing dimensionality since it recognizes the importance of each component [19, 20] Due to the Massive Numbers, random forest is a more successful prediction method than decision tree, although it is more difficult to over-fit than choice tree [18]. Random forests can be used to rank the importance of variables in a regression or classification problem in a natural way. At each split in each tree, the improvement in the split-criterion is the importance measure attributed to the splitting variable, and is accumulated over all the trees in the forest separately for each variable [18].

3 Results and Discussion

This study used data of weather and bike sharing use collected from June to October 2021 in Budapest, Hungary. Weather data contained temperature, humidity, pressure, wind speed, precipitation, and sun hours that are summarized in Table 1. Bike sharing use data includes the number of bikes used per day and total daily trips per user groups.

Table 1. Average, standard deviation, minimum, and maximum vales of weather parameters

Weather parameter	Average value	Standard deviation	Minimum	Maximum
Precipitation	1.11 mm	0.31 mm	0.00 mm	33.5 mm
Temperature	19.4 °C	5.9 °C	6.0 °C	33.0 °C
Humidity	65.1%	9.1%	45%	93%
Sun hours	13.8 h	1.9 h	10.0 h	16.0 h
Pressure	1017.14 hpa	0.42 hpa	1005 hpa	1033 hpa
Wind speed	6.8 km/h	2.6 km/h	3 km/h	16 km/h

It is found that Saturday and Sunday are the most attractive day for irregular users with an average of 88 and 77 trips respectively. The difference between weekends and weekdays based on the number of users, bookings, rentals and trips were 160% for all the values. This indicates a concentration of using the bike sharing system in weekends more than weekdays for occasional and visitor users. Moreover, average number of bookings (1.1) and rentals (1.4) per user remained stable. On the other hand, the total daily trips per user fluctuates from day to day. The highest ratio is on Tuesday with 3.3 trips per user, while the lowest is on Thursday with 2.5 trips per user.

It was noted that visitors pay more for bike sharing service than occasional users. It is found that the daily average booking cost is 7.8 and 5.5 Euros, respectively. The average daily revenue and booking values per day are presented in Fig. 1.

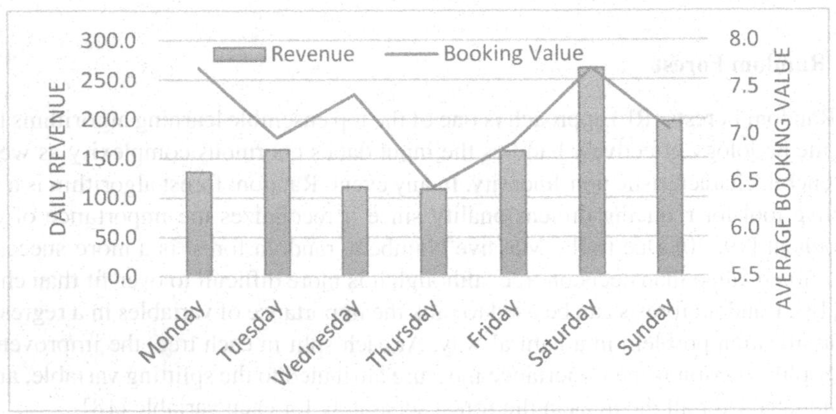

Fig. 1. Average daily revenue and booking cost per day

A seasonal pattern was noted over the investigated period. We applied Exponential Smoothing (ETS) to forecast future values of trips and bikes. We used a smoothing parameter Alpha of 0.25, which means that higher number of observations taken into consideration of forecast. Two analyses were conducted; the average bikes used, and trips per user. The results showed that during the forecasted 5 months, the average number of bikes used could reach 3.3% increase after one year, and the trips per user could reach 20% increase for the same period of time, see Figs. 2 and 3.

It is found that the average number of daily bookings on clear days is 11% higher than on rainy days. The wind speed higher than 10 km/h causes a significant drop (−40%) in the average number of bookings (Fig. 4). This is expected due to the stability and comfort of riders in their daily trips. However, even higher wind speed does not further reduce the number of bookings. It may be because wind speed does not impact experienced bikers.

It was found that temperatures below 15 °C and over 27 °C have a negative impact on the number of bookings (Fig. 5). This may be explained by the adverse effect of cold and hot weather. Finally, a negative correlation was found between the humidity and the average daily booking. Consequently, increasing humidity significantly decrease the comfort of cycling.

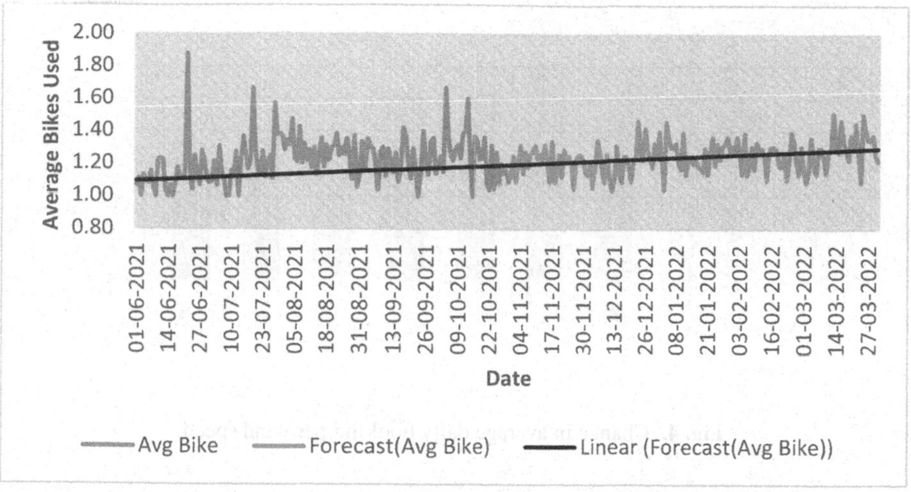

Fig. 2. Historical and forecasted average bikes used per day

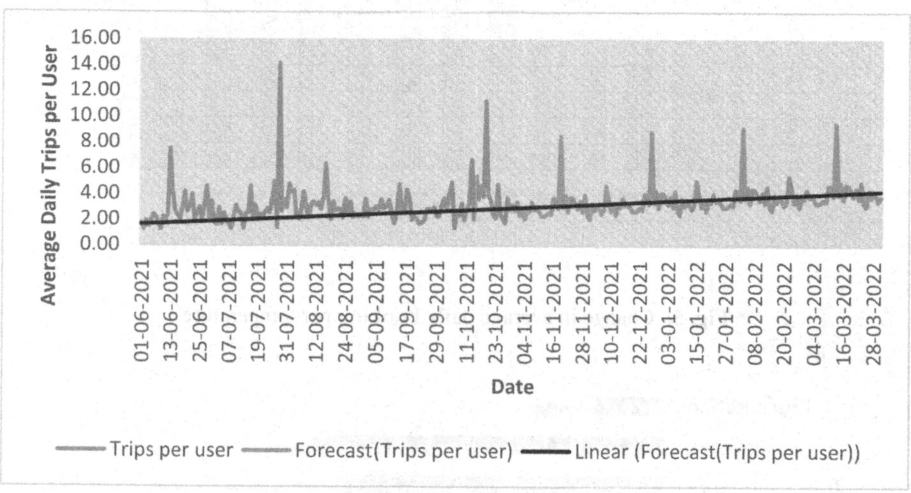

Fig. 3. Historical and forecasted average daily trips per user

For the random forest analysis, the models have used 140 trees to get the results for the bookings and 300 trees for the trips of bike sharing. The results showed almost similar importance ranking between the daily trips and booking numbers. For the bike sharing trips of irregular users, the length of sun hours is the most affecting variable, while temperature is the second. Unexpectedly, precipitation is the least important variable. This indicates that visitors or occasional riders use the bike sharing system in rainy days as normal ones. For the number of bookings, the top ranked variable is length of sun hours as well, while secondly is the type of day (weekend or weekday). The least important variable is precipitation. See Fig. 6.

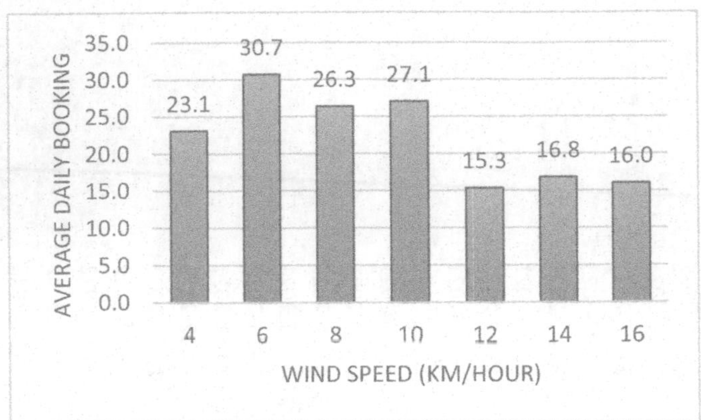

Fig. 4. Change in average daily booking per wind speed

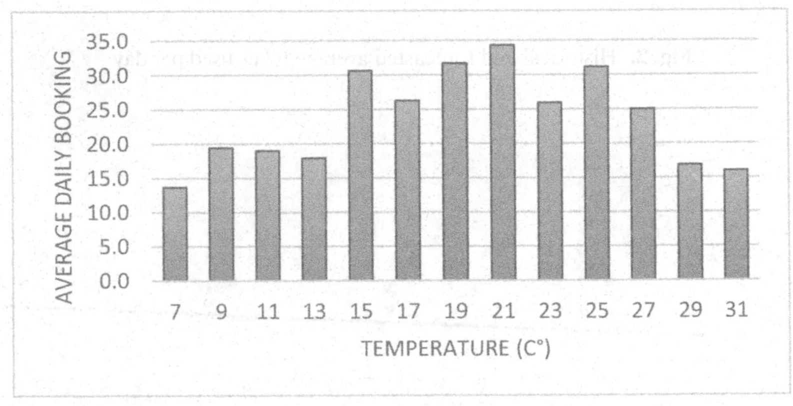

Fig. 5. Change in average daily booking per temperature

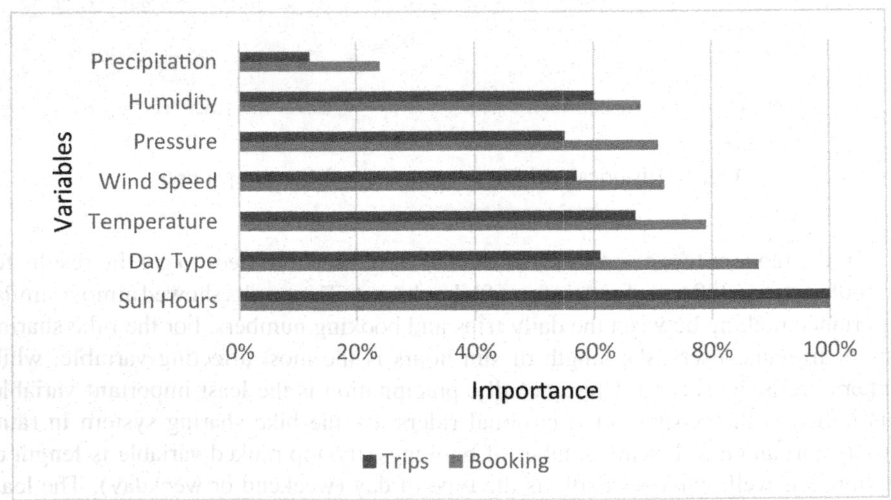

Fig. 6. Importance of temporal variables on bike sharing trips and booking

In order to evaluate the performance of random forest, the following indices are used: Root Mean Squared Error (RMSE), and Coefficient of Variation (CV). RMSE stands for the sample standard deviation of the residuals between the observed and the predicted values. Large errors can be identified using this measure and the fluctuation of model response regarding variance can be evaluated. Besides, CV estimates the overall prediction error corresponding to the mean value of the target. Larger CV value denotes that a developed model has a largest error range. These formulas are shown in the Eqs. (1) and (2), where A_i is the actual values, P_i is the predicted value, and n is the total number of cases (days).

$$\text{RMSE} = \sqrt{\frac{1}{n}\sum\nolimits_{i=1}^{n}(A_i - P_i)^2} \tag{1}$$

$$\text{CV} = \text{RMSE}/\text{Mean} \tag{2}$$

In the random forest analysis, RMSE for booking is 5.27 while it is 20.6. The Coefficient of variation estimates are: 19%, and 28%, respectively. These values are somehow high, but relatively accepted [21].

In comparison with other studies, [22] found that occasional trips are not sensitive to weather conditions. It may be because only smaller ranges of weather conditions were observed during a shorter period (1 month). Compared to research with random forest approach; Irregular users of Budapest bike sharing system have similar behavior with the results of [13–16] as temperature. As bottom ranked, our study findings indicated that humidity level is not highly significant which is in line with a European study of [16].

4 Conclusions

Bike-sharing is becoming a common mode of mobility. This research found that they tend to use the service on weekends more than on weekdays especially on Saturdays, whereas weekdays have more variations and extremes. Users, bookings, and rentals have all been found to have consistent ratios between each other over the investigated period. Visitors pay more for bike-sharing than occasional users. For forecasting purposes, an exponential smoothing analysis was performed. It is estimated that bike-sharing services will be used more frequently in the extended period of next months in Budapest. Moderate temperature, low humidity, precipitation, and wind speed are the ideal conditions for irregular users. Based on the Random Forest techniques, the top ranked variables influencing trips and booking are sun hours and temperature, while the least is the precipitation. This research helps decision-makers to predict the number of bookings and plan maintenance. Consequently, it also supports the implementation of a dynamic tariff system to reduce the demand fluctuation. Future research shall focus on spatial distribution.

Acknowledgment. The authors gratefully acknowledge the support provided by the Budapest University of Technology and Economics (BME) and the Faculty of Transportation Engineering and Vehicle Engineering through Scholarship awarded to the first author.

References

1. Eren, E., Uz, V.E.: A review on bike-sharing: the factors affecting bike-sharing demand. Sustain. Cities Soc. **54**, 101882 (2020). https://doi.org/10.1016/j.scs.2019.101882
2. Wei, X., Luo, S., Nie, Y.: Diffusion behavior in a docked bike-sharing system. Transp. Res. Part C Emerg. Technol. **107**, 510–524 (2019). https://doi.org/10.1016/j.trc.2019.08.018
3. Cai, S., Long, X., Li, L., Liang, H., Wang, Q., Ding, X.: Determinants of intention and behavior of low carbon commuting through bicycle-sharing in China. J. Clean. Prod. **212**, 602–609 (2019). https://doi.org/10.1016/j.jclepro.2018.12.072
4. Murphy, E., Usher, J.: The role of bicycle-sharing in the city: analysis of the Irish experience. Int. J. Sustain. Transp. **9**(2), 116–125 (2012). https://doi.org/10.1080/15568318.2012.748855
5. Kabak, M., Erbaş, M., Çetinkaya, C., Özceylan, E.: A GIS-based MCDM approach for the evaluation of bike-share stations. J. Clean. Prod. **201**, 49–60 (2018). https://doi.org/10.1016/j.jclepro.2018.08.033
6. Xu, Y., Chen, D., Zhang, X., Tu, W., Chen, Y., Shen, Y., Ratti, C.: Unravel the landscape and pulses of cycling activities from a dockless bike-sharing system. Comput. Environ. Urban Syst. **75**, 184–203 (2019). https://doi.org/10.1016/j.compenvurbsys.2019.02.002
7. Bieliński, T., Kwapisz, A., Ważna, A.: Bike-sharing systems in Poland. Sustainability **11**(9), 2458 (2019). https://doi.org/10.3390/su11092458
8. Zhang, L., Zhang, J., Duan, Z.-Y., Bryde, D.: Sustainable bike-sharing systems: characteristics and commonalities across cases in urban China. J. Clean. Prod. **97**, 124–133 (2015). https://doi.org/10.1016/j.jclepro.2014.04.006
9. Fishman, E.: Bikeshare: a review of recent literature. Transp. Rev. 1–22 (2015). https://doi.org/10.1080/01441647.2015.1033036
10. Fishman, E., Washington, S., Haworth, N., Mazzei, A.: Barriers to bikesharing: an analysis from Melbourne and Brisbane. J. Transp. Geogr. **41**, 325–337 (2014). https://doi.org/10.1016/j.jtrangeo.2014.08.005
11. Fuller, D., Gauvin, L., Kestens, Y., Daniel, M., Fournier, M., Morency, P., Drouin, L.: Use of a new public bicycle share program in Montreal, Canada. Am. J. Prev. Med. **41**(1), 80–83 (2011). https://doi.org/10.1016/j.amepre.2011.03.002
12. Buck, D., Buehler, R., Happ, P., Rawls, B., Chung, P., Borecki, N.: Are bikeshare users different from regular cyclists?: A first look at short-term users, annual members, and area cyclists in the Washington, D.C., region. Transp. Res. Rec. **2387**(1), 112–119 (2013). https://doi.org/10.3141/2387-13
13. Ashqar, H.I., Elhenawy, M., Rakha, H.A.: Modeling bike counts in a bike-sharing system considering the effect of weather conditions. Case Stud. Transp. Policy. **7**(2), 261–268 (2019). https://doi.org/10.1016/j.cstp.2019.02.011
14. Sathishkumar, V.E., Park, J., Cho, Y.: Using data mining techniques for bike sharing demand prediction in metropolitan city. Comput. Commun. **153**, 353–366 (2020). https://doi.org/10.1016/j.comcom.2020.02.007
15. Sathishkumar, V.E., Cho, Y.: Season wise bike sharing demand analysis using random forest algorithm. Comput. Intell. 1–26 (2020). https://doi.org/10.1111/coin.12287
16. Ruffieux, S., Spycher, N., Mugellini, E., Khaled, O.A.: Real-time usage forecasting for bike-sharing systems: a study on random forest and convolutional neural network applicability. In: Intelligent Systems Conference (IntelliSys), pp. 622–631 (2017). https://doi.org/10.1109/IntelliSys.2017.8324359
17. Jaber, A., Juhász, J.: Measuring and forecasting of passengers modal split through road accidents statistical data. In: Sierpiński, G. (ed.) Intelligent Solutions for Cities and Mobility of the Future. LNNS, vol. 352, pp. 14–26. Springer, Cham (2022). https://doi.org/10.1007/978-3-030-91156-0_2

18. Breiman, L.: Random forests. Mach. Learn. **45**, 5–32 (2001). https://doi.org/10.1023/A:1010933404324
19. Chen, X., Ishwaran, H.: Random forests for genomic data analysis. Genomics **99**(6), 323–329 (2012). https://doi.org/10.1016/j.ygeno.2012.04.003
20. Deng, H., Runger, G.: Gene selection with guided regularized random forest. Pattern Recogn. **46**(12), 3483–3489 (2013). https://doi.org/10.1016/j.patcog.2013.05.018
21. Al-Hyari, L., Kassai, M.: Development and experimental validation of TRNSYS simulation model for heat wheel operated in air handling unit. Energies **13**, 4957 (2020). https://doi.org/10.3390/en13184957
22. Noland, R.B., Smart, M.J., Guo, Z.: Bikeshare trip generation in New York city. Transp. Res. A: Policy Pract. **94**, 164–181 (2016). https://doi.org/10.1016/j.tra.2016.08.030

Analysis of the Tasks of Control Room Operators Within Chinese Motorway Control Rooms

Linyi Jin[1], Val Mitchell[1(✉)], Andrew May[1(✉)], and Mei Sun[2,3,4(✉)]

[1] Design School, Loughborough University, Loughborough LE11 3TU, UK
{l.jin,v.a.mitchell,a.j.may}@lboro.ac.uk
[2] Chengdu University, Chengdu, China
sunmei@cdu.edu.cn
[3] Tsinghua University, Beijing, China
[4] Wuliangye Yibin Company Limited, Yibin, China

Abstract. This paper develops an understanding of the tasks that provide a basis for generating reliable design recommendations for the introduction of future technologies into Chinese motorway traffic control room systems. Studies involving comprehensive and practical task analysis of the operations in motorway control rooms face a significant research gap. This study aims to broaden the understanding of Control Room Operator tasks related to motorway safety. Building on existing documents, a field study was conducted in two motorway control rooms in China. Eighteen operators and four engineers participated in the study. The study uses a user-centred approach to investigate the operators' tasks in terms workflow, goals, sub-goals and related cognitive aspects. Four categories of tasks stakeholders believed related to motorway safety were presented in the form of a hierarchy and goal-based and cognition-based description were identified. The analysis revealed the unexpected importance placed on reporting tasks by the Control Room Operators and associated stress, as well as providing an in-depth description of the tasks involved in responding to incidents.

Keywords: Motorway control room · Experience · Task analysis

1 Introduction

1.1 Background

It is important to understand the workflow and the cognitive demands of the tasks given to Control Room Operators (CROs), because these two factors impact system safety and human performance (Hollnagel 2002) and task analysis is a key method for achieving this. For example, Wahlström et al. (2016) developed usability design goals for a future ship operation systems using the Core-Task Analysis method. In the domain of the road traffic control room, Starke et al. (2017) undertook a Hierarchical Task Analysis (HTA) to decompose the task of 'respond to incident' into goals and sub goals, to provide

H. Krömker (Ed.): HCII 2022, LNCS 13335, pp. 526–546, 2022.
https://doi.org/10.1007/978-3-031-04987-3_36

the foundation for investigating operator's visual behaviours. However, analysis of the work of CROs requires a more holistic approach as CROs undertake multiple tasks to monitor traffic flow and respond to incidents. Moreover, little work has been done to investigate the operators' cognitive tasks. Such investigations are highly relevant to motorway safety, because the high mental workload of the motorway operator may cause human errors (Fallahi et al. 2016). In general, studies involving comprehensive and practical task analysis of the operations in motorway control rooms have received inadequate empirical coverage in the literature.

1.2 Literature Review

Task analysis (TA) is concerned with identifying and examining any task process that must be performed in the workplace (Kirwan and Ainsworth 1992, p.vii). HTA has endured as a popular branch of TA (Salmon et al. 2010). It offers a means of describing a system in terms of goals and sub-goals, with feedback loops in a nested hierarchy (Stanton 2006). HTA can be traced back to the scientific management movement advocated by researchers such as Gilbreths and Frederick Taylor in the early 1900s. Early HTA investigations were concerned with setting and achieving goals, in response to the changing nature of industrial work process, within which tasks were becoming more cognitive. Therefore, in addition to the in-depth goal-based description provided, it also attempted to describe the related cognitive and physical processes (Salmon et al. 2010).

Understanding the cognitive demands imposed by tasks is crucial in work associated with supervision and control of complex automated (Jin et al. 2020) systems (Dadashi et al. 2013). Cognitive task analysis (CTA) is a set of methods for capturing cognitive knowledge and defining the mental demands, that are needed in order to complete the task proficiently (Militello and Hutton 1998). Salmon et al. (2010) argued that HTA and CTA can provide highly complementary outputs, implying that combining the analysis of physical and cognitive elements can produce more comprehensive results.

1.3 Aim

The aim of this research is to provide comprehensive and practical understanding of significant CRO tasks using data gathered from two field studies in Chinese motorway control rooms. This task analysis has been undertaken as part of a wider research project that is seeking to enhance CRO engagement within Chinese motorway traffic control rooms (Jin et al. 2020).

The research questions that set the structure for this work were:

- Which tasks have the potential to influence current motorway safety systems from the stakeholders' perspectives?
- What are the goals and sub-goals of these significant tasks and their corresponding cognitive aspects?
- How should the workflows of task analysis be organized to aid other research which is related to the design of motorway control systems?

This paper answers these questions by reporting on a study that involved interviews and card-sorting (CS) to investigate and understand significant tasks. The target tasks are presented in the form of a clear hierarchical structure, and the goals of the tasks and sub-tasks as well as the corresponding cognitive thinking have been identified. In addition, this paper presents key lessons from the end-users' perspective, it shows the real situation of the operator performing safety-related tasks and points out areas for improvement. Finally, this study suggests guidelines for task analysis for related studies of control rooms, which can be used to examine actual working conditions for controlling other transport systems.

2 Methodology

To produce this TA, a review of previous research and official Control room documentation was conducted. Semi-structured interviews and CS were then used to collect data. A combination of Cognitive Task Analysis (CTA) and HTA was used in the task analysis. The role of CS in this research was to help participants express their experience and thoughts about tasks by selecting from a collection of tangible cards; cards are usually regarded as being useful in aiding the design process and providing information (Roy and Warren 2019). CTA terminology is used to specify the cognitive skills and mental demands needed to complete a task (Militello and Hutton 1998). HTA offers a method of presenting a system goal and sub-goal hierarchy (Stanton 2006).

There were three separate steps in this study: the first one was a review of existing related documents. The second one focused on checking consistencies in the description of control room tasks in official documentation, relevant literature, and the contexts of real-life traffic control rooms. The third step aimed to identify target tasks.

2.1 Participants

Eighteen operators and four engineers participated in the two case studies. The participating operators consisted of eight males and ten females, between 25 and 50 years old. All of them possessed more than three years' working experience. The engineers were responsible for designing the flow and content of the operators' tasks in the software and had a deep understanding of these tasks. Participation was voluntary and no financial incentives were given. Two field studies were conducted in two active motorway control rooms based in Guizhou, China during December 2018.

2.2 Identify Target Tasks

This study was concerned with identifying which tasks in the Chinese motorway control room should be targeted according to their influences to motorway safety and traffic flow, based on existing documents related to operator tasks and according to operators' perceptions. All 18 operators from two motorway control rooms participated in these three steps during this study, and four engineers participated only the third step.

In the first step, official documents in the traffic control rooms were reviewed for the description of procedures and the content of tasks, including four categories: emergency plans, operator handbooks, operator recruitment and software operation manuals. This documentation was retrieved from motorway control rooms in Chongqing, Sichuan and Guizhou. Secondly, due to regional and other contextual differences, descriptions of tasks can vary between different control rooms. To identify the core content of tasks in traffic rooms in general, a range of literature (e.g., Mat and Rawidean 2000; Falk 2003; Starke et al. 2017) related to motorway control rooms was reviewed.

In the second step, the first semi-structured interview was used to check consistencies between the descriptions of control room tasks in official documentation and literature and in the task descriptions used in the context of real-life traffic control rooms. Each operator was interviewed individually. At the beginning, a pilot study with four operators was conducted to test the feasibility of the interview questions. The researcher provided a task name to the operator, and then asked the operator whether he or she had performed this task as part of their work, and if so, how they had performed it. Then the researcher gradually came to realize that terminologies used by operators and in the documentation to describe the same task could differ, making it difficult for operators to recognize a task just by the official names of the task. The study therefore utilized a summary of the content, procedures, and purposes of each task as described in the official documents and literature, and used the summary when talking to an operator to ensure that they understood which task was being referred to. Then the operator was then asked to describe whether he or she had ever performed a task similar to the one that had been described. If so, he or she was invited to identify any differences or similarities between the task they had performed and the one just described. Every task was investigated in this way.

In the third step, the CS was used to identify the target tasks and generate a ranking of tasks according to the influence of the tasks on motorway safety and traffic flow. This step was conducted immediately after the preliminary interview so that operators could sort and rank tasks based on clearer task definitions. During the CS, each operator was encouraged to provide explanations for his or her ranking and sorting choices. They were told that it was unnecessary to rank these tasks one by one, for example, if an operator thought several tasks influence motorway safety equally, they could put these tasks on the same level. They were always asked to explain why they had ranked tasks in these ways.

2.3 Investigate Target Tasks

After the target tasks have been identified, the second semi-structured interview was designed to explore with 18 operators in two motorway control rooms how the target tasks should be decomposed, and how to understand the participants' goals and sub-goals for each task and their cognitive thinking in these tasks. However, many of the participants found it difficult to articulate their tasks in this way and were reluctant to answer the questions which were similar to the questions already asked in the preliminary semi-structured interview. To ease this problem, the researcher drew from data collected in the preliminary semi-structured interview to explain the procedures of the target tasks using process charts (e.g., Fig. 1). These process charts were used to visually help participants communicate their understanding of tasks. A total of ten process charts were developed. The task procedure in each process chart was firstly verified by each operator. Secondly, the operator would be asked to share a typical experience about how he or she coped with this task, and the way they described their tasks indicated their thoughts, goals, experience, understanding, and the knowledge that they considered necessary for completing the particular task.

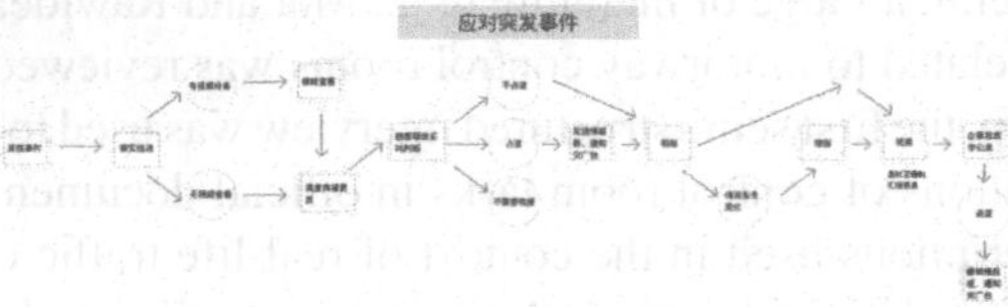

Fig. 1. A typical process chart used in the second semi-structured interview

2.4 Analysis

Both sets of interviews were recorded, transcribed, and imported into QSR NVivo software for qualitative thematic analysis. This was used to identify, analyse and report patterns, and to create meaning within data (Braun and Clarke 2006). Relevant statements from participants were tagged and clustered into two main themes, the first theme being task procedures, and the second theme the cognitive demands imposed on tasks and sub-tasks. Under the first theme, the statements were separated into the task goal and sub-goals of each task and used to generate awareness of how different contexts affect tasks and sub-tasks. Under the second theme, the transcriptions were coded according to participants' thoughts, experience, frustrations and skills when completing tasks and sub-tasks. Themes derived from participants' responses were merged and ordered according to their frequency and importance.

3 Results

Participants confirmed that two types of tasks have a significant impact on motorway safety, tasks related to accident prevention and accident handling. Participants perceived the influence of these two task types upon motorway safety and traffic flow to be interrelated. For example, participant G described how efficient accident handling minimised the risk of further accidents: "I think it is particularly important to know real-time conditions on a motorway in order to prevent accidents risks. Because risks can be minimised immediately when abnormalities are found, accidents can be avoided. In addition, the handling of emergencies is also very important, because if these emergencies are handled successfully and immediately, the motorway can be restored to smooth operation in a short time." The impact of these two types of tasks on motorway safety is also related to the external environment, such as traffic conditions and time. For example, participant F said, "The focus of the operator varies because different traffic conditions depend on geography. In the sections with high incidence of accidents, I think handing accidents urgently has a greater impact on motorway safety than other interventions. But in the areas with fewer accidents, prevention must be more important". And participant D said, "On workdays, it is certainly more important to deal with accidents promptly, otherwise many subsequent accidents would be caused. And it is difficult to prevent accidents by our current technical means on workdays; for example, we can rarely detect the risks by CCTV at ordinary times. However, during holidays, I think it is very useful to prevent or detect accidents, which can greatly affect the traffic flow, by close monitoring of CCTV".

From the thematic analysis, four categories of tasks that have direct or indirect impact on motorway safety were marked as target tasks, namely Emergency response, Organizing and transmitting information, Monitoring the everyday situation of the motorway and Routines. In the two control rooms these tasks were generally alike with slight differences in detail. The specific tasks are described below, based on different task categories. The target task flows in the four categories were presented in the form of a hierarchy of procedures, indicating the goals and sub-goals of the operator in each task, and the conditions that require subordinate procedures to be carried out. In all the figures below, a circle represents a condition, a capsule shape represents cognition, and a rectangle represents a specific goal or sub-goal.

Emergency Response. For the operator's chief task of 'Emergency response' (goal 0) (Fig. 2), the operator's goal was to follow a standard procedure when transferring incident information to help to deal with the emergency and to restore traffic flow. This task usually made the operator nervous and tired. Because it often happened unexpectedly and suddenly, and the superior department attached great importance to this task, and therefore set very detailed and strict regulations and limited completion times for the implementation of this task. So the operators found this task challenging. The operators hoped that the situation could be resolved as soon as possible. But more importantly, operators tried their best not to make any mistakes in emergency response, otherwise they would be held accountable. For example, participant J mentioned that "You can't make mistakes in submitting information during emergency response, because if you make mistakes, you will be deducted points". Lower points mean a decrease of salary for the operators. The task procedure was generally similar in the two control rooms. It was divided into eight sub-goals which were identified and are shown with the full HTA in Fig. 2 and described in the text below.

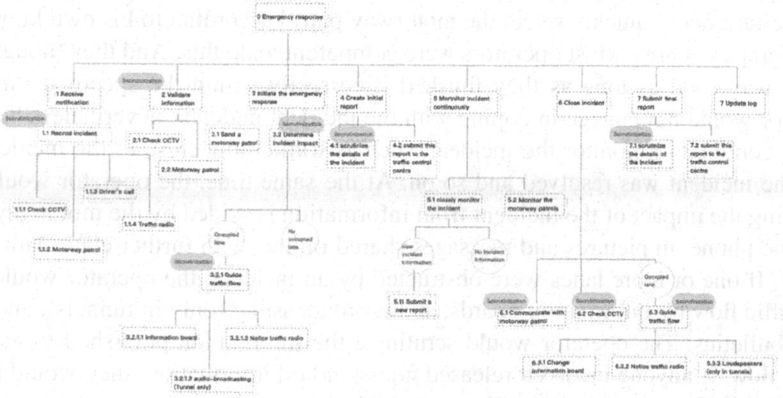

Fig. 2. Emergency response

Subgoal 1: [Receive notification]. The operator typically responded to an incident notification as soon as the information was received. The notification could arrive through different sources (CCTV, motorway patrol personnel, a driver's call, traffic radio, etc.). The operator carefully and swiftly recorded the incident location, incident types, road condition and so on. And he or she confirmed these details carefully with the person providing the information to avoid any mistakes. The operators were very serious and devoted to this step. They hoped they could concentrate on collecting information and didn't want to be disturbed by others. As participant A mentioned "When I answer the phone, I must listen carefully. If the first step is wrong, the following steps will be wrong. At this time, my colleagues won't talk to me and disturb me".

Subgoal 2: [Validate information]. The operator would make sure that the notification was from a credible source. He or she would then track and investigate the information of this incident based on the clues collected from the previous notifications. He or she would use a CCTV camera close to the incident or ask a motorway patrol to track or check the incident. The operator would collect field information according to the template designed by the managers, including incident type, location, and impact. Then the operator would use his or her rescue experience to assess whether the information was correct. The operator would be very focused because the information about the incident would be used in the next possible initial incident report. And if the submission was wrong, it might hinder the rescue, and he or she would be held accountable. For example, participant F said, "You must carefully verify and collect information, because if you pass the wrong information on to others, you may delay the rescue, and you will be punished". Then if the response to the incident met the required standard according to the assessment of the operator, the emergency procedure would be initiated. However, if a fatal accident occurred, the operator would need to report it to the superior department for handling.

Subgoal 3: [Initiate the emergency procedure]. One or more motorway patrols would be sent to the scene by the operator to deal with the incident once the emergency procedure has been initiated. The operator would select the motorway patrol according to the jurisdiction of the motorway patrol and the location of the incident. This step requires that the operator could quickly select the motorway patrol according to his own knowledge of geographical area. Most operators were competent to do this. And they thought their action was good as long as they finished it correctly within the specified time. The operator would not engage in coping with the incident in detail, nevertheless he or she would continue to monitor the incident, such as traffic flow close to the incident, and how the incident was resolved and so on. At the same time, the operator would keep assessing the impact of the incident from information provided by the motorway patrol over the phone, in pictures and messages shared online, with further clarification from CCTV. If one or more lanes were obstructed by an incident, the operator would guide the traffic flow by information boards, audio-broadcasting (only in tunnels), and traffic radio bulletins. The operator would scrutinize the information published to guide the traffic flow. If anyone involved released non-standard information, they would be held accountable. Just as participant C reported "Every time I send text to the information board, I have to check it myself and discuss it with my colleagues when I am not sure.

I am particularly afraid of making mistakes in this step because the information we publish will be assessed".

Subgoal 4: [Create Initial report]. The operator would scrutinize the details of the incident, including incident location, road condition, incident type and the accuracy, formatting and grammar of the text in the report, to exclude any mistakes. Then the operator would carefully edit the information and enter it into a template and submit this report to the traffic control centre. This is necessary because if a wrong submission occurs, the operator would be held accountable. As reported by participant F "Every time, before submitting information, I will check whether the content and format of my information are correct, because once there is an error, it is a big mistake for me, and I will be held accountable and deducted points". Those CROs with experience in the role felt less nervous than inexperienced colleagues, but still reported that this was a stressful activity and were very careful to create and file the reports correctly.

Subgoal 5: [Monitor incident and motorway patrol at the scene]. The operator would closely monitor the incident to check if the incident had been resolved and whether the motorway patrols were handling incidents according to the standard procedures. If some new incident information appeared, for example, if another lane became obstructed or new incidents occurred, the operator would need to carefully assess this new information and swiftly submit a report about these changes to the control centre. Many operators mentioned that they were uneasy before an event was over and always wondered if there was something unfinished. For example, participant D said, "Sometimes when an event is not over, I still think about it after work. Sometimes I call my colleagues at home to ask about the event". This might be because an incident was taking longer to resolve than expected due to unforeseen circumstances or because the incident was continuing for a scheduled reason, such as road works.

Subgoal 6: [Close the incident]. An incident is considered to be closed, once the motorway patrol tells the operator the incident has been resolved. Then the operator would scrutinize the incident situation by CCTV to confirm the information provided by motorway patrol and that traffic is flowing normally again close to the incident. The operator would be relieved to know that the incident was over, as participant E exemplified: "My mood becomes relatively relaxed when I know that the task has been completed". And if one or more lanes had been obstructed during the course of the incident, then the operator now needs to cancel the text on the information board that he or she had previously displayed to guide the traffic flow. This step was relatively easy and less error-prone. In addition, the operator would tell the road-users by means of loudspeakers (only in tunnels) and traffic radio bulletins that the lane was now unblocked.

Subgoal 7: [Submit final report]. The operator submits the final report to the traffic control centre, to confirm that the incident had been resolved. Before doing this, the operator carefully reviews the information uploaded by him or her in case of any mistakes. At this time, the mood of the operator was also relatively relaxed, because everything has been determined, the probability of error was limited, and it was only necessary to complete the work according to the defined procedures.

Subgoal 8: [Update the log]. The operator creates an incident log to record the incident. This step was very easy; the operator only needed to record the information according to the template. And because the incident was completely over, the operator again felt relaxed.

Organizing and Transmitting Information. Report the previous day's information on the roads.

The task of "Report the previous day's information on the roads" belonged to the category of organizing and transmitting information. The goal of this task was to conclude what happened on the motorway within the jurisdiction of the previous day and share the information to the relevant agencies. During this whole process the operator felt calm because this was the daily work that he or she was already very familiar with. Since there was no strict time limit for this task, it was generally executed at the end of the day. The operator usually had plenty of time to complete it. This task was methodical, tedious and less challenging, as participant E noted "It doesn't make sense to do this kind of task every day. I don't think anyone will read these reports that I summarized. This task is too boring and simple. I feel that there is no need to learn. Children could do it". The goal and experience of the operators in the two control rooms were basically the same, but the procedures were slightly different.

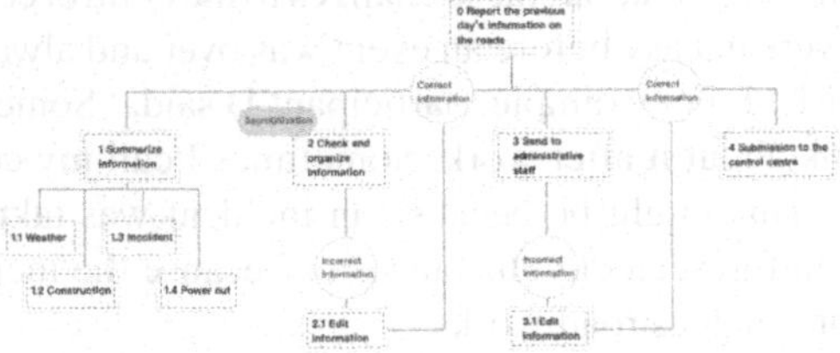

Fig. 3. Report the previous day's information on the roads

This task analysis in control room 1 was demonstrated in Fig. 3 for the following four subgoals.

Subgoal 1: [Summarize the information]. The operator would summarize the information from the records of weather, construction, incidents, and power cuts.

Subgoal 2: [Check and organize information]. The operator would edit information and enter it into a template according to the required format. The operator also needed to scrutinize the accuracy of the content, language, grammar, spelling, logic, and formatting. If the content was accurate, the next step would be initiated, otherwise the operator needed to edit it again.

Subgoal 3: [Send to administrative staff]. The operator's submission would be checked by the administrative staff. If there were any mistakes, the operator would correct them.

Subgoal 4: [Submission to the control centre]. The operator would submit the report to the control centre.

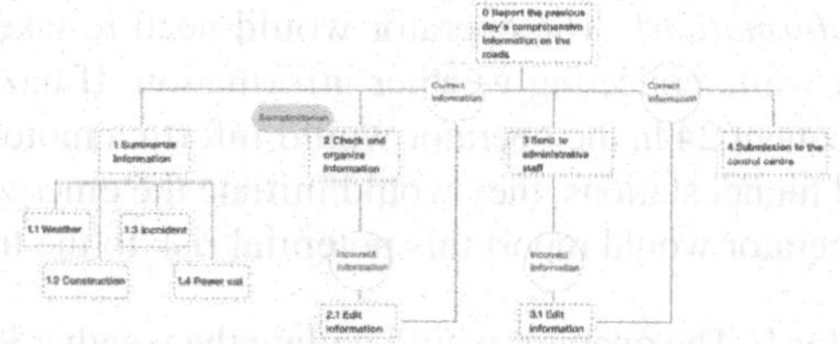

Fig. 4. Report the previous day's information on the roads

In control room 2, the procedure was almost the same, except that the operator in control room 2 was not required to send the information to the administrative staff (Sub-goal 3 in Fig. 4) before submission.

Monitoring the Everyday Situation of the Motorway. The purpose of this task category was to detect dangers or potential risks on the road to make preparations for preventing any emergencies as early as possible. The procedure referred to collecting, verifying, recording and submitting information. There were three tasks in this category, including Monitor weather, Monitor CCTV and Survey traffic flow.

Monitor Weather. In control room 1, the goal "Monitor weather" (Fig. 5) was to collect the next day's weather forecast (from 00:00–24:00) to prepare for possible emergencies if the weather was likely to make the road hazardous. The operator normally conducted this task in a systematic way when he or she was not busy. However, this task became important in seasons when bad weather was expected. As participant A noted "In normal times, this is a routine task that I complete when I am not busy. But in winter and summer this task is more critical, because bad weather is often encountered in these two seasons. The weather forecast allows us to prepare early". The following three sub-procedures were identified (the full HTA is shown in Fig. 5).

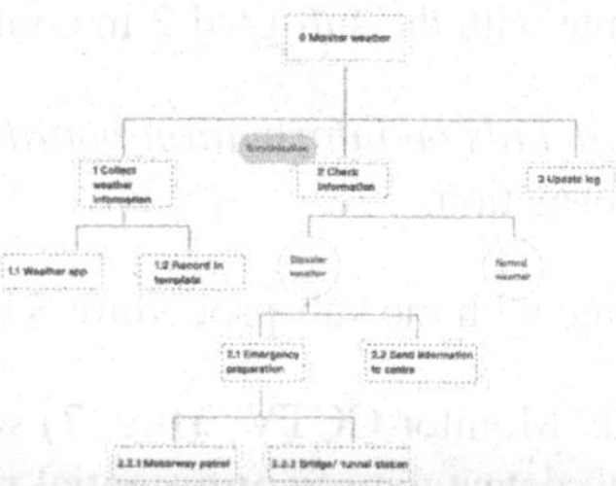

Fig. 5. Monitor weather

Subgoal 1: [Collect weather information]. The operator would collect information about temperature and weather conditions in the subsequent 24 h from a weather app.; then this information was recorded in a templated document.

Subgoal 2: [Check information]. The operator would need to take note of any abnormal weather forecast while collecting weather information. If hazardous weather was expected in the subsequent 24 h, the operator would inform a motorway patrol and colleagues at bridge and tunnel stations, they would initiate the emergency preparation. At the same time, the operator would report this potential risk to the traffic control centre.

Subgoal 3: [Update log]. The operator would update the weather log, then the task was completed.

The task "Monitor weather" (Fig. 6) was different in control room 2; the operator would collect real-time weather information to initiate emergency preparedness when road conditions were deteriorating and inform drivers about the weather conditions using the information boards. The following four sub-goals were identified.

Fig. 6. Monitor weather

Subgoal 1: [Collect real-time weather information]. This information would include temperature, weather conditions indicated by weather instruments near the road every couple of hours, and recording these in a template.

Subgoal 2: This step was same with the sub-goal 2 in control room 1.

Subgoal 3: [Publish weather details on information boards]. The operator would release real-time weather information.

Subgoal 4: This step was same with the sub-procedure 3 in control room 1.

Monitor CCTV. The aim of "Monitor CCTV" (Fig. 7) was to check road conditions over the whole control area to detect danger or potential risks, and to ensure the satisfactory operation of the CCTV system. The operator conducted the CCTV inspection several times per day. The frequency would be decided by the traffic load, for example during the festivals when the traffic was heavy, the operator would inspect the roads by CCTV every 30 min. On working days with normal traffic flow, twice a day would be enough. This work might not be carried out when the operators were busy and the traffic load on the motorway was low. In addition, the attitude of the operator toward this task would be affected by the different road environments. The operators thought it was difficult to stay aware of critical traffic situations using CCTV in the absence of special circumstances, such as holidays or extreme weather. At this time, continuously reviewing all the CCTV screens was a routine and unexciting task for them, and the priority given to this task was not high. However, when the traffic flow was heavy, the operators would survey the motorway very actively and seriously, because they thought it was easy to find the dangers on the motorways by means of CCTV at this time. As participant D said, "It is difficult for us to find abnormal traffic situations using CCTV, but it is very important to continuously monitor CCTV during holidays. Accidents were usually found within half an hour. At this time, we will check the roads more frequently".

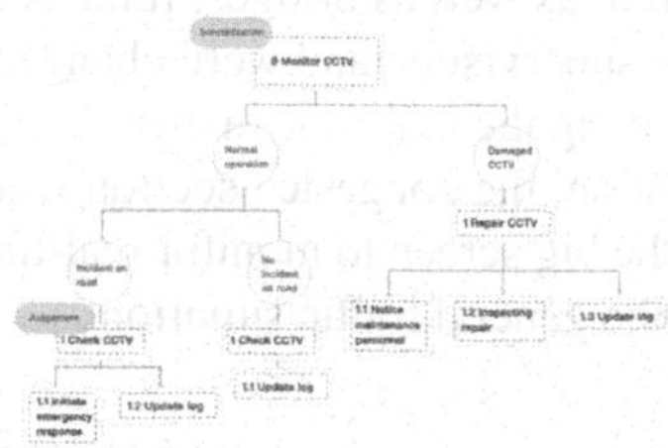

Fig. 7. Monitor CCTV

There were three situations to be considered: (i) CCTV in normal operation with no incident, (ii) CCTV in normal operation when there is an incident, and (iii) working with damaged CCTV. The procedures in two control rooms were the same.

For the condition of CCTV in normal operation with no incident:

Subgoal 1: [Check CCTV]. The operator would check the CCTV screens one by one in the control area and update the log with details of the road condition and the checked locations.

For the condition of CCTV in normal operation with an incident:

Subgoal 1: [Check CCTV]. The operator would check for any congestion or incident on the road. If he or she spotted any congestion, they would check the videos around the congestion to see what had happened. Otherwise, if an incident was spotted directly, the operator would judge whether it was serious enough to require a response; if so an emergency response would be initiated. Then the operator would update the log with an entry about the road condition and the checked locations.

For the condition of damaged CCTV:

Subgoal 1: [Repair the CCTV]. If the operator detected damage to the CCTV system, he or she would inform the maintenance personnel. The operator would check the repair once it had been resolved. A repair log would be created.

Monitor Traffic Flow on the TV Wall. The purpose of this task was to continuously enable the operators to check some key situations on the motorways. "Monitor traffic flow on the TV wall" was a routine and frequent task for operators. Most operators said that when they were not busy, they would look up at the road on the TV wall from time to time and pay special attention to any important events. For example, Participant J said, "Some construction works are often displayed on the TV wall, and I will look up to check these works when I am free. In fact, this is also my habit".

In the control room 1, the TV wall was hung out in front of the operator all the time (Fig. 8). The TV wall is composed of a large screen and an electronic map, and they were usually used together if the budget allowed. As in Fig. 8, on the left and on the right were large screens which were used for showing some selected risky road sections, such as where most accidents occurred, as well as bridges, tunnels and road construction sites. These spots were selected by supervisors; and were changed regularly. The middle part was an electronic map, displaying the real-time distribution of traffic flow in the control area. If there was any congestion, the congested section would turn to red within a few minutes. The operator used the big screen to monitor real-time traffic flow in detail, and the electronic map to check the general traffic situation.

Fig. 8. .

The situation is similar in control room 2, while there was only a large screen in control room 2 to show the important spots on the motorways (Fig. 9). Apart from the difference in information resources, this task procedure (Fig. 10) was generally the same in both control rooms with respect to the monitoring of CCTV, so one description is sufficient for both. The detailed descriptions about goals and sub-goals were shown in Fig. 10.

Fig. 9. .

Monitoring Risky Spots on the Motorways. The task category of "Monitoring risky spots on motorway" aimed to monitor potential risks on roads such as those caused by roadworks and power cuts using information provided by road-side assistance personnel. The procedure included collecting new information from road-side assistance personnel, comparing new information with recorded information which the operator had already

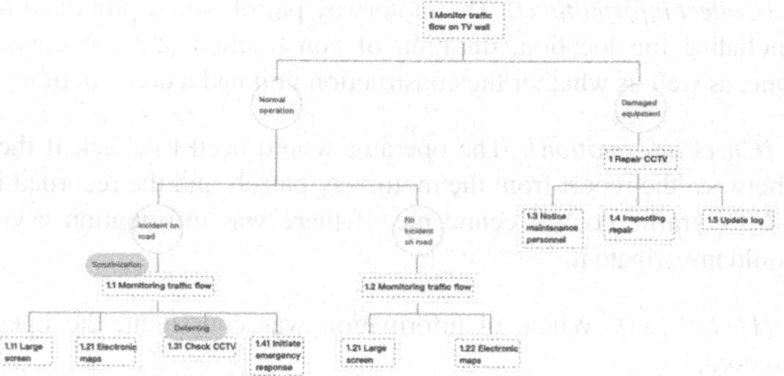

Fig. 10. Monitor traffic flow in TV wall

received. The operator logged information to conclude the task. These were the daily duties of the operator. As long as there was no error in the collected information, the operator would feel calm, as participant I said: "We need to carefully record information from road-side assistants to avoid any mistakes. What we fear most is that the collected information does not match the information I have, then there must be an error in some link". Two tasks were performed in this category, one was "Monitor roadworks" this task collected information from the motorway patrol's report – and the other was "Monitor construction and power cuts". For this task reports from bridge and tunnel stations were required. Because the management of the two control rooms was different, these tasks are generally similar but slightly different in two control rooms.

Monitor Roadworks. The goal of the task "Monitor roadworks" was to collect construction information from the motorway patrol's report to monitor road construction activities. This goal of this task has three sub-goals (Fig. 11). This task procedure was the same in the two control rooms.

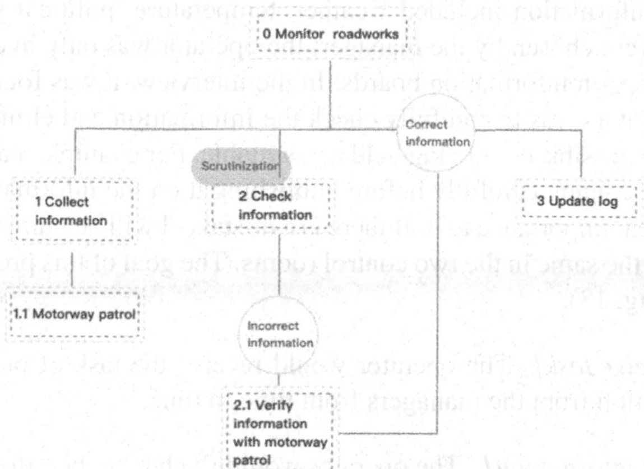

Fig. 11. Monitor roadworks

Subgoal 1: [Collect information]. The motorway patrol would provide a report to the operator, including the location, duration of construction and the condition of the occupied lane, as well as whether the construction unit had a construction permit.

Subgoal 2: [Check information]. The operator would need to check if there was any difference between the report from the motorway patrols and the recorded information from the CCTV, traffic control centre etc. If there was information asymmetry, the operator would investigate it.

Subgoal 3: [Update log]. When all information was consistent, the operator would update the record.

Monitor Roadworks and Power Cuts. This task only existed in control room 1, with the aim of collecting information about construction and power cuts at tunnel and bridge stations. In addition to information from other sources (Fig. 12). The task procedure was almost the same as the task "Monitor roadworks".

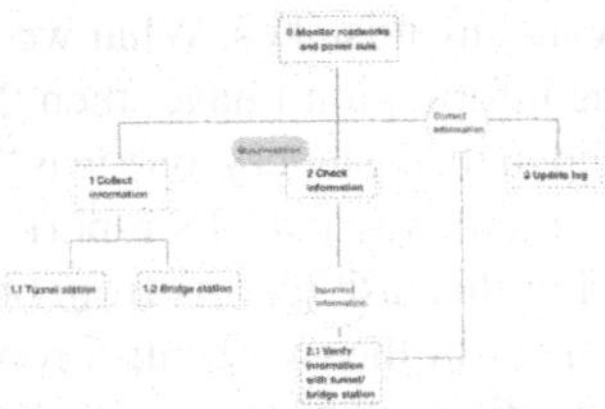

Fig. 12. Monitor roadworks and power cuts

Routines – Release Predefined Information. The purpose of "Release predefined information" was to transmit predefined information to road users in non-emergency situations. The information included weather, temperature, political signs and safety slogans, which were chosen by the manager; the operator was only in charge of releasing these messages on information boards. In the interview, it was found that the main focus of the operators was to carefully check the information and eliminate any errors, so as to avoid the possibility of being held accountable. For example, participant H said, "I will scrutinize content carefully before publishing it on the information boards. Our leaders attach great importance to it. If there is a mistake, I will be punished". This task's procedures were the same in the two control rooms. The goal of this procedure included four subgoals (Fig. 13).

Subgoal 1: [Receive task]. The operator would receive the task of publishing various kinds of information from the managers from time to time.

Subgoal 2: [Edit information]. The operator wouldn't change the information content; he or she would invest efforts in choosing the formatting and colours. Any mistakes were penalised.

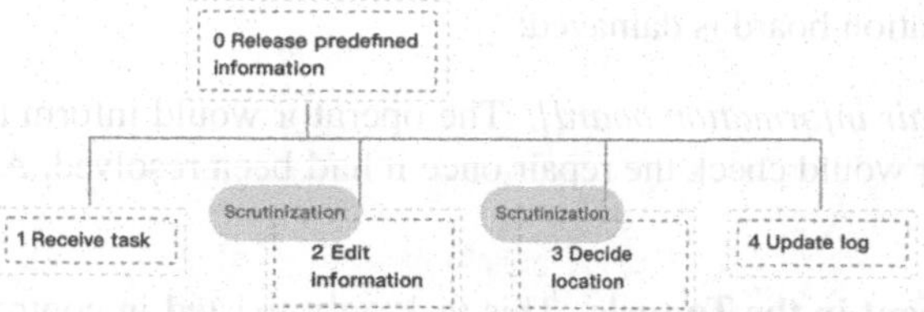

Fig. 13. Release predefined information

Subgoal 3: [Decide location]. The operator would publish message to selected information boards; he or she was extremely careful to avoid making mistakes.

Subgoal 4: [Update log]. The operator would update the record of displayed information.

Inspect Information Boards. The operator inspected the information boards to check the accuracy of the displayed information and ensure the normal operation of the information boards. The operator did this task step-by-step twice per day. Although this task did not require very complex knowledge to complete, it required the operator to be careful. There were two conditions in this task (Fig. 14).

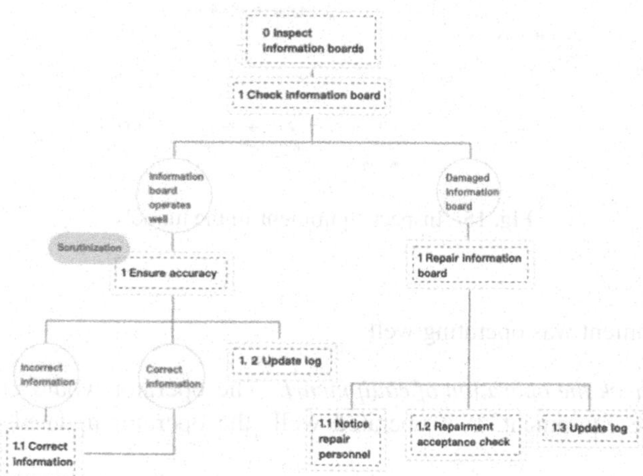

Fig. 14. Inspect information boards

If the information board operates well:

Subgoal 1: [Ensure accuracy]. The operator would check the running status of each information board and the displayed information. If the information board operated well, the operator checked whether each message matched its location, the text formatting, and colours; the operator would correct any problems. The operator would update the information board record.

If the information board is damaged:

Subgoal 1: [Repair information board]. The operator would inform the repair personnel. The operator would check the repair once it had been resolved. A repair log would be created.

Inspect Equipment in the Tunnels. This task only existed in control room 2 since it was responsible for controlling tunnels. The purpose of this task was to ensure normal operation of the equipment in the tunnel. The operator inspected equipment such as illumination, broadcasting, fans, variable speed limit signs and ventilation blowers in the tunnel twice per day. This was also a routine for the operators. It did not demand high technical knowledge and tight time constraints, and the operator often completed this task easily. There were two conditions affecting this procedure (Fig. 15).

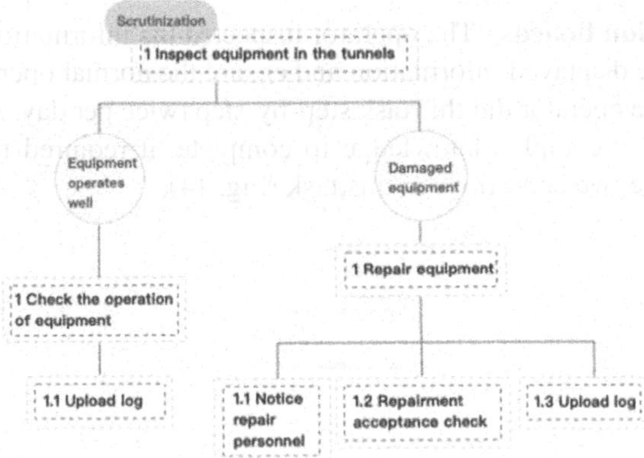

Fig. 15. Inspect equipment in the tunnels

If the equipment was operating well:

Subgoal 1: [Check the operation of equipment]. The operator would check the operation of all the equipment. If it operated well, the operator updated the inspection record.

If the equipment was damaged:

Subgoal 1: [Repair equipment]. The operator would inform the repair personnel. The operator would check the repair once it had been resolved. A repair log would be created.

4 Discussion

This study contributes a comprehensive understanding of the significant tasks related to motorway safety in actual motorway control rooms, including goal-based descriptions, related physical processes and cognitive thinking. Previous research in the domain of road control systems only reported analysis of some tasks without detailed cognitive descriptions (e.g., Starke et al. 2017). This improved task analysis provides a basis for new design recommendations for motorway control room design to underpin future research.

Previous studies have limited their research scope to the analysis of emergency tasks in the domain of the traffic control system (e.g. Dadashi et al. 2013; Starke et al. 2017), and the analysis of routine tasks is rarely reported, even some of them are related to traffic safety. This study identified a series of target tasks in four categories which have the potential to improve motorway safety from the perspectives of operators and engineers. Although it is widely believed that traffic control rooms should contribute to maintaining road safety (Fallahi et al. 2016), the analysis of tasks and workflows in this study, suggest that operational procedures in motorway control rooms are not always achieving the intended results. This situation is caused by two reasons. Firstly, it is difficult for the operator to effectively grasp the real-time motorway conditions due to the two following objective reasons. There are only two types of information source: (i) equipment, including CCTV systems and electronic displays for monitoring traffic flow, and weather stations. (ii) the other source is personnel, including roadside assistance personnel and road users. However, due to the instability of equipment and the limitations of manual data collection, the information collected through these two channels is often incomplete or even delayed. Secondly, the operators in these two control rooms are not authorized to directly intervene in traffic. For example, operators were only allowed to monitor rescues rather than guiding them during the emergency response.

This study presents the goals, sub-goals, cognitive strategies and user experience of the identified target tasks for the CROs. Compared to the task of emergency response often reported in the literature (e.g. Starke et al. 2017), it is reported in a similar fashion in this study. However, the discussion of emergency response in the literature encourages the operator to judge and deal with the incident; the operator may be responsible for guiding the traffic flow by assessing the cause and impact of an incident and by changing the road signs. By contrast, in the task of emergency response observed in this study, much of the CROs' attention was paid to whether the information collected by them met the requirements of the supervisory department and whether they (the operators) transmitted the information to relevant agents (i.e. the traffic control center, media agencies and other motorway control rooms) on time. This may be due to the limitation of technology - as explained before, it is difficult for the CROs to understand real-time traffic flow information efficiently. As it is easier for them to ensure that reporting is carried out, this also can explain why one of the focuses of the monitoring work observed in these two control rooms is that of transmitting information. Consequently, regarding the cognitive aspects of the tasks, one of concerns of the CROs seemed to be to avoid punishment as a result of transmitting incorrect information. For example, in the interviews, the CROs often mentioned the need to carefully check the information they were reporting, to avoid being held accountable for mistakes, but few mentioned the impact of their work on traffic safety. This emphasis on reporting weakens the original intention of the highway monitoring room, that is to enhance motorway safety (Dobson 2015).

The significant tasks were organized in the form of a hierarchical structure with goals, sub-goals and corresponding cognitive demands; this is because interaction between cognitive and physical elements decides the success of the performance of tasks (Shepherd 1998). What's more, the combination of HTA and CTA can facilitate the understanding of individual activities, goals, information needs and motivations (May et al. 2014). Related studies can benefit from this task analysis when reviewing workflow and corresponding cognitive aspects.

4.1 Contribution

Many previous studies about road control systems only use task analysis results, but the detailed presentation of the process of task analysis is omitted (e.g., May et al. 2014; Starke et al. 2017). The absence of information about the process may lead to obstacles when executing similar task analysis investigations. This study presents the detailed process of implementing the combination of HTA and CTA in the domain of road traffic control systems. This could potentially be used as a reference for studying the control room CROs experience within other transportation systems.

4.2 Limitations and Future Work

This study is based on data collected from related documents and interviews. It is generally recommended that multiple sources of information are used in task analysis (Stanton 2006). Taking observation (Clark et al. 2012) as an example, observational research techniques have advantages in capturing objective data, such as roles and behaviour (Walshe et al. 2012). However, in the case of complex systems, researchers who lack a sufficient understanding of the CRO's task may have difficulty in collecting useful data, because the critical steps may happen rarely or the observer may not be sufficiently aware of the origin of and motivation behind the behaviors (Clark and Estes 1996).

What's more, the belief is apparent in literature (e.g. Sarikan and Ozbayoglu 2018; Formosa et al. 2020) that advanced technologies based on the application of highly reliable sensors and sophisticated algorithms should ensure that CROs always efficiently monitor, intervene and control traffic flow. These applications may change the procedures of tasks, suggesting that the challenges discussed in this study are only temporary. However, it is needed to properly understand the current control room system and tasks so that the new technology is designed to enhance the role of the operators, improve their user experience and most importantly how effectively they perform their role. In addition, the introduction of cutting-edge technology is bound to bring great changes to working practices in control rooms. Because of the serious implications of working habits in the control room for motorway safety, the culture in the control room tends to be somewhat conservative (Savioja et al. 2013). Therefore, future research should consider this culture by designing tasks in such a way that the application of these technologies is gradual and stable and implemented in a way that is acceptable to the CROs and managers, for example, reducing unnecessary stress.

Finally, the interviewees were working for a company operating in Guizhou, China. Therefore, it is reasonable to assume that the task analysis presented here may not be representative of every motorway control room and culture, and further similar research may be required to extend the applicability of the findings.

5 Conclusion

This study has looked systematically at the wider role of the CROs and uncovered other aspects of the role that they consider important and can be stressed by. It examines their behaviour and the corresponding cognitive demands of different tasks and subtasks. Furthermore, this comprehensive task analysis presents goals and sub-goals for each task and condition. It highlights the real situation of the tasks being performed. This contributes to an understanding of where improvements are needed. What's more, this research provides a useful understanding of tasks in the current motorway control room tasks that can benefit future research in this and related fields.

References

Braun, V., Clarke, V.: Using thematic analysis in psychology. Qual. Res. Psychol. **3**(2), 77–101 (2006). https://doi.org/10.1191/1478088706qp063oa

Clark, R.E. et al.: The use of cognitive task analysis to improve instructional descriptions of procedures. J. Surg. Res. **173**(1), e37–e42 (2012). https://doi.org/10.1016/j.jss.2011.09.003

Clark, R.E., Estes, F.: Cognitive task analysis for training. Int. J. Educ. Res. **25**(5), 403–417 (1996). https://doi.org/10.1016/S0883-0355(97)81235-9

Dadashi, N., et al.: Practical use of work analysis to support rail electrical control rooms: a case of alarm handling. Proc. Inst. Mech. Eng. F J. Rail Rapid Transit **227**(2), 148–160 (2013). https://doi.org/10.1177/0954409712465709

Dobson, K.: Human factors and ergonomics in transportation control systems. Procedia Manuf. **3**, 2913–2920 (2015). https://doi.org/10.1016/j.promfg.2015.07.815

Falk, H.: Review of road traffic control strategies. In: Proceedings of the IEEE, pp. 2041–2042 (2003). https://doi.org/10.1109/JPROC.2003.819606

Fallahi, M., et al.: Effects of mental workload on physiological and subjective responses during traffic density monitoring: a field study. Appl. Ergon. **52**, 95–103 (2016). https://doi.org/10.1016/j.apergo.2015.07.009

Formosa, N., et al.: Predicting real-time traffic conflicts using deep learning. Accid. Anal. Prev. **136** (2020). https://doi.org/10.1016/j.aap.2019.105429

Hollnagel, E.: Cognition as control: a pragmatic approach to the modelling of joint cognitive systems. Control **9**, 1–23 (2002)

Jin, L., Mitchell, V., May, A.: Understanding engagement in the workplace: studying operators in Chinese traffic control rooms. In: Marcus, A., Rosenzweig, E. (eds.) Design, User Experience, and Usability. Design for Contemporary Interactive Environments. LNCS, vol. 12201, pp. 653–665. Springer, Cham (2020). https://doi.org/10.1007/978-3-030-49760-6_46

Kirwan, B., Ainsworth, L.: A Guide to Task Analysis. CRC Press (1992). https://doi.org/10.1201/b16826

Mat, I., Rawidean, M.: The design of intelligent traffic management system with user centred approach. In: 2000 TENCON Proceedings Intelligent Systems and Technologies for the New Millennium (Cat. No. 00CH37119). IEEE, pp. 244–247 (2000). https://doi.org/10.1109/TENCON.2000.888741

May, A., Mitchell, V., Piper, J.: A user centred design evaluation of the potential benefits of advanced wireless sensor networks for fire-in-tunnel emergency response. Fire Saf. J. **63**, 79–88 (2014). https://doi.org/10.1016/j.firesaf.2013.11.007

Militello, L.G., Hutton, R.J.B.: Applied cognitive task analysis (ACTA): a practitioner's toolkit for understanding cognitive task demands. Ergonomics **41**(11), 1618–1641 (1998). https://doi.org/10.1080/001401398186108

Roy, R., Warren, J.P.: Card-based design tools: a review and analysis of 155 card decks for designers and designing. Des. Stud. **63**, 125–154 (2019). https://doi.org/10.1016/j.destud.2019.04.002

Salmon, P., et al.: Hierarchical task analysis vs. cognitive work analysis: comparison of theory, methodology and contribution to system design. Theor. Issues Ergon. Sci. **11**(6), 504–531 (2010). https://doi.org/10.1080/14639220903165169

Sarikan, S.S., Ozbayoglu, A.M.: Anomaly detection in vehicle traffic with image processing and machine learning. Procedia Comput. Sci. **140**, 64–69 (2018). https://doi.org/10.1016/j.procs.2018.10.293

Savioja, P., Liinasuo, M., Koskinen, H.: User experience: does it matter in complex systems? Cogn. Technol. Work **16**(4), 429–449 (2013). https://doi.org/10.1007/s10111-013-0271-x

Shepherd, A.: HTA as a framework for task analysis. Ergonomics **41**(11), 1537–1552 (1998). https://doi.org/10.1080/001401398186063

Stanton, N.A.: Hierarchical task analysis: developments, applications, and extensions. Appl. Ergon. **37**, 55–79 (2006). https://doi.org/10.1016/j.apergo.2005.06.003

Starke, S.D., et al.: Workflows and individual differences during visually guided routine tasks in a road traffic management control room. Appl. Ergon. **61**, 79–89 (2017). https://doi.org/10.1016/j.apergo.2017.01.006

Wahlström, M., et al.: Designing user-oriented future ship bridges: an approach for radical concept design. Ergon. Des. Methods Tech. **1**, 219–233 (2016). https://doi.org/10.1201/9781315367668

Walshe, C., Ewing, G., Griffiths, J.: Using observation as a data collection method to help understand patient and professional roles and actions in palliative care settings. Palliat. Med. **26**(8), 1048–1054 (2012). https://doi.org/10.1177/0269216311432897

Gender Inclusiveness in Public Transportation: Social Media Analysis

Umi Kulsum(✉), Achmad Nurmandi, Isnaini Muallidin, Mohammad Jafar Loilatu, and Danang Kurniawan

Department of Government Affairs and Administration, Jusuf Kalla School of Government, University of Muhammadiyah Yogyakarta, Yogyakarta, Indonesia
Umikullsum.1997@gmail.com

Abstract. This study aims to analyze how social media informs women's facilities in public transportation. Public transportation is one of the facilities provided by the government for its people to facilitate public access. However, there are problems in public transport, one of which is women who are sometimes the objects of crime in public transportation. Therefore, special facilities for women are needed in public transportation. In today's era of social media, a policy will be more easily conveyed to the public. Social media, especially Twitter, is needed in delivering women information services in public transportation. This study used a Qualitative Data Analysis Software (QDAS) approach to Nvivo 12 Plus. This research data used Twitter through several busway accounts such as BRT Semarang, Trans Jakarta, and Trans Surabaya. The results indicated that information about women's and safe women's facilities had received special attention from the public service providers but was less intensely discussed in the Twitter accounts of BRT Semarang, Trans Jakarta, and Trans Surabaya. The results of the word frequency showed that the greeting word "sis" was used more often on Twitter. They used Twitter as a medium to receive suggestions, criticisms, and complaints from the public through #continuetocleanup, which is a step to continue improving busway services to become comfortable and safe public transportation for the community.

Keywords: Social media · Gender inclusiveness · Women's facilities · Public transportation

1 Introduction

Public services are categorized as poor when they fail to accommodate the population's needs, and women are marginalized by the limited transportation services available [1]. Due to gender inclusion, women and youth have a higher probability of using public transportation than cars/private vehicles [2]. Moreover, there are more female passengers on public transportation than male passengers. Urban women, in general, are more concerned about eco-friendly mobility and use private cars less often than men unless traveling with children under 14 years old [3]. However, most systems are not

H. Krömker (Ed.): HCII 2022, LNCS 13335, pp. 547–556, 2022.
https://doi.org/10.1007/978-3-031-04987-3_37

designed for women's gender inclusion [4]. Therefore, women are vulnerable to negative experiences around bus stops and stations [4].

The problem of passenger density, traffic congestion, poor service quality, unhealthy vehicles, mobility of women, and rampant sexual harassment in public transportation arise in the transportation sector [5]. Mobility is necessary for the whole community, so the availability of public transport is vital to meet the demands or needs of the community [6]. A policy program is essential to measure its influence on gender norms, roles, and relations in the society in which they operate to respond to unexpected consequences in public transportation [7].

Transportation service problems related to poor infrastructure, low service levels, discriminatory planning policies, and public transportation that are not friendly to women create various barriers to daily travel across the city [8]. Gender inclusion women are more likely to pay attention to public transportation in terms of the convenience of the transit environment (for example, temperature, density, and security, especially at night). At the same time, men are more likely to be interested in electronic payment services, transit systems and traffic incident reporting [9].

Regarding gender differences in perceived security, women (especially younger women) feel less secure during transport interchanges [10]. However, gender and gender factors have not been considered when assessing innovative and sustainable urban mobility. Therefore, a gender-sensitive perspective is needed to increase the possibility of using sustainable modes of transportation to improve the quality of life of urban communities [3].

Previous studies explained that the gender gap in mobility still occurs. This issue also occurs in developed countries. Thus, a policy is needed that can close the gap and meet the mobility needs of women [11]. Improving information and facilities in public transportation is the most crucial thing to increase accessibility, especially for female passengers [12]. There is a need for a better sustainable transportation policy by improving women's gender inclusion services in public transportation [13]. These innovative policies must be directed at efficiency and service improvement to the community [14] because public transportation plays an essential role in the city's sustainability.

For transportation policies that are inclusive of women's gender to the community, social media is needed as a place to share information and at the same time as a place for passive community participation [15, 16]. In Indonesia, the inclusive transportation policy has been implemented in several KAI Commuter Lines, Light Rapid Transit (LRT), Mass Rapid Transit (MRT), and Bus Rapid Transit (BRT) with the availability of women-only carriages. Therefore, this study will describe how social media, especially Twitter, informs policies or programs for women's facilities available in public transportation—seeing how community participation through Twitter in informing the women's gender-inclusive program is part of passive participation. In the current era of social media, Twitter is also used as a medium to inform a public service policy.

2 Literature Review

2.1 Social Media and Public Transportation

Social media is an internet-based application built on the ideological and technological foundations of web 2.0 [17, 18]. Social media has five functions: (a) to share real-time information and consultation services with the public; (b) provide the public with information on services, tariffs, updates on ongoing and upcoming projects, and in particular service-related information; (c) engage with the people based on their feedback and sentiments through social media analysis. (d) a means to promote public transport services and increase passengers; (e) collect data from social media to advocate for organizational goals and manage them.

A transportation system responsive to public demand can be achieved using the social media approach [19] because there is an interaction between public transportation service providers and passengers [20]. Public transportation can frame its services through social media to attract people to use public transportation services [21, 22]. Thus, public transportation service providers must use a social media approach to frame services and build dialogue with the community [23].

2.2 Gender Equality and Social Inclusion

Gender equality and social inclusion (GESI) is the concept that addresses unequal power relations between women and men and between social groups that focuses on the need for action to rebalance these power relations, equal rights and respect for all individuals [24, 25]. IDPG (2017) stated that Gender Equality and Social Inclusion (GESI) is intended to address the inequality of power relations experienced by the society based on language, gender, wealth, location, wealth, or a combination of all these dimensions and focuses on the need for action to rebalance these power relations, reduce inequality and ensure equal rights, opportunities and respect for all individuals regardless of their social identity.

Some priorities must be considered regarding this diversity and equal access regardless of gender or social status. The researchers focus on women's facilities in public transportation and its relation to the concept of gender equality and social inclusion, the availability of inclusive facilities on public transportation. An effort is being made to provide equal access to women to avoid assaults while using public transportation.

3 Research Method

This study used a Qualitative Data Analysis Software (QDAS) approach to Nvivo 12 Plus. Nvivo 12 Plus is a tool used for (1) capturing data, (2) importing data, (3) coding data, (4) classifying data, (5) displaying data [25]. Nvivo's analysis process displays data in graphs and tables. An analytical model is called five steps analysis [26]. Data from social media is considered relevant for users to see how the information conveyed through Twitter is used to voice women's facilities on public transportation. Capturing data used N-Capture by selecting an account and hashtag in Table 1. The account and hashtag were chosen because they could integrate information on women's facilities on public transportation.

Table 1. Twitter accounts and description

Account	Description
@Transsemarang	This account is used to inform about BRT
@transjakarta	This account is used to inform about Trans Jakarta
@transsurabaya	This account is used to inform about Trans Surabaya

4 Results and Discussion

Public transportation is a facility provided by the government for the mobility of its people, but the place is often the target of crime, especially for women. Crimes against women in public transportation occur in Indonesia around 46.8% [27]. Crime acts that often occur in public transportation include violence, crime, sexual harassment, and rape of women. Sexual harassment that occurs in public transportation can be physical, verbal, and visual harassment.

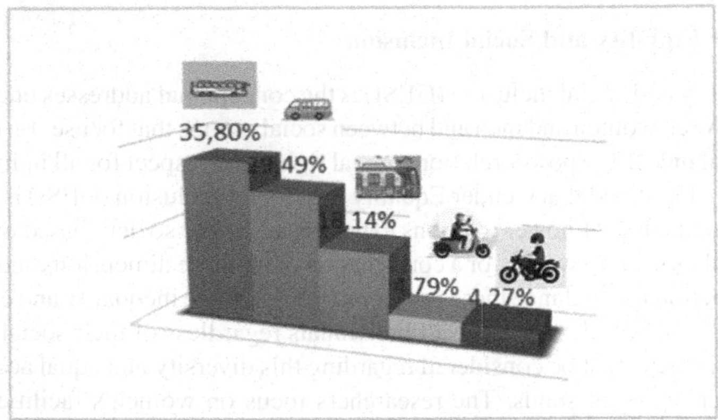

Fig. 1. Sexual harassment in public transportation. Sumber: [27]

Based on Fig. 1, more acts of sexual harassment occur on buses (35.80%). The second position with the highest incidence of sexual harassment occurs in angkot (mini-van) (29.49%), and the lowest incidence of sexual harassment occurs in conventional motorcycle taxis (4.27%). Regarding Fig. 1, the bus is the type of public transportation with the highest percentage of sexual harassment. This research focuses on women's facilities on the busway. A facility for women to facilitate their activities using public transportation and feel safe, some of the facilities provided include priority seats for women and one door specifically for women in and out of public transportation. According to a study by Asher and Lyric Fergusson, Spain is the safest country globally, including safe for women who do activities alone. When compared, the existing public transportation modes in Indonesia, judging from the results of a Reuters survey in 2014, Jakarta (Indonesia) is included in the 16 most dangerous countries, including public transportation problems that are not safe for women [28]. Indonesia, which still lacks women's facilities, especially in public transportation, must be of particular concern in providing public facilities.

Inclusive Transport Communication Model

In Indonesia, public transportation services currently use social media to communicate between transportation service providers to the public regarding all transportation access and other related information. This condition can be seen in the activity of transportation service providers in their respective social media. Updated service information will help users determine whether the state of public transportation is crowded, queues, or congestion situations [29]. BRT Semarang, Trans Jakarta, and Trans Surabaya's Twitter accounts see how intensely they tweeted on their respective accounts. Second, the researchers look at the number of activities on their separate Twitter accounts, Tweet and Retweet. Third, from the hashtags they often use on their respective Twitter accounts.

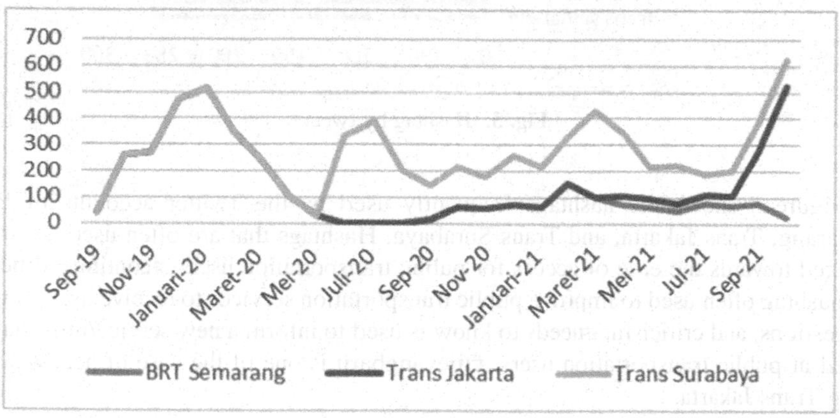

Fig. 2. Tweets by month

Figure 2 shows that the Trans Surabaya Twitter account is more active through twitter media, while the less active BRT Semarang account tweets on Twitter. The Semarang BRT account also shows that they have just joined and tweeted the youngest among Trans Jakarta and Trans Surabaya, only in March 2021. Meanwhile, the Trans Surabaya account has been using Twitter for a long time since September 2019. The researchers refer to the beginning of its operation busway, Trans Jakarta, which operated first in 2004, BRT Semarang in 2009, and Trans Surabaya only operated in 2018. However, it was Trans Surabaya who could use their Twitter account as a medium of information for their passengers.

The Trans Jakarta Twitter account tweets more often, with a total of 3249 tweets. Meanwhile, the BRT Semarang account has made 3241 tweets, and Trans Surabaya has tweeted the fewest compared to Trans Jakarta and BRT Semarang with 2821 tweets. However, the Trans Surabaya account is the only account that frequently retweets with a total of 420 retweets compared to BRT Semarang and Trans Jakarta accounts that have not retweeted. The BRT Semarang, Trans Jakarta, and Trans Surabaya accounts have a good relationship pattern with Twitter users, either through tweets, retweets, or hashtags used as direct communication media between public transportation providers and the public on Twitter.

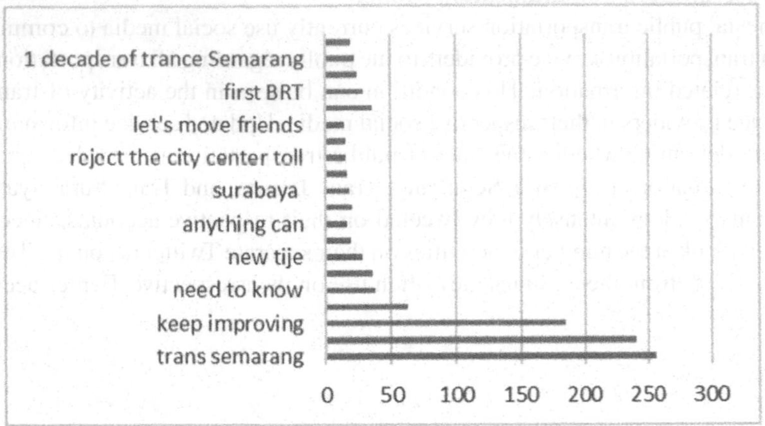

Fig. 3. Hashtag by tweet

Figure 3 shows the hashtags frequently used by the Twitter accounts of BRT Semarang, Trans Jakarta, and Trans Surabaya. Hashtags that are often used are more directed towards the ease of access for public transportation users. #continueberbenah is a hashtag often used to improve public transportation services to receive users' input, suggestions, and criticism. #needs to know is used to inform a new service/information aimed at public transportation users. #tijeyangbaru is one of the ease of access when using Trans Jakarta.

What Is the Difference in Information on Each Public Transportation Twitter Account?

This section shows that in Figs. 5, 6, 7, women's gender inclusion has become an aspect that service providers consider, both from BRT Semarang, Trans Jakarta, and Trans Surabaya accounts seen from words that are often used by the accounts of these public transportation providers, such as the mention of the phrase women's facilities and safe women in their Twitter activities.

Word frequency in Figs. 4, 5, 6 shows that information about safe women's and women's facilities has become a concern but is less intensely discussed in the Twitter accounts of BRT Semarang, Trans Jakarta, and Trans Surabaya. The results of the word frequency show that the greeting word "sis" is the one they use more often on their Twitter. Low information about women's facilities resulted in the public and busway passengers not being aware of these services. It will result in the lack of achievement of the purpose of women's facilities in public transportation.

Figure 7 shows that the Trans Surabaya Twitter account often shares information about women's facilities, women's doors, safe women, and #continue to improve. Meanwhile, Trans Jakarta's Twitter account provides the least amount of information about

Fig. 4. Word cloud BRT Semarang

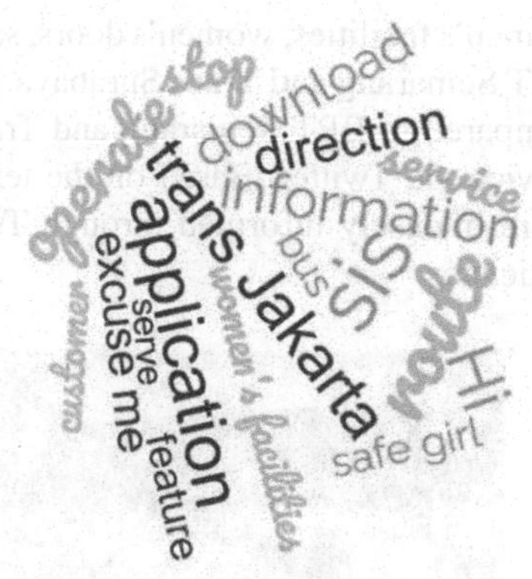

Fig. 5. Word cloud Trans Jakarta figure

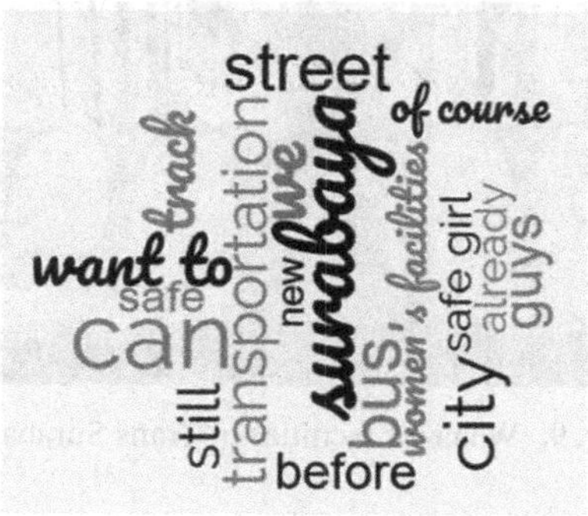

Fig. 6. Word cloud Trans Surabaya

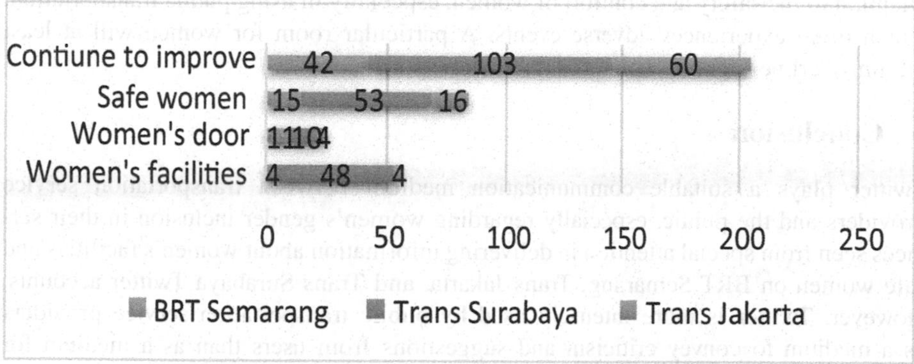

Fig. 7. Text search for woman information in public transportation

women's facilities, women's doors, safe women, and #continues to improve compared to BRT Semarang and Trans Surabaya. Even though most passengers are in Trans Jakarta, compared to BRT Semarang and Trans Surabaya, Trans Jakarta is the least informing service via Twitter. Based on the text search, Fig. 7 shows that #continueberbenah is more intensely informed through Twitter. Through Twitter, they receive suggestions, criticisms.

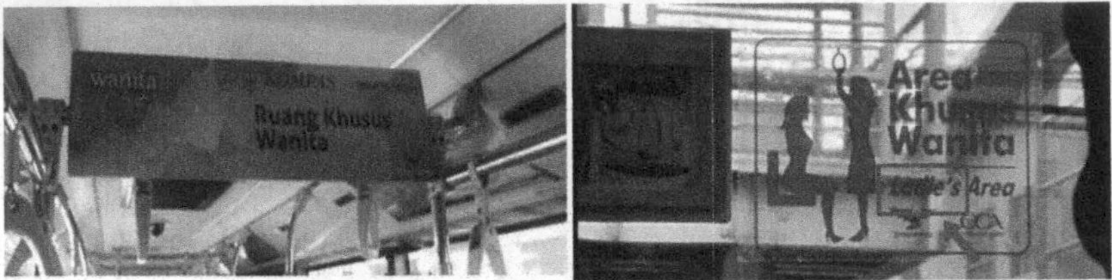

Fig. 8. Women's facilities in Trans Jakarta

Fig. 9. Women's facilities in Trans Surabaya

Figure 8 shows that Trans Jakarta already has women's facilities in the form of a women's room, as can be seen from a symbol or information board that reads "ladies area". Figure 9 shows that in Trans Surabaya, women's facilities have been provided in unique chairs for women with a pink seat symbol. So this indicates that there is special attention to the safety and comfort of women, especially in using public transportation, which often experiences adverse events. A particular room for women will at least minimize crimes against women in public transport.

5 Conclusion

Twitter plays a suitable communication medium between transportation service providers and the public, especially regarding women's gender inclusion in their services seen from special attention in delivering information about women's facilities and safe women on BRT Semarang, Trans Jakarta, and Trans Surabaya Twitter accounts. However, Twitter is more intensely used by public transportation service providers as a medium to convey criticism and suggestions from users than as a medium for women's service information. This study indicates that information on women's facilities is less intensely intensified through Twitter, but #continuetocleanp is more intensely disseminated.

References

1. Iqbal, S., Woodcock, A., Osmond, J.: The effects of gender transport poverty in Karachi. J. Transp. Geogr. **84**, 102677 (2020)
2. Harbering, M., Schlüter, J.: Determinants of transport mode choice in metropolitan areas the case of the metropolitan area of the Valley of Mexico. J. Transp. Geogr. **87**, 102766 (2020)
3. Kawgan-Kagan, I.: Are women greener than men? A preference analysis of women and men from major German cities over sustainable urban mobility. Transp. Res. Interdiscip. Perspect. **8**, 100236 (2020)
4. Chowdhury, S., van Wee, B.: Examining women's perception of safety during waiting times at public transport terminals. Transp. Policy **94**, 102–108 (2020)
5. Hoor-Ul-Ain, S.: An empirical review of Karachi's transportation predicaments: a paradox of public policy ranging from personal attitudes to public opinion in the megacity. J. Transp. Heal. **12**, 164–182 (2019)
6. Mutiarin, D., Nurmandi, A., Jovita, H., Fajar, M., Lien, Y.-N.: How do government regulations and policies respond to the growing online-enabled transportation service (OETS) in Indonesia, the Philippines, and Taiwan? Digit. Policy Regul. Gov. **21**(4), 419–437 (2019)
7. Gupta, M., et al.: Impact of a rural drowning reduction programme in Bangladesh on gender equity, norms and behaviour: a mixed-method analysis. BMJ Open **10**(12), 1–11 (2020)
8. Kerzhner, T., Kaplan, S., Silverman, E.: Physical walls, invisible barriers: palestinian women's mobility in Jerusalem. Reg. Sci. Policy Pract. **10**(4), 299–314 (2018)
9. Luo, S., He, S.Y.: Understanding gender difference in perceptions toward transit services across space and time: a social media mining approach. Transp. Policy **111**, 63–73 (2021)
10. Lois, D., Monzón, A., Hernández, S.: Analysis of satisfaction factors at urban transport interchanges: Measuring travellers' attitudes to information, security and waiting. Transp. Policy **67**, 49–56 (2018)
11. Hortelano, A.O., Grosso, M., Haq, G., Tsakalidis, A.: Women in transport research and innovation: a european perspective. Sustainability **13**(12), 6796 (2021)
12. Jayanti, R.A., Joewono, T.B., Rizki, M.: Aksesibilitas Stasiun Kereta Rel Listrik Commuter Line Berdasarkan Persepsi Wanita. J. Transp. **21**(1), 63–72 (2021)
13. Jin, H., Yu, J.: Gender responsiveness in public transit: evidence from the 2017 us national household travel survey. J. Urban Plan. Dev. **147**(3), 04021021 (2021)
14. Nurmandi, A.: Inovasi Organisasi Publik: Implementasi Knowledge Management mendorong Inovasi. J. Kebijak. dan Adm. Publik **10**(2), 133–148 (2015)
15. Charalabidis, Y., Loukis, E.N., Androutsopoulou, A., Karkaletsis, V., Triantafillou, A.: Passive crowdsourcing in government using social media. Transform. Gov. People Process Policy **8**(2), 283–308 (2014)
16. Loilatu, M.J., Irawan, B., Salahudin, S., Sihidi, I.T.: Analysis of twitter's function as a media communication of public transportation. J. Komun. **13**(1), 54 (2021)
17. Kaplan, A.M., Haenlein, M.: Users of the world, unite! The challenges and opportunities of Social Media. Bus. Horiz. **53**(1), 59–68 (2010)
18. Roengtam, S., Nurmandi, A., Almarez, D.N., Kholid, A.: Does social media transform city government? A case study of three ASEAN cities: Bandung, Indonesia, Iligan, Philippines and Pukhet, Thailand. Transform. Gov. People Process Policy **11**(3), 343–376 (2017)
19. Ni, M., He, Q., Gao, J.: Forecasting the subway passenger flow under event occurrences with social media. IEEE Trans. Intell. Transp. Syst. **18**(6), 1623–1632 (2016)
20. Cottrill, C., Gault, P., Yeboah, G., Nelson, J.D., Anable, J., Budd, T.: Tweeting transit: an examination of social media strategies for transport information management during a large event. Transp. Res. Part C Emerg. Technol. **77**, 421–432 (2017)

21. Das, S., Trisha, N.F., Sener, I.N., Walk, M.: Uses of Social Media in Public Transportation. Texas A&M Transportation Institute Texas A&M Univ. Syst. Coll. Station. Texas (2021)
22. Nisar, T.M., Prabhakar, G.: Trains and twitter: firm generated content, consumer relationship management and message framing. Transp. Res. Part A Policy Pract. **113**, 318–334 (2018)
23. Arwanto, A.: Public participation, transparency- the utilisation of social media Bandung City. J. Stud. Pemerintah. **9**(1), 1–26 (2018)
24. Bagale, S.: Gender equality and social inclusion in technical and vocational education and training. J. Train. Dev. **2**, 25–32 (2016)
25. Budhathoki, P., Sapkota, B., Maharjan, R., Bista, S., Gosain, A.: Empowerment of diversity in the Nepalese corporate sector. Quest J. Manag. Soc. Sci. **1**(1), 96–118 (2019)
26. Brandao, C.: P. Bazeley and K. Jackson, qualitative data analysis with NVivo (2nd ed.). Qual. Res. Psychol. **12**(4), 492–494 (2015)
27. KRPA: Survei Pelecehan Seksual di Ruang Publik, Indonesia (2019)
28. BBC Indonesia: 100 Women: Apakah moda transportasi khusus perempuan kurangi pelecehan? BBC News Indonesia, Indonesia (2017)
29. Purnomo, E.P., et al.: How public transportation use social media platform during covid-19: study on Jakarta public transportations' twitter accounts? Webology **18**(1), 1–19 (2021)

Robust Linear Regression-Based GIS Technique for Modeling the Processing Time at Tourism Destinations

Ali Mahdi(✉) and Domokos Esztergár-Kiss

Department of Transport Technology and Economics, Budapest University of Technology and Economics, Műegyetem rkp. 3., Budapest 1111, Hungary
alijamalmahdi@edu.bme.hu

Abstract. Tourist attractions are dispersed across wide geographic areas even within the cities making the data collection prohibitively expensive. For these reasons, information on tourism destinations should be collected automatically. Recently, the collection of particular data on destinations has become easier with the growing popularity of location-based applications. Based on Google Popular Time (GPT), behavioral data are collected to investigate the actual tourist behavior. The statistical analysis clearly shows the presence of outliers in the collected data. Consequently, a regression model based robust approach is used to study the tourists' processing time (i.e., the time spent) at various tourism destinations in Budapest. Such spatial parameters are adopted as car parking, public transport station, and location. The statistical outcomes present that the availability of car parking or public transport stations significantly affects the tourists' processing time at the tourism destinations. The findings demonstrate the benefit of using GPT and other online resources to analyze and predict individual behavior. Furthermore, current study reveals that location-based services provide a principal option for tourists during their journeys.

Keywords: GPT · GIS · Behavioral data · Robust regression · Tourism · Processing time

1 Introduction

Tourism is defined as tourists traveling for leisure purposes and staying outside their usual environment for a period of time that does not exceed one year. Tourism industry includes entertainment destinations (e.g., recreation, culture, or sport activities), food establishments (e.g., restaurants, cafes, and taverns), lodging (e.g., hotels, motels, and campgrounds), transportation (e.g., airplane, rail, bus, or car), shopping facilities, and several other facilities (Theobald 2013). Visitors devote 24 hours of the day to various activities based on their limits and preferences. The choices regarding the processing time or the time spent determine the individual activity patterns (Arentze and Timmermans 2004). The travelers' expected preferences are usually indicated by ratings assigned to products or services, which reflect how much the tourists like them. Visitors must balance

H. Krömker (Ed.): HCII 2022, LNCS 13335, pp. 557–569, 2022.
https://doi.org/10.1007/978-3-031-04987-3_38

their interests in the destinations with other factors (Ashiru et al. 2004). The decision on visiting a tourism destination is a complex issue because of the variety of alternatives and the influencing factors (Mahdi and Esztergár-Kiss 2021). The variables connected to the visitors, the geographical features of destinations, and the trip circumstances are identified as three key categories that make an impact on visiting the tourism destinations (Mahdi and Esztergár-Kiss 2020).

Despite the prevalence of the location-based services (LBS) in the tourism sector and the benefits they provide to visitors, an inadequate number of studies is conducted on the spatial factors that influence the tourists' behavioral intentions. LBS can detect the individuals' locations and provide tourists with relevant information and services based on their physical location. Approximately 74% of adults owning smartphones have already used LBS to get directions or other information (Zhou 2017). Tourists are eager to obtain relevant information which solves their travel problems because the destinations are unfamiliar environments to them (Hur et al. 2017). Based on the LBS data, (Freytag 2007) reveals that tourists in Heidelberg have a particularly concentrated spatial behavior with the majority visiting the old town and some places garnering solely little attention. In the same vein, (Hwang et al. 2006) studied the spatial activities of international tourists in US cities and they demonstrated that route patterns have significant implications on destination aggregation. Another study by Modsching et al. (2008) proposes a method for tracking and analyzing the tourists' spatial behavior based on the LBS data. This method can visualize the display and analysis of the tourists' activity areas serving as examples for subsequent activity area identification. Additionally, (Larson et al. 2005) use radio frequency identification (RFID) tags on customers' shopping carts to track their movements in a supermarket. The method works by storing and retrieving data via RFID transponders. The monitored journeys are grouped together to determine typical grocery store routes.

Mobile phone data are identified as possible sources of information due to the large amount of datasets provided (Grantz et al. 2020). Location-based applications are becoming more and more popular as smartphones with GPS are more prevalent (Choi et al. 2015). Google Popular Times (GPT) is the most widely used application as a source of collecting vast amount of information in large geographical areas (Kaosiri et al. 2019). According to GPT (2021), GPT gives information on previous visits as well as the current amount of visits in a given area. It may be feasible to observe and forecast individuals' behavior based on the collected data from GPT (Holland and Mandry 2013). However, rarely can be found studies on GPT by other researchers in the transportation and tourism sectors. Based on the collected data from GPT, Mahajan et al. (2021) investigate activity and demand patterns at different destinations in Munich during the Covid-19 pandemic. The study reveals that transportation characteristics, such as the parking space and public transport (PT) stop distance, have an impact on the number of desertions by visitors. In the same city, Möhring et al. (2020) utilize GPT to investigate real tourists' behavior. Bivariate linear regression and correlation analysis are used by the researchers. The quantity of submitted images and Google scores are found to be connected to an estimate of tourist numbers in the study area.

Previous studies recognize that time plays an important role in people's behavior, decisions, and activity patterns (Kitamura 1990; Ashiru et al. 2004). Individuals allocate time to different activities based on constraints and preferences (Arentze and Timmermans 2004). Processing time is viewed as an entity where individuals make decisions on each activity, and leads to the concept of the activity-based model (Esztergár-Kiss 2020). In activity-based travel behavior analysis, it is hypothesized that travel demand is formed from the motivation to participate in activities, and that knowledge about activity participation should be used to understand travel behavior (Zhicai and Xianyu 2010). The activity-based model is the primary foundation of the time allocation decision, and it is the most appropriate to replicate the travelers' decisions (Castiglione and Bradley 2015; Pendyala and Goulias 2002). However, merely a few studies explore the correlation between activity timing and the quantity of time allotted to it. Zong et al. (2013) develop a model for assessing commuters' daily activity and travel patterns. The ordered probit model is applied to forecast the journey time and the activity duration. Similarly, Bowman and Ben-Akiva (2001) use the multinomial logit model to forecast people's daily travel departure timings. Another study by Zhicai and Xianyu (2010) applies the hazard model to estimate the daily journey time. The researchers investigate the relationships between the daily trip duration, the travelers' socio-demographic parameters, and the activity and travel characteristics.

Most of the studies focus on the travelers' socio-demographic variables (e.g., age, sex, education, marital status, and income) or on the trip circumstances, such as travel time, travel cost, and transport mode. However, current study pays more attention to the spatial factors surrounding the tourism destinations. Furthermore, using the traditional approaches for collecting the relevant data, which requires cost and time, is avoided. In this study, we use an up to date approach for collecting the relevant information instead of using the traditional method.

2 Methodology

Due to lifting the lockdown restrictions in the study area, a developed Python code by Mahajan et al. (2021) is run for 24 h a day and seven days a week to collect tourism destination information and behavioral data form Google. A sample of 1346 tourism destinations in Budapest were collected in July, 2021, which is the peak tourism season of the city (Pinke-Sziva et al. 2019). The collected data include the names of the destinations, the coordinates (i.e., longitude and latitude), the types of the destinations, and the processing time at the destinations. GIS-based destination coordinates are used to obtain such spatial parameters as car parking availability, PT stations, and location parameters. According to Gasco and Gattiglio (2011), most transit agencies use a 400 m walking distance as comfortable and applicable distance. As a result, the availability of car parking and public transport stations is divided into three categories: high, medium, and low (based on the comfortable walking distance). Buffer analysis within the GIS technique is used for this purpose. A 400 m or less buffer is applied to indicate the destinations high class, while 400–600 m distance refers to the medium class. The low class represents the destinations with more than 600 m to reach car parking or public transport stations. It is worth mentioning that the location factor is obtained based on the spatial categorization analysis of GIS. This factor has three classes according to the distance from the CBD of Budapest: good location (i.e., within the CBD), medium location (i.e., 400–800 m distance from the CBD), and low location (i.e., more than 800 m away from the CBD).

After collecting and preparing the relevant database, a multiple linear regression is applied to model the processing time. The goal of the linear regression analysis is to determine how a dependent variable is linearly related to a set of regressors. The linear regression model is represented as follows (Uyanık and Güler 2013):

$$Y_i = \alpha + \beta_1 X_1 + \ldots\ldots\ldots \beta_p X_p \tag{1}$$

where Y_i is the vector including the values of the predicated variable, and X_i represents the vector of the explanatory variables, α is the intercept, and β_i refers to those unidentified regression coefficients that should be determined. It is possible to fit the dependent variable by using the estimated parameter $\hat{Y}$ and to calculate the residuals $\hat{R}$, as shown in the following equation:

$$\left.\begin{array}{c} \hat{Y} = X\hat{\beta} \\ \hat{R} = Y_i - \hat{Y}_i \\ \text{for } 1 \leq \text{i} \leq \text{n}. \end{array}\right\} \tag{2}$$

The ordinary least-squares (OLS) method is one of the most used methods for predicting the values of β_i. This method, which is particularly sensitive to the outliers, is applied to estimate the parameters by minimizing the sum of the squared residuals (Khan et al. 2021). Three types of outliers affect the OLS estimation in linear regression (Fig. 1). Vertical outliers, bad leverage points, and good leverage points are the terms used to describe the three types of outliers (Rousseeuw and Leroy 2005). The vertical outliers are observations with outlying values on the Y-axis but no outlying values in the independent variable (X-axis). The vertical outlier affects the OLS estimation, specifically the predicted intercept. The good leverage points can be represented by the observations outlying in the domain of the independent variable and near the regression line. They have no effect on the regression analysis, but they have an impact on the statistical inference since they reduce the predicted standard errors. The bad leverage points are data outlying in the space of the independent range and far from the regression line. Both the intercept and the slope are considerably influenced if the bad leverage outliers are found in the OLS estimation. In fact, the statistical analysis demonstrates the presence of outliers in the collected data. Consequently, the robust regression approach is used instead of OLS to predicate the processing time. In other words, the robust regression is used, which is not affected by the outliers (Rousseeuw and Leroy 2005).

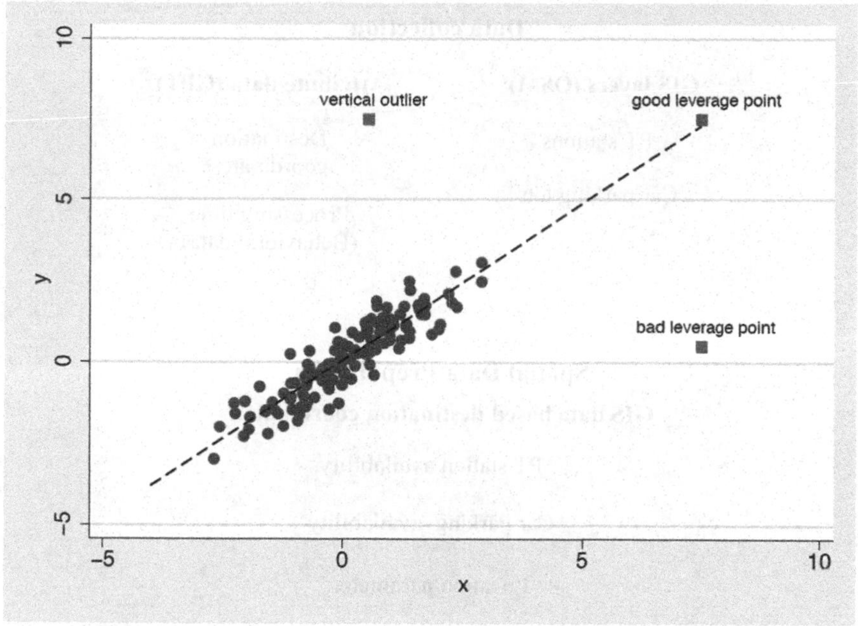

Fig. 1. The expected outliers in the linear regression estimation (Verardi and Croux 2009)

The outcomes are obtained by conducting a linear regression analysis based-robust approach to determine whether the independent spatial variables in the robust approach predict the processing time at the tourism destinations (Yu and Yao 2017).

$$\hat{\beta}_{OLS} = argmin_{\beta} \sum_{i=1}^{n} R_i^2(\beta) \tag{3}$$

where $R_i(\beta) = Y_i - \beta_\circ - \beta_1 X_{i1} - \ldots\ldots\ldots \beta_p X_{ip}$ for $1 \leq i \leq n$. Figure 2 depicts the proposed general flow chart for a better understanding of the calculating approach of the processing time at the tourism destinations at tourism destinations in Budapest city.

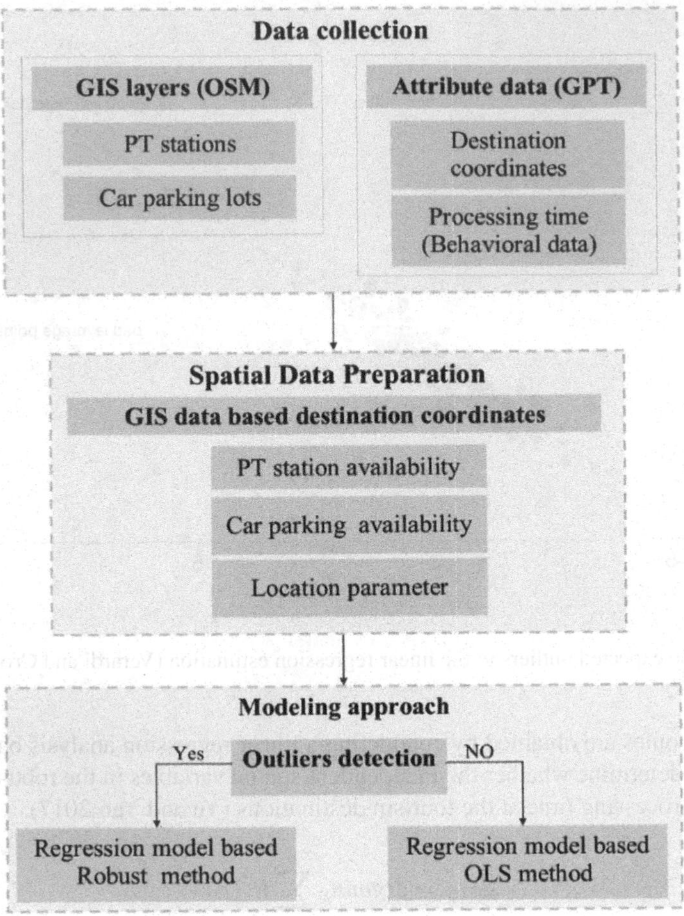

Fig. 2. The methodological approach

3 Results and Discussion

Budapest is chosen as the location of the case study to analyze the behavioral data at tourism destinations. Generally, Budapest plays a significant role in Hungary's tourist industry: almost every third guest night is recorded in the capital, and the city generates approximately three-quarters of the country's foreign tourism revenues (Ratz et al. 2008). Budapest is organized into 23 districts (Fig. 3) with distinct economic, social, and cultural characteristics. The city is located on both banks of the River Danube (Smith et al. 2019). The city's tourism industry, attractions, services, and facilities are generally concentrated in the city center and in the inner-urban residential quarters (Kovács and Wiessner 2004).

Fig. 3. Spatial distribution of tourism destinations in the study area

The spatial parameters are prepared by using GIS techniques. The results of the spatial analysis are illustrated in the following figures. Figure 4 shows the analysis area divided into three primary sections to indicate the location parameter. The distance from the city center determines the three primary groups for the location variable: the inner region, the inner-suburbs, and the outer-suburbs region.

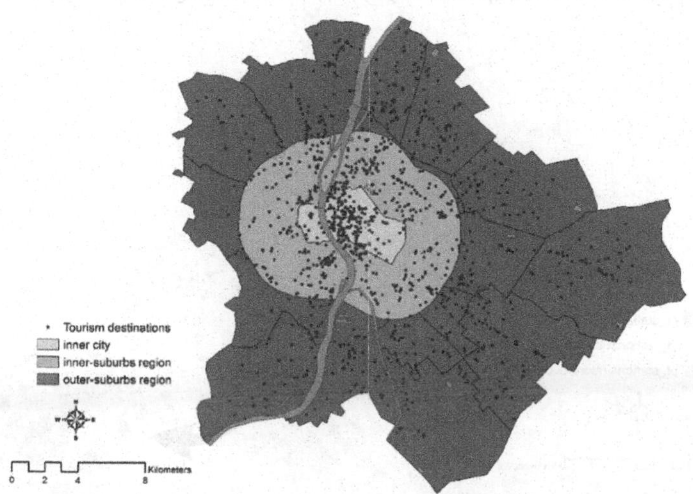

Fig. 4. The location parameter and spatial distribution of tourism destinations

Although the study focuses solely on off-street parking, the availability of parking areas around the majority of tourism destinations is noticeable from the results of the geographical analysis (Fig. 5). Furthermore, PT stations are well-distributed throughout the research region, and most tourism destinations are within 600 m of a PT station. As an illustrative instance, in Fig. 6, the destinations in the yellow region acquire the maximum value (3) indicating that the individual walk fewer than 400 m to reach the destination. Meanwhile, the medium and low values are assigned to the destinations identified in the grey and green zones, respectively.

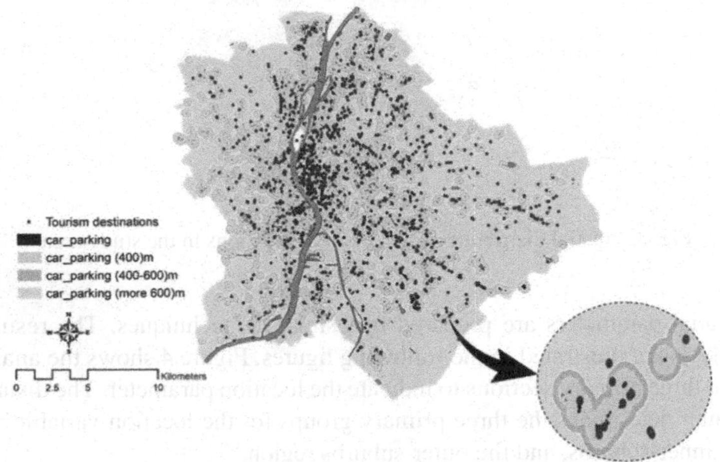

Fig. 5. The results of the spatial analysis for the car parking availability parameter

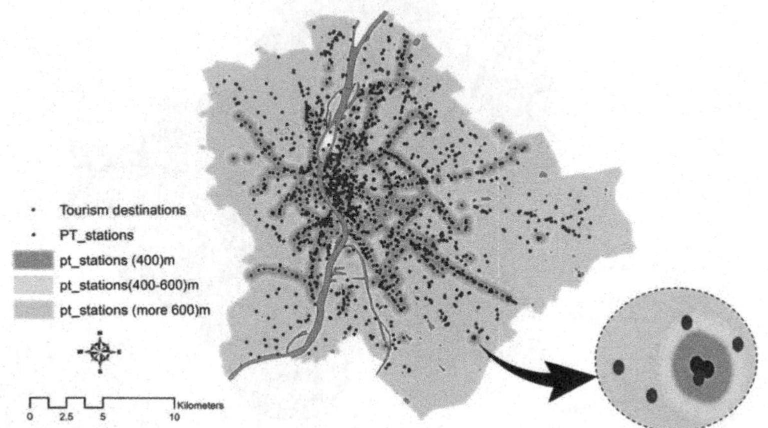

Fig. 6. The results of the spatial analysis for the PT stations availability parameter

In order to model the tourists' behavioral data at tourism destinations, the outlier detection step is conducted. Based on the outcomes of the statistical analysis, the outliers are observed in the collected data. The outliers have an impact on the classical regression (i.e., the OLS method); hence, using outlier-insensitive techniques is essential. As a result, full robustness can be achieved by approaching the regression problem from a different viewpoint. Generally, two approaches are employed to address this issue: the diagnostic approach and the robust procedure. The diagnostic approaches use diagnostic statistics to discover the odd observations and to remove them from the data. Afterward, traditional procedures, such as OLS, can be applied to clean the dataset. In fact, the diagnostic approach is not valid in current case due to the extremely large values in the response variable, as shown in Fig. 7. This method is effective in case of simple data or if there are solely one or two outliers. On the other hand, the method is inefficient in case of complicated datasets with a large number of outliers (Garcia 2010).

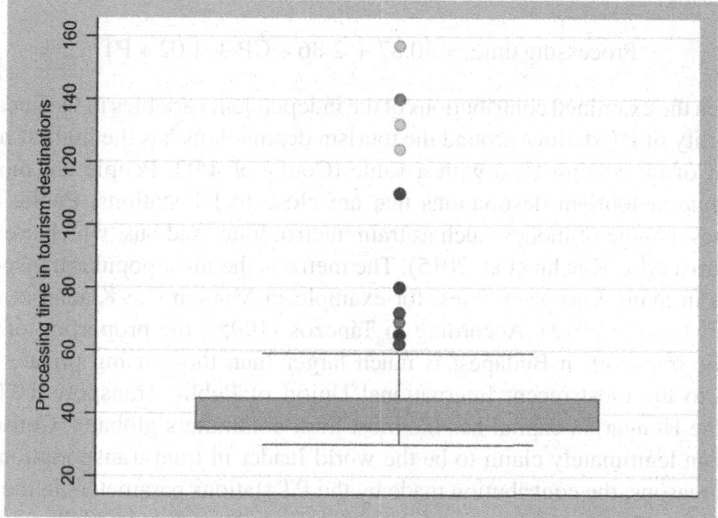

Fig. 7. Boxplot indicating the outliers of the processing time

The opacity degree of the red circle markers in Fig. 7 refers to the concentrated number of outliers, where about 10% of the database involve outliers. Accordingly, to predict the processing time, the robust regression method is adopted instead of using OLS. The statistical outcomes by applying Eq. (1) based robust approach Eq. (3) clearly shows (Table 1) that the availability of car parking or public transport stations significantly predicts the processing time at tourism destinations, where the p-values equal 0. On the other hand, the location parameter is not significant. It is worth mentioning that the degree to which the model explains variance in the dependent variable R2 is 0.712. Based on these results, it is possible to conclude that the model accurately predicts the processing time at a tourism destination.

Table 1. The robust linear regression analysis related to the processing time at a tourism destination.

Parameters	Abbreviation	Coefficient	Std. error	t-test	p-value
Car-parking	CP	2.86	0.16	18.16	0
Public transport stations	PT	4.02	0.13	30.75	0
Location	LO	0.19	0.18	1.06	0.23
Constant	–	30.87	0.33	93.44	0

R-squared: 0.712
Adjusted R-squared 0.711

According to the outcomes of the regression analysis, the developed regression model is the following:

$$\text{Processing time} = 30.87 + 2.86 * \text{CP} + 4.02 * \text{PT} \tag{4}$$

Based on the examined contributions of the independent variables in the linear model, the availability of PT stations around the tourism destinations has the highest impact on the amount of processing time with a value (Coef.) of 4.02. People are more likely to spend time at tourism destinations that are close to PT stations. Public transport encompasses a range of modes, such as train, metro, tram, and bus, which are the most used by tourists (Le-Klaehn et al. 2015). The metro is the most popular transport mode for tourists in many European cities, for example in Munich (Le-Klaehn et al. 2014) and in Paris (Simon 2012). According to Tánczos (1995), the proportion of travelers using public transport in Budapest is much larger than those using private vehicles. According to the most recent International Union of Public Transport (UITP 2022) statistics, the Hungarian capital has the most tram commuters globally. Consequently, Budapest can legitimately claim to be the world leader in tram transportation. For the mentioned reasons, the contribution made by the PT stations parameters in the model is more significant than car parking availability. The intersect value is 30.78, which refers to the value of the dependent variable when the independent variables equal 0. However, in current research, the explanatory variables cannot take the value 0 because if a tourism destination is located in the worst conditions (i.e., away from car parking or PT stations), the explanatory variables are 2.86 and 4.02. Nevertheless, the intersect value confirms the reasonability and reliability of the developed model, where the processing time of more than half of the collected database ranges between 30 to 35.

4 Conclusion

The tourists' actual behavior is extracted from GPT. Python code is run for 24 h a day and seven days a week to collect tourism destination data and behavioral data from GPT in the peak season of Budapest. The tourists' behavior is expressed by the processing time at various tourism destinations. The statistical analysis detected the existence of outliers extensively in the collected data. Therefore, a robust linear regression model is applied in this study to examine the effect of the built environment parameters on the tourists' processing time. The environment parameters are represented by such spatial parameters as the location, the availability of car parking spaces, and the availability of PT stations around the tourism destinations. GIS-based destination coordinates are applied to develop these spatial parameters. Various points related to the processing time are emphasized based on the statistical findings. All factors are significant in the regression model, except for the location, which has large p-values (more than 0.05). The degree to which the model predicts variance in the dependent variable is 0.712. Based on the statistical findings, it can be stated that the model accurately predicts the dependent variable.

In conclusion, the findings provide evidence on the importance of the built environment parameters in travel behavior. It is found that the availability of PT stations around the tourism destinations has the highest impact on the processing time with the value of 4.02. The outcomes show the value of using GPT and other web resources to assess and anticipate individual behavior. The main contribution of this article is to analyze the spatial parameters and the tourists' behavior in Budapest. A similar study determining the processing time at the destinations while considering more variables and a larger sample is recommended to be conducted.

Acknowledgments. The linguistic revision of this article is prepared by Eszter Tóth.

Funding. This research was supported by the János Bolyai Research Fellowship of the Hungarian Academy of Sciences (BO/00090/21/6).

Conflict of Interest. The authors declare no conflict of interest.

References

Arentze, T.A., Timmermans, H.J.P.: A learning-based transportation oriented simulation system. Transp. Res. Part B: Methodol. **38**(7), 613–633 (2004)

Ashiru, O., Polak, J.W., Noland, R.B.: Utility of schedules: theoretical model of departure-time choice and activity-time allocation with application to individual activity schedules. Transp. Res. Rec. **1894**(1), 84–98 (2004)

Bowman, J.L., Ben-Akiva, M.E.: Activity-based disaggregate travel demand model system with activity schedules. Transp. Res. Part a: Policy Pract. **35**(1), 1–28 (2001)

Castiglione, J., Bradley, M., Gliebe, J.: Activity-Based Travel Demand Models: A Primer (2015)

Choi, S.J., Park, S.-B., Kim, K.-Y.: Estimating category of POIs using contextual information. Indian J. Sci. Technol. **8**(S7), 718–723 (2015)

Esztergár-Kiss, D.: Trip chaining model with classification and optimization parameters. Sustainability **12**(16), 6422 (2020)

Freytag, T.: Städtetourismus in Europäischen Grossstädten: Eine Hierarchie Der Standorte Und Aktuelle Entwicklungen Der Übernachtungszahlen. DisP Plan. Rev. **43**(169), 56–67 (2007)

Garcia, D.: Robust smoothing of gridded data in one and higher dimensions with missing values. Comput. Stat. Data Anal. **54**(4), 1167–1178 (2010)

Gasco, I., Gattiglio, M.: Geological map of the middle Orco valley, Western Italian alps. J. Maps **7**(1), 463–477 (2011)

GPT. 2021. Popular Times, Wait Times, and Visit Duration (2021). https://support.google.com/business/answer/6263531h?hl=en

Grantz, K.H., et al.: The use of mobile phone data to inform analysis of COVID-19 pandemic epidemiology. Nat. Commun. **11**(1), 1–8 (2020)

Holland, C.P., Mandry, G.D.: Online search and buying behaviour in consumer markets. In: 2013 46th Hawaii International Conference on System Sciences, pp. 2918–2927. IEEE (2013)

Hur, K., Kim, T.T., Karatepe, O.M., Lee, G.: An exploration of the factors influencing social media continuance usage and information sharing intentions among Korean travellers. Tour. Manag. **63**, 170–178 (2017)

Hwang, Y.-H., et al.: Multicity trip patterns: tourists to the United States. Ann. Tour. Res. **33**(4), 1057–1078 (2006). Elsevier

Khan, D.M., et al.: Applications of robust regression techniques: an econometric approach. Math. Probl. Eng. **2021** (2021). Hindawi. https://doi.org/10.1155/2021/6525079

Kitamura, R.: Trip chaining behavior by central city commuters: a causal analysis of time-space constraints. In: Developments in Dynamic and Activity-Based Approaches to Travel Analysis (1990)

Kovács, Z., Wiessner, R.: Budapest: restructuring a European metropolis. Europa Reg. **12**(1) 22–31, (2004). DEU

Larson, J.S., Bradlow, E.T., Fader, P.S.: An exploratory look at supermarket shopping paths. Int. J. Res. Mark. **22**(4), 395–414 (2005)

Le-Klaehn, D.-T., Gerike, R., Hall, C.M.: Visitor users vs. non-users of public transport: the case of Munich, Germany. J. Dest. Mark. Manag. **3**(3), 152–161 (2014)

Le-Klaehn, D.-T., Hall, C.M.: Tourist use of public transport at destinations–a review. Curr. Issues Tour. **18**(8), 785–803 (2015)

Mahajan, V., Cantelmo, G., Antoniou, C.: Explaining demand patterns during COVID-19 using opportunistic data: a case study of the city of Munich. Eur. Transp. Res. Rev. **13**(1), 1–14 (2021)

Mahdi, A., Esztergár-Kiss, D.: Modelling the accommodation preferences of tourists by combining fuzzy-AHP and GIS Methods. J. Adv. Transp. **2021**, 16 (2021). Hindawi. https://doi.org/10.1155/2021/9913513

Mahdi, A.J., Esztergár-Kiss, D.: Variables Associated with the Tourists' Activity Chain: Definition, Grouping, and Measurement Approaches (2020)

Modsching, M., Kramer, R., Ten Hagen, K., Gretzel, U.: Using location-based tracking data to analyze the movements of city tourists. Inf. Technol. Tour. **10**(1), 31–42 (2008)

Möhring, M., Keller, B., Schmidt, R., Dacko, S.: Google popular times: towards a better understanding of tourist customer patronage behavior. Tour. Rev. (2020). https://doi.org/10.1108/TR-10-2018-0152

Kaosiri, N., Yeamduan, L.J., Fiol, C., Tena, M.A.M., Artola, R.M.R., Garcia, J.S.: User-generated content sources in social media: a new approach to explore tourist satisfaction. J. Travel Res. **58**(2), 253–265 (2019)

Pendyala, R.M., Goulias, K.G.: Time use and activity perspectives in travel behavior research. Transportation **29**(1), 1–4 (2002)

Pinke-Sziva, I., Smith, M., Olt, G., Berezvai, Z.: Overtourism and the night-time economy: a case study of budapest. Int. J. Tour. Cities **5**(1), 1–16 (2019). https://doi.org/10.1108/IJTC-04-2018-0028

Rátz, T., et al.: New places in old spaces: mapping tourism and regeneration in budapest. Tourism Geographies **10**(4), 429–51 (2008). Taylor & Francis. https://doi.org/10.1080/14616680802434064

Rousseeuw, P.J., Leroy, A.M.: Robust Regression and Outlier Detection, vol. 589. Wiley, Hoboken (2005)

Smith, M.K., et al.: Overtourism and resident resistance in budapest. Tourism Plann. Dev. **16**(4), 376–92 (2019). Taylor & Francis. https://doi.org/10.1080/21568316.2019.1595705

Simon, G.: Walking and the underground train: study of intra-urban movement of tourists under the prism of the 'adherence.' RTS-Recherche Transports Securite **28**(1), 25 (2012)

Tánczos, K.: Organising and financing urban public transport in budapest. Sustainable Transport IN Central AND Eastern European Cities, p. 309 (1995)

Theobald, W.F.: Global Tourism. Global Tourism. Routledge (2013). https://doi.org/10.4324/9780080507446

UITP: The International Association of Public Transport. Budapest, Hungary (2022). https://www.uitp.org/

Uyanık, G.K., Güler, N.: A Study on multiple linear regression analysis. Procedia Soc. Behav. Sci. **106**, 234–240 (2013)

Verardi, V., Croux, C.: Robust regression in stata. Stand. Genomic Sci. **9**(3), 439–453 (2009)

Yu, C., Yao, W.: Robust linear regression: a review and comparison. Commun. Stat.-Simul. Comput. **46**(8), 6261–6282 (2017)

Zhicai, J., Xianyu, J.: Daily travel time analysis with duration model. J. Transp. Syst. Eng. Inf. Technol. **10**(4), 62–67 (2010)

Zhou, T.: Understanding location-based services users' privacy concern: an elaboration likelihood model perspective. Internet Res. **27**(3), 506–519 (2017)

Zong, F., Hongfei, J., Xiang, P., Yang, W.: Prediction of commuter's daily time allocation. PROMET-Traffic&Trans. **25**(5), 445–455 (2013)

Enabling Knowledge Extraction on Bike Sharing Systems Throughout Open Data

Francisco J. Marquez-Saldaña[1(✉)], Gonzalo A. Aranda-Corral[2], and Joaquín Borrego-Díaz[1]

[1] Departamento de Ciencias de la Computación e Inteligencia Artificial, E.T.S. Ingeniería Informática – Universidad de Sevilla Avda. Reina Mercedes s.n., 41013 Sevilla, Spain
{framisal,jborrego}@us.es

[2] Departamento de Tecnologías de la Información, Universidad de Huelva, Crta. Palos de La Frontera s.n., 21819 Palos de La Frontera, Spain
gonzalo.aranda@dti.uhu.es

Abstract. Bike Sharing Systems (BSS) have changed urban mobility patterns. Their study as part of the overall transport system in cities is attracting growing attention in recent years. Nevertheless, some deficiencies such as the lack of convention in data serving tools and the absence of historical information difficult the analysis and improvement of realistic BSS digital platforms. Additionally, other challenges related to the Big Data nature of the analysis, have hindered an integral data analysis. This paper outlines solutions for both problems, based on a sound addressing for the Big Data Extraction-Transformation-Loading (ETL) problem of storing historical BSS data. In particular, consumption tools have been provided. They not only allow handling recorded information but also allow enhancing BSS knowledge. This way the overall system can manage other relevant information (KPIs and statistics in nature). The Big Data-inspired solution proposed in this paper solves this kind of issue, showing how it can manage more data collected during a period of about six years and from twenty-seven systems. Such data have been stored and enabled for both machine-machine communication and Human-Computer Interaction.

Keywords: Data acquisition · Big data in mobility · Bike sharing platforms · ETL

1 Introduction

Bike Sharing Systems (BSS) represent a driving force for transforming people's urban mobility behavior in the last years. From their observation, data analysis and the study of the effect of decision-making process become necessary

Supported by *Agencia Estatal de Investigación* project PID2019-109152GB-I00/AEI/10.13039/501100011033 and FEDER 2014-2020, Junta de Andalucía and Universidad de Huelva, project UHU-1266216.

H. Krömker (Ed.): HCII 2022, LNCS 13335, pp. 570–585, 2022.
https://doi.org/10.1007/978-3-031-04987-3_39

for understanding its role in city mobility. This need is key in the *smart cities* projects. Due to its interest, multiple approaches -to address different problems and challenges- for information management and exploitation exist: modeling network growing [15] solving optimization issues [7] supporting strategic decisions [13], multiagent modeling [4,14], and prediction [9], among others.

The analysis of data from BSS can also serve to estimate how this type of service can help to reduce the carbon footprint associated with urban mobility. Therefore, it is a necessary challenge for the analysis of smart city projects [10].

1.1 ETL and (Big) Data Issues

In contrast to projects which are focused on a particular city (e.g. [9]), to study and compare the global nature of phenomena, it would be necessary to tackle the problem of *Variety* and *Volume* that data from BSS systems (e.g. based on docks versus dockless [8]) represents [1].

The number of BSS has significantly increased in the last decade, each of them with its particular data structure, definition, business model, and operating methodology. Data variety comes from the lack of convention (and standardization practices) between the organizations responsible for the systems. Thus, researchers do not only have difficulties in analyzing a specific system but also to compare them. In addition, existing APIs just provide information about BSS or station current status. That historical data absence brings the necessity of a unified and historical Bike Sharing System data repository. Despite efforts focused on Data Interoperability (mainly by the Open Data community [6]), commercial nature of municipal concessions does not encourage these practices.

Therefore, the first aim towards a global analysis (from the Big Data realm) focuses on unifying, storing, and serving historical data about BSS. That is the required Extraction-Transformation-Loading (ETL) phase for Data Science Projects. Another goal would be to provide information for supporting several applications (ranging from information apps for smartphones to machine learning systems for prediction and diagnosis dashboards). In particular, this type of ETL can provide new windows of information for the so-called smart city control rooms [11].

1.2 Aim and Structure of the Work

This work aims to describe a system that supplies the aforementioned needs. Currently, it covers twenty-seven BSS around the world. The solution is also able to store extra related data, such as weather records and metrics (commonly used when analyzing user behavior). In addition, it is presented a general concept of station status with available bikes to rent, remaining docks to return a bike, and the overall capacity of the stations, including the two just mentioned and not working stands (relevant for health and state analysis). All of them are under Open Data Common Attribution (ODC-BY1) and Creative Commons (CC-BY 2.02) licenses.

The structure of the paper is detailed as follows. First section is devoted to describing the rationale behind the unified data collector as a solution to the lack of both data interoperability and historical information storage for BSS. In particular, our proposal for database schema is outlined in Sect. 2.4. Section 3 concerns the data consumption tools designed to facilitate both the machine-machine and human-machine communication. The system includes a number of System User Profiles and Uses Cases that have been described in Sect. 4. In Sect. 5 we discuss some general considerations on the system. Lastly, in Sect. 6 some conclusions on the overall work and future work are provided.

2 Unified Data Collector

Dealing with the lack of convention in BSS, the dataset provided by managers involves several aspects that must consider. Therefore, it is necessary to handle variable notation differences as well as to address the discrepancies in similar concept definition between several data storage systems (semantic heterogeneity). For instance, consider the term *available stands*. On the one hand, it may refer just to the aggregation of *available docks* and *available bikes*. On the other hand, it could include not working stands that are not recorded as "available docks" to show *Quality of Service* (QoS) measures. The absence of semantic commitment obstructs truly robust Data Science-based services.

Moreover, there have been observed diverse update time frequencies observed not only between several data access points but also through different stations of the same system. This phenomenon makes the analysis and comparison task enough, demanding to limit the number of systems to be studied at the same time (as the recorded time will not be matched from one dock to another). In addition, this problem worsens when it is necessary to include external factors such as weather variables or other traffic data in the process as it comes from a different origin with no fixed time range neither.

Furthermore, another deficiency could disable the study of the system in the medium and long term: no historical records are directly available from the original data sources. Currently, BSS information platforms only allow researchers to retrieve the current system status, requiring periodically relevant high-frequency data extraction tasks to avoid information loss. This feature increases the *Velocity* requirements of the Big Data System.

On top of that, there is an extra difficulty concerning the *Volume* of data to store that has been previously mentioned as a Big Data ETL problem. Even when saving frequency -five minutes- might not be considered as latency low, as the total number of docks in the unified collector system is about 4425 (from twenty-seven cities worldwide), from which 12 measurements are extracted per hour for six years, resulting in approximately 2.8 billion records. As a result, the designed data collector and distribution architecture is shown in Fig. 1.

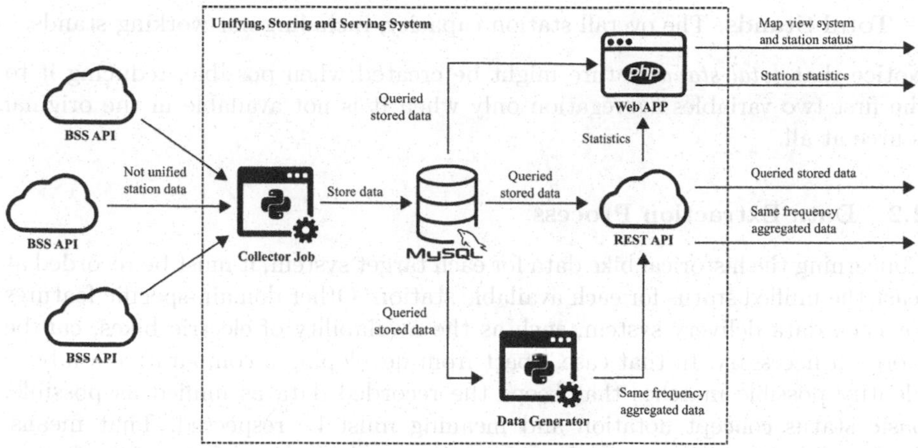

Fig. 1. Full system functional diagram

2.1 Unified Station Status Concept

It has been addressed the aforementioned syntactic and semantic heterogeneity among manager information delivery systems. It has been designed a specification for station information aiming to simplify its status representation at a certain time. It just includes just those fields that describe all relevant information for knowing the overall station evolution through time. This way, it facilitates system integration and interoperability of different data assets. To achieve this goal has been analyzed data delivery solutions from several system owners such as JCDCaux[1].

It has been found two concepts that are widely used by all available information systems studied. Additionally, they do not have any meaning discrepancies: the number of available docks to return a bike, and the total bikes ready to rent at a certain time. Despite those features could report the whole bike movement history of the station, they can not describe other features, such as broken stands. This information could be useful for future Quality of Service analyses (driven by the total capacity station including not working stands). Unfortunately, depending on the system, that field may not include this information cause, it just represents the aggregation of the first two features, is included in a different variable, or even is not available, representing one of the main difficulties to achieve the unified status. It is handled in the extraction process by including the domain knowledge of target systems.

As a result of the previous analysis, the station status, at a certain time, will be specified by the following triple:

- **Available Docks**. As the number of empty stands for returning a bike.
- **Available Bikes**. Bikes that can be taken without taking into consideration its kind (mechanical, electrical, etc.).

[1] https://developer.jcdecaux.com/#/home.

- **Total Stands**. The overall station capacity, including not working stands.

Notice that *total stand* feature might be created when possible, reducing it to the first two variables aggregation only when it is not available in the original source at all.

2.2 Data Extraction Process

Concerning the historical bike data for each target system, it must be recorded at least the unified status for each available station. Other domain-specific features for each data delivery system, such as the availability of electric bikes, can be stored if necessary. In that case, apart from developing a comparative study to identify possible matches that keeps the recorded data as unified as possible, basic status concept notation and meaning must be respected. That means, for example, that electrical bike availability could be stored as a new feature whenever it is always included in the available bike field. Consequently, historical data could be defined as a set of statuses, which includes unified criteria and any other relevant specific variables during some period.

In relation to data nature, it is necessary to make the difference between static and dynamic data: whether it is not supposed to change over time or not. Concerning the second one, it is clear that could be defined as the set of historical status records. In relation to static information, as the unification system is thought to include and aggregate data from several systems, it is necessary to keep the relevant meta-data that describes each of them as well as other station information. This makes the relation with the system or may result interesting for future analysis. Then is shown the static data registered by the system whenever possible:

- **System**
  - Inner identifier
  - Original identifier
  - Commercial name
  - Country
  - Time zone
- **Station**
  - Inner identifier
  - Original identifier
  - Commercial name
  - Latitude
  - Longitude

Point Data Access Analysis. Once defined what data will be recorded by the presented extraction system, it is necessary to define how this information could be accessed from the original manager data source. The manager normally supplies a RestFul API that allows to get both static and dynamic data previously defined. In general, the API's response follows JSON format as the current trend in overall machine to machine communication nowadays. Concerning XML format, its use has been reduced with old SOAP APIS system less frequent now. In addition, despite this format is available in some APIs, they delivery both including JSON. Consequently, it has been chosen RestFul APIs with JSON format as the preferred access point to data. Nevertheless, it could be possible to define special cases for other extraction methodology if needed.

Concerning the data extraction process, it is focused on solving different needs. It involves reading original information and processing it for improving and enhancing value. Also, it is necessary to adapt to the defined common structure and to store it in the centralized database for the different bike systems. It has been developed as a Python solution to bridge the variety of available libraries for dealing with APIs, data structures, and databases. As each system data could be delivered by different APIs, it must be defined one specific extractor per API considered. Each extractor had to be implemented taking into account specific knowledge of the source, to be able to map original data into the unified solution to upload it to the database. Therefore, the overall extraction system is defined as the set of all specific extractors.

A quite important feature of the extraction system is the execution frequency, which directly influences in the quality of integrated data and information loss. It is desirable that, on the one hand, the process runs regularly enough to not miss any change in station status but, on the other hand, the execution frequency does not overload server storage and computing capabilities keeping in mind that it must be enough time window between each call for the system to be able to run potential new extractors in the future. To optimize time this parameter it has been studied station information time updates for several systems concluding that, despite most of them has a very low update periodicity, there are others that change its status more often arriving near ten-minute frequency. As a result, the full extraction will be run using a Unix cron task every 5 min for each station in order to reduce information loss.

As referenced above, this periodicity conduces to a Big Data problem, namely, to avoid system storage overload. The solution comes from representation optimization. Although the system reads the current station status every 5 min, the extractor checks the centralized database before inserting new data. The system only inserts the requested status if and only if there is any change compared to the last record. This decision solves both, to avoid repeating information and to alleviate storage overload for low-frequency update stations. In fact, it reduces the total register from 2.8 billion to 220 million approximately (more than 10 times smaller size), which represents an important storage efficiency improvement.

Despite it is not supposed to be changed, static data could be found variation issues in practice. For instance, when BSS managers modify some contracts or update their metadata. Such kind of modification could include variations in fields used in the final data consumption process such as commercial names or other essential ones. This could affect original identifiers, critical for the extraction process to run properly. Therefore, the extraction logic has been implemented not only to detect and update centralized database metadata when needed, but also to warn the extraction system administrator if any critical change has been found.

2.3 Data Storage Architecture

Extracted data is stored in the centralized database together with other relevant information for future analysis such as weather factors or traffic data. To select the database engine, it has been studied two available alternatives driven by the open-source criteria as the project. Moreover, to enhance this analysis about bike data storage methods for historical records, it has been chosen two engines that represent both sides of the actual data architecture paradigm, MySQL[2] (SQL) and MongoDB[3] (NoSQL). It is worth mentioning that, although emergent architecture solutions including Data Lakes have not been taken into consideration (due to current server hardware limitations), it could be possible to be analyzed and make a system migration in future work.

It has been selected one-year data of the BSS with a total of 260 stations with more than four million records (over the mean). It has been performed charge tests for both previously mentioned engines to check the storage space and query time performance. These metrics could be considered the best ones to drive the concerning optimization problems, such as potential large number of records (close to Big Data solutions) or real-time data consumption.

Concerning disk space, MongoDB shows much better results than MySQL (70 against 330 MB). Here could be notice the power of first one BSON[4] comprehension tool for when time series collection is used, reducing more than four times MySQL storage space.

Nevertheless, regarding the query time performance, MongoDB keeps raising regularly as the number of records increases, see Fig. 2, whereas MySQL reaches the stability from about two to four million records, apart from showing a lower curve tendency, resulting in a considerably better performance than the first one in this metric.

Consequently, despite MongoDB seems better for dealing with Big Data problems mentioned in this study, the query time-analyzed suggests that data consumption service could be affected, especially for long record number queries. In addition, MySQL lower performance in storage space can be handled by the current system server even for future potential data income. Therefore, MySQL has been chosen as the database engine for storing historical bike data.

2.4 Database Schema

To reduce the storage space in the centralized database, it has been separated static and dynamic data in the final schema, as shown in Fig. 3. Concerning the first one, it has been created two tables for allocating each bike sharing system and station metadata such as commercial names, source identifiers, or station location.

[2] https://www.mysql.com/.
[3] https://www.mongodb.com/.
[4] https://www.mongodb.com/json-and-bson/.

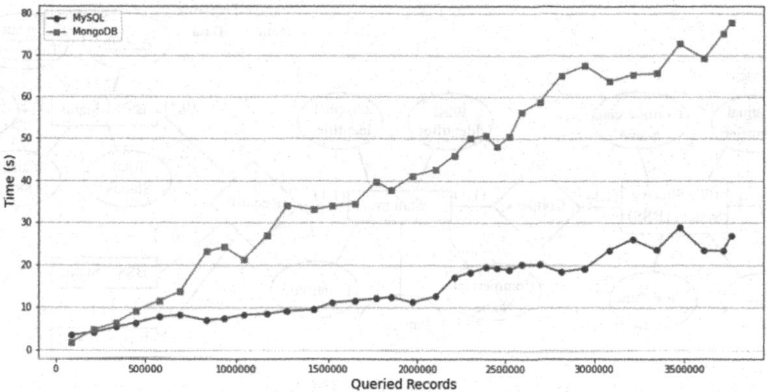

Fig. 2. Database engine query time comparison

Regarding dynamic data, MySQL tables are capable of storing a considerable number of records (2^{32})[5] enough to handle historical station status data for more than one hundred years in the same table. However, the final installation of server hardware could drive into problems in the time necessary to solve queries on long-size tables. As a result, it has been created a *status* table, which contains all station status data per system. This design reduces the table size in those cases where over mean station number needs to be stored.

Furthermore, in each table is included at least three unified status features to ensure data comparison between the systems to be possible. Apart from that, other relevant system domain-specific information could be included to enhance the final system value. However, please note that no new variable is stored without considering if it really improves the final solution and without checking a match in meaning with yet registered ones. Then, a new one adaptation becomes necessary to maximize unification.

As a result, the defined storage architecture reduces static data replication to only station system identifiers. That prevents for overloading disk space with unnecessary information. In addition, as the methodology is system-based, only a few queries are necessary for comparing several systems, resulting in a better query time performance. Nevertheless, the update timestamps do not match even between stations of the same system, which implies an important difficulty for studying and comparing the information. Nevertheless, it is solved by the data consumption tools developed in the project.

[5] https://dev.mysql.com/doc/refman/8.0/en/table-size-limit.html.

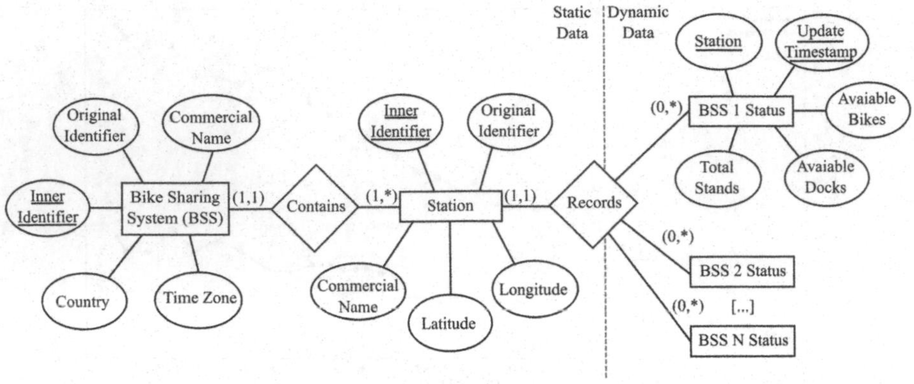

Fig. 3. Database entity relation diagram

3 Data Consumption Tools

For making unified data available, several tools for data processing and both human and machine communication services has been developed. They not only solve several previously mentioned problems concerning data reduction but also enrich the information delivered value.

3.1 Data Generator

The designed storing solution is not able to provide user-friendly information that enhances and reduces the comparison process time as the recorded timestamps do not match from one station to another. To solve the difficulty, it has been implemented a Python solution that can generate same-frequency status data. This way the users are able to define a step window, 20 min for instance, and the returned data by this process shows real statuses at a fixed time (00:00, 00:20, 00:40, ...) during the requested date interval.

The tool only records status changes, even if no data is stored for several hours. Consequently, the status at a fixed time is the same as the last previously recorded. As a result, frequency interpolated information is generated by first querying all recorded data between the requested dates. Second, constructing step window interval timestamps. Finally, assigning the most recent status to each generated instance.

As a result, the system is able to deliver unified data, not only about the status concept itself, but also in a fixed time to enhance future comparison processes. It is worth to mention that the tool is designed as an inner part of the system, it cannot be directly accessed by the final user. Instead, these options are included in the final developed RestFul API.

3.2 API Rest

For handling access to collected data to external users programmatically, a RestFul API has been developed. It can serve information about systems and stations metadata, and the status history in a certain period. It is based on Python Flask[6] Library as it can be used with all Python data suite libraries to enhance functionality. Moreover, as commonly used now, JSON format has been chosen as the returned response format for unifying its use.

Concerning URI naming patterns, it has been following the convention commonly accepted[7]. Information must be accessed hierarchically from the systems to stations. Therefore, systems, stations, and statuses sources have been defined. Any other requested filters must be included as HTTP parameters for the request. In addition, while meta-data from different sources can be extracted at once, it is only possible to request status information for a single station. That makes necessary to iterate over them to extract full system status.

As a result, the following are the actions available from the API at the time of publication of this work[8]:

- Get meta-data for all systems and a specific one.
- Get meta-data for all stations or a specific one located in a certain system.
- Get the status of a certain station at any time within the collected data.
- Get all recorded statuses of a certain station (just changes) between two dates.
- Get all recorded statuses of a certain station with the same frequency timespan between two dates. Here is where the previously mentioned data generator occurred and can be exploited by external users.

3.3 Web Application

To handle with Human Computer Interaction (HCI) and brings an user-firendly data access, it has been implemented as a Web Application[9]. It not only presents recorded content, but also adds extra knowledge for reducing future analysis tasks difficulties.

For that purpose, it should describe two main views, designed to ensure most use cases are being covered. These tools draw a clear distinction between end-user types. On the one hand, referring to those who only need to check current station status. On the other hand, others who require more deep information and knowledge about a station's behavior for future research or maintenance tasks.

[6] https://flask.palletsprojects.com/en/2.0.x/.
[7] https://restfulapi.net/resource-naming/.
[8] It must be mention that this API is in experimental status at the publication of this study assuming that it could be future changes in the future or it may present unexpected behaviour.
[9] http://opendatalab.uhu.es/~tfgbicis/.

In relation to check the system status whenever the time available in the storage database -including the current status- it is presented a map view of the selected system by the user. Each station status is presented as a point placed in its real location and coloured from green to red based on high or lower available bikes or docks, depending on user selection. In addition, consumers could check station status trend for a selected day by clicking on station point displayed. For implementing that map view it has been used existing open source solutions, such as Open Streep Map[10] and Leaflet.js[11]. They brings more useful functionalities apart from just displaying a map and follows open source philosophy.

Regarding a more advanced usage, it has been designed a simple dashboard where users could check relevant monthly statistics for each station. Selected metrics are those we have considered as interesting, and commonly used for researching and maintenance. The rationale behind its creation is to reduce the final consumer effort of processing using returned data from API. These indicators are presented as charts, by using the well-known Javascript open-source library Chart.js[12], of several types and focused on the following aspects:

- **Weekday average activity** base on the total changes of the status. That can help to determine in which week period the station is used the most.
- **Hourly average activity** base on the total changes of the status, for helping to get what time of the day the station is used the most.
- **Not working stands tendency** over the months, measures as total stands − (available bikes + available docks) for monitoring the quality of service.
- **Whole station status trend** over months for a more detailed station status evolution over time.

Moreover, inside this application it has been designed a handler tool for dealing with the developed API to make it easy to understand its use and even accessing data without the necessity of programming tasks.

4 System User Profiles and Uses Cases

Recording historical data from BSS comes useful in a wide range of areas and may be interesting for diverse types of users. For that, this work focuses on covering as much functionality as possible. Not only for scientific purposes but also for improving the overall bike-sharing system, and, hence, the urban mobility experience. Consequently, it has been defined four potential users of the tools presented in this work, as it is shown in Fig. 4.

System-affiliated users have to be considered as they are supposed to exploit the bike service. They are allowed to access relevant information such as the bike station or dock availability near both their start and end journey location.

[10] https://www.openstreetmap.org/.
[11] https://leafletjs.com/.
[12] https://www.chartjs.org/.

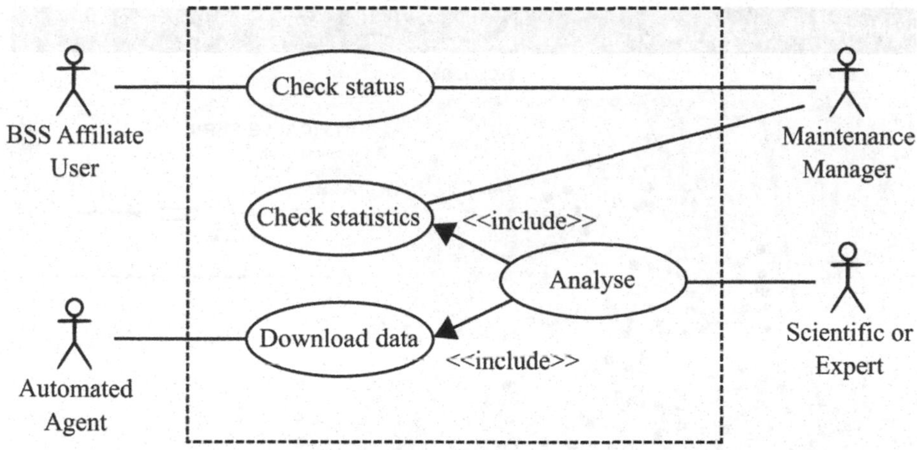

Fig. 4. Full system uses cases

Additionally, as one more step, to compute an estimation of how a station could be someday at a certain time (for example, each Monday at 09:00), based on the observation of previous statuses at the same condition.

In the case of the maintenance manager, the system could help to discover common unbalanced system patterns within several systems and conditions. They can also detect not working docks. Even they could monitor how these deficiencies affect the overall service, depending on the area.

Other relevant actors could be automated (intelligent or software) agents. Its aims could be focused on keeping up to date with bike information or republishing. Furthermore, it could be more advanced tasks, such as feeding existing models for forecasting services with new data. All that could be handled through the developed RestFul API.

Finally, more scientific/expert profiles from urban mobility researchers to a traffic analyst must be taken into account for the importance of the influence of the BSS in their work. Therefore, they could use the implemented tools for checking statistics measures, supported by six-year historical data, of interesting activity patterns of system stations. Moreover, they could find a wide range of systems to analyze and compare for future research in the field.

5 Results

First of all, and as the main contribution of the presented work, is the designed ETL methodology that has been working, in earlier versions, since December 2015. More than six years of station status historical data has been recorded from near thrifty bike sharing systems around the world.

Moreover, the unifying concept explained could put a bridge between others available alternatives that have been analyzed, by merging the basis of the station status essence. This, joined with all historical data retrieved, brings the

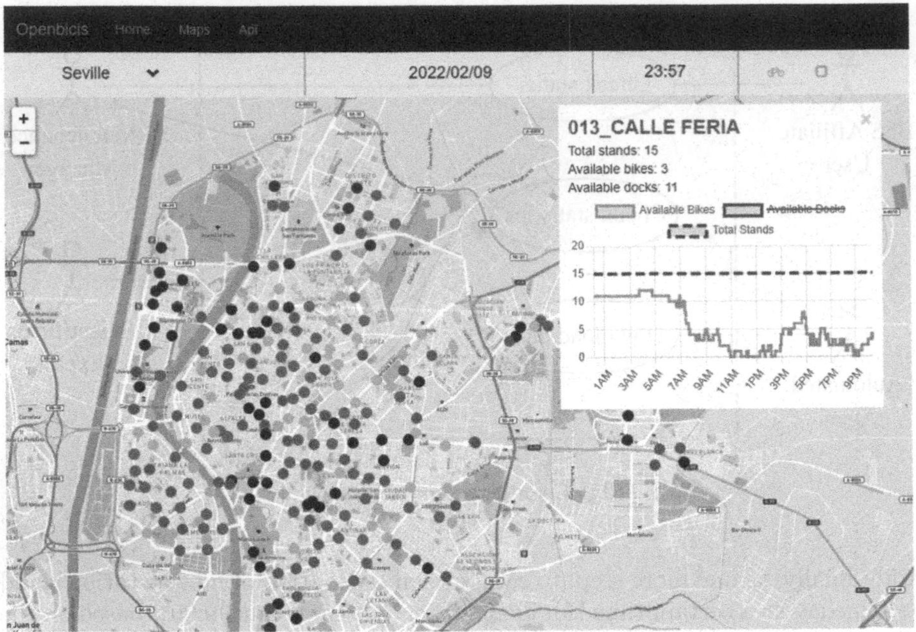

Fig. 5. Map view with system status at certain time showing station status evolution for that day.

opportunity to compare and analyze the behavior between systems by using the same source and tools. That simplifies future research efforts in the field.

In relation to data storage difficulties for storing historical system information (the Big Data facet of the problem), the refined storage methodology used in this study results in a 93% record number reduction (from 2.8 billion to 220 million approximately). Furthermore, as this methodology increases comparison difficulties between systems, the implemented data generator allows to create datasets with real information presented in a target needed frequency to help future analyses.

Concerning to the stored data access issue, both sides of the problem, machine-machine communication and Human-Computer Interaction, have been covered. They are the RestFul API and Web Application respectively. It has been taken into consideration several types of end-users. On the one side, for casual users, it brings general information of the target system or stations, as it is shown in Fig. 5. On the other side, a more detailed view is given for helping research and maintenance tasks, presented in Fig. 6, including relevant statistics information from historical station activity.

Finally, by providing unified and usable information, the system facilitates data to be consumed by other software solutions for several problems, as would be:

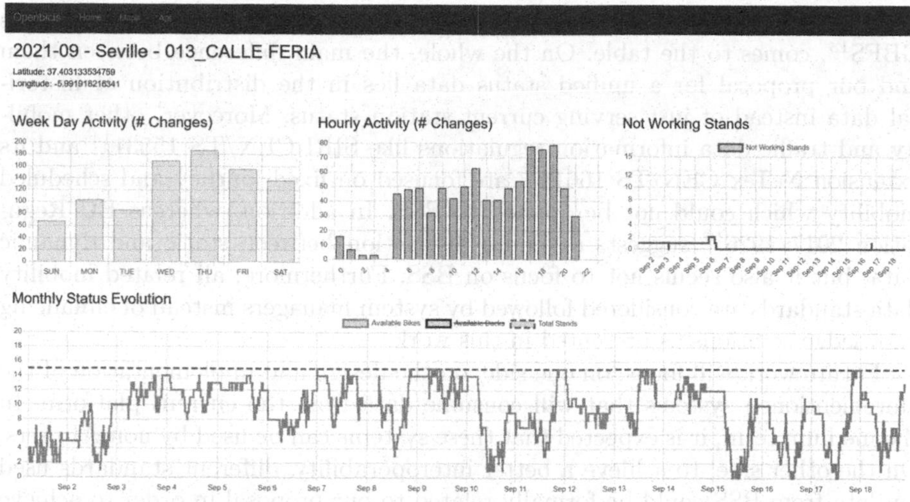

Fig. 6. Charts of stations KPIs and status evolution for one moth view.

- To add new functionality to the Smart City Control Room Dashboard with bike mobility information
- Smartphone apps. For example, by providing a prediction on bike availability near to the user (in the line of [9]).
- Data Solutions for global analysis of smart sharing in cities (topology of sharing in urban networks), and more ambitious goals, such as the estimation of carbon footprint reduction.
- To complement other data science studies on the urban realm [5]. For example, as an aggregated information system for others that also work with data extracted from third party agents (e.g. [12]).
- Machine Learning solutions for predicting user demand (near or long term). See, e.g., [3] as a first case study, and [2] as example to emulate in the case of BSS.
- Monitoring Quality of Service of the system.

6 Conclusions and Future Work

In this paper, a BSS service data collection platform has been described. The main motivation of its design and implementation is to provide data for the consumption of different systems based on Artificial Intelligence models that the authors are designing: service usage prediction (Machine Learning), predictive simulation of usage (Multiagent Systems), enhanced HCI systems for monitoring, etc.

The difficulties intrinsic to the use of massive data both in the ETL process and in its processing for use cases have also been pointed out.

Comparison with other standards used for serving BSS information, such as GBFS[13], comes to the table. On the whole, the main difference between them and our proposal for a unified status data lies in the distribution of historical data instead of just serving current station status. Moreover, other mobility and traffic data information regulations like SIRI CEN/TS 15531[14] and its extension NeTex CEN/TS 16614[15] are focused on fixed journey and scheduled mobility which could not be applied to BSS. In addition, whereas EU Regulation 2017/1926[16] suggests a similar distinction between static and dynamic data, but it also seems not to focus on BSS. Furthermore, all related mobility data standards are considered followed by system managers instead of enhancing knowledge solutions as presented in this work.

Future work will focus, on one side, on the design and implementation of the aforementioned systems that will consume data from the current platform. In the medium term, it is expected that these systems can be used by non-AI users. On the other side, to achieve a better interoperability, different standards used on data from BSS could be formally related to our proposal in order to achieve truly Linked Open Data. Moreover, new upcoming data storing methodologies or architectures could be considered to improve the implemented solution with other Big Data ETL state-of-the-art solutions. Finally, improving the implemented consumption tools with new features will be also considered.

References

1. Andrienko, G.L., et al.: (So) big data and the transformation of the city. Int. J. Data Sci. Anal. **11**(4), 311–340 (2021)
2. Aranda-Corral, G.A., Borrego-Díaz, J., Galán-Páez, J.: Synthetizing qualitative (logical) patterns for pedestrian simulation from data. In: Bi, Y., Kapoor, S., Bhatia, R. (eds.) IntelliSys 2016. LNNS, vol. 16, pp. 243–260. Springer, Cham (2018). https://doi.org/10.1007/978-3-319-56991-8_19
3. Aranda-Corral, G.A., Rodríguez, M.A., Fernández de Viana, I., Arenas, M.I.G.: Genetic hybrid optimization of a real bike sharing system. Mathematics **9**(18), 1–18 (2021)
4. Barbet, T., Nacer-Weill, A., Yang, C., Raimbault, J.: An agent-based model for modal shift in public transport. CoRR, abs/2107.11399 (2021)
5. Borrego-Díaz, J., Galán-Páez, J., Miguel-Rodríguez, J.D.: Building knowledge layers and networks from urban digital information. In: International Conference Virtual City and Territory. 9° Congresso Città e Territorio Virtuale, pp. 216–228 (2014)
6. Charalabidis, Y., Zuiderwijk, A., Alexopoulos, C., Janssen, M., Lampoltshammer, T., Ferro, E.: Open data interoperability. In: The World of Open Data. PAIT, vol. 28, pp. 75–93. Springer, Cham (2018). https://doi.org/10.1007/978-3-319-90850-2_5

[13] https://github.com/NABSA/gbfs.
[14] https://www.transmodel-cen.eu/siri-standard/.
[15] https://netex-cen.eu/.
[16] https://eur-lex.europa.eu/eli/reg_del/2017/1926/oj.

7. Chemla, D., Meunier, F., Calvo, R.W.: Bike sharing systems: solving the static rebalancing problem. Discret. Optim. **10**(2), 120–146 (2013)
8. Costa, E., Silvestri, F.: On the bike spreading problem. In: 21st Symposium on Algorithmic Approaches for Transportation Modelling, Optimization, and Systems, ATMOS 2021, volume 96 of OASIcs, pp. 5:1–5:16 (2021)
9. Froehlich, J., Neumann, J., Oliver, N.: Sensing and predicting the pulse of the city through shared bicycling. In: Proceedings of the 21st International Joint Conference on Artificial Intelligence, IJCAI 2009, pp. 1420–1426 (2009)
10. Makarova, I., Shubenkova, K., Pashkevich, A., Boyko, A.: Smart-bike as one of the ways to ensure sustainable mobility in smart cities. In: Magno, M., Ferrero, F., Bilas, V. (eds.) S-CUBE 2016. LNICST, vol. 205, pp. 187–198. Springer, Cham (2017). https://doi.org/10.1007/978-3-319-61563-9_16
11. Marazzini, M., Mitolo, N., Nesi, P., Paolucci, M.: Smart city control room dashboards: big data infrastructure, from data to decision support. J. Vis. Lang. Sentient Syst. **4**, 75–82 (2018)
12. De Miguel-Rodríguez, J., Galán-Páez, J., Aranda-Corral,G.A., Borrego-Díaz, J.: Urban knowledge extraction, representation and reasoning as a bridge from data city towards smart city. In: 2016 Intl IEEE Conferences on Ubiquitous Intelligence Computing, Advanced and Trusted Computing, Scalable Computing and Communications, Cloud and Big Data Computing, Internet of People, and Smart World Congress (UIC/ATC/ScalCom/CBDCom/IoP/SmartWorld), pp. 968–974 (2016)
13. Orozco, L.G.N., Battiston, F., Iñiguez, G., Szell, M.: Data-driven strategies for optimal bicycle network growth. R. Soc. Open Sci. **7**(12), 201130 (2020)
14. Shimizu, S., Akai, K., Nishino, N.: Modeling and multi-agent simulation of bicycle sharing. In: Mochimaru, M., Ueda, K., Takenaka, T. (eds.) ICServ 2013, pp. 39–46. Springer, Tokyo (2014). https://doi.org/10.1007/978-4-431-54816-4_5
15. Szell, M., Mimar, S., Perlman, T., Ghoshal, G., Sinatra, R.: Growing urban bicycle networks. CoRR, abs/2107.02185 (2021)

Perception of Incidental Social Interactions During Independent Travel on Public Transport: An Exploratory Study with Adults with Intellectual Disability

Hursula Mengue-Topio(✉), Séléné Conrad, Laurie Letalle, and Yannick Courbois

Univ. Lille, ULR 4072 - PSITEC - Psychologie : Interactions Temps Émotions Cognition, 59000 Lille, France

hursula.mengue-topio@univ-lille.fr

Abstract. People with intellectual disability (ID) face a variety of barriers to independent travel in their communities. Barriers to independent mobility are related to both individual characteristics and the physical and social environment. This exploratory study explores the perceptions of people with ID about social interactions that may occur during their travels in the community and particularly when using public transportation. Using social information processing theory, we assessed the reading and interpretation of appropriate versus inappropriate social interactions (in the context of bus travel) of 19 adults with ID from 8 video vignettes. Results revealed that ten out of nineteen participants (52.63%) correctly identified all inappropriate social interactions. Eighteen out of nineteen participants (94.73%) correctly identified all appropriate social interactions. Finally, nine out of 19 participants (47.36%) made no identification errors with appropriate and inappropriate social interactions. In addition, there was a tendency for participants to better analyze appropriate, adapted social interactions compared to inappropriate social interactions. Social interactions with other passengers of public transport can be a source of anxiety during travel for people with ID and are one of the reasons why people themselves and those around them (families, professionals) restrict travel. This social dimension, also needed during travels, should further be integrated into mobility training in order to teach problem solving skills to ID people.

Keywords: Intellectual disability · Mobility · Public transportation · Social interactions · Videos · Virtual reality

1 Introduction

Transportation plays a critical role in the social inclusion of people with disabilities, including individuals with ID. In fact, the vast majority of these people do not have a driver's license or a personal vehicle and irrevocably need public transport to access the various places in their community: work, training and education, social life and leisure, health care facilities, administrations, etc. However, using public transport remains a real

H. Krömker (Ed.): HCII 2022, LNCS 13335, pp. 586–599, 2022.
https://doi.org/10.1007/978-3-031-04987-3_40

challenge for many people with ID: difficulties in planning journeys, in continuing the journey in the event of connections, difficulties in managing unforeseen events, and in interacting with other users during their journeys [1]. Indeed, it can be difficult for them to interact with someone they do not know, ask for help when needed, and react appropriately to some users' inappropriate behaviors such as mockery, embarrassing looks, and scornful comments. Similarly, these people report feeling anxiety when traveling on public transport. They declare that relationships with other users are among the situations considered to be anxiety-provoking. These types of problematic situations strongly discourage them from using public transport again. [2–5]. The objective of this exploratory study is to examine the perceptions of ID individuals about unplanned, incidental social interactions situations close to those usually observed in daily life and specifically during public transportation trips. This study makes use of an experimental protocol based on video vignettes illustrating appropriate versus inappropriate social interactions given the context, i.e. a bus ride. Participants are asked to describe the scenes and then to judge the appropriateness or inappropriateness of the exchange between the protagonists. Faced with the specific difficulties related to social interactions during travel reported through literature, professionals and families are still helpless and do not have appropriate tools to prepare people with ID for this dimension of travel. From this point of view, this work also wishes to discuss the potential contribution of technological tools such as virtual environments in order to help professionals prepare social scenarios allowing them to reflect on the different social interactions likely to be observed during public transport travel and how to deal with them.

1.1 Intellectual Disability: Definitions, Diagnostic, and Particularities of Social Information Processing

ID is a disability characterized by significant limitations in both **intellectual functioning** and in **adaptive behavior**, which covers many everyday social and practical skills. This disability originates **before the age of 22** according to the Diagnostic and Statistical Manual of Mental Disorders (DSM)-5th edition [6] and the American association on intellectual and developmental disabilities (AAIDD) [7]. According to AAIDD intellectual functioning refers to abilities such as reasoning, planning, abstract thinking, understanding complex ideas, and problem solving. Adaptive behavior refers to the set of conceptual skills (language, reading, writing, concepts of number, etc.), social skills (interpersonal skills, social responsibility, gullibility, etc.), and practical skills (personal care, use of money, occupational skills, health care, travel/transportation, etc.). All of these conceptual, social, and practical skills allow the individual to function on a daily basis in his or her usual life context. The causes of ID are multi-factorial and this population presents a very high heterogeneity [8]. Indeed, the levels of severity of ID are based on the description of the person's daily functioning by considering the conceptual, social, practical domain and the level of support they need. There are then 4 levels of ID severity: mild, moderate, severe, or profound [6]. In the absence of appropriate support, individuals with ID would then encounter difficulties in fulfilling the requirements of personal independence and social responsibility based on their age and the socio-cultural norms present in their environment [6, 8]. These difficulties, then significantly hinder one or more areas of daily life.

Much of the work done with individuals with ID focuses on the development and functioning of their social skills in everyday life and different life contexts. Social skills are considered to be the ability to pursue personal goals in social interaction while maintaining positive relationships with others across time and situations [9]. One of the skills deployed during interactions with others corresponds to social information processing [10]. During social situations (situations involving two or more protagonists), the individual must mobilize his or her ability to read and interpret verbal and non-verbal cues on the social and emotional level. This reading of the situation is based on the individual's internal states and the external context of the situation, which allows him/her to analyze the situation and give meaning to it. After this interpretation of the cues, the individual can clarify the purpose of the behavior, generate several alternative responses, choose a specific response, and evaluate the outcome of his or her behavioral response [11–13]. Thus, different cognitive processes are involved when individuals have to make sense of a social situation and elaborate a behavior in response to it: processing socio-perceptual information to recognize the emotions expressed by the gaze, the voice of others; considering the beliefs, perspectives, intentions of others, soliciting pragmatic language and our social knowledge to anticipate and solve social problems, etc. [11, 12]. Social information processing develops in infancy, during the child's socialization, and over the years [14–16]. Its development is linked to the opportunities and occasions provided by the environment, which in turn promotes better social interactions and the individual's social adaptation [17]. In the context of ID, this process may be delayed (comparison by developmental age) or deficient (comparison by chronological age). Indeed, people with ID may have difficulty understanding whether a social situation is appropriate or not, or in solving a social problem in an appropriate manner. This may be due to various factors: brain abnormalities, genetics, the severity of cognitive, motor, or sensory deficits, social and emotional skills, language difficulties (production and comprehension), non-verbal reasoning. Other factors such as the context of interaction, the behavior of others, and low exposure to learning opportunities, i.e. fewer confrontations with various social situations, can explain difficulties in the processing of social information in people with ID [18].

1.2 Intellectual Disability and Transportation: Specificity of Social Interactions During Travel

Using public transport requires confronting rapid changes in a dynamic environment and performing a sequence of behaviors [19, 20]. Traveling by public transport also requires the ability to deal with the complexity of routes, schedules, scheduling of unfamiliar destinations, and the cognitive load associated with these issues [21]. Information processing and decisions must be made quickly [2]. Certain skills such as time management, problem solving, access to reading, maintaining attention [21], as well as reasoning and memory skills [2] are necessary to successfully travel by transit alone. Work on the mobility of individuals with ID shows that their travel is highly restricted and limited to routine trips made in the vicinity of the institutions they attend [22, 1]. Cognitive difficulties, safety issues, as well as adaptation to the environment, and reluctance from relatives are barriers to learning and performing independent travel for these individuals [21–24]. Although ID individuals are able to memorize routes in known environments [23, 25], other difficulties are observed when using public transportation: fatigability, concentration problems, stress-related to schedules, changes, unexpected events, and problems related to information reception [2]. Moreover, these people themselves declare that they have difficulty solving a problem during travel, whether it is an unforeseen problem related to technical equipment or human error [1].

The literature contains numerous studies on the teaching of safety rules to people with ID during their travels [20, 26, 27]. Similarly, many recent studies emphasize the contribution of new technologies for these individuals when using public transport, particularly the bus [21, 28]. The same is true for the study of spatial representations during travel among individuals with ID in the environment, which is increasingly studied [29–31]. On the other hand, few studies have addressed the social dimension of mobility and specifically the perception of social interactions that may occur during travel; Yet, moving around on a daily basis also corresponds to a social situation that requires to interact with other users in the public realm in an appropriate manner [32, 33]. However, some available data show difficulties related to social interactions during travel for people with ID. Indeed, in a survey on adults with ID who worked in a sheltered workshop [3], they report difficulties in "interacting with someone unknown," "carrying on a conversation, reacting to an unexpected event" (p. 60), and even "asking for help in case of an unexpected problem" (p. 65). Half of the survey participants said they "feel anxiety when traveling on public transportation," and that dealing with other passengers is among the situations deemed anxiety-provoking. "The other difficulty cited is that when there are many people, it is difficult to get on and off the bus, as people do not move aside and block entry or exit" (p. 63). Similarly, "situations of interaction with other people can also cause anxiety, for example, when the person takes a long time to validate the ticket" (p. 65). Similarly, "the presence of groups of young people who are too noisy, who do not always respect the equipment and the rules, and who are sometimes mocking" is a source of anxiety" (p. 66). Other field studies with support staff have confirmed these findings [5, 33–35]. Some works highlight the use of avoidant coping strategies in adults with mild intellectual disabilities to deal with stressful social interactions, [36].

Moving around independently (without the help of another person) and autonomously is essential for the social inclusion of people with ID, yet the daily mobility of these people is hampered by several factors that force relatives, professionals, and the people themselves to restrict their trips. Among other factors, the quality of social interactions, which may be inadequate, during travel is one of the reasons for this restriction. Such situations are described by people with ID and their relatives as sources of anxiety that may explain the restrictions on travel to familiar environments. Furthermore, it is essential to analyze and interpret social situations correctly in order to resolve any interpersonal problems that may arise during travel. To this end, it is necessary for people to identify inappropriate social interactions in the context of travel, to define them correctly, and to develop and choose alternative strategies to solve the problem. All these steps related to the processing of social information require the mobilization of cognitive, emotional, and behavioral resources. However, many studies show an under-functioning, weak mobilization of such resources in people with ID. The objective of this exploratory study is to examine the identification of problematic and non-problematic social interaction in public transport, interactions that are usually unplanned, i.e. the first stage of information processing in social situations in adults with ID.

2 Method

In this exploratory study, we adopted an experimental procedure based on 8 video-vignettes depicting social interactions (appropriate social interactions and inappropriate social interactions) between users during travels in public transportation. Each scenario was presented to adults with ID and they had to answer several questions about their understanding and their interpretation of the interactions between users the video vignettes used in this study describe specific situations developed by the research team to illustrate the social skills necessary for travel, skills that are otherwise described in the literature [32, 33].

2.1 Participants

19 adults (11 women and 8 men) aged between 24 and 69 years (mean age: 47.8 years; standard deviation: 13.8 years) with ID participated in this study. the participants with ID were living in one of the community-based residential facilities of "Papillons Blancs de Lille", a Care organization of people with ID in Lille, France. They were previously diagnosed with ID. For the recruitment of people with ID, support staff helped to recruit adults who had sufficient language abilities skills (in relation to the level of comprehension and expression) and who did not have severe behavioral or emotional problems that would make participation too demanding for them. We focus on intellectual disability in order to study its impact on the processing of social information in the context of independent travel. Therefore, Participants with other disorders associated with intellectual disability (mental health disorders, sensory disorders such as blindness, deafness; etc.), as well as those with an identified syndrome (autism spectrum disorders, Down syndrome, etc.) were excluded from the group. These adults, all living in residential homes, presented diverse profiles in terms of public transport use: some had previously used public transport to go to work, others still use it when they are with their families and others are not very familiar with the use of public transport.

2.2 Material

The experiment procedure was based on eight video-vignettes filmed on a bus. The framework for shooting and editing the videos was inspired by current recommendations for making educational videos [38]. The vignettes were shot in a bus loaned by the local public transport company of the city of Lille (Hauts-de-France region). The scenes and sound recordings took place in the outdoor environment. The actors (non-professionals) were two women and two men and were strangers to the participants. Each video-vignette depicted social interactions (verbal and/or non-verbal) between three actors. A fourth actor, always the same in each video-vignette, played the role of the third person who observes the scene without intervening. The different video-vignettes (presented in Table 1) show scenarios of social interactions (verbal and non-verbal) that can occur during a bus ride. Four video-vignettes present appropriate social interactions (ASI) and four video-vignettes present inappropriate social interactions (ISI) in the context of travel. In constructing the scenarios, we drew on Dever's (1997) taxonomy of community living skills, including travel-related skills.

Table 1. Description of the content of the video vignettes.

Designation of the video-vignette	Nature of social interaction	Description of the video vignette
Verbal abuse	Inappropriate Social Interaction (ISI-1)	A female bus passenger accidentally steps on another passenger's foot. The passenger who was the victim of the situation became angry and verbally abused the person who stepped on his foot
Bullying	Inappropriate Social Interaction (ISI-2)	A bus passenger asks a young girl for her phone number. She refuses. Despite this refusal, the passenger insists strongly
Mockery	Inappropriate Social Interaction (ISI-3)	A passenger gets on the bus, misses a step, and almost falls off. Two other passengers on the bus openly mock him by looking at him and laughing
Impoliteness	Inappropriate Social Interaction (ISI-4)	While boarding the bus, a passenger shoves two others who want to get off
Obeying traffic rules	Appropriate social interaction (ASI-1)	A passenger gets off the bus and politely asks a person to step aside to access the door and exit the bus
Necessary interactions with other passengers	Appropriate social interaction (ASI-2)	A passenger accidentally steps on another passenger's foot while getting off the bus and apologizes. The other passenger accepts the apology
Respect for behavioral constraints	Appropriate social interaction (ASI -3)	A passenger's phone rings during a bus ride in the presence of other passengers. The passenger answers the phone in a whisper and cuts the discussion short. He explains to the caller that he will call back at another time because he is on the bus
Respect for conversational constraints	Appropriate social interaction (ASI -4)	Two passengers are facing each other on the bus and one passenger starts a discussion about the weather with the other passenger who replies cordially

2.3 Procedure

The experiment took place in a quiet space within the specialized establishment. It lasted about 20 min. The experimenter was seated next to the participant, a computer was placed in front of them on the table. The test started with an explanation of the instructions and the overall content of the videos. The videos of an average length of 30 s were presented to the participant, twice consecutively, in a random order after counterbalancing. At the end of each video vignette, the experimenter asked several questions to ensure that the participant understood the content and perceived the situation:

Question 1: "What is happening in this video?". This question allowed participants to describe the scene. This was an initial identification of the nature of the social interaction.

Question 2: What can we say about this situation? What do you think of this situation, what impression does this exchange between the people present in this scene gives you? If necessary (depending on the participant's reaction), the experimenter provided an additional clarification such as: for you, is there a problem in this scene or not? give your reasons in your own words as if you were to tell the scene to someone else. The second question clarifies the participant's reading of the social interaction he or she has just seen.

The scenes with so-called problematic situations referred to inappropriate social interactions. These are the scenes related to "verbal aggression (ISI-1)", "Bullying (ISI-2)", " Mockery (ISI-3)", and "impoliteness (ISI-4)". Scenes showing appropriate social interactions in travel correspond to videos on "obeying traffic rules (ASI-1)," "necessary interactions with other passengers (ASI-2)," " Respect for behavioral constraints (ASI-3)," and "obeying conversational constraints (ASI-4).". Regarding the rating, the identification of a video-vignette is considered correct if the participant identifies videos 1, 2, 3, and 4 as problematic, inappropriate, and vignettes 5, 6, 7, and 8 as appropriate exchanges in the study context. The participant's response is given in verbal form. Following a manual content analysis of the response and recording of the response, it is scored 1 when the response is correct and 0 if the response is incorrect.

3 Results

Since the conditions of normality of the distribution of errors and homogeneity of variances were not satisfied, we then favored non-parametric methods for data analysis. An observation of the correct identification judgments indicated contrasting results according to the nature of the situations: ten participants out of nineteen (52, 63%) correctly identified all inappropriate social interactions. Eighteen out of nineteen participants (94.73%) correctly identified all appropriate social interactions. Finally, nine out of nineteen participants (47.36%) made no identification errors on all videos featuring appropriate and inappropriate social interactions.

The analysis of social interactions indicated a higher percentage of correct identification for appropriate, adapted social interactions (ASI: 94.73%) compared to inappropriate social interactions (ISI: 52.63%). This difference between the two types of social interactions tends to be significant (Wilcoxon test for paired samples; $W = -8.5$; $p = .052$). Table 2 shows the number and percentage of correct identification of each of the video vignettes reflecting appropriate and inappropriate social interactions.

Table 2. Distribution of the number and percentage of correct identification according to the type of social interaction

	ISI-1	ISI-2	ISI-3	ISI-4	ASI-1	ASI-2	ASI-3	ASI-4
Number of correct responses (n = 19 participants)	18	12	15	18	18	19	18	19
Percentage of correct answers	94,74	63,16	78,95	94,74	94,74	100	94,74	100

Friedman's ANOVA for k non-independent samples performed on the identification of appropriate social interactions showed vignettes no statistically significant difference between the four videos-vignettes (Chi^2 Anova (3, N = 19) = 3; p < 0.39). In contrast, analysis of inappropriate social interactions (Friedman's ANOVA for k non-independent samples) showed a statistically significant difference between the four videos-vignettes (Chi^2 Anova (3, N = 19) = 11.88; p < 0.0078). The least identified social interactions were those related to verbal harassment and mockery.

Video-vignette 2, featuring verbal harassment (A bus passenger asking a girl for her phone number insistently) was the least identified: 7 out of 19 participants did not identify any problems in this scene. Participant 2 was able to say "he asks for the number, I don't know. I think there's no problem. Participant 7 expressed that "Yeah it's going well. He talks to the lady". According to participant 11, "It's going very well. Mister, he is happy, he wants the phone." Participant 14 explained that "It's going well, the gentleman he says please! He asks the lady for her number, it's fine.

Scene 3 features a mockery (A passenger getting on the bus misses a step and almost falls off., Two other passengers, on the bus openly mock him by looking at him and laughing). 4 participants did not note the inappropriateness of this situation: Participant 3 said, "The man, he laughs, but I don't know why. He is nice. It's going well". Participant 9 was able to say, "It's fine here. The lady gets on the bus and the man laughs because he is happy". Participant 14 said, "The man is laughing but I don't know why. It's going well". Finally, according to participant 17, "the lady gets on the bus and the man laughs but we don't know why. He's happy, so it's fine".

4 Discussion

The aim of this study was to explore ID individuals' perceptions of social interactions that may occur while traveling on public transportation (buses). Appropriate social skills need to be developed for independent travel since social interactions are frequent when using Transit. Among social skills, it is important to recognize potential danger from others in the environment, learn rules of safety when dealing with strangers. At the same time, independent travelers are often required to initiate a conversation with others, ask leading questions regarding location, route, and transit systems or respond appropriately to other users' questions [32]. Identifying the nature of social interactions and interpreting them is important because it is the first step in the process of interpersonal problem solving [39], a skill necessary for travel alone on public transport in particular. To this end, adults with ID were recruited and asked to estimate whether or not a given social interaction seemed appropriate to them (in a travel context). The overall results indicate that less than half of the group of participants was able to correctly evaluate the nature of the social interactions presented.

4.1 Social Information Processing and Cognitive Limitations Associated with Intellectual Disability

An analysis of the situations revealed that appropriate social interactions were better identified than inappropriate ones. The analysis of the participants' verbal responses to each video-vignette led to the observation that in several cases, the situations in which the interaction is verbal (appropriate or inappropriate social interactions) could be more difficult to identify for our participants. Indeed, video-vignette n°2 (a passenger asks a female bus passenger for her phone number, and despite her refusal, the passenger insists strongly), involving only verbal interaction and no physical contact, is the least well interpreted by the participants. Similarly, video-vignette n°3 describing a mockery (A passenger getting on the bus misses a step and almost falls. Two other passengers on the bus openly mock him by looking at him and laughing) is also less well-identified and interpreted than others. In addition, it should be reported here that several participants - despite a correct response - were unable to explain their response for video-vignette n°8 (two passengers are on the bus. One of them starts a discussion about the weather, the other passenger replies cordially). In these situations, communicative skills are questioned. Difficulties in language skills (pragmatic, productive, or receptive language) frequently encountered in individuals with ID [40] may explain these results. Furthermore, the analysis of the content of the responses suggested that some participants did not perceive certain details or, conversely, privileged them, failing to interpret the situation as a whole, hence a failure to identify the inappropriateness or otherwise of certain social interactions presented. This difficulty was illustrated in video-vignette n°5 (a passenger gets off the bus. Two people who are about to get on the bus, back up and apologize so that he can get off the bus easily). Some participants initially identified this interaction as inappropriate, justifying the presence of a problem by the jostling, despite the other passenger's apology. Participants focused their attention on a salient element of the situation (the shoving) at the expense of its outcome (the apology). These results are reminiscent of those of [41] concerning the attentional, visual scanning, or processing speed difficulties associated with ID. These results could probably explain the difficulties in perceiving certain details in the videos, leading to an erroneous interpretation of the whole scene.

4.2 Limitations

This exploratory study marks the first step and raises many questions that could be explored in future studies. However, to strengthen the validity of this future work, several limitations observed at this stage should be noted. First, the rather small sample size and heterogeneous nature of our sample in terms of the opportunities to be exposed to the situations presented in this study (high variability in the use of public transportation among participants) may lead to different results being observed with a larger sample with other characteristics. Regarding the use of the video material, although it was made based on scientific rules [38], it has not been previously validated in other clinical groups or in people without ID. It is therefore conceivable that among the scenes involving physical contact, some are more salient than others. The same is true for scenes involving verbal interaction. It is possible that the physical contact between the actors in some of the scenes provides an additional cue to the identification of the problematic social situation, in contrast to the scenes showing verbal mockery and bullying, which may be more complicated to perceive or identify in this study. Nevertheless, the use of videos is an asset for our study. Indeed, this medium allowed us to stage social interactions in a more concrete way with numerous cues (voices, movements, facial expressions of the protagonists). Thus, the video medium seemed to be more conducive to the perception and identification of social situations than an image or a text describing the context and the social interactions observed. Validation of our material with a control group without ID would ensure that the video-vignettes are perfectly identifiable by all. Contrasting the perceptions collected from people with ID and those without ID is important in order to confirm or not the particularities observed in the first group regarding perceptions of social interactions in public transport. Similarly, we studied situations that were definitely opposed (problematic versus adapted), but in everyday life certain social situations experienced can be relatively ambiguous and therefore require the mobilization of cognitive and emotional resources to identify their nature and move on to the other stages of the interpersonal problem solving process.

4.3 Futures Research Directions

This study has contributed to exploring social interactions occurring during travel and specifically in Mass Transit. Many studies on spatial navigation of people with ID in their environment focus on the cognitive dimension (elaboration of spatial representations such as landmarks, routes, configurations; memorization, verbal description of routes, planning of trips; wayfinding performances) and the use of assistive technologies to allow some people with ID to move around alone, according to their needs and by adapting to their abilities. Very few scientific works, to our knowledge, address the processing of social information in this context in people with ID.

However, these people (adolescents and adults), their families, and the professionals on the field have been regularly mentioning, through qualitative studies, this factor linked to interactions with other users in public space and specifically in transport. Thus, inappropriate behavior by other users (teasing, annoying looks, inappropriate comments), whether actual or perceived, clearly constitutes an obstacle to the achievement of independent travel. Beyond the study of the processing of social information in our population, it is necessary to provide precise work tools to professionals, families, and people themselves, that could be integrated during the training of independent mobility. In this respect, virtual reality (VR) could offer opportunities to researchers and professionals in the field to plan scenarios prefiguring the social interactions that may take place during travel. Indeed, this tool can simulate a variety of environments as close to natural environments as possible (classroom, supermarket, cafeteria, roadway, subway train, bus…) and that can mimic the tasks of everyday life. This possibility offered by VR makes it possible to reinforce the ecological validity of assessments and learning or remediation sessions compared to what can be observed in traditional assessments [46], which is very appreciable in our context. Thus, this tool would allow the simulation of social scenarios for the assessment of perceptions and learning of behaviors to prevent and resolve interpersonal problems that may occur during travel.

Another advantage of VR is that it allows researchers to strictly control the parameters of the designed environments while offering flexibility that is valuable for studying a wide variety of social scenarios, unlike physical environments. Environments designed using VR can be generated as many times as needed, which improves the standardization of protocols (by allowing different participants to repeat the same scenarios and benefit from the same instructions) and strengthens both the validity and reliability of studies (maintaining control of study variables and measurement) [42]. Namely, VR can help to enrich the number and nature of the social interactions, which were rather limited in this study, in order to integrate certain dimensions that were not included here and that can be difficult to study in real environments with video vignettes: perception of insecurity tied to the presence of crowds, noise; environmental conditions like day/night, weather; simulation of errors linked to the person or not, etc. All these parameters could be easier to experiment conditions with different for the same scenario, and provide the perfect replicability of the scenarios.

Finally, Virtual Reality has been used for many years in studies conducted with people with ID whose etiology is not identified, or very specific syndromes such as Down Syndrome, William syndrome, or other neurodevelopmental disorders such as autism spectrum disorders. Regardless of the syndrome studied, these studies on different subjects point to similar characteristics, namely: information is presented in a sequential manner, responses (feedback) are given to individuals immediately, and they can learn at their own pace and repeat the learning as many times as necessary [43, 44], which is particularly appropriate for these populations. Another strength of VR mentioned in the work with these individuals is their acceptance of the tool, their strong involvement in the proposed tasks, and the satisfaction expressed at the end of the experimental procedure. This motivation is even more pronounced in children and adolescents compared to adults [42].

5 Conclusion

Access to and use of public transportation is an essential community resource for the quality of life and social participation of people with ID [45]. Indeed, these people do not always have the necessary resources to get around on a daily basis and often depend on their entourage and public transportation to access the services and resources available in their environment [28, 21]. Independent mobility training that integrates as much as possible public transport-centered facilities, technical know-how, and social perceptions related to transport use is essential for this field to become a real vector of social inclusion for ID people.

Acknowledgments. This study was funded by the Conseil Régional Région Hauts-de-France. We are grateful to all the participants and Staff support for their help in recruitment.

References

1. Mengue-Topio, H., Courbois, Y.: L'autonomie des déplacements chez les personnes ayant une déficience intellectuelle : une enquête réalisée auprès de travailleurs en établissement et service d'aide par le travail. Revue Francophone de la Déficience Intellectuelle **22**, 5–13 (2011)
2. FIT: Cognitive Impairment, Mental Health and Transport: Design with Everyone in Mind, Éditions OCDE, Paris (2009). https://doi.org/10.1787/9789282102183-en, Accessed 15 Nov 2021
3. Alauzet, A., Conte, F., Sanchez, J., Velche, D.: Les personnes en situation de handicap mental, psychique ou cognitif et l'usage des transports. https://www.lescot.ifsttar.fr/fileadmin/redaction/1_institut/1.20_sites_integres/TS2/LESCOT/documents/Projets/Rapp-finalPOTASTome2.pdf, Accessed 17 Oct 2021
4. Bascom, G.W., Christensen, K.M.: The impacts of limited transportation access on persons with disabilities' social participation. J. Transp. Health **7**, 227–234 (2017)
5. Mengue-Topio, H., Letalle, L., Courbois, Y.: Autonomie des déplacements et déficience intellectuelle: Quels défis pour les professionnels? Alter-Eur. J. Disabil. Res. **14**(2), 99–113 (2020)
6. American Psychiatric Association (APA): Diagnostic and statistical manual of mental disorders, 5th edition. American Psychiatric Association, Arlington, VA (2013)
7. American association on intellectual and developmental disabilities (AAIDD). https://www.aaidd.org/intellectual-disability/definition, Accessed 15 Nov 2021
8. Inserm, Institut national de la santé et de la recherche médicale: Déficiences intellectuelles. Collection Expertise collective. EDP Sciences. Montrouge (2016)
9. Rubin, K.H., Rose-Krasnor, L.: Interpersonal problem solving and social competence in children. In: Van Hasselt, V.B., Hersen, M. (éds.) Handbook of Social Development: A Lifespan Perspective, pp. 283–323. Springer, Heidelberg (1992). https://doi.org/10.1007/978-1-4899-0694-6_12
10. Nader-Grosbois, N.: Vers un modèle heuristique du fonctionnement et du développement social et émotionnel. In: Nader-Grosbois, N. (éd.) La théorie de l'esprit: Entre cognition, émotion et adaptation sociale, pp. 45–63. De Boeck Supérieur, Louvain-la-Neuve (2011)
11. Nader-Grosbois, N., Houssa, M., Jacobs, E., Mazzone, S.: Comment soutenir efficacement les compétences émotionnelles et sociales d'enfants à besoins spécifiques en milieu préscolaire et scolaire. Bulletin de Psychologie **544**, 295–315 (2016)
12. Crick, N.R., Dodge, K.A.: A review and reformulation of social information-processing mechanisms in children's social adjustment. Psychol. Bull. **115**(1), 74–101 (1994)
13. Huré, K., Fontaine, R., Kubiszewski, V.: Traitement de l'information sociale et profils dans le harcèlement scolaire chez les adolescents. Eur. Rev. Appl. Psychol. **65**(2), 83–91 (2015)
14. Shure, M.B., Spivack, G.: Interpersonal problem solving as a mediator of behavioral adjustment in preschool and kindergarten children. J. Appl. Dev. Psychol. **1**(1), 29–44 (1980)
15. Shure, M.B., Spivack, G.: Interpersonal problem solving in young children: a cognitive approach to prevention. Am. J. Community Psychol. **10**(3), 341–356 (1982)
16. Downey, G., Walker, E.: Social cognition and adjustment in children at risk for psychopathology. Dev. Psychol. **25**(5), 835–845 (1989)
17. Shure, M.B., Spivack, G.: Interpersonal cognitive problem solving and primary prevention: programming for preschool and kindergarten children. J. Clin. Child Psychol. **8**(2), 89–94 (1979)
18. Hickson, L., Khemka, I.: The role of motivation in the decision making of people with mental retardation. In: Switzky, H.N. (ed.) Personality and Motivational Differences in Persons with Mental Retardation, pp. 199–255. Lawrence Erlbaum Associates Publishers, Mahwah (2001)

19. Neef, N.A., Iwata, B.A., Page, T.J.: Public transportation training: in vivo versus classroom instruction. J. Appl. Behav. Anal. **11**(3), 331–344 (1978)
20. Page, T.J., Iwata, B.A., Neef, N.A.: Teaching pedestrian skills to retarded persons: generalization from the classroom to the natural environment. J. Appl. Behav. Anal. **9**(4), 433–444 (1976)
21. Davies, D.K., Stock, S.E., Holloway, S., Wehmeyer, M.L.: Evaluating a GPS-based transportation device to support independent bus travel by people with intellectual disability. Intellect. Dev. Disabil. **48**(6), 454–463 (2010)
22. Slevin, E., Lavery, I., Sines, D., Knox, J.: Independent travel and people with learning disabilities: the views of a sample of service providers on whether this nee is being met. J. Learn. Disabil. Nurs. Health Social Care **2**(4), 195–202 (1998)
23. Golledge, R.G., Richardson, G.D., Rayner, J.N., Parnicky, J.J.: Procedures for defining and analyzing cognitive maps of the mildly and moderately mentally retarded. In: Pick, H.L., Acredolo, L.P. (eds.) Spatial Orientation: Theory, Research, and Application, pp. 79–104. Springe, Boston (1983). https://doi.org/10.1007/978-1-4615-9325-6_4
24. Gomez, J., Montoro, G., Torrado, J.C., Plaza, A.: An Adapted wayfinding system for pedestrians with cognitive disabilities. Mob. Inf. Syst. **2015**, 1–11 (2015)
25. Courbois, Y., Mengue-Topio, H., Blades, M., Farran, E.K., Sockeel, P.: Description of routes in people with intellectual disability. Am. J. Intellect. Dev. Disabil. **124**(2), 116–130 (2019)
26. Steinborn, M., Knapp, T.J.: Teaching an autistic child pedestrian skills. J. Behav. Ther. Exp. Psychiatry **13**(4), 347–351 (1982)
27. Batu, S., Ergenekon, Y., Erbas, D., Akmanoglu, N.: Teaching pedestrian skills to individuals with developmental disabilities. J. Behav. Educ. **13**(3), 147–164 (2004)
28. Mechling, L., O'Brien, E.: Computer-Based video instruction to teach students with intellectual disabilities to use public bus transportation. Educ. Train. Aut. Dev. Disabil. **45**(2), 230–241 (2010)
29. Courbois, Y., Mengue-Topio, H., Sockeel, P.: Navigation spatiale et autonomie dans les déplacements, apports des environnements virtuels. In: Broca, R. (ed.) La déficience intellectuelle face aux progrès des neurosciences: Repenser les pratiques de soin, pp. 214–223. Chronique sociale, Lyon (2013)
30. Mengue-Topio, H., Courbois, Y., Farran, E.K., Sockeel, P.: Route learning and shortcut performance in adults with intellectual disability: a study with virtual environments. Res. Dev. Disabil. **32**(1), 345–352 (2011)
31. Letalle L., et al.: Ontology for mobility of people with intellectual disability: building a basis of definitions for the development of navigation aid systems. In: HCI in Mobility, Transport, and Automotive Systems. Automated Driving and In-Vehicle Experience Design. HCII 2020. Lecture Notes in Computer Science, vol. 12212, pp. 322–334. Springer, Copenhagen (2020). https://doi.org/10.1007/978-3-030-50523-3_23
32. Dever, R.B.: Habiletés à la vie communautaire : Une taxonomie. Presses Inter universitaires, Québec (1997)
33. LaGrow, S., Wiener, W., LaDuke, R.: Independent travel for developmentally disabled persons: a comprehensive model of instruction. Res. Dev. Disabil. **11**(3), 289–301 (1990)
34. Kersten, M.L., Coxon, K., Lee, H., Wilson, N.J.: Traversing the community is uncertain, socially complex and exhausting: autistic youth describe experiences of travelling to participate in their communities. J. Transp. Health **18**, 100922 (2020)
35. Lubin, A., Feeley, C.: Transportation Issues of adults on the autism spectrum findings from focus group discussions. J. Transp. Res. Board **2542**, 1–8 (2016)
36. Deka, D., Feeley, C., Lubin, A.: Travel patterns, needs, and barriers of adults with autism spectrum disorder: report from a survey. J. Transp. Res. Board **2542**, 9–16 (2016)
37. Hartley, S.L., MacLean, W.E.: Coping strategies of adults with mild intellectual disability for stressful social interactions. J. Mental Health Res. Intell. Disabil. **1**(2), 109–127 (2008)

38. Pfund, Y., Petitdant, B.: Dix règles simples pour réaliser une vidéo éducative. Kinésithérapie, la Revue **17**, 33–37 (2017)
39. D'Zurilla, T.J., Goldfried, M.R.: Problem solving and behavior modification. J. Abnorm. Psychol. **78**(1), 107–126 (1971)
40. Gremaud, G., Petitpierre, G., Veyre, A., Bruni, I.: L'entretien de recherche avec des personnes ayant une trisomie 21. Spécificités du discours et réflexions sur les soutiens. Travaux Neuchâtelois de linguistique **60**, 121–136 (2014)
41. Cornoldi, C., Vecchi, T.: Visuo-spatial abilities in genetic syndromes. In: Cornoldi, C., Vecchi, T. (eds.) Visuo-spatial Working Memory and Individual Differences, pp. 109–118. Psychology Press, Hove (2003)
42. Bioulac, S., et al.: Qu'apportent les outils de réalité virtuelle en psychiatrie de l'enfant et l'adolescent ? L'Encéphale **44**(3), 280–285 (2018)
43. Moore, D., McGrath, P., Thorpe, J.: Computer-aided learning for people with autism – a framework for research and development. Innov. Educ. Train. Int. **37**(3), 218–228 (2000)
44. Knight, V., McKissick, B.R., Saunders, A.: A review of technology-based interventions to teach academic skills to students with autism spectrum disorder. J. Autism Dev. Disord. **43**(11), 2628–2648 (2013)
45. Abbott, S., McConky, R.: The barriers to social inclusion as perceived by people with intellectual disabilities. J. Intellect. Disabil. **10**(3), 275–287 (2006)
46. Bon, L., et al.: Cognition sociale et autisme : Bénéfices de l'entraînement aux habiletés sociales chez des adolescents présentant un trouble du spectre de l'autisme. Revue de neuropsychologie **8**(1), 38–48 (2016)

Corporate Mobility Budgets as a Contribution to the Enforcement of Sustainable Mobility

Markus Schlegel(✉) and Ulrike Stopka

Chair of Information and Communication Business Management and Economics, Technische Universität Dresden, Dresden, Germany
markus.schlegel@mailbox.tu-dresden.de,
ulrike.stopka@tu-dresden.de

Abstract. Companies are looking for solutions to meet the challenges of growing urbanisation, climate change and the achievement of carbon and particulates reduction by changing the mobility behaviour of their employees. One way to encourage employees to use environmentally friendly means of transport such as bikes/e-bikes, bike- and car sharing, velomobiles or e-scooters instead of their own cars or company cars is to implement mobility budgets. Today, isolated mobility solutions for individual employees or groups of employees such as company cars, job tickets, fuel vouchers or BahnCards still predominate. In the meantime, however, more convenient solutions in the form of corporate mobility budgets are becoming popular on the market. Based on a market overview of national and international mobility budget offers, the paper examines mobility budgets' fundamental features and design possibilities. It discusses the functions of the different partners of a mobility budget (role model), the prerequisites, and implementation requirements. The paper presents a configurator tool for corporate mobility budgets. It includes decision criteria before introducing such a measure, namely for the determination of the service design, the utilisation options, the selection of the suitable provider, the billing modes, and company-specific features of mobility budgets. This tool facilitates the management decision-making processes. Finally, the authors conclude by focusing on the impacts of corporate mobility budgets on the involved stakeholders.

Keywords: Corporate mobility budget · Mobility behaviour · Decision tool

1 Motivation and Definition of the Term "Corporate Mobility Budget"

In the last years we can see an increased demand for alternative forms of mobility in companies. In 2020 the implementation of corporate mobility budgets in Germany has increased to 31% compared to the previous year (10%) and a further 21% of the companies surveyed are planning to introduce such a concept in the next three years (cf. Arval Deutschland GmbH 2021, p. 55). These are primarily companies that have a

H. Krömker (Ed.): HCII 2022, LNCS 13335, pp. 600–617, 2022.
https://doi.org/10.1007/978-3-031-04987-3_41

particularly high proportion of employees with their own company car. It is important to consider how the company cars are currently financed. Companies that already rely on a leasing model, in which a monthly instalment has to be paid for each vehicle, are more inclined to switch to a mobility budget with a fixed monthly amount too.

A mobility budget can be both, a mobility service for employees, where they can spend a monthly allowance for different means of transport at the expense of the company, be it for business or private purposes, as well as the replacement of the classic company car through a flexible use of intermodal mobility services. The company defines a financial framework, the so-called mobility budget, within which employees are entitled to organise their mobility with alternative means of transport in an individual manner (Intelligent Apps GmbH 2021).

In this definition, the mobility budget itself is described as a "mobility service", whereby an "allowance" is granted by the company for the use of not very precisely defined means of transport. The group of users is generally defined as employees. This represents a major difference to the definitions in other publications where the mobility budget is explicitly seen as an alternative to users of personal company cars:

- The basic idea of the mobility budget is that the classic company car is replaced by a flexible mobility offer. The company defines a financial framework, the so-called mobility budget, within which the employees entitled to a company car can individually organise their mobility (Klimaschutz-Unternehmen 2021).
- A mobility budget is an offer for a company's employees that enables them, instead of a personal company car, to make business as well as private journeys with alternative means of transport of their choice within an agreed budget framework (VCD Verkehrsclub Deutschland e.V. 2021).

Derived from the definitions above, the definition valid for this paper is as follows: The (corporate) mobility budget is a fixed amount of money that is made available by the employer to the employee for a fixed period of time to pay for mobility services. Employees can choose from a previously defined portfolio of means of transport. The aim of the mobility budget is to induce a change towards multimodal travel behaviour and more climate friendliness.

The choice and booking of transportation means, the tracking of expenses, the management of the mobility budget and billing are carried out via mobile devices and apps. The design of mobility budgets can be very manifold. Table 1 provides a better understanding what mobility services could be used.

Table 1. Overview of mobility services (cf. Mobiko GmbH 2020, p. 6)

Mobility category	Mobility types and service providers
Public transport	Single ticket, monthly abonnement, etc.
Train	RE, RB, ICE, IC, etc.
Taxi	Uber, FreeNow, taxi receipts, etc.
Long-distance bus	Flixbus, BlaBlaCar bus, etc.
Car sharing	ShareNow, Clevershuttle, BlaBlaCar, etc.
Scooter sharing	Lime, VOI, Tier, etc.
Bike sharing	Swapfiets, Nextbike, Jump, DB Bike, etc.
Car rental	Avis, Sixt, Hertz, Europcar, etc.
Flight	All airlines
Mountain and water transport	Ferry, boat ride, cable car, mountain railway, etc.

2 Role Models and Target Groups

After the definition of the corporate mobility budget, the presentation of the different actors involved in the practical implementation of the mobility budget follows. Three different role models can be distinguished, covering the basic structure and interactions of the involved parties. Within the role models, the stakeholders are the employers, the employees and the mobility budget providers (MBP). They are also the most important target groups for the corporate mobility budget approach.

MBPs act as service providers to facilitate the introduction of corporate mobility budgets. These can be public transport companies, various private mobility service providers, platform providers or railway companies that consider corporate mobility budgets as an additional field for their businesses. But also newly founded companies whose core business is the realisation of corporate mobility budgets are active on the market.

The companies that decide to introduce a mobility budget for their employees act as the customers of the MBPs and the employees are the users of the mobility budget. As a rule, they have only low influence on the choice of the MBPs and the framework conditions, such as the amount of the mobility budget or its period of validity. These features are set by the employers. Nevertheless, the acceptance of the employees is decisive for the success and the benefits of a corporate mobility budget. Especially the younger generation of employees represent an important target group. As part of a survey commissioned by Ford-Werke GmbH, the mobility behaviour of people aged 18 to 23 was analysed (cf. Rauch 2020, p. 10). It showed that for young people mobility primarily means flexibility, while at the same time there is a strong price and environmental awareness for mobility (cf. ibid., p. 10). When asked about their awareness of services such as e-scooter sharing, ride pooling, bike sharing, car sharing and carpooling, at least 61% of respondents answered with “I know about them, but I haven’t used them yet” or “I know about them and I have already used them” (cf. ibid., p. 27). This means the change in mobility behaviour does not have to be brought about by the mobility budget, since it already fits the behaviour of the younger target groups.

The following paragraph presents three role models for mobility budgets. The implementation of the first mobility budget type takes place exclusively within the company (cf. Fig. 1). No other parties such as MBPs are involved.

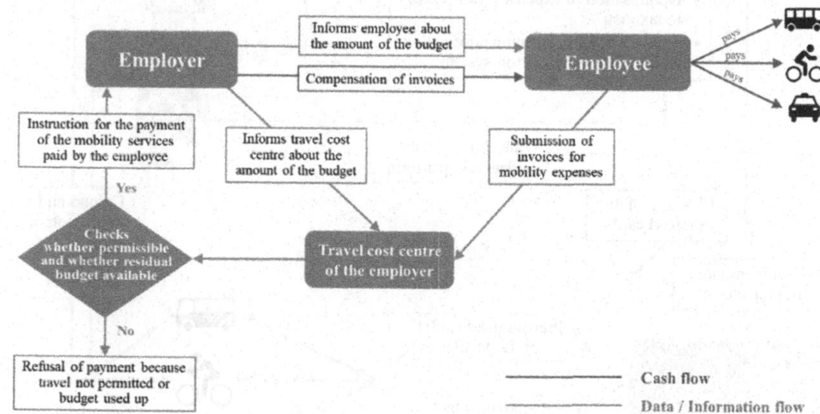

Fig. 1. Role model I – mobility budget within the company (in-house)

For this purpose, the employer informs the employee about the amount of the mobility budget available to them. With this knowledge, the employee initially pays for his mobility services privately and must subsequently submit the invoices to the travel cost centre of his company (cf. Beutnagel 2021). In addition to the employee, the travel cost centre is also informed about the amount of the budget, as it is responsible for checking, recording, and accounting the employee's expenses. After receiving the employee's invoices, the travel cost centre has to check whether the service paid for is permissible and whether the employee's remaining budget is not yet expanded. If both questions are answered with "yes", the feedback to the employer is to compensate the costs for the invoices paid by the employee (cf. ibid.). This can be done via the monthly payroll.

The second type of mobility budget integrates a third actor, the mobility budget provider (MBP). The MBP is mandated by the employer and provides him with a platform and an app for managing the mobility expenses of the employees (cf. Fig. 2).

The employer enters the individual mobility budgets for the employees onto this platform (cf. Mobiko GmbH 2021a). The employees can view the current amount of their budget in the corresponding app of the MBP. In order to use the available budget for mobility services, two options exist on the market. On the one hand, the employee makes a prepayment and gets the uploaded and submitted invoices compensated by the employer (cf. Mobiko GmbH 2021b). On the other hand, the MBP offers a prepaid debit card which can be covered by the employer with any amount of money (cf. belmoto mobility GmbH 2021). In both cases, the invoices for the mobility expenses are then stored in the app. The MBP uses this information to ensure tax-optimised accounting for the employer, which can be entered directly into the employer's payroll system (cf. Mobiko GmbH 2021a).

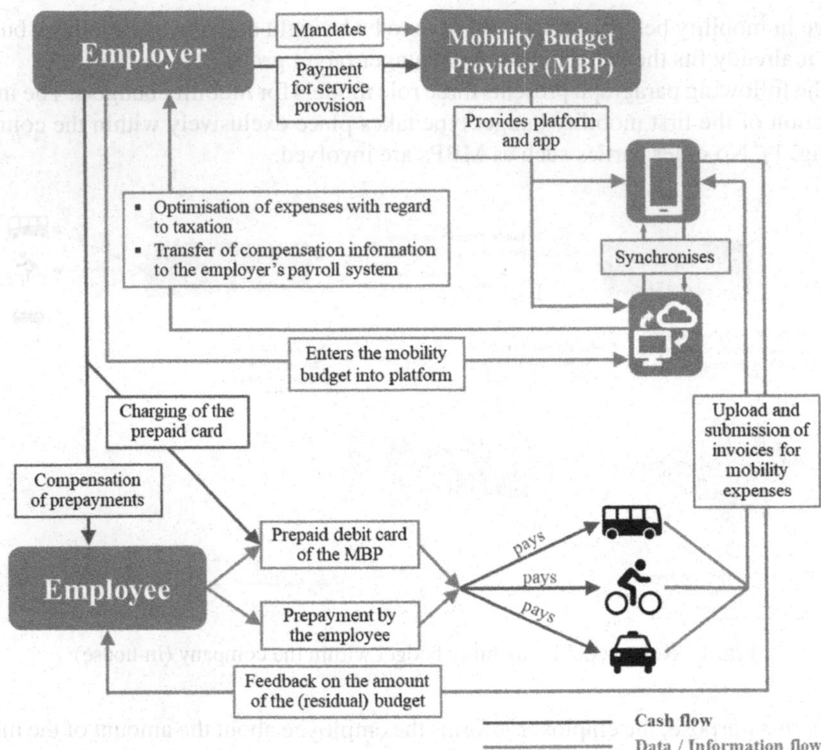

Fig. 2. Role model II – Mobility budget with billing and settlement via MBP

The advantage of this option is that the employer only has to take care of setting up the individual mobility budgets for the employees once, covering the budget on the debit cards or compensating the invoices of the employees. The MBP carries out the checking and the (automated) tax-optimised accounting. The latter point in particular would be difficult to implement in practice if the travel cost centre had to manually check each of the employees' invoices. In this case, the different invoices would probably be taxed at a flat rate and not optimised.

The third type of mobility budget implies the least complexity from the perspective of the employees and employers, whereby another actor is integrated as well (cf. Fig. 3). Like in type II, the employer mandates an MBP who provides the platform and app (cf. Intelligent Apps GmbH 2021). The employer must enter the mobility budgets of the individual employees into the system and cover the costs through the MBP, so that the budget is available in the user account of the employees' apps (cf. ibid.). The employee can then book and pay the desired mobility service directly via the app (cf. ibid.). This eliminates the step of prepayment by the employee and subsequent compensation by the employer. Nevertheless, offers with a direct booking function may have the disadvantage that only a certain selection of mobility services can be used. In addition to the three described types of role models, mixed forms also exist in practice.

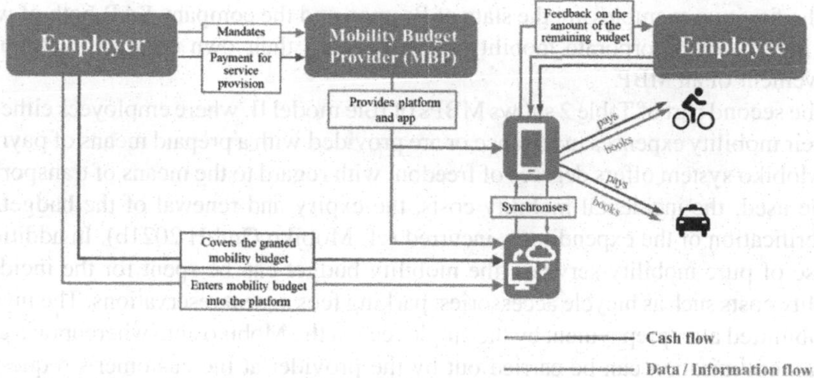

Fig. 3. Role model III – Mobility budget with direct booking functionality

3 Market Overview of Corporate Mobility Budget Providers and Concepts

3.1 National Providers

Table 2 shows the actual MBPs in Germany. The table follows the classification of the different role models presented in Sect. 2.

Table 2. Mobility budget providers in Germany

Provider	Product name
Role model I	
State of Bremen	Corporate mobility concept
SAP SE	Flexible Mobility
Role model II	
Mobiko GmbH	Mobiko
Lofino GmbH	Lofino Mobility
Moovster GmbH	Mobility budget
Movever GmbH	Digital mobility budget
Belmoto Mobility GmbH	(Belmoto) Mobility Card
XXImo GmbH	(XXImo) Mobility Card
1st Mobility AG	Mobility meets Benefit
Role model III	
Deutsche Bahn Connect GmbH	Bonvoyo/hvv-m
Intelligent Apps GmbH	Free Now For Business – Mobility management
Rydes GmbH	Mobility budget

The first two examples are the state of Bremen and the company SAP, both of which have introduced a corporate mobility budget within their own company without the involvement of an MBP.

The second part of Table 2 shows MBPs of role model II, where employees either pay for their mobility expenses in advance or are provided with a prepaid means of payment. The Mobiko system offers degrees of freedom with regard to the means of transport that can be used, the incidental mobility costs, the expiry and renewal of the budget, and the verification of the expenditures incurred (cf. Mobiko GmbH 2021b). In addition to the use of pure mobility services, the mobility budget can be spent for the incidental mobility costs such as bicycle accessories, parking fees or seat reservations. The invoices are submitted after prepayment by the employee via the Mobiko app, whereupon a check and tax optimisation can be carried out by the provider at the customer's request (cf. Mobiko GmbH 2021a).

Lofino offers a similar system, where the payment is made in advance by the employee. The user uploads the invoices via app, and a tax check is carried out by Lofino (cf. Lofino GmbH 2021a). The difference to Mobiko, however, is that the mobility budget is only one part of Lofino's offer (cf. Lofino GmbH 2021b). In addition to a mobility budget, the employee can be provided with further budgets, e.g. for meal or sport course expenses, which are submitted and billed via the same app (cf. ibid.).

At Moovster, in addition to the classic billing model, as offered by the two previous MBPs, the use of mobility services is assessed via the Moovster app (cf. Moovster GmbH 2021). In this process, employees collect points for particularly multimodal and sustainable mobility behaviour, which can be redeemed for rewards such as vouchers at partners (cf. ibid.). Such a gamification approach is a novelty in the field of mobility budgets and represents an additional attraction especially for the younger generation (cf. Wuttke 2019, p. 68 f.).

Besides the possibility of submitting expenses made by the employee via an app, there are also MBPs that issue their own prepaid debit cards, which are covered by the employer. The other three providers in the second part of Table 2 fall into this category. Belmoto, for example, offers the possibility of using mobility services with its "Mobility Card", based on Mastercard, given that the partners accept it as a means of payment (cf. belmoto mobility GmbH 2021). The "Mobility Card" from XXImo has a very similar structure, with the difference that it is a debit card from Visa (cf. XXImo GmbH 2022a). It can also be used for nearly any kind of service, insofar as the employer approves the corresponding category, e.g., public transport or taxi (cf. XXImo GmbH 2022b). The third MBP with prepaid means of payment, 1st Mobility, differs in its concept from the previously mentioned providers by offering a platform under the label "Mobility meets Benefit". The platform can be used to pay for mobility services and other goods within a given budget (cf. 1st Mobility AG 2022). Using the same platform, the employer can also allocate budgets to employees for company cars or "mobility equipment" such as company smartphones or laptops, which are subsequently configured and ordered directly via the platform (cf. ibid.).

Thc MBPs in the third part of Table 2 offer either only direct booking or a combination of direct booking and prepayment, thus representing a mixture of role model II and III.

The brief overview of the national market has shown that several MBPs are already present on the market and that their offers differ in certain aspects. For comparison purposes, the most important characteristics are depicted in the following diagrams. Figure 4 clearly shows that the model of prepayment by the employees is the most common one amongst the twelve national mobility budget offers considered.

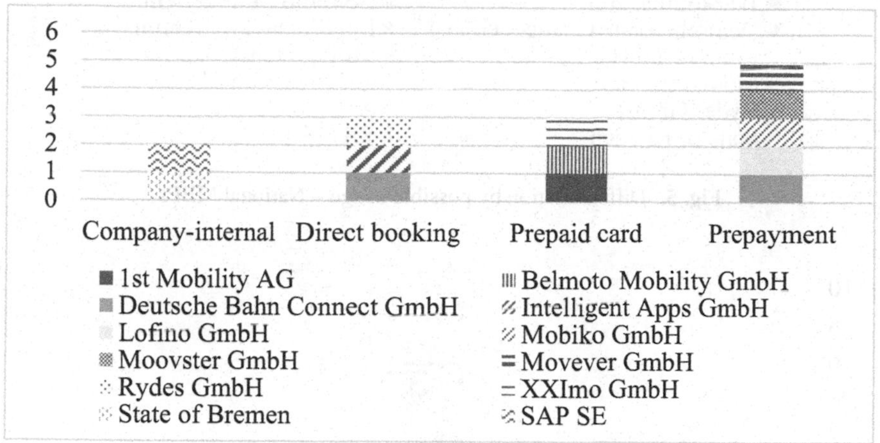

Fig. 4. Differentiation by billing method – National MBPs

Figure 5 shows what the mobility budgets can be used for. First of all, it is not surprising, mobility services can be paid for in every case. In five out of twelve cases, incidental mobility costs can also be charged. These must arise in direct connection with the mobility service and in order to contribute to the goal of "inducing a behavioural change towards multimodal travel behaviour" as defined. However, the use for other completely unrelated goods must be viewed critically.

Figure 6 shows a clear picture regarding the commitment to cooperation partners. It depicts that only in two cases, the choice of mobility services is restricted by the MBP. In the other cases, the employees are free to choose which mobility services they use for their journeys.

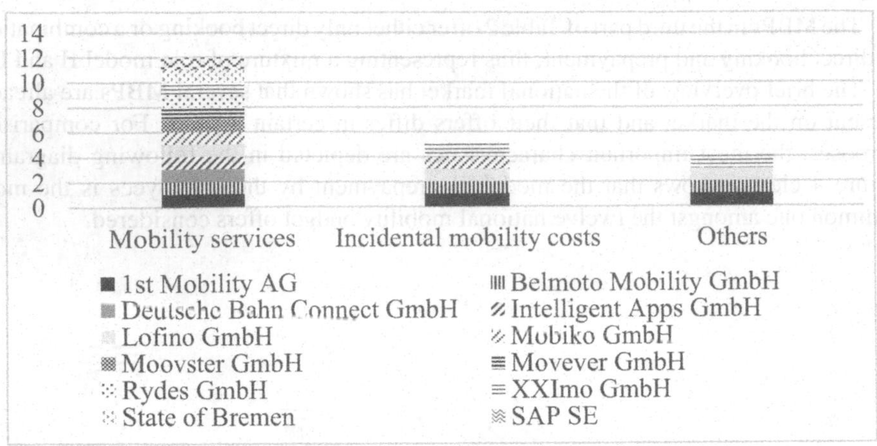

Fig. 5. Differentiation by possible usage – National MBPs

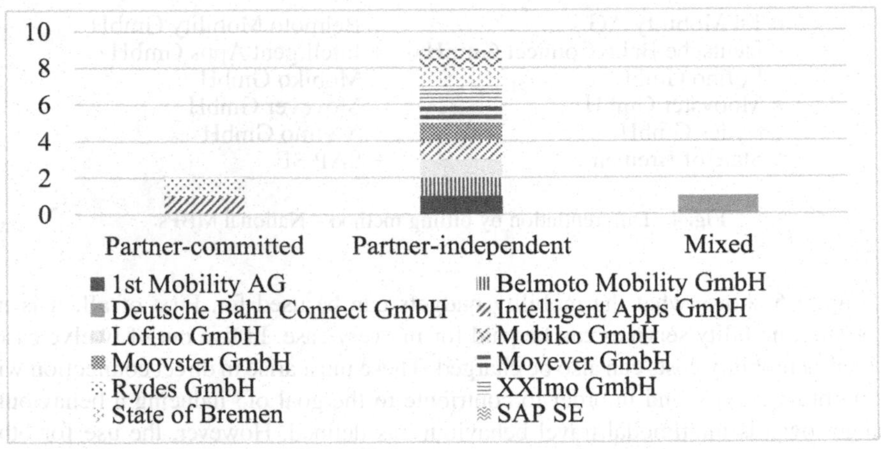

Fig. 6. Differentiation by partner commitment – National MBPs

Finally, in Fig. 7, two other relevant features of the various MBPs are considered: tax optimisation and the availability of an app. It can be seen that all MBPs make an app available. Only the two mobility budgets according to the in-house role model I do not have their own app, as already described in Sect. 2. In practice, this can lead to acceptance problems if the submission of invoices is more complicated compared to the apps of the MBPs. Furthermore, only half of the MBPs optimise the expenses for tax purposes instead of invoicing all services as a lump sum. This can be a competitive advantage if it results in significant cost differences for the employees.

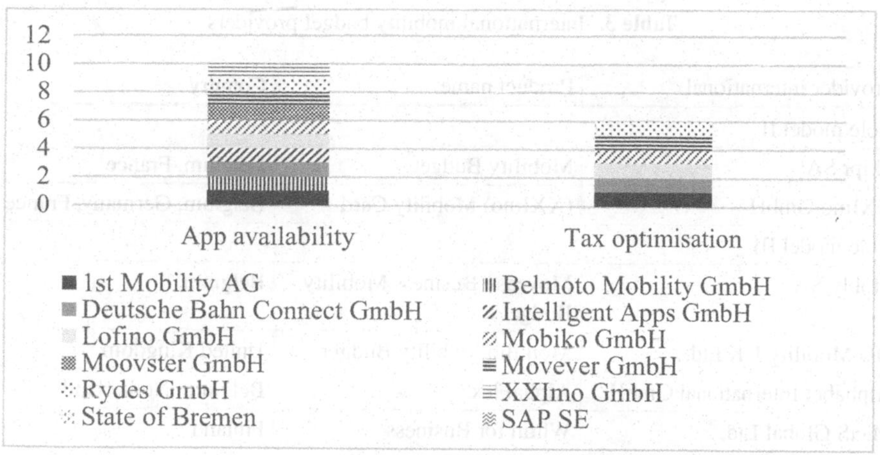

Fig. 7. Other characteristics – National MBPs

After looking at the providers on the national market the following Sect. 3.2 looks at individual providers outside of Germany and compares which similarities and differences exist.

3.2 International Providers

When looking at the international market, it is remarkable that no comparable model could be found outside of Europe in the course of this research. Therefore, only European providers outside of Germany are considered in this section. Table 3 shows a selection of international MBPs, which are divided into providers with and without direct booking and payment functions[1]. In-house company concepts[2] are not presented here.

The first MBP with prepaid offers is Skipr, where the employees are provided with a prepaid means of payment that can be used for mobility services and selected incidental mobility costs (cf. Skipr SA 2020). In addition, it is possible to have unused budget paid out at the end of the month (cf. ibid.). In Belgium, according to legislation (cf. KPMG Law 2019), mobility services paid by mobility budgets are completely tax-free for the employee and the payment of the surplus is tax-privileged. The first provider in Table 3 where employees can book mobility services within the app is Mobly with its Moveasy Business product (cf. Mobly SA 2021). With Moveasy, in addition to direct booking, employees can submit invoices for other mobility services to increase flexibility. Mobillio Mobility Budget also offers the option of direct booking as well as a prepayment option (cf. OD Mobility UK Ltd. 2021). The AlphaFlex product in addition to direct bookings is able to record bookings with mobility companies that are not integrated in the app (Alphabet Belgium Long Term Rental N.V. 2022). Whim for Business by MaaS Global Ltd. corresponds predominantly to a mobility budget according to role model III (MaaS Global Ltd. 2022).

[1] This corresponds to the role models II and III in Sect. 2.

[2] See role model I in Sect. 2.

Table 3. International mobility budget providers

Provider international	Product name	Country
Role model II		
Skipr SA	Mobility Budget	Belgium, France
XXImo GmbH	(XXImo) Mobility Card	Belgium, Germany, France
Role model III		
Mobly SA	Moveasy Business Mobility Budget	Belgium
OD Mobility UK Ltd.	Mobillio Mobility Budget	United Kingdom
Alphabet International GmbH	AlphaFlex	Belgium, Netherlands
MaaS Global Ltd.	Whim for Business	Finland

Analogous to Sect. 3.1, the mobility budgets are briefly summarised and compared below. It is noticeable that the offers that allow direct booking are most represented internationally, whereas prepayment schemes only occurred once (Fig. 8). This represents a clear difference to the providers on the national market, who currently predominantly rely on the system of prepayment by the employees with subsequent compensation.

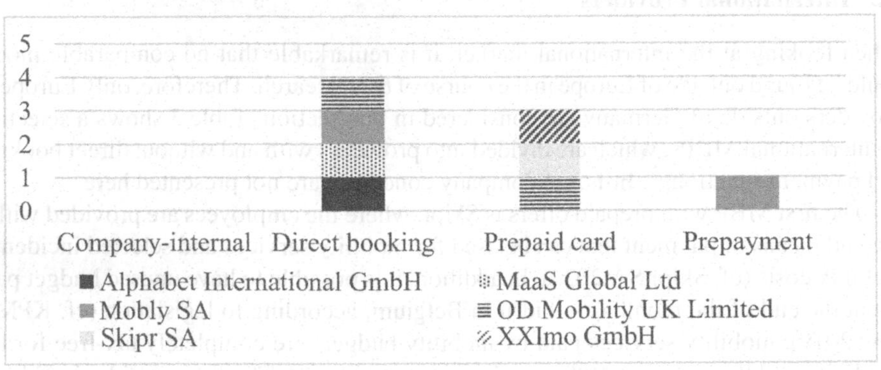

Fig. 8. Differentiation by billing method – International MBPs

The deployment options in Fig. 9 shows a similar picture to that of the national providers. All mobility budgets offer the possibility to pay for various mobility services, whereby some of the providers also allow the payment of incidental mobility costs or the purchase of other goods.

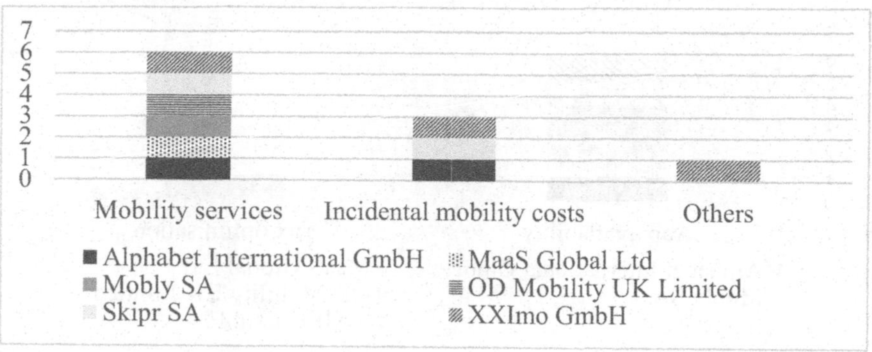

Fig. 9. Differentiation by possible usage – International MBPs

In terms of partner commitment (Fig. 10), there is once again a difference to the offers on the national market. Most providers on the international market have a mixed commitment with a partner-committed and partner-independent component. On the national market, the partner-independent system predominates.

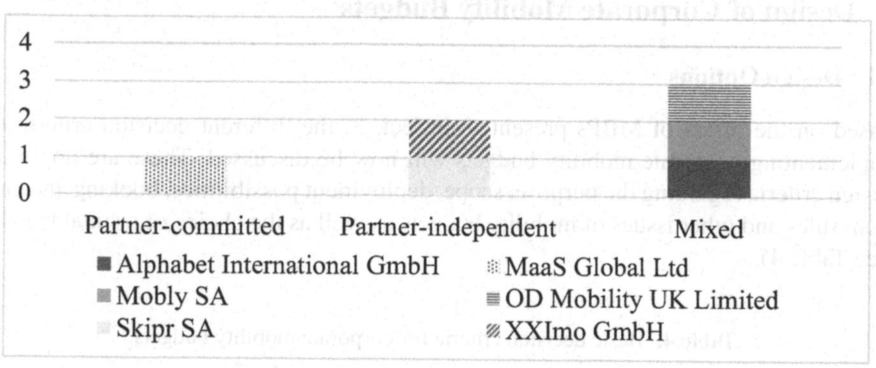

Fig. 10. Differentiation by partner commitment – International MBPs

Finally, the other two characteristics "App availability" and "Tax optimisation" are considered in Fig. 11. Every international MBP provides an app, whereas tax optimisation is only carried out by one provider, OD Mobility UK Ltd (cf. OD Mobility UK Ltd. 2021). On the national market 50% of the providers carry out such optimisation. This is mainly due to the fact that two thirds of the international MBPs considered operate on the Belgian market, where the mobility budget is already anchored in law and thus no tax optimisation is necessary.

The overview of providers of corporate mobility budgets shows that a large number of concepts are already offered both in Germany and in Europe. Although all concepts correspond in their basic structure to one of the role models described in Sect. 2, most of them differ in individual special features. These include e.g. the possibilities to pay for incidental mobility costs, to combine direct booking with uploading and submitting invoices, to set additional incentives for climate-friendly mobility behaviour, to transfer

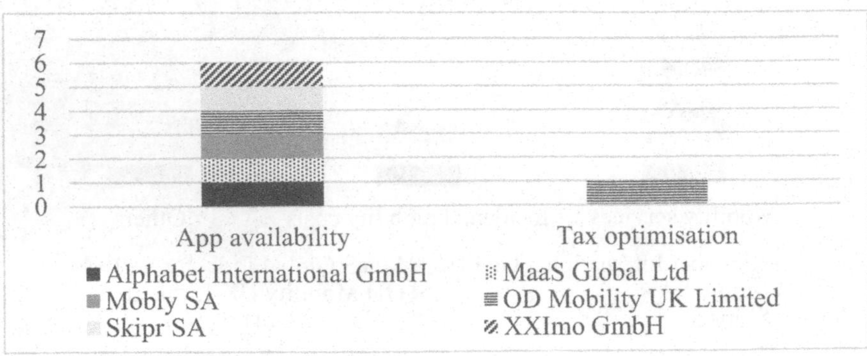

Fig. 11. Other characteristics – International MBPs

a fixed share of the budget to other areas such as fitness. This allows the MBPs to differentiate themselves on the market and the employers to choose and implement the concept that suits their company and their employees best.

4 Design of Corporate Mobility Budgets

4.1 Design Options

Based on the offers of MBPs presented in Sect. 3, the different decision criteria for implementing corporate mobility budgets will now be discussed. These are important design criteria regarding the purpose, scope, deployment possibilities, booking and payment rules and other issues of mobility budgets as well as the choice of a suitable MBP (see Table 4).

Table 4. Basic decision criteria for corporate mobility budgets

Decisions before introduction	Decisions for provider choice	Decisions for deployment set by the employer
· Intended purpose · Involvement of third parties	· Region of deployment · Payment options · Possible usage of the budget · Billing and settlement · Dashboard · App · Special features	· Validity · Budget carry-over · Handling of remaining budget · Transferability to third parties

Before implementing a mobility budget, it is necessary to determine how the budget will be deployed. According to the definition (see Sect. 2), it does not have to lead to a total replacement of a company car. Instead, it can be seen as incentive to switch to more fuel-efficient, cheaper company or electric cars and to get rewarded with the price difference. In addition, the mobility budget offers the employer the possibility to provide each employee with a budget, even if they were not previously entitled to a company car. This increases the company's attractiveness for the staff. Furthermore, it must be determined in advance how the mobility budget is to be implemented in the company. As described in the role models in Sect. 2, this can be done internally or with the involvement of an MBP. If the employer decides to involve an MBP, further questions regarding the features of the mobility budget and its' specifications have to be answered in advance in order to select the provider whose product meets the company's needs best. MBPs with an exclusive direct booking function are often regionally limited due to their commitment to local mobility partners. They are therefore not suitable for the use throughout Germany or Europe. In the case of providers whose billing scheme works by invoice upload, there are technically no limits to the area of application. The only hurdles can be exchange rates, the non-availability of internationally recognised means of payment and any foreign transaction fees that may be charged. A solution for these problems is the choice of an MBP offering a debit card, insofar as this allows payment in foreign currency. Furthermore, the payment and billing rules have to be determined. As explained in Sects. 2 and 3, a distinction can be made between prepayment by the employee, payment using a means of payment of the MBP, and a direct booking function. The decision for one or a combination of the mentioned payment possibilities can be important for the acceptance of the mobility budget by the employees.

Another decision concerns the question, for which services the mobility budget may be spent: exclusively for mobility services, or also for incidental mobility cost, for example, accessories or repairs for the bicycle, seat reservations for the train, expenses for fuel, parking fees or the car wash. The latter makes it more difficult to achieve the original goal to change the employee's behaviour towards multimodal travel chains. Alternatively, the share allowed to be spent on a company car could be limited.

Most MBPs offer employers an interface (dashboard) for setting up and controlling the mobility budget. Besides the option of not having a dashboard at all, the possibility of entering the individual budgets of the employees is the simplest form. Furthermore, it is possible to set the general conditions such as the renewal or the period of validity. More comprehensive dashboards also offer the option to permit user-individual utilisation of the budget.

In addition to the dashboard for the employer, the app is relevant for the employees as users of the mobility budget. The range of the app features varies depending on the MBP. It can have a purely informative function, e.g. about the amount or validity of the mobility budget. In addition, various functions can be integrated with regard to the payment functions, for example, the invoice upload with scan function and/or a direct booking functionality. It is also possible to transfer an amount of money from the mobility budget to the app of the mobility service company. In this case, the users might need apps from several mobility service companies.

The last important decision for the choice of MBP concerns additional features. As discussed in the provider overview in Sect. 3, this could be bonus programs that reward particularly multimodal and sustainable transport behaviour with points that can subsequently be converted into rewards.

The last column of Table 4 shows the decisions of deployment set by the employer. First of all, this concerns the validity, i.e., for how long a mobility budget is allocated. This can vary from a monthly, quarterly, annual to a flexible allocation for an individual period.

Depending on this, the way of budget carry-over must be defined: What happens to the remaining budget when the validity period expires? Can the budget be accumulated over several months or years and spent on a larger trip?

In this context, the question of transferability to third parties arises, i.e., whether the mobility budget may only be used for budget holder or also for fellow travellers.

The last decision concerns the unused remaining budget, which cannot be carried over further. In practice, there are various options to handle this. The most common way is to pay out the unused budget via the payroll at the end of the month, quarter, or year, depending on the period of validity of the budget. Alternatively, the mobility budget can also expire and be transferred back to the employer, for example, if it has already been deposited in a means of payment. A third option is to invest these unused budgets for a specific purpose, e.g., in sustainable projects for environmental protection.

4.2 Decision Support Tool for Employers

In order to support the decision-making process for the most appropriate design of corporate mobility budget, an Excel-based tool was created within the framework of this paper. The tool is a selection mask implemented in Microsoft Excel, which contains almost all of the above mentioned decision criteria (see Sect. 4.1) and their characteristics, divided into three sections: pre-implementation decisions, provider selection decisions and decisions for deployment set by the employer like in Table 4.

The first section of the tool (see Fig. 12), in contrast to Table 4, only asks for the purpose of use, since a decision to integrate an MBP is the reason for using the tool and is therefore assumed. The user can select which purpose(s) of use he or she envisages and, if necessary, make a multiple selection.

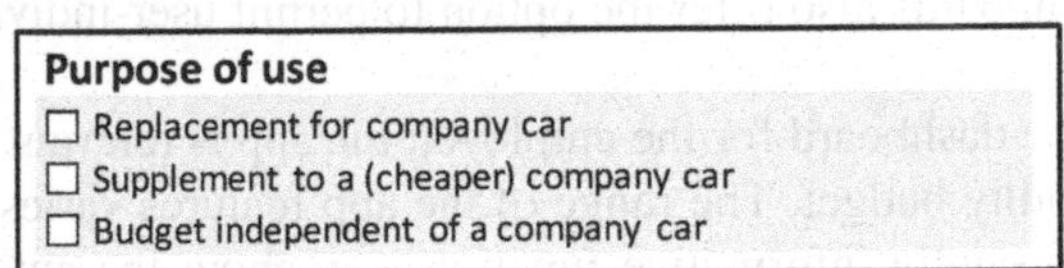

Purpose of use
Replacement for company car
Supplement to a (cheaper) company car
Budget independent of a company car

Fig. 12. Section 1 – Decision criterion and its characteristics before the implementation of mobility budgets

Section 2 concerns the decisions for the choice of MBP and has the highest relevance for the issued recommendation, since the various mobility budgets show the strongest difference in the characteristics of this section (see Fig. 13). The section contains fields that allow only single choice and fields with multiple choices. The reason for this is that a characteristic such as "Europe-wide" necessarily also contains "Germany-wide" as an attribute for the region of deployment.

Decisions for provider choice

Region of deployment
☐ Regional
☐ Germany-wide
☐ Europe-wide

Payment options
☐ Prepayment by employees
☐ Means of payment of the MBP
☐ Direct booking functionality

Possible usage of the budget
☐ Mobility services
☐ Incidental mobility costs
☐ Company car
☐ Other purchases

Billing and settlement
☐ Lump sum as a benefit of kind
☐ Differentiated consideration of means of transport

(Employer) Dashboard
☐ Not available
☐ Setting the budget
☐ Setting the framework conditions
☐ Limitation of usable services

App
☐ Not available
☐ Information function
☐ Invoice upload
☐ Direct booking
☐ Credit booking

Special features
☐ Bonus programme
☐ Other budgets possible
☐ All-in-One-Solution

Fig. 13. Section 2 – Decision criteria and their characteristics for MBP selection

The third section contains the criteria set by the employer and the technical possibilities of budget implementation (see Fig. 14). For example, if a budget transfer to the next month or an expiration of the remaining budget is technically not possible, the product may not be the best recommendation for the employer.

Vailidity
☐ Monthly
☐ Quarterly
☐ Annually
☐ Flexible

Budget transfer
☐ Into next month
☐ Into next year
☐ Flexible

Unused remaining budget
☐ Expiration
☐ Corporate investment
☐ Payout to the employee

Transferability to third parties
☐ Non-transferable
☐ Transferable in conjunction with budget-holder (limited)
☐ Transferable in conjunction with budget-holder (unlimited)
☐ Fully transferable

Fig. 14. Section 3 – Decision criteria their characteristics set by the employer

Figure 15 first lists the providers currently available on the market and shows in the last column their level of conformity with the previously selected characteristics, which is additionally supported by a colour differentiation according to the traffic light logic[3] (see Fig. 15).

The level of conformity is calculated according to the following scheme:

$$\frac{\sum \textit{Characteristics that mobility budget fulfills}}{\sum \textit{Selected characteristics}}$$

Each selected characteristic is considered in the same way: A fulfilled characteristic equals 1, an unfulfilled characteristic equals 0. The number of characteristics in the denominator of the equation equals the sum of all selected characteristics, whereby each characteristic enters the calculation unweighted. A 100% match thus means that the corresponding mobility budget meets all the selected characteristics.

[3] The highest level of conformity is marked in dark green, the level of conformity at the 0.5 quantile is marked in yellow and the lowest level of conformity is marked in red (with different shades of the respective colors for values in between).

MBP recommendation:

Company	Product name	Conformity
Mobiko GmbH	Mobiko	80%
Deutsche Bahn Connect GmbH	Bonvoyo/hvv-m	80%
Intelligent Apps GmbH	Free Now For Business - Mobilitätsbudget	67%
Belmoto Mobility GmbH	(Belmoto) Mobility Card	73%
XXimo GmbH	(XXimo) Mobility Card	60%
Moovster GmbH	Mobilitätsbudget	53%
Rydes GmbH	Mobilitätsbudget	53%
Movever GmbH	Digitales Mobilitätsbudget	40%
Lofino GmbH	Lofino Mobility	53%
1st Mobility AG	Mobility meets Benefit	80%

Fig. 15. Example of a mobility budget recommendation by the decision tool (Color figure online)

The Excel tool is on the current data status at the time of writing this paper. A regular data check-up has to be carried out in order to generate the best possible recommendation. Nevertheless, it gives users, especially employers, an initial recommendation of a suitable mobility budget for their company.

5 Summary

The implementation of mobility budgets instead or in addition to more fuel-efficient company cars constitutes a significant contribution to a better environmental performance of a company. This can have a practical impact on the value of the company in the case of an environmental certification (ISO 14001). The introduction of a general mobility budget can help to augment the employer attractiveness. Employers have better cost control through fixed occurring costs. Variable components such as fuel costs for company cars are eliminated. Before introducing a mobility budget, its acceptance in the company has to be evaluated carefully in order to decide whether the mobility budget should replace the company car or only supplement it. If necessary, individual solutions can be agreed upon depending on the work tasks.

Employees who have not yet received a budget for mobility services could generally benefit from the introduction of a mobility budget. Employees who previously had a personal company car will have to adapt their mobility behaviour if the mobility budget completely replaces the company car. However, according to Zijlstra (2016, p. 129), there is a high probability that the elimination of a company car will result in the purchase of an (additional) private vehicle for a large proportion of subjects interviewed in this study. In any case, there is a need to address multimodal mobility behaviour. Furthermore, the locations of the company site as well as the places of the employees' residences influence the acceptance of corporate mobility budgets. There must be a sufficient offer of alternative mobility services, otherwise it leads to problems, especially in rural areas.

For the MBPs, such as public transport companies or any kind of private mobility service companies, the increasing awareness and use of mobility budgets implies an increasing demand on the market. The resulting competition can be an accelerator for innovations. Furthermore, different cost models are necessary to present an attractive mobility solution for small companies with few employees as well as for large companies with a high number of users.

References

1st Mobility AG: Das Leistungsspektrum von "Mobility meets Benefit" (2022). https://1stmobility.com/de/leistungsspektrum. Accessed 10 Jan 2022

Alphabet Belgium Long Term Rental N.V.: Alphabet Mobility App (2022). https://www.alphabet.com/en-be/products/alphabet-mobility-app. Accessed 11 Jan 2022

Arval Deutschland GmbH: Mobilitäts- und Fuhrparkbarometer Deutschland 2021 (2021)

Belmoto mobility GmbH: So profitieren Sie und Ihre Mitarbeiter von der belmoto Mobility Card (2021). https://www.belmoto.de/de/mobility-card. Accessed 03 Jan 2022

Beutnagel, W.: Löst das Mobilitätsbudget den Dienstwagen ab? (2021). https://www.automotiveit.eu/mobility/mobilitaetstrends/loest-das-mobilitaetsbudget-den-dienstwagen-ab-225.html. Accessed 03 Jan 2022

Intelligent Apps GmbH: Eine Definition des Mobilitätsbudgets (2021). https://free-now.com/de/business/blog/das-mobilitaetsbudget-die-zukunft-der-mobilitaetsstrategie-in-unternehmen/. Accessed 15 Dec 2021

Klimaschutz-Unternehmen (Die Klimaschutz - und Energieeffizienzgruppe der Deutschen Wirtschaft e. V): Flexibel einsetzbares Budget. - Statt starrer Dienstwagenregelung (2021). https://www.klimaschutz-unternehmen.de/erfolgsrezepte/mobilitaetsbudget/. Accessed 15 Dec 2021

KPMG Law: Mobility budget (2019). https://www.kpmglaw.be/news/posts/2019/march/mobility-budget/. Accessed 11 Jan 2022

Lofino GmbH: LOFINO Mobility - ein Budget, alle Möglichkeiten (2021a). https://www.lofino.de/produkte/mobility/. Accessed 06 Apr 2022

Lofino GmbH: LOFINO – alle Benefits für Ihr Unternehmen in einer App! (2021b). https://www.lofino.de. Accessed 06 Jan 2022

MaaS Global Ltd.: For businesses (2022). https://whimapp.com/helsinki/en/forbusinesses/. Accessed 11 Jan 2022

MOBIKO GmbH: Mobilitätsreport 2020 (2020)

MOBIKO GmbH: So funktioniert Mobiko für Arbeitgeber (2021a). https://www.mobiko.de/mobiko-fuer-mitarbeiter/. Accessed 03 Jan 2022

MOBIKO GmbH: So funktioniert Mobiko für Mitarbeiter (2021b). https://www.mobiko.de/mobiko-fuer-mitarbeiter/. Accessed 03 Jan 2022

Mobly, S.A.: Moveasy - mobility made easy (2021). https://moveasy.be. Accessed 11 Jan 2022

Moovster GmbH: Wir machen mehr aus Deiner Mobilität (2021). https://www.getmoovster.com/index_de.html?id=83. Accessed 06 Jan 2022

OD Mobility UK Ltd.: Introducing Mobility Budgets To Your Organisation (2021)

Rauch, C.: Mobility Zeitgeist Studie - Die mobile Generation Z (2020)

Skipr, S.A.: Increase your employees' income and flexibility thanks to the Mobility Budget (2020). https://www.skipr.co/pages/mobility-budget. Accessed 11 Jan 2022

VCD Verkehrsclub Deutschland e.V.: Mobilitätsbudget statt Dienstwagen (2021). https://www.vcd.org/artikel/mobilitaetsbudget-statt-dienstwagen/. Accessed 15 Dec 2021

Wuttke, R.: Mobilität in der Tasche. In: Flotten Management (2019)

XXImo GmbH: XXImo-Mobilitätskarte (2022a). https://www.xximo.de/xximo-mobilitatskarte/. Accessed 07 Jan 2022

XXImo GmbH: Mobilitätsoptionen (2022b). https://www.xximo.de/optionen/. Accessed 07 Jan 2022

Zijlstra, T.: On the mobility budget for company car users in Flanders. Doctoral thesis. University of Antwerp (2016)

A Tangible Based Interaction- and Visualization-Tool for the Analyzation of Individual Mobility Data on an Augmented Reality Table

Waldemar Titov(✉) and Thomas Schlegel

Institute of Ubiquitous Mobility Systems (IUMS), Karlsruhe University of Applied Sciences, Moltkestrasse 30, 76133 Karlsruhe, Germany
{waldemar.titov,iums}@h-ka.de

Abstract. The use of new technologies for the control and presentation of information is being researched in many areas. In addition to the usual, widely widespread methods of touch input or the classic buttons, there are many other forms of interaction. Thanks to the constant progress of technology, new possibilities appeared the use of which is being researched and their suitability for different use-case. The goal of this work is to evaluate the representation of individual mobility data collected by individuals using an app-based mobility diary on an Augmented Reality (AR) Table. In [1] we introduced the AR-Table and its presentation and interaction use-cases. Additionally, to the presentation, an interaction concept using tangibles is developed and evaluated. Via tangibles, the presented data can be filtered and thus varied. The tangibles offer new ways and ideas to explore data, thereby attracting new user groups. The representations of the individual traffic routes were designed and a layout for the representation of the route relationships on a map and its interaction was created. The dynamic generation of the routes allows for immediate analysis of the information for the users.

Keywords: Tangible interaction · Visualization of mobility data · Evaluation

1 Introduction

The development in the use of new technologies for interaction with applications is progressing. It is now normal to deviate from the familiar interaction via touch and to use other interaction techniques. In addition to control by gestures, tangibles are also used in some areas. Control by gestures allows a free and distanced operation of the application. In contrast, tangibles combine physical objects with visualizations on the output device. Tangibles are physical, i.e. tangible, objects. Tangibles can have different shapes and sizes. The physical elements can serve as interactive controls through their changeable spatial representation. The content of this paper revolves around the display of traffic data on a repurposed AR-Table, prior introduced in [1], in addition to the design of an

H. Krömker (Ed.): HCII 2022, LNCS 13335, pp. 618–636, 2022.
https://doi.org/10.1007/978-3-031-04987-3_42

interaction concept with tangibles. The data comes from the results of a traffic survey using our MobiDiary mobile application that was prior introduced in [2]. Over a period of time, users were encouraged to record their trips in a trip diary within the app. Thus, in addition to spatial and temporal characteristics, additional context parameters were recorded. The data analysis and preparation of the information had already been carried out in a previous project. Through this preliminary work, the focus can now be placed on visualization. The different routes are to be displayed on a map section of the city of Karlsruhe in Baden-Württemberg, Germany. It should be possible to filter the data set according to different properties of the path relationships. These include, among other things, the purpose of the path, the traveled distance and the duration of the path. This filtering is to be achieved with the help of the tangible interaction. In the course of the project, a concept will be developed that changes the filters by influencing the tangibles and adapts them to the user's specifications.

Based on this data set, the visualizations are applied to individually collected mobility data introduced in the next section. After implementation, the visualizations and the interaction concept will be evaluated within a user study described in chapter six. Thereby, the type and representation of the routes are queried. At the same time, the interaction with the tangibles will be observed and subsequently recorded in a questionnaire. The focus of the work is on the one hand on the development of a visualization concept and its implementation in the program, on the other hand the use the development of a tangible based interaction concept to control the interactions with the visualized content.

The work is based on the research project KATZE[1], which was conducted by the University of Applied Sciences in Karlsruhe. Because of the project, an AR-Table was assembled and equipped with individual sensors and features further described in Sect. 1.2. This AR-Table setup introduced in [1] was used for the current work. The findings on the handling of tangibles and visualization presented in section eight can be used for further research projects.

The elaboration is structured as follows. After the introduction to the topic and the identification of the objectives, the first chapter presents the current state of research. Thereby all relevant works and contents are summarized. In the following chapter, the conception of the interaction with the tangibles and its implementation will be discussed. This is followed by the presentation and the related ideas. The penultimate section deals with the preparation and implementation of the evaluation. The evaluation gives an overview of the results and findings of the evaluation.

1.1 MobiDiary Data Description

In [2] we introduced our mobility evaluation tool MobiDiary an instrument for multi modal mobility analysis. As described in more detail in [3] we conduct annual mobility analysis of student's mobility. Following the standardized method for accessing travelers' mobility designed by the German ministry of traffic and infrastructure [4] our android application captures start time, chosen transport mode, transfer time, time of arrival

[1] Research project KATZE url: https://www.h-ka.de/ivi/projekte/katze.

and the purpose of the taken route. Additionally, the app is able to track additional context information. The app queries the current weather and links the Information to the recorded routes. The app also checks the audio jack, and records, if headphones are connected. Furthermore, the app asks the user to state their mode of transport after each stage of their way. Simultaneously, the Google Awareness API automatically identifies the modes. This allows verifying the provided data from the users and vice versa, the identification Google provides. Similar we handle the purpose of the route. As stated above user initially provide the purpose of the route. Additionally, we also use the Google nearby Places API to identify the purpose automatically. Finally, MobiDiary enables the users to add a description of the situations in which they made a transport change decision. We use this information to validate the specifications on the purpose of a trip given by the app users. If for example, a user indicated that the route purpose is free time when being located in a university building, the given information might be wrong.

1.2 AR-Table Description

The campus of Karlsruhe University of Applied Sciences is undergoing an architectural rearrangement. To support the planning phase for these changes, we developed a demonstrator that is able to show changes of the buildings as well as changes in the mobility to, from and on the campus. The ambitious overarching goal of the project was the establishment of a CO_2 neutral campus until 2030. An additional goal was enhancing the quality of stay and several other requirements and constraints were also in place. Due to the multitude of goals and responsibilities, many different participants and stakeholders were involved in the planning process. Those were civil engineers, architects, traffic engineers, computer scientists, students, employees, representatives of the city of Karlsruhe, the local transport and transportation sharing companies and many more.

Therefore, the field of participants was very heterogeneous. Because of that, we searched for a suitable possibility to bring these different disciplines together and to provide a basis for a joint discussion. Our approach was the construction of an interactive demonstrator using interactive spatially augmented reality. For the development of the demonstrator, we pursued a prototyping approach.

The AR-Table is used for meetings with stakeholders, presentations, explorative surveys and participation workshops. During the planning process, new ideas were constantly being added, which influenced the planning. In the course of the project the concept was adapted and further developed in several steps. Thus, an important requirement for the demonstrator was to be able to visualize new ideas and measures quickly and easily. In addition, it should also be ensured that as much information as possible can be understood and memorized by those involved. The demonstrator should be able to display spatial data, architectural data, data concerning the mobility on campus and visualizations of key figures.

Looking for a suitable medium for this purpose, we decided to develop a construction with an architectural model as centerpiece onto which information is projected with video mapping. Already the old Egyptians used physical models to design and communicate [5]. Physical models make it easier to understand and evaluate forms and at the same time present spatial relationships and proportions. According to Stanford Hohauser, architectural models are the most easily understood presentational technique [6]. Especially for people that are not familiar with a project it can be difficult to perceive a planning clearly. Architectural models can directly communicate ideas to the stakeholders and public and therefore facilitates understanding. At the same time, the campus reconstruction project does not only focus on architectural changes. Due to the goal to achieve a CO_2 neutral campus, mobility and energy information is also relevant. These data are related to buildings and other architectural aspects of the campus, but cannot easily be displayed on an architectural model on its own. The video mapping can augment the architectural model and integrate additional data with architectural information.

2 Related Work

The topic offers different approaches, which could be the basis for the research. This is because the number of papers dealing with the same topic is small. For the summary of the current state of technology and research, two areas were therefore examined separately. On the one hand, works with augmented reality and their use of tangibles were researched and on the other hand, the focus was on the visualization of traffic data. The results are summarized below.

As a first point of view, the use of tangibles as markers for augmented reality application is discussed. Therefore, first the work, which was done in the course of the already described project [1], was analyzed. The work mainly deals with the design of the AR-Table. Different developments for a zero-emissions campus are displayed on an underlying 3D model. The paper has studied the interaction of users with markers. The representations changed based on the actions taken with the tangibles on the 3D model of the table. Different information and visualizations were displayed for each interaction. The content was displayed in the form of videos, images, or graphics. In addition to the basic presentation of the content, the extent to which users can absorb and digest all the information was investigated. With the interaction timeline, videos and images for the individual time steps are displayed in addition to the content on the model. The simple and self-explanatory operation allows immediate use even by people not familiar with the subject. During the course of the project, it became apparent that gray tones are difficult to distinguish. Therefore, light colors were used and the layout was designed in black with white lettering, which was found to be more recognizable in the evaluation. The evaluation found that users were very poor at answering questions about the diagrams presented. The abundance of information and the limited display duration are decisive for the poor perception of the users. For the most part, the interface was rated as understandable and almost everyone liked the display with the demonstrator.

Next, we will look at implementations of augmented reality using marker interaction. The first work by Billighurst et al. [7] is about collaboration based on virtual representation of objects. In the work, they mainly focused on the possibilities of tangibles in conjunction with augmented reality. In this approach, each physical marker is associated with a corresponding object, which is shown to the user via a projection. According to the work, the advantage is the possibility to change the virtual objects by physical movements. Problems that arise due to the separation of interaction and representation in tangible user interfaces. This allows several users to work on different objects at the same time and the results are visible to all users. Due to the virtual representation and the natural movement of physical objects, the use did not cause any problems even for inexperienced users. The work has shown how the tangibles simplify interaction and what physical control options they offer. These movements, already familiar to the user, facilitate interaction.

These initially rather general works on tangibles related to augmented reality are complemented by further works focusing on the representation of geographic data or traffic data. For this purpose, Park et al. [8] developed a first concept, which is similar to our setup in parts. In addition to the content on the interface itself, the user sees information on additional screens here. Via a camera, the movements with the tangibles on the table are captured and the geographical data is adjusted. In addition to the 2D position, the rotation of the objects is also recorded. A comparison of control with a joystick has shown that both effectiveness and user satisfaction are better with the tangibles.

Dalgaard et al. [9] developed their augmented reality application on a transparent surface. The interaction is comparable, the position and rotation of the tangibles is also captured. The distinctive feature of this work is that the tangibles are included as a representation tool and render content. The physical objects either blend into the background or provide a contrast. Several markers are used to change the displayed geographical data on a map. By positioning them, certain areas on the map can be enlarged or reduced. This allows content to be retrieved in detail. The project shows that the combination of the different markers allows an almost unlimited variation of content. The markers can be connected by their spatial properties and always present different and new data. For a smooth user acquisition, the reduction of inconsistencies and graphical errors has to be minimized.

The second section focuses on the representation of traffic data on maps. Here, the aspects and applications to be considered are listed. For this, Chen et al. [10] provides a good basis in their work. The possibilities and approaches for the representation of traffic data are explained in detail. A distinction is made between temporal, spatial and temporal-spatial representation. All three aspects are examined and the possibilities of their representation are shown. The spatial representation can be shown by line segments. This allows the relationships between start and destination to be displayed on a map, for example. The individual coordinates are connected and distinguished from each other by color coding. A problem of this approach is seen as the overlapping at a certain amount of elements. This so-called clustering must be avoided for better recognizability. By clustering elements that belong together, the number can be minimized, thus ensuring clarity.

Another work on this topic deals with visual analytics based on transportation and mobility data [11]. In this work, the different types of data and their representation are discussed. For the complex traffic data and its complex problems, solutions are sought in the work. The different approaches of the last years are pointed out in the work and their impact on the future use of intelligent transportation systems are described. In addition to the basic structure of the data and its processing, the work covers different aspects of mobility. These include "Movement and Transportation Infrastructure", "Movement and Behavior", and "Modeling and planning". Similar to the previous work, the presentation of the data is discussed. In this case, the spatial events describe the positional changes of individual objects in the system. For this purpose, time sequences of these spatial events are represented. A representation form represents thereby the connecting of the events. The lines show not only the spatial changes but also the temporal differences. Depending on the goal of the visualization, the work provides information about the possible representations of the path relationships. For example, the paths can be differentiated by color depending on the means of transportation. In order to better compare the spatial conditions, it is also possible to display only certain routes based on a geographic selection made.

A first evaluation approach of the mobility data collected by out mobility evaluation tool MobiDiary evaluating student's mobility before and after the covid-19 pandemic was conducted in [12]. We performed our mobility behavior analysis and compared the collected mobility data from October 2018 (before the corona virus pandemic) and October 2020 (after the outbreak of SARSCoV-2). In both measuring periods, students were asked to record their daily mobility over a two-week period with our mobility evaluation tool "MobiDiary". The mobility data set collected in 2018 contained data from 38 students. Overall, 308 ways with a sum of 4.954 km in over 89 h of travel time were collected. Thereby the density of tracks traveled around campus and its outposts were significant. In 2020, the number of participants rose by three person up to 41. However, the collected data decreased by more than 50% down to 150 ways. The distance of collected tracks decreased by over 63% to the amount of 1.760 km in 74 h travel time. Due to online and distance lectures, the necessity of visiting lectures at the campus disappeared.

The research on the different areas has shown that there are many different approaches in the area of Tangibles User Interfaces. The interaction and its implementation differ. In terms of representation, the work provides important insights for visualization.

3 AR-Table Construction

The structure already described by Hansert et al. [1] serves as the basis for this work. Therefore, the hardware itself will no longer be discussed, but only briefly the individual components and their relevance to the topic being worked on. The AR table used can actually no longer be considered as such, because the physical backgrounds in the form of the 3D model have been dismantled. The table is now used exclusively for rendering the images. This is because using the tangibles for interaction is not a use of augmented reality.

The surface has a height of 60 cm. This consists of a white wooden plate with a length of 2.50 m and a width of 1.40 m. The use of the table is later on the longer side of the table. A camera and a beamer are installed above the table surface. The stereo depth camera from Intel RealSense is used to capture the situation in an image and evaluate it in the program. For each time step, a black and white image of the camera is created and passed on to the program. For this purpose, the image, which is distorted, is first transformed to a normal view so that an evaluation can take place. The program reads the markers and their positions from the individual images. In addition to the markers for interaction, markers are recorded at each corner of the table. The position of these is calculated and thus the necessary transformation of the images is worked out. If one or more markers are not recognized, a wrong transformation is chosen and the image to be displayed is distorted. The beamer generates the display of the generated content. For this purpose, the image is overwritten and re-projected several times a second. In the process, the original image is first converted to the beamer's view of the table. This means that the pixels of the new image are also transformed again.

In addition, the tangibles are important components of the structure. Markers are applied to the surface of these elements. Markers are combinations of black and white squares, similar to a QR code. The markers were created and stored via the public ARuco library. The library provides predefined codes for each marker ID for different sizes. Markers from the 6×6 library are used for the theme. Thus, the width and length of the markers are six squares each. However, the subsequent size of the markers may vary. Depending on the camera used, the markers can be reduced in size as desired. The recognition of the markers is easier and faster with increasing size.

For the display, the mobility data available in json format is loaded into the system. The MobiDiary app [2] was used to collect information about routes taken by students and staff for a period of two weeks in October 2018. In addition to querying the means of transport, purpose of the journey and other data, the app also includes the automatic collection of other information. This includes relevant values such as the time and position but also data that is not interesting for this work, such as the use of the headphone jack of the smartphone. For each route, this data is stored in the file provided. The processing of the data was already done in a separate project. In this, the file was read in and the data prepared for further processing. The relevant information was stored within a data frame. This project status serves as the basis for the interaction concept and the visualization. The AR-Table is shown in Fig. 1.

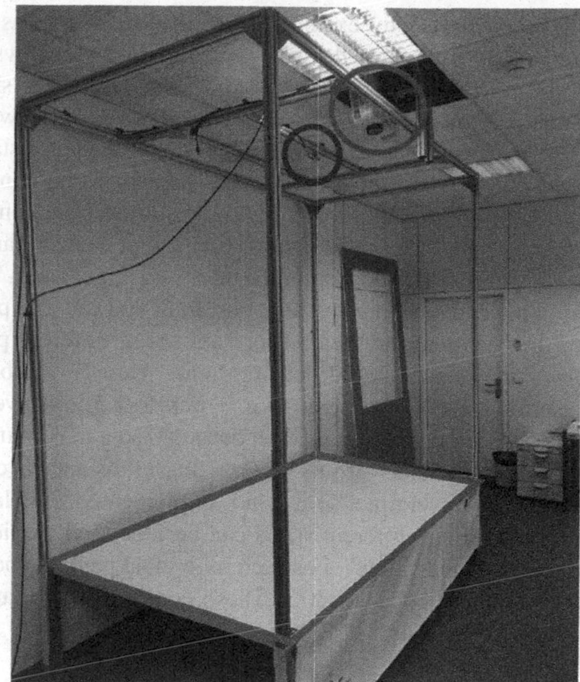

Fig. 1. Structural design of AR-Table with camera, projector and table surface

4 Concept of Interaction

The following section explains the development and implementation of the interaction. In order to make the subsequent interaction more understandable, the existing data must first be discussed for this purpose. The application has collected the following relevant information:

- track id,
- time: start and end time of track,
- position: longitude and latitude with corresponding timestamps,
- means of transport,
- purpose of way,
- travel distance in meters,
- travel time in hours/minutes/seconds and
- prevailing weather conditions.

Based on the collected data, a concept for interactive presentation had to be developed for the routes. For this purpose, only a part of the data was taken into account so that the users could still process the information. In addition to the means of transport and the purpose of the journey, the duration of the journey and the weather were taken into account in the implementation. In order for the information to reach its full potential, the different aspects are linked together. Thus, routes with different means of transport and purposes are to be displayed, for example, when the sky is overcast and the travel time is a maximum of 30 min. This flexible choice of factors allows differentiated representations of the collected data. The study area is limited to Karlsruhe due to the positions of the paths. The number of means of transport is very high with 13 different modes of travel. However, this also includes airplanes, ships, long-distance trains and long-distance buses. These modes of transportation are not to be considered for the study area. In addition, streetcars, suburban trains, and subways are combined into one mode of transportation, "rail." The same applies to cabs, passenger cars (drivers) and passenger cars (passengers), which are combined into "passenger cars". This leaves five means of transport in the end: walking, cycling, bus, train and car. The purposes, which could be specified for each way, are kept. There are seven different purposes: work, education, shopping, bring/fetch, errand, leisure, home. Here, a combination has not been considered useful. Travel time ranges from 1 min to 2.5 h. However, the longer travel times can only be partially represented on our map, so a maximum travel time of 60 min is assumed in the remainder of this section. Travel distance is comparable and provides similar results as travel time, so it is not implemented. The last aspect to be considered is the weather. Four different states can be identified. Besides "clear" and "cloudy" there are "foggy" and "rainy". For each individual path, the position is stored in latitude and longitude at intervals of 30 s. These coordinates are later used for the representation of the path relations.

4.1 Tangibles and Markers

The prototype of our AR-Table allows an easy use of tangibles. As described by Hansert et al. in [1] the previous project used a low fidelity tangible interaction concept for data visualization. Therefore, the recognition of the markers and the output of the position already existed. However, to handle all factors via the one existing marker is not possible, so the existing interaction concept was extended. The existing concept only had the possibility to retrieve predefined images based on marker positions. However, due to the large variation and combination of data, this form would have made the creation of the images very time-consuming. For this reason, a dynamic evaluation of the positions of the markers is developed and the data is used directly for the application of the filters. This means that each image is created and loaded anew and no images have to be created in advance. To ensure that the variance is as large as possible, a separate tangible is created and produced for each means of transport. For each means of transport, the corresponding marker is stuck on one side of the cube. This means that this one side must always be on top of the table for recognition. Therefore, for the means of transport five different markers are created. For the transportation purposes, the idea is different. Since the trip purposes are considered individually and there is, for example, not a summary like the environmentally friendly transportation types (walking, cycling, bus, train), only three tangibles with one marker each are designed. These can then combine up to three aspects simultaneously according to their position. The travel time, a slider controls i.e. the duration of a trip. Here, too, a tangible with a marker is needed. The position of the tangibles on the slider should represent the maximum travel time. This can be determined by the position. Thus, the travel time setting remains very flexible. The weather is controlled by a tangible with four different markers. Each side selects a different state. Care must be taken to ensure that the side markers are not detected by the oblique angle of the stereo depth camera.

Different materials were used for the tangibles. The means of transport were each to be represented in a different color. Therefore, these five Tangibles were assembled with LEGO building blocks. This allows the color representation to be made directly. At the same time, the tangibles can be changed at any time. For example, their size and shape can be easily adjusted. The tangible for the weather was also implemented using a cube with LEGO. In this case, the even size of the sides was especially important. This can prevent the favoring of one state. The remaining four tangibles were made independently from wood. Care was taken to ensure that the tangibles had a tangible and pleasing shape. The size of each top was determined to be seven to eight centimeters. The size allows easy gripping without becoming unwieldy. This makes it possible to apply the markers later in a size of five by five centimeters. This also leaves enough space for a white border. This is intended to simplify recognition of the markers and at the same time make them more reliable. The size and width of the markers vary. Only the marker for the weather has the same length sides everywhere. The markers are shown in Fig. 2 and 3.

Fig. 2. Tangibles for transportation modes

Fig. 3. Tangibles for path purposes

4.2 Marker Detection and Filters

In the following section, the program itself and the function of the marker detection and the associated filters will be discussed. The markers are captured in a black and white image via the stereo depth camera. The evaluation of the marker IDs and their position have already been implemented. In the program, the function for the output of the markers is called permanently within a loop. This function outputs each time a list with the IDs and the corresponding coordinates of the markers. The coordinates correspond to the table dimensions. A data frame object is now created from the contents and the information is evaluated with it. Data frames are organized in tables and thus allow access to specific positions of a row or column. Because of the easy access and the unlimited size it was decided to store the paths in data frames [13]. A new data frame is now created throughout with the currently visible marker IDs. Now follows the verification of the position of the markers or rather the tangibles. For this purpose, different polygons are defined for the individual factors. These polygons are based on the assigned areas in the interaction area. There is no limitation for the transport factors. They can be placed on the complete surface and be recognized as active. All other markers are recognized as active only in predefined areas. In the function it is queried for each marker whether it is active, more precisely whether the coordinates are in the previously defined areas. The result of the query is stored for all markers (state). The active filters are then gradually applied to the complete json file of the app. For this purpose, the file has already been upgraded in another project and the filter functions for all aspects have been implemented (filter_mode, filter_purpose). In the following, the object state is run through in several if-conditions and in each case it is checked whether the individual means of transport, path purposes or weather are active (1 = active, 0 = inactive). The filters are then applied accordingly to the entire data frame of all paths. Finally, all data frames are merged and the final data frame object is used for the map display.

5 Data Visualization

With regard to visualization, a distinction must be made between several levels. Primarily, this includes the layout on the table surface. The ratio of the table sides is decisive here. The longer tableside is chosen as the interaction side so that the interaction and display can show the information in more detail. Thus, on the map, which represents Karlsruhe, the section can be selected as large as possible. Similar to our table, the cityscape of Karlsruhe is more extended in east-west direction than in north-south direction. The layout consists of the map itself and the drawn paths. Below is the interaction area. For general understanding, the contents on the map are once again summarized in the form of a title. The remaining parts of the surface refer to the individual factors, which are influenced by the tangibles. The means of transport are each assigned to a color by the label and a separate icon. The assignment is done by the legend. The textual and pictorial description should prevent possible misunderstandings and allow a clear assignment. The color selection is based on the common color codes. The choice of colors is limited by the tangibles from Lego. For pedestrians, the color black is chosen because it stands out well in contrast to other possible colors. For bicycles, green is chosen, which at the same time should convey the emission-free use of this means of transport. For the trains, yellow is used, which is also reflected in the color choice of the vehicles in Karlsruhe. The tangible, which represents the routes taken by bus, is given the color blue. The last means of transport are the cars, which are drawn with the color red. The negative effects of mass car use and the intended tendency to use alternatives should be expressed in this way. So that the assignment to the corresponding markers can be achieved more quickly, the assigned tangibles have been created in the same colors. The freedom of interaction and activation of the means of transport is also reflected in the layout. In this, no fixed fields are provided for the means of transport. The legend is shown in Fig. 4.

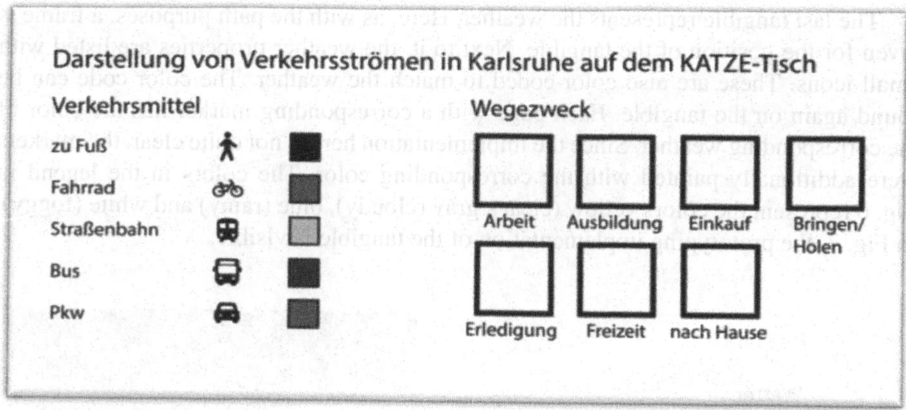

Fig. 4. Interaction bar with means of transport and track purposes. (Color figure online)

In contrast, fixed areas are defined for the respective path purposes. For a clear and understandable use, further color codes were omitted here. In addition, an assignment using different forms of the tangibles for the path purposes is very prone to error. Since only three tangibles are used for seven path purposes, a color assignment is also not possible. Due to the fixed position of the frames, the active path purposes can be recognized at any time based on the position of the tangibles, shown in Fig. 4. The choice and color of the tangibles does not matter with respect to the factors in this case.

The same tangibles or one of these pieces of wood is also used for setting the travel time. Here, the desired maximum travel time is clearly displayed via a time bar. The bar is similar to a zoom function in Google Maps or similar maps. At the beginning and at the end, the limits are indicated and in between, individual steps are also labeled. This is to ensure intuitive operation of the travel time by users. The color of the bar is chosen so that it stands out but at the same time does not catch the eye. The height of the bar can fully encompass a tangible. This leaves the edges of the bar visible in the background, shown in Fig. 5.

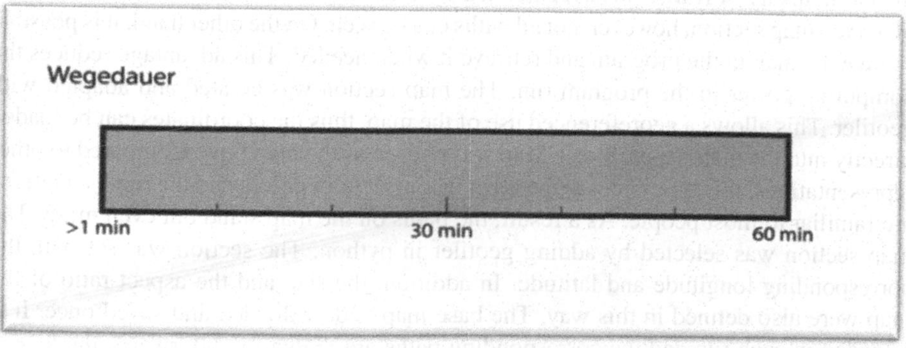

Fig. 5. Slider for setting the maximum travel time.

The last tangible represents the weather. Here, as with the path purposes, a frame is given for the position of the tangible. Next to it, the weather properties are listed with small icons. These are also color-coded to match the weather. The color code can be found again on the tangible. Each page with a corresponding marker has the color of the corresponding weather. Since the implementation here is not quite clear, the markers were additionally painted with the corresponding color. The colors in the legend in Fig. 6 represent the colors yellow (clear), gray (cloudy), blue (rainy) and white (foggy). In Fig. 7, the prototyping implementation of the tangible is visible.

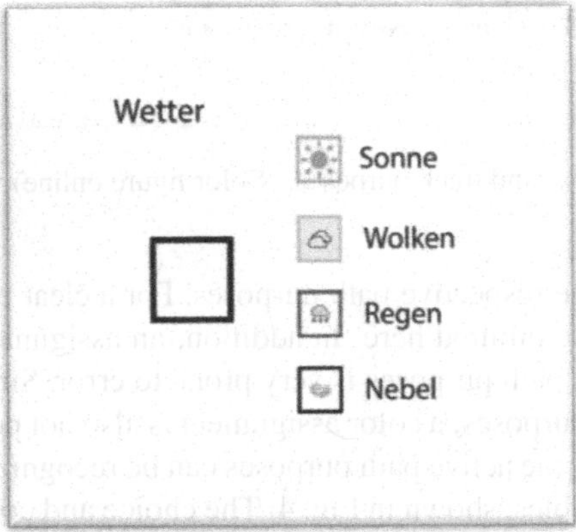

Fig. 6. Legend of the four weather types (Color figure online)

Fig. 7. Tangible for the weather.

5.1 Map

In addition to the layout, the map was also adapted for display on our surface. So that the map and especially the paths are later proportional to the table dimensions, the ratio of the page lengths was also applied here. The map section was defined beforehand and includes most of the paths within the city of Karlsruhe. The section was set to the shape of the German city of Karlsruhe and extended by a ten-kilometer radius. Due to the choice of a fixed map section, however, not all paths can be seen. On the other hand, it is possible to save the map in the program and retrieve it when needed. This advantage reduces the computing power in the program run. The map section was created and adapted with geotiler. This allows a georeferenced use of the map, thus the coordinates can be loaded directly into the map. Open-Street-Map was chosen as the map type. Compared to other representations, this type chooses the most inconspicuous colors and the representations are familiar to most people. As a result, the paths on the map stand out even more. The map section was selected by adding geotiler in python. The section was set with the corresponding longitude and latitude. In addition, the size and the aspect ratio of the map were also defined in this way. The base map is downloaded and saved once. It is reloaded in each run and the corresponding paths are drawn in. Afterwards the legend is added and placeholders fill the remaining areas. The complete map is saved anew in the program each time and permanently updated.

5.2 Tracks

As the last point of visualization, the paths themselves are now viewed on the map. The visualization is done by connecting the individual coordinates with lines. A function loads the current data frame and determines the coordinates. The access takes place in the data frame. A previously defined column "coordinates" is accessed. However, the output from the application is swapped compared to the output on the table. Therefore, the X and Y coordinates must be swapped using the "swap" function. The points are then lined up one behind the other and then connected to each other via a line (cv2.line). After the coordinates have been output, the basic image is loaded. The following conversion of the color scale allows an application according to BGR scale. The color selection of the lines is chosen according to the length of the paths. The color is varied depending on the travel time. For this purpose, the paths are divided into three equal time ranges. This allows additional information to be displayed graphically. The line thickness was determined on the basis of the test runs (thickness). This allowed the different line thicknesses to be compared and the thickness with the best detectability and simultaneous overview to be selected. No dashing or differentiation of the line types was done. These factors are difficult to recognize or distinguish on the display. The implementation in the program is done with OpenCV in Python. The result of all paths of a certain travel time are shown in Fig. 8.

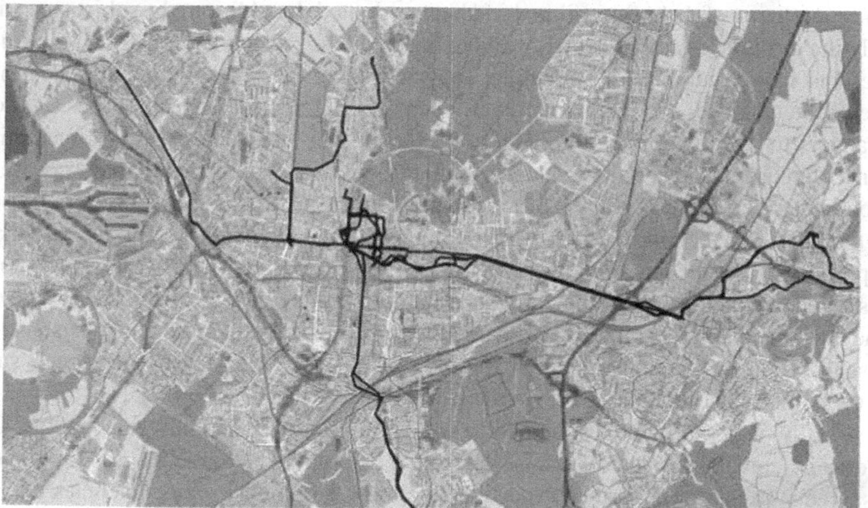

Fig. 8. Map section of Karlsruhe with paths filtered by travel time $\geq$ 30 min.

6 Evaluation

For a meaningful assessment of the interaction and visualization, the application is evaluated within a user study. The user test is intended to reveal the deficiencies and ambiguities in the interaction. At the same time, the color representations and their perception will be evaluated. The study will simulate the use of the application in the real world. In the following, the structure and the realization of the study will be described.

6.1 User Study Design

The conducted user study served as a first evaluation of the developed AR-Table as a whole system. Due to the unique equipment, the study was conducted in the laboratory. All subjects were selected so that all participants could be assigned to a similar technology-savvy group. As a result, the results are readily comparable. The subjects are all in their early twenties and are either students or professionals. The same age allows a conclusion to be drawn about technical aptitude, as they all grew up with a smartphone or own one. In order to obtain a meaningful result, it is important to conduct the study with only one group of people. In future projects, a comparison with another group of people is conceivable. The study can be structured as follows. After the introduction by a questionnaire, the task with the individual processing parts was explained in writing. For this, first the age and the knowledge about Augmented Reality and Tangibles were asked. It could be seen that AR is known to most and many know what it means. Tangibles, on the other hand, are unknown to most and its use is new territory for all.

The task consists of two parts. One is a brief introduction of what the study is about and the other is the actual tasks. The study is methodologically classified as observation. The completion of the tasks is filmed and later evaluated. In addition, the subjects receive only the most necessary information about the study. It is only mentioned that the study presents traffic data and that it can be analyzed using tangibles. The assignment and use of the tangibles are intentionally left open. The interaction structure aims to allow strangers to use the application without problems. All tasks deal with the interaction concept in different ways. The degree of difficulty of the tasks increases in the course of processing. The first tasks only look at individual means of transport or journey purposes. In the later course, comparisons of travel times and weather follow. The five tasks are kept short so that the maximum time required does not exceed 20 min. Questions are not answered during the processing, only in case of problems or wrong results help is given. The interaction is not evaluated later based on time, but of problems and inconsistencies. Visualization itself is not explicitly explored in the tasks. However, visual aspects such as the choice of colors play a role in the learnability of the interaction.

Finally, users in two questionnaires evaluate the interaction and visualization. The questions can be answered on a scale from "I completely agree" to "I completely disagree". In addition, further expected functions, comments, or deficiencies can be specified.

6.2 Studies Implementation

The study was conducted with eight subjects of the described group of people. In addition to four males, four females also participated. The loading time of the images was reduced as much as possible for the use of the application. Nevertheless, clear visible delays can still be perceived. The test subjects were made aware of the resulting waiting times. Next to the table surface, the possible tangibles were placed on a side table as shown in Fig. 9.

To avoid confusion with the wooden tangibles, the marker for the travel time was already placed on the table. Some subjects had problems with the interaction at the beginning. However, the operation was quickly memorized in the course of the tasks. The study leader only had to intervene at a few points because incorrect assumptions were made. Care was taken to provide the same assistance for the same errors. The subjects found the interaction with the unfamiliar technology consistently interesting.

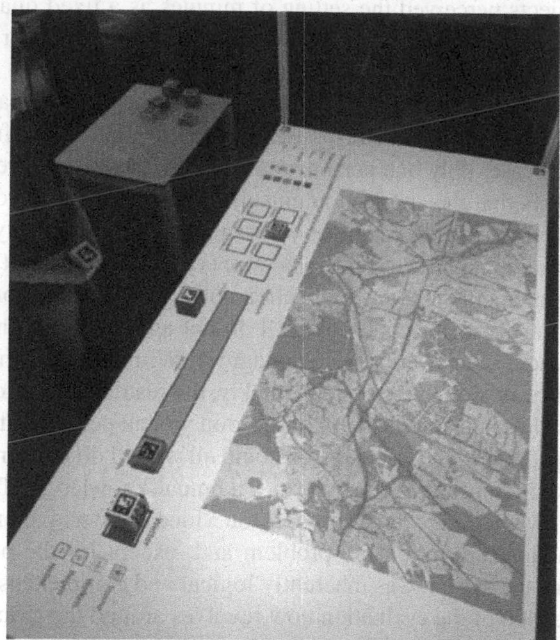

Fig. 9. User study evaluating prototype of AR-Table with tangible interaction.

7 Results

The results of the evaluation were recorded separately in the video recordings and the questionnaires. While the first questionnaire was dedicated to the interaction, the second one deals with the graphical representations. For the evaluation, in addition to the observations during the study, the results of the questionnaires are also addressed. The evaluation of the results is structured according to this order.

At the beginning, the interaction was difficult for all of them at first. The tangibles, which were unknown to all subjects, could not be directly assigned to the interactions and the effects. Therefore, there was a lot of "trial and error" at the beginning. Nevertheless, all subjects recognized the color assignment of the means of transport and also applied them correctly. However, over half of the subjects placed the tangibles for the mode of transportation in the squares of the path purposes. This misunderstanding was resolved after clarification of the different markers. However, it should be noted that the placement of the transportation tangibles without a fixed marked area is problematic, resulting in incorrect actions. Except for this misunderstanding, all other markers were always placed in the correct positions. The area to the right of the icons or below the timeline was chosen for the means of transportation. In addition, three subjects were not aware of the possibility of combining means of transportation. Therefore, they always considered the means of transport separately until this further possibility was pointed out to them. All correctly recognized travel time in its function. However, the meaning of the setting differed. Two subjects perceived the setting of minutes as a fixed quantity. They have thought with it all ways with exactly the travel time are indicated. For both travel time and weather, the possible positions of the tangibles were clear.

In addition to the general observations, the results of the questionnaire are discussed below. There was a wide range of responses to the question about future use of this interaction. In each case, only one person would use the technology regularly or not at all. This result shows that the application must be used meaningfully depending on the context. The interaction with the Tangibles was evaluated very positively. The interaction was easy for all of them and the test persons were confident in using it without the help of others. To the statements that the application contains too many contradictions or is cumbersome, four or five subjects checked "I do not agree at all". The remaining test persons chose the neutral answer or "I do not agree". With regard to the ability of other people to find their way around the system quickly, the results tended to be neutral. Half of the test persons chose the middle here. In addition, not all perceived the self-confident working with the program. The last question could all with "I do not agree at all" answer. This question asked about the required prior technical knowledge. The questionnaire confirmed the knowledge perceived through the videos. After a short familiarization period, the interaction did not pose a problem and, except for the positioning of the means of transport, the system was inherently logical and comprehensible.

The second section of the evaluation now revolves around the graphical representations. These features cannot be derived directly from the video recordings. Therefore, the findings in the first section come from post-study communication. The overall layout has been positively evaluated by the subjects. The clarity and the simple colors have been emphasized. Regarding the interaction, only the color choice and implementation of the weather were criticized. Here everyone wished for a clearer recognition of the respective marker. The map was not particularly considered in the evaluation, it was however to be recognized that two persons had difficulty recognizing the ways and/or not to confuse with colors of the basic map. The different color of the paths was only partially perceived and if then it could only be clearly assigned by two subjects. In any case, these should be revised and color coded according to the means of transport as indicated by most of the test persons.

As for the interaction, the results of the questionnaire are now still considered. The questionnaire for the design and visualization is structured as for the interaction. The results of the questionnaire represent the visualizations as a whole positively. All users rate the overall layout and the choice of background map as useful and appealing. Except for one person, the recognition of the paths was also perceived positively by all. The same result applies to the design of the interaction bar itself and the color choice of the tangibles. As was already recognized during the study, however, the color gradations of the paths are hardly recognizable and cannot be correctly interpreted by most people. The result is also reflected in the questionnaire. The ratings here are neutral but not bad. A similar picture emerges for the color-coding of the tangibles. Whereas the weather was hardly assigned correctly and therefore rated worse. The color selection of the means of transport makes sense and can be understood quickly.

The time delay of four to five seconds is a disadvantage. In the additional comments, six test persons addressed this problem and revealed their problems with it. As a result, the subjects criticized the fact that it is not clear whether the current interaction is already displayed or not. It is not apparent to the subjects whether the input has already occurred because they do not know the content goal of the task. In the study, the leader could always confirm the result or ask for patience. These possibilities are omitted in a real-world application. Here, a loading icon or a display of the current active factors was desired. This could indicate the current means of transport, route purposes, etc. at the top of the screen. This would make it possible to see at any time whether the application is still loading and whether the desired filters have already been applied.

8 Summary and Outlook

The result of this work illustrates that the use of tangibles for the presentation of information offers new possibilities for interaction. A comprehensive concept was developed, which in its basic features also allows strangers to interact easily. Using Python, the interaction was implemented on a converted AR table. Ideas were also developed and graphical elements designed for the visualization and presentation of the information. The concepts were then evaluated in a user study. It has been worked out that for an error-free interaction, the assignment of tangibles for the respective function is indispensable. The interaction could be fundamentally understood and applied within a short period of time by persons not familiar with the subject. The representations were for the most part intuitively perceived correctly by the subjects and supported the interaction. Our prototype has shown to what extent traffic data can be represented with the help of these tangibles. The application in this form could also explore discussion and presentation in a larger group of people in future scenarios. In further work, the interaction with the application can be revised and especially the loading time can be reduced.

Acknowledgments. The authors wish to thank the participants of the user study for their time and valuable input. In Addition, we would like to thank Kai Schwägerl and Valentin Hecht for their excellent contribution to the project.

References

1. Hansert, J., Trefzger, M., Schlegel, T.: Interactive AR models in participation processes. In: Chen, J.Y.C., Fragomeni, G. (eds.) HCII 2020. LNCS, vol. 12190, pp. 50–62. Springer, Cham (2020). https://doi.org/10.1007/978-3-030-49695-1_4
2. Trefzger, M., Titov, W., Keller, C., Böhm, F., Schlegel, T.: A context aware evaluation tool for individual mobility - extended abstract. In: Hands on Sustainable Mobility. International Students Workshop and Conference, Karlsruhe, Deutschland, 19–24 May 2019

3. Böhm, F., et al.: Toolbox for analysis and evaluation of low-emission urban mobility. In: Krömker, H. (ed.) HCII 2020. LNCS, vol. 12213, pp. 145–160. Springer, Cham (2020). https://doi.org/10.1007/978-3-030-50537-0_12
4. BMVI: Article describing the inquiry of mobility data by the German ministry of traffic and infrastructure (2019). https://www.bmvi.de/SharedDocs/DE/Artikel/G/deutschesmobilitaetspanel.html. Accessed 27 Oct 2021
5. Smith, A.: Architectural Model as Machine – A New View of Models from Antiquity to the Present Day. Elsevier, Oxford (2004)
6. Hohauser, S.: Architectural and Interior Models, p. 6. Van Nostrand Reinhold, New York (1970)
7. Billinghurst, M., Kato, H., Poupyrev, I.: Tangible augmented reality. In: ACM SIGGRAPH ASIA, p. 7 (2008)
8. Park, Y., Woo, W.: The ARTable: an AR-based tangible user interface system. In: Pan, Z., Aylett, R., Diener, H., Jin, X., Göbel, S., Li, L. (eds.) Edutainment 2006. LNCS, vol. 3942, pp. 1198–1207. Springer, Heidelberg (2006). https://doi.org/10.1007/11736639_150
9. Dalsgaard, P., Halskov, K.: Tangible 3D tabletops: combining tangible tabletop interaction and 3D projection. In: NordiCHI von Association of Computing Machinery, New York (2012)
10. Chen, W., Guo, F., Wang, F.-Y.: A survey of traffic data visualization. IEEE Trans. Intell. Transp. Syst. **16**, 2970–2984 (2015)
11. Andrienko, G., Andrienko, N., Chen, W., Maciejewski, R., Zhao, Y.: Visual analytics of mobility and transportation: state of the art and further research directions. IEEE Trans. Intell. Transp. Syst. **18**, 2232–2249 (2017)
12. Titov, W., Schlegel, T.: Analysis of the daily mobility behavior before and after the corona virus pandemic–a field study. In: Stephanidis, C., Antona, M., Ntoa, S. (eds.) HCII 2021. Communications in Computer and Information Science, vol. 1498, pp. 552–557. Springer, Cham (2021). https://doi.org/10.1007/978-3-030-90176-9_71
13. Vander Plas, J.: DataScience mit Python: Das Handbuch für den Einsatz von IPython, Jupyter, NumPy, Pandas, Matplotlib, Scikit-Learn. Frechen: mitp (2018)

Author Index